THE STORY OF THE FAITH

THE MACMILLAN COMPANY
NEW YORK · BOSTON · CHICAGO
DALLAS · ATLANTA · SAN FRANCISCO

MACMILLAN AND CO., LIMITED
LONDON · BOMBAY · CALCUTTA
MADRAS · MELBOURNE

THE MACMILLAN COMPANY
OF CANADA, LIMITED
TORONTO

The Story of the Faith

A SURVEY OF CHRISTIAN HISTORY

FOR THE UNDOGMATIC

By *William Alva Gifford*

1946

THE MACMILLAN COMPANY · NEW YORK

PREFACE

This book is written for those many persons who read history but have never read the history of the Christian religion. Some millions profess it; other millions are mildly interested in it; and many, whose numbers I shall not guess, are critical of it, often without being enlightened critics. Here, then, is the story of the faith, for friend and foe alike.

A word of caution! No true story of the faith can be a primer; for the Christian Church is a part of all that she has met. Whatever may have been her faith at first, she gathered many things from many sources as the generations passed. At length she arrived at Catholic Christianity, then set her face against further change; but already there had been incorporated into Catholic Christianity Greek philosophy and Roman law, Oriental ritual and German folklore, not to speak of ancient Jewish hopes and fantasies. These all make up "the Christian mind" to-day. These all constrain the pen of anyone, who will write with candour the story of the faith. I therefore set the Christian Church, from first to last, in the contemporary scene, and particularly amidst those nations of Europe whose life she directed for a thousand years.

To attempt the story of the faith in one volume imposed stern limitations. I have kept to the highway, stopping long enough with the greatest characters and movements to introduce them properly to the reader; and writing for the western world, I have said nothing of the Greek and Eastern Churches, after the lamentable separation of East from West. This exclusion is regrettable; but the historian who labours to be more inclusive, while keeping to one volume, ends by writing an ecclesiastical dictionary.

Again, I have described the twentieth century only in terms of forces and tendencies in religious life and thought; for the "Christian Church" has strictly ceased to exist. In its place are "churches," very many of them, and each with a history of its own. This is especially true in the United States. The history of Christianity there is now the history of denominations, to be written in a multitude of monographs. This is not my undertaking.

vii

And I have not written for scholars; though I hope scholars will respect what I have written. As a concession to them, I have indicated the general sources of my information. For the very studious reader, who is yet not a scholar, I have added footnotes and appendices, that he may pursue the subject further. Indeed, he may well read Appendix I before beginning the text itself. This will refresh his memory as to the ancient Mediterranean world, into which both Judaism and Christianity were born.

An essay at prediction! The future, the distant future, of organized Christianity depends on its ability to renew itself at the source. It is now being transmuted and diminished into Service Clubs. A useful but pedestrian service, not quite consonant with either the history of the churches or their present pretensions! Organized Christianity greatly needs its Lord, that it may live again among elemental things. "Even so: come, Lord Jesus."

WILLIAM ALVA GIFFORD

Divinity Hall,
Montreal
May, 1945

ACKNOWLEDGMENTS

I AM in debt to many earlier explorers, in the general domain of this book and contiguous areas, but cannot hope to recall now all whose labours have advanced my own. I shall not consciously overlook anyone whose help has been considerable.

First, I acknowledge gratefully the contribution of two great scholars, whose object was similar to mine—to survey a vast range of history and make it intelligible to the general reader. One of these is J. H. Breasted, whose *Ancient Times. A History of the Early World*, Ginn and Company, is scholarly, ornate and readable. The other is H. A. L. Fisher, whose *History of Europe*, Edward Arnold & Co., London, is a monumental record of three thousand years, since the coming of the ancient Greeks to the coastlands of Asia Minor, the Aegean isles and the land that is now called Greece.

Of another sort, but of great merit, is a volume of essays by British scholars, *The History of Christianity in the Light of Modern Knowledge*, Blackie & Son, London and Glasgow.

For Old Testament times in Palestine I have consulted, among other texts, two small volumes of *The Clarendon Bible*, Clarendon Press, Oxford. These are W. L. Wardle, *History and Religion of Israel*, and W. F. Lofthouse, *Israel after the Exile*. For New Testament times, and the transition from Old to New, I am chiefly indebted to Shailer Mathews, whose *New Testament Times in Palestine*, often reprinted by The Macmillan Company, remains quite the best work in its field.

For the inter-relations of primitive Christianity and ancient Graeco-Roman life and thought, two volumes have been especially useful. These are W. R. Halliday, *Pagan Background of Early Christianity*, Hodder and Stoughton, and Edwin Hatch, *Influence of Greek Ideas and Usages upon the Christian Church*, Williams and Norgate.

For the Middle Ages the best text is still that illuminating work of Duruy, *Histoire du Moyen Age*, which, often translated and revised, retains its charm in the translation by G. B. Adams, published by Henry Holt & Co., as *The History of the Middle Ages*.

For the development of Christian theology, an incomparable text is that by the late A. C. McGiffert, published in two volumes by Charles Scribner's Sons, under the title *A History of Christian Thought.* Of equal merit, in a more restricted field, is the same author's *Rise of Modern Religious Ideas,* The Macmillan Company.

For the philosophical backgrounds of theology, I have had helpful suggestions from my friend Dr. B. W. Brotherston, Professor Emeritus of Tufts College, who is not responsible, however, for any blunders I may have made. Of texts, especially useful has been a fine abbreviation of western philosophy by A. K. Rogers, *A Student's History of Philosophy,* The Macmillan Company. I have found help, too, in E. A. Burtt, *Types of Religious Philosophy,* Harper and Brothers.

And I would mention with gratitude two indispensable volumes of selections and translations, from the limitless source materials for Church History. These are J. C. Ayer, *Source Book for Ancient Church History,* and Thatcher and McNeal, *Source Book for Mediaeval History,* both published by Charles Scribner's Sons. The second of these is of exceptional merit, in both its choice of materials and their translation. In a narrower field I have used, in both teaching and writing, Wace and Buchheim, *Luther's Primary Works,* Hodder & Stoughton.

William Alva Gifford

CONTENTS

xi

MAPS

CHAPTER I

THE ANCIENT HEBREWS AND THEIR FAITH

GREAT religions have their source in the recesses of one solitary, timeless, inexplicable soul. Nothing in the era and the place, the people and their ways, can quite account for him. He is a breach in history, an exotic from an unknown land. But the efforts of men to understand, to appropriate, to conserve and disseminate the timeless thing in him, turn it into a religious system. The system has a history; and if one would know it, one must go with anchorites to desert places and mitred men to conclaves, with saints in ecstasy and canon lawyers with their codes, with knightly figures on crusades and kings in palaces, and not least with common folk at work and prayer.

So with Christianity. It was born of the ineffable goodness of Jesus, but has acquired many things, from many men, of many lands since then. Indeed it is with Christianity as it is with persons: some forces that were to fashion it were already working before the birth. The story of the faith begins twelve hundred years before Jesus, with Hebrew tribes, emerging from a nomad to an agricultural society.

The ancestral home of the Hebrews was Arabia, which is really three deserts, set in a vast expanse of arid steppe, the whole being encircled by a belt of fertile land. This belt is, in the north, extensive enough to sustain a great population; and scholars now call it the Fertile Crescent. At one end of it lies the delta of the Nile, at the other the Tigris-Euphrates valley, while between are Palestine, Syria and Mesopotamia. Into this crescent the desert peoples irrupted century after century, driven by the meagreness of desert life and the needs of a growing population, or drawn by the greater opulence of the Fertile Crescent. Thus out of Arabia came all the Semitic nations—Babylonians and Assyrians, Amorites and Canaanites, Aramaeans (or Syrians) and Phoenicians,

Hebrews, Abyssinians and the rest. This is now the most widely accepted theory of Hebrew origins.[1]

The Hebrews moved into Canaan (later called Palestine [2]) when the neighbouring powers, Egypt and the Hittites of Asia Minor, had worn themselves out with fighting. The international situation gave the Hebrews two centuries, about 1200 to 1000 B.C., in which to overrun Canaan and establish themselves there. It was not longer than was required to overcome resistance within Canaan itself, from the earlier inhabitants, the Canaanites, and from the Philistines of Crete,[3] who were entering south-west Canaan while the Hebrews were overrunning the rest of the country.

The religion of the Hebrews had been that of ancient Arabia; but during the conquest of Canaan the tribes from Arabia came into contact with the higher religion of another Hebrew tribe, or tribes, that had been in Egypt and that had left that land for Canaan under the leadership of Moses. Moses had had an extraordinary religious experience, that had led him to enter into an exclusive covenant with Jehovah, or Yahweh, a storm god of Midian. Moses had also succeeded, during a long delay on the trek to Canaan, a delay in and around the oasis of Kadesh, in organizing and consolidating his followers in the service of Yahweh. In time all Hebrew tribes worshipped Yahweh. Moses thus did for the Hebrews what Mahomet was to do for the Arabs eighteen centuries later. He lifted them above the near-heathenism of Arabia and its inter-tribal warfare, into the worship of one god, whom he conceived to be good and gracious, and whose will for them was that they should be good and gracious with each other. All later Hebrew traditions agree in this. Their ancestors had accepted Yahweh as their one, their only god; and their religious duties were to include mutual consideration and goodwill, at least within the nation's borders.

The gradual concentration of Hebrew religious devotion upon Yahweh, and the gathering of social idealism around him, were the first steps towards both Judaism and that later Christianity which began

---

[1] It is not the traditional theory, preserved in the first six books of the Bible, the *Hexateuch;* but both Jewish and Christian scholars now recognize that the *Hexateuch* is not dependable as history. See Appendix II.

[2] Palestine means "Philistine-land," a name first applied to the whole country by Herodotus.

[3] Some think they were Carians or Lycians from Asia Minor.

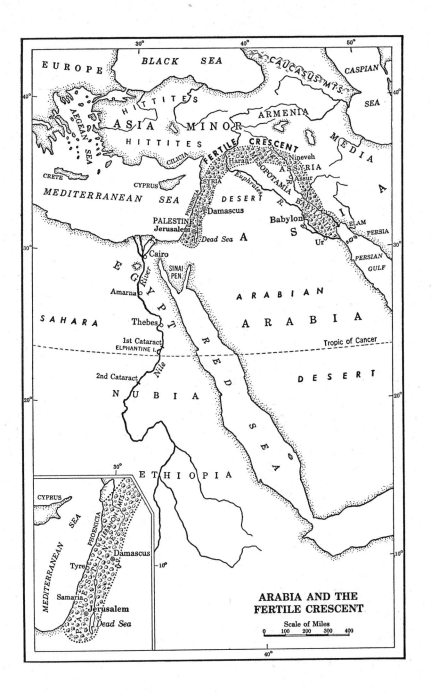

ARABIA AND THE
FERTILE CRESCENT

Scale of Miles
0   100   200   300   400

as an evangelical movement within Judaism. Students of these religions may therefore begin with Moses and the conquest of Canaan.

Canaan, or Palestine, is a little mountainous country, set between northern Arabia and the Mediterranean Sea. It greatest length is about one hundred and fifty miles, its greatest width less than one hundred. Such area as it has is not all productive. The valleys of the north are fertile; but the desert encroaches upon southern Palestine, Jerusalem itself being set among barren limestone hills, while the lack of summer rains tends to scant harvests. Ancient Palestine was also cut off from the sea; for all harbours lay in the north and were held by the Phoenicians. Palestine had little chance for political greatness, or even for peace; for it formed the corridor through which travel passed east and west, between Egypt and the world of the Euphrates and the Tigris; and in its markets strange faces were seen, strange dialects heard, strange wares exchanged. On its soil, too, strange armies contended. Egypt, Babylonia, Assyria, Chaldea and Persia, the Greeks and the Romans, all held Palestine in turn.

Conditions in Palestine during the generations of the Hebrew conquest may be gleaned from the Old Testament, supplemented by evidence from outside sources.[4] External influence was still chiefly that of Egypt. Southern Palestine is easy of access from Egypt, and relations between the two can be traced back to approximately 3000 B.C. From then until the Hebrew conquest, Egyptian authority over Palestine fluctuated but never failed; and when the Hebrew invasion began, Egypt was still the leading power in the Near East, Palestine was generally recognized as a province of the Egyptian Empire, the petty kings of its city-states were in doubtful allegiance and were flirting with Babylonia, and an important commerce flowed along the caravan routes through Palestine, connecting Egypt with Mesopotamia.

The *Book of Joshua* represents the Hebrew conquest of Palestine as having been short and sharp; but this is refuted by the testimony of *Judges,* and by contradictions within *Joshua* itself. The writer is using conflicting traditions. The truth is that the petty Canaanite kings kept

[4] The correspondence of the Pharaoh Akenaten with vassal kings in Palestine, the famous letters found in 1887 at Tell-el-Amarna, south of Cairo, are very informative about Palestine; as is also the history of Egypt two centuries later, under Merenptah, about 1225 to 1215 B.C., who was probably the Pharaoh of Moses and the Exodus.

up resistance generation after generation. The Hebrew invaders were never united in attack; and the conquest of various districts was achieved by individual tribes. After a century the Hebrews held only the hill country, while the Canaanites still dominated the plains, their war chariots and city walls being insuperable obstacles.[5] Then a new obstacle was encountered in the Philistine invaders, who had just been foiled in an attempt to settle in the Nile delta.

We read of these perilous times in *Judges*. We read also of heroes who arose—Deborah and Barak, Gideon and Abimelech and Jephtha—to rescue the people of their neighbourhood from one danger or another; but there was no Hebrew nation, no common action against the foe. The one common bond was religion; all Hebrews were worshippers of Yahweh. Even that bond was threatened, because here and there Hebrews and Canaanites were living at peace with each other, intermarrying, and combining their religious rites.

At length the Hebrew tribes were compelled by the threat of disaster to sacrifice something of their tribal independence and submit to unified leadership. A beginning was made when several tribes rallied at the call of Deborah and Barak, to meet the threat of a Canaanite league under Sisera.[6] Something more was needed. The Philistines were growing in strength, and were now more dangerous than the Canaanites. The Hebrews had no military leader, and no national figure except the old priest Eli, of the central sanctuary at Shiloh; and he was too timorous to protect the sanctuary itself against defilement by his own sons. In this situation the Philistines moved to make the land of the Hebrews a province of Philistia. The Hebrews, ill-equipped for a struggle, carried into battle the sacred ark, in which the power of Yahweh was believed to reside; but the ark was captured by the enemy, and Shiloh itself seems to have been taken and sacked. In the crisis men turned hopefully to a young man Saul, of the tribe of Benjamin, who had once rallied his clans-

[5] The successful resistance of the Canaanites presented a problem to Hebrew writers long afterwards; and they offer various explanations. Yahweh, they say, suffered the Canaanites to survive, to give Israel practice in war (*Judges* 3: 2); or to discipline Israel (*Joshua* 23: 13); or to subdue wild beasts until the Hebrews could occupy the whole land (*Exodus* 23: 29).

[6] The result was decisive for north-central Palestine. The Canaanites were routed in the Plain of Esdraelon, being overwhelmed by a deluge that turned the brook Kishon into a flood. The Hebrews interpreted the event as an intervention of Yahweh, who came from his desert home to their aid (*Judges* 4–5).

men to rescue the town of Jabesh in Gilead, that had been taken by the Ammonites. Popular enthusiasm for Saul was ratified by the priest Samuel, who succeeded Eli at Shiloh; and Saul was anointed king.[7]

Saul justified the people's confidence. Raids from the desert peoples were stopped, and Philistia held in check for years. Central Palestine and part of Trans-Jordania were united into a real kingdom. In the end, however, Saul fell in battle with the Philistines at Mt. Gilboa, taking his own life after witnessing the defeat of his army and the death of his sons. His fame was sung in a certain *Book of Jashar,* one of whose odes is preserved in II *Samuel* 1: 19–27.

In his later years Saul had attached to his person a young man, David, of the tribe of Judah; for "when Saul saw any mighty man, or any valiant man, he took him unto himself." David was a skilful harpist as well; and his music relieved the melancholy into which the old king sometimes fell. Soon the land was filled with stories of David's exploits. These stories were gathered by editors long afterwards, and pieced together into a rather confused account of David's career. It is told first in the closing chapters of I *Samuel* and all of II *Samuel.* A later account in I *Chronicles* is based on *Samuel.*

It is related that Saul grew jealous of David, who became the darling of the soldiers, the bosom friend of the king's son Jonathan, and the lover of his daughter. In the end Saul attempted the young man's life; and David was thenceforth an exile from the court. In the famous "cave of Adullam" he was joined by some hundreds of his own clansmen and of bankrupt debtors, and became a sort of Robin Hood to cities beleaguered by the Philistines and by desert marauders. When Saul fell at Mt. Gilboa, David was the one hope of the Hebrews. Saul's son Ishbaal was no leader. David therefore consulted an oracle and at Hebron, a place of great sanctity, declared himself "king over the house of Judah," about 1010 B.C. Saul's commander-in-chief, Abner, transferred his allegiance from Ishbaal to David. That was decisive. The ten tribes of the north swore allegiance; and David was king of all Israel. Seven years later he captured Jerusalem, which the Hebrews had failed for two centuries to re-

[7] There are contradictory traditions of this event. According to one, Saul is chosen by Yahweh to deliver his people, and is anointed by Samuel at Yahweh's command (I *Samuel* 9, 10). In a later tradition, anti-monarchical in temper, the elders of Israel ask for a king, Yahweh, the true king of Israel, is offended but instructs Samuel to assent to the elders, to teach them a lesson (I *Samuel* 8: 4–22).

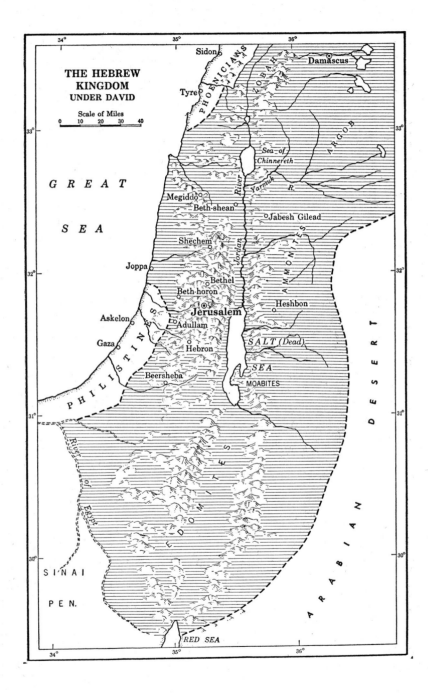

THE HEBREW
KINGDOM
UNDER DAVID

Scale of Miles
0   10   20   30   40

34°   35°   36°

Sidon

PHOENICIANS

Tyre

ZOBAH

Damascus

33°

ARGOB

GREAT

Sea–of
Chinnereth

SEA

River Jordan

Yarmuk R.

Megiddo

Beth-shean

Jabesh Gilead

Shechem

32°

AMMONITES

Joppa

Bethel

Beth-horon

Jerusalem

Heshbon

PHILISTINES

Askelon

Adullam

Gaza

SALT (Dead)

Hebron

SEA

Beersheba

MOABITES

DESERT

31°

PHILISTINES

River of Egypt

EDOMITES

ARABIAN

30°

SINAI

PEN.

RED SEA

duce; and the capital was transferred there from Hebron. It was an act of statesmanship. Jerusalem was more central, less identified with the tribe of Judah, and more acceptable to the northern tribes. David strengthened the fortifications, built himself a palace, and transferred to Jerusalem the ark, for which a special tabernacle was prepared. Jerusalem thus became the religious as well as the political centre of the nation.

The armies of David were consistently victorious over the neighbouring kingdoms, Moab and Ammon and Philistia. In time his kingdom included all Palestine, and seems to have extended northward beyond Palestine, to the Orontes, and to have included a part of Syria—a greater dominion than the Hebrews were ever again to possess. When, after a reign of forty years, David "slept with his fathers," he was remembered as the ideal king. Centuries later, when no one but God could help Israel, it was believed that He would send a deliverer, the Messiah, of the family of David.

David was no saint and it may seem strange that religious hopes should gather around him; but he must be judged by the standards of his time. He was a truly religious man, loyal to Yahweh, reverent to prophet and priest; and his establishment of a united Hebrew kingdom was a genuinely great achievement, which his people were likely to remember later, when they were conquered and scattered. David was, besides, a man of some poetic gift, interested in literature and in the history of the nation. Hebrew tradition attributes to him about half the national hymnbook, the Psalter, and credits him with having appointed a court historian.[8]

David's son Solomon set himself to consolidate what his father had won. This would require security abroad and wealth at home. For the former, Solomon trusted to alliances rather than warfare. He provided against Egyptian aggression by securing for his harem a royal princess of Egypt. He entered into alliances with Moab and Ammon and Sidon; and as this implied an alliance of Yahweh with their gods, Solomon built altars to their gods in Jerusalem.[9] This policy was successful; Solomon's long reign was free from foreign wars.

For wealth, Solomon devoted himself to trade and commerce. He entered into partnership with king Hiram of Tyre in building a fleet

[8] II *Samuel* 8: 16, 17.
[9] II *Kings* 23: 13.

for trade with Mediterranean nations; though Tyre provided the sailors, as Hebrews had no taste for the sea. This policy, too, was successful. Jerusalem became an imposing city, and Solomon an oriental sultan. He built for Yahweh a splendid temple, though not so splendid as the palace he built for himself, of which the temple was really the royal chapel.

The work of building was extended throughout the country. Provincial towns were fortified and garrisoned. Taxes were heavy; the people were poor; and discontent gathered force. The splendour of Solomon proved the beginning of national dissolution. The kingdom held together while he lived, only to fall apart under his son Rehoboam. The ten tribes of the north withdrew and chose a king of their own, "Jeroboam, the son of Nebat, an Ephraimite." [10] Thereafter there were two Hebrew kingdoms, *Israel* (also called Ephraim), with a capital at Shechem,[11] and *Judah,* whose capital remained Jerusalem. The kingdom of David had lasted less than a century.

Older forces were at work in all this. Tribal loyalties had been an obstacle to political unity from the beginning; and other divisive tendencies were developing. Long association with the Canaanites and with neighbouring nations had been making changes in Hebrew life. Most Hebrews abandoned the nomadic life. They built houses and exchanged their garments of sheepskin for coloured wool. They accommodated themselves to Canaanite religious rites. They intermarried with Canaanites.[12] The changes, however, were less pronounced in the south. There among the Judaean hills many Hebrews continued devoted to the old desert customs; and shepherd nomads still wandered with their flocks and dwelt in tents. There also the Hebrews were more exclusively devoted to Yahweh. They therefore lived in uneasy relations with their less austere kinsmen of the north.

The story of the next three centuries, to the close of Hebrew national history in Palestine, is related in the two books of *Kings,* which are the court annals of the time, as edited long afterwards. They are supplemented by the two books of *Chronicles,* which are a still later reinterpre-

[10] I *Kings* 12.

[11] A later king, Omri, built a new capital, Samaria, on an almost impregnable site. The country, therefore, is frequently called *Samaria* in the Old Testament.

[12] It was thus the Hebrews acquired the type of face which the Canaanites had acquired by intermarriage with the Hittites, especially the prominent nose still common among Jews.

tation of the annals by religious idealists. The sympathies of the editors
are entirely with Judah; and the importance of Israel, or Ephraim, is
therefore obscured. It was more extensive, more populous, more progressive than Judah, more influential in international affairs, though less influential in the history of religion.

Jeroboam I of Israel was an able king, and devoted his ability to making permanent the separation from Judah. He built temples at Bethel
and Dan, and established a priesthood independent of Jerusalem. The
editors of *Kings* refer to him with horror as "he who caused Israel to
sin," and tell us almost nothing of his reign.

The royal line changed frequently in Israel, usually by conspiracy and
assassination; but in the succession were able men. So we learn from
other sources than *Kings* and *Chronicles*. The editors of these books, for
example, tell us only this of king Omri, that he built Samaria and "did
that which was evil in the sight of Yahweh." From Assyrian annals we
learn that the fame of Omri spread far beyond Israel, which was known
in Assyria by his name for nearly two centuries. There Israel was Omri-
land (*Bit Humri*). From excavations also in Palestine we learn that
Omri's new capital Samaria was a great piece of building, comparable
with that of David at Jerusalem. Like David, too, he strengthened his
country by alliance with Tyre and secured a Tyrian wife, the princess
Jezebel, for his son Ahab.

So also with Ahab, a wise and able ruler, gallant in war, but whose
history in *Kings* and *Chronicles* is darkened by his admission to Israel
of the worship of the Baal of Tyre. It was such a thing as Solomon had
done, and was not inconsistent with his own loyalty to Yahweh; but religious leaders were now more anxious for the purity of Yahwism. The
action of Ahab led to revolutionary movements and a change of dynasty,
encouraged by the prophets Elijah and Elisha.

Thus the life of Israel went on for two centuries. She was more exposed than Judah to the cupidity of imperial neighbours; and so king
followed king in rapid succession, several dying violent deaths, according as the pro-Egyptian or pro-Assyrian party gained the upper hand.
Hoshea, last of the kings of Israel, paid tribute to Tiglath-pileser of Assyria, only to intrigue with Egypt as soon as he died. This brought down
upon Israel the wrath of Assyria; and after a siege of two years Samaria
fell to Sargon in 722 B.C. Sargon carried off much of the population to

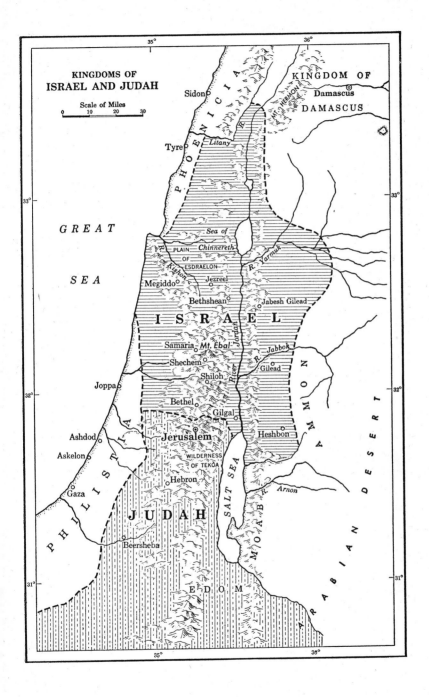

KINGDOMS OF
ISRAEL AND JUDAH

Scale of Miles
0   10   20   30

35°   36°

Sidon   KINGDOM OF
                         Damascus
                         DAMASCUS
Tyre   *Litany*

P H O E N I C I A

G R E A T   MT. HERMON

33°   33°

Sea of
PLAIN   *Chinnereth*
OF
ESDRAELON
Kishon
Megiddo   Jezreel   R. *Yarmuk*
S E A

Bethshean   Jabesh Gilead

I S R A E L

Samaria Mt. Ebal   *Jabbok*
Shechem   R. Gilead
Shiloh   A
Joppa   M
32°   32°
Bethel   M
Gilgal   O
Ashdod   **Jerusalem**   Heshbon   N
Askelon WILDERNESS   D
         OF TEKOA   E
         Hebron   S
Gaza   SALT SEA   E
P H I L I S T I A   M   R
J U D A H   O   T
                            A *Arnon*
Beersheba   B

31°   A   31°
        E D O M   R
                            A
                            B
                            I
                            A
                            N

35°   36°

Assyria; and Israel disappeared from history, being gradually absorbed into the peoples of the East.[13] Assyria brought colonists from other lands, and "placed them in the cities of Samaria instead of the children of Israel." They were soon in trouble; the god of the land was clearly angry; and the alarmed colonists appealed to the king of Assyria, who sent back one Hebrew priest, to teach them the religion of Yahweh.[14]

The Hebrew remnant throughout Samaria intermarried with the new colonists, and lost completely the racial purity they had already compromised by intermarriage with the Canaanites. They lived out of touch with later religious developments in Judah, and were thus unorthodox. The *Samaritans*, as they were called, came to be despised in Judah. Even a story about a good Samaritan became in time an offence to pious Jews; there were no good Samaritans.

Many things must have happened in the history of Israel, of which we should like to know something. This we do know, there were devoted champions of Yahweh there as in Judah; for Elijah and Elisha were prophets of Israel. And of the later, "the great prophets," Hosea, most gentle and tender of all, was a native of Israel. There was literary activity as well. That history of the Hebrews which is known among scholars as *E*, and which is one of the chief documents used by the compilers of the *Hexateuch*, was written in Israel, as were some of the Psalms.

We must now enquire more closely concerning the religion of the Hebrews, for most of whom national history had now closed, a fate that was soon to overtake the remainder as well. And to be accurate, there is strictly no "religion of the Hebrews." The Hebrews differed widely, according to the proportions in which four elements mixed in their beliefs and practices—the primitive religion of the Hebrews in Arabia, the Yahwism of Moses, the religious practices of the Canaanites in Palestine, and the monotheism of a very few prophets and the inner circles of their disciples. The one constant element was Yahwism; all Hebrews were worshippers of Yahweh. They differed as to what precisely Yahwism was, and how far participation in foreign cults was consistent with it.

[13] There are no "lost ten tribes," just as there are in modern England no lost Britons, Romans, Anglo-Saxons, Danes, Normans; they are absorbed into one new people, the English.
[14] II *Kings* 17: 24–26.

Out of their desert home the Hebrews brought with them animism. That is to say, they thought of trees and streams, whatever conferred special favours upon them, as animated by spirits, who were to be kept friendly and who might be consulted in emergencies. Spirits spoke to them in the rustling of the leaves and in the movement of the waters; and these spirits easily became deities in popular thought. Certain trees were therefore sacred to the Hebrews in Palestine, especially the oak; all the more because Canaanite shrines had already been under their branches. There the Hebrews worshipped Yahweh, but with rites so like Canaanite rites that they tended to polytheism. It was this the prophets meant when they complained that Israel "played the harlot" under every green tree.

Similarly with water, especially "living" or running water, which fertilized the land and sustained animal life. In Palestine, as in Arabia, waters continued to be regarded as divine, and sometimes as giving oracular instruction. In an ancient song preserved in *Numbers* 21: 17, 18, a well is addressed as a person; and the oasis of Kadesh was called *En-mishpat,* the spring of judgment. It was with the Hebrews as with the Greeks, who had their Nereids and Nymphs, and their oracular springs at Hierapolis and Dodona, Daphne and Delphi.

Sacred stones also had been regarded in Arabia as dwelling-places of deities; and this belief came with the Hebrews into Palestine. Upright stones sometimes stood beside Hebrew altars, often hollowed at the top to receive offerings to the indwelling deity, offerings of oil or wine or blood. Such a stone was called a *Massebah;* and the awe with which it was regarded is seen in the story of Jacob, who sleeps in the open at Bethel, with a stone for a head-rest, and learns in a dream that it is a dwelling-place of deity. Jacob therefore sets the stone on end, and pours upon it an offering of oil.[15]

These are only a few of the ancient religious practices of Arabia that persisted in Yahwism, to the great disquiet of generations of religious reformers. Side by side with them were magical practices, of a semi-religious character, such as were common throughout the Near East and of which Babylonia was especially prolific. When, in the last days of the kingdom of Judah, reformers set themselves to banish these things, they listed divination, augury, sorcery, wizardry, necromancy and other

[15] *Genesis* 28.

---

magical arts as "abomination unto Jehovah." [16] Strangely the casting of lots, to discover the will of God, survived through all Jewish history and into early Christianity.

Such was the religion of the Hebrews when they came under the spell of Moses, one of those few great souls whom some new insight carries far in advance of his contemporaries, so that in him the ordinary course of evolution is broken and a new beginning is made. Religion calls such a new insight a "revelation"; but it is probably not different in character from that sudden flash of insight familiar to scientists, when the phenomena one is poring over come together in some unity that has never been seen before. Then the whole science concerned is lifted by the new discovery to a higher level. The religious reformer, too, is a discoverer; but as the matters of his observation and reflection are life itself and destiny, his discovery may cross all geographical and social lines, and create in time a great fellowship of belief and experience. This actually happened through Moses.

It is difficult to say with precision what the Yahwism of Moses was. He was the first great religious leader and law-giver of the Hebrews; and it became the practice of Hebrew law-makers to attribute their codes to him. His name would give authority to whatever religious reforms were called for. So there are in the first five books of the Bible, the Pentateuch, five law-codes, widely separated in time, increasingly elaborate, and all attributed to Moses. The first is the Decalogue, found in *Exodus* 20, which does seem to have come from Moses himself, though probably in some simpler form. The second is the code found in *Exodus* 21-23, which scholars call the Book of the Covenant, because it is so described in *Exodus* itself, and whose contents identify it with the time of the "Judges." The third is the Deuteronomic Code. It is based on the Book of the Covenant, and is a reform code promulgated by King Josiah of Judah in 621 B.C. (*See* page 22). The other codes of the Pentateuch are the Code of Holiness found in *Leviticus* 17-26, and known among scholars by the symbol *H;* and the Priests' Code, *P,* interwoven by the editors through the Pentateuch, in an effort to interpret all Hebrew history as a supernatural movement, leading up to the Jewish Church. These codes together represent a legislative development of eight or nine hundred years, but all are attributed to Moses.

[16] *Deuteronomy* 18: 10-14.

Original Yahwism is the reduction to a system of the religious experience of Moses and the inferences he drew from it. He had been with
other Hebrews in Egypt. Tradition says that he escaped their oppression
and hardships, but that he witnessed it, and his conscience and emotions
were deeply stirred. In the end Moses was roused to violent resistance,
and had to fly for his life. He took refuge in a Midianite settlement in
Arabia, near the head of the *Yam Suph,* now called the Gulf of Akaba.
The Midianites were kinsmen of the Hebrews; and Moses became a
shepherd in the service of Reuel, or Jethro, the chief priest of the tribe.
His duties lay in the neighbourhood of the volcanic Mt. Sinai, in a
country sometimes shaken by earthquakes. It is not strange that the
Midianites believed the mountain to be the seat of a storm god, Yahweh;
nor is it strange that Moses thought Yahweh alone could succour his
people and was best trusted to do so. It is unlikely that Moses was a
monotheist, or even consciously looking towards monotheism. The Hebrew religious tradition is rather that Moses pledged his people to mo-
nolatry, or henotheism, the worship of one god while recognizing that
there are others. Henotheism did lead on to monotheism in time; but
that was long afterward.[17]

More significant than the henotheism of Moses was his conviction
that the will of Yahweh was wholly moral. Moses had brooded on the
sufferings of his people, and had seen the majesty of Yahweh on his
smoking mount. Yahweh, he thought, must be offended, as he was offended, by the wrongs men do to each other. There could be in Yahweh
no caprice, no selfish will, but only moral concern and moral activity.
The Hebrews, therefore, must not invoke his name for any evil undertaking. They must honour father and mother, avoid murder and adultery
and theft, give no false testimony nor covet a neighbour's property. They
must observe a day of rest for man and beast, a sabbath unto Yahweh. All
this was included in the covenant of Moses with Yahweh, on behalf of
the people. When in the future, under the influence of neighbouring religions, Yahwism acquired an elaborate ritual and sacrificial system, it
was an embarrassment to the priests that the prophets could quote Moses
against them. Yahweh, great prophets said, had never asked of Moses

[17] Five hundred years after Moses, the prophet Micah could still describe the religious
duty of the Hebrews in henotheistic terms: "For all the peoples walk every one in the
name of his god: and we will walk in the name of Jehovah our God for ever and ever"
(*Micah* 4: 5).

bloody sacrifices and burnt offerings; nor had he any taste for ritual sights and sounds and odours.[18] But the prophets were always a small, protesting minority; and when the Golden Age of prophecy closed, the priests were still attributing their rituals, the rituals of *Exodus* and *Leviticus* and *Deuteronomy,* to Moses himself. Even psalms of prophetic spirit were edited, to make them support ritual practices.[19]

The ethical henotheism of Moses was bound to have a precarious existence in Palestine. It had a rival, as we have seen, in the more primitive religion of the Hebrews in their desert home. Indeed the Hexateuch discloses that, even in Mosaic times, the Hebrews continued to worship divinities that dwelt in rocks and trees and fountains. The tendency would be strengthened in Palestine. The Canaanites, inhabitants of Palestine for a thousand years, had developed a civilization more advanced than that of the Hebrews, drawn largely from Egypt and Babylonia; and they had no national deity. Instead they had many local gods, or Baalim, whose favour was believed to give fertility to the soil. The Baalim were specially honoured at three great festivals, at the beginning and end of the wheat harvest and at grape gathering. These festivals were times of eating and drinking without restraint, debased by the licentious worship of the Ashtaroth, or goddesses of human fecundity. The Hebrews tended to accommodate themselves to Canaanite rites, worshipping the local divinities on the hilltops and under the evergreen trees. So that henotheism was an honourable tradition, rather than an actuality, to the very end of Hebrew history in Palestine.

Into the confused religious situation here described the great prophets came. They appeared first in the last troubled days of the kingdom of Israel, which were perilous for Judah as well. Great souls, we learn from *Kings* and *Chronicles,* were distressed at the position of their people. Devout servants of Yahweh were distressed at the spread of Canaanite

---

[18] *Amos* 5: 21–25; *Micah* 6: 6–8; *Jeremiah* 7: 22, 23.

[19] Thus a psalmist writes:

"Thou delightest not in sacrifice; else would I give it:
Thou hast no pleasure in burnt offering.
The sacrifices of God are a broken spirit:
A broken and a contrite heart, O God, thou wilt not despise"

to which an editor adds—

"Then wilt thou delight in the sacrifices of righteousness,
In burnt offering and whole burnt offering:
Then shall they offer bullocks upon thine altar" (Psalm 51: 16–19).

rites. Devout lovers of the past were distressed at the rise of town life, the increase of luxury, the oppression of the poor, so different from the simple equality of their nomadic ancestry. Devout lovers of the national life were disturbed about the international situation, which threatened both Hebrew kingdoms. First the two kingdoms warred against each other; then both were threatened by the Syrian kingdom of Damascus. When Damascus itself fell to Assyria, the Hebrews were exposed to more deadly perils still; for Assyria had long been bent on the conquest of all lands between the desert and the Mediterranean. It was these perils that produced the great prophets; and they had one view of the national tragedy—it was the fruit of disloyalty to Yahweh.

Prophecy in lower forms had existed long before. It was then but an ecstatic frenzy, in which the prophet was believed to be the medium of spirits or gods. We hear of such prophets in *Samuel*. The great prophets were quite different. They were men who observed life, brooded over it, prayed about it, until they saw more clearly than anyone else.[20] They were very great men indeed, these Hebrew prophets, quite as great in religion and ethics as were the greatest of the Greeks in philosophy and science and the arts. Neither Judaism nor Christianity has yet appropriated all the truth the prophets taught concerning life and religion. Their spiritual heirs are few, as indeed they themselves were few.

The earliest of the great prophets was Amos, a native of Judah, a "herdsman and dresser of sycamore trees" and a representative of the simpler life of the past. Amos appeared dramatically at Bethel, a city of Samaria, about 750 B.C., denouncing the sins of the northern kingdom. He had more than once visited the ancient sanctuaries, Bethel and Gilgal and Beersheba, to sell wool in their markets; and what he saw there made him sick at heart. The change from agricultural to commercial life had brought riches, and with riches had come great evils. The worship of Yahweh was hardly to be distinguished now from that of the Baalim; nor did religion seem to improve morals. The sanctuaries were

[20] It is a misfortune that prophecy has been persistently misunderstood. It became very early a synonym for inspired prediction, and remains so to this day, with the result that both Jews and Christians have busied themselves ever since interpreting and reinterpreting ancient prophecies, to find some sense in which they have been or will be fulfilled. The particular spiritual achievement of the prophets was insight, not the supernatural foresight popularly attributed to them. When the great prophets predicted the future they were frequently wrong, and such foresight as they had grew out of their understanding of the present and its inevitable consequences.

thronged for the appointed religious festivals; but scrupulous worshippers were unscrupulous in business and oppressed the poor. So great was the moral confusion that Amos thought men would never find the way until they abandoned such religious rites entirely and sought God through Nature—"Seek not Bethel, nor enter into Gilgal, and pass not to Beersheba . . . seek him that maketh the Pleiades and Orion, and turneth the shadow of death into the morning" (5: 5–8). Amos had discovered that quiet nights under the stars illuminate the mind and make God real to the human spirit.

Several things became clear to the prophet, as he watched the life of his times and brooded on what he saw. First, he was sure that right conduct in one's daily relations is dearer to God than religious punctiliousness. Yahweh was weary of the sights and sounds and smells of worship, while righteousness failed among men. If men would please him, they must "let justice roll down as waters, and righteousness as a mighty stream" (5: 21–24). In this Amos was in the Mosaic tradition, but he went further; he saw that existing standards of righteousness must be revised. Senseless slaughter was thought right, if only one were slaughtering the worshippers of other gods than Yahweh. Amos knew better. His soul sickened at the mutual hatred and destruction of the nations. Yahweh, he said, would punish them all. And as for the gods, there were no national gods, and no Semitic Olympus, where the gods strove with each other. Amos was not thorough-going in this monotheism. It was the god of the Hebrews, he thought, who was god of all and was partial to Hebrews; but his sway did extend beyond them and embrace all the children of men (4: 13).

It is not to be thought that Israel accepted the teaching of Amos and a younger contemporary Hosea, who continued his work. The days were those of king Jeroboam II, and quite the most splendid in the whole separate history of Samaria. The northern kingdom was prosperous; and Hebrew orthodoxy declared prosperity to be a sign of Yahweh's favour. The declaration of Amos and Hosea that Assyria would be used by Yahweh to punish the Hebrews seemed particularly mad; Yahweh was their god and could not go over to the enemy. They were not persuaded when the prophet Micah raised his voice with the rest. Assyria was already on the march. Her violence would fall first upon Israel. That, Micah said, would be the vengeance of Yahweh (1: 6). While he was still prophesying, Samaria fell to Assyrian arms, and the kingdom of Israel came to an end.[21]

The last years of the northern kingdom were years of great anxiety for Judah. If Damascus and Israel should fall before Assyria, what would become of Judah? When they did fall, Sennacherib of Assyria was not long in turning his eyes towards the south. Some twenty years after the fall of Samaria, he came into Judah and reduced all her fortified towns except Jerusalem. Hezekiah, king of Judah, stripped the temple of its adornments and emptied the royal treasury to pay the tribute demanded; but this did not satisfy the invader. An Assyrian army appeared before Jerusalem itself and demanded its surrender. Then the court went into mourning, the king did penance in the temple and sent to Isaiah the prophet, to learn the will of Yahweh in the crisis.[22]

Isaiah, a contemporary of Amos and Hosea and Micah, had long been giving advice to Judah. He was of noble birth, at home in the royal circle; and he endeavoured particularly to guide Judah's foreign relations. Speeches of Isaiah, covering many years of public life, may be found in the first thirty-nine chapters of the *Book of Isaiah*. They helped to steady the government and prevent a foolish alliance with Egypt. Isaiah regarded Assyria as the "rod" of Yahweh, which Judah must endure for her sins. When, however, Sennacherib now undertook the destruction of Jerusalem, Isaiah called for resistance. Yahweh did not will the destruction of Jerusalem.

The issue of events seemed to vindicate the policy of Isaiah. Before the main forces of Assyria could be brought against Jerusalem, a pestilence swept through the camp, and Sennacherib withdrew to Assyria. The "angel of Yahweh" had saved Jerusalem, which was to stand for a century longer.[23]

With the retreat of Sennacherib, Isaiah disappears from history. His prophetic activity had continued through forty years, and he had seen Judah safely through three great crises—a combined attack of Damascus and Israel upon her in 734, the fall of Samaria in 722, which Isaiah had foretold, and the invasion of Sennacherib in 701. Always the policy of Isaiah for Judah had been to trust Yahweh and avoid entangling al-

[21] *See* p. 12.
[22] II *Kings* 19: 1, 2.
[23] II *Kings* 19: 35, 36.

liances. He had joined also in the demand of earlier prophets for social reform, had shared their antipathy to the elaborate sacrificial cult of the priests (1: 10–17), and was the earliest of the prophets to preach the Messianic hope. In other words, he believed that God would yet raise up a Messiah, someone of the family of David, called and consecrated to save His people once for all (9: 2–7).

The national reformation for which Isaiah worked did not come. For eighty years heathenism reigned unchecked. Altars to the Baalim were everywhere, even in the temple of Yahweh. The lewd worship of the Ashtaroth flourished, and human sacrifices were offered. Life in Judah was like that of the peoples about her. Prophets protested in vain. They had so little effect that their names were not preserved for posterity.[24]

But the work of Isaiah did have a profound effect on the future. He had been an aristocrat; for many years he had been the adviser of the king; in critical moments his policy had been right. A school of reformers now gathered about his name; there arose a prophetical party, which included some of the priests. Many years they worked silently, preparing a religious constitution for the State, which should embody the Mosaic tradition of life and worship, and also the lofty principles of the great prophets. Their work is embodied in *Deuteronomy,* which means "the second Law." It is written in the form of a series of discourses, spoken by Moses near the end of his life. In the Arabah, the deep valley of the Dead Sea, "Moses spake unto the children of Israel, according to all that Jehovah had given him in commandment to them." He told them of a second covenant, later than that at Mt. Sinai, into which he had entered with Yahweh on their behalf. The terms of the new covenant had been "written with the finger of God" on two "tables of stone," and embodied a code of life and worship to be adopted in Palestine. A later chapter of *Deuteronomy* contains yet another covenant, "which Jehovah commanded Moses to make with the children of Israel in the land of Moab," just before his death and their entrance into Palestine.[25]

It was thus reformers in Judah tried to effect their reforms. The new constitution, they believed, expressed the will of Yahweh for his people. They would win popular assent to it by attributing it to Moses, and

[24] II *Kings* 21: 10–14.
[25] *Deuteronomy* 1: 3; 5: 2, 3; 9: 9; 29: 1.

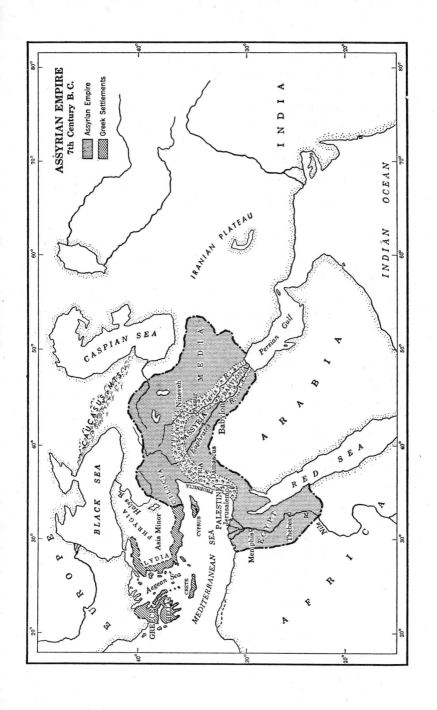

ASSYRIAN EMPIRE
7th Century B.C.

Assyrian Empire
Greek Settlements

through Moses to Yahweh himself. Such things were not unknown in the ancient world. The Spartans attributed their laws to Apollo, the Cretans to Jupiter, the Etruscans to Tages. Hammurabi of Babylonia attributed his code to Shamash, the god of justice, though men would know that it was his own codification of various legal systems, in use by the commercial centres of the empire at his accession. Hammurabi would mean only that he had been inspired by Shamash in the compilation of his Code; though in time the Code came to be accepted as of divine origin, as did *Deuteronomy* and the whole of the Old Testament scriptures.

There are things in *Deuteronomy* of which Amos and Hosea, Micah and Isaiah would not have approved. It is a working compromise between Moses and the prophets on one side, and priestly developments of many generations on the other, a compromise almost inevitable in the circumstances.

The disciples of Isaiah accomplished nothing for a generation or more, until the reign of Josiah. In the eighteenth year of the new reign, 621 B.C., the king "sent Shaphan . . . the scribe to the house of Jehovah," with the wages of workmen repairing the temple. Shaphan found the high priest Hilkiah greatly excited. In making repairs Hilkiah had come upon "the book of the Law." He delivered it to Shaphan, who carried it to the king. Josiah was deeply distressed. "The book of the Law" contained a covenant with Yahweh, which the nation had neglected. The matter must come before the people. A popular assembly was therefore summoned to the temple, and there the covenant was publicly read. The king himself swore to observe it, and the assembly confirmed the oath. An official reformation of religion throughout Judah was undertaken. The symbols of Baal worship, and of the worship of the sun and the constellations, were removed from the temple and burned in the valley of the Kidron; and royal officers traversed the land, destroying the altars of the Baalim and bringing the priests to Jerusalem, where they probably became servants of the temple.[26]

The reformation of Josiah, which seems to have extended to Samaria as well, followed the lines of *Deuteronomy*. It is clear that the newly discovered "book of the Law" was *Deuteronomy,* in whole or in part; and its acceptance by the nation made it the first canonical book, of what was to grow into a collection of canonical books, the Old Testament.

[26] II *Kings* 22, 23.

The future was to show that the population was by no means converted to the higher ideals of *Deuteronomy;* but at least those ideals were now officially accepted. They were the rule, the canon, by which conduct was to be judged. The teachings of the great prophets, in so far as they were incorporated in *Deuteronomy,* were now orthodox.

After the reformation the little kingdom of Judah moved swiftly to destruction, though not at the hands of Assyria. The day of Assyria was closing. Her policy of colonizing conquered lands had expatriated so many Assyrians that there was no longer at the heart of the empire a dependable body of citizens. The unity of the empire depended too much on the personality of the sovereign himself; and the last emperors were unequal to their task. Fierce Scythians raided the lands of Assyria; Chaldeans wrested from her Babylonia in the south; Medes seized the north, including proud Nineveh, the capital. The Hebrew prophet Nahum celebrated the fall of Assyria in a war song, which was included among the sacred writings when the Old Testament was formed.

To Nahum the destruction of Assyria was an act of Yahweh, intervening on behalf of his people. It was not so. Once more tiny Judah was caught in the conflict of empires. Pharaoh-necoh of Egypt thought to profit by the misfortunes of Assyria, and made his way to the Euphrates. His movements brought him into Judah. "King Josiah went against him; and Pharaoh-necoh slew him at Megiddo." [27] The rest is soon told. King followed king in rapid succession in Judah; and each "did that which was evil in the sight of Jehovah." In other words, they did not worship Yahweh alone, nor follow the tradition of Moses and the prophets. The prophet Jeremiah broken-heartedly pronounced the doom of the nation, until his "jeremiads" put him in prison and men demanded his death.

Jeremiah belonged to a priestly family of Anathoth, some six miles north of Jerusalem. A man of property and education, he transferred his prophetic activity to Jerusalem. The Deuteronomic reformation occurred early in his public life there; but Jeremiah nowhere mentions it. Its humanitarian provisions would appeal to him; but they probably seemed quite inadequate, and he would certainly reject its sacrificial system. [28]

[27] II *Kings* 23: 29.
[28] *Jer.* 7: 21–23.

Jeremiah was therefore opposed by priests and prophets alike; and only the influence of friends preserved his life. A sensitive, shrinking, reluctant prophet, grieved for his people, he found them resentful and violent. He abandoned hope for a covenant nation, and turned to the slower task of converting individuals to Yahweh. Jeremiah was the first great preacher of personal religion. In international relations, too, he was a consistent pacifist. Even when Chaldean forces surrounded Jerusalem, Jeremiah still preached non-resistance. To repent and trust Yahweh was the duty of Judah, in any crisis. The nation would have none of it.

Chaldea, as soon as her conquest of Babylonia was complete, moved to enforce her will against Egypt and the west. Egypt was soon subdued; and Judah, which was flirting with Egypt, was isolated. Nebuchadnezzar, the Chaldean king, came against Jerusalem in 597. At his approach king Jehoichin of Judah went out to meet him, surrendering himself, the royal family, and the treasures of both the palace and the temple; and Nebuchadnezzar carried away to Babylon many hundreds of the leading people of the nation, including the prophet Ezekiel.

Zedekiah, the unhappy king's uncle, was left to reign in Judah. After nine years he rebelled; and Nebuchadnezzar came and laid siege to Jerusalem. It offered desperate resistance for nearly two years, until broken by famine. An attempt of Zedekiah and his men to escape from the city by night was foiled by the enemy. "They took the king and carried him up unto the king of Babylon to Riblah; and they gave judgment upon him. And they slew the sons of Zedekiah before his eyes, and put out the eyes of Zedekiah, and bound him in fetters, and carried him to Babylon" in 586. Jerusalem was burned, and other hundreds of the leaders deported. Gedaliah, a scion of a noble Hebrew family, who had probably disapproved of the revolt, was made governor of the leaderless community, and undertook the reorganization of Judah. Hebrew refugees began to return from the neighbouring kingdoms of Ammon and Edom and Moab. But Gedaliah soon fell beneath the daggers of assassins; and in fear of Chaldean vengeance, thousands of the population fled to Egypt, taking with them the prophet Jeremiah.[29]

[29] II *Kings* 24, 25.

It has commonly been thought that virtually the whole population of Judah went into exile, and the idea is somewhat encouraged by the account in II *Kings* 24, 25. It is, however, a later account. Jeremiah, a contemporary, fixes the number of those deported at

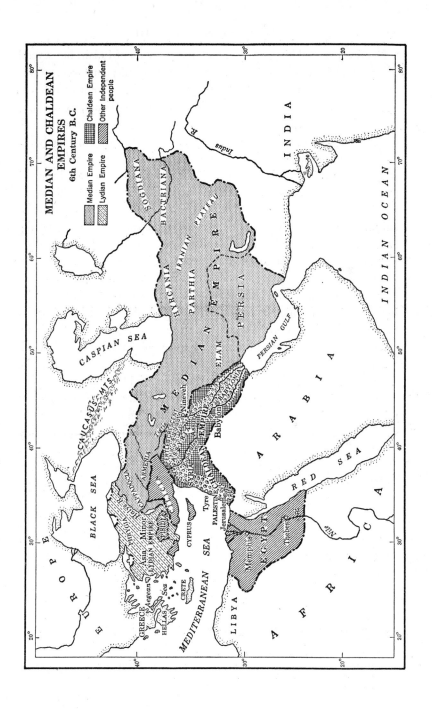

MEDIAN AND CHALDEAN
EMPIRES
6th Century B.C.

Median Empire
Lydian Empire
Chaldean Empire
Other Independent
people

Hebrew national history closed with the conquest of Judah; but several things in Hebrew religion were of permanent vitality and were to survive in Judaism and Christianity. The first was the movement towards monotheism. It was never achieved by the Hebrew nation, as we have seen. Hebrew religion did not go beyond henotheism, even in ideal, except in small prophetic circles. Monotheism had to wait until the Exile, and afterwards. Even then it was compromised; for Hebrew religious thinkers promoted their ancient national god Yahweh to the throne of the universe, and he continued to be partial to Hebrews. But the future would refine this crude monotheism. And religion can hardly survive in enlightened society unless it attains to monotheism. The belief that the universe expresses, and mankind must answer to, one Mind and Will, not many, is as essential in religion as the belief in one Ultimate Reality, whether material or spiritual, is essential to philosophy and science.

Another element of Hebrew religion that was to survive was the incorporation of ethics in religion. Prophets had said, elaborating the teaching of Moses, that the central religious requirements were kindly feelings, just dealings, and humility of spirit, all under the eye of God. Some of this prophetic conviction was incorporated in *Deuteronomy,* the first Bible of the Hebrews. It was an aspect of Hebrew religion that civilization would not outgrow. The last demand of an enlightened mind concerning God is not that He shall be all-powerful but that He shall be supremely good, that He can neither commit nor approve any evil thing, so that in being true to conscience one is being loyal also to God, and to educate the conscience is to increase the knowledge of God. Indeed, one may say that being and doing good does not become happy and tireless until it is regarded as achieving in time some eternal purpose of the Ultimate Will.

Hebrew mysticism, too, was to survive. True mystics are a minority in all religions. Most men of all faiths simply join in public worship, observe the conventional requirements of their religion, and are reasonably satisfied if the habit of life commended by their religion brings them

---

3,023 in 597, and 832 in 586. He mentions a further deportation of 745 persons five years later. These numbers include only men; and the exiles in Babylonia, including women and children, may have been a community of nearly 20,000. It would be perhaps a tenth of the population of Judah. The exiles were, however, the foremost people of the nation; and naturally regarded themselves, and were regarded by Jeremiah and Ezekiel, as the trustees of the future. *See Jeremiah* 42, 43, 52: 28–30.

some substantial rewards. But religion does profess to deal with ultimate things, with personal salvation and the hereafter and the Supreme Being; and even conventional persons need some modest confidence that their religion is effective for all worlds. In other words, religion, if it is to endure, must have the aroma of sainthood, the assurance of immortality, and some present experience of the supernatural. Hebrew mysticism did exhibit two of these things. If Hebrew poets and prophets had little assurance of immortality, they did live the saved life; and they had learned that the Ultimate Reality does respond to him who faithfully observes and meditates and submits himself to the good. They could say with Wordsworth:

> I have felt a presence that disturbs me
> With the joy of elevated thoughts.

It was a true religious experience, authenticated by the spiritual energy and moral courage and intellectual insight it conferred.

CHAPTER II

THE JEWS AND JUDAISM

THE destruction of Jerusalem and the removal of the leaders of the community may well have seemed to them the end of all things. That it was not so, is one of the miracles of history. The nation had always been small. Palestine is slightly larger than Wales, or the State of New Jersey. It is but a thumb-mark on the map of the Mediterranean world; and the Kingdom of Judah was hardly a third of its area. The population of Judah, at the time of the first deportation to Babylonia, was perhaps 250,000, and that of Jerusalem 25,000. After three deportations to Babylonia and an extensive migration to Egypt, Judah was a disorganized community of not more than 150,000, whose neighbours—the Ammonites and Moabites, the Edomites and Philistines—encroached upon her lands almost at will. These peoples were all subject to Babylonia, which would care little where they fixed the petty boundaries between themselves. As for Jerusalem, it was now an unwalled and ruined town, whose people had neither the courage nor the resources to rebuild. They did offer sacrifices on the site of the Temple and maintain some sort of national religious life; and the obliteration of the old political boundary between Judah and Samaria seems to have brought Samaritans back to worship at Jerusalem. But at best Judah was now a dishevelled poor relation among the nations.

The future of the Hebrews lay with the Dispersion. Hebrews were probably to be found almost everywhere throughout the Near East. There were many in Egypt. It was easy of access; and both commercial advantage and mercenary service had drawn Hebrews thither generations before the Exile. Hebrew settlements in Egypt were now enlarged by those thousands who, against the advice of Jeremiah, took refuge there after the assassination of Gedaliah. Hebrew prophets had consistently fought against Egyptian influence, partly because they saw that Egyptian aid would not avail them against Assyria and Chaldea, partly because Hebrews there yielded too readily to foreign influences. The Deuteronomic legislation was not observed in Egypt. Hebrews there worshipped other gods as well as Yahweh; and a colony at Elephantiné, far up the Nile, had a temple of its own. It was Babylonian Hebrews that kept their civilization and religion distinctive during the Exile, and that produced Judaism.

The story of exile in Babylonia is epic. Here were cities, beside which Jerusalem was a country town. Here were temples, beside which the temple of Solomon was ordinary and the rural sanctuaries contemptible. Here were gods, Marduk and Ishtar, worshipped with a magnificence that far outshone the solitary splendour of Yahweh. And here the exiles were as insignificant, numerically and socially, as the Jews of modern London or New York. It would not have been strange if they had been swallowed up, as those had been who were deported by Sargon to Assyria. And indeed many of them were. They worshipped the gods of Babylonia, side by side with their own, even as their ancestors had worshipped the Baalim in Canaan. But others held together and held to the past. They could not forget Jerusalem and the Temple and the national hopes. They were homesick for the rugged land across the desert which, if meagre, had at least been their own and the land of their fathers. So much we learn from Ezekiel's moving apostrophes to the "mountains of Israel," and from the dirges in *Lamentations,* as well as a Psalm or two.

> By the rivers of Babylon,
> There we sat down, yea, we wept,
> When we remembered Zion.
> Upon the willows in the midst thereof
> We hanged up our harps.
> For there they that led us captive required of us songs,
> And they that wasted us required of us mirth, saying,
> Sing us one of the songs of Zion.
> How shall we sing Jehovah's song
> In a foreign land? Psalm 137: 1–4

Grief held the exiles together in Babylonia as nowhere else in the Dispersion. They had been the foremost people of Judah. Life in Judah had been kinder to them than to others; they had had more "stake in the country." And they understood better than others the superiority of the great spiritual traditions of their race. No other people had had a Moses, an Elijah, an Amos or Hosea, a Micah or an Isaiah. Men who had once known these realized now that the magnificent idols of Babylonia were just absurd. Men who had caught the social meaning of the prophets, who had known *Deuteronomy,* were unawed now by the commercial and industrial greatness of Babylonia, and her ancient Code of Hammurabi. In short, to a Hebrew aristocrat, Babylonian civilization was Philistinism; and it was not impossible for him, an exile, to think of himself as one of an elect people, with an exclusive destiny.

Some beliefs, however, would require to be revised. All the ancient hopes had been falsified. The crude popular faith in Yahweh as champion of Israel had been disproved; he seemed to have gone over to the enemy. Isaiah and his school had been discredited in this, that the holy city had not proved inviolable, as they had taught. If men were still to hope, some better word must be spoken. Jeremiah had believed that exile would come when others had not believed it; and his word had come true. It was remembered now that he had also believed in Yahweh's forgiveness of his people and their restoration after seventy years. Perhaps that also was true. From Egypt he was now sending assurances that already the judgment of Yahweh had gone forth against Chaldea, that in time Babylon would fall and the exiles be free.[1]

Some of the exiles fed on these words, and the work of comfort and reconstruction was carried forward by Ezekiel in Babylonia. He assured the exiles of restoration, when punishment should be complete. He painted bright pictures of the future, when they should come again into their own land. The unfaithful shepherds, false prophets and priests and princes, would all be brought to their duty by one shepherd, of the family of David. The exiles in Assyria would be restored, as well as those of Judah in Babylonia; and all together they would form a holy nation, faithful to Yahweh. Ezekiel described minutely the future division of the land among the tribes, and gave details of the temple that was to be, its dimensions and appointments and ritual.[2]

These were greater hopes than would ever be realized. The exiles of

[1] *Jer.* 25: 11, 12; 29: 4–14; 30: 1–11, 51.
[2] *Ezek.* 20: 33, 34; 34: 23, 24; 37: 15–28.

Samaria would never return, nor the family of David rule over a united
Israel. But such hopes were congenial to the devout, and helped to keep
them a compact body in Babylonian society.

A different word came, in the later years of exile, to an unknown
prophet, who is called Deutero-Isaiah, or the second Isaiah, and who is
the author of much of *Isaiah* 40–66. He had brooded particularly on the
problem of suffering. Sensitive minds were troubled that Israel should
have to endure the oppressions of other peoples, equally sinful but still
prosperous. They were troubled that the righteous within Israel should
suffer equally with the unrighteous. Deutero-Isaiah tried to set forth the
inner meaning of this moral chaos. His explanation is this—Israel is not
so much the favourite son as the special servant of Yahweh, in the work
of saving all mankind. Israel is thus called to great duties, and is made
fit for his duties by suffering. Deutero-Isaiah saw that the things one
willingly suffers for others discipline one's own soul and accredit one to
those for whom one suffers. The nations now derided stricken Israel; in
time they would acknowledge that he suffered for them:

Surely he hath borne our griefs, and carried our sorrows; yet we did esteem
him stricken, smitten of God, and afflicted. But he was wounded for our
transgressions, he was bruised for our iniquities; the chastisement of our
peace was upon him; and with his stripes we are healed.   *Isaiah* 53: 4, 5

This teaching was not accepted by even the devout; but it was laid
up in a few hearts, and was never quite forgotten in Israel.

Meanwhile important religious developments were taking place
among the exiles, in both Egypt and Babylonia. In the former, as we have
seen, Hebrew immigrants adjusted themselves to the new situation, worshipping Yahweh, but not to the exclusion of Egyptian deities. This
susceptibility was to mean that when, two centuries later, Egypt would
be brought within the Greek empire of Alexander the Great and Hellenized, Hebrews there would adopt the Greek language and customs,
and there would arise what is known as Hellenistic Judaism.[3] Meanwhile the religious developments of most significance for exilic times,
and indeed for all time, were taking place in Babylonia. There too

---

[3] Egyptian Jewry then translated the Hebrew scriptures into Greek, the Septuagint;
and later still Jewish thought accommodated itself to Greek, in the philosophy of Philo,
a Jew of Alexandria. This Alexandrian philosophy became influential in Graeco-Roman
society and in the Christian Church.

changes were inevitable; but they took the direction of a zealous codification of Hebrew law and elaboration of the religious ritual. The leaders
in Babylonia were not accommodating themselves to contemporary
situations; they were poring over the past, planning for the future, confident that the future was with them. In other words, the religion known
as Judaism was taking form in Babylon, and was to change the very
name of the Hebrews. They would be known as Jews, adherents of
Judaism. This was to happen also in Judah and Egypt and everywhere.
Such was the influence of the Babylonian community.

The first significant movement towards Judaism had begun before
the Exile, with the creation of *Deuteronomy* and its adoption as the law-
book of Judah. The will of Yahweh was now to be learned from an
inspired book, not from inspired men. Jeremiah was the last prophet
of the old school.

Deuteronomy established legalism in Hebrew life. Society had been
guided by ancient tribal custom. In special situations it had also had for
its guidance "torah," or instruction, and "mishpatim," or judgments.
"Torah" was a priest's instruction concerning the ritual, and a prophet's
instruction as to the principles of true living, or the right policy for a
crisis. A "mishpat" was a decision given by the king, or by the elders
assembled at the town gate, or by any person of prestige, on some question of right submitted to him. Such a decision was not strictly a law; it
was rather a precedent. There were in early Israel no law courts, in the
modern sense; but there were very ancient precedents, and Hebrew
tradition said they had originated in decisions of Yahweh himself, transmitted by Moses.

The appearance of Law Codes changed the situation, by converting
some precedents and principles into laws. An ancient and simple Code,
as we have seen, is the Book of the Covenant, *Exodus* 21–23; but the
decisive early code is *Deuteronomy,* or more accurately the legal part of
that book, chapters 12–26.

Life under *Deuteronomy* was an advance on the past. It purified worship, and turned some of the moral teachings of the prophets into laws.
But ecclesiastical legislation, having consolidated past gains, tends to
stand in the way of future progress. Nothing new, it thinks, can be
divine, since it is not in the inspired book. In other words, a religious
law-book, like a creed, is static and becomes a substitute for living in-

sight, which is a growing thing. Deuteronomic ethics were better than those of the past, but not so good as the future would require. For example, the humanitarian regulations of *Deuteronomy* were applicable to Israel alone; wrongs might be done to a foreigner that must not be done to a fellow Hebrew. And, contradicting the great prophets, *Deuteronomy* left rites and ceremonies as important as justice and mercy and truth. When religious pedants in the future should have worked out all the implications of their law-book, piety would tend to become mere punctiliousness.

The new legalism was carried further during the sixty years of the Exile and the century following. Old laws were codified and new laws constructed. The ritual of worship was elaborated. Thus *Genesis, Exodus, Leviticus,* and *Numbers* came into being. They were added to *Deuteronomy* and, like *Deuteronomy,* were attributed to Moses. These five books, the Pentateuch, are still known as the Five Books of Moses.[4]

The man most influential in this development was Ezekiel, who has been called the first of the scribes, or professional interpreters of the Law. Ezekiel was of priestly birth and training; and the times were suited to his genius. The king was gone, and the activities of the court, politics and the conduct of the war. These were the things that had chiefly engaged the prophets; and with their passing the classical age of prophecy closed. The priest remained, without a temple or an altar. It is a tribute to his tenacity and his courage that he survived; but it is easier to pore over ancient institutions than to work through dark days for a new and better world. Ezekiel set himself to elaborate the ritual of *Deuteronomy;* and his work was carried forward by his school. Their plan for the nation that was again to rise in Palestine is seen in the last nine chapters of *Ezekiel.* The civil ruler, in that ideal state, will concern himself chiefly with making proper provision for the priests and the cultus. The Temple will be surrounded by two courts instead of one, being doubly protected against all possible pollution. Its services will be performed by the priestly family of Zadok alone; and the care of the Temple will be committed to other consecrated persons, the Levites. It had previously been cared

---

[4] The years of exile were years of great literary activity. From them come not only the writings of Ezekiel and Deutero-Isaiah, but the history of the Hebrew nation found in *Judges, Samuel* and *Kings.* In them the court annals and other literature of the past were collected, preserved, and re-edited, to provide encouragement for the exiles and to be ready for use in the restored community.

for by slaves of foreign birth, provided by the king; but thenceforth only consecrated persons would fill all offices connected with the sanctuary, and laymen would be excluded. The old national festivals, which had been times of feasting and rejoicing before Yahweh, would now be purifying rites.

Thus in Ezekiel the priestly view of religion triumphs, and the teaching of the prophets is reversed; it is now sanctity, not common goodness, that will be rewarded in the Golden Age, the Messianic Kingdom.

Gradually the school of priest-scribes, following Ezekiel, developed the ritual into that more elaborate code set forth in the central section of the Pentateuch, *Exodus* 24 to *Numbers* 9. Some of this ritual is probably ancient; but everything is brought into harmony with the view of Ezekiel. The essence of all sin is ceremonial uncleanness, the loss of sanctity. Laws concerning worship therefore overshadow laws promoting justice. Not that moral wrongs are no longer reproved; it is only that they are *relatively* less serious than the prophets had thought, no more serious than ritual irregularities. In the mind of Ezekiel and his disciples, business dishonesty, the shedding of innocent blood, the oppression of the poor and the helpless, are all of a piece with the handling of sacred vessels by unauthorized persons, the eating of meat wrongly prepared and the cutting of one's beard.

A religion so unreal and remote from life would suffer many vicissitudes; and Judaism had its troubles. It always had opposition from within; and in later centuries it had to fight for its life against the influence of alien civilizations, superior in some ways to that of the Jews and more attractive. But Judaism remained essentially what Ezekiel and his priest-scribes made it.

We cannot say how much of Judaism came into effect during the Exile. It could not be established in its entirety until the Jews could return to Judah and rebuild the Temple.[5] The opportunity came after sixty years. A cataclysmic event happened in the international world. We are to remember that when Assyria was crushed, the Chaldeans had seized only her southern province, Babylonia, and her lands along the Euphrates. Most of the Assyrian Empire had lain farther north and east, beyond

---

[5] Indeed Ezekiel's plan for Israel's economy never came wholly into effect. It was rather the ideal; it determined the lines along which the leaders of Judaism moved, and the spirit animating them.

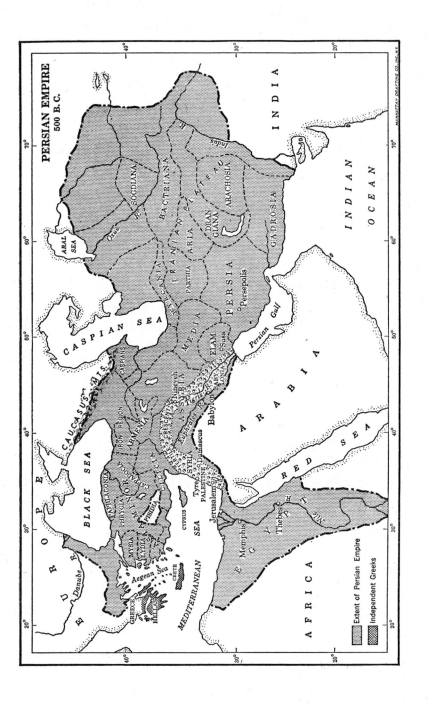

the Tigris. These lands had fallen to the Medes. The Median power spread more rapidly than the Chaldean, and soon stretched from Asia Minor to the frontiers of India. Then an event within the Median kingdom changed the face of the world. The petty king of a single tribe, Cyrus the Persian, revolted and embarked upon a career of conquest more astonishing than any other in history, except that of Alexander the Great. Within five years he had established himself on the throne of Media, pushed her borders westward through Asia Minor to the Mediterranean, then on his way east had overrun much of the Chaldean kingdom, including Babylon itself. Belshazzar, the regent, surrendered the capital in 539 B.C. A few years later Egypt succumbed, and Jewry everywhere was within the dominions of Persia.[6]

All nations watched with alarm the swift conquests of Cyrus; and a shiver of expectancy ran through Babylonian Jewry. The prophet Deutero-Isaiah was exultant. To him the advance of Cyrus was an intervention of Yahweh on behalf of his people. The exiles would return, he cried, a token of Yahweh's forgiveness. Jerusalem would rise again, and the Temple; and Cyrus would bring it to pass.[7]

It is not wholly strange that Deutero-Isaiah so thought. The religious policy of Cyrus was astonishingly liberal for the times. He seems to have proclaimed a general amnesty to all subject peoples and their religions; and he himself, when in Babylon, comported himself as a servant of the Babylonian deity Marduk.

Events fulfilled the prophet's prediction. In the year when Cyrus established his authority in Babylon, he authorized the return of the exiles and the rebuilding of the Temple. Cyrus commanded that those who did not wish to return should support the project with gifts, and himself set the example by restoring the treasures of the Temple, carried off by Nebuchadnezzar.

We may assume that much of Babylonian Jewry felt little enthusiasm for the return to Judah. Sixty years had passed since the first, fifty years since the second deportation. Babylonia was now the native land of

[6] For two centuries, until Alexander the Great, all Jewry was under the suzerainty of Persia. It was the most beneficent foreign rule that Jewry was ever to know; and is generally less esteemed now than it deserves. The history of the period is known chiefly from Greek sources, especially Herodotus and Thucydides; and we tend to judge ancient Persia by the reverses at Marathon and Salamis. Persia in fact remained a great empire, respected and feared by the Greeks, for more than a century after Salamis.

[7] *Isaiah* 40: 1, 2; 44: 24–28.

most Jews who dwelt there; and doubtless many had prospered. They would take a benevolent interest in the project of restoration, like those wealthy Jews who to-day subscribe to Zionism but have no intention of removing to Palestine. Cyrus, however, did his part, appointing a Jew, Sheshbazzar, to be governor of Judah. Sheshbazzar departed with an escort; and we hear nothing further about him. He probably achieved little by way of restoration in Judah. Patriotism and religious conviction would require some time to rally. Nearly twenty years later, in 520 B.C., the second year of Darius I, a few thousand Jews of Babylonia set out across the desert for "Jerusalem and Judah, everyone unto his own city." They were led by the Jewish prince Zerubbabel, who was to be governor, or pasha, and by Joshua as high priest.[8]

In Judah the returned exiles were a small band, scattered among a considerable population, whom their coming disturbed. To the north were the Samaritans, that mixed population of Canaanites, Hebrews and Assyrian colonists, all nominal worshippers of Yahweh, but out of touch with the new Judaism of Babylonia. So placed, the returned enthusiasts were in sorry case. Their history may be gleaned from *Ezra* and *Nehemiah*. They speedily took charge of the altar, amidst the ruins of the old Temple, offered the required sacrifices, and observed the required feasts. In the second year they began the rebuilding of the Temple, with solemn ritual and profound emotion. Native Jews were unsympathetic. They had got along for many years without a temple, and probably grudged both the money and the labour for the enterprise. The Samaritans, however, offered to co-operate. The offer was refused. The returned exiles would keep themselves racially and religiously separate; and to them the Samaritans were a mongrel people, whose religion was a corruption of Yahwism. This attitude aggravated the hostility of both the natives of Judah and the Samaritans, who had thwarted an earlier attempt at rebuilding by arousing Persian suspicions of Jewish loyalty. Now, however, the work of rebuilding was seriously undertaken, encouraged by the prophets Haggai and Zechariah.

On hearing the news, Tattenai, Persian governor of Syria, sent to Darius for instructions. "Search was made in the house of the archives"; and the decree of Cyrus was found and confirmed. In 516 B.C., some twenty-two years after the first return from Babylonia under Sheshbaz-

---

[8] II *Chronicles* 36: 22, 23; *Ezra* 1: 1–2: 1.

zar, the new temple was finished amidst great rejoicing. It was a modest structure, this second temple, to the few who remembered the glory of Solomon's temple; but it was the centre of their life and the symbol of their hopes.

Haggai and Zechariah prophesied a glorious future for the restored community. Their hopes were not realized. The country was harassed by raids from Edom. The population was disinclined to rigid religious observances. Foreign cults began to appear. Seventy years after the dedication of the Temple a distressing report of conditions reached the ears of Nehemiah, a Jewish cupbearer of Artaxerxes I of Persia. His grief touched the heart of his master; and he was given passports to Judah, with the status of local governor, a sort of mayor of Jerusalem and the neighbourhood.

Nehemiah set out, in 444 B.C., with the purpose of making Jerusalem again a walled city, capable of exclusiveness and the defence of its sanctity. Reaching the city, he found his coming resented by Sanballat, governor of Samaria, as an encroachment upon his authority, and unwelcome to many of the natives, who had lived in fellowship with Samaria and did not wish to see Jerusalem once more a walled city, isolated and estranged. But Nehemiah was a Jewish Cromwell and not easily daunted. He inspected the ruined walls by night, then roused the local leaders to undertake their restoration. Fifty-two days the work was pressed with vigour, the people working in families, at many points at once, and armed against attack as they worked. At the end of that time the restoration was complete, all sections having been rebuilt and joined together; and the wall was dedicated with rejoicing. Nehemiah "appointed two great companies that gave thanks and went in procession" upon the wall, part to the right and part to the left, meeting at the Temple, where "they offered great sacrifices that day, and rejoiced . . . so that the joy of Jerusalem was heard even afar off." [9]

Nehemiah now undertook the organization of the community and the enforcement of religious observances. The twelve years of his governorship were filled with reforms. Then he returned to the Persian court, only to hear very soon that disloyal men in Judah were falling away. Samaritans were being accepted as members of the community. A certain Tobiah, a friend of Sanballat, had even been permitted by the

[9] *Ezra* 6–10; *Nehemiah* 1–6, 12.

High Priest to establish a residence in the Temple precincts; and a son of the High Priest had married a daughter of Sanballat. Many others married foreign wives; and the children could not speak their father's tongue. Levites were not receiving their dues, and were therefore deserting their posts and spreading through the country. Labour and traffic profaned the sabbath.

Nehemiah returned and dealt sternly with these derelictions. He expelled Tobiah from the Temple precincts, throwing his goods out after him, and requiring the priests to reconsecrate the place. He chased the son-in-law of Sanballat from the country, whipped others that had married foreign women, and exacted from them an oath that their children would not follow their evil example. He recalled the Levites, required them to purify themselves, and posted them at the city gates, to see that no traffic passed through on the sabbath. When traders squatted outside the closed gates, Nehemiah drove them away with threats; and soon "came they no more on the sabbath." [10]

With Nehemiah's account of his "purge" of Jerusalem, his vivid memoirs close; and for us the curtain falls upon the community, not to rise again until the arrival from Babylonia, a generation later, of a priest-scribe Ezra, some of whose memoirs also are preserved in the books of *Ezra* and *Nehemiah*.[11]

We cannot determine what precisely was Ezra's position and authority at Jerusalem; but he brought with him and promulgated a still more elaborate code of laws. Much of *Deuteronomy* was now out of date, because unsuited to conditions in both the Dispersion and the new Judah. Its social ethics and humanitarianism, less important at any time to the

---

[10] *Neh.* 13.

[11] The author of *Chronicles, Ezra,* and *Nehemiah,* commonly called the Chronicler, making use of the memoirs of Ezra and Nehemiah but writing long afterwards, is confused as to the order of events. He sometimes represents Ezra and Nehemiah as contemporaries and collaborators, whereas there is no mention of Ezra in the memoirs of Nehemiah. Elsewhere the Chronicler makes Ezra precede Nehemiah; and this is further suggested by the order of the books in the Old Testament. A careful examination of the whole material of the Chronicler leads to the conclusion that Ezra is later than Nehemiah; and this is confirmed by certain of what are known as the Asswan, or Assuan, papyri. These are documents from a military colony of Jews in south Egypt, living partly at Asswan, partly on the neighbouring island of Jeb, or Elephantiné, on the Nile. The documents cover the fifth century B.C., are written by Jews in Aramaic, like the language of Ezra; and the communities are under Persian rule.

The weight of the evidence is that Nehemiah came first to Jerusalem in 444 B.C., the twentieth year of Artaxerxes I; and Ezra in 397 B.C., the seventh year of Artaxerxes II.

priest-scribes than the rules for worship, may well have seemed almost irrelevant now, as such matters were dealt with by the Persian governors. The legislation of Ezekiel, too, was rather a dream, or ideal, than a practical scheme of organization. It was influential, but had not been made canonical. There was room for a new edition of "the law of Moses," providing further safeguards for the sanctity of the Temple and the racial purity of the population. The guild of scribes in Babylonia had been engaged in the work; and Ezra now appeared in Jerusalem, with a large following, to promulgate the new laws.

The people were assembled to "the broad place that was before the water gate"; and Ezra brought forth "the book of the law of Moses" and "read therein . . . from early morning until midday." The people wept to hear that they and their fathers, during all the centuries since the first entrance into Canaan, had disregarded a divine law. A second day the reading was continued; and "they found written in the law, how that Jehovah had commanded by Moses, that the children of Israel should dwell in booths in the feast of the seventh month." This feast of booths, or tabernacles, they thought, had been neglected until now. So the people brought branches of trees and bushes, and "made themselves booths, every one upon the roof of his house, and in their courts, and in the courts of the house of God, and in the broad place of the water gate, and in the broad place of the gate of Ephraim." The people confessed the sins of their national history, and entered into a covenant to "walk in God's law, which was given by Moses," to avoid marriage with the people of the land, to refuse trade with them on the sabbath and on holy days, to observe each seventh year as a sabbath for the land, to pay annually a poll tax and tithes for the maintenance of the Temple services, the priests and the Levites.[12]

The "book of the law of Moses," thus brought from Babylonia and published at Jerusalem, seems to have been what is known among modern scholars as the Priests' Code, and comprises most of the legal section of the Pentateuch. It is the last important codification of law in the development of Judaism; and is the second, as *Deuteronomy* is the first, Bible of the Jews.[13]

[12] *Neh.* 8–10.

[13] It in turn became part of a larger work, which opens with the first verse of *Genesis,* interprets creation itself in such a way as to make the Jewish sabbath a divine institution, describes the history of the Hebrews as a supernatural preparation for Judaism, and carries

With the promulgation of the Priests' Code the legal system of Judaism was completed; and the ideals of Ezekiel were triumphant. The Temple sacrifices were increased and enlarged, and the people undertook to provide more liberally for the Temple priesthood. Ezra, more exacting than even Nehemiah, required that all existing mixed marriages be dissolved; and some hundreds of foreign wives were sent away. The community became fixed in the policy of racial and religious exclusiveness; though that policy continued to call forth some protests, as two writings of the Old Testament indicate. The *Book of Ruth* is a liberal tract, reminding Jews that Ruth, an alien from Moab, had adopted the country and religion of the Hebrew Naomi, and through her filial devotion had become foundress of the royal Davidic line. Similarly the wonderful *Book of Jonah* is a parable, in which Jonah is Israel, who is recalled to the mission assigned her by Deutero-Isaiah, of carrying to the nations the knowledge of God. And indeed priests themselves, even high priests, sometimes abandoned the policy of exclusiveness; but that policy prevailed. In Judah "the people of the land" continued to the end a despised people. Union of the Jews with the Samaritans also became impossible, the final breach coming a century after Nehemiah. The governor of Samaria under Darius III, another Sanballat, gave his daughter in marriage to Manasseh, brother of the High Priest at Jerusalem. The leaders there demanded the annulment of the marriage. Manasseh refused. Instead he removed to Samaria, where Sanballat built him a temple on Mt. Gerizim, and secured from the Persian king his appointment as high priest there. The schism between Jew and Samaritan thus became permanent.[14]

We must now enquire more particularly concerning the essential nature of Judaism. What is that mysterious inner strength that has enabled it to endure the most terrible vicissitudes, and to outlive the empires to which it so often seemed an insignificant and irritating fanaticism? Part of the answer is that Judaism grew out of a great per-

the whole sacrificial system of Judaism back to Moses, to whom it was revealed by God Himself. The larger work, combining the Priests' Code with a history, is known among scholars as the Priestly Document, and designated by the symbol *P*.

[14] More conservative in one regard than the Jews, the Samaritans never admitted to their sacred scriptures any other writings than the Pentateuch; and today, nineteen centuries after the cessation of sacrifices at Jerusalem, the sacrifices prescribed in the Pentateuch are still offered on Mt. Gerizim.

sonal experience. In this it is like the other higher religions of the world. The founders of religions all pass first through a spiritual crisis; and however differently they interpret it, they all know that at that moment they sense the final truth of life. They speak the truth they have sensed; disciples gather; the experience is repeated in them; an establishment grows up; a new religion is launched.

This is what happened in Judaism. It arose upon foundations laid in the experience and teaching of Moses. In the flaming outbursts of Mt. Sinai and the earthquake shudders that ran through the land of Midian, Moses felt a presence that disturbed and awakened him. Here was a power before which man was helpless and with which he must come to terms, a power that all the gods of Egypt could not tame. The inhabitants of Midian attributed the phenomena of volcanic eruption and earth-quake to the emotions and activities of Yahweh, a storm god. Moses did not reject their conclusion; but in essence his experience was that of communion with the Universe and appeal to the Universe from the decisions of men and circumstances. This is an element of all human experience on the most effective levels, life is there renewed by daily contact with the Universal.

This element of nature mysticism never quite failed in Judaism. If it was seldom dominant, it was always present, in a few seers and poets, and in humble folk whom we do not know. And when the altars reeked most with blood, or the stench of social injustice was in the nostrils of men, there was always someone to call them back to the elemental— "Seek not Bethel, nor enter into Gilgal, and pass not to Beer-sheba: . . . seek him that maketh the Pleiades and Orion, and turneth the shadow of death into the morning, and maketh the day dark with night; that calleth for the waters of the sea, and poureth them out upon the face of the earth."

Another enduring element was built into the foundations of Judaism when Moses concentrated all his devotion upon Yahweh, invoking him as the deity of the Hebrews. If Yahweh would lead the Hebrews out of Egypt, and protect them on the way, the Hebrews would worship only Yahweh and do his will alone. This solemn undertaking Moses embodied in a covenant. It was a greater event than Moses himself knew. It opened a door of escape from the moral and political confusion of polytheism, with its many gods and their conflicting wills. It is true that monotheism came slowly; but in time men came to believe that there is but one God in all the Universe. His will, they saw, is the final law for all men, His approval the highest good of all. This probably became the faith of most Jews before the Exile closed.

One result of the emergence of monotheism was a distinctive doctrine of sin. The religious life under polytheism tended to be an elaborate matching of wits with the capricious powers that sustained or menaced the lives of men; and misfortunes were attributed to neglect of the ritual or a wrong technique in its use. There was something of this in Judaism also; but that was an aberration of priests. Through all legal developments there persisted, as an inheritance from Moses, a sense of sin as national disloyalty to a beneficent Deity, whose will for his people was only their good, and who was wounded by their disloyalties. "My people are bent on backsliding from me. . . . How shall I give thee up, Ephraim? . . . Mine heart is turned within me. . . . O Israel, return unto the Lord thy God." [15]

When the national life was interrupted, the sin of individuals came to be similarly regarded; it was a personal offending against a personal Deity, who himself had always been compassionate and understanding. This was of great moral consequence. For sin so regarded is not irreparable; broken personal relations can be restored by repentance and forgiveness.

Here is something that was lacking, not only in the crassness of polytheism but even in the higher thought life of Greece, where wrongdoing tended to be conceived as lack of conformity to Nature. For such lack there was no forgiveness; even future amendment could be no more than the salvaging of so much of life as remained. The Jew had far more. Confession and forgiveness were open to sensitive souls.

> I acknowledged my sin unto thee, and mine iniquity have I not hid:
> I said, I will confess my transgressions unto the Lord;
> And thou forgavest the iniquity of my sin.   Psalm 32: 5

Another and strange result of the emergence of monotheism is that the Jews came to think of themselves as an elect people, dearer to God than other peoples, and having a unique national destiny. That is to say, having become monotheists, they advanced their own god Yahweh to

[15] *Hosea* 11: 7, 8.

the throne of the Universe, and interpreted their ancient covenant with Yahweh as a covenant with God. Marduk and Ishtar, Isis and Serapis, were no more; but Yahweh was God, and they were still his people.

Nothing contributed more to the enduring strength of Judaism than this doctrine of an elect nation. As well in exile or in the Ghetto as in Palestine, the Jew was the favourite child of heaven. All nations would yet acknowledge it. The Jew could wait.[16] He still waits. Disciplined by misfortune, educated in endurance, he is still God's chosen and Palestine his promised land, though the Jew has held independent sovereignty there only one century since Ezekiel and Ezra.[17]

Another element of strength in Judaism, an inheritance from Moses, is the conviction that the will of God is wholly moral. Doing the will of God is to honour father and mother, to avoid murder and adultery and theft, to give no false testimony nor otherwise to wrong one's brother man. It was to this Moses had pledged Israel in his covenant with Yahweh. The greatest prophets of later centuries were in no doubt about it. Even the jurists, who gave Israel the later editions of the Law of Moses, did not consciously depart from his teaching that the will of Yahweh is wholly moral. They thought of their successive codes—the Book of the Covenant, the Deuteronomic Code, the Code of Ezekiel, the Code of Holiness, the Priests' Code of Ezra—as faithful elaborations of the Law of Moses, to meet new times and circumstances. When at last all these codes were brought together into one compendium of Jewish legislation and history, the Pentateuch, the scribes quite honestly described it as the Five Books of Moses. They intended it to be so.

The moral earnestness that lay at the heart of Judaism, obscured by successive schools of jurists, was later to be brought to the surface by hard necessity. Jews of the Dispersion could not fulfil the ritual requirements of the Law. Perforce they stressed its more domestic and social features. When at last the Temple sank in flames, never to rise again, and the

[16] Nothing works more powerfully to keep the Jews alive and separate than this sense of being a unique, a chosen people. Beside a religious faith so exalted and so ancient, the Nordic myth and the British-Israel myth must appear to Jews as bastard upstarts, as indeed they are. Nevertheless the Jewish doctrine of a chosen people is a social handicap; it tends to a certain arrogance and acquisitiveness, an insensitiveness to the rights of others, that makes very many Jews social misfits.

[17] The heart of the British problem in Palestine is that Jews still think of Palestine as a land given them by God, while the Arabs won it in a crusade, a holy war, for Allah. To the Arab it may well seem that Allah's gift of Palestine has been confirmed by twelve centuries of unbroken occupancy.

Temple worship was outlawed, Jews everywhere could yet fall back on the ethical ideals of Judaism. Then the Graeco-Roman world became aware of the diligence of the Jew, his personal purity, the dignity of his domestic life, his sensitive regard for childhood. These things tended to make the Jew a stable element in a dissolving world.

Moreover, if the Law overlaid and obscured for centuries the ethical idealism of Moses and the prophets, it did provide the Jews with a discipline. Here was the will of God, set forth in explicit, if exacting, terms. Doing the will of God, and doing it together, the Jews acquired an *esprit de corps* such as the legal decisions of Mahomet, under Jewish influence, gave to the armies of Islam centuries later.

The regulative institution of Judaism was the Law; and it was not complete even when the Pentateuch was finished. For the scribes were always busy, interpreting, elaborating, applying. So that the authoritative Law received an authoritative interpretation, which grew from generation to generation, until it covered the smallest details of life and duty. This authoritative interpretation is that "tradition of the elders," which one meets in the New Testament. Taught in the synagogues, it was discussed in the streets and in the homes, and pondered by devout men "in the night watches."

Two other institutions were also focal points of Judaism. These were the Temple and the synagogue. The Temple had been the one legitimate centre of public worship in pre-exilic Judah, after the reformation under Josiah. During the Exile there was no temple, and it was possible that it might never rise again; for Jeremiah taught that no temple was necessary to the right worship of Yahweh. But Judaism, as we have seen, followed the priest Ezekiel. Jerusalem, he declared, would rise again, and the Temple be again the one centre of public worship. The High Priest would be the head of the community, indeed of the whole nation; for the Dispersion would also look to him. Three times a year all adult male Jews would make the ancient pilgrimages to Jerusalem. They would present the offerings prescribed in the Law, and participate in the feasts of the Passover and Pentecost, commemorating the exodus from Egypt and the giving of the Law on Sinai, and the feast of Tabernacles, in thanksgiving for the harvest.

But a religion centring in the Temple could never be wholly effective.

It would be impossible for many Jews in Egypt and Babylonia, and difficult for many in Judah, to come thrice a year to Jerusalem. And so there arose the synagogue, we hardly know when or how, to be a second centre of Judaism. In time every city and village had one or more synagogues, where the faithful met for prayer and praise and for instruction in the Law. And the religious exercises in the synagogues gradually overshadowed the sacrificial ceremonial at Jerusalem. The synagogue was close to common life, and it was democratic. The Ruler of the Synagogue was a layman; and he could ask whom he would to take part in the service. People heard the Pentateuch and the Prophets read aloud, and made comprehensible to all. So that unconsciously Temple and synagogue became rivals. The priest in the Temple was supplanted in popular esteem by the scribe, a student and teacher of the Scriptures, a layman and a democrat, as close to the people as the priest was aloof. Judaism became an ancient Protestantism, the religion of a book, under the leadership of the scribes.

The two religious observances by which the Jew was most easily distinguished from his Gentile neighbours were circumcision and the observance of the Sabbath. Circumcision had been an ancient tribal mark, common to the whole group of peoples to which Israel belonged; but Judaism explained it as the sign of an ancient covenant with God, the neglect of which deserved death. In time Judaism came to think it celestial in origin. The higher orders of angels, Jews said, were created circumcised. As for the Sabbath, it seems to have been at first a lunar festival. In *Deuteronomy* it became an institution of social relief, a day of rest for man and beast. In Judaism it was explained as an ancient institution, appointed by Yahweh to be a distinguishing mark of Israel; and violation of the Sabbath was to be punished by death. Judaism made circumcision and the observance of the Sabbath a sort of minimum of piety, without which one had no standing whatever in Israel.

Such was the religion built up during the Exile, and put into effect among the restored community in Jerusalem and Judah. It became the religion of the Jew everywhere.

Little is known of the history of Judah during the century after Nehemiah and Ezra. It must have been a time of social distress. The cleavage between Jews and "the people of the land" would continue to divide

society; and the fostering power of Persia was failing. She was engaged
in a long struggle with Egypt. Battles were fought in Syria; and armies
marched through Judah. Then came the Greek menace. A successful revolt of the Greek cities of Asia Minor, and Greek victories at Marathon,
Thermopylae and Salamis, had long since saved the Greek world from
Persia. Now Hellenism, under Macedonian leadership, was itself aggressive and carrying the war into Asia. And there was no Cyrus, no Darius
the Great, to lead Persian resistance. So Persia fell an easy prey to
Alexander the Great. His victory at the river Granicus, 334 B.C., breached
the walls of the Persian Empire. In an incredibly short time Greek
arms had triumphed on the Euphrates, the Tigris and the Nile. The
whole Persian Empire lay prostrate. Judah and the Jewish Dispersion
once more changed masters; and the policy of the new master, unlike
that of Persia, was to establish Greek life everywhere. This policy of
Hellenization was not checked by the untimely death of Alexander
the Great. Though his empire speedily fell apart, his generals still ruled
in all parts of the old Persian dominions, the Ptolemies in Egypt, the
Seleucids in Asia.

Greek civilization, in the age of the Ptolemies and the Seleucids, was
not far past its Golden Age. The Jews could not rival the Greeks in
philosophy, the sciences, or the arts. They had no Pericles in the science
of government, no historian like Herodotus, no architect like Ictinus, no
sculptor like Phidias. In most of the arts of civilization the Jews were a
backward people. This had not mattered so long as Jew and Greek lived
far apart; but the conquests of Alexander the Great brought Greek
civilization forcibly to the attention of the Jews. Centres of Greek culture
sprang up on all sides of Judah. Antioch and Alexandria, great new
cities, were Greek. Jews traded with them, settled in them, acquired
citizenship, adopted Greek habits, took Greek names, spoke the Greek
language. In Egyptian Jewry the change was so complete that the Scriptures would have become a closed book to Jews, had they not been translated into Greek, the Septuagint.

Judah herself could not continue immune. She had to trade with
Antioch and Alexandria. And Jews of the Dispersion, revisiting Judah,
brought back the ways of the Greeks. The Seleucids planted Greek
cities in Palestine, and Hellenized existing ones. In the cities Greek tended
to become the language of the people; and Hebrew, long since displaced

in common speech by Aramaic, was in danger of becoming obsolete. In Jerusalem itself a gymnasium arose, where Jewish youths indulged in Greek games and discussed every new thing, like the Greeks.

Judaism, already in uneasy relations with "the people of the land" and the Samaritans, was itself sharply divided by Hellenism. On one side were the Sadducees, or Zadokites, who seem to have received their name from Zadok, the High Priest of Solomon's temple, in whose family the office became hereditary sometime after the Exile. The Persian kings had granted the High Priests considerable authority. They were therefore in some degree secular rulers, and their families a Jewish aristocracy. They and the priests, who grew rich from the tithes and offerings prescribed in the Law, soon lost the zeal that had produced Judaism. They became a thoroughly worldly party, the Sadducees. Their natural affinity was for any power to which they could look for the security of their privileges. They cultivated the favour of Persia during the Persian period; they now cultivated the Seleucids. And with them stood the Sanhedrin (Greek *Sunedrion*), an aristocratic body of priests and elders, which acted with the High Priest in the rule of the Jewish community.

More closely in touch with the people were the scribes, a body of lay teachers or Rabbis, as we have seen, expounding the Law in the synagogues. As the Sadducees became worldly, the scribes took up the work of the ancient prophets. They were the new defenders of the true worship of God against Hellenic innovations; and many of them, with their disciples, became a sort of Puritan party, the *Chasidim,* or Pious, greatly respected by the masses of the people.

The influence of the synagogues and the Chasidim could not stop the advance of Hellenism. Within a century of the death of Alexander the Great all the Orient had yielded to Greek influence except Judah; and her submission seemed imminent. The charm of Greek life was felt everywhere. There was that, too, in the higher thought life of Greece that was consonant with the best that the Hebrew prophets had reached. Stoics and Epicureans both taught that there is a Law of Nature, and a duty that is laid upon all men, without regard to national boundaries. The theology of the great prophets had tended in that direction.

Persecution saved Judaism. Antiochus Epiphanes, Seleucid king of Syria, half genius and half madman, became impatient of Jewish conservatism and determined to hurry the assimilation of Jewish to Greek

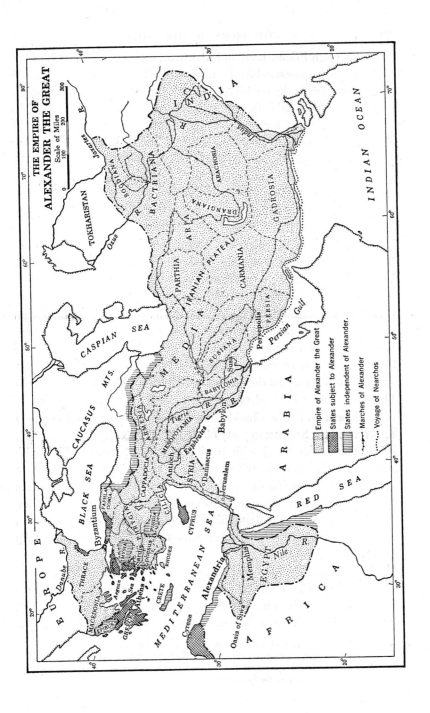

THE EMPIRE OF
ALEXANDER THE GREAT

Scale of Miles
0   100   200   300

Empire of Alexander the Great
States subject to Alexander
States independent of Alexander.
Marches of Alexander
Voyage of Nearchos

EUROPE

THRACE

MACEDONIA

EPIRUS

GREECE

Athens

Aegean Sea

CRETE

Byzantium

BLACK SEA

PAPHLAGONIA

BITHYNIA

PHRYGIA

Sardis

LYDIA

CARIA

RHODES

CYPRUS

MEDITERRANEAN SEA

Cyrene

Alexandria

CAUCASUS MTS.

CASPIAN SEA

ARMENIA

CAPPADOCIA

CILICIA

Antioch

SYRIA

Damascus

Jerusalem

MESOPOTAMIA

Tigris

Euphrates

BABYLONIA

Babylon R.

Susa

SUSIANA

PERSIA

Persepolis

Persian Gulf

MEDIA

PARTHIA

IRANIAN PLATEAU

CARMANIA

ARIA

DRANGIANA

ARACHOSIA

GADROSIA

BACTRIA

SOGDIANA

Oxus R.

Jaxartes R.

TOKHARISTAN

INDIA

PERSIA

Indus R.

ARABIA

RED SEA

Nile R.

Memphis

EGYPT

Oasis of Siwa

AFRICA

INDIAN OCEAN

life. Two High Priests, Jesus and Menelaus, co-operated. The Chasidim and the synagogues stood in the way. So Antiochus determined, in 168 B.C., to exterminate the Jewish religion. He forbade circumcision and the observance of the Sabbath, abolished Jewish worship, erected heathen altars in the cities of Judah, and converted the Temple into a temple of Zeus. Jerusalem was turned into a Greek city, and a Syrian garrison placed in the citadel to discourage resistance. Royal officers traversed the country, enforcing the law. Many Jews deserted their faith; many others, especially the Chasidim, chose martyrdom. They were whipped; they were torn to pieces. Mothers were crucified, their strangled infants hanging about their necks.

Persecution only increased the devotion of the Chasidim to the Law. Their devotion found expression also in a new anonymous literature of visions and prophecies, written to encourage the faithful with explanations of the present distresses and pictures of a glorious future.[18]

At length rebellion flared up. At Modin an aged priest, Mattathias, an Asmonaean, or descendant of Asmon, when commanded to offer sacrifices to Zeus, slew the king's officers and fled with his five sons to the mountains. There they were joined by other men zealous for the Law. Mattathias died and left the leadership to his son Judas the Maccabee, or Hammer. Under his leadership the Asmonaeans (later called Maccabees), supported by the Chasidim, made war upon the Seleucid power of Syria and the Sadducean party of the High Priest.

Fortunately for the Jewish patriots, Syria was pre-occupied with Persia and distracted by civil war. Fifteen years the Asmonaeans kept up the fight. Judas fell fighting in 161 B.C.; but his brother Jonathan stepped into his place. In time Jonathan became ruler of a united Palestine, in alliance with the Republic of Rome. The Maccabean power was firmly consolidated by his brother Simon, and by Simon's son, John Hyrcanus, 135–106 B.C.

The success of the Maccabean revolt advanced the cause of the synagogue and the Chasidim. It was they that had aroused the people to resistance, when the High Priest held aloof or supported the alien. Thenceforth the Temple became subordinate to the synagogue, the

[18] This literature is part of what is now called *The Inter-Testamental Literature*. It is apocalyptic. That is, it attempts to remove the veil of the future and reveal the destiny of the world, of the Jewish nation, of the individual. It is thus eschatological as well; for eschatology is the doctrine of the last things.

priest to the scribe. The Temple services continued because they were prescribed in the Law; but the emphasis had shifted, and the priestly cultus was overshadowed by the study and practice of the more personal and domestic features of the Law.

As this tendency advanced, there arose within the Chasidim a new party, the Pharisees. They were a fraternity, calling themselves simply *Chaberim,* neighbours. Admission was by the laying on of hands. Their aim was perfect righteousness; that is, the perfect performance of the Law and "the tradition of the elders." What the scribes and Chasidim were experts in interpreting, they would be expert in doing. Outwardly the Pharisees were noticeable by reason of their scrupulous avoidance of whatever the Law regarded as unclean. They removed chance defilements by frequent washings, of themselves, of their garments, of the dishes they used. They avoided all contact with "the people of the land," who still lived outside the Law or in very loose relations with it. They were "the separated ones." Indeed, the word "Pharisees" is the Hebrew *Perushim,* the separated. In them the legalism of Ezekiel bore its finest fruit. They were the saints of Judaism.

The scribes and Pharisees put their trust in the Maccabees. If the Maccabees should fail them, they would be again as that desolate but faithful minority that had wept by the waters of Babylon. And the Maccabees did fail them, turning gradually from religious idealism to worldliness and political scheming, until civil war between Maccabean princes gave Rome an excuse for intervention. Most of Asia Minor had already fallen to her arms; and her great general Pompey was now stamping out resistance in the Seleucid kingdom. He came into Palestine in 63 B.C., received the submission of Jerusalem and stormed the Temple, the last centre of resistance. He put an end to the Maccabean monarchy, and set up a High Priest, subordinate to the Roman governor of Syria.

Once more Jewish independence was lost, and the hopes of Jewish idealists defeated. A new Jewish Dispersion began, this time through the Latin West. Jewish communities spread along all trade routes. Jewish quarters sprang up in the cities. The synagogue appeared in Rome itself. The purity of Jewish life, and the monotheism taught in the synagogues, attracted earnest men everywhere. Disliking the Jew, they were nevertheless drawn to his faith; and Judaism in adversity became, rather unwillingly, a missionary religion.

In Judaea, as the Romans called Judah, authority fell into the hands of Antipater, son of a governor of Idumea under the Maccabees. Antipater had been useful to Julius Caesar, in his struggle with Pompey for control of the Roman world, a struggle largely fought out in Syria and Palestine; and on Caesar's triumph Antipater was made procurator of Judaea. When he died by poison, his son Herod was made king of all Palestine. Herod was Semitic enough to understand Jewish prejudices, and politic enough to work with the Roman authorities. He seemed best fitted to stand on Rome's eastern frontier, facing the Parthians.

The reign of Herod the Great, 40–3 B.C., is important for the history of Judaism. He began a magnificent new temple, in place of the modest post-Exilic structure; and he respected its sanctity. He was adroit enough to cultivate Pharisaic good will, as a means of conciliating the masses. It served his purposes to reduce the old Sadducean aristocracy to harmlessness; so he quarrelled with the Sadducees and broke their power, by executing forty-five leaders and confiscating their property. There were material services also, for which Herod could justly expect public gratitude. He reduced the taxes, suppressed the numerous robber bands, kept the frontiers secure, and improved the water supply of Jerusalem.

But there were activities of quite another sort. Herod was an eager Hellenist, with a flair for Roman magnificence; and he set out to rival Augustus himself as a builder. He built a splendid new city on the seacoast, which he named Caesarea in honour of the Emperor, and another in his honour at Sebaste. He built Antipatris and Phasaelis in the Jordan valley, naming them in honour of his own father and brother. He rebuilt Samaria, which John Hyrcanus had rased to the ground, for its sympathy with Syria against the Maccabean cause. He made Jerusalem the finest city of the East, but a Graeco-Roman city, with a theatre and an amphitheatre, where games were celebrated quadrennially in honour of Augustus. And so throughout all Palestine. Heathen temples arose in Jewish cities, and colonnades, all the outward marks of Graeco-Roman life; and the non-Jewish population, at home in this new Palestine, steadily increased.

In the end such a policy could only affront the Jews; and Herod prepared against revolt by establishing fortified posts throughout the country. Pious Jews were distressed. The enmities of Jew and Gentile increased. Some sentiment for the Asmonaeans survived. They were at least Jews, and recalled the brief glory of the Maccabean adventure. One by one Herod accomplished their death. An Asmonaean princess, beautiful Mariamne, had become Herod's wife; but her cold contempt enraged his family and encouraged false accusations concerning her faithfulness. Herod took her life, and thereafter became subject to fits of melancholy, when a sort of madness and blood-thirst possessed him. In old age he became thoroughly intolerant. Jewish feelings were inflamed; and among the Pharisees there arose a party of violence, the Zealots. No Messiah had come, no kingdom of God by peaceful means; the Zealots would again try revolution.

Herod received from Augustus permission to bequeath his kingdom, and left it to his three surviving sons. Archelaus became king of Judaea, which Augustus soon extended to include Samaria and Idumea. Herod Antipas became tetrarch of Galilee and Perea. Philip became tetrarch of certain remote districts north and east of the Sea of Galilee, which had been conquered by the Asmonaeans or given by Augustus to Herod the Great. Interspersed through the two tetrarchies was a federation of Graeco-Roman cities, the Decapolis, like those leagues of free cities in Europe in the Middle Ages. The cities of the Decapolis were centres of a vigorous anti-Semitism.

King Archelaus was a worthless fellow; and the Kingdom of Judaea soon fell into anarchy. The Pharisees demanded a theocracy, under the scribes. The Jewish population broke into rebellion and seized the Temple. Its cloisters were fired to expel them; and the defenders perished in the flames. The revolt was crushed, and two thousand Jews executed. So great was the disorder and distress that chief men carried an appeal to Augustus at Rome; and Archelaus was banished to Gaul, 6 A.D., where he died.

The kingdom of Archelaus now became the Roman province of Judaea, ruled by a procurator at Caesarea. The people were required to take the oath of allegiance to the Emperor. High Priests were appointed and removed by the procurator, and thus became tools of the governing power. The Sanhedrin at Jerusalem was required to raise the Roman tribute; and local Sanhedrins, in the eleven toparchies into which the country was divided, collected the taxes for the Roman officers. The customs were farmed out to collectors, the Publicans. But in all this, regard was had to Jewish sensibilities; and daily life among the Jews was

little affected by the Roman administration. The Sabbath was officially
recognized, and the sanctity of the Temple guaranteed. The Jerusalem
Sanhedrin, seventy-two men of pure Jewish blood, was respected. It was
under the presidency of the High Priest, and members of the high-
priestly families took precedence; but most of the members were Pharisees, and this increased its moral authority. The Sanhedrin was the
supreme court, for the trial of all cases coming under the Mosaic Law.

But whether in the tetrarchies of Herod Antipas and Philip, or in
Judaea under the procurators, the Jews were unhappy. The situation was
particularly strained in Judaea. The foreign procurators were less en-
durable than the family of Herod, who as Edomites were at least descendants of Abraham through Esau, and were therefore kinsmen of the
Jews. Besides, Roman policy, though generous in intention, was sometimes defeated by the procurators. Rome was often badly served by her
representatives, and never more so than in Palestine, where their task
was particularly difficult and the population particularly disliked. One of
the early procurators, Pontius Pilate, 26–36 A.D., treated the Jews with
contempt. He provoked frequent riots, and crushed them mercilessly.
Executions were frequent, sometimes wholesale. The Samaritans complained at last to Vitellius, governor of Syria; and Pilate was sent to Rome
for trial and condemned. Things were a little better when, in 41 A.D., the
Emperor Claudius gave Judaea to Herod Agrippa I, a grandson of
Herod the Great and Mariamne. He had already received the two
tetrarchies, on the death of Philip and the banishment of Herod Antipas.
So that once more there was a king of the Jews, whose dominion in-
cluded all Palestine. But Herod Agrippa died in 44 A.D.; and then all
Palestine came under procurators, usually corrupt and violent men. They
dealt with troublesome patriots by the method of wholesale crucifixion;
and some patriots degenerated into common assassins, the *Sicarii,* or
Dagger Men. Society was disintegrating. The Jewish community in
Palestine was moving to its doom.

There were religious enthusiasts who thought it was not so. They
were very sure of God; and they still refuse to doubt that He had a gracious purpose for Israel. Their dauntless faith broke forth in new forms of
prophecy. It had always been so. The prophets had been called forth by
national perils or national sufferings. At such times thoughtful men are
thrown back on the ultimate questions of life; and those among them

who receive light and give guidance are the prophets. So here in Israel's final crisis. Men tried to interpret the present and forecast the future; and that literature of vision and prophecy of which we have spoken (p. 50) continued to appear, from the time of Antiochus Epiphanes until the close of the first Christian century. It was the answer of earnest men to such questions as these: Were the national hopes of the past vain, and the promises of the prophets an illusion? Why has Israel suffered beyond other peoples? And why do the righteous within Israel suffer with the unrighteous? Is it well with the righteous dead? Has God any plan for the world?

It was the pressure of questions like these that produced the Inter-Testamental Literature. In its visions the last end of the righteous, of the Jewish nation, of mankind, of the world itself, is disclosed. The literature is sometimes anonymous, because it was dangerous to the author to make himself known; it is sometimes pseudonymous, to attract attention. Since revelation was thought to be complete in the Law, a writer would not be accepted as inspired unless writing under the name of some ancient worthy who had been thought inspired. So the Inter-Testamental Literature is usually cast in the form of visions, or apocalypses, given to Enoch and Noah and Baruch and Ezra. The earliest of these apocalypses, the *Book of Daniel*, was admitted to the Old Testament. Others are in the Apocrypha. Still others, some of them now seen to be very important, are I *Enoch*, II *Enoch*, *The Testaments of the Twelve Patriarchs*, *The Psalms of Solomon*, and II *Baruch*.

The Apocalyptists were like the wise of all ages in their refusal to disbelieve in the goodness of God; for faith in the goodness of God, whether He is conceived as the One or the Many or the Universe itself, is as necessary to the good life as is the scientist's faith in the rationality of the Universe. Indeed faith in the goodness that lies at the heart of things, and faith in their rationality, are two sides of the same thing. When, however, men try to imagine how the Divine goodness will manifest itself, they can think only in such forms as their blood, their religion, their history and their present tragedies suggest. Some of the expectations of the Apocalyptists were weird, lurid, impossible. Indeed much of Jewish apocalypticism is prophecy in hysterics.

Apocalypticism, however, was an advance on Old Testament teaching in this, that the Apocalyptists worked out a philosophy of world history, where Old Testament writers tended to be satisfied with an explanation of Jewish history. And there are other doctrines, either new or differently developed, in the Apocalyptists.[19] The first is the doctrine of personal immortality. In the Old Testament the dead pass to Sheol, the shadowy home of all departed souls, where they drag out a semi-conscious existence which is hardly existence, and where no providence of Yahweh can reach them (*Psalm* 88: 3–5). The doctrine of a blessed hereafter does not appear in the Old Testament until the *Book of Job,* about 400 B.C., and a very few Psalms of late date. It is a minority view, and it is late. In the Inter-Testamental writings, however, a confident faith in personal immortality appears.

The Apocalyptists differ also from Old Testament thinkers concerning the kingdom of God. The Hebrew prophets had thought of it as a Golden Age for the nation, when king and people would be blessed because wholly obedient at last to Yahweh. That would be a true kingdom of Yahweh, encompassed by his law, obeying his living voice through the prophets. The kingdom would then endure forever; and its citizens would live lives of patriarchal duration. Such teaching, however, offers nothing to those already dead; and so the early Apocalyptists enlarge the doctrine. The kingdom of God will include the righteous dead, whom God will call from the grave, to enjoy the kingdom with their brethren. This teaching is everywhere in the writings of the second century B.C., supporting the faith of those who face martyrdom under Antiochus Epiphanes and later.

In all this there are many differences in detail. Some thought that God would set up the kingdom suddenly, and with great convulsions in the natural world, stars falling, the earth quaking, the sun obliterated. Others thought He would do so by the gradual transformation of Nature and mankind. Most thought that righteous Gentiles would share the blessings of the kingdom; the finest spirits could no longer exclude all their Gentile neighbours.

In the next century, the last before Christ, great changes came over the Apocalyptists, reflecting the decay of the Maccabees, the new subjec-

---

[19] It may be that these doctrines are not quite original with the Jewish Apocalyptists. Similar doctrines appear in Zoroastrianism, the religion of Persia, under whose protection Judaism grew up. However that may be, the Apocalyptists introduce us to beliefs that are not found in the Old Testament, and that are to meet us again in the New Testament and in Christian history.

tion to Rome, and the general despair. There is no longer hope of a kingdom of God on the earth. There will be instead a temporary kingdom on the earth, under the Messianic king. The resurrection of the dead and the judgment day will take place at its close. Then will come the eternal kingdom of God, in the heavens, to which only the spirits of the dead will rise, not their bodies.

One extraordinary exception appears in the literature of this century, in I *Enoch,* a book that foreshadows more than one doctrine of the New Testament. The author conceives that neither the present earth nor the present heaven is fit for the kingdom of God, which will require a new heaven and a new earth, united in one, in which the righteous will have many mansions, according to their merits. In I *Enoch* is a new conception also of the Messiah. He is here called for the first time the *Son of Man,* which in apocalyptic symbolism generally signifies a being from heaven. Repeated disappointments had brought disillusionment concerning an earthly Messiah; and long contact with Persia and Zoroastrianism had familiarized Jews with the idea of heavenly beings. A Messiah from these heavenly hosts was a possibility.[20]

The author of I *Enoch,* chapters 37–71, looks for such a supernatural Messiah; and he is described in terms that, in the New Testament, are used of Jesus Christ. The Son of Man is "the righteous One," "the Elect One"; he pre-existed from the beginning with God; his dominion is universal; all judgment is committed to him.

The faith of the author was not shared by many of his contemporaries. The Pharisaic party reverted to the hope of a warrior Messiah, of the family of David. He would banish strangers from Jerusalem and destroy ungodly nations by the breath of his mouth. Those that survived would then submit to him. In the *Psalms of Solomon,* also called the *Psalms of the Pharisees,* it is said:

[20] Or there might be no Messiah. He was never so central in Jewish thought as Christians usually assume. The ancient prophets had no difficulty in conceiving the kingdom without the Messiah; and to such as speak of him he is but the ideal king, of the Davidic line, coming very soon. To the Apocalyptists of the second century B.C., Messiah is to be from Levi, the tribe of the Maccabees, because the hopes of the nation are now fixed on them. The debasement of the Maccabees again affected the Messianic hope, and I *Enoch* looks for a supernatural Messiah. But some later Apocalyptists, in the first Christian century, abandon the doctrine of a Messiah and a Messianic kingdom. Their hopes are now fixed on heaven itself, the abode of God. Individual Jews are thinking of their own future, as the nation moves to destruction. This is the case in *Philo,* II *Enoch,* I *Baruch,* IV *Ezra,* and in *Josephus.*

Behold, O Lord, and raise up unto them a king, the Son of David,
At the time in the which Thou seest, O God, that he may reign over Israel
    Thy servant.
And gird him with strength that he may shatter unrighteous rulers,
And that he may purge Jerusalem from nations that trample her down to
    destruction.   47: 23–25

Pharisees inspired by such hopes were committed to political action; and with them stood many of the people.

In such a situation a deliverer might appear in any one of several forms, and adopt any one of several plans. He might raise the standard of revolt. If he were of the family of David, Messianic expectations and enthusiasm would almost certainly be aroused. Indeed Messianic hopes could gather around any man, famed for both prowess and piety. But such a movement would certainly end in disaster. No Maccabee could triumph now. The Caesars were mightier than the Seleucids.

But one might refuse the appeal to force, and reach leadership through a reputation for piety. There were men, even in the most distant Dispersion, who strove after that perfect performance of the Law attempted by the Pharisees, men like Saul of Tarsus and that "Tobit, son of Tobiel," a Jew of Nineveh, who left us the strange apocryphal "Book of Tobit." Such piety was in great repute. To extend it, men thought, would bring in the kingdom of God. There was a saying current among the scribes, "If all Israel keep the Law but a single day, Messiah will come." The difficulty was that society was incapable of such piety. The requirements of the Law were quite beyond most people. Weariness and disillusionment would once more arrive before the kingdom of God.

But, rejecting both military adventures and laborious piety, one might win Jewish society by turning to account the hopes raised by the Apocalyptists, by coming on the clouds, a heavenly being, like the Son of Man of I *Enoch*. Any dramatic or mysterious appearance would carry conviction, if followed by the supernatural signs and wonders expected of a supernatural being. Men were ready to believe that a supernatural ministry would end in an intervention of God himself, the destruction or transformation of the earth, and the establishment of a society of the saints, in a new heaven or a new earth or both. The popular agitation stirred by such hopes would of course be repressed by the Jewish authorities, because it might lead to intervention from Rome and the loss of such autonomy as Israel enjoyed. And, even if unrepressed, such hopes would wear themselves out in time, in weary expectation. God does not intervene in the world apocalyptically.

Finally, one who heard in his soul the call of God, might come as the greatest prophets had come, teaching new truth about life and religion, and inviting men to enter with him by self-dedication into a new society, the kingdom of God. Such a teacher would be feared by the rulers, disliked by the saints, and followed fitfully by the multitude. A few would come to his feet, and lay up his truth in their hearts, and try to express it in deeds. It would be a slow process, which many vicissitudes would delay and only a distant future would vindicate. Meanwhile it would seem a poor, an impossible substitute for the vivid and urgent hopes of the Jews.

The policy of the Zealots, the policy of revolution, prevailed. It was to culminate in the fall of Jerusalem and the destruction of the nation. The final disaster was delayed until 70 A.D., as we shall see. Before it overwhelmed the nation, Jesus of Nazareth had lived and spoken, and the generation that knew him was rapidly passing away.

CHAPTER III

JESUS OF NAZARETH

JESUS OF NAZARETH was born in the last years of Herod the Great, 7–5 B.C. The records of his life may be read by anyone; for practically everything that is to be known is in the four Gospels. There are certain Apocryphal Gospels that tell us a great deal about Jesus; but they do not repay examination. The earliest is perhaps a century later than Jesus; and, with the exception of the *Gospel according to the Hebrews,* none seems to rest on reliable traditions.[1] As for contemporary Greek and Roman historians, they tell us nothing. Jesus' movement was not of the sort in which they were interested.

The writings of most importance for the life of Jesus are the three Synoptic Gospels [2]—*Matthew, Mark* and *Luke.* Of less importance are the Fourth Gospel, *John,* and the Epistles of St. Paul. Paul might have given us considerable information. He was at Jerusalem shortly after the crucifixion of Jesus. He took part in the first systematic effort to suppress Jesus' movement, and was himself converted. He conferred immediately with disciples of Jesus at Damascus, and after three years went up to Jerusalem to consult "James, the Lord's brother." Fourteen years later he was there again with the Apostles, assuring himself as to the accuracy of his own teaching.[3] But Paul was interested chiefly in the crucifixion, resurrection and expected return of Jesus; he tells us nothing of the life of Jesus before Passion Week. As for the Fourth Gospel, it was written later than the Synoptic Gospels, and probably dates from the first decade of the second century. Besides, it is a philosophy, not a biography; and such narrative as it contains conflicts seriously with that of the other Gospels.

[1] These may be read in M. R. James, *The Apocryphal New Testament,* Clarendon Press.
[2] Synoptic means "taking the same view," as contrasted with the Fourth Gospel, which is rather a special thesis about Jesus than a biography.
[3] *Acts* 9: 1–30; *Galatians* 1: 18, 19; 2: 1, 2.

One must look chiefly to the Synoptists therefore; and a serious student ought to read them all together.[4] If *Matthew* and *Luke* are placed in parallel columns, with *Mark* between, one sees that sometimes all three, sometimes two, report the same event or teaching in practically the same words. Sometimes they report the same thing, but in different words and with a different sense. Sometimes only one Gospel reports an event or teaching. The problem presented by these agreements and differences is called the "Synoptic Problem," which is discussed in Appendix III. Here one need only note that New Testament scholars are in general agreement as to the credibility of the Synoptic Gospels. If their authors had little, if any, personal acquaintance with Jesus, they knew those who had. They report in the Gospels what eye-witnesses have told them, together with some little popular tradition, less valuable as evidence.

From these Gospels one learns, as we have said, that Jesus of Nazareth was born in the last years of Herod the Great. His parents, Joseph and Mary, or Miriam, belonged to Nazareth, a village of southern Galilee; but Augustus ordered a census throughout the kingdom of Herod, and this necessitated that Jews go to their native places to register. Joseph and Mary went south for this purpose to Bethlehem, a small city six miles from Jerusalem. There at a khan, or inn, Mary's eldest son was born; and a week later he was called Jesus, a Greek form of Joshua, and a name common among the Jews. Long afterwards it was believed in some circles that Jesus was born without a human father, and that his birth was accompanied by miraculous events. There is no mention of these things in *Mark,* the earliest of the Gospels; nor in the Fourth Gospel. Even *Matthew* and *Luke,* which tell of the virgin birth, trace the genealogy of Jesus through Joseph, not Mary.[5] Joseph belonged to the ancient and royal Davidic line; but his family was one of the many whose genealogical records had been lost.[6] Perhaps that is why Joseph lived in Galilee, not with the exclusive group, or guild, of Davidic families in Jerusalem.

[4] There are numerous "Harmonies" of the Gospels, works in which they are printed side by side. A serviceable one is Stevens and Burton, *A Harmony of the Gospels,* Scribner.

[5] The "virgin birth" appears now to have been the best explanation that simple folk could give, long after the event, of the origin of one who seemed to them to be more than human. New Testament writers do not attach such importance to the manner of Jesus' birth as did the Christian Church later.

[6] The genealogies in *Matthew* and *Luke* cannot be made to agree; but the Davidic descent of Jesus is unquestioned throughout the New Testament.

Shortly before the birth of Jesus, a son, John, was born to Elizabeth, a kinswoman of Mary, whose husband Zacharias was a priest, living in the highlands of Judaea. We are not told that Jesus and John ever saw each other in childhood. They were as widely separated as Galilee and Judaea; and a tradition preserved in *Luke* 1:80 says that John was an anchorite even in childhood, living in that desolate wilderness where the highlands of Judaea run steeply down to the chasm of the Jordan and the Dead Sea. Jesus, however, grew up in the home at Nazareth, which stood in the loveliest district of Palestine, among the hills of Galilee. Four other sons were born to Joseph and Mary—"James and Joses, and Judas and Simon"; and there were at least two sisters. We hear in the Gospels of cousins also; for Mary's sister Salome married Zebedee, a fish merchant doing business around the Lake of Galilee; and their sons, James and John, became disciples of Jesus in manhood.

Only one incident in the life of Jesus is reported, between his infancy and his public ministry. That is a visit to Jerusalem at twelve years of age, the age at which a Jewish boy was regarded as entering upon manhood. Jesus accompanied his parents for the first time, on their annual pilgrimage to Jerusalem to the Feast of the Passover. There the intelligence and devout spirit of the boy attracted the attention of some scribes; and his feeling for the Temple disconcerted his parents. He had taken so seriously the teaching of the synagogues concerning the fatherhood of God that the Temple seemed the house of his Father and the natural place for a boy to stay.

No story has come down to us from the following twenty years, probably because there was little to tell. The stream of his life ran quiet and deep. But some things may be inferred from conditions in Palestine, and some from incidents of his later life. Jesus was apprenticed to his father's trade, that of a carpenter. It was a respected vocation, offering modest independence. While working as a carpenter Jesus was also receiving the normal education of a Jewish boy. Schools were attached to the synagogues; and there boys were introduced to the Old Testament Scriptures. Jesus learned the history of his nation, the great thoughts of the prophets as to her divine mission, the national hymns, the duties enjoined in the Law, and the strange apocalyptic hopes that were beating in the hearts of devout men. He would learn something of the archaic Hebrew language, the language of the Scriptures; but he spoke Aramaic,

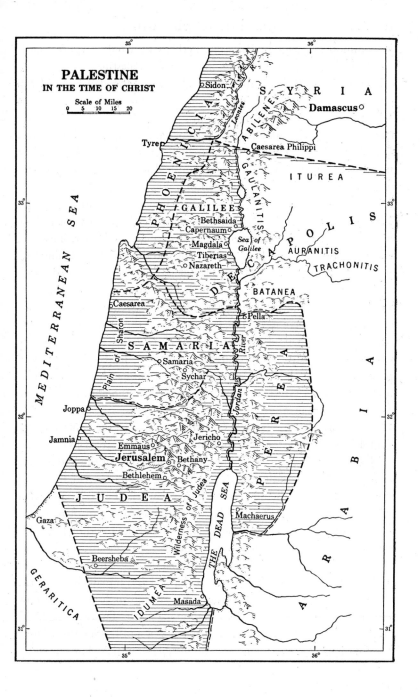

PALESTINE
IN THE TIME OF CHRIST
Scale of Miles
0   5   10   15   20

MEDITERRANEAN SEA

SYRIA

Sidon

Damascus

PHOENICIA

Leontes R.

ABILENE

Tyre

Caesarea Philippi

GAULANITIS

ITUREA

GALILEE

Bethsaida

Capernaum

Sea of Galilee

AURANITIS

Magdala

TRACHONITIS

Tiberias

Nazareth

DECAPOLIS

BATANEA

Caesarea

Pella

Plain of Sharon

SAMARIA

Samaria

Sychar

Jordan River

PEREA

Joppa

Jamnia

Jericho

Emmaus

Jerusalem

Bethany

Bethlehem

Wilderness of Judea

J U D E A

Gaza

THE DEAD SEA

Machaerus

ARABIA

Beersheba

GERARITICA

IDUMEA

Masada

the common language of Palestine. Perhaps he would acquire a little Greek, the language of the Syrian merchants in Palestine.

They were troubled days for the Jews. In the childhood of Jesus, Herod the Great died. The worthless Archelaus then ruled over Samaria, Judaea and Idumea; and his kingdom soon fell into anarchy. Not long before the visit of the boy Jesus to Jerusalem, a Jewish rebellion flamed up and two thousand rebels were executed (p. 53). It was at about the time of the visit that Archelaus was banished by the Emperor; and his kingdom became the Roman province of Judaea, ruled from Caesarea by a procurator, under the general supervision of the Roman governor of Syria. Soon the governor, Quirinius, came to take a census of Judaea, in preparation for the taxes to be paid as tribute to Caesar. This had not been foreseen when Judaeans appealed to the Emperor against Archelaus; and the presence of Gentile officials was hotly resented. Once more Jewish fanaticism blazed up in rebellion, this time under Judas the Galilean and Sadduk, a Pharisee. Once more rebellion was stamped out; but sullen disaffection persisted throughout the country, and tax-gatherers were in bad odour. Throughout Jesus' youth, therefore, Judaea was smarting under the procurators, who met Jewish bigotry with contempt and brutality. Galilee, under Herod Antipas, had some chance for peace; but its Greek cities were centres of anti-Semitism, and disorder was never far off.

No echo of these things breaks the silence in which the youth of Jesus is enfolded; but we know that sometime during these years Joseph died, and Jesus, the eldest son, would become the mainstay of the home. Like the prophet Amos, tending sheep and dressing sycamore trees, he would be engaged, without being absorbed, by his work. There is work that encourages meditation. The work of a village carpenter is of this sort; and the future was to show what thoughts filled the mind of Jesus. He pondered the tragic history of his people, and recalled what the prophets had taught concerning the national destiny. He thought of the Law, the religion of his people, how it fulfilled and how it thwarted the will of God. He thought of the sufferings of the simple poor, and how God must feel as He watched. He thought of the far-away goal, the kingdom of God, for which good men yearned and hot men conspired, and from which foolish men hoped impossible things. As Jesus brooded, saw clearly, and followed the light, there came a deep sense of his own complete accord with God, and a sense that the purposes of God were somehow committed to him for fulfilment.

While Jesus thus brooded, going forward with present duties while awaiting God's call, the call came to his anchorite cousin. John's youth, like that of Jesus, is enveloped in silence. What made him an anchorite we do not know. Perhaps he had been thrilled as a child by the story of that ancient anchorite Elijah, who was justly honoured in Judaism. He doubtless knew those ascetics of his own time in Judaea, the Essenes. They are not mentioned in the New Testament; but the Jewish historian Josephus makes much of them. Whatever the explanation of John's asceticism, he too, in the wilderness, had come to complete identification with the will of God. But God's will never appears the same to the solitary as to the socially minded. The latter, being an observer of human life, may make new discoveries about life and God's will for it. It is the socially minded men, therefore, who lead new movements. When a religious solitary leads a movement, it is a return to the past, not an advance.

So it was with John the Baptist. "In the fifteenth year of the reign of Tiberius Caesar, . . . in the high-priesthood of Annas and Caiaphas, the word of God came unto John the son of Zacharias in the wilderness"; and he came forward as a preacher. The Messiah, John said, was at hand; and the kingdom of God was just round the corner. But to be a Jew would give one no standing with either the one or the other. God could make Jews out of pebbles. Messiah would begin with an act of judgment. Those found righteous would be preserved for the kingdom of God; but the unrighteous would be swept out, like chaff from the threshing floor. John summoned men to his hermitage by the Jordan, to repent and give proof of repentance by submitting to baptism. Men came in great numbers from Jerusalem and Judaea. John scorched them with denunciations of their sins, and searched them for signs of repentance. Without that, they were but as vipers, fleeing before fire in the grass. When penitents asked what they must do, John enjoined common honesty and justice and brotherliness. It was a quite conventional demand. The new thing was the tremendous moral earnestness of the preacher, and the fact that, like most of the prophets, John concentrated upon the moral requirements of the Law. It was not in the disregard of rites and ceremonies that religion was deficient; it was in the lack of common human goodness.

There was tremendous excitement throughout the south. Messianic hopes once more flamed up. Multitudes came for baptism. The news reached Galilee; and among those who came the four-days' journey to the confluence of the Jordan and the Dead Sea was Jesus of Nazareth. He seems to have come quietly among the throng, receiving baptism like the rest; [7] but he came wondering whether the preaching of John might not be the call of God, for which he was waiting. At the moment of baptism there came a profound experience of God's favour. Jesus knew that he was God's son, as the king had been called God's son in the great days of the past. He was called to great services. Some great deliverance was to be wrought out through him. He went away as quietly as he had come, to ponder and pray in the wilderness.

The so-called "temptation in the wilderness" was the wrestling of the new leader with the problems of leadership. What was the kingdom of God, which he was to advance? What means should he use to advance it? Should he be influenced by self-interest?

Many days Jesus remained "with the wild beasts" in the wilderness of Judaea, the wilderness that is still so desolate, so dreadful to a luckless traveller, by reasons of prowling hyenas and jackals. There Jesus fought through terrific spiritual conflicts. In the language of that day, he was "tempted of Satan," the superhuman being, the tester of men, imported into late Jewish thought from Persia. The special temptation that comes to every sensitive soul, in the reaction that follows great spiritual exaltation, is to doubt the reality of the experience through which he has just passed. Such doubt swept in upon Jesus and threatened to engulf him. It was suggested to him that if he really was the son of God, as he had thought in his great moment, he could prove it by very simple tests. Why not try out the new spiritual energy, that had surged for a day within him, by making bread out of stones, to satisfy his hunger? Why not test God's love, and convince the public in a moment, by leaping from a wing of the Temple, when the people were assembled for the

---

[7] The story of the baptism in *Mark* and *Luke* is simple and brief. *Matthew* adds that John demurred, thinking it unfitting that he should baptize Jesus; but this is almost certainly a later accretion, with a theological bias.

evening sacrifice or for some annual festival? Why not use his great
spiritual insight to further the kingdom of God by beating the world
at its own game, winning "all the kingdoms of the world" by astuteness
and enlightened self-interest?

There were good precedents in Jewish religious history for attempting
all these things; but there were the best of reasons for rejecting such
methods. One who feels himself encompassed by the divine love can
only give himself to his duty, and live by whatever love provides; for
self-interest obscures duty and is fatal to all the finer relationships,
whether human or divine. The putting of love to the test is equally fatal.
Pure love asks no proofs, and is wounded in its inmost being when
proofs are demanded. Besides, miracles of self-interest could not advance
the kingdom of God. Jesus saw already that the kingdom of God is the
kingdom of goodness; and men are not helped to goodness by "signs
and wonders." As for trusting to worldly wisdom, in the end it is fatal
to one's spiritual integrity. Jesus determined to take the long way. He
would make no demands for himself; he would not advertise; he would
not compromise. He would trust to the truth and worth of his cause, and
leave both himself and the result in the hands of God.

Jesus emerged from the wilderness, his principles fixed, his plans
awaiting divine guidance. The time is fixed for us by the very explicit
statement in *Luke* 3: 1, 2. It was in the autumn of 27 A.D.; and Jesus was
then thirty-three or thirty-four years of age. A very few weeks were spent
in Judaea and Perea, in touch with the mission of John. That work
closed abruptly, when Herod Antipas ordered John's arrest and imprisonment in the fortress of Machaerus.

The arrest of John and the popular excitement led Jesus to retire to
Galilee, where he settled at Capernaum, in the populous region around
the Lake of Galilee. Thenceforth the north was the scene of most of his
ministry until its close. How long that ministry lasted we cannot say,
except that it was either somewhat more or somewhat less than two
years.

Some fame had preceded Jesus north from Judaea; and he was invited
immediately to read the Scriptures and address the people in the synagogue at Capernaum. With Capernaum as a centre he also preached in
the open air around the lake; and crowds "pressed upon him, and heard
the word of God" from the first. His opening message was that of John

—"The time is fulfilled, and the kingdom of God is at hand; repent ye, and believe the good news." But the announcement of the kingdom soon passed into a body of teaching, made vivid by parables, concerning the real nature of the kingdom, what it offered to men, and how they became fitted for it.

There was nothing sensational about Jesus' methods, and he deprecated excitement; but his teaching compelled attention. Men knew that he spoke out of his own insight, "as having authority, and not as the scribes." They were attracted as well and subdued by his moral majesty. It was not that he was stern and ascetic like John; it was rather that in him sweetness and light, and the moral energy of utter disinterestedness, spoke to their hearts. The effect was increased by miracles, which, however, were not performed as proofs of his authority. To others they were "signs"; to him they were natural expressions of his spirit. Society in the East, especially among the poor, is disease ridden. Mental disorders were particularly prevalent in Palestine, with hysteria and paralysis and epilepsy, aggravated by the meagreness of life and its insecurity. These were just such torments as a calm and victorious spirit could relieve. That Jesus should relieve them was inevitable. It was as impossible that he should be indifferent to suffering as that a mother should desert her sick child.

And a ministry of healing was inevitable for another reason. Mental disorders were regarded as the work of evil spirits or demons.[8] Their defeat would be one evidence that the reign of God had begun. Jesus so regarded the matter: "If I by the spirit of God cast out demons, then is the kingdom of God come upon you." And what Jesus did other men would do, he thought, when they felt within themselves the new energies of the kingdom of God.

[8] Of course other miracles than the cure of mental disorders are attributed to Jesus, some involving power over the forces of Nature and even the ability to raise the dead. If the evidence for an alleged miracle is satisfactory, we are not free to say that it did not happen because such things are impossible. We do not know what things are possible. One may properly doubt the raising of Lazarus from the dead because the evidence is not satisfactory. It is reported in the Fourth Gospel as having happened in Bethany, close to Jerusalem, in the family of Mary and Martha, well known to the disciples. It is such an event as would become common knowledge, and indeed is declared to have precipitated a meeting of the Great Sanhedrin and a decision to compass the death of Jesus. Yet no one of the Synoptists mentions the matter. It is either a legend that grew up in the seventy or eighty years before the Fourth Gospel was written, or it is a misunderstood parable.

Jesus soon determined to carry his message beyond Capernaum and the lake, and to make a preaching tour of the synagogues of Galilee. But first, from among the fishermen around the lake, he drew into his service two men of Capernaum, Simon and Andrew, earnest brothers who had been with John until his arrest. Immediately thereafter he called his own cousins, James and John, the sons of Zebedee and Salome. These would occasion no surprise. In Palestine, as in Greece, any man with repute as a teacher could attract to himself travelling disciples. But the next one whom Jesus drew into his circle was Matthew, a publican; and his inclusion would arouse hostility. For tax-collectors in Galilee, though directly in the pay of Herod Antipas, were indirectly servants of the Roman Government.

The call of Matthew was symptomatic of an attitude that was bound to involve Jesus in conflict with the scribes and Pharisees. Obedient to the Mosaic Law, they avoided contact with irreligious persons, keeping themselves clean for the kingdom of God. To Jesus it seemed a duty to extend the kingdom of God by seeking out the irreligious and winning them to the kingdom. His instinct was against the orthodox view.

The tension was increased by Jesus' feeling for humanity in general. Of course Judaism itself showed a fine concern for the poor and needy; but relief work was hampered by the ceremonial law. One must be careful with whom one came into contact; and one must suspend works of mercy on the Sabbath. This was God's day, and His will must then be man's concern. Jesus knew that God must come first, on all days; but he felt also that God is best served when one cares for God's children. He had turned back from the Levitical view of the Sabbath, as a day of self-denials and taboos, to the Mosaic view of the Sabbath as a day of social relief. He declined, therefore, to rebuke his disciples when, passing through a field of ripe wheat on the Sabbath, they plucked and ate, though the tradition of the elders regarded this as a form of threshing. Jesus declined also to stay his hand when, teaching in a synagogue on the Sabbath, he saw a man with a withered hand and healed him.

This incident in the synagogue aroused the Pharisees. The tendency of Jesus' teaching and conduct was clear; and piety took alarm. The view of the scribes and Pharisees was that the kingdom of God could only be brought in as men observed the Law. The new teacher encouraged men to break the Law. It was the duty of religious leadership to see that he was silenced. So "the Pharisees went out, and straightway with the Herodians took counsel against him, how they might destroy him."

The threatening danger called for special divine guidance, and Jesus spent whole nights alone in the open in prayer; but he did not withdraw from Galilee. Instead, he transferred his mission back from the synagogue to the seashore, where greater crowds than ever attended him. People were coming now, not simply from Galilee and Judaea but from the Phoenician cities of the coast, from Perea, and from Idumea in the far south. A great movement was under way. Jesus prepared for it by enlarging the inner circle of disciples to twelve, who were to become more than disciples; they were to be apostles, or emissaries, carrying on work of their own under his direction.

Jesus opened the larger mission by taking the apostles with him on a tour of the cities and villages of Galilee. What he saw of the masses moved him deeply. They were "distressed and scattered as sheep not having a shepherd." So he multiplied the mission by dividing the missionaries. He sent out the twelve in pairs. They were to take with them no money, nor even the wallet in which the beggar was accustomed to receive and conserve his food. They were to accept such hospitality as was offered, sure that the spiritual help they could give in return would repay their hosts. They were to exhibit the spiritual energies that Jesus possessed, healing even as he did, and concentrating on their fellow Jews. They went their several ways, and found that the energies of the kingdom were indeed working by them also: "They cast out many devils, and anointed with oil many that were sick, and healed them."

The more widespread activity aroused uneasiness in Herod Antipas. He had recently put John the Baptist to death. A superstitious fear now seized him that the new preacher was no other than John, risen from the dead. When Jesus heard of John's death and Herod's alarm, he sought seclusion across the lake in the territory of Philip.

It was now impossible, however, to escape the crowd. They followed on foot around the lake; and Jesus "welcomed them, and spake to them of the kingdom of God, and them that had need of healing he healed." Then sending the apostles across the lake to Bethsaida, Jesus dismissed the multitude at the close of the day, and himself spent some hours on a hillside in prayer. He knew that a crisis was approaching. The alienation of the religious leaders had been growing more and more complete. The reasons for this are clear when one thinks of his teaching, the main body of which comes down from these months. Here belongs the so-called Sermon on the Mount, with its departures from the Law. Other departures, which could only increase the hostility of the scribes and Pharisees, were involved in his acts of mercy. In Capernaum he healed the servant of a Roman centurion, Gentile dog as he was, and made the faith of the centurion the text of a sermon to his unbelieving countrymen. In the house of Simon, a friendly Pharisee, he accepted loving services from a fallen woman, who had been reclaimed by his purity and tenderness and who now, coming weeping behind him as he reclined at dinner, anointed and kissed his feet. When scribes and Pharisees came from Jerusalem to observe his work, and immediately complained that his disciples were ceremonially unclean and offended against religion, eating food without first washing their hands, Jesus replied by rejecting the whole Jewish idea of cleanness and uncleanness. Man is not defiled, he said, by the things he eats, but by the evil things that nest in his heart.

The crisis was now upon Jesus. The countryside was astir; the civil power was disturbed and hostile; the religious leaders were alienated. The future was not clear. So Jesus retired for a short time, apparently alone, to Phoenicia and the Mediterranean coast, in the territory of the Roman governor of Syria.

Before we go farther we must consider more carefully what Jesus taught. On examination it proves to be surprisingly limited in extent. Jesus assumed the existence of God; there was no need to prove it to Jews. Besides, Jesus had his own immediate experience of God. It was so profound and so sacred that attempts at proof would have seemed a desecration. In this Jesus is like religious mystics in general. They do not argue; they testify. As to the character of God, Jesus conceived Him very much as the great prophets had done. God was simply more humane and familiar and dear to him than to them, more utterly worthy of love and trust.

Jesus therefore speaks very often about faith, faith that men can be delivered from sickness and suffering by the power of God, faith that even the inescapable evils of life do not disprove the goodness of God. If a sparrow falls dead to the ground, God is not indifferent. If a man endure hunger and thirst and nakedness, nevertheless the very hairs of his head are numbered; and in the end human goodness will receive its legitimate reward, and the goodness of God be vindicated.

Jesus believed, with the Apocalyptists, in the approaching intervention of God in the world. The world was growing old. It had long been under the sway of evil Powers. The sickness and suffering of his fellow Jews, not to speak of the tragedies of the nation, were proof enough of that. God would intervene, and that very soon. Indeed, Jesus' own healing power, and that of his disciples, seemed to him an evidence that the victorious energy of God was already at work. Men need only have confidence in Him to find Him present and active.[9]

The intervention of God would come through the Messiah, or Christ, whom Jesus conceives to be, not an earthly prince of the Davidic line, but the supernatural Son of Man of I *Enoch,* who will come on the clouds of heaven. He will introduce the kingdom of God, or the kingdom of heaven, as it is called alternatively in the Gospels.[10]

The whole ministry of Jesus was devoted to showing men what the kingdom of God was like, and what character and conduct made one ready for it. It was the pearl of great price, the treasure hidden in a field, for which the wise man would part with everything else. And now was the time for action. When the kingdom was actually upon them, it would be too late. Besides men need not await its final establishment, in order to experience some of its blessings. They might know in their souls the peace, the moral victory, the love and trust and forgiveness of the kingdom, before it was finally set up. In this sense the kingdom of God was within them. But men could neither enjoy the life of the kingdom in the present, nor enter into it in the future, unless they were good.

When Jesus set about making men good and exemplifying goodness in his own conduct, it was soon apparent that his idea of goodness was not that of his time. It was not simply that he thought the children of the kingdom must go farther in goodness than even the best men went. If that had been all, he would not have aroused in the scribes and Pharisees so deadly an enmity. Men will endure, will even be grateful for, a summons to do better what they have always believed to be right; but to

[9] *Matthew* 9: 7, 8; *Mark* 9: 23; *Luke* 11: 20.
[10] *Matthew* 24: 29-31; 25: 31-33; *Mark* 13: 24-27; *Luke* 17: 22-30; 21: 25-28.

be told that one's goodness is not good, that even the light that is in one is darkness, is quite another matter. And this is just what Jesus thought and said. Good men, even the best men, had missed the way. They were on the wrong road. If they went ever so far in their direction, they would not arrive at true goodness. For Jesus felt that goodness, in its inmost being, is love, in the sense of active concern for others, while contemporary religious thought emphasized the meticulous observance of religious laws. One may be very meticulous and very unloving, very blind. Indeed, religious persons may be more blind to real human needs in proportion as their religion is elaborate and exacting. This, Jesus thought, had actually happened to the Pharisees. They were too blind to have desire to see; and, as blind leaders of the blind, they had led men with them into the ditch.

It is not easy to realize how tremendous was the religious revolution involved in such teaching. Indeed many rise from a study of the Gospels, disappointed that so little in the teaching of Jesus seems original. Most sentiments attributed to him may be found elsewhere. This is not so strange as it seems. The essential human relationships are permanent. So that even cave men, if they had been able to write about life and society, would have written about fatherhood and sonship and brotherhood, about duty and mutual aid and love; but they would have meant by all these things something strange to our minds. The same relationships take on new meanings as mental and moral standards advance; they never mean to ordinary people what they do to individuals of some special refinement of feeling and insight. Jesus transformed everything he touched. For those who understood, fatherhood and sonship and brotherhood, duty and mutual aid and love, would thenceforth be quite different things.

The moral revolution was the more complete because Jesus saw that if love is real and active, it is not simply one of the qualities of a character, it is the central and controlling one. Wherever he himself went, the active love within broke through social conventions. Rules for the regulation of the Sabbath, of one's association with other people, of eating and drinking, of prayer and worship—rules accepted as of divine origin and authority—all broke down in his practice. So the social action of Jesus was cataclysmic.

Let us think, for example, of his teaching concerning the nature of success. Jewish thought conceived of success as we do, as long life and riches and honour. These things were the gifts of God, the rewards of religious devotion. Jesus saw that the pursuit of these things is inimical to love. One will not go far in active good will if one is deeply concerned about personal safety, or the acquisition of riches, or the achievement of distinction. One keeps one's life forever, Jesus said, by spending it freely in great causes; one gains "treasure in heaven" by refusing material riches; one achieves true distinction by giving oneself to the service of others without craving distinction.

At no point was Jesus more explicit and more in conflict with common opinion than in his doctrine of riches. The desire for riches, he thought, is at best a foolish thing; they satisfy no real need of the soul. But, deeper still, Jesus saw a "deceitfulness of riches" that puts the soul to sleep as to its own condition. There is almost no poverty of soul that riches cannot hide from the rich man. One comes easily to regard himself as a superior man, with the right to control others, though he may have no spiritual qualifications for control. One easily persuades himself that he desires riches in order to serve God with Mammon, when in reality he is labouring to serve both God and Mammon. So double-mindedness, the pursuit of contrary ideals, darkens the inner light, obscures the higher vision of the soul, and confuses the moral life. A camel, sweatily labouring to pass through a needle's eye, was not too strong a figure, Jesus thought, to describe the difficulty with which the rich would enter into the kingdom of God.

Such teaching was as little welcome then as it is now. It shifted the attention from those "sins of the flesh," whose evil all men acknowledged, to other sins of the spirit, of which men were not and are not ashamed. Jesus saw in them the deadliest enemies of the kingdom. They were the negation of that active good will, which was central in goodness.

The final result of such teaching, in the Palestine of that day, would be either religious revolution or the death of the teacher. At first Jesus seems to have hoped for the former; but the hope faded as opposing forces drew together against him. What should he do? He had determined at the outset to be loyal to the truth that was in him, and leave the result in the hands of God. His loyalty had now brought him where he faced the fate of John the Baptist. How could that serve the ends of the kingdom of God?

It was the pressure of that problem that took Jesus outside Palestine, "into the borders of Tyre and Sidon." There in Phoenicia he would be beyond the jurisdiction of the two Herods and Pilate, and outside the immediate influence of the scribes and Pharisees. He would have opportunity for thought and prayer.

We do not know how long Jesus was absent. Only one incident of his retirement is reported, the healing of the daughter of a Greek-speaking woman of Phoenicia. He was back soon, teaching and healing by the sea of Galilee. His duty was becoming plain. From the first he had been looking for the kingdom of God, as something to be ushered in by the action of the Messiah, whom he clearly identified with that heavenly being, the Son of Man of I *Enoch*. We cannot say with certainty whether he had thought himself to be the Son of Man; but now he speaks definitely in that sense. Retiring once more, this time to the northern extremity of Palestine, after another clash with the Pharisees, he found himself with his disciples in the region of Caesarea Philippi, the city that Herod Philip had just built, or was building, in honour of the Emperor. There Jesus asked his disciples what conclusion men were reaching about him. They replied that men differed. When asked what they themselves thought, Peter said, "Thou art the Christ." Jesus assented, and from that time "began to teach them that the Son of Man must suffer many things, and be rejected by the elders, and the chief priests, and the scribes, and be killed, and after three days rise again." [11]

This was a new departure in Jewish thought. Judaism had no doctrine of a suffering Messiah.[12] Jesus had come to it through the pressure of circumstances. He had felt himself divinely called to preach the kingdom of God. In loyalty to that call he had now reached the point where he

[11] *Mark* 8: 27–31 (*Luke* 9: 18–22; *Matthew* 16: 13–21). The Account in *Mark* and *Luke,* of Jesus' question concerning his identity and Peter's reply, is very simple and direct. It is elaborated in *Matthew,* and complicated by statements about Peter himself and the "keys of the kingdom of heaven," which are almost certainly a later interpolation, in support of "the Petrine theory" of the Church.

[12] *Isaiah* 53, interpreted by Christians as Messianic, has never been so interpreted in Judaism. There Isaiah's "suffering servant of Yahweh" is understood as having been the Jewish people, or the devout minority within the nation, or some man of the Exile whose humble and unflinching devotion to Yahweh had become a symbol.

must either desist or die. To desist would be treason and moral catas-
trophe. But, to die! What could that be but defeat? Defeat seemed the
more incomprehensible and terrible, because he could not now fall back,
as John had done, on the Messiah, who would take up the cause if he
perished. He was himself the Messiah. That was the conclusion to which
he had come, as he struggled against the general spiritual darkness and
moral frailty and rebellion. He and the Father were alone in a community of understanding. Only God understood him; only he understood God. Without him men would never find God. God had committed, or would commit, to him the work of the Messiah. His death,
therefore, would be the death of the Messiah, or the Messiah designate.
One of two things, then, God would do. He would either prevent the
death or annul it. Jesus rested at last in the conviction that he was to
die, but that God would raise him from the dead and receive him into
the heavens, whence he would return as the Son of Man, to establish
the Messianic kingdom. This consummation would not be long delayed. Believing that, Jesus went forward to death.[13]

The death and resurrection, the exaltation and return of Jesus, were
later to become central in Christian thought, quite overshadowing his
earthly life and teaching concerning the kingdom of God. Yet the four
Gospels do not provide us with materials for a complete doctrine of these
things. Almost no explicit teaching concerning the death survives, for
which the authority of Jesus himself can be claimed. Christian theology
was to find the explanation in the sacrificial system of Judaism; his
death was to be the one grand sacrifice that would meet the Divine requirements forever. It is almost certain that Jesus himself did not think
so. He would be in sympathy with that view of the greatest prophets and
some of the Psalmists, that God never ordained the sacrificial features
of Judaism. The clue to Jesus' thought is to be found in words uttered immediately after Peter's declaration and his own acknowledgement of his
Messiahship. Jesus then not only predicted death for himself; he exalted
it into a general principle of conduct that the citizens of the kingdom
must not refuse to die for it. He who is too anxious to live does not live.
To play safe is to sell life itself, its strength and beauty and peace, for a
whole skin. And further, as one saves oneself by giving oneself, so also
does one save others. Two later utterances of Jesus set forth this doctrine.

[13] *Mark* 8: 38–9: 1; *Matthew* 16: 27, 28; *Luke* 9: 26, 27.

In one he places himself in the succession of those great prophetic souls of the past, who had continued to speak the truths by which men are saved, though at the price of their own desolation and rejection. In the other he says to two ambitious youths that true human greatness is utter devotion to the common good, even as he himself had come, not to get anything for himself, but to give himself for others, and by so doing to save many.[14]

Here is a philosophy of life and a method of redeeming it. It is the function of the prophet, Jesus says, and of all great souls, to work out the real issues of life for mankind. They see the evil that most men do not yet see; they support the good that most men do not yet acknowledge. By willingness to suffer for what they see, they clarify the thinking of others, accredit the new cause, win others to it, and so redeem them. What good men will die for, other men will one day acknowledge and adopt. It is thus the good become a "ransom for many."

When once Jesus had clearly foreseen and accepted death, events moved swiftly. He set his face towards Jerusalem, as the place where he would naturally bear his final witness. Moving southward east of the Jordan, he and his disciples were soon in Perea, in the neighbourhood of John's early ministry. There multitudes thronged him once more. Pharisees were soon down from Jerusalem, to trick him into some contradiction of the Law of Moses. They had heard of his chivalrous view of womanhood and the indissolubility of marriage, and attacked him at that point; for the Law required only that a man, who wearied of his wife and put her away, should give her a certificate to that effect. Jesus affirmed that the Law was not in harmony with the original intention of the Creator, and that a man could not rightfully put away his wife. The declaration served the purpose of the Pharisees and also disturbed the disciples, who thought a marriage so binding was not attractive. They were further disturbed when a rich young man of good reputation was advised to part with his riches before committing himself to the kingdom of God.

The disciples were thus in doubt and bewilderment when Jesus led them across the Jordan, for the last march to Jerusalem. On the way he took the twelve aside and forewarned them again that he would be

[14] *Mark* 8: 34–38 (*Matthew* 16: 24–27; *Luke* 9: 23–26); *Luke* 13: 31–33; *Mark* 10: 35–45 (*Matthew* 20: 20–28).

condemned by the Jewish authorities, and delivered by them to the Roman procurator for execution; though his death would not be the end. Approaching Jericho, followed by a crowd, Jesus healed a blind man, and in the city shocked pious sentiment by going to rest in the house of a well-disposed publican.

From Jericho, set in the plain, they took the road that climbs steeply up to Jerusalem, through bare limestone hills, unrelieved by shade or greenness. Its rocky pass had an evil reputation for violence and robbery; and its desolation would somehow consort with the doubt and depression of the disciples and the growing isolation of Jesus. After fifteen miles they came, by way of the Mount of Olives, to the village of Bethany, the home of Martha and Mary, where they rested.

It is impossible now to reconstruct accurately the happenings of the succeeding week, "Passion Week," spent in and around Jerusalem; but the general direction of events is clear. Leaving Bethany the next day, Sunday, Jesus approached the capital, riding on an ass, for which arrangements had been made. The manner of his coming corresponded with a prediction of the prophet Zechariah concerning the expected Messianic king; and at the news of his approach a crowd of pilgrims, already in Jerusalem for the Passover, came forth to welcome him. Jesus neither encouraged nor discouraged them; but he wept as the city came into view across the valley of the Kidron. Reaching the city, he dismounted and entered the Temple, looking around silently upon the traffic that profaned it. As evening approached he withdrew with the twelve to Bethany; but next morning, Monday, he was back in the city, in the Temple. The Temple market was busy again, pilgrims exchanging foreign coins, with their pagan symbols, for the Jewish shekel, and buying therewith birds and beasts certified by the priests to be without blemish and fit for sacrificial offerings. The court of the Gentiles, the one place in the Temple where non-Jewish worshippers could pray, was thus a place of profitable business, of confusion and animal filth. Jesus drove out the traders, saying, "Is it not written, My house shall be called a place of prayer for all the nations? but ye have made it a den of robbers." It was not an act of violence, which Jesus was in no position to exercise if he would; it was a successful exercise of moral authority. The traffic in the Temple had been a public scandal; and the purging of the Temple was such an act as would be expected of any prophet or reformer. The priests and the temple guards, however, were furious, though prevented by fear from arresting Jesus; "for the people all hung upon him, listening." At nightfall Jesus again left the city, to find seclusion, perhaps at Bethany, perhaps in a garden of olives on the hillside.

On Tuesday morning Jesus was once more in the Temple teaching. The Jewish authorities were now thoroughly aroused. "The chief priests, and the scribes, and the elders" came, demanding to know whose authorization he had for interfering in Temple affairs. He replied by asking whose authorization John the Baptist had had. When they would not answer, he declined to justify himself. They themselves, he knew, believed that the prophetic reformers of the nation had always acted by a more-than-human authority. Without making any defence, therefore, Jesus warned the authorities in a parable that God's vineyard had been a long time in their hands for cultivation, and that when God's servants had come, one after another, requiring of them fruit, these servants had been rejected with violence. God's last messenger, a "beloved son," was now to die by their hands. That would be the end of the husbandmen also. The vineyard would thenceforth be entrusted to others.

Again the Jewish authorities would have arrested Jesus, but were deterred by fear of public disorder. They must wait until they could take him alone. Meanwhile they would lead him into some offence against the Roman power, in order that, when they did arrest him, the procurator might have his own reasons for condemning him. To effect this, Pharisees and Herodians came, encouraging Jesus to condemn payment of tribute to Rome. The ruse failed; but the battle of wits went on all that day. Before the day closed Jesus publicly condemned the scribes, their fondness for distinctive dress, for deferential greetings in the street, for places of honour in the synagogues; their formalism, their meticulous observance of little things and blindness to great moral wrongs.

At sunset, as Jesus was leaving the Temple, a disciple remarked its magnificence. It was the greatest structural achievement of that great builder, Herod the Great. Almost fifty years it had been in course of construction, and was not yet complete. The Temple proper, a building of marble and gold, stood on a lofty terrace, surrounded by cloisters of marble, and approached by a gateway 150 feet high. Beneath, and surrounding all, were the walls of the Temple enclosure, faced with massive blocks of stone, pure white. As Jesus looked, he said, "There shall not be left here one stone upon another that shall not be thrown down." The disciples seem not to have been greatly astonished. They were accustomed now to startling news; and the lurid expectations of the apocalyptic writers were not unknown to them.

That night, as Jesus sat on the Mount of Olives, looking across at the city, some of the twelve came and asked him privately, "When shall these things be? and what shall be the sign when all these things are about to be accomplished?" Then Jesus spoke at length of the future. His own interest and duty had been to teach men what manner of life would enable them to "inherit the kingdom of heaven." He had left to the Father the determination of the method and the moment of its formal appearance. Even now Jesus confesses ignorance of the time, but speaks of the method, of God's intervention.[15]

Discarding the more lurid details, found only in *Matthew*, the picture of the future, in all three Gospels, is still thoroughly Jewish; and it would seem that Jesus had assumed all along that the intervention of God in the world would be catastrophic, as the Apocalyptists thought.[16] He does warn the disciples against being too credulous. There will be rumours and wars and disturbances in the physical world. The disciples will be subjected to violence in the synagogues, and will be brought to trial before Jewish and Roman tribunals. They must continue nevertheless to trust God and preach the gospel of the kingdom, until Jerusalem is "compassed with armies" and the Roman standards profane the sanctuary itself. Then such of the disciples as are in Judaea are to "flee unto the mountains"; and mankind will endure unprecedented tribulations. Nature will be convulsed; "the sun shall be darkened, and the moon shall not give her light, and the stars shall be falling from heaven, and the powers that are in the heavens shall be shaken. And then they shall see the Son of man coming in clouds with great power and glory. And then shall he send forth the angels, and shall gather together his elect from the four winds," into the Messianic kingdom. All these things will come

---

[15] *Mark* 13; *Matthew* 24, 25; *Luke* 21: 5–38.

[16] Modern scholars are by no means agreed about this. Some think that the future here pictured is not consistent with the spirit and teaching of Jesus, and that even the earliest account, that in *Mark*, is an elaboration and distortion of some simple utterance of Jesus, misunderstood from the first. Other scholars think that Jesus did share current apocalyptic hopes of the future; and certainly the first generation of Christians lived in the expectation that these hopes would be realized.

to pass while the generation of Jesus still lives; but only God knows the day and the hour. Meanwhile they are to be always ready.[17]

After a night on the hillside, Jesus probably appeared again in the Temple teaching. We cannot say with certainty. It seems to have been late that day that he retired again to Bethany with the twelve, and took supper in the house of Simon the leper. There a woman disciple, perhaps Mary of Bethany, came with a flask of costly pistachio ointment, which she poured upon his head as he sat at meat. There was some indignation among the disciples. They said, not quite sincerely, that the ointment, if sold, would have provided much alms for the poor. Jesus defended the woman. Impulsive devotion in rare moments is as fragrant and useful as the calculated givings of a wise philanthropy. Indeed it may leave a longer afterglow in tired and lonely hearts. This grateful woman, Jesus said, had but done in advance what bereaved Jews did for their dead.

For Judas of Kerioth this was too much. He was the single Judaean of the twelve. Perhaps he had always felt a little ill-at-ease among Galileans. Certainly he shared the general doubt and dismay at the turn events were taking. He would now end this unpractical dallying, and hurry the crisis that Jesus himself was predicting. Judas went from the supper to the chief priests, and offered to guide their agents to Jesus. They were glad and promised to give him money.

Throughout Thursday Jesus seems to have remained quietly at Bethany, or perhaps on the Mount of Olives. He had perceived the collapse of Judas, and was now awaiting the end. During the day he sent two of the twelve to an affluent disciple in Jerusalem, perhaps the father of that John Mark who wrote the Gospel of Mark, asking that the guest chamber be prepared for an evening meal; and when evening came he sat down to supper with the twelve. According to the tradition preserved in *Mark,* and repeated in *Matthew* and *Luke,* it was the day of the Passover, and this was the regular Passover meal. A different account is given in the Fourth Gospel, where the supper occurs on the day of the "Preparation of the Passover," that is the day before; and the authorities are careful that the arrest and trial and crucifixion of Jesus shall all be over before the Passover, which was always a holy day and fell that year on the Sabbath as well. The account in the Fourth Gospel is

[17] *Mark* 13: 24–32; *Matthew* 24: 29–36; *Luke* 21: 25–36.

generally accepted as the true one. The "last supper" was the ordinary evening meal, on the day of the Preparation; and Jesus sat down with the twelve, knowing that he would not live to eat the Passover itself.

When the twelve had eaten, Jesus instituted a new rite. He took bread and wine, which he gave to all, saying, "Take ye, this is my body," and "This is my blood of the covenant, which is shed for many."

Opinions differ as to the meaning of the rite and of the words of institution. The earliest account is that of St. Paul in I *Corinthians* 11:23-26. Paul writes some twenty years after the event; but he is repeating what he was taught at his conversion, perhaps a few months, at most five or six years after the crucifixion. What he says is this:

I received of the Lord that which also I delivered unto you, how that the Lord Jesus in the night in which he was betrayed took bread; and when he had given thanks, he brake it, and said, This is my body, which is for you: this do in remembrance of me. In like manner also the cup, after supper, saying, This cup is the new covenant in my blood: this do, as often as ye drink it, in remembrance of me. For as often as ye eat this bread, and drink the cup, ye proclaim the Lord's death till he come.

Matthew, Mark and *Luke* are in general agreement with Paul; though *Matthew* adds a phrase, "unto remission of sins," which introduces a foreign idea. Men's minds were full of the Passover; and lambs slain for the Passover were not propitiatory sacrifices, "unto remission of sins." They were for a feast of thanksgiving, to commemorate a great deliverance. It is thus that the Supper of the Lord was conceived at the first. The rite was to be observed until Jesus should return in glory, to establish the Messianic kingdom. Until then Jesus' sacrifice of himself was to be remembered as the visible symbol of God's gracious purpose to deliver them, even as in ancient Israel covenants with both God and men were ratified with sacrifices.

At table Jesus let them all know that he expected betrayal by one of their number. They fell into sorrow and confusion at his words. He spent an hour or two with them in sacred confidences and admonitions. He had, earlier in the evening, performed a servant's duty, washing their feet, as a last lesson in humility. He exhorted them to love each other, assured them that the spirit of God would be their strength until his own return in glory, and prayed for himself and them. They sang, according to custom, the second half of the *Hallel, Psalms* 95–98, and withdrew to the Mount of Olives. There they entered an enclosure called Gethsemane, oil press; and Jesus said to the disciples

"Sit here till I pray." But he took Peter and James and John along with him; and as he began to feel appalled and agitated, he said to them, "My heart is sad, sad even to death; stay here and watch." Then he went forward a little and fell to the earth, praying that the hour might pass away from him, if possible. "Abba, Father," he said, "thou canst do anything. Take this cup away from me. Yet, not what I will but what thou wilt." [18]

Three times, in the intervals of praying, Jesus turned to the three for comfort, only to find them asleep, exhausted with sorrow. At length Judas appeared, accompanied by an armed band. A greeting and a kiss from Judas, then Jesus was seized and led away, protesting only that the manner of his arrest was unnecessary. Someone standing by intervened to rescue him, drawing and striking with a sword; but Jesus deprecated any use of force. Thereupon the disciples fled, and with them a young man, perhaps John Mark, who had followed secretly from the place of the supper.

Jesus was taken first to the house of Annas, who had been High Priest and seems to have remained leader of the high priestly party. Peter followed, and another disciple who was probably John; and they stood with the officers and servants around a fire of coals in the chilly court, awaiting the dawn. Annas questioned Jesus, then sent him bound to his son-in-law Caiaphas, who was High Priest that year. There, in the official residence of the High Priest, Jesus was brought to trial in the early morning before the Sanhedrin, while Peter again sat with the officers around a fire in the court, awaiting the result. The testimony of the witnesses was conflicting; and there were crude misunderstandings that Jesus had said he would destroy the Temple and build another in three days without physical means. Jesus stood silent; it was no use teaching here. But when he was asked directly whether he were the Christ, Jesus said that he was and that they would see him "sitting at the right hand of power, and coming on the clouds of heaven." This was declared to be blasphemy, and Jesus was pronounced worthy of death.

The Sanhedrin had no power to pass sentence of death; that was re-

[18] *Mark* 14: 33–36; Moffatt's translation.

served for the Roman governor. Pilate was in the city, having come from Caesarea to guard against disorder during the Passover festival. To him the Sanhedrin took the prisoner. But first there were difficulties to be overcome. Pilate would care nothing about blasphemy, or apocalyptic ideas, or any other question of Jewish religion. The charge against Jesus would therefore require to be changed; and he was accused of being seditious, of condemning the payment of tribute, of declaring himself a king. Questioned by Pilate, Jesus answered that his kingdom was not of this world.

Here, Pilate thought, was another of those incomprehensible and irritating questions of Jewish religion, about which he knew nothing and cared less. So, knowing that Jesus was a Galilean and that Herod Antipas was in the city, Pilate sent Jesus to Herod, who might express some view of the case. The Sanhedrin followed, pressing its accusations; but Jesus made no defence. Thereupon Herod, failing to extract anything from the prisoner or to induce him to perform a miracle, made sport of him and returned him in royal apparel to Pilate, who determined to scourge him and set him free. But a crowd of Jerusalemites had assembled before the praetorium, clamouring for the usual Roman amnesty at feast times. Pilate offered them Jesus, but with irritating taunts about "the king of the Jews." They shouted for Barabbas, a violent patriot, in prison for insurrection. His sturdy lawlessness, perhaps, seemed better than the far-away hope of a Messiah and a kingdom of God, both of which, as Jesus preached them, they found incomprehensible. Pilate gave amnesty to Barabbas, and condemned Jesus to death by crucifixion.

Crucifixion was a form of special punishment acquired by Rome from the Phoenicians, and was meant to be as humiliating as possible. It was always preceded by whipping; and the condemned man carried to the place of execution the cross-beam to which he was to be nailed, where it was fastened to a permanent upright. When in position, the cross raised the head of the sufferer hardly two feet higher than the bystanders, who came to witness such spectacles. A piece of wood above the head of the victim, whitened to receive an inscription, published his crime. Strong men sometimes lived two days on the cross, and their legs were broken to hasten the end. All was ghastly, appalling, except that gentle women sometimes brought drugged wine, to dull the senses of the crucified ones.

Pilate witnessed the scourging of Jesus, then left him to the soldiers. They subjected him to every indignity, then led him forth, too broken to carry his cross-beam, which was forced upon a Jew from North Africa, Simon of Cyrene. Arrived at Golgotha, the place of execution outside the city, the soldiers crucified Jesus, placing above him the inscription "The King of the Jews," as one more jibe at the nation. He was offered, but refused, the drugged wine; he would die in his right mind. Six hours, from nine in the morning until three in the afternoon, he survived among the jeering rabble. Through all there stood by the cross four women— his mother, her sister Salome, Mary the wife of Clopas, and Mary of Magdala—together with John, the beloved disciple, while others watched from a distance. From noon the sky was covered with an unnatural darkness. At the ninth hour, three o'clock, Jesus cried out in agony, in the words of the twenty-second Psalm, "My God, my God, why hast thou forsaken me?" Then, being thirsty, he received a sponge of vinegar, held up on a reed by a friendly hand. Another agonized cry, then he said: "It is finished; and he bowed his head, and gave up his spirit."

Strange thoughts had been rising in the Roman centurion. Now he was deeply moved. He said: "Truly this man was a son of God." Others too were deeply moved; as the crowd melted away, men smote their breasts.

As sunset approached, Joseph of Arimathaea, a rich and devout mem- ber of the Sanhedrin, ventured to approach Pilate alone and ask for the body of Jesus. He would forestall the coarse and common burial by soldiers. Pilate granted the request; and Joseph took away the body to a garden not far off, where was a new tomb, hewn in the rock. There he was joined by Nicodemus, another member of the Sanhedrin, a secret disciple of Jesus. Together they wrapped the body in new linen, putting spices in the folds, then laid the body in the tomb, rolling a great stone to the doorway, to foil wild beasts or a thief. Women disciples watched the entombment from a distance, among them Mary of Magdala, and Mary, "the mother of James the less and of Joses," and Salome.

The friends of Jesus, obedient to the Mosaic Law, waited decorously through the Sabbath; but the two Marys and Salome had purchased spices to anoint the dead, and at early dawn on Sunday they hurried to the tomb. The accounts of what followed are conflicting in almost all details, the most circumstantial being that in the Fourth Gospel. It says that Mary of Magdala came "while it was yet dark," to find that the stone had been removed. She ran to Peter and John, who hurried to the tomb. These two entered in, and found only the grave clothes there. They "went away again unto their own home," John believing that Jesus had risen. Mary remained outside the tomb weeping; and as she stooped and looked in, she saw "two angels in white sitting, one at the head and one at the feet, where the body of Jesus had lain." They reproved her tears; and, turning back, she saw, as she thought, the gardener standing. Inquiring for the body of the Lord, she was answered by Jesus himself, who spoke her name and said "cling not to me; for I am not yet ascended unto the Father; but go to my brethren, and say unto them, I ascend to my Father and your Father, and my God and your God."

There followed a series of experiences, continuing throughout forty days. Here also there is no agreement in the Gospels; nor do they agree with Paul's account in I *Corinthians* 15. It is clear that when the Gospels were written, Christian communities had different traditions as to the events of the forty days.

The last event is as enshrouded in mist as the rest. *Matthew* says that Jesus appeared last to the disciples on a mountain in Galilee, and tells nothing of an ascent into heaven. *Mark* closes abruptly without mention of the forty days; for the original ending of that Gospel is lost. The present ending says, "the Lord Jesus, after he had spoken to them," evidently somewhere in Galilee, "was received up into heaven, and sat down at the right hand of God." *Luke* describes an interval of only one of two days, spent, not in Galilee but in and around Jerusalem, the ascension taking place from Bethany.[19] The Fourth Gospel locates the experiences in and around Jerusalem, and closes with no mention of the ascension. All that we can confidently conclude from the Gospels is that, after the burial of Jesus, the tomb was found empty, and the disciples for some days had experiences which satisfied them that he was alive.

The crucifixion is the visible symbol of the incompatibility of Judaism and Jesus. He could not be incorporated within the national religion. His kinship was with three minority movements—prophetism, mysticism and apocalypticism. They had all been in uneasy, somewhat un-

---

[19] Later, when Luke wrote *Acts*, he had become acquainted with the tradition of the forty days. *Acts* 1: 1–14.

natural relations with Judaism. Prophetism had died slowly as Judaism developed. In other words, as the codification of law advanced, the voice of individual inspiration died away. Why should individuals expect inspiration, and why should society heed inspired individuals, when it already had an inspired book, elaborate enough to cover all the relationships of life? So Judaism stifled prophecy; and, having stifled prophecy, it was inevitable that it should cast out Jesus of Nazareth, who lived and spoke by his own insight, "as having authority, and not as the scribes."

As for mysticism, no one familiar with the *Psalms* can doubt that Judaism had its mystics; but, like the prophets, who indeed were mystics also, they were loosely attached to the national religion. That religion promised, in the name of God, substantial rewards to those who discharged the multitudinous obligations of the covenant; the mystics received their reward daily in the experience of God's present help and the hope of endless life with Him. And Jesus was the supreme mystic. He knew God so intimately, lived by his grace so completely, that nothing contractual could exist between them. All was uncalculating, spontaneous, self-giving, as the finer personal relationships always are. Jesus was not a child of the Law; and those who learned his way could not naturally express their devotion through a code.[20]

As for Jewish apocalypticism, it too belonged to the fringe of Judaism. One can read the Old Testament entire and be hardly aware of the strange hopes of the Apocalyptists. One doctrine of apocalypticism, however, had become part of the common faith, the doctrine that man survives the grave, not simply as an immortal soul but as a resuscitated body. The scene of the resurrection was to be Jerusalem; and devout Jews wished to be buried on the western slope of the Mount of Olives, to be close at hand on the great day. This is about all that Jewish orthodoxy absorbed from apocalypticism, this and the related doctrine of a judgment to come.

As for eschatology, as a doctrine of the last state of the world itself, it affected orthodoxy hardly at all. So that, whatever may be the truth as to Jesus' eschatological ideas, they would give him no effective contact with Judaism. The pilgrims who escorted Jesus in triumph into Jerusalem

---

[20] Mysticism, in all living religions, tends to live in detachment. The mystic may submit to the discipline and discharge the obligations of institutional religion; but his heart is elsewhere "in the secret place of the Most High."

were animated by ideas of a Davidic Messiah and by worldly hopes, such hopes as he did not share and would never fulfil.

These things, however—his prophetic insight, his consciousness of God, his apocalyptic ideas—which did not prevail in his Palestinian mission, worked together to give Jesus a following among the Jews of the Dispersion and the Gentiles. They explain why, during the next four centuries, Jesus came gradually to be confessed throughout the Mediterranean world as both universal Saviour and "Very God of Very God." More powerful still was the impression he had made of an ineffable goodness. His conception of the right had been so direct and simple and profound that it cut through the ethical underbrush of centuries. And what he conceived to be right, he himself seemed to men to embody. During his earthly life Jesus had drawn men to his feet in tears; after his death his ineffable goodness acquired theological significance. It was more, men thought, than an ideal to be pursued by those who also aspired to goodness; it was a revelation of the goodness of God, and a way of salvation. "Him who knew no sin, he made to be sin on our behalf, that we might become the righteousness of God through him."

CHAPTER IV

THE INFANCY OF THE CHRISTIAN CHURCH

AFTER the crucifixion of Jesus, life in Palestine went on as before for another forty years. It is doubtful that most men saw any special significance in what had happened. Judaea was the centre of both social and religious life; and Jesus had been a Galilean, whose activities seldom brought him into Judaea. He was not the first, the Sadducees would say, to encourage wild dreams in simple minds; he would not be the last. Nor was he the only one to die for having done so.[1] They would know how to deal with any recurrence of such folly.

As for the disciples of Jesus, after the crucifixion they returned to their homes in Galilee. It was there the visions of Jesus were seen. When these ceased, the disciples made their way back to Jerusalem. They thought the return of Jesus and the end of the Age would not be long delayed; and Jerusalem was the place to wait. The number of disciples was growing. The attraction of the cross was felt; and among the first to be drawn were Jesus' own brothers, who had held aloof during his public life. The leader of the company, however, was Peter. He would give place to others in time, as careful thought and organization became more useful than his impulsive enthusiasm.

The disciples went daily to the Temple, and met also in such homes as were open to them, talking together of their great hopes, praying together, eating together, and at the close of the common meal taking bread and wine in commemoration of the Last Supper. They were expectant and eager. The Lord might come any day, this time as the victorious Messiah.

What followed, for some thirty years, we learn from the book of *Acts*,

---

[1] There were several Messianic pretenders in the last fifty years of Jewish national life in Palestine. Josephus, one of the many conservative Jews who thought it politic to stand well with Rome, complained bitterly of disturbers. "Cheats and vagabonds caused rebellion and total subversion of society, under the pretension of being divinely inspired. They infected the common people with madness." *Wars of the Jews,* ii. 13: 4.

with some additional light from the letters of St. Paul. The author of *Acts* was Luke of Antioch, a physician who travelled with Paul in his later years. Luke wrote *Acts* as a companion volume to his *Gospel;* and both are addressed to Theophilus, a Greek enquirer concerning the new movement.[2]

From *Acts* we learn that a few days after the return to Jerusalem, some seven weeks after the crucifixion, the Feast of Weeks came round, or Pentecost, the Jewish harvest home. Jerusalem was again thronged with pilgrims, "devout men from every nation under heaven." The disciples met as usual, but more expectant than ever. As they waited and prayed there came a profound emotional experience, not uncommon in religious revivals. It confirmed the hopes of the disciples. They believed that Jesus, having been "by the right hand of God exalted, and having received of the Father the promise of the Holy Spirit," had now "poured forth" the Spirit upon them. The New Age was upon them; the Messianic hope was now realized, in the form in which the prophet Joel had held it:

And it shall be in the last days, saith God,
I will pour forth of my Spirit upon all flesh:
And your sons and your daughters shall prophesy,

.   .   .   .

And I will show wonders in the heaven above,
And signs on the earth beneath;
Blood and fire and vapour of smoke:
The sun shall be turned into darkness,
And the moon into blood,
Before the day of the Lord come,
That great and notable day:
And it shall be, that whosoever shall call on the name of the Lord shall
    be saved.   *Acts* 2: 17–21

[2] *Acts*, as a history, has serious limitations. The most disappointing is that it tells so little about the twelve Apostles. After the first few chapters they disappear from view; and *Acts* becomes virtually a biography of St. Paul, and therefore a history of only part of the Christian movement. A second limitation is that in *Acts*, as the name suggests, Luke was more concerned with the doings than the doctrines of the Apostles. It is hard to discover from *Acts* what was distinctive in the doctrines of Paul. And there is this further limitation, that Luke wrote at first without direct knowledge. It is not until the sixteenth chapter that he begins to describe events in which he himself participated. For earlier chapters he depends on the testimony of others, and that testimony is not always consistent. So Luke quotes one tradition of the ascension in his Gospel, and a different one in *Acts*. (Cf. *Lk.* 24 and *Acts* 1.)

Fired by their great experience, the disciples now began an eager, courageous mission to bring others to faith in the Messiah, before the end should come. Many people in Jerusalem responded; and the mission spread through the country. The new preaching, accompanied as it was by acts of healing, roused uneasiness in the Jewish authorities; and the Sanhedrin arrested Peter and John. They were dismissed, however, with a warning. The first sanguinary clash with the authorites did not come until Greek-speaking Jews, or Hellenists, showed themselves especially hospitable to the Gospel. They were always in Jerusalem in considerable numbers, transient pilgrims and elderly Jews of the Dispersion who came to spend their last years in the Holy City. They had been broadened by contact with the outer world; and, besides, the devout spirit that brought them to Jerusalem may have been gratified in the eager, brotherly company of the disciples more than by the worldliness of the Sadducees and the formalism of the Pharisees. So Hellenists speedily became a considerable element in the new brotherhood. Indeed, when it became necessary to appoint men to supervise the distribution of relief among disciples who were far from their homes, six of the seven chosen were Hellenists; the seventh was Nicholas, a Greek from Antioch, a proselyte to the synagogue there.

The appointment of the seven was a new departure. They were more than relief officers. Some immediately became preachers and missionaries like the Apostles. One of them, Stephen, preached with great power in the synagogues of the Hellenists, and soon drew the fire of the Jewish authorities. His teaching was found dangerous to Judaism and the Law. An excited crowd brought him before the Sanhedrin, where his defence did not help matters. He accused his nation of having persecuted its prophets, rejected their predictions of a Messiah to come, and of having now become his "betrayers and murderers." At that the mob rushed upon the prisoner, hustled him outside the city walls, and stoned him. Persecution began in Jerusalem; and the Hellenist converts scattered throughout Judaea and Samaria. The Apostles, however, were untouched. The movement, so far as they were concerned, was still regarded as a movement within Judaism. It was the first gesture towards the wider world that had stirred up persecution.

The Hellenists who fled through the countryside preached everywhere, and to such good purpose that the Jerusalem disciples soon heard that

Samaria was astir. Philip, another of the seven, was there, winning great numbers to the faith; and Peter and John went down from Jerusalem to see what was happening. They found many converts, already baptized into the name of Jesus, but without the Pentecostal experience. The two Apostles "prayed for them, that they might receive the Holy Spirit. . . . Then laid they their hands on them, and they received the Holy Spirit." Thus Peter and John were themselves led into a wider work than they had intended. On the way back to Jerusalem to report, they "preached the gospel to many villages of the Samaritans" (*Acts* 8).

The activities of the fugitives stimulated the persecutors. Repression followed the evangelists through the country. A young Jew of Tarsus, called Saul, was particularly active. He had been at the stoning of Stephen, and immediately thereafter became a sort of inquisitor-general for the Jewish authorities. His work was of little avail. Disciples were soon preaching the gospel up and down the Phoenician coast, in the island of Cyprus, and finally in Antioch.

As the infection spread, Saul became more active and more angry, "breathing threatening and slaughter against the disciples of the Lord." He seems to have heard bad news from Damascus; for he asked and received from the Sanhedrin a special commission to arouse the synagogues there against the disciples. The result, to Saul himself, was extraordinary; and we must digress here to learn something of Saul and of Tarsus.

Tarsus, the chief city of Cilicia, in southern Asia Minor, stood in a fertile plain less than ten miles from the Mediterranean; and through it the river Cydnus flowed. Ships had long sailed up the Cydnus from the sea, to discharge famous voyagers, like Cleopatra, within the walls of Tarsus. Having safe access to the sea, it also held the southern end of the great highway, along which both trade and war flowed across the Taurus Mountains to central Asia Minor. Tarsus had already been a great commercial city under the Seleucids, two centuries before Christ. It had long been enthusiastic for Greek culture, and was one of the three great university centres of the Mediterranean world, rivalling Athens and Alexandria; and it was a free city, with power to make its own laws. A Greek city, it was not wholly Greek; it was rather a meeting place of Greeks and Orientals. And it had a large Jewish colony; for the Seleucid kings placed Jewish colonists everywhere in the cities.

All this was left unchanged when Rome conquered Asia Minor and

Syria, some sixty years before Christ. Tarsus was confirmed in her ancient privileges, and Tarsan poets and philosophers were soon highly esteemed at Rome itself. The Tarsan Stoic, Athenodorus, became tutor to the young Augustus, who later appointed him to reform the government of Tarsus. There Athenodorus ruled long and honourably, highly respected by the Roman governors of Syria.

Such was the environment in which Saul of Tarsus grew up. He would hear in childhood about Athenodorus; he would know his worthy successor, the philosopher Nestor. And Saul himself came of a worthy family. Tarsus had many inhabitants but few citizens; for Athenodorus had made citizenship the reward of merit. Saul was a citizen. It was a satisfaction to him, to the end of his days, to be able to say, "I am a Jew, a man of Tarsus in Cilicia, a citizen of no mean city." Saul was as well a Roman freeman. His father had been granted Roman citizenship for some service to the State; and the son bore the Roman name Paul (*Paulus*) in addition to the Jewish Saul. More than once, in later perils, Saul's Roman citizenship stood him in good stead.

Strangely this Roman citizen, native of a Greek city, was brought up in the strictest Jewish piety, "a Hebrew of Hebrews; as touching the Law, a Pharisee." Saul was educated for the work of a Rabbi; but with Jewish thrift he was taught how to earn his bread, if need arose, as a weaver of tent-cloth.

Such were the conflicting elements in Saul's life. A Roman citizen and an heir to Greek culture, therefore disposed to be broad and tolerant; a pure Jew and a Pharisee, therefore taught to be narrow, exclusive, and sternly moral. Such elements, in one subconscious mind, meant either mental and moral confusion, or open war and victory.

This young Roman, Greek, Jew was in Jerusalem soon after the Crucifixion, studying for the rabbinate. He soon heard of certain Hellenists, preaching a new Messianism, dangerous to Judaism. Saul was disturbed, and was in the crowd that hurried Stephen to death.

After a brief, stern pursuit of disciples in and around Jerusalem, Saul set out, as we have seen, to carry the inquisition to Damascus. On the way he was overwhelmed by a religious cataclysm, which turned him into a follower of Jesus. Luke in *Acts* gives three accounts of the matter, not quite consistent with each other; and there are several references in the letters of Paul, only one of them explicit: "it was the good pleasure of God . . . to reveal his Son in me, that I might preach him among the Gentiles" (*Gal.* 1:15-17). Here is a clue. Saul, as a Tarsan, could not escape a decision some day on two questions—his Gentile neighbours and the nature of religion. So far his life with the former had been hampered by his conception of the latter. One had no mission to neighbours whom religion required one to avoid. But what if religion were faith and love, not obedience to the Mosaic Law! Then one's life and conscience would be liberated. Liberation had long been going on among Jews of the Dispersion. Some were achieving a sort of freedom by abandoning religion. Saul would never do that. He was too deeply religious to drift. What liberated him was the discovery, in Jesus and his followers, that one might love the Gentiles without ceasing to love God. Whatever had overtaken these new enthusiasts, Saul knew it was not irreligion; it was religion of another sort. Saul would require years to work out a system of thought to describe the new religion; but meanwhile he perceived that the new was better. The conflict between his training and his present observation was settled; the latter had won.

Shaken and dazed, Saul was led by his companions into Damascus. Disciples were already there, driven by the persecution. Saul joined himself to them. They received him with some uncertainty and baptized him. Henceforth we may call him Paul, as he and his new associates did.

Luke's account of Paul's first years as a disciple is confused, but is corrected by the explicit statement of Paul himself. After his conversion he went into retirement in the desert east of Damascus, perhaps for only a few weeks, perhaps for some months. Returning to Damascus, he participated for three years in the life of the disciples there. Preaching in the synagogues, he "confounded the Jews that dwelt in Damascus, proving that this is the Christ." Orthodox Jews plotted against his life; but he escaped over the city wall by night and made his way to Jerusalem. There he consulted Peter about the details of the new faith. Instructed and reassured, he left Jerusalem after fifteen days and retired to Tarsus, whence he was soon to go on extensive missionary travels with Barnabas and others. Paul was not to see Jerusalem again for fourteen years.[3]

The effort of the Jerusalem authorities to suppress the new movement seems to have been suspended after the conversion of Paul. "The Church

[3] *Galatians* 1: 15-2: 1; *Acts* 9: 8-31.

throughout all Judaea and Galilee and Samaria had peace, being edified; and, walking in the fear of the Lord and in comfort of the Holy Spirit, was multiplied." On a journey to the seacoast Peter found companies of disciples at Lydda and Joppa, and remained some time in the latter place, a guest of Simon a tanner. There another unexpected event happened. The news of Peter's presence spread north to the Roman fortress of Caesarea; and a centurion there, a proselyte to the synagogue, sent servants to Joppa, asking for the Gospel. Peter's religious scruples were overcome by a dream, or vision. He would not be made unclean, he was persuaded, by contact with a Gentile. He therefore went to Caesarea and, in the home of Cornelius, preached the Gospel to a Roman family, and received them by baptism into the Messianic community.

This was a new and startling departure. Peter himself drew back later when he found what was involved; but for the moment he saw that "God is no respecter of persons; but in every nation he that feareth him, and worketh righteousness, is acceptable to him." It was different at Jerusalem. There was consternation there at the news that Peter had consorted with Gentiles. He was upbraided on his return; but Peter told his story and it carried conviction. His own scruples, he said, had been overcome by the facts. As he preached in the house of Cornelius, the Pentecostal experience had been repeated there; and he had remembered the words of Jesus, how he said, "John indeed baptized with water; but ye shall be baptized in the Holy Spirit." Who was he, that he should reject those whom God baptized? The Jerusalem disciples were convinced. "They held their peace and glorified God, saying, Then to the Gentiles also hath God granted repentance unto life." Like Peter, they would never work out the new principle consistently, and were later to fall into confusion.

Other disciples, in flight from the persecution about Stephen, were now very far afield, preaching everywhere but only to Jews. Some of them, however, Hellenists from the island of Cyprus and from Cyrene in North Africa, were soon led like Peter into new ways. Coming to Antioch of Syria, perhaps as early as Peter to Caesarea, they preached to Greeks; and "a great number that believed turned unto the Lord." So much so that when the news reached Jerusalem, the disciples there sent Barnabas, a converted Levite of Cyprus, to observe and report what his fellow Cypriotes were doing. What he saw convinced him, as Peter had been convinced. Gentiles could not be excluded. Instead Barnabas went to Saul, in retirement at Tarsus, and brought him to Antioch, to assist in a mission to Jews and Gentiles alike. Converts were soon numerous enough to be conspicuous, and to receive a new name. They were called Christians, or Christ-ones. For some time the disciples throughout the world did not themselves use the name; but it stuck.

In two cities of the world, Jerusalem and Antioch, the community of disciples was now strong enough to be called a church; and of these two the Jerusalem church was to diminish steadily in importance, as Christianity spread among the Gentiles outside Palestine. The Antioch church was to grow in importance, as the mother church of Gentile Christianity.

Antioch of Syria was the third city of the Roman world, being surpassed in importance by Rome and Alexandria alone. The Greek Seleucids had built Antioch on the river Orontes, a few miles from the Mediterranean, as a more suitable capital for Syria than ancient Damascus. It stood just where the great trade routes from the Euphrates and the far East break through the Syrian mountains and debouch upon the coast. The city backed up the slope of Mt. Silpius; and nearby was Daphne, a grove sacred to Apollo. The city was thoroughly Greek in form, but with a mixed population and a large Jewish colony. When Pompey and the Roman legions came, Antioch was made a free city; and during the next century Julius Caesar, Augustus, Tiberius, Herod the Great of Palestine, and others, continued to adorn it with theatres, baths and columned streets. In the time of Christ Antioch was capital of the Roman province of Syria, which included Palestine. The praefect at Antioch had general supervision of Pontius Pilate and the later procurators of Judaea.

The Gospel must have reached Antioch in the very first days of the Christian movement. We have seen that Nicholas, "a proselyte of Antioch," was one of the distributors of relief among the disciples at Jerusalem, and that other disciples reached Antioch during the persecution that arose about Stephen. Now Barnabas and Paul were directing a vigorous mission there. The church in Antioch was soon strong enough to send them on a mission to other cities. They sailed from Seleucia, the seaport of Antioch, to the neighbouring island of Cyprus, taking with them John Mark of Jerusalem, a nephew of Barnabas, who was later to write the Gospel of Mark. They traversed the island, preaching in the synagogues, then sailed north to the mainland. There John Mark lost courage and returned to Jerusalem; but Paul and Barnabas pressed on into the interior, to Antioch of Pisidia, where they were welcomed to the synagogue and soon had the country town astir. The attendance of Gentiles at their preaching, however, alienated most Jews and led to the expulsion of Paul and Barnabas, but not before "the word of the Lord was spread abroad throughout all the region" (*Acts* 13).

It was the same at Iconium, Lystra and Derbe, little cities in a mountainous district, sparsely populated and not highly civilized. Public order was unstable, orthodox Judaism easily inflamed, the petty magistrates easily influenced. The apostles preached in the cities and the surrounding country, everywhere making converts, everywhere pursued at last by a howling mob and saving their lives by flight. When the storm subsided they retraced their steps, "confirming the souls" of the converts, then made their way home to Antioch, where they remained for some time. In several cities they had left a church, including Gentiles, and had made the beginnings of an organization, appointing elders in every church, on the model of the synagogue.

What was the Gospel to which the new converts were being won? It was that men need no longer wait for the Messiah; he had come. True he had been crucified; but that did not disprove his messiahship. He had died in fulfilment of God's plan; and God had raised him from the dead. The first disciples had seen him alive again; they were now having emotional experiences which meant, they were sure, that Christ was sending down the Spirit upon believers. One day, very soon, the Messiah would manifest himself to all men; for he would come on the clouds of heaven.

Why then had Christ died? It was, they believed, "that the scriptures might be fulfilled." In them prophets had foretold a "Day of the Lord," to be followed by the "Age to Come," when "this evil Age" would pass away. The prophecy had now been fulfilled in Jesus. He had exhibited on earth the spiritual energy and illumination of the New Age; he had now by death passed into the New Age. And all who so believed, and who repented of their sins, would pass with him at last. But every man must first appear before "the judgment-seat of Christ" (also called "the judgment-seat of God"), that he may "receive the things done in the body, according to what he hath done, whether it be good or bad." For judgment the dead will be raised; and all men, living and dead, will exchange their natural bodies for spiritual bodies. Then Christ will rule until he overcomes all evil things, after which he "shall deliver up the kingdom to God, even the Father." [4]

This was the Gospel that Paul preached throughout the Mediterranean world. It was the Gospel already being preached before his conversion. Paul was careful to inform his hearers that he was proclaiming to them what he himself had received at the first, and what Peter and James and John had later approved. And indeed one can find it for himself in *Acts,* in several speeches of Peter. These are not stenographic reports of Peter's utterances; but the author of *Acts* must be assumed to have known what sort of Gospel Peter was preaching.

The Gospel of St. Paul was essentially the Gospel preached, first and last, by the Christian evangelists, during the two generations covered by New Testament writings. It is the Gospel that long afterwards became the Rule of Faith and the Apostles' Creed, when the scattered Christian congregations of the world were drawing together into one Catholic Church.

There were, of course, some modifications of the Gospel even in apostolic times. The first disciples had expected the immediate return of Christ. To them his resurrection, ascension, and second advent were all parts of one divine event. When years passed and Christ did not appear, men still clung to the belief that he would. When Paul wrote I *Thessalonians* he still expected the second advent soon; when he wrote II *Thessalonians* he was trying to adjust himself to the unexpected delay. In the very latest writings of the New Testament, such as the *First Epistle of John,* men still hoped. Nevertheless resurrection, ascension and second advent came to appear, not one divine event but two. The substance of the Gospel still was that God had visited and redeemed his people; but the confirmation of that, the second advent, was another crisis, yet to come.

The delay of the second advent had another effect, the deterioration of the hope itself. Men began to think of the future in forms more

[4] *Galatians* 1: 4; *Romans* 14: 10; I *Corinthians* 5: 10, 15: 24.

Jewish and less Christian. This tendency first appears in II *Thessalonians*. It is completed in the New Testament Apocalypse, the *Revelation of John*, whose temper and imagery are entirely those of Jewish apocalypticism. The fierce Messiah of the Apocalypse is not the Jesus who went about doing good; nor is the God of the Apocalypse the Father of whom Jesus had spoken. One is back in the atmosphere of *Daniel, Enoch, Baruch,* and II *Esdras*.[5] Thus the Gospel was changing in the matter of eschatology, even in the first two Christian generations.

But there is much in the New Testament beside the Gospel. Indeed there is not a writing there, not a biography or epistle or philosophy or apocalypse, of which it can be said that it was produced in order to commit the Gospel to writing. Everyone knew what the Gospel was. What men did not know was the facts of the life of Jesus, what he had said about life and duty, how his disciples ought to conduct themselves as husbands and wives, as servants and masters, as citizens and fellow Christians. In all these things Jesus was still their teacher and lord. So men wrote down what they knew, or could learn, about him and those who had been with him. Thus, side by side with the Gospel, there was taught in the churches a manner of life worthy of the Gospel, learned from Christ himself. "Put on therefore, as God's elect, holy and beloved, a heart of compassion, kindness, humility, meekness, long-suffering; forbearing one another, and forgiving each other, if any man have a complaint against any; even as the Lord forgave you, so also do ye . . . let the peace of Christ rule in your hearts. . . . Let the word of Christ dwell in you richly in all wisdom. . . . Whatsoever ye do, work heartily, as unto the Lord, and not unto men . . . ye serve the Lord Christ" (*Col.* 3: 12–24).

This may be described as the morals of the kingdom of God. It is clearly distinguished in the New Testament from the Gospel. The latter was an announcement, or proclamation (Greek *kerygma*), as by a herald or town crier (*keryx*); the former was teaching (*didaché*) or exhortation (*paraklesis*). The Gospel was received by faith; morals were acquired by study, observation, self-discipline, and the contagion of

---

[5] The so-called "Little Apocalypse," in *Mark* 13, which echoes the famines, earthquakes and political disturbances in the East during the reigns of Claudius and Nero, attributes to Jesus himself an outlook upon the future that has long been recognized as inconsistent with the rest of his teaching.

like-minded persons. The primitive Christian evangelists found it easier
to make converts to the Gospel than to introduce them to a life worthy
of the Gospel, as the Epistles of St. Paul testify. Human frailty and for-
getfulness, passion and perversity, set strongly against the new way of
life; and the world in which it was to be lived was very perplexing, even
to the most thoughtful and courageous. The Christians were taught
therefore to seek the help of God, for themselves and for each other, in
their pursuit of the way, "with all prayer and supplication praying at
all seasons in the Spirit, and watching thereunto in all perseverance and
supplication for all the saints."

They became conscious of other supernatural aid as well. As the
second advent of Christ retreated farther and farther into the future, a
mystical presence of Christ came more and more into the present consciousness of believers. And one can see, from *Acts* and the *Epistles,* how
this came about. The loving fellowship of the first weeks of waiting, and
the emotional experience of the Day of Pentecost, an experience constantly repeated in the preaching missions, had seemed from the first
a supernatural thing, "the gift of the Holy Spirit." Here was life of a new
quality, hopeful and joyous and free, such as prophets had foretold:

> This is that which was spoken by the prophet Joel;
> And it shall be in the last days, saith God,
> I will pour forth of my Spirit upon all flesh.

The last days might be prolonged, but they were here nevertheless; and
men were living by the power of the Spirit, sent in advance by Christ
himself. He, "being by the right hand of God exalted, and having received of the Father the promise of the Holy Spirit," had "poured forth"
the Spirit upon his disciples. And, more wonderful than all the abnormal phenomena that followed, was the love or charity (Greek *agapé*)
that resulted, a reproduction in the Church of what men had seen in
Jesus himself. As St. Paul reflected upon this, he came to believe that the
Spirit was none other than the Lord himself; and this received a prominent place in his preaching—"The Lord is the Spirit"; to be "in the
Spirit" is to be "in Christ"; and the Church is in some sense "the body of
Christ," an extension of his personality on earth. The triumphant life
that believers now lived was the triumph of Christ in them.[6]

[6] I *Corinthians* 1: 1–9; II *Corinthians* 3: 17, 18; *Romans* 6: 1–11.

This Christ-mysticism, as it has been called, became prominent in the preaching of St. Paul in proportion as the second advent became more remote. Where once he had said to believers "the Lord himself shall descend from heaven, with a shout, with the voice of the archangel, and with the trump of God," he now prays rather "that (they) may be strengthened with power through his Spirit in the inward man." The advent hope remained, was indeed to survive into modern times, reviving whenever the times are critical and the minds of men confused and hopeless. Meanwhile there was a presence of Christ in the Church, that was a much surer foundation for right living in the world than were naïve expectations of catastrophic events to come.

This, then, was the Gospel; and these were the teachings of the primitive Church. They were both eschatological, the Gospel in the sense that Christ would come again and the world be transformed, the teachings in the sense that the life of the Age to Come was already being lived in the Church.

The Gospel and the teachings were both to raise difficult questions. What was to be the attitude of Gentile Christians to the Law of Moses? And how could the Christian beliefs be fitted into a general view of the Universe? The answer to the former question was to divide the Church, separating Gentile from Jewish believers. The answer to the latter was to develop into Catholic Christian theology.

While the Gospel was spreading outside Palestine, the Jerusalem church was enduring great trials. On the death of Herod Philip and the banishment of Herod Antipas, the Roman government had given their territories to Herod Agrippa I, grandson of Herod the Great and his Jewish wife Mariamne. To further placate the Jews the government added to his kingdom Judaea and Samaria, withdrawing the procurator. Herod Agrippa I (41–44 A.D.) was now king of all Palestine. He found throughout the land a Christian Church, grown strong enough in the twelve or thirteen years of its existence to attract attention; and its accommodation of itself to Gentile converts was complicating its own position within Judaism. Suppression of the Church, Herod thought, would be popular with the Jews. So he executed James, the brother of John, in the week before the Passover, when Jerusalem was again filled with pilgrims. Popular approval encouraged the king to arrest Peter also;

but his trial and execution were delayed by the Passover. In the interval Peter escaped from prison, it seemed by a miracle; and Herod Agrippa, returning to Caesarea, soon died of a loathsome disease. His death was attributed by the Church to a judgment of God. Palestine thereafter was ruled by a succession of procurators, two of whom, Felix and Festus, meet us in *Acts*.

During these years the relations of the Jerusalem and Antioch churches were becoming strained. Jerusalem disciples were holding fast to the Mosaic Law, all the more because Pharisees were now entering the church there. Some of them went down without authorization to Antioch, and taught that converts could not be admitted without circumcision. The Messianic kingdom, they thought, was only for the people of God; and Jews were the people of God; men must therefore become Jews if they were to enter the kingdom of God.

The visitors disturbed the peace of the Antioch church, which therefore appointed Paul and Barnabas to carry an appeal to Jerusalem. Paul's account of the matter indicates that it was his teaching that had been singled out for attack; and that he felt some disquiet, lest he should have been in error. So he and Barnabas went to Jerusalem, taking a certain Titus with them. Paul wanted a private consultation; and the church at Jerusalem was therefore not assembled. Only the apostles and elders met, in what is known as the Apostolic Council of Jerusalem, fourteen years after Paul's previous visit and probably about 49 A.D. Paul and Barnabas told "what signs and wonders God had wrought among the Gentiles through them"; and Peter reminded the Council once more of his own experiences, and how God had given to his Gentile converts the Holy Spirit, even as to Jewish converts. James, the brother of the Lord, was convinced and spoke the deciding word. The Council agreed to write to Antioch, asking only that Gentile Christians refrain from practices offensive to Jewish consciences. They were to avoid food that had been offered to idols, and to abstain from eating flesh from which the blood had not been drained off, since blood is held by Jews to be the material element of life and is therefore consecrated to religious uses. They were asked also to avoid the sexual laxity that was too common in Gentile society.[7]

The Council chose two Jerusalem leaders, "Judas, called Barsabbas,

[7] *Acts* 15; *Galatians* 2: 1–10.

and Silas," to return with Paul and Barnabas to Antioch, with a friendly letter setting forth the decision of the Council. The letter gave great satisfaction to the Antioch church; and the distress was allayed.

The decision of the Council, however, did not meet the whole difficulty. It was generous to Gentile, but difficult for Jewish, believers. The Gentile Christian need not be circumcised; but what then of the Jewish Christian? If he sat at meat with uncircumcised Christians, he compromised his orthodoxy as a Jew; if he refused to do so, he disturbed the fellowship of the Lord's Supper. The situation was too complicated for even Peter. He came down from Jerusalem to Antioch, and mingled freely at first with Gentile Christians; but when others came from Jerusalem "he drew back and separated himself, fearing them that were of the circumcision." Other Jewish Christians followed his example; and even Barnabas wavered. Paul publicly rebuked Peter for his double-mindedness. Paul now saw that the Law and the Gospel were not compatible, that one must choose between them. For himself he was satisfied that "a man is not justified by the works of the Law but through faith in Jesus Christ."

Time was to vindicate Paul. As for Peter, he practically disappears from primitive church history. Having set his hand to the plough, he was looking back and could not plough a straight furrow in the new field. The church at Jerusalem, led by James the brother of Jesus, also declined, as we shall see later.

The friendship of Paul and Barnabas must have been strained by the wavering of Barnabas; but they planned a further visit to the churches established during their mission to southern Asia Minor. Unhappily they now differed sharply about John Mark, whose earlier desertion made Paul unwilling to take him on a second mission. So Barnabas took Mark with him, and went home to Cyprus. Paul took Silas; and, after visiting churches that had sprung up in the neighbourhood of Antioch, they set off overland to southern Asia Minor. At Lystra they picked up Timothy, son of a Christian Jewess and a Greek father; and Luke, a converted Syrian of Antioch, was also a member of the party, at least on occasion, for in writing *Acts* he begins now to write in the first person (16:11).

Paul and his party completed a visitation of the young churches, then looked for unbroken ground to cultivate. They pressed north-westward to the Aegean at Troas, near the site of ancient Troy, and there awaited guidance. It came to Paul in a dream, in which a man of Macedonia besought him, "Come over into Macedonia and help us." The party set sail from Troas, and two days later were in Macedonia at Philippi. They were committed now to preaching the Gospel in Europe.

Philippi was a Roman colony. Outside its walls, in 42 B.C., Octavian, soon to become Augustus, had overwhelmed the republican forces of Brutus and Cassius and avenged the murder of his foster-father Julius Caesar. It was in honour of Caesar that Philippi was made a Roman colony; and its earliest citizens were members of the bodyguard of Augustus. As a Roman colony, Philippi was now organized on the model of Rome itself. It had its senate, and magistrates who were attended in public by lictors bearing *fasces,* or bundles of rods; and it enjoyed the *jus Italicum,* exemption from the land tax imposed upon conquered countries.

In this Roman city Jews were so few that they had no synagogues in which one might begin a Christian mission; but outside the city, by the river, Paul found a place where Jews came together for prayer. There on a Sabbath day he sat and spoke informally to a few women; and there the first known convert on European soil was made, Lydia, a seller of purple stuffs. Her family embraced the faith with her; and her house soon became the meeting-place of a new church.

Paul must have been at Philippi several weeks when an unfortunate incident involved him with the authorities. A demented girl was being exploited by a syndicate. Her dementia passed for spirit-possession; and a person so possessed was thought to be the passive instrument of the possessing spirit, "the slave of the god." People at Philippi paid fees to consult the spirit. The mad girl came to know Paul and his company. To her disordered mind they also were slaves, "slaves of the Most High God"; and as they passed daily to the place of prayer, she would follow them, shouting this to the populace. Distressed one day, Paul turned and commanded the evil spirit to depart; and the dementia of the girl was subdued. She was thus ruined as an oracle, and her owners would lose their fees. They dragged Paul and Silas to the Forum, the great open space on which the law-courts looked, and brought them before the magistrates, as disturbers of the peace and men who practised illegal rites. Paul and Silas were disrobed and beaten by the lictors, by order of

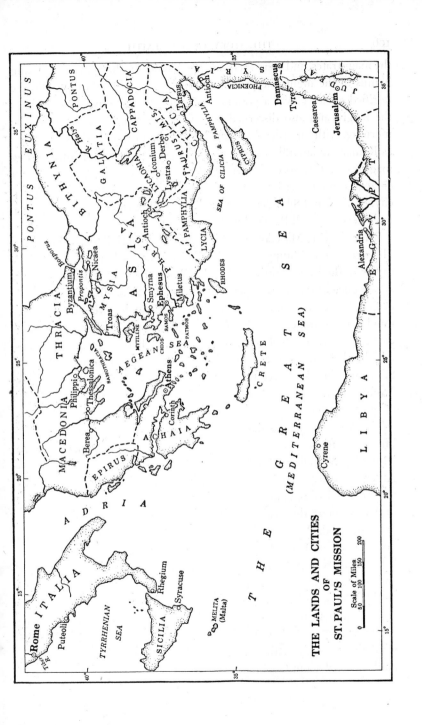

THE LANDS AND CITIES
OF
ST. PAUL'S MISSION

Scale of Miles
0   50   100   150   200

the magistrates, and were then cast into prison. As they prayed and sang hymns in the night, the prison was shaken by an earthquake. To the terrified gaoler it was a portent; and it led to his conversion. Perhaps the magistrates also discerned a portent. They sent the lictors in the morning, with an order for the release of the prisoners. Paul and Silas, as Romans unlawfully beaten, would not accept private dismissal. The magistrates, therefore, disturbed at the news that they were Roman citizens, came in person and set them free, requesting them to leave the city. So Paul and Silas departed, leaving a young church at Philippi, the most devoted of all Paul's churches.

Before leaving Macedonia, Paul attempted to work in two other cities. He went from Philippi to Thessalonica, the modern Saloniki, then capital of the Roman province of Macedonia. There Paul again found a synagogue, where he was permitted on three Sabbaths to address the people. Some Jews and many Greek proselytes believed, including a number of prominent women; but orthodox Jews raised an uproar, and converts conveyed Paul and Silas by night to Beroea. Again, however, they left behind a church; and the experience was repeated in Beroea. Silas and Timothy stayed there for a time; but Paul was worn out with labour and adversity, and friends took him by sea to Athens for a period of quiet and rest.

The Athens of Paul's day was a city of little commercial or political importance; but it was still a great university center. Men who loved leisure and intellectual pursuits came to Athens from everywhere. Athenian society was hospitable to all manner of ideas, and therefore to all manner of religions. As Paul landed at Piraeus and made his way to Athens along the road called Hamaxitos, he would pass many altars to strange gods. Entering the city by the Piraeus gate, he would pass the noble temple of Theseus on his way to the *Agora*.

In seclusion in Athens Paul was distressed by the prevailing idolatry, and was soon drawn from retirement, to reason in the synagogues and in the *Agora*. Epicurean and Stoic idlers came upon him there, and brought him to the *Areopagus* or Mars Hill, that overshadowed the *Agora* on the south. It was a favourite resort for all sorts of folk, who were always ready "either to tell or to hear some new thing." There Paul reasoned about God, the coming judgment, and the resurrection of the dead. But Athenians were not noted for their moral earnestness; and while they were familiar with the doctrine of immortality, the Jewish idea of a physical resurrection seemed to them grotesque. "When they heard of the uprising of the corpses, some mocked"; the rest postponed consideration to some later date. So Paul moved on to Corinth; but he left in Athens a few disciples, including "Dionysius the Areopagite, and a woman called Damaris" (*Acts* 17: 32–18: 1).

Corinth was a city of great importance for anyone contemplating the evangelization of Europe. It was the capital of the Roman province of Achaia, the ancient Greece, and the seat of the proconsul. It was commercially important, as lying on the great central route from Italy to the Orient. Standing on a narrow isthmus, with a foot planted on two seas, it was easy of access from both east and west. Many a traveller from Italy landed at one harbour, *Lechaeum,* and crossed the isthmus to sail from the other, *Cenchreae,* for Asia. The Romans had destroyed ancient Corinth in the general conquest of Greece; but Julius Caesar had re-founded it in 46 B.C. and made it a Roman colony. So most names connected with Corinth in the New Testament are Roman. But Corinth had a large Greek population also, as well as strangers from many lands and a considerable Jewish community.

In Corinth Paul found a Jew and his wife, Aquila and Priscilla, lately expelled from Rome by an anti-Jewish edict of the Emperor Claudius, 49 or 50 A.D. Suetonius informs us that the edict was provoked by persistent disturbances in the Ghetto, "instigated by one Chrestus." He probably means *Christus,* as the name of Christ is more than once confused in Roman usage. The disturbances at Rome may well have been a controversy between Christian Jews and the orthodox; and Aquila and Priscilla may have been Christians before coming to Corinth. In any case they offered Paul hospitality; and their house became his home. They were fellow craftsmen; and together they pursued their trade as weavers. If Aquila and Priscilla were not already Christians, they now became so; and to the end of Paul's days they were his trusted friends and helpers. When he left Corinth for Ephesus, they accompanied him. Their house in Ephesus became a meeting place for the Christians of that city. Aquila was a Jew of Pontus; but Priscilla bears a good Roman name, and may have been a Roman lady of wealth.

For some weeks after reaching Corinth, Paul "reasoned in the synagogue every Sabbath," until Silas and Timothy came on from Macedonia. Then the mission was intensified, and the Jews became hostile; so much so that Paul publicly renounced his Jewish mission and transferred his teaching to the home of a certain Titus Justus, a Roman proselyte. For a year and six months Paul carried forward a Gentile mission in Corinth, winning many converts, including a few Jews.

While Paul was at Corinth, Junius Gallio came from Rome to be proconsul of Achaia. He was brother to the philosopher Seneca, and a high-minded man, with a great reputation as a wit. Seneca says of him that "no mortal man was so gracious to anyone as he was to everyone." He and Seneca were both to fall victims to the madness of Nero; but meanwhile Claudius had appointed him proconsul of Achaia, influenced perhaps by his urbanity and his thorough Greek culture.

The coming of Gallio was to prove of importance to Paul. The Jews, relying perhaps on the complaisance of the new proconsul, dragged Paul before him; but Gallio promptly dismissed the case. It was, he saw, a Jewish religious controversy, which he was indisposed to judge. The mission to Corinth was therefore relatively secure.

During the long stay at Corinth, apparently in 51 or 52 A.D., I *Thessalonians* was written, the first of the known Epistles of St. Paul and the earliest of all New Testament writings. A little later II *Thessalonians* was written. Paul had found reason for anxiety concerning the young church at Thessalonica, and had sent Timothy to investigate and report. Timothy returned to Paul at Corinth, bringing "glad tidings of the faith and love" of the Christians of Thessalonica, and of their longing for Paul's return; but they had fallen into doubt. They were particularly disturbed about friends who had recently died and would therefore not be here when Christ returned. Paul writes to reassure them. "The dead in Christ shall rise first," when "the Lord shall descend from heaven, with a shout, with the voice of the archangel, and with the trump of God." After that, "we that are alive, that are left, shall together with them be caught up in the clouds, to meet the Lord in the air; and so shall we ever be with the Lord." Meanwhile the Christians at Thessalonica were exhorted to go on with the business of living, and remain loyal to the teaching of Paul.

Some time after the affair with Gallio, Paul determined upon a visit to Jerusalem. In some moment of peril or spiritual crisis, he had made a vow; and the time was approaching when he must fulfil it. It was a Jewish practice to make a vow to God, when in sickness or in danger. In such cases, the last month before the fulfilment of the vow was a month of special consecration, when the hair was clipped and wine avoided. Paul began the month by shaving his head at Cenchreae, then set sail for Caesarea, taking with him Aquila and Priscilla. These two left the ship at Ephesus and remained there; but Paul pressed on to Caesarea and thence to Jerusalem. Having greeted the church and fulfilled his vow in the Temple, he went down to Antioch to see the friends of earlier years. He was soon off again, visiting the centres of his missionary journey with Barnabas. He went overland, "through the region of Galatia and Phrygia, establishing the disciples," then made his way back to Ephesus, where he was to labour more than two years.

Ephesus, though not the capital, was the chief city of the Roman province of Asia, that part of Asia Minor bordering on the Aegean Sea. In all the East only Antioch and Alexandria passed it in importance. It was the sea end of the great highway from Italy to the East; and many roads converged there upon the main route. Close to Ephesus, under the brow of a little hill, was an ancient temple of Asian worship. There long before the Greeks came the Asiatics had worshipped a goddess of fecundity. The Greeks later identified her with the chaste Artemis (Roman *Diana*), but without changing the cultus. It was orgiastic in character, and included ceremonial prostitution. The Greeks had built for the goddess a splendid temple; but its priests remained the centre of the conservative Asiatic section of the population. The goddess herself was represented by a rude statue, believed to have fallen from heaven, a tradition attached to many such statues.

In the weeks or months before Paul reached Ephesus, Apollos, an eloquent Jew of Alexandria, came to Ephesus. Somewhere he had learned about Jesus, and believed him to be the Messiah. In the synagogue at Ephesus he undertook to persuade his fellow Jews. Aquila and Priscilla welcomed him, and "expounded unto him the way of God more accurately." Apollos soon crossed to Greece and began to work in Corinth, with such effect that some Christians there thought him superior to Paul; and the church was divided. Paul felt it necessary to write the Corinthians, reminding them that none were to be of Paul, none of Apollos, but all of Christ.[8]

While Apollos was at Corinth, Paul came on to Ephesus from southern Asia Minor. There were probably converts in Ephesus already; there were certainly disciples of John the Baptist. Paul instructed them in Christian beliefs; and they received Christian baptism.[9]

For three months Paul worked through the synagogue; but the Jews were sharply divided. When the dissension grew too sharp, Paul withdrew his disciples to a lecture-room for Sophists, "the school of Tyrannus," where he continued teaching for two full years, with great effect, his influence being enhanced by a reputation for exorcism. The Gospel began to spread from Ephesus throughout the province of Asia; so much so that a generation later, when the Jerusalem church was at an end, Ephesus and the province became the centre of Christianity, overshadowing even Antioch.

During the years at Ephesus Paul carried a growing burden of anxiety concerning his young churches everywhere. One detects it in three letters written from Ephesus—*Galatians,* and I and II *Corinthians.* The *Epistle to the Galatians* was called forth by the news that visitors from Jerusalem were disturbing the churches in southern Asia Minor. The Christians throughout Galatia were being drawn back to the belief that one must be obedient to the Mosaic Law in order to be a Christian. Paul writes with deep emotion. He knows that the Law and the Gospel are incompatible, that where the former is revived the latter will be lost. As to the church at Corinth, Paul learned that party feeling had again raised its head there; and also that Christians, unable to settle their differences among themselves, were going to law before pagan courts. Worse still, Paul hears that pagan morals still persist, and Christian living is not what it ought to be. So Paul writes I *Corinthians,* and sends it by the hand of Timothy. The Epistle includes a panegyric on Christian love, one of the most beautiful things in the Scriptures. Love, Paul says, is the greatest of all human achievements, and the most enduring.

The evils at Corinth continued, and were aggravated by a visit from

[8] *Acts* 18: 24–28; I *Corinthians* 1: 10–13.
[9] *Acts* 19: 1–7.

those "Judaizers" who had disturbed the churches of Galatia. So Paul wrote another letter, stern and threatening, and sent Titus to Corinth. The letter has long been thought lost; but it is now believed to be the last four chapters of II *Corinthians*.

The influence of the Christian movement at Ephesus finally involved it with the tradesmen. The profitable business of making little silver images of Artemis was injuriously affected by Paul's teaching against the worship of idols. The guild of the silversmiths raised an uproar that convulsed the city. A mob rushed into that great amphitheatre that modern excavations have uncovered; and Paul was with difficulty dissuaded from entering and addressing the crowd. The uproar died away in time; and an officer of the municipal council dismissed the people, with warnings about the heavy hand of the proconsul.

The mission to Ephesus was successful; but the perils were greater than are told in *Acts*. From Paul himself we learn that he had "fought with wild beasts at Ephesus," perhaps literally, perhaps only figuratively. His life was saved by Aquila and Priscilla at the risk of their own. It was time for change and relief. Paul had planned, even before the rioting, to revisit the churches in Macedonia and Greece, and had sent forward Timothy and a certain Erastus to prepare for him. After that he would visit Jerusalem. Then he hoped to preach the Gospel at Rome itself.[10]

When, therefore, quiet was restored at Ephesus, Paul said an affectionate farewell to the Christians and set out overland for Greece, with a special thought to Corinth. On the way he tarried long enough among the churches of Macedonia to gather money for the church at Jerusalem, and to hear from Titus at Corinth. Titus came at last with news that the Corinthian church had come to a better mind and was now longing for Paul's return. He was soon at Corinth, where he spent the winter, probably of 57 A.D.[11]

Delegates from Macedonia were to join Paul at Corinth, to accompany him to Jerusalem with the collection for the poor. The assembling of the delegates would take time; and Paul had three months of quiet. He used it to write the *Epistle to the Romans*, the longest of his letters and the most carefully reasoned statement of his teaching. Paul had

[10] I *Cor.* 15: 32; *Rom.* 16: 3, 4; *Acts* 19: 21.
[11] II *Cor.* 2: 1–13; 7: 5–7.

longed to visit Rome. Soon he would do so; and the letter would prepare the way. After the visit to Jerusalem, he would close his work in
the East and turn to the West, carrying the Gospel to Rome and on to
Spain.[12]

The *Epistle to the Romans* opens a window upon the churches of
Corinth and Rome. At Corinth "Erastus, the treasurer of the city," is
now a Christian, and a certain Gaius, sufficiently affluent to be host to
Paul and the whole Church. As for Rome, Aquila and Priscilla are settled there again; and one of several Christian groups meets in their
home. In Rome also are Christian Jews, Andronicus and Junias, who had
been converted in Palestine before Paul himself and were well known
to the apostles. There is the household of Aristobulus, deceased brother
of Herod Agrippa I; and the household of Narcissus, favourite of the
Emperor Claudius, who was to die by Nero's command. Some of the
names in *Romans* may still be read on the walls of the catacombs, where
the first Christians laid their dead; others are in sepulchral inscriptions
along the Appian Way. The Gospel at Rome was surmounting all barriers of race and class.

In the spring Paul set out with a company from Corinth for Jerusalem. A Jewish plot prevented them from going by sea, and sent them
overland through Macedonia, to sail from Philippi. Thence following
the Asiatic shore, with many stops, they came in a few weeks to Miletus.
In haste to reach Jerusalem for Pentecost, Paul had declined to land at
Ephesus and visit the church; but "from Miletus he sent to Ephesus, and
called to him the elders of the church." They made the toilsome journey
of twenty-five miles across the mountains; and Luke tells very movingly
the story of their last meeting with Paul, who knew he was never to see
them again. Weeping they brought him to the ship. The travellers
coasted along and, rounding Cyprus, crossed the sea to Tyre. Christians
in Tyre tried to keep Paul there, fearing for his life; but after seven
days he pressed on with his company to Caesarea. Philip, once fellow
evangelist of the martyr Stephen, was still at Caesarea, an old man now,
with four daughters who preached the Gospel with him. These all besought Paul with tears not to go on to Jerusalem. When he could not be
dissuaded, several men of Caesarea accompanied him, as well as a certain

[12] *Rom.* 15: 22–28.

"Mnason of Cyprus, an early disciple," who had a home in Jerusalem ready for the travellers.

The sixty-five miles to Jerusalem would be accomplished in two days; and Paul and his company were warmly welcomed by James, the brother of the Lord, and by the elders, who listened thankfully as Paul told how many Gentiles had been won to Christ. But there were serious difficulties to be discussed. Believers were not all Gentiles. Palestinian Jews, thousands of them, had accepted Christ, while still loyal to the Law of Moses. They had heard that Paul was encouraging Jews of the Dispersion to abandon the Law. This placed Jewish Christians in a painful position. Some public proof that Paul was still devoted to the Law, James thought, would reassure the Jewish Church. Four Jewish Christians in Jerusalem were even then under a vow. The time for its fulfilment was near, when they would present offerings in the Temple, shave their heads and cast the hair into the sacrificial fire. Let Paul publicly associate himself with them, and pay for the offerings, two lambs and a ram for each man. If Paul would do this, everyone would know that he was still a devout Jew.

Paul agreed. He went next day to the Temple with the four, and added his vow to theirs. The vow was to be discharged in seven days. Within that time Paul was seen in the streets in company with a Greek, one of his travelling companions, whom Jewish pilgrims from Ephesus recognized as a certain Trophimus of that city. So Paul's appearance in the Temple after seven days created an uproar. It was assumed that Greeks were with him and that the Temple was defiled. The news spread through the city. A mob gathered quickly to the Temple; and Paul was dragged out and beaten in the Temple area. Near-by was quartered the Roman garrison, a cohort of six hundred men with cavalry. The tribune Claudius Lysias was soon down the castle steps with a guard of soldiers; and Paul was borne in chains towards the fortress. He was, the tribune thought, an Egyptian Jew, who had recently led thirty thousand enthusiasts to the Mount of Olives, in expectation of the Messianic kingdom. They had been dispersed with many casualties and were now, it seemed, wreaking vengeance on the deceiver.[13]

[13] Josephus, *Wars* II. xiii. 5; *Acts* 21: 27-40.

Paul spoke to the tribune in Greek, declaring himself a citizen of Tarsus, and received permission to address the crowd. When silence was secured, he spoke from the castle steps in Hebrew, the language of the sacred Scriptures. That, he thought, would dispose the crowd to listen. It was of no use; there was further violence. An appearance of Paul next day before the Sanhedrin, under military protection, achieved nothing but still further violence; and he was soon on his way back to Caesarea, under strong guard, to be tried by Felix, the Roman procurator.

Felix (52–60 A.D.) was one of the procurators who governed all Palestine after the death of Herod Agrippa I. They were generally brutal and corrupt; and the land fell into hopeless disorder. Romans and Jews provoked each other to violence. The Jewish Sicarii, or Dagger men, took to systematic assassination. Felix himself hired them to murder the high priest Jonathan.

Such was the man to whom Paul must now look for justice. Happily Paul had more than once used his Roman citizenship to good effect with Roman officials; and in Caesarea, though under guard, he was permitted to receive his friends, while Felix dallied two years, hoping for a bribe. Felix lost his position, however, on the accession of the Emperor Nero; and Festus, a very different man, became procurator. The trial of Paul was now hurried on. But he was weary of the long imprisonment, doubtful of receiving justice, and had resolved to exercise a citizen's right to appeal to the emperor. Having appealed, no lower court could try him; and Paul was ordered sent to Rome.

The months at Caesarea, wearisome to Paul, were nevertheless important for Christian history. It may be that some of Paul's latest letters, "Epistles of the Imprisonment," were written from Caesarea. In any case, Luke would there gather some of the materials for his Gospel, and perhaps for the early chapters of *Acts*. For Philip the Evangelist had been thirty years at Caesarea, and many other Christians unknown now by name. Some had known the Lord himself; many would remember the events of the first years after the crucifixion. The library of Christian antiquities at Caesarea became one of the most valuable sources of information concerning the primitive Church; and the first Church History was written by Eusebius, bishop of Caesarea, in the fourth century.

Paul sailed from Caesarea in charge of Julius, a centurion of the Augustan cohort. Luke was of the party, and Aristarchus, a Macedonian convert who had been with Paul through the riots at Ephesus. They sailed in a coasting vessel to Myra, on the southern tip of Asia Minor, and there transferred to a government corn ship, on its way from Egypt to Italy. The wind was contrary, and many tedious days brought the ship only to Crete. The season for shipping was soon to close; and both captain and shipowner thought it wise to coast along to Phoenix, the best harbour in Crete, and there winter. The decision, on a government ship, would rest with the centurion; and the ship sailed, only to be driven out to sea and thrown helplessly about for a fortnight, with neither sun nor stars to direct her course. A terrific north-east wind seemed likely to drive her across the sea upon the Syrtis, the great sands off the coast of Africa; but by lessening sail and throwing out cargo, the ship was held westward, and one day at midnight found herself in shallow water. The sailors "let go four anchors from the stern, and prayed for the dawn." Paul's courage steadied the ship's company. In the grey dawn they broke a long fast by taking bread, after Paul had given thanks to God before them all; and at daybreak they found themselves near a sandy beach. They cut away the anchors, threw out wheat to lighten the ship, and hoisted the foresail to beach her. When the ship struck and began to break up, they were near enough to swim ashore or float in on the wreckage; and the company of two hundred and seventy-six were all saved. The land proved to be Malta.

Three months were spent in the island; then the centurion sailed with his prisoner for Italy, in another corn ship that had wintered in Malta. In a few days Paul was landed at Puteoli. There were Christians in the town, who gave hospitality for seven days to him and his company. Then they went forward on the Appian Way towards Rome. Forty miles from the city, at the Market of Appius, and thirty miles, at the Three Taverns, the travellers were met by Christians from Rome. Among them would be some whom Paul had mentioned in the *Epistle to the Romans* —Aquila and Priscilla perhaps, and Andronicus and Junias, as well as members of the households of Aristobulus and Narcissus. Warmed by their love and solicitude, Paul "thanked God and took courage."

In Rome Paul was delivered by the centurion to the *stratopedarch,* the liaison officers between the legions of the provinces and the imperial authorities. Paul was allowed lodgings of his own, though bound by light chains to a soldier. His Roman citizenship would accomplish this, and perhaps the affluence of friends. However that may be, Paul did not lack money; else he could not have appealed to Caesar, a proceeding as costly as most appeals to supreme courts.

The churches in Rome were not Paul's first concern. They were strong enough to regard him as an honoured guest, without looking to him for direction. Paul gave himself immediately to a last effort to win his fellow Jews. They came by invitation to his dwelling, "to whom he expounded the matter, testifying the kingdom of God, and persuading them concerning Jesus" (*Acts* 28: 17-28). A few believed; most disbelieved. To Paul it seemed the final refusal. The Gospel, he concluded, was meant for the Gentiles.

Business in the supreme court at Rome must often have been congested; and delays would be common. Paul continued under guard two years, awaiting trial, but living in a dwelling of his own and preaching the Gospel to all who came. Very strangely Luke tells us no more than this, closing *Acts* abruptly and without explanation. We should have expected him to tell of the death of Paul; but he was probably interrupted by sickness, or persecution, or some duty at a distant church, and was never able to resume writing. Nor is it strange that Paul wrote so little during the four long years in prison at Caesarea and Rome. He was not in quiet retirement, as with Aquila and Priscilla at Corinth; and the churches were older now and better able to direct themselves. Paul's work was nearly done. So there are only four "Epistles of the Imprisonment" —*Ephesians, Colossians, Philemon,* and *Philippians.*

It is disappointing that we know so little of Paul's last days. We may infer from Luke's silence that he was not tried and condemned at the end of the two years' imprisonment at Rome. If the biography closed because the hero died, the biographer would have said so. It is likely that Paul's accusers did not appear against him, and that the charge dropped automatically. Jewish leaders in Palestine were too busy with tragic affairs there to press accusations, now four years old, against one far away. In any case, there are in the "Pastoral Epistles"—I and II *Timothy* and *Titus*—glimpses of further labours of St. Paul, after the imprisonment. We read of a mission to the island of Crete, and a journey up the coast of Asia Minor and across to Macedonia. Soon Paul was re-arrested and brought back to Rome, probably because of fresh disorders provoked by his preaching. Before all this happened, he seems to have visited Spain, as he had long wished to do. The *First Epistle of Clement of Rome,* a document of the late first century, reports such a visit.

There are enthusiasts who think Paul visited Britain; but this is wishful thinking. Britons, living at Rome, may have been converted before the death of Paul. The poet Martial, 70 A.D., writes of a beautiful, gifted British princess, Claudia, living at Rome. She wedded a noble Roman, Pudens; and Martial celebrates the event in verse:

> Claudia, from far-off climes, my Pudens weds;
> With choicest gifts, O Hymen, crown their heads!

Excavations at Rome disclose that the house of Pudens, in the late first century, was used for Christian worship, and that it had been bought from Aquila and Priscilla. The Church of St. Pudentiana now stands on the site. As for Claudia, names of the Gens Pomponia, to which she belonged by adoption, are found in an early Christian catacomb. It seems clear that the Pudens and Claudia of Martial are the Pudens and Claudia of II *Timothy*—"Eubulus saluteth thee, and Pudens, and Linus, and Claudia, and all the brethren." But this does not prove that Paul visited Britain.

An unbroken Christian tradition, as ancient as Clement of Rome, says that both Paul and Peter were martyred at Rome; and Clement was a late contemporary of both. But we cannot tell when Peter came to Rome. He was not yet there during Paul's first imprisonment; and his stay must have been brief. The story that Peter was founder and first bishop of the church of Rome, and that he ruled twenty-five years as bishop, is an ancient invention. Paul, in the *Epistle to the Romans,* and Luke in *Acts* would not have been silent about so important a fact.

The consensus of tradition and legend is that Peter and Paul died under Nero, whether in the persecution of 64 or later we cannot tell. In the summer of 64 fire broke out in Rome. The flames spread through the narrow, winding streets, overwhelming multitudes of people and beasts. Incendiaries heaped fuel on the flames, whether by order of the emperor or in the hope of plunder was not known. The fire was arrested after six days, only to break out afresh, this time reaching higher levels and destroying many ancient temples and priceless treasures.

Nero remained outside Rome at Antium until the poorer parts of the city were destroyed, then became active in fighting the fire and in works

of relief. A new city was planned and hurried forward with prodi-
gious efforts. Nero first extended his own domain, to provide for a
more magnificent palace, set among fields and woods and lakes.
Then a new city was laid out, with broad, straight streets, detached
houses, set on arches of stone and fronting porticoes. But no prodigies
of labour or excellence of planning could quell the popular anger, or
remove the suspicion that Nero had planned the destruction of the
city, in order to build a new one and give it his name. The mad,
lascivious emperor seemed capable of such a crime. Nero therefore
determined, so Tacitus says, "to transfer the guilt to others." "He found
a set of profligate and abandoned wretches, who were induced to confess themselves guilty, and, on the evidence of such men, a number
of Christians were convicted, not indeed upon clear evidence of having
set the city on fire, but rather on account of their sullen hatred of the
whole human race." What Tacitus means is that Christians absented
themselves from state worship, the gladiatorial contests, and the obscene
shows of the time, and gathered alone in small conventicles, thus coming
to be thought anti-social and guilty of evil practices. Nero turned to his
own account the popular dislike of Christians. "They were put to death
with exquisite cruelty, and to their sufferings Nero added mockery and
derision. Some were covered with the skins of wild beasts and left to
be devoured by dogs; others were nailed to crosses; numbers were burnt
alive; and many, covered over with inflammable matter, were lighted up
when the day declined, to serve as torches during the night." "At length
the cruelty of these proceedings filled every breast with compassion.
Humanity relented in favour of the Christians. It was evident that
they fell a sacrifice, not for the public good, but to glut the rage and
cruelty of one man only." Four years later, deserted by the legions and
with Rome falling into anarchy, the mad emperor fled and took his own
life.[14]

Sometime during these years, 64–68, Paul died, as we have said, dying
by the sword, as a Roman citizen. A spot on the Ostian road, outside the
city, was early fixed as the place of his martyrdom; and the splendid
church of *St. Paul outside the Walls,* with its twenty-four columns of
Phrygian marble, stands where he is said to have been buried. Peter
died the meaner death by crucifixion, asking to be crucified head down-

[14] Tacitus, *Annals* XV, xxxiii–xliv, trans. E. H. Blakeney, Everyman's Library.

ward, as unworthy to die like his Lord. Such was the tradition current
in the churches a century later.

We have written as if the story of the primitive Church were the
story of St. Paul. This was inevitable. The twelve Apostles speedily
disappear from Christian history. The New Testament tells us practically nothing of them after the first twenty years; and the so-called
Apostolic Fathers, the earliest surviving Christian writings outside the
New Testament, tell us nothing at all. In the early fourth century, when
Eusebius, bishop of Caesarea, undertook to write the first history of
the Christian Church, he could find almost no reliable information about
the Twelve outside the New Testament. Eusebius could have told many
things about them, on the authority of apocryphal Gospels, Acts,
Epistles, Revelations; but the Church had rejected these writings. They
were neither good literature, nor good religion, nor good history.

Eusebius, as a scrupulous historian, contents himself with repeating
what traditions concerning the Twelve he can find in earlier writers.
He treats them as traditions; he knows that he has no certain information. But according to these traditions, St. John went to Asia Minor, to
the Roman province of Asia, which did become in fifty years a more
important Christian centre than even Antioch; and St. Peter preached
throughout Asia Minor, in the provinces mentioned in I *Peter.* Most of
the Apostles, however, are said to have gone beyond the frontiers of the
Roman Empire, to Parthia, Scythia, India, and in Africa to Ethiopia.
In the apocryphal *Acts of Thomas* it is related that Jesus appointed St.
Thomas to preach in India and that the apostle went there, to the court
of the Parthian king Gundophorus. There was indeed at that time a
Parthian king of that name, whose dominions extended into north-west
India. There is nothing incredible therefore in the claim of the ancient
Christian settlement around Madras, that they were first evangelized by
St. Thomas.

The Twelve would naturally go east, not west like St. Paul. Jews of
the Dispersion were very numerous in the East, especially in Mesopotamia, and were in close contact with Palestine. The Gospel there,
however, had little permanent result. The evangelists would preach in
the synagogues, laying stress on the expected return of the Messiah and
the speedy end of the age. When these things did not happen, most

converts would be re-absorbed into orthodox Judaism. There was no Christian theologian in the East, like St. Paul, to interpret the Christian facts in a wider and permanent way.

Apart from St. Paul and the Twelve, there were, of course, many preachers of the Gospel, unknown by name, of whom we hear faint echoes in *Acts*. Soon after the crucifixion of Jesus there were in Jerusalem, for the feast of Pentecost, Jews of the Dispersion, "devout men, from every nation under heaven." Among them were Jews from Parthia and Media and Syria, from Mesopotamia and Asia Minor, Egypt and Africa, Crete and Italy. Three thousand of them are said to have believed and been baptized. They would return to their homes with news of the crucifixion and resurrection of Jesus, of his expected return and the enthusiastic hopes of the disciples. This explains why disciples were already in the great centres of population—Damascus and Antioch, Ephesus and Rome—when Paul first reached there. It helps also to explain how, in a century, the new faith spread through the whole Roman world.

CHAPTER V

THE CHURCH LEAVES HOME

WHEN Peter and Paul died at Rome, their nation in Palestine was moving swiftly to its doom. Within five or six years the streets of Jerusalem were running with blood and the Temple sinking in flames. The story is told at great length by the Jewish historian Josephus, in *The Wars of the Jews*. The outrages committed by Florus, the Roman procurator, provoked a desperate rising of Zealots in Jerusalem in May, 66 A.D. They determined to fight the Roman Empire itself; and Pharisees and Sadducees together could not restrain them. The Roman garrison was butchered; and Cestius, governor of Syria, brought an army from Antioch, only to be repulsed from Jerusalem and routed in retreat near Beth-horon. Messengers carried the bad news to Nero; and his great general Vespasian was soon on the way to Palestine with a powerful army.

In this perilous situation many prominent citizens left Jerusalem; but most men still hoped. Jerusalem therefore was not abandoned to the mad Messianism of the Zealots. The party of the Sanhedrin took control, under the direction of Ananus, a former high priest. They organized Jerusalem and the country for defence, thinking that, if capable of resistance, they could treat more successfully for peace. Generals were appointed for the armed forces already forming throughout Palestine, Josephus being made governor of Galilee. He organized the administration there, and trained sixty thousand men in Roman methods of warfare. He would carry resistance just far enough to win favourable terms. The Zealots among the recruits, however, would fight to the death. So Josephus had trouble with men like John of Gischala, leaders of small bands of desperate patriots. Jewish strategy was thus confused, to the advantage of the enemy.

Vespasian and his son Titus fought their way over all Galilee in the summer of 67, Josephus saving his own life by cunning. His garrison in

Jotapata, perishing from famine and thirst, had determined to die by their own hands. The order of their dying was fixed by lot, Josephus contriving to be the last. He surrendered instead to Vespasian, and saved his life by posing as a prophet and predicting Vespasian's elevation to the imperial throne. John of Gischala kept up the fight until only his city remained to the Zealots in all Galilee. Then he fled with his men to Jerusalem, to join the Zealots there.

Judaea was subdued more slowly, and was more thoroughly devastated on that account. Vespasian and Titus fought their way down the coast plain, the Plain of Sharon. Caesarea, Jamnia, Azotus, all the fortified posts, fell in turn; and when the Passover of 70 approached, Roman armies were nearing Jerusalem. Meanwhile Vespasian was proclaimed Augustus by the legions in Palestine and Egypt and returned to Italy, the mad Nero having fled from perils at home and taken his own life. So Titus was left to reduce Jerusalem.

Within Jerusalem ghastly conditions already prevailed. Moderate men, led by Ananus, thought it necessary to treat for peace; John of Gischala and the Zealots would fight to the end, expecting an intervention from heaven, as some apocalyptic enthusiasts had taught. Violent men from the country, Sicarii, crept into Jerusalem, bringing pillage and murder. Civil war broke out. The party of Ananus succeeded in shutting up the Zealots and Sicarii in the Temple area; but these sent word to Idumea that Ananus intended to betray Jerusalem to the Romans, and twenty thousand Idumeans came to their aid. Admitted at night by treachery, they carried carnage through the darkened streets and into the Temple area. The Idumeans wearied of slaughter at length and left the city; but Ananus had already been slain and his policy defeated.[1]

Deserters from Jerusalem kept Titus informed of the carnage there; and he delayed the assault, in hope of a bloodless victory. But the city was not to be had without fighting; and every known engine of war, every stratagem, was brought against it. Two of the three walls were breached. Titus still offered peace, and sent Josephus to negotiate with the defenders. It was of no use. Madness had seized the Zealots. Tortured by famine, they fought on. The inmost wall was breached at last. Again Titus offered peace; again it was refused. Titus fired the gates of the Temple area; and, against his orders, the Temple itself was fired. Men

---

[1] Josephus, *Wars,* III. vii; IV. ii, v.

fought through the blazing cloisters and round the great altar itself. With the Temple in ruins, the upper city, a separate fortress, soon fell; and Titus ordered the demolition of the entire city and Temple, except three towers and the west wall, preserved for garrison purposes. The siege had lasted five months, from spring until autumn, 70 A.D.

A force of Sicarii remained in Machaerus, east of the Dead Sea, a fortified seat of Herod the Great, in whose dungeons John the Baptist had died. Another survived in Masada, a fortress on a lofty plateau, standing close to the Dead Sea on the south-west. The Maccabees had first built a fortress there; and Herod the Great had turned it into one more royal palace and surrounded the plateau with a wall of white stone, intersected by thirty-eight towers. The plateau was fertile; and the Sicarii, when they got the fortress by treachery, found great stores of corn and wine, of oil and dates, as well as an arsenal of weapons for ten thousand men.

Titus left the reduction of these strongholds to others, and himself returned to Rome, to share with his father an imperial triumph. The pageants baffled description. Most spectacular of all was that of the Temple at Jerusalem, with the treasures seized there, the golden table and the golden candlestick with its seven lamps, and the Book of the Law.

As for Palestine, Machaerus surrendered by agreement; and the garrison marched out under a safe conduct. Masada, whose garrison was led by an adventurer Eleazar, held out for two years. The Roman commander Silva improvised towers of great height, iron-clad, to overlook the defenders and force them from the walls. His battering-rams breached the walls at last; and a secondary defence, hastily made of timbers, was fired. There was no way of escape for the garrison; and they resolved to die by their own hands. One morning, when the legions rose to the attack, the fortress was silent. They raised a shout; and there came forth from an underground cavern an old woman, and a younger one with five children, a kinswoman of Eleazar himself. They were the only survivors. Husbands, they said, had tenderly embraced wife and children, then slain them. They had then lain on the ground, their arms about their dead, and been slain by ten men, chosen by lot, who then slew themselves. Nine hundred and sixty had died. Two women preferred life.

Thus tragically closed Jewish national history in Palestine. The cost in human life had been terrible. Josephus says eleven hundred thousand died in Jerusalem, by famine and pestilence and the sword. It is possible; for pilgrims to the Passover were in the beleaguered city. Ninety-seven thousand persons were carried away captive, the fairest youths for the triumph of Rome, others as gifts to provincial governors, to die in amphitheatres by the sword or by wild beasts, still others to slave in the mines of Egypt. Other multitudes had fled from the country when rebellion flared up, fearing the worst.

Judaea was now a wilderness; and Vespasian took the land for himself, to endow the new dynasty. His agents offered it for sale, except certain lands around Emmaus, reserved as a home for aged veterans. An imperial decree diverted from Jerusalem the temple-tax, the half-shekel. It was to be paid into the imperial treasury thereafter, by all Jews of the Roman world. To crown all, Vespasian, "having now by Providence a vast quantity of wealth," built at Rome a temple to Peace, adorned with priceless things from all lands, among them the spoils of the Jewish Temple. The Book of the Law and the "purple veils of the holy place" were reserved for the imperial palace.[2]

When the tide of war receded from Palestine, the Jews lifted tired faces and looked once more for the sunrise. The nation was vanquished; but the land itself remained, even though men must hold it on lease, as tenants of the Emperor. And with the land there survived that other indestructible treasure, the Law of Moses. Men fixed their devotion upon that, and turned for direction to the Pharisees who had loved it. The Temple was gone, and the priestly aristocracy. The Zealots were discredited; they had brought on the war that engulfed the nation. Only the Pharisees remained; and they had a program of spiritual reconstruction already thought out and waiting.

The rabbi Johanan, son of Zacchai, leader of the Pharisees, asked and received from the Roman commander the town of Jamnia (or Jabneh), near Joppa, to be a new centre for Judaism. It became a miniature Jerusalem, but without a temple. A rabbinical school arose there, and a supreme court that appropriated the old name Sanhedrin. Synods of rabbis laboured to overcome past divisions and consolidate the faith.

[2] *Ibid.*, VI. ix; VII, v, vi.

Scholars like Shammai and Hillel had differed about the oral law. The rabbis now undertook its unification. They also fixed the limits of Holy Scripture, excluding the Apocalyptists. These had come too late for Divine inspiration, which was thought to have ceased in the Persian period; and they had contributed to the national destruction by raising false hopes.

The ritual of synagogue worship was recast and a section added, condemning apostates, especially the Nazarenes, as Jewish Christians were called. On Sabbaths and holy days lessons from the Law and the Prophets were read, then translated into the native Aramaic and explained. And there were services daily, wherever a company of ten adult males was assured. This was impossible in the villages; but on Mondays and Thursdays, when villagers came to the city market, short lessons from the Law were read for them there, by anyone who could do so and who was of good character and suitably garbed. The scrolls of the Law, wrapped in linen, were kept in a chest called the Ark; and other chests held the other books of Scripture. When required for worship, they were taken from the chest by the sexton, under supervision by the ruler of the synagogue, and placed on the reading desk.

Every synagogue had a Bible school, and an advanced school for the study of tradition. There girls were taught as well as boys, though education was compulsory only for the latter. Instruction was free to the poor and fatherless. If the fees of teachers were insufficient, the deficit was made up from the public funds.

In each Jewish community, large enough to have one hundred and twenty male adults, a law-court of twenty-three judges was formed, and an administrative council of seven men. The seven were called *parnasim,* managers, or *tobe ha-'ir,* best men of the town. They were installed by the judges, or by some noted rabbi; and were required to be persons of dignity and integrity. They supervised trade and commerce, weights and measures and wages, sanitation and charity and public order. They maintained the courts and schools, and public baths with basins for ritual baptism.

The work of reconstruction was rudely interrupted a generation after the Jewish War. The Emperor Trajan was fighting in the East, extending the frontiers of the Empire to India. Jewish Zealotism, alive still in the Dispersion, seized the opportunity in 116 and raised an insurrection against Rome and the Greek population, in Egypt and Cyrene and in the Island of Cyprus. Multitudes fell, both Greeks and Jews. The rebellion was suppressed by Trajan's general Turbo, and Cyprus was completely cleared of Jews; but those in Mesopotamia rose, only to be crushed with barbarous cruelty by Trajan's general Quietus. Palestine had little, if any, part in this Second Jewish War; but the brutal Quietus was sent there as governor, and a terrible depression of spirit fell upon Palestinian Jewry. Brides were forbidden by the rabbis to wear bridal dress; the study of Greek was banned; the old Greek translation of the Scriptures, the Septuagint, was rejected, because used by the Nazarenes; and a new and more rigid translation was made by Aquila of Pontus.

Trajan's eastern campaign collapsed after a defeat in Arabia; and his successor Hadrian drew in the frontier to the Euphrates. In Palestine he projected a Roman city in place of Jerusalem, frustrating Jewish hopes for a new Temple; and revived an ancient law against the mutilation of the body, thus making circumcision illegal. It seemed an attack upon Judaism; and the Third Jewish War flamed up in 132, inspired by the great rabbi, Akiba, and led by Simon of Cozeba, better known as *Bar Cochba,* Son of the Star, because he seemed to fulfil an ancient prophecy, "There shall come forth a star out of Jacob." Akiba believed him to be the Messiah; and all Palestine struck once more for freedom. Waging guerrilla warfare from strongholds and caves and ravines, the rebels baffled the governor, Rufus, and captured Jerusalem. Hadrian sent his great general Severus at last, recalling him from Britain; and the rebels were hunted down and destroyed. Jerusalem was retaken, and the war was over by 135. Judaea was now a desert. A thousand villages lay in ruins. Five hundred thousand Jews are said to have perished, and Roman losses were very heavy.

The ruins of Jerusalem were now cleared away, the earth ploughed in token of a new beginning; and a Roman city was built, *Aelia Capitolina.* There were temples to Bacchus, Serapis and Venus; and on the site of the sanctuary itself rose the temple of Jupiter Capitolinus. Jews were forbidden to visit the city; and spies were set, to prevent the exercise of their religion. Nevertheless each year, on the ninth of Ab (August), pilgrims came from everywhere, bribing the Roman guards to permit them to linger and weep. They weep there still; and still they hope.[3]

What of the Nazarenes during the last desperate years in Palestine? They could not support the Zealots in violence, nor the Sadducees in an orderly defence. The former was precluded by the teaching of their Master, the latter by their own belief that the tragedies of the nation were a judgment of God. The Nazarenes seemed therefore, to patriots of all parties, to be traitors to the national cause. What happened to them is recorded by Eusebius of Caesarea in the *Ecclesiastical History*. Those of Jerusalem, as the Roman legions drew nearer, were "commanded by a revelation" to seek refuge across the Jordan at Pella, a town in the mountains of Gilead. They retired therefore to Pella, where they continued to observe the Law of Moses, praying for the conversion of the nation, and awaiting the return of the Messiah. They were led by various members of the family of Jesus, in a sort of caliphate. The simple Nazarenes thought it more important that their leaders should be of the Messianic family than that they should have been disciples of Jesus himself, who understood his mind. So the church at Jerusalem had at the outset preferred James, the brother of the Lord, before all the apostles; and after his martyrdom [4] they chose Simeon, a cousin of Jesus, who was to die under Trajan. We are told also of two grandchildren of Jude, a brother of Jesus. They came under suspicion in the reign of Domitian, 81–96; but when they proved to be men whose hands were hard with toil and who possessed together only thirty-nine acres of land, they were discharged. Domitian accepted their assurance that the kingdom of Christ, which they expected, "was not a temporal nor an earthly kingdom, but a heavenly and angelic one, which would appear at the end of the world, when he should come in glory to judge the quick and the dead." [5]

[3] For later developments in Judaism see Appendix IV.

[4] Eusebius relates the martyrdom of James the Just, brother of the Lord. He had been the recognized leader of the church at Jerusalem for many years, and had as well a great reputation for ascetic piety. His knees had become hard, like a camel's, through long praying in the Temple for the nation. In a popular disturbance at the Feast of the Passover, James was thrown from a pinnacle of the Temple, was stoned where he lay, and was killed at last with a fuller's club. *Ecclesiastical History*, III. 20, 23, 31.

[5] *Ibid.*, III. 5, 11, 20.

Nazarenes drifted back to Palestine in time, like other Jews; but their position was incredibly hard. They were faithful to the Law of Moses, and so were separated from the growing Christian churches of the Mediterranean world; and they were heretics to their fellow Jews, who cursed them thrice at each Sabbath assembly in the synagogues. They yearned for the friendship of Gentile Christians; and some crept into the churches. A diminishing few remained, faithful to the Law, hostile to St. Paul who had led so many away from the Law, and rejecting the general view of Jesus as divine, Son of Man, Son of God. Jesus, they said, was a man like themselves, but dedicated at his baptism to the Messianic office.

The reactionary party became so small at length, so insignificant, that people called them, and they called themselves, *Ebionim,* "the poor folk," the forgotten ones of God. After a few generations they disappeared.

Meanwhile the Christians were less and less associated with Judaism. When Jerusalem fell, most Christians were already Gentiles; and Gentiles had taken over the leadership in the churches. Very few of them are known to us now.[6] Indeed the fifty years following the fall of Jerusalem have been called "the Age of the Nameless Ones." During these years the Gospels were written and the *Acts,*[7] lest all who had known Jesus should die and their knowledge perish with them; but the authors tell us nothing about contemporary events. Something is to be learned from *The Apostolic Fathers,*[8] a collection of writings whose authors are thought to have had some first-hand knowledge of one or other of the apostles. Some of these are as early as the Age of the Name-

[6] Most of the apostles were dead. James, the brother of John, had long since been put to death by Herod Agrippa I, in 43 or 44 A.D. Peter and Paul and James the Just all died in the years between 60 and 70. Others of the original apostles may have lived on; but they were strangers to the churches of the Roman Empire and are lost to history, except the apostle John. He lingered on at Ephesus until the end of the century, and died when a hundred years old. Strange, beautiful legends are told of his end. *Acts of John,* in M. R. James, *Apocryphal New Testament.*

[7] *Mark* was written shortly before Jerusalem fell; *Matthew, Luke* and *Acts* in the twenty years after. A little later, in the last troubled years of Domitian, the *Revelation of St. John the Divine* was written; and early in the second century, in the reign of Trajan, the *Gospel of John.*

[8] These may all be had in English, with the Greek text also, in Kirsopp Lake, *The Apostolic Fathers,* 2 vols., Heinemann.

less Ones. And out of desolate Palestine comes a collection of reminiscences left by Hegesippus, a Hebrew Christian, whom Eusebius often quotes.

There are also certain non-Christian sources of information. Josephus was writing and Plutarch lecturing at Rome in the reign of Domitian, when Christians were enduring persecution there. Pliny the Younger was governor of the province of Bithynia under Trajan, and was finding it impossible to coerce Christians there into worshipping the ancestral gods. The historian Suetonius was Hadrian's literary secretary; and that great man of letters, Tacitus, lived from Nero to Hadrian. They all tell us a little about the Christians, good people, but with unreasonable prejudices and holding aloof from society.

From many sources we gather that the Church was growing. In Rome, as early as the reign of Nero, the Christians, according to Tacitus, were "a great multitude." Elsewhere in the Latin West they were not very numerous until the second century was well underway; but in the Greek East Christianity went steadily forward from the days of St. Paul. Pliny says that in Bithynia Christians were numerous in both town and country, so much so that in some places pagan temples were deserted and worship discontinued. It is reasonable to assume that the situation was much the same throughout all Asia Minor. Farther east, also, along the Roman frontier, were Christian churches, whose mother church was at Antioch; and the Mesopotamian kingdom of Edessa was being Christianized.

Everywhere converts were being made from all social classes. There is no evidence for the view so widely held, that Christians were drawn chiefly from the peasantry and the proletariat. Christianity did appeal to the depressed classes. It offered them fellowship, and supported their self-respect. At the Holy Supper all men were brothers. But the churches drew many from the class of freedmen also; and freedmen were commonly persons of capacity and education and skill. It was because of this they had been carried into slavery; and it was often because of special services they were given freedom. They were active in industry and trade and in the governmental services, the ablest rose to the highest positions in the State; and the future of the Empire was largely in their hands. And Christians were drawn, too, from among Roman citizens, even from the greatest families. In the reign of Domitian the consul Acilius Glabrio was a Christian; and the Emperor's cousin Flavius Clemens suffered for the faith, as did his wife Domitilla.

It is not strange that people were thus drawn from every class. There was a general need of something Christianity could supply. Things were not well with Rome in the Age of the Nameless Ones. The ancient Republic had come to an end with the rise of Julius Caesar a century before. His adopted son, Octavian, had continued one-man rule without much difficulty. After a hundred years of revolution and civil war under the dying Republic, most people welcomed the principate. Even the ancient senatorial families were content, so long as they were treated, as they were, with respect. Indeed, it was the Senate that made Octavian *Princeps* and *Augustus,* and gave him control of the army; and Augustus justified the new order by giving the Mediterranean world forty-four years of peace. When he died in 14 A.D. the general well-being continued, under his stepson Tiberius. Tiberius was an able soldier and administrator; but he despised both the Roman nobles and the populace, ignored the Senate, made himself thoroughly unpopular, and died, soured and disillusioned, in 37 A.D.

Rome was now to know the tragedy of one-man rule, when the one is unfit for rule. Gaius Caesar, a great-grandson of Augustus, was made Emperor by his soldiers, who had named him Caligula, "little boot." Long dissipation, and the new experience of unchecked authority, soon turned Caligula into a madman. He embarked upon crazy building enterprises, squandered the wealth of the State, indulged in confiscation and murder, made his favourite horse a consul, and was put to death after four years by his military officers. All this was happening just when Christianity began to appear in the chief cities of the Empire.

After Caligula the imperial guards placed upon the throne his uncle, Claudius. He was weak in body and in character; but the Senate dared not object. Claudius did his best for thirteen years, 41–54; but he could not control the court itself. In the end Agrippina, last of his wives, pushed his eldest son aside and secured the succession for her own son Nero, with whom a violent night settled upon Rome. The popular decadence that had destroyed the Republic was now accelerated by the evil example of the monarch; and no degradation was so pathetic as that among the ancient noble families. The ill-suppressed horror in the writings of Seneca is unconscious self-portrayal, the rich man and the philosopher, debased and longing for death. Tacitus, too, looks back with horror to his childhood under Nero.

One sees portrayed in Seneca and Tacitus a society at Rome greedy for gold, acquired by every means, only to be squandered or filched away. It is a society sunk in gross luxury, envious, treacherous and cruel, with jaded nerves, its capacity for self-indulgence exhausted. Some great souls survive; but they go in daily fear of death. In some senatorial families men never reach middle life, because of the suspicion of the Emperor. And the hand of the destroyer reaches them everywhere, even when on service in distant provinces. Men of noble ancestry sink into cringing servility. They have seen their wives defiled, or compelled to expose themselves in public shows. They themselves have been forced to exhibit themselves in pantomime, or fight in the arena. Men who once wore the mantle of the consulship have been compelled to run as footmen beside the imperial chariot, or wait as slaves at the Emperor's feet through dinner. And some, alas, find Nero's debauchery attractive. They go to school to the Emperor, share his obscene revels, laugh at virtue, and make self-indulgence a fine art.

There were, of course, aristocratic families that kept their honour unsullied, aloof from the court, in rural retreats in Tuscany and Lombardy. Men like Persius and Pliny and Tacitus practised the ancient Roman virtues, and cherished the Stoic ideal. Nevertheless it was as Pliny said: "The world readily conforms its life to that of one man, if that man is head of the State"; and the shame of Rome was a taint in the blood everywhere.

The death of Nero and the accession of Vespasian brought a brief respite. Vespasian observed the simple life he had learned from his Sabine ancestors, in the old farm house at Reate; and with him came men from the provinces, with clean blood and purer manners. An age of repentance seemed at hand. But Vespasian and his son Titus were both gone in little more than a decade; and power passed into the hands of another son, Domitian, 81–96. Domitian was morose, disloyal and cruel. He maintained an unresting and unscrupulous inquisition, impeached and plundered the old families, and was profoundly indulgent to the army and the populace of Rome. His low and costly shows finally bankrupted the State. Things were little better than under Nero.

Domitian was followed by the blameless Nerva; but he died too soon to achieve permanent reform. Reformation came with Trajan, 98–117. Under his strong and temperate rule virtue lifted its head everywhere; but thoughtful men were not optimistic. The ancient Republic was gone forever. Too much depended now upon the character of one man.

During the sixty years from Caligula to Trajan the Christian Church was offering a new life and a future of hope to its converts. The way had been prepared for it by the Synagogue. People of many races had long been finding in the Synagogue a religion of confident faith and hope, and had become proselytes to Judaism. There men and women who had grown doubtful about the many gods of Greece and Rome could worship one God, and that without idolatry. His will, unlike the will of Zeus and Jupiter, was conceived to be moral and beneficent. It was set out, too, in a venerable Law, and could be known quite explicitly. And there was taught in the Synagogue a view of history that relieved its tragedy, discerning purpose and direction in the long travail of mankind. Above all, because God was good and there was hope in Jewry, there was moral cleanness also.

All that Judaism had offered, the Christian Church now gave. It, too, had one God, whom it had received from Judaism; and the same ancient Scriptures. Indeed God had spoken again, this time more clearly than in the Law and the Prophets, and more humanely. In Christ, the Church believed, God had said the final word. The end was not far off. And the Church went beyond the Synagogue in this, that the former had no hesitancy about receiving converts from all races and faiths, while Gentile converts were never quite incorporated into Jewry. The rabbis had been uneasy about accessions from the heathen world. Ezekiel, they knew, would not have approved; nor Ezra; nor Nehemiah. And it was hard to interpret the Law of Moses as including aliens. So the rabbis thought of proselytes as "the leprosy of Israel." It was not so in the Church. There it was said to all believers, "There can be neither Jew nor Greek, there can be neither bond nor free, there can be no male and female: for ye are all one in Christ."

Tension was thus inevitable between the Church and Judaism. It was inevitable, too, between the Church and society at large. Christians could not participate in violence, nor attend obscene shows, nor even join good men in the public worship of the gods. They held aloof, disliked for this exclusiveness, and often suspected by reason of their secret assemblies. When, therefore, Nero required to divert the rage of the mob in Rome, it was easy to turn it against the Christians. They suffered terribly, as we have seen, both in the capital and in certain cities of the East.

After Nero the Christians were never safe. Everyone now knew that Christianity was not Judaism. It therefore lost the legal protection extended to national religions. In the eyes of the law Christianity was a "superstition," or a "wandering faith," not a "permitted religion"; and sometimes there was persecution and slaughter.

Such a situation could not continue indefinitely. The Church was growing in spite of persecution. Violent suppression was not always and everywhere practicable. The position of the Church required legal definition.

Christians could reasonably expect from the State a certain friendliness. They themselves were disposed to be amenable to political authority. Their Master had said, "Render therefore unto Caesar the things that are Caesar's." Saint Paul had said, "Let every soul be in subjection to the higher powers." And Rome, on her part, was religiously tolerant. She respected the national sentiments of subject peoples, and therefore their national religions. She asked of such peoples only this, that they respect her gods as well as their own. Judaism had always presented a special problem. Jews were monotheists. For them there were no other gods, but only God. Rome met their difficulty, however, by excusing them from participation in the State religion. Christianity, at first, shared this immunity; but, as we have seen, Church and Synagogue parted company, and Christianity ceased to be associated in the public mind with Judaism or any other national faith. Her converts were drawn from all races and classes. Were they, too, to be exempt from the religious obligations of people in general?

The difficulty was aggravated by the Christians. They did not simply ask immunity; they regarded Christianity as the absolute religion. All other religions were superstitions, all other gods false gods. Christians were therefore intolerant, in principle. They believed, too, that the existing political and social order must pass away. Only one empire was permanent, the empire of Christ. Christians longed for his coming; and his coming would involve the fall of Rome. Christianity thus undermined virtue; for virtue, to the Romans, meant devotion to the State.

Matters came to a head under Trajan. His representative in Bithynia, Pliny the Younger, found the province infested with Christians. They were offering no sacrifices, and were absenting themselves from the temples; so much so that the temples were virtually deserted. And this at a time when Pliny was trying to promote a religious revival!

Pliny invoked a law against associations dangerous to the State, haled many Christians to court, and subjected some to torture. He found that "the sum of their guilt or their error amounted only to this, that on a stated day they had been accustomed to meet before daybreak and to recite a hymn among themselves to Christ, as though he were a god, and that, so far from binding themselves by oath to commit any crime, their oath was to abstain from theft, robbery, adultery, and from breach of faith." Pliny, therefore, released all who would renounce their faith, executed those who refused, not for their religion but for their "obstinacy," and sent some to Rome for trial, as they were Roman citizens. He asked the Emperor for further instructions.

Trajan approved the action of the procurator. There was, he said, to be no inquisition; and anonymous accusations were to be ignored. But if legal complaints were laid against Christians, they must be brought to trial. Those found guilty were to be given opportunity to recant; if they refused, they were to be executed.[9]

The legal position of Christians continued for two centuries as here defined. During all that time they were never quite secure. Much depended on political conditions and the temper of provincial governors; but accused Christians, if faithful, were guilty of treason. Many died under Trajan, in several provinces. Two are still known by name. Simeon, son of Clopas, head of the church of Jerusalem after James, was crucified when very old. He was the last, so far as we know, of those who had known Jesus of Nazareth. And Ignatius of Antioch was sent to Rome, and given to the beasts in the amphitheatre.[10]

As often as persecutions devastated the churches apocalyptic hopes revived. Jesus would soon come on the clouds of heaven, to rescue his people, to judge the world and bring it to an end.[11] But always the crisis

---

[9] *Letters of the Younger Pliny*, X. xcviii, xcix.

[10] Eusebius, *Ecclesiastical History*, III. 32, 36.

[11] The persistence of apocalypticism, with the second-advent expectation, is an extraordinary phenomenon. Judaism excluded most apocalyptic writings from the Old Testament;

passed, Jesus did not appear; and Christians settled again to the sober business of living. Gradually adjustments were made to this world that refused to come to an end. The churches learned to present a common front to the State, to build an ecclesiastical constitution, to consolidate themselves. Before the Age of the Nameless Ones closed, the movement towards "one Holy, Catholic, Apostolic Church" was well under way.

One step towards unifying Christianity was the examination and sifting of its literature. By the time of Trajan there were in existence many writings of Christian origin. All that later became known as the New Testament had come into being. Other writings, as we have seen (p. 128), were the so-called *Apostolic Fathers*,[12] of which some were as early as Trajan, as were also some of those many writings that still exist, in fragmentary form, as the Apocrypha of the New Testament. All these writings came slowly, as circumstances dictated. So far as we know, none of the apostles except John ever saw a written Gospel. They repeated the oral traditions concerning Jesus. It is these Paul means when he writes the Christians of Thessaly, "Hold fast the traditions which ye have received" (II *Thess.* 2: 15). Writing began as conditions in the scattered churches called for letters of advice and instruction; it continued for all sorts of reasons.

None of the Christian literature that thus grew up was regarded as Scripture. The Bible of the Christians was still the Old Testament, which they read in the Greek translation, the Septuagint, as did Jews of

---

but the Christian Church included in the New Testament the *Book of Revelation,* which is a thoroughly Jewish apocalypse, except for its identification of Jesus with the Messiah. And to-day, after nineteen centuries, many Christians still expect a second coming of Christ and a catastrophic end of the world by divine intervention. Such a hope answers well to the sense of human helplessness in the presence of the almost irretrievable disasters that the sin and folly of mankind sometimes bring upon the race. At such times apocalyptists have their day; for apocalypticism, as we have said, is prophecy in hysterics, unable to discern the signs of the times, unable to extract any comfort from the present, conjuring up lurid, abnormal pictures of the future.

Thoughtful Christians, in increasing numbers, are aware that there will be no end to the physical world except such as science predicts, probably by the exhaustion of its central fires; that long before then the human race will have passed away forever, so far as the earth is concerned; that Jesus will never come again, except as he is always coming, always present—as a gracious memory, or the mystic companion and guide of the good; and that it is impossible now to know with certainty what was his own eschatology, except that he felt himself to be the incarnation and vehicle of an eternal truth, an ultimate good, that God would preserve alive forever.

[12] I *Clement, The Epistles of Ignatius, The Epistle of Barnabas,* The *Didaché* (or *Teaching of the Twelve Apostles*), and the *Shepherd of Hermas,* are as early as Trajan.

the Dispersion. And the Bible, whether in Hebrew or Greek, was in the form of a collection of parchment or leather rolls, kept in the synagogues and the churches; it was not privately owned. The Christian writings, too, were not privately owned. They circulated among the churches as papyrus rolls, written in columns of colloquial Greek, the sheets varying in size as the letter or treatise required. Sheets of papyrus could be bought in the shops. They were reasonably durable, and much less expensive than parchment.[13]

The Christian writings were read in the churches. Public worship consisted of prayer, including always the Lord's Prayer; Divine teaching —lessons from the Old Testament; human teaching—the repetition of the Gospel story, perhaps an exhortation, or the reading of an important letter or treatise; and the Lord's Supper. Thus Christian writings appeared in public worship, along with the Scriptures and the Gospel tradition. The more edifying they were, the more consonant with Christian ideals, the more likely they were to be read, lent to other churches, and copied. The less suitable writings disappeared from public worship and instruction, not by official decision of a synod or council, but because of their unsuitability.

We learn from three great men how far this sifting had gone by the beginning of the second century. They were three bishops, in three widely separated cities—Clement of Rome, Ignatius of Antioch, Polycarp of Smyrna. They were themselves greatly revered in after days, as men who had known one or other of the apostles; and all three wrote letters that were sometimes read in the churches, and that are preserved in *The Apostolic Fathers.* These three together disclose what writings were then authoritative. They were substantially the books of our New Testament.[14] These were not yet thought of as Scripture; they were not in the Bible; but they had become authoritative nevertheless. Erroneous teaching and individual idiosyncrasy could be corrected by these catholic standards.

A further check on individual idiosyncrasy (and initiative) came by

---

[13] After two centuries, when certain writings had become "Holy Scripture," they were transcribed to the more durable parchment.

[14] Eusebius examined the matter at length and found that the writings universally accepted in these early days were the books of the present New Testament, except that II *Peter,* the *Apocalypse,* and *Hebrews,* were each rejected by some churches. *Eccl. Hist.,* III. 3.

the development of a church constitution. Whatever unity may have existed among the primitive churches, in their beliefs and hopes and moral ideals, there was little in organization. Indeed, organization must have seemed at first a matter of no consequence. Why organize a brotherhood so soon to be translated to the skies? What was needed was rather teachers who had known Jesus, or had a religious experience of their own to report and a good example to set, men who could prepare them all for the great event.

So the church at Jerusalem was at first a brotherhood, led by all the apostles, of whom Peter was chief, by reason of his greater enthusiasm and preaching power. When it became necessary to supervise the distribution of relief, the whole brotherhood chose seven suitable men. They were a sort of administrative council, like the managers (*parnasim*) of Jewish communities of the Dispersion, but without their authority. They were servants of the church, for special duties.

When the twelve apostles scattered from Jerusalem and Palestine, carrying the Gospel wherever duty called, a permanent leadership at Jerusalem passed to James, the brother of the Lord. Only his martyrdom after some twenty-five years and the destruction of Jerusalem, prevented the establishment of a Christian caliphate there, hereditary in the family of Jesus.[15] But the church of Jerusalem provided no model for churches elsewhere. It was too devoted to the Law of Moses, too hesitant about admitting Gentile converts.[16]

The fall of Jerusalem made Antioch, for a brief space, the capital city of Christianity. The church there had not followed the Jerusalem model. It had been founded by Hellenist Jews, refugees from persecution in Palestine; and it very soon admitted Gentiles.[17] It had no apostles to lead it, except during their visits to the city; and seems to have had no officials whatever during the first generation. One hears only of "prophets and teachers" in the *Acts;* and this simple model influenced the neighbouring churches of Syria, to the end of the first century.

Things were different in the churches founded by Paul and Barnabas

[15] It is interesting to speculate what effect such a development would have had on the later theory that Peter was divinely appointed Head of the Church.

[16] When a new city rose on the site of Jerusalem, and a church came again, it was a Gentile city and a church of Gentiles.

[17] The church of Antioch still claims Peter as its founder, with little reason, but with more reason than the church at Rome.

in Asia Minor. Here the first preaching was in the synagogues, the converts were Jews, and the churches became independent by expulsion from the synagogues. It was natural that they should adopt the constitution to which they were accustomed; and each synagogue had among its officials a group of elders, or presbyters. Paul and Barnabas therefore appointed elders in the churches. They were to be the guardians, or overseers, of the churches, supplementing the oversight that visiting apostles could give only intermittently. Their office and duty are indicated in Luke's account of Paul's last meeting with the elders of the church at Ephesus: "And from Miletus he sent to Ephesus, and called to him the elders of the church. And when they were come to him, he said unto them, . . . Take heed unto yourselves, and to all the flock, in which the Holy Spirit hath made you guardians,[18] to feed the church of God, which he purchased with his own blood" (*Acts* 20: 17, 18, 28).

The first churches on European soil, being Gentile and less influenced by the synagogues, had not even the eldership. They acknowledged the spiritual authority of apostles, of their assistants, like Timothy and Titus, of great preachers like Apollos; but these were not officials appointed by the churches. They were men engaged in a calling.

The evidence for this statement is negative, but quite convincing. In the letters of St. Paul to the churches at Corinth, Thessalonica and Rome, there is no mention of officials; and St. Paul was not the man to write letters to churches and ignore their officials. The courtesy of the salutations is a feature of Pauline letters. It is to be assumed, therefore, that these churches were still unorganized fellowships, in which some were more influential than others but none were officials.[19]

It was different at Philippi. The church there, when Paul wrote *Philippians,* was more than ten years old and had found it desirable to organize. So there were in the church at Philippi guardians, like the elders in the Jewish churches, and deacons, like the Seven in the first

[18] The Greek word is *episcopoi,* which is accurately translated *overseers,* or *guardians,* or *superintendents,* but not *bishops,* which for many centuries has meant only one kind of ecclesiastical superintendent, the episcopal, and is therefore too narrow in meaning. The word *episcopos* (plural *episcopoi*), used in the New Testament to describe the function of the elders, is equally applicable to all forms of ecclesiastical superintendency.

[19] At Cenchreae a certain Phoebe had a household establishment substantial enough to give hospitality to travelling evangelists; and the family of Stephanas at Corinth could do likewise for the whole church there. *Romans* 16: 1, 2; I *Cor.* 16: 15, 16.

days of Jerusalem.[20] This is as far as constitutional developments went during the lifetime of St. Paul. *Philippians* is one of his last letters, an Epistle of the Imprisonment.

The diversity exhibited in the New Testament, in the matter of ecclesiastical organization, continued to the close of the first century.[21] This is discoverable from the *Didaché* and the *Letters of Ignatius*,[22] and from other sources. The *Didaché* was written at Antioch, at about 90 A.D., and was circulated by the church there among its daughter churches in the towns and villages of Syria, to standardize their organizations. The simplicity of earlier days was becoming a snare. The apostles had passed away, but some wandering evangelists still called themselves apostles; and there were prophets now who made a business of prophecy, and expected too much hospitality in return. The time had come for a resident officiary, locally chosen and responsible. So the *Didaché* urges upon the churches of Syria what had existed in Philippi since St. Paul, and now existed in other churches: "Appoint for yourselves, therefore, guardians and deacons . . . despise them not, for they are your honourable men, along with the prophets and teachers" (xi: 3; xv: 1).

We cannot discover precisely how far this advice was accepted by the churches of Syria, or how far the Philippian model had been adopted by the churches everywhere; but the *Didaché* at least indicates that in the last decade of the first century the ministry of gifts was being displaced by the ministry of officials—elders or presbyters, to be guardians, deacons to be administrators of the churches. And this is confirmed by a letter from the church at Rome to that at Corinth, just after the assassination of the Emperor Domitian in A.D. 96. The letter is the *First Epistle of Clement to the Corinthians*. It makes clear that in both these churches government was now by guardians and deacons; and it advances the

[20] *Philippians* 1: 1.
[21] This is quite as we should expect, and would be a fact of little consequence, had not present-day denominations been disputing about it for four centuries. The main types of church organization—Episcopalian, Presbyterian, Congregational—have each claimed to be the truly primitive, apostolic, and therefore divinely authorized, form of organization. Scholars have now pretty well exhausted the subject; and those who are open to conviction are aware that there was constitutional diversity in primitive Christianity, and that all types can appeal to ancient precedents. An exhaustive treatment of the subject is that by the late Canon B. H. Streeter, *The Primitive Church*, Macmillan, 1929.
[22] See footnote 12, p. 135.

interesting theory that the presbyters as guardians are the legal successors of the apostles.[23]

A further development would inevitably follow. When the presbyters met to exercise their guardianship, someone must preside. He would be the senior presbyter, or one of superior piety and wisdom, or the one of proven capacity for the presidency. No divine inspiration known to history has been sufficient to make all men, even good men, efficient chairmen and executives; and before any theory required it, the practice would already have begun, of making one man permanent president of the presbyters. It would be as president that Clement wrote to Corinth, on behalf of the church at Rome.

From the permanent presidency it is but a short step to the place where the president is, in a special sense, the guardian, or *episkopos,* of the church; though the step was not taken in the early churches without stern opposition. The chief surviving documents of the conflict are the *Letters of Ignatius,* written some twenty years after *First Clement,* when Ignatius was on the way from Antioch to Rome, to die a martyr's death. After Ignatius one can with propriety translate *episkopos,* or guardian, by the English word bishop. He had become, rather shakily, what we mean by bishop. Ignatius was president of the presbyters at Antioch; and, whether or not the authority of the presidents had been accepted in other churches, Ignatius had been having a hard fight to establish that at Antioch elders might be elders, but he alone was guardian, or bishop. The letters were written under great nervous strain. Ignatius had the neurotic variety of "the will to power"; and in the prospect of early martyrdom he was proclaiming hysterically a fixed idea—"We ought to have respect to the bishop, as to the Lord Himself." "The bishop presiding after the likeness of God, and the presbyters after the likeness of the council of the Apostles" have their distinctive functions. If the church is divided on this issue, the true church, Ignatius says, is that part that adheres to the bishop—"Wheresoever the bishop shall appear, there let the people be; even as where Jesus is, there is the Catholic Church."

The fortunes of this constitutional war would be different in different places. The earlier ecclesiastical democracy, we may be sure, did not surrender without a fight; but there were good reasons for the concentra-

[23] This is the effective beginning of the Catholic doctrine of the Apostolic Succession of bishops.

tion of authority, and these reasons were to become more pressing as the second century advanced. When the Age of the Nameless Ones closed, the elders were no longer bishops; only the president of the elders everywhere was bishop, though he had no diocese, only a single church, to rule.

CHAPTER VI

THE CHURCH COMES TO TERMS WITH THE WORLD

WHEN the Age of the Nameless Ones closed the Church was a hundred years old. There were many Christians now whose parents and grandparents had been born within the Church. And she had a somewhat better world in which to live. The reforming emperors, Trajan and Hadrian, had done something to bring back the glories of the Augustan Age. The frontiers were now secure, and the Empire at peace. The frontiers were held by legions recruited from all the peoples of the Empire—Britons, Gauls and Spaniards, Egyptians, Moors and Syrians, and what not. They did more than hold the frontiers; they built roads and bridges and aqueducts, and public buildings in the cities.

Here, then, was a commonwealth of some seventy or eighty millions, encircling the Mediterranean, embracing many peoples, of different colours and customs and creeds, but bound together in a genuine community of interest. The magnificent Roman roads ran everywhere, paved with massive stones, smooth as a city street. On the sea, too, the old-time pirates were gone, good wharves and lighthouses made navigation safe, and comfortable ships sailed from the Tiber to Gaul and Spain, North Africa and Egypt, Syria and Asia Minor and Greece. Egypt was the granary of Italy; and government corn-ships, carrying several thousand tons of grain and several hundred passengers, plied regularly between Alexandria and Italian ports.

Tourists from Italy visited Greece and Asia Minor, Syria and Egypt, as we visit Italy. These were their ancient world. They felt a justifiable pride in the achievements of Rome in the older lands, and especially when they visited the flourishing cities of Syria. There east of the Jordan a wilderness of nomads had become a land of prosperous towns, with imposing public buildings, that are awe-inspiring to-day in their ruin. These towns were linked together by fine roads, linked also with Rome by highways that ran through the Taurus Mountains, across Asia Minor and the Balkan Peninsula, to cross the Alps into Italy. Rome had done wonders everywhere.

The whole Mediterranean world took on something of the Roman character. Though East was East and West was West, the influence of Roman ideals was at work everywhere. Rome was materialistic. There was truth in Juvenal's satire, "No deity is held in such reverence among us as Wealth; though as yet, O baneful money, thou hast no temple of thine own." The Roman, too, was generally unimaginative. So there was little refinement of feeling, or good taste, to guide his social conduct. Gluttony was a characteristic vice. All vices tended to grossness. Worst of all was a certain hardness and cruelty, encouraged by slave labour in the households.

The conquered peoples were influenced by all this, but in turn influenced the conquerors. Nowhere was this more manifest than in the city of Rome itself. Rome was the most magnificent monumental city of the age; but her treasures were stolen [1] or acquired by imitation. Architecture, sculpture, painting all followed Greek models. Latin literature, too, was imitative. The originality of the Augustan Age was lost; there was no Horace now, no Virgil. Leadership in literature returned to Athens, where the emperors endowed the four schools of philosophy and made them a State University. In short, the Roman imperialist was compelled to look, for the refinements of life, to people whom he regarded as inferiors.

Popular education in the second century may be described as debased Greek. In Greece itself popular education had begun five centuries before. Its special quality had been due to circumstances. It did not develop the physical sciences, probably because Greece lost her political independence. She turned for intellectual satisfaction from the study of Nature to her own ancient literature, where Greece was still supreme. Grammar and Rhetoric therefore, by which were meant acquaintance with literature and the art of cultivated speech, became the hall-marks of the educated man. A quotation from Homer, or from a tragic poet, was apposite on all occasions and in all social circles; and the power of extempore speech, on every subject, was the supreme cultural achievement.

[1] Everywhere were beautiful statues, whose empty pedestals were in the cities of Greece.

To Grammar (or *Belles Lettres*) and Rhetoric was added Philosophy, but in the new sense of Logic, or Dialectic, the art of discussion. That is to say, the philosopher had been succeeded by the trained debater who, far from pursuing truth for truth's sake, could uphold equally well both sides of a question.

Such were the educational ideals acquired from Greece, and current in the Roman world in the second century. There were grammar schools in most towns, and advanced instruction by eminent professors at Rome and Athens, Ephesus and Smyrna, Antioch and Alexandria, Marseilles and Bordeaux. Municipalities and the State encouraged teaching by establishing endowments and granting teachers exemption from civil duties. The professor was a familiar figure in social life. At any elaborate dinner one met the professor of Grammar, reciting and expounding poetry; the professor of Rhetoric, speaking on whatever subject was proposed; and the professor of Philosophy, reading a discourse on morals. The philosopher was most fashionable of all, a sort of domestic chaplain in great houses and the pet of great ladies. Lucian satirizes the professor who travels with my lady's lap-dog, discourses on temperance while her hair is being dressed, and suspends the discourse while she answers a clandestine letter from a lover.

Lucian exaggerates, as satirists are prone to do; but education in the second century was artificial. And Christianity itself was to be affected, as we shall see, by the intellectual ideals of the converts it made. Men of Greek education, when they became Christians, would be different from those of the first generation. Men who had admired Rhetoric would have less taste for the uncultivated earnestness of lay preachers. Men to whom the expression of ideas had been more important than the ideas themselves, would be less steady in pursuit of a truth to live by.

Professional philosophers and artificial education did not, of course, commend themselves to all men. There were small circles in which the best traditions of Greek philosophy were still maintained.[2] Stoicism survived; and in the five hundred years since Zeno brought it from the island of Cyprus and set up as a teacher in the Stoa, or painted corridor on the north side of the market-place of Athens, Stoicism had produced a type of character nobler than any of the other schools. Virtue, it said,

---

[2] For a brief sketch of Greek philosophy see Appendix V.

was the highest good; and virtue was conformity to Nature. But Nature was not a mere collection of atoms, but a living soul, of which each human soul was a part.

By the second century Stoicism had been refined by the long tragedy of Greece into a religion of hope. Nature tended to become a Person, and all men her children. The lame slave Epictetus, greatest of the Stoics, could say like any Christian: "Dare to look up to God and say: 'Deal with me for the future as thou wilt; I refuse nothing that pleases thee.'"

Greek philosophy in general had long been yielding more and more to the need for religion; and when a new development came, just after the close of the second century, it was thoroughly religious. This was Neo-Platonism, the last great system of Greek philosophy. Its founder was a certain Ammonius Saccas of Alexandria, whose fame, however, was soon overshadowed by that of his pupil, Plotinus. Plotinus crossed to Rome, and acquired a great reputation as a teacher. His philosophy was an attempt to deal with the contemporary sense of sin and need for salvation. And, like other redemptive schemes of that day, it explained the moral conflict in man as the human phase of a wider conflict in the universe. All matter, it said, is evil and the enemy of spirit. In human life therefore, "the flesh lusteth against the spirit"; and salvation does not begin until physical desires are exterminated and, rising above all normal feelings and emotions, one lives the pure life of the soul.

The authority of Plato could be claimed for such doctrine. He had disparaged the life of the senses and praised the life of contemplation. Plotinus went farther. It is not enough, he said, to rise above the body and sensation; one must get beyond thought as well. No intellectual process will bring us into that touch with God which is salvation. We cannot say what God is; we cannot think what God is. So that something more than the cultivation of the mind is necessary to him who would know God. He must yield to the feeling of something real that is beyond all thought. The reward is ecstasy, in which thought, consciousness, individuality itself, fall away; and one melts into unity with the Absolute.

All this reminds us that there were good men in the second and third centuries, and clever men, who were not Christians. Some were active critics of Christianity, the ablest being three men, Lucian and Celsus and Porphyry of Tyre, whose names are well known still. Lucian was a witty, polished Greek scholar and man of letters, who was an agnostic and a critic of all religions.[3] Celsus was a Platonist, but chiefly a man of the world, whose religion was the Roman Empire. He was an able critic of the whole Christian system, dangerous enough to draw a weighty reply a generation later from Origen of Caesarea, the greatest Christian scholar of the third century. Porphyry of Tyre, more feared by the Church than either Lucian or Celsus, was a Greek scholar and Neo-Platonist, a disciple of Plotinus at Rome and his interpreter after his death. Porphyry was, in relation to Christianity, what may be called a Higher Critic. He analyzed the Christian Scriptures and showed their contradictions. It was an attack to which the Church was then little equipped to reply.

Christianity, however, did not lack defenders; and as the Church has kept their names alive, we know them better than we know her critics. There were Quadratus, bishop of the Christians at Athens, and Aristides a philosopher, who presented apologies, or reasoned defenses, of Christianity to the Emperor Hadrian, on his visit to Athens in 125. There was Justin, a native of Samaria, who, having tried the philosophical schools, was attracted at length by the earnestness and enthusiasm of Christians, and became a wandering Christian teacher. He presented two apologies to Hadrian's successor, Antoninus Pius, died a martyr, and is therefore known as Justin Martyr. And Melito, bishop of the Christians at Sardis and influential throughout all Asia Minor, presented an apology to Marcus Aurelius, successor to Antoninus. And greatest of all the Christian apologists was Origen (184–254), the first great writer born of Christian parents.

A native of Alexandria, Origen became famous as a teacher and scholar, winning intellectuals to the faith. Called to Greece, to arbitrate a difficulty among the churches there, and passing through Palestine, Origen visited Caesarea, where he ultimately settled, devoting his life to study and authorship. He was the first to survey the whole field of Christian thought and state its problems. His educational method was dictated by a fearless love of truth. He read pagan literature, attended the

---

[3] His orations, biographies, satirical dialogues, are still read in the colleges. Of them all, the *Life of Peregrinus* is the most sustained attack upon Christianity.

lectures of the Neo-Platonists, and may be described as the first great Christian Modernist.[4]

The attack of educated paganism upon Christianity was many-sided. The Christians were charged with credulity, in expecting great things from a simple Galilean, and with absurdity, in incorporating him in a doctrine of God and the universe. They were charged with atheism, because they did not worship the Roman gods; with immorality, on the ground of their secret assemblies; with treason, because they looked for a kingdom of Christ; and with hatred of the human race, because of their aloofness from society. Neither attack nor defence is very convincing to modern ears. The charge of atheism was manifestly false, as against any monotheist, whether Jew or Christian. The Jewish and Christian rejoinder also, that pagans worshipped stocks and stones, was only a half-truth. Early Stoicism condemned idolatry, later Stoicism rationalized it. The attitude of educated pagans of the second century, to idolatry and to religious art in general, was not very different from that of Roman and Greek Christians to-day.

In general, the Christian defence was as competent as the pagan attack; but the true strength of the Church lay in the character of the Christians and their hopes. The case was put by a nameless apologist, in a letter to a certain Diognetus, perhaps the tutor of Marcus Aurelius: "What the soul is in the body, that the Christians are in the world. . . . The soul dwells in the body, but is not of the body; and Christians dwell in the world, but are not of the world. . . . The soul dwells immortal in a mortal tabernacle; and Christians sojourn among corruptible things, waiting for the incorruptibility which is in heaven. The soul when evil treated in food and drink becomes better, and Christians when buffeted day by day increase more. God has appointed them to so great a post, and it is not right for them to decline it."

[4] Other apologists were Tatian, an Assyrian who became a disciple of Justin at Rome and then a Christian evangelist to Syria; and Irenaeus, a disciple of Polycarp at Smyrna, who travelled widely and became at length a bishop in Gaul; and Clement, an Athenian who, after wandering in search of truth, became a disciple of the Christian Pantaenus at Alexandria, and settled there to a life of quiet study and teaching, thus becoming known to history as Clement of Alexandria. He was the teacher of Origen.

These were all Greek-speaking Apologists; but Latin Christianity contributed one in Tertullian, son of a Roman centurion at Carthage, who married a Christian woman, was converted to Christianity, and became an elder. Trained to the practice of law, indifferent to poetry and art, contemptuous of philosophy, Tertullian contributed a vigorous, but not very Christian, invective to the defence of the Church.

The post was not very perilous in normal times; and times were normal for long periods. The Roman Empire was singularly fortunate in the character and capacity of the emperors of the second century. Four great men ruled in succession, from the beginning of the century until the year 180. They were Trajan and Hadrian, and the first two Antonines—Antoninus Pius and Marcus Aurelius. Thoughtful men may have discerned a portent in the fact that none of these was of Roman, or even Italian, birth. All had to be found in the provinces.[5] But if Rome and Italy were no longer producing emperors, the age of the Antonines was nevertheless the happiest in the history of the Empire. The Roman genius for government had received its reward. In Gaul and Spain and distant Britain, in Africa and Syria, the earlier tribal life, with its village centres, had become a life in towns. The amenities of civilization were more available there, and the imperial taxes more easily gathered. But the genius of Rome is shown in that she preserved the ancient tribal districts, or cantons, establishing a town to be the centre of each, and providing it with magistrates and a senate, on the model of Rome. The new officers were the earlier chiefs; but now they bore Roman names, *duoviri* and *quaestores,* and sat in a senate.

Very little literature survives, to tell us of life in these provincial towns; but there are monuments and inscriptions. Deciphering them, we see a multitude of urban communities, electing magistrates each year, who pass after their term as magistrates into a permanent senate of advisers. The magistrate must be a man of wealth, because the tradition of the office is that he pay a fee on his accession, provide public games during his term, give feasts to the populace, or distribute money. And the magistrate wishes also to immortalize himself by endowing a school, or erecting a theatre, or a bath, or an aqueduct. Gradually the magistracy is thus impoverished, men decline the office; and the senatorial class decays. More serious still, the populace learns to look to the rich for its comforts and pleasures, not to its own industry and thrift. The larger towns acquire amphitheatres, on the model of the Colosseum at Rome; and pleasures become increasingly inhuman, associated with dying gladiators and contests with caged beasts. And more and more the

---

[5] Trajan and his cousin Hadrian came from Spain. Titus Antoninus, called after his accession Antoninus Pius, came from Nismes in southern Gaul, as did his nephew and adopted son, Marcus Aurelius Antoninus. Nismes, now Nîmes, still honours Antoninus Pius with a statue, in the *Place Antonin.*

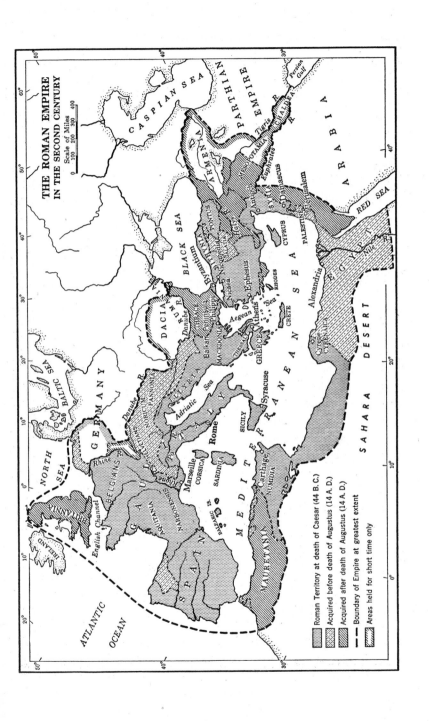

THE ROMAN EMPIRE
IN THE SECOND CENTURY

Scale of Miles
0 100 200 300 400

Roman Territory at death of Caesar (44 B.C.)

Acquired before death of Augustus (14 A.D.)

Acquired after death of Augustus (14 A.D.)

Boundary of Empire at greatest extent

Areas held for short time only

imperial government becomes paternal, an increasing providence to towns increasingly improvident.

Such social health as existed was chiefly among the workmen. Members of similar trades and callings were associated in guilds, each licensed by the central government at Rome. The associates were more than craftsmen; they were searchers after fellowship, anxious too that at death they should not be cast into a common grave and forgotten. The guilds would provide decent burial and a simple monument, where friends "would bring the annual offering of wine and flowers."

On the whole, life in the provincial towns would be a pleasant one, so long as the frontiers of the Empire were securely held. And the Empire was well guarded while Trajan and Hadrian lived. Vigilance lapsed under Antoninus Pius. Diligent and dutiful as he was, he seems to have thought that Hadrian's frontiers would stand of themselves. Before he died German tribes were threatening the Rhine-Danube frontier; in the days of Marcus Aurelius they swarmed across the Danube, and even broke through the Brenner Pass into Italy. Roman resistance was weakened by a plague, one of the most terrible in history, recently brought by the legions from the East. Thirteen years were required to expel the invaders from Roman territory. Marcus Aurelius died in camp at Vienna before the task was completed, leaving a worthless son Commodus, with whom the long decline of Roman power began. The burden of self-defence was too great for progress; and the monarchy became more absolute and government more centralized; the people were over-taxed and the middle classes ruined. Depopulation began; and an attempt to remedy it by settling barbarian invaders within the frontiers was perilous. Rome walked unsteadily.

Meanwhile Christianity was slowly changing, in such ways as would naturally follow its migration from Semitic to Hellenic soil. Some Christian beliefs and practices of the second century would have seemed strange and alien to Jesus, some even to Paul. The Church was assimilating Hellenic philosophy and ethics and social forms, Roman ideas of law and government.

Change is seen in the Christian method of interpreting the Scriptures. Contemporary Greece reverenced the past, and believed in the divine inspiration of her ancient literature. Poetry was regarded as a sort of philosophy, presenting in attractive dress the principles of wise living. Homer was quoted as we quote the Bible, to enforce all sorts of moral truths. The immoralities in his writings were excused on the ground that he pictured life as it is, that the good in Homer outweighed the evil, that poets sometimes speak by inspiration of the Muses, sometimes by their human knowledge only. But the most convincing argument was that hidden meanings lay beneath the surface of Homeric poetry, that the narratives were symbolical. The gods were the powers of Nature; their assemblies and amours were the interaction of natural forces; their battles were the conflict of natural forces.

Symbol, or allegory, became the favourite device for interpreting ancient literature and religion in such a way as to bring them into harmony with the higher ethical ideals and the monotheistic tendency in philosophy. All the great literature of the past became a literature of riddles; and the grammarians were their interpreters.

Christians employed the current method. There were many things in the Old Testament that offended the Christian conscience. This, it was explained, was because there is a human, as well as a divine, element in the Old Testament; and because Moses, like Homer, wrote in symbols, to conceal his meaning from the foolish. The prophets, too, wrote not in plain words but in pictures, whose meaning was purposely obscure. Indeed it might be unknown to the prophets themselves; for prophets were passive agents of Deity, the lyres through which the Spirit breathed.

Thus the allegorizing of ancient literature went on apace. Greek philosophers read their systems into Homer; Hellenist Jews read Moses into Homer; Christian theologians read Jesus and Paul and John into the Old Testament. It is so in Justin Martyr and Clement of Alexandria, Irenaeus and Tertullian, and their successors until modern times. The method carried conviction to ancient society; it carries conviction still, among uncritical people.

Gradually Christian scholars applied the same method to the New Testament. The life of Christ was as difficult for Christian philosophers as was the Old Testament. How could one conceive a human being, of humble origin, as at the same time the Word (*Logos*), who was in Stoic thought the soul of the world, and in Philo [6] the agent of God in both creation and revelation? The difficulty could be overcome by represent-

[6] *See* Appendix V.

ing the life of Christ as the symbolic presentation of superhuman events, written in code.

Sober Christian scholars at first denounced the application of such a method to the Christian Scriptures; but it was suited to the times and secured a firm footing, first in the great school at Alexandria, where the influence of Philo was strongest, then throughout the churches.

The effect of Hellenism upon Christian preaching was equally marked. Literary culture and appreciation were widely diffused in the second century; and the most characteristic product of the contemporary culture was Rhetoric, whose vogue was all the greater because of the growing devotion to ancient literature. Rhetoric had once been a training for the pleading of actual cases in the law courts; it now became a training in formal oratory. It was known as Sophistic. Its standard of excellence was dramatic consistency, or a style appropriate to the theme and the occasion.

Sophistic thus grew out of Rhetoric, but it was related also to Philosophy; for its utterances were often discourses on morality and theology. But the new Sophists differed from true philosophers in that they did not profess allegiance to what they described. They were professional public talkers. Sometimes they spoke in private houses, sometimes in theatres, sometimes in regular lecture halls, like that "school of Tyrannus" at Ephesus, where Paul debated Christianity for two years.

Christian writers spoke scornfully of Sophistic; but it influenced Christian practice nevertheless. Primitive preaching had been called "prophesying." It was spontaneous utterance, not by church officers but by men having a divine gift (*charisma*), who needs must utter what had come to them. Such utterance ceased in the second century. As the churches drew together, freedom of utterance was curtailed. Confederation of the churches was impossible without doctrinal agreement; and men who spoke spontaneously would not always speak alike. So prophesying was discouraged as rapidly as the Catholic Church increased. It gave place to preaching, which was restricted to officials. Those who, like the Montanists (pp. 164–166), insisted on freedom of utterance became heretics.

This preaching, or prepared utterance by Christian officials, is the origin of the sermon, which has continued until now. Best known of the

early preachers was Origen of Caesarea, who delivered carefully prepared sermons daily, drawn from the Scriptures, quite as the Sophists
around him drew homilies from Homer and other ancients. The
greatest preachers of the next century—Basil the Great, Gregory
Nazianzen and John Chrysostom—had all been teachers of Rhetoric.
Their prepared utterances came to be known by the name used in the
schools—discourses, or disputations, or speeches. The preacher, like the
rhetorician, sat in an official chair, with his hearers before him,
frequently interrupting him with shouts of approval.[7]

The value of the new instruction was somewhat neutralized by the
sophistry it encouraged. Rhetoric had already degraded philosophy, because the rhetorician valued fine phrases more than the philosophic life.
Rhetoric was now to affect Christian preaching for the same reason.
Christian officials would often speak, not because some truth was pressing for expression, but because the time had come for another sermon. A
Christianity so communicated would be different in quality from that
communicated by either the testimony of Christians or their example.

The Christian Church acquired also a philosophy. The habit of discussion, as we have seen, was general in Graeco-Roman society. Under
the name of Dialectic, which was regulated conversation, it had a
prominent place in both the schools of Philosophy and Rhetoric and in
ordinary life. Conversation tended to be Dialectic and Dialectic to be
logical. And as rapidly as original thinking declined, so rapidly was the
moral obligation to find the truth obscured by the obligation to discuss
logically whatever the Masters had thought true.

All this had lain outside primitive Christianity. In it moral considerations were supreme. It inherited the mentality of Palestine, which was
concerned, not with abstract questions but with the practical problems of
human life. It appealed first to classes that philosophy did not reach;

[7] This applause troubled the conscience of high-minded men. "There are many
preachers," said John Chrysostom, "who make long sermons: if they are well applauded,
they are as glad as if they had obtained a kingdom; if they bring their sermon to an end
in silence, their despondency is worse, I may almost say, than hell. It is this that ruins
churches, that you do not seek to hear sermons that touch the heart, but sermons that
will delight your ears with their intonation and the structure of their phrases. . . . I am
not speaking at random; when you applaud me as I speak, I feel at the moment as it is
natural for a man to feel. . . . And then when I go home and reflect that the people who
have been applauding me have received no benefit, and indeed that whatever benefit they
might have had has been killed by the applause and praises, I am sore at heart, and I
lament and fall into tears." *Homilies*, xxx.

and it quoted authorities, the prophets and Jesus, that Greek philosophy did not know. The Gospel would have a strange sound in Hellenic ears; and it is noteworthy that St. Paul, when first he crossed to Europe and visited Athens, changed the method of his preaching. Encountering Epicurean and Stoic philosophers on the Areopagus, he preached in philosophic terms, alluding to an Epicurean dogma that "God needs nothing," and quoting a Stoic poet, "For we are his offspring."

The adoption by Christianity of the philosophic dress was the more possible because some ideals of Greek philosophy were identical with its own. Both commended justice and fraternity, chastity and sobriety, repentance and faith. So much so that both critics and defenders of Christianity thought it necessary to account for this kinship. Celsus said Christianity was only a crude Platonism; Tertullian said Greek poets and sophists had "drunk at the fountain of the prophets."

This kinship of ideals made Christianity congenial to many of the nobler minds in the Graeco-Roman world. So Greek philosophy entered the Church; and simple Christians became uneasy. Clement of Alexandria deplores "the ignorant timidity" of those "who think that philosophy will prove to have been introduced into life from an evil source, . . . for the ruin of men."

Conflict within the Church was inevitable. It was as impossible for her to ignore the philosophical inheritance of her converts as it is for the churches now to ignore the physical sciences. The struggle went on throughout the second century; and gradually both extremities dropped away from the main body of Christians. Old fashioned Christians went out as Montanists; speculative extremists went out as Gnostics (pp. 159–161). The main body of the Church compromised. Rejecting certain speculative ideas, it retained the speculative habit. Instinctively it adopted the popular practice of expressing its ideas in philosophical form and testing its facts by philosophical principles. Christian Apologists borrowed Greek theories of the *Logos,* the nature of spirit, and what not, and met their opponents with the weapons of Dialectic. In short, Christianity was being adopted by men of Greek education, who retained as Christians the habit of mind in which they had grown up. It gradually became the mind of the Church. It showed itself in a tendency towards definition and speculation. Primitive Christians had been content to believe in God and to worship Him; Catholic Christians had to define Him, to draw inferences from their definitions, to weave the inferences into a system, to test beliefs by their logical consistency with the system. Gradually correct views became more important than trust in God and a holy life. Indeed, the new definitions were included among the things that had been divinely revealed to the Church. Thenceforth, until the present day, men who would discover chemistry and physics by observation and experiment were to be required to accept metaphysics as supernaturally revealed.

Hellenic influence is as clearly seen in Christian ethics. The ethical ideal of Graeco-Roman society was acquired from the Stoics. Right conduct was conduct befitting one's station and relationships. Rarely was conduct put on that higher plane, where goodness is uncalculating, spontaneous, done for the pure love of God and humanity. It was on this higher plane the primitive Christians had tried to live. They were to love their enemies, to forgive until seventy times seven, to give without counting the cost, to esteem others better than themselves, that they might be true sons of the Father in heaven. But this was air too rarefied for those who no longer had before them the example of Jesus and St. Paul, or the vivid expectation of a judgment to come. Christian ideas of righteousness and holiness were displaced by Stoic ideas of virtue, and spontaneous beneficence by conduct worthy of one's station. In time Stoic ethics became thoroughly at home in the Church; and bishop Ambrose of Milan incorporated it in a book which became the great text-book of moral philosophy in the Middle Ages.[8] Thus the ethics of the Sermon on the Mount was transmuted into the rights and duties of reputable Roman citizens.

While the Church was thus accommodating herself to Hellenism, she was meeting competition from other religions. And indeed Christianity had something to fear from those who offered an alternative religious experience. It was a satisfying experience that men craved, an experience of victory over circumstances, of stability in an unstable world, of immortality. Here Stoicism and Neo-Platonism offered little or nothing to the common man. They asked of him a detachment from society and a sustained intellectual effort of which he was incapable, and offered him an admirable example which he could not follow. It was not so with

[8] *De officiis ministrorum.*

certain mystery religions, born in the Orient but long since at home throughout the Empire. These gave to mortal man the experience of saving union with a more-than-mortal Saviour; and before the rise of Christianity, many earnest Greeks and Romans, like Cicero, could already say of the mystery religions, "From them we have learned the rudiments, as they are called, which are in fact the fundamental principles of living, and thereby have received a rule not only of happy living, but of dying with a better hope."

Several Oriental gods—Adonis and Isis, Osiris and the Phrygian Cybele—all had their worshippers in Rome itself.[9] Their cults differed from the ancient state religion in this, that they were not restricted to any racial group and concerned themselves with the relation of the individual to God. They had, too, a solemn emotional liturgy, performed by a consecrated priesthood, majestically garbed. The Roman magistrates, who presided over the jovial festivals of the ancient state religion, had no spiritual authority to match these new hierarchies from the Orient, where learning was the distinctive prerogative of the priesthood and supernatural sources of information were believed to guarantee its infallibility. The worshippers acquired also from the East a sense of sin and an ideal of holiness, suitable at all times, and never more so than in the period of the Empire.

The ritual of corporate worship in some, perhaps most, of the mystery religions consisted centrally in lamentations over the death of their god, followed by ecstatic celebrations of his resurrection. The dying god was often represented in effigy, as in Roman Catholic and Orthodox services for Good Friday and Easter Sunday. The ritual went back to a primitive vegetarian magic, to ensure and celebrate the rebirth of Nature in spring, after the apparent death of winter; but in the Mysteries the resurrection of Nature had been changed into the resurrection of the worshipper, which was thought to be guaranteed by the resurrection of his god. Death and resurrection are the theme of the mystery religions. Initiation itself was regarded as death to sin and rebirth to righteousness; and the

[9] Better known to-day is the cult of Mithras, a Persian deity, whose name indeed appears much earlier in Indian religion, in the Vedas. Mithraism, however, was not more important than other mystery religions. It is better known because of the researches of a distinguished French scholar, M. Cumont. Its strength was on the frontiers, in the legionary centres, partly because of its special fitness for the military life, partly because in pre-Roman days it was deeply rooted in Asia Minor, the chief recruiting centre for the legions in all the East.

frequent use of subterranean chapels was, sometimes at least, symbolic of descent into the grave and resurrection to immortality.

In the mystery religions, as in philosophy, there was a disposition to monotheism. All claimed to worship the Supreme Power of the Universe, whatever name they might give Him. So that the Mysteries were rivals in the worship of God, not cults of rival gods. Indeed, men were frequently initiated into several of the Mysteries.

Rites of initiation into the Mysteries were secret; but one fairly complete account, of initiation into the cult of Isis, survives in a novel of Apuleius, the *Metamorphoses*. The hero of the novel is Lucius, who lives for a time in the temple precincts at Corinth with the priests, is initiated, and returns to Rome a thankful devotee of Isis. "My voice is too poor in utterance to tell what I feel concerning Thy majesty. . . . Therefore will I strive to do all that a poor, yet faithful servant may. I will guard the memory of Thy divine countenance and of Thy most holy godhead within my heart's inmost shrine, and their image shall be with me forever."

Many highly cultivated gentlemen were devoutly attached to the Mysteries. The aim of the ritual was to create, not a realistic illusion but an emotional experience, which did, in fact transform many a new convert. In other words, a psychological revolution, accompanied by a moral transformation, did take place, and is justly described as conversion in the religious sense.

Contemporary movements, that had so much in common as had the Mysteries and Christianity, would affect each other. They were parts of one great religious revival in the Graeco-Roman world. They were alike in their aim to worship one God, to live pure lives, to cultivate fraternity here and the hope of life hereafter. Men passed from the Mysteries into the Church, bringing with them religious ideas and ritual tendencies. Christian apologists were in time disturbed by the similarities between practices in the Mysteries and those in the Church. Justin Martyr thought the communion service in Mithraism, commemorating the last meal of Helios and Mithras together on earth, was an imitation of the Supper of the Lord, inspired by demons.

Similarities increased after the late second century, until Christian ritual owed as much to the Mysteries as Christian theology owed to Greek philosophy, and Christian ethics to Stoicism. For example, primitive Christianity had had no secrets. Its rites were simple and its teaching open to the public; but now the Church acquired mysteries of her own, some doctrines being imparted only to the initiated.

The change is seen best in baptism. At first Christian baptism had followed immediately upon conversion, the ritual was of the simplest kind, only water being used; and no minister or priest seems to have been necessary. This continued to the end of the first century; [10] but by the time of Justin Martyr all is changed. The whole vocabulary of baptism is now that of the Mysteries. Baptism is itself a "mystery," the one who performs it a "mystagogue." Baptism comes only after a long preparation; [11] and Christians are now divided into two classes, those who have and those who have not received baptism, the catechumens. A few days before baptism the catechumens receive a pass-word, or "symbol," composed of a Creed [12] and the Lord's Prayer. These are now mysteries. The giving of the pass-word is an impressive ceremony. In some churches the baptized are crowned with garlands, just as the initiated had worn mystic crowns at ancient Eleusis. And as the gods there had been thought to watch the initiations from the midst of brilliant light, so John Chrysostom and Cyril of Jerusalem describe the white-robed bands of the newly baptized, approaching the doors of Christian churches on Easter-eve amidst blazing illuminations.

So also with the Lord's Supper. It is difficult to determine from the New Testament the precise form of the Supper at the beginning; but the *Didaché* describes it a generation or two later. There was thanksgiving for the bread, and then for the wine; after which the communicants ate and drank, only those participating who had been baptized. Another thanksgiving followed, and a prayer of supplication.

Further developments of the ritual of the Supper, in the early second century, are described in an ancient collection of documents, the *Apostolic Constitutions*. A deacon now announces the exclusion of catechumens and those baptized persons who confess any fault or lapse. These go out, quite as uninitiated and the ceremonially impure were excluded from the Mysteries. In the late second century the holy table becomes an altar; and still later the offerings placed upon it become

---

[10] *Didaché* 7.
[11] *Apostolic Constitutions*, 8.32.
[12] To-day the technical name for a Creed is still *symbol*, or *pass-word*.

"mysteries" and the minister becomes a priest. After the fifth century a great mystical writer, the Pseudo-Dionysius, whose influence is still traceable in Catholic treatises on the Mass, describes the whole Supper in terms applicable only to the Mysteries. It is no longer in any real sense the Supper of the Lord; it is a "thearchic mystery," into which only the celebrating priest wholly enters.[13]

The visible form of Christianity, in public worship and sacraments, was thus changing from generation to generation. The elaborate ceremonial of the Mysteries entered the Christian Church, which moved farther and farther from the simplicity of Galilean days. This alien element is present still, unrecognized as alien, in the splendid ceremonial of Catholic Christianity.

The Church was less hospitable to another movement in the Graeco-Roman world, the movement called Gnosticism. It was one aspect of the Orientalism that was first introduced into Europe through the conquest of the Near East by Alexander the Great. Orientalism seriously influenced Greek thought in Stoicism, an influence later revived in Neo-Platonism. It influenced Judaism next, in those world-renouncing desert-dwellers, the Essenes, to whom John the Baptist may have belonged. It reached Christianity, under the name of Gnosticism, through certain false teachers of Colossae. There are echoes in the New Testament of disturbances caused by the doctrine that Christ and Jesus are not the same, that Christ did not have a true human body, and therefore did not die on the cross.[14] From the early second century such doctrines were openly proclaimed in the churches, and won a considerable following among Gentile Christians. A few exponents built elaborate Gnostic systems, the foremost being Basilides and Valentinus.

The Knowledge (Greek *Gnosis*), from which Gnosticism received its name, was believed to come by divine revelation. To receive this divine Gnosis was to be saved. The Gnosis was presented in the form of mysteries; and initiates were often united in associations, as in the mystery religions.

It is impossible now to do justice to Gnosticism, unless one remembers the religious unrest of that age, the eagerness to appropriate fruitful

[13] Dionysius Areopagiticus, *Ecclesiastical Hierarchy*, ch. 3, par. 1.
[14] *Colossians* 2: 1–9; I *John* 2: 22; 4: 2, 15; 5: 1, 5; 2 *John* 7.

ideas from anywhere, and the necessity, for the Greek mind, to harmonize them. Orientalism was an attempt to unite philosophical and religious principles from different sources. Gnosticism differed from other Orientalism in that it drew upon Christianity for its doctrine of redemption. It was a number of schools of philosophy, Oriental in their general character, but all accepting the Christian doctrine of redemption through Christ.

The difficulty of all this for the Church was that the Gnostics did not appropriate other Christian doctrines; and even the doctrine of redemption, as they taught it, was different. The Gnostics regarded redemption as the victory of wise men over matter, not the redemption of mankind from sin. Indeed Gnosticism was rather a philosophy than a religion. Its central problem was this, Granting that human redemption comes through Christ, how shall we fit him into a total view of the universe? The Gnostic schools did not give the same answer; but a general average of Gnostic teaching was somewhat as follows:

Spiritual beings first came into existence through emanations from the Absolute, as in Neo-Platonism. From these came other emanations, and from them still others, farther and farther from their source in the Absolute, until at length the bridge between the spiritual and the material was crossed, spirits came into contact with matter.

It is next explained that matter is essentially evil. Alexandrian Gnostics conceived it in the Platonic way, as something inert and unsubstantial, in which spirits, remote emanations from God, are imprisoned. Syrian Gnostics conceived it in the Zoroastrian fashion, as an active and evil power, intruding upon the world of spirits. In both views matter was evil. Gnosticism in general therefore held ascetic views, regarding the body as evil and all the appetites as seductive.

As for creation, it was the work, not of the Supreme God but of a Demiurge, one of the angels, who was the Jehovah of the Old Testament. He was the imperfect instrument of God in creation; and he bungled the work. A redeemer was therefore necessary, to mend what he had done.

As for the redeemer, one who came to redeem men from matter could not himself come in a material body. So that Gnosticism sometimes held that, while the manhood of Christ was real, his body was but the garment of a spiritual being who dwelt within, having entered the body at the baptism of Jesus and departed before his crucifixion. The redeemer therefore was not crucified. Another, and more consistent view, however, was that Christ had no real body; he only seemed to eat and drink and die.

As for the redeemed, they were few indeed. Only a remnant of the spiritual world, a colony of heaven, exists in the material world. For men were created of three grades, according to the degree of their spiritual endowment and redeemability. There were hylic men, the heathen world, without spiritual endowment, to be overwhelmed at last in the general destruction of the world. And there were psychic men, the Jews and ordinary Christians, moderately endowed and destined for a shadowy existence hereafter, like the Sheol of the Hebrews. And there were a few pneumatic men, the Gnostics, the true prophets and philosophers, who had been adequately endowed and who would return at last to their home in the spirit world, the Pleroma of divine beings, into whom the Absolute had unfolded himself.

It was a true instinct that led the Church to cast out the Gnostics. It could adopt Greek exegesis and oratory, metaphysics and ethics; it could take over ritual forms from the Mysteries, and yet remain Christian. But Gnosticism was another matter. What became of Jesus, his teaching and example, if his presence was a phantom and his parables a set of allegories, comprehensible only to the wise? What became of redemption through the cross, if Christ was not there, but only a shell from which he had departed? What was the use of the Gospel, and where was the hope of overcoming the world, if most men were irredeemable? In Gnosticism the reinterpretation of the Gospel went so far that there was no Gospel left. And so when Marcion, devout Christian but a Gnostic, met Polycarp at Rome and asked for recognition, Polycarp said, "I recognize the first-born of Satan."

Gnosticism, however, left its mark upon the developing Catholic Church. Christian scholars can trace its influence still in the sacramental ritual, in Christian asceticism, and in the Catholic principle that religious beliefs must be rationalized, becoming thus speculative dogmas.[15]

[15] Gnosticism survived outside the Catholic Church. Valentinus established a sect, a cultured and aristocratic one, that continued for several generations. He had been an earnest Christian, a diligent student of the Gospels, especially the Gospel of John. His disciples, Ptolemaeus and Heracleon, wrote Bible commentaries that were quoted by Cath-

Out of all the movements and forces here described Catholic Christianity emerged. It was an amalgam of Greek philosophy and mental habits, Oriental ritual and methods of salvation, Stoic ethics and Roman law. That is, it was so much of current life as ecclesiastical leaders thought the Church could absorb, without compromising its own inheritance from Judaism and Jesus. That it did in fact compromise was as clear to some Christians then as now. Men protested and suffered expulsion from the Church rather than conform. Two of the protesting movements were Marcionism and Montanism.

Marcion was a rich shipowner and a Christian, of Sinope, on the south shore of the Black Sea. He came to Rome about A.D. 140, put before the church there strange views of the Scriptures, was expelled, and established in Rome a church of his own. From Rome he travelled far and wide, winning many converts, and labouring to bring the whole Catholic Church to his views. Marcionite churches continued to spring up for a hundred years, and were a dangerous threat to Catholicism.

Marcion was a Bible reader, at a time when Christians knew little of the Bible. For the Bible was still the Old Testament. Jews heard it read in the synagogues, in the Greek version, the Septuagint. Christians did not attend the synagogue services, did not own the Septuagint, and were interested anyway in little except the prophecies that were thought to refer to Christ. There were, of course, the Christian writings as well, accepted as authoritative, though not yet in the Bible. In the time of Marcion Christians were generally agreed that the four Gospels and twelve epistles of St. Paul were authoritative.[16]

The Bible was not privately owned. Bishops and presbyters probably had access to it, in the archives of the larger churches; but there were very few "Bible readers." The Christian writings also, in separate rolls of papyrus, were costly, difficult to collect, and sometimes banned by law. Christians accepted both the Bible and the Christian writings on the authority of the bishops and a few scholarly presbyters, who were themselves uncritical in the use of the Bible.

It was an awkward moment to assert the right of private judgment

---

olic Fathers. Another disciple, Bardaisan of Edessa, was very influential in the churches of Syria. He wrote a noble Christian poem, *The Hymn of the Soul*, that has been described as a *Pilgrim's Progress* of antiquity.

[16] Official approval of all writings of the New Testament was not given until a Council of Carthage in 397.

and encourage a Bible-study movement. This was what Marcion did. He had access to the Scriptures, perhaps because he was rich enough to buy the Old Testament and send copyists to Christian centres, to copy the Christian writings. And Marcion was also a realist. His mind rejected naïve allegorical interpretations of Scripture. It was as clear to him as to St. Paul that the Mosaic Law and the Gospel were incompatible. Believing in the divine inspiration of ancient writings, he could only conclude that Law and Gospel were inspired by different gods. And learning from the Old Testament that Jehovah was often angry, sometimes changed his mind, repented even that he had made man, Marcion said Jehovah was not the Supreme God, the Father of Jesus Christ. Jehovah was the Demiurge, of whom Marcion had heard from the Gnostics and elsewhere.

As for the Gospel, only Paul, of all the apostles, had rightly understood it. Marcion would bring the Church back to Jesus and Paul. To do this, he not only rejected the Old Testament; he edited the New Testament. Marcion denied the genuineness of the Pastoral Epistles, and excluded from *Luke* what he thought were later interpolations. Very courageously, if crudely, he anticipated by eighteen centuries the "Higher Criticism."

There is much else in Marcion; but it was his Bible-study that mattered most in his day. The Church had been moving for a century towards catholicity, in the sense of uniformity in doctrine and worship and government. Catholicity of that sort is inconsistent with the right of private judgment. It requires "churchmen," submissive to the institution, not individualists. And indeed the Church was then incapable of individualism, was indeed to become less and less capable, as society sank slowly in culture and the Church with it. If the Catholic Church was to survive, men must accept doctrines on its authority. They did so. The Bible became a closed book. Catholic theology took its place. Christians were not, in any large numbers, to "search the Scriptures" until fourteen centuries later, and then only through the Protestant revolt. And indeed after four centuries of Protestantism, the problem of Marcion is unsolved. It is not in the interest of ecclesiastical unity that a solution should be attempted.[17]

[17] History has seen four attempted solutions of Marcion's problem. Judaism said Old Testament and New Testament were not both from God, and rejected the New Testa-

As for Montanism, it was an attempt to return to the simplicity and spontaneity of the first Christians, and especially to recover the emotional experience associated with the Day of Pentecost. The leader of the movement, a certain Montanus, had been a priest of Cybele, whom the Romans called the Mother of the Gods. Her worship originated in Phrygia, a lofty tableland of Asia Minor, remote from the cities of the coast and untouched by Hellenic culture. There, at the forest sanctuaries of the goddess, Montanus had participated in her highly emotional rites. Converted to Christianity, his religious life continued to be marked by the emotionalism of the Phrygian villages.

Montanus appeared, in the first years of Marcus Aurelius, at Ardabau, on the border of Phrygia, preaching revelations from the Holy Spirit. The Church, he said, was growing cold. She had taken into her heart too much of the world. Christians were committing their religious duties to officials. They must return to the spirit of prophecy. God was ready to restore to his people the gift of prophecy, to "pour forth of (his) Spirit upon all flesh." Indeed this had happened to Montanus. It was not he who was preaching, but the Spirit through him.

Montanism spread through the Phrygian villages, in the form of a wild revivalism; and in more moderate forms it reached Italy and Gaul and North Africa some twenty years later.[18] The flame was fanned by persecutions then being endured by the churches. The general distress was regarded as a sign of the speedy return of Christ and the end of the

---

ment. Marcion said they were not both from God, and rejected the Old Testament. Catholic Christianity has said both are from God, and has reconciled them by allegory. Protestant Liberalism says both are from God, and solves the problem involved by saying that divine revelation is a historic growth, a "progressive revelation." This, as a solution of the problem of the Scriptures, is a palpable makeshift, inspired by reluctance to change. It is directly refuted by the fact that most of the higher conceptions of the Old Testament are in the earlier, not the later, literature.

A defensible doctrine of the Bible is that it is the record of the long search for God by the Jews, the classic people of religion, a search in which the supreme event is the life of Jesus, in whom the ultimate truth of life is revealed, the ultimate goodness realized.

Meanwhile many simple, devout Christians continue to read the Scriptures, suspending judgment about the contradictions they find, leaving the problem to God for solution, and poring over the many things in both Old and New Testaments that do support the higher life.

[18] Two prophetesses, Prisca and Maximilla, were especially ardent in the work; and Tertullian was won. Montanism lasted two centuries in Phrygia, then slowly died out in the East. It is still strong in the West, being present in some degree in most Protestant churches, while several small sects—Millennialists, Pentecostalists, and what not—are Montanists under other names.

for truth, as undoubtedly containing what the churches received from the Apostles, the Apostles from Christ, Christ from God.[21]

The substance of the Rule of Faith at Rome, and presumably therefore in other apostolic churches, may be learned also from Tertullian:

One Lord God does she acknowledge, the Creator of the Universe; and Christ Jesus born of the Virgin Mary, the Son of God the Creator; and the resurrection of the flesh; the Law and the Prophets she unites in one volume with the writings of Evangelists and Apostles, from which she drinks in her faith.[22]

From this and other summaries it is clear that, in answer to Marcion, there was in the churches of the late second century, a fixed canon of Scripture, including the Old Testament and a New Testament much as at present, though differing slightly from church to church. There was also in each church, in answer to the Gnostics, a Creed which grew out of the confession that had been made by the first Christians at their baptism,[23] that confession being expanded, somewhat differently in different churches, by materials drawn from the Rule of Faith. The local forms of the Creed, in the second century, cannot now be known. They were, according to a paraphrase by Tertullian, an affirmation of belief in

One God, the Almighty, the Maker of the world; and His Son, Jesus Christ, born of the Virgin Mary, crucified under Pontius Pilate, on the third day raised again from the dead, received in the heavens, sitting now at the right hand of the Father, coming to judge the quick and the dead also, through the resurrection of the flesh.[24]

Such a creed is less a theology than a re-affirmation of certain historical facts and hopes. And indeed for a long time there was no theologian

---

[21] *De Praescriptione,* 20, 21, in Ayer, *Source-Book for Ancient Church History,* pp. 114, 115.

[22] *Ibid.,* 36, in Ayer, p. 116.

[23] This primitive Baptismal Confession may be inferred from the *Didaché* and from *Matthew* 28: 19. It was substantially this: "I believe in God, in Jesus Christ, and in the Holy Spirit."

[24] *De Virginibus Velandis,* 1, in Ayer, p. 125. The so-called Apostles' Creed was developed out of these second-century Creeds, but not until the fifth century. It had from the first nothing to do with the Apostles, except that it was the authorized summary of the teaching of Christ, transmitted by the Apostles, and preserved in the churches. The Apostles' Creed is, however, primitive in the sense that a careful student can gather most of its contents still from the first Church History, that of Luke in his Gospel and the *Acts.*

capable of carrying forward the work begun by St. Paul and the author of the Fourth Gospel. Further development had to wait until the third century. Then Christian theology received an impetus from outside the Church, from Neo-Platonism. It arose in Egypt, as we have seen (p. 145), the work of Ammonius Saccas of Alexandria. His most distinguished disciples were Plotinus, who gave to Neo-Platonism its lasting fame, and Origen of Caesarea, who turned it to the service of Christianity.

The new philosophy was Platonism, influenced by the best things in other systems. It was one more composite creation of the Hellenistic Age, with its eagerness for religious satisfaction from any source. A disciple says of Plotinus: "His end and aim was to be united with the God who is over all; and four times, while I was with him, he attained this aim." [25]

Neo-Platonism is thus best described, for our purposes, as a mysticism that conceives the universe pantheistically, as animated by a divine soul, and that sees also, beyond the universe, a transcendent Being, the Absolute, who cannot be intellectually perceived and described but may be known in mystical ecstasy.

There is much in Neo-Platonism that Catholic Christianity could not assimilate; and it was unnecessary anyway that the average Christian have a philosophy of religion. Origen himself thought that the teaching of Holy Scripture, summarized in the Rule of Faith, was quite enough for most Christians, and did not dream of incorporating philosophy into the Creed and imposing it upon the conscience. But Origen knew the thoughtful man's necessity to unify his thinking. It was impossible that he hold in religion views that were in conflict with views he held in philosophy and science. It was equally impossible that he remain forever dumb about the implications of his religion, in the schools of Grammar and Rhetoric and wherever bright men indulged in the delights of Dialectic. In other words, the religion of thoughtful men inevitably includes also some theology, or philosophy of religion; and religious teachers require it in emergencies.

Origen undertook the task of making the Christian faith possible to thoughtful men, by providing it with a comprehensive philosophy of the universe. Attempts had been made in the second century, by men like

[25] Porphyry, *Life of Plotinus*, 23.

Justin Martyr and Tatian, Irenaeus and Clement of Alexandria; but now Christian theology advanced rapidly under the leadership of Origen, who has been called "the father of theological science." When he died in 254 the Catholic theology was well launched; but unfortunately his successors did not distinguish as he did between what one must believe in order to become a Christian and what one may think in order to satisfy the mind and answer an enquirer.

Meanwhile Christianity was engaged in recurring struggles with the State for the right to live. The Roman Empire, as we have seen, was already threatened with disintegration in the second century; and periods of social insecurity are dangerous to dissenters. Political leaders tend at such times to make scapegoats of unpopular minorities; patriots become resentful of any active opposition to ancient ideas and methods; and disorderly elements in the population break out in deeds of violence against those they dislike.

It was so with the Christians in the last troubled days of Marcus Aurelius. They had been relatively safe, in the general security of Hadrian's reign and that of Antoninus Pius; but now that pestilence and the barbarian stalked through Roman lands, and there was uneasiness everywhere, the populace could not quite forget that there were those among them who held aloof from the common life, objected to military service, and talked of another kingdom than that of the Caesars. Above all, they did not worship the gods of Rome; and their impiety had gone unpunished by the authorities. Well, men saw now where impiety led! The favour of the gods was withdrawn; and calamity was overtaking the world.

So Christians were assaulted in the streets, charged before the courts, condemned to death. Tertullian complained, as repression swept through North Africa, "If the Tiber rises too high, or the Nile does not rise high enough, or if there be drought, or earthquake, or famine, or pestilence, then straightway 'The Christians to the beasts!'" Unreason was in control. At Rome Justin Martyr and a company of disciples were tried before the prefect of the city, condemned to death and beheaded. At Smyrna eleven Christians were given to the beasts; and when the crowd in the arena shouted for Polycarp, he was burned there at the stake. In Gaul the storm broke over the churches in 177. Mobs stoned and plundered the Christians at will. Thousands were thrown into prison and tortured to recant. Bishop Pothinus, ninety years of age, was attacked in the streets and died of his injuries. Blandina, a slave girl, endured incredible tortures in the arena, and died confessing, "I am a Christian, and there is nothing evil done among us." The local authorities appealed to the Emperor for a ruling as to the thousands in prison. Marcus Aurelius, gentle and dutiful, sent commands for the release of all who would deny the faith, death by the sword for all steadfast ones who were Roman citizens. Those who were not citizens were to be given to the beasts.

None can persecute so terribly as those who conceive it to be the will of God. So the sands of the arenas of Gaul were soon red with the blood of Christians. Their bones were burned and their ashes scattered, to destroy the Christian hope of a resurrection.[26]

Such things never go on interminably. Reason resumes control, and humanity sickens of slaughter. The Church grew steadily for seventy years after Marcus Aurelius. Then German tribes again broke the frontiers. The Empire was in danger. It was the duty of all good citizens to support the Emperor; but the Christians would not lift a hand. Some even welcomed the barbarians, thinking that by them God was avenging the Christian martyrs. So the Emperor Decius, and after him Valerian, concluded that it was time to check disloyal societies, and undertook systematic repression, designed to stamp out Christianity everywhere.

There were terrible scenes again. Multitudes died; multitudes denied the faith. Christians everywhere were profoundly impressed. Apocalyptic expectations flamed up; the end of the world was at hand.

Persecution flagged at length, and died away, leaving the Church once more refined by suffering, though impoverished in leadership.[27] Peace continued for a generation. It was not that the emperors were friendly; they were busy with the barbarians and with mutinies in the legions. So the Church grew until it reached every part of the Empire. The Christians were still a minority; but they were attracting the best elements in society, and were influential beyond their numbers. When the third century closed, the moral vigour of the Empire was largely

---

[26] Eusebius, *Ecclesiastical History*, IV, xiv, xv, V, i.

[27] Christian literature for the next generation, 260–303, is very scanty, because few great leaders survived.

within the Christian Church. Then the Emperor Diocletian (284–305) issued the final challenge. Was it to be Caesar or Christ?

Diocletian, exemplary in his life, deeply religious and devoted to the past, first strengthened the imperial power by establishing a college of emperors. Now there were four emperors, administering the Empire from four centres, as circumstances might dictate. The Church profited, as did all other institutions, by the re-establishment of public order. Stately churches arose. Christians came to high civil position. There were Christian officials at the imperial courts. Then, after nearly twenty years, Diocletian consulted an oracle at Miletus and determined upon repression. An edict in 303 commanded that Christian churches be destroyed, the Christian Scriptures burned, Christian officials removed from office and deprived of citizenship.

This time there was widespread resistance. Fires, thought to be incendiary, broke out in the imperial palace at Rome; and panic spread through the city. In the provinces, too, there were commotions. Diocletian died without seeing his policy effective; and his colleagues continued repression in vain. There were scenes as horrible as the earlier orgies in Gaul; but the persecution was neither sufficiently widespread nor sustained. The conscience of heathenism revolted; and in Italy itself the mob turned to the Christians within two years. A few years later repression had failed everywhere; and in 311 three of the emperors united in an edict of toleration. They had, they said, wished to restore the ancient glory, including the religion of the fathers; and so had forbidden innovations. But things had not turned out well. The Christians would not worship the ancient gods, and could not worship their own. The State thus lost the merit of their prayers on both counts. The Christians, therefore, might rebuild their churches and resume the customary worship. It would be their duty in return to pray to their own God for the welfare of the State.[28]

Civil war among the emperors made permanent the new freedom of the Church. Constantine, who administered Gaul, had long been monotheistic in thought and friendly to Christianity. Maxentius, of Italy and Spain, was hostile. It was between these two that the decisive battle was to be fought; and Constantine, looking round for allies, bethought him of the Christians' God. Encouraged by a cloud formation in the sky at noon, cruciform in shape, Constantine took the Christian cross as a

---

[28] Eusebius, *Ecclesiastical History*, VIII, xvii.

military standard, and under it fought on to victory.[29] There followed the famous Edict of Milan, in 313, granting religious liberty throughout the Roman world, "that whatever heavenly divinity exists may be propitious to us and to all that live under our government."[30] It was only a political device; but it soon made the Chrisian Church the favourite son of the State—a doubtful gift, though it seemed at the time a very great one.

Delivered from danger from without, the Church was soon torn by theological dissension within. This had become inevitable, by reason of the changed character of Christianity. Having assimilated Hellenic philosophy and ethics and social forms, she had also come to a new frame of mind, shifting the emphasis from conduct to belief. In no single thing is the change more visible than in the contrast between the Sermon on the Mount, which comes at the beginning, and the Nicene Creed, which comes at the end of this period. The former is an ethical sermon, presenting a new law of conduct; the latter is a metaphysical creed, un-related to conduct.

The incorporation of theology in the Creed was meant to support unity and catholicity; but the more theology invaded the Creed, the more Christians were required to believe, the sharper became their dif-ferences. For, once admitted to the Creed, theological opinions became a matter of life and death.

Ecclesiastical controversy accompanied the theological developments that began with Origen. The first serious strife came with an attempt to include in the Creed a philosophical definition of the being of Christ and his relation to God the Father. The doctrine that Christ was the Logos, or spoken Word, of God, could be variously interpreted. Stoics thought of the Logos as the soul or reason immanent in the universe itself. For them there was no other God than the Logos. Platonism thought of the Logos as subordinate to God, who was outside and above the world, the Absolute with whom Plotinus sought communion. If then Christ was the Logos, was he identical with God or an intermediary between God and man?

The question was very serious. Enlightened pagans had converted the

[29] Eusebius, *Life of Constantine*, I, xxvii, xxviii, xxix.
[30] Eusebius, *Ecclesiastical History*, X, v.

ancestral gods into Logoi, subordinate agents of Deity. Was Christ also one of the gods, and Christianity a new polytheism? If not, if Christ was truly God, what became of the unity of the Godhead? Jesus could hardly be identical with either the heavenly Father to whom he had prayed or the metaphysical Absolute of Greek thought.

The question was serious enough to engage the attention of the Emperor and lead to a council of the churches. Constantine, having lifted from Christianity the heavy hand of the law, and looking to it hopefully as a stabilizing force in the Empire, almost immediately found the Church itself divided as to the true doctrine of Christ. The controversy was especially sharp at Alexandria, where a scholarly presbyter, Arius, had been expelled by his bishop for maintaining that Christ the Son is subordinate to God the Father.

The theological war spread far and wide. Was Christ like God (Greek *homoiousios*) or identical in essence with God (*homoousios*)? Constantine understood the issue as little as Pilate and Gallio; but he knew that division threatened. So, after a letter to Alexandria, vainly exhorting the controversialists to repent of such foolishness, he summoned a council of the churches, the first General Council, to meet at Nicaea, one of the imperial capitals, in 325.

The Council met in the imperial palace, and was opened by the Emperor himself. The leadership in discussion was taken by the historian Eusebius, a disciple of Origen and bishop of Caesarea. He proposed that the baptismal confession used in his church be adopted as the Creed of all the churches. It was a comparatively simple statement; but it went beyond the Rule of Faith in defining the Person of Christ theologically. It spoke of him as "incarnate," "the Logos," "God of God, Light of Light." It went too far for those who felt that theological definitions ought not to be introduced into the Creed and laid upon the conscience of Christians. It did not go far enough for the theologically minded. Most members of the Council agreed, however, that there ought to be a pronouncement against Arianism, which seemed to make of Christ a sort of demigod.

In the end the Council adopted a creed that may be described as the first edition of the present "Nicene Creed." [31] It was as follows:

[31] The original Nicene Creed was further elaborated by the Council of Constantinople, called by the Emperor Theodosius the Great in 381. The new council reaffirmed the Nicene

We believe

In one God, Father Almighty, maker of all things visible and invisible;

And in one Lord Jesus Christ, the Son of God, begotten of His Father, only begotten, that is of the substance of the Father, God of God, Light of Light, true God of true God; begotten, not made, of one substance with the Father, by whom all things were made, both things in heaven and things in earth;

Who for us men and for our salvation, came down from heaven and was made flesh and was made man; suffered and rose again on the third day, ascended into the heavens and comes to judge the living and dead.[32]

Nicaea did not bring peace. The churches were torn by controversy all the way from Arabia to Spain. Emperors changed sides, in efforts after peace. Theological leaders were excommunicated and restored, exiled and recalled, as the battle line swayed this way and that. Christians who had so recently won the right to live now lost the right to think. Fortunately for the Catholic Church the privilege of thinking became less and less important, as steadily as the Roman world collapsed and its culture with it.

Creed, enlarging it to condemn several parties that had arisen since Nicaea. This Nicaeo-Constantinopolitan Creed, as it is called, is the recognized Creed of the Greek Church still. The present "Nicene Creed" of western Christianity is the Nicaeo-Constantinopolitan Creed, with further changes, made in the early Middle Ages and never accepted in the East.

[32] Socrates, *Ecclesiastical History*, I, 8, as in Ayer, p. 306.

CHAPTER VII

IN THE TWILIGHT OF THE EMPIRE

AFTER three centuries there were Christian churches everywhere, though unevenly distributed, throughout the Mediterranean world. In Palestine, strangely enough, they were not numerous, and were largely confined to the Greek cities. The tenacious Jews had crept back to their ancient land, displacing the Gentiles and the Christians among them.

To the north, in Syria, native Christians were few. The capital city, Antioch, had been a centre of Christianity from the beginning, and had now a famous school of theology; but the Christians were Greeks. Northeastward, however, between the upper waters of the Tigris and the Euphrates, the city of Edessa was largely Christian and a centre of missionary activity for all Mesopotamia.

Westward in Asia Minor Christians were more numerous than anywhere else. Paul and Barnabas had preached there, and probably most of the Apostles; and the Fourth Gospel was written at Ephesus. It is estimated that half the population of Asia Minor, in the days of Constantine, were Christians; and the most influential leaders of Catholicism dwelt there.

In Africa, too, Christians were numerous. Alexandria was the great educational centre of all Christendom; and the bishop there had a certain patriarchal authority over the churches of Egypt. And westward along the Mediterranean were Christian churches, the strongest being at Carthage.

As for Europe, we know little of the churches in Greece and the Balkans; but there were many in Italy. Rome, long before Constantine, had a bishop, forty-six presbyters, and more than a hundred minor clergy.[1] Some millions of Christians already lay buried in the catacombs, when freedom was won for the faith.

In Gaul Christians from Asia had established churches in Greek

[1] Eusebius, *Ecclesiastical History*, VI, xliii, 11.

cities like Marseilles and carried the Gospel up the Rhone, preaching to the Gallic population as well. And from Roman Britain three bishops came to Gaul, to the Council of Arles, in 314.

We know little of early Christianity in Spain, though a council of the churches at Elvira, in or about 303, included clergy from all parts of the peninsula.

It is probable that, through the whole Roman world in the time of Constantine, one person in ten was a Christian.

The victory of this minority must have seemed complete, after the Edict of Milan and the Council of Nicaea. All the world knew its recent struggle for the right to live. Now the position was reversed; it was the ancient paganism whose doom was sealed. The Edict of Milan was the open confession that the life had gone out of it. The historian Eusebius could not restrain his joy when Constantine, having summoned the Council of Nicaea, dined the bishops at the palace, many of them still bearing the scars of persecution.[2]

The moral danger to Christianity was very great. There was now no refining fire of persecution to burn out the dross of the Church, no cold wind of unpopularity to discourage self-seekers from entering her; and doctrinal tests are uncertain tests of morality.

The privileges and prerogatives of the Church grew steadily during several reigns. If emperors did not act like Christians, they had a keen apprehension of what Christianity was doing for the Empire in this world and might do for themselves in the next.

Constantine himself went little beyond admitting Christianity to equality with the State religion. If he called a Council of the Church and enforced its decision, he still remained *Pontifex Maximus,* high priest of the State religion. Constantine did, however, command public officials everywhere to encourage Christianity, *pro bono publico;* and late in life he transferred to the Church some of the many pagan temples in the eastern Empire.

Constantine ruled alone in his last years and built a new capital, Constantinople, on the site of ancient Byzantium, where he could keep a sharp eye on the Euphrates and Danube frontiers. When he died in 337, the Empire reverted to Diocletian's plan of a college of emperors; and

[2] Eusebius, *Life of Constantine,* III, xv.

the three sons of Constantine ruled together—Constantius at Constantinople, Constans in Italy and Africa, Constantine II in Britain, Gaul and Spain.

Violent edicts were now issued against paganism. To offer the ancient sacrifices was made a crime, and even to visit the temples; though exceptions had to be made for Rome and Alexandria, where the old families were still influential and devoted to the past. Elsewhere temples were devastated, Christians participating in the violence. We have records of these sorry events from three Church historians, who are quite complacent about them.[3]

A brief respite came to paganism when the sons of Constantine died. They had assassinated most of their kinsmen, to rid themselves of possible rivals. In time Constans, the youngest, was killed by his brother Constantine, who was himself slain by a usurper. Only Constantius remained; and he was suffering military reverses in Asia, at the hands of the Persians. German tribes seized the occasion to carry devastation through Gaul. Hard pressed, the Emperor summoned his cousin Julian from philosophic studies at Athens, to command the legions in Gaul. Julian expelled the barbarians, repaired the frontiers, and on the death of Constantius became sole emperor in 361.

Revolted by the conduct of his imperial cousins, and disliking the clerical influences under which he himself grew up, Julian reverted to paganism. Returning from Gaul to Constantinople, he reopened the pagan temples as he advanced, then set himself to restore the rights of paganism everywhere and reduce Christianity to the position of a tolerated religion.

Such a policy may well have seemed promising. Roman history and tradition still reminded men that the great days of the Empire were the days of its paganism. The Classics—Homer and Horace and Virgil—that were still the literature of educated men and the text-books in schools of rhetoric and philosophy, were full of the gods. Neo-Platonism had done something to rehabilitate pagan philosophy. The old families in

[3] These are the last three of the so-called Greek Ecclesiastical Historians, all of them continuators of Eusebius of Caesarea, who wrote a history of the Church from the beginning until 324. The three continuators, who carried the history through a further century, are Socrates, an advocate of Constantinople; Sozomen, a wealthy Christian of Palestine, who also became an advocate at Constantinople; and Theodoret, a native of Antioch, who became bishop of Cyros, a small city east of Antioch.

the cities, and remote country folk, were still pagan. There seemed a chance to bring back the past.

It was too late. The minds of men had rejected polytheism; and the decadence of pagan society had advanced too far. A Christianity that lacked discipline and often forgot its ideals was better than that. Julian died in 362, knowing that he had failed. His last words—so runs a legend—were these, "Thou hast conquered, O Galilean."

Succeeding emperors reverted to the policy of the sons of Constantine. Gratian laid down the office of *Pontifex Maximus*. Theodosius the Great, a clean, stern man from Spain and a devoted Christian, gradually stopped the ancient worship, closed the temples, and made idolatry treasonable through all the Empire. In the East Christian mobs, sometimes incited by their bishops, destroyed pagan temples. When a mob under bishop Theophilus wrecked the Serapeum, the great temple of Isis at Alexandria, and when the earth did not open and the Nile cease to flow, as ancient oracles had foretold, all omens seemed favourable to Christianity.

By 450 the State religion was officially dead; though remote districts like the Peloponnesus were still solidly pagan. The old religion was now the religion of peasants, *pagani,* a fact to which it owes its later name, *paganism.*

One educational centre of paganism remained, the University of Athens. It was closed in 529 by the Emperor Justinian, in the interest of Christian schools at Constantinople. That was the death-knell of paganism. As for the scholars of Athens, they fled to Persia, where their descendants became leaders of the literary and scientific life of Islam, at Bagdad and other centres.

Justinian assumed the headship of the Church. Imperial edicts regulated public worship, directed ecclesiastical discipline, and even dictated theological doctrines. The Church had to submit for a time to "Caesaropapism," a papacy of the Emperor.

What of society itself throughout the Empire? Decay had begun, as we saw, before the second century closed. It was retarded, but only retarded, by the administrative genius of men like Diocletian and Constantine the Great. They divided the Empire into four prefectures,[4] each

---

[4] The prefectures were the East, Illyricum, Italy and Gaul.

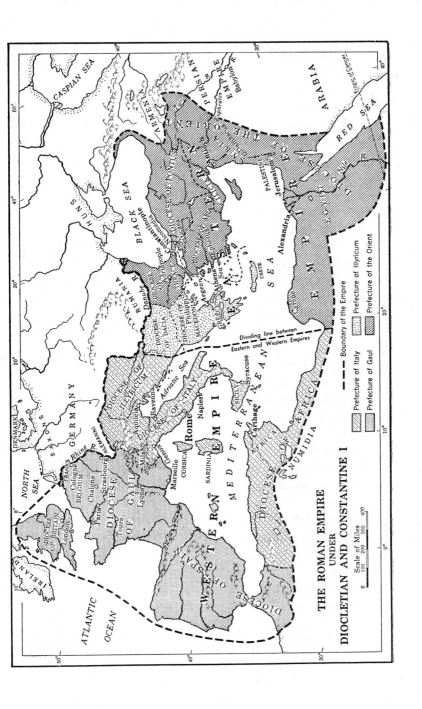

THE ROMAN EMPIRE
UNDER
DIOCLETIAN AND CONSTANTINE I

Scale of Miles
0   100   200   300   400

Boundary of the Empire
Prefecture of Illyricum
Prefecture of the Orient
Prefecture of Italy
Prefecture of Gaul

Dividing line between
Eastern and Western Empires

CASPIAN SEA

ARMENIA

PERSIAN EMPIRE

Euphrates R.

Babylon

Tigris R.

ARABIA

RED SEA

Tropic of Cancer

THE ORIENT

PALESTINE

Jerusalem

EGYPT

Nile R.

Alexandria

Cyrene

BLACK SEA

HUNS

DIOCESE OF PONTUS

Constantinople

Nicomedia

DIOCESE OF ASIA

DIOCESE OF THRACE

Adrianople

CRETE

Aegean Sea

Athens

GREECE

DIOCESE OF MACEDONIA

Philippi

DIOCESE OF DACIA

Danube R.

ROUMANIA

VINDALS

EASTERN

MEDITERRANEAN SEA

ATLANTIC OCEAN

IRELAND

ENGLAND

DIOCESE OF BRITAIN

London

NORTH SEA

DENMARK

SAXONS

GERMANY

FRANKS

Cologne

Rhine R.

ALEMANNI

BELGIUM

Paris

Strasbourg

Chalons

Tours

Lyons

DIOCESE OF GAUL

Marseille

DIOCESE OF SPAIN

WESTERN EMPIRE

DIOCESE OF ILLYRICUM

Aquileia

Milan

Genoa

Ravenna

DIOCESE OF ITALY

Rome

Naples

SICILY

Syracuse

CORSICA

SARDINIA

Adriatic Sea

DIOCESE OF AFRICA

Carthage

NUMIDIA

DIOCESE OF EGYPT

under a prefect, who published the Emperor's decrees, saw to the collection of his taxes, and supervised the conduct of imperial officers in the subdivisions of his prefecture.

The prefectures were divided into dioceses, each governed by a vice-prefect. There were sixteen dioceses in the Empire, themselves divided into one hundred and twenty provinces, under officers differing in name and authority, according to the circumstances of the province.

All this was civil administration; and in addition there was a military administration, under a master of cavalry and a master of infantry, stationed at Constantinople. Under them were counts and dukes, commanding the troops on the frontiers and in the provinces.

Each town of the Empire still had its own senate, or curia, composed of landowners, the curials; but all was not well with these municipal governments. The needs of the imperial government were very great; and its rapacity equalled its needs. The curials were required, not simply to collect the taxes but to pay what they could not collect. It was always a terrible day when the swarm of fiscal agents descended once more upon the towns.

Overburdened curials took refuge in the army, the clergy, and certain privileged orders; but there was no escape. They were arrested and brought back to their duties; and their children were born to their office. Despair often drove them to a roving existence in the forests, or to life among the barbarians.

In addition to the privileged orders, who constituted the new nobility, and the curials, there was a third social class—the free men. They were merchants and artisans, and landowners with less than fifteen acres. The artisans were associated in corporations for self-protection; but the government treated them as it did the curials. So the corporations became a servitude; and the children of artisans were born into it. As for the petty landowners, what they did not lose by barbarian raids they tended to lose through the scheming of great proprietors; and they became *coloni* of the rich, with few of the rights of free men. So the morale of the free man was destroyed. He had no heart, either to work or to fight.

Beneath all were the slaves, whose lot, however, had been improved through the influence of Stoicism and Christianity. Slaves were now human beings; and to kill them was homicide. By the improvement of their lot and the degradation of free men, the two classes had become much alike. Both were serfs.

There was decadence everywhere, except among those elevated by philosophy and the Church. In general, ancient society had fallen very low. Because there was little courage there was little genius. So there were no really great writers and artists, only sophists and rhetoricians like Libanius, mediocre poets like Claudian, and very poor ones, rich men who wrote *epithalamia,* trifling verses for wedding feasts. Such vigour as remained in literature was in the practical and impassioned words of Christian bishops like Ambrose and Augustine, and of Lactantius, "the Christian Cicero," who was tutor to Constantine's son Crispus. And as for art, when emperors at Constantinople undertook the adornment of their new city, they had to pillage older cities for monuments. Paganism was too much disparaged, and Christianity too otherworldly, to depict in art the beauty of human life.

The army was recruited more and more from those without money or work, and from the barbarians. The legions on the frontiers were reduced in size. Having in theory six thousand men, they often had less than two thousand. The legionaries were degraded, too, by the branding of their bodies, and affronted by the favours lavished upon the idle guards of the palace, the *palatins.* Such men had little incentive to defend the frontiers; and, without that, no fortifications could avail.

So decadence within and danger without increased together. Everywhere on the frontiers were potential enemies. In Africa desert tribes of Moors disturbed the sleep of Roman officials. In the East the Persians often made war on Rome, for a disputed frontier. The most pressing dangers, however, were in Europe, along the Rhine-Danube frontier. There German peoples stretched all the way from the Black Sea to the Baltic. Along the Danube they were Goths. Between the upper reaches of Danube and Rhine, facing Hadrian's Wall, they were Alemanni. Along the lower Rhine, in what is now the Netherlands, they were Franks, a confederacy of tribes.

Back of this frontier there were other German tribes—Jutes, Angles and Saxons, Vandals, Burgundians and Lombards, and what not.

Behind this second line of Germans were other peoples, crowding them westward. There were Slavs, themselves being pushed from the Volga by Asiatic hordes; and Huns, a Tartar-Finnish race, with brown, tattoed bodies, bony faces, slit eyes and flat noses. The pressure of these peoples upon the Germans left them little choice. They must some day break through into Roman lands.

As early as the first century a great Roman man of letters, Tacitus, had observed the contrast between German freedom and simplicity and the servility and degeneracy of Roman life, and embodied his observations in a book, the *Germania*. Within the Empire was discipline, to the point of slavery; among the Germans was individual freedom and voluntary devotion to chosen leaders. War was not a drab duty, but an adventure, for glory and for booty. Boys became citizens as soon as they could bear the shield and javelin; and every citizen was a soldier, attached to some chieftain, whose service he chose. It was a voluntary tie, made secure by a sense of honour.

Despotism was impossible here. Government was by an assembly of all citizens, an assembly originated, they thought, by the gods them-selves. The assembly met in the open air, on a height or in a grove, on sacred days, like those of the new moon and the full moon. Members of the assembly were armed; and the clashing of shields indicated their ap-proval of what was proposed.

In the German pantheon the chief god was Woden, who descended each night to ride through the air, with the warrior dead of his people. All who died in battle ascended to his paradise, Walhalla, forever to drink there with him and to fight. "One thing alone does not die," said the Germans, "the memory of the famous dead." So bards were held in great honour; and men laughed in the face of death.

There were gracious deities, too, like Holda, the goddess, who flew through the air all in white, on a winter's night, scattering snow as she went. And there was Hertha, the earth; and Sunna, the sun; and her brother Mani, the moon; and the stars. In the song of the Niebelungen, a thousand years later, one still hears the dear myths of the ancient gods.

The Germans, in the earliest times, thought little of agriculture; and individuals had no property rights in the land. The magistrates dis-tributed each year, to the villages and the families, the land they were to cultivate. Villages were scattered huts of earth, each surrounded by the field to be cultivated; but hunting and fishing, and the wild fruitage of nature, brought more food than the fields.

Purity of life was general. "Good habits," said Tacitus, "are here more effectual than good laws elsewhere." The great vice was drunkenness. German feasts were carousals, where men drank each other's health in the skull of a vanquished enemy and sometimes ended by killing each other. Here was a coarseness, however, that could be refined and that was less hopeless than the moral exhaustion of Roman society.

In the late fourth century the pressure of Slavs and Huns upon the German peoples was becoming irresistible; and the Germans anyway were in need of more land. The growing depopulation of Roman provinces was a standing invitation to them to come.

Other forces also had long been drawing them. Germans enlisted in the legions from the earliest times of the Empire. Some commerce flowed back and forth across the Rhine-Danube frontier. German legionaries and traders returned to their villages, to tell great tales of the magnificence of Roman cities, of the fertility of Roman lands, and perhaps of the softness of Roman youths.

Rome, too, was now less exclusive. Her two dominant philosophies were both against Roman pretensions. Stoicism spoke of a world commonwealth, crossing all frontiers of race and class. Neo-Platonism was an eclecticism, appropriating truth from anywhere, especially the Orient. And in the Christian Church men were taught that there was no "Greek and Jew, circumcision and uncircumcision, barbarian, Scythian, bondman, freeman"; Christ was to be "all, and in all."

Some of the Germans, at least along the Danube, received Christianity. In the time of Constantine there were already shadowy beginnings of a Church among the West Goths, or Visigoths. "Theophilus, bishop of Gothland," was one of those at the Council of Nicaea. The work of Christianization went forward through the fourth century. The great apostle to the Goths was Ulfilas, who had been converted to Christianity at Constantinople and was consecrated Bishop of the Visigoths in 341, by Bishop Eusebius of Nicomedia. Ulfilas laid the foundation of Christian civilization among the Goths; and his translation of the Bible into Gothic was the beginning of German literature.

For all these reasons the Germans were not likely to be excluded forever from Roman lands; and decisive movements began late in the fourth century. There was an irruption of Huns from the great plains of central Asia. They made their way to the shore of the Black Sea, where the East Goths, or Ostrogoths, submitted to them. The Visigoths, however, retreated to the Danube, and asked the Emperor Valens for asylum on Roman soil. He dared not refuse; and in 376 they were admitted to the province of Moesia, south of the Danube, and enlisted in the legions. Soon the arrogance of their Roman officers provoked a revolt; and Valens himself was defeated and slain, in battle at Adrianople in 378. His successor, Theodosius the Great (378–395), suppressed the disorders, entered into treaties with the Visigoths, distributed some of them through the Eastern Empire, and engaged others to defend the Danube frontier.

The march of the German peoples had begun; but instead of moving southward, across the Danube and through the Balkan mountains, they went westward to Gaul and Italy. The Eastern Empire thus stood for another thousand years, until submerged in the rising tide of Islam; but the Western Empire was gone in less than a century.

The invasion of the West began on the death of Theodosius the Great. The Visigoths, under their great leader, Alaric the Bold, revolted again, ravaged Macedonia and Greece, then rounded the Adriatic Sea into Italy. The only man who could save Italy was Stilicho, a stately Vandal, who had married a niece of Theodosius and was commander for his worthless son Honorius, emperor of the West. Indeed the best generals and ministers of the Empire, both East and West, were now Germans, as were the best soldiers in the legions.

Honorius listened to evil tales about Stilicho, and ordered his destruction. Roman legionaries followed the example of the emperor and murdered the wives and children of Germans in the legions. Some thirty thousand Germans thereupon went off in a rage to the camp of Alaric; and he and his Visigoths were soon at the gates of Rome. Completely surrounded, cut off from supplies of food, the city opened its gates and was given over to pillage in 410. The barbarians respected only the Christian churches.

The "eternal city" had not been sacked since an incursion of the Gauls, eight hundred years earlier. At the news of its present peril, the legions in Britain set out to the rescue. They were too late, and never got back to Britain, where the defenceless population was soon being overrun by Angles and Saxons.

Alaric died in south Italy; and his followers buried him there, turning the river Busento from its channel, entombing the conqueror, surrounded by the spoils of war, then restoring the river, to conceal his resting place. His brother Athaulf (or Adolf), still in awe of the Empire, offered his services to Honorius, to restore order in southern Gaul and Spain. But Athaulf died by assassination at Barcelona in 415; and his people remained in Gaul and Spain as conquerors.

A decade later the Vandals, on the shore of the Baltic Sea, began a migration through Gaul, fought their way through Spain, and crossed to Africa. The whole Roman province of Africa was overrun in ten years of "Vandalism," Carthage falling in 439.[5] The Vandals, untouched as yet by Christianity and wholly barbarous, spread terror around the Mediterranean, once crossing to Italy and sacking Rome, which was saved from destruction by the moral authority of bishop Leo and an embassy of Christians.

Three years before, in 452, the Huns had threatened Rome. Gaiseric, king of the Vandals, had been in conspiracy with the Huns, for an assault upon the Empire from all sides at once. The Huns, having come out of Asia, had settled for fifty years in central Europe, holding the Ostrogoths and southern Slavs in subjection. Now they turned to new conquest, under Attila, who called himself the "scourge of God" and swore that no grass should grow where his horse trod.

Attila led six hundred thousand men into Roman Gaul. Twenty cities were destroyed; and Attila moved on Orleans, key to the south. There he was opposed by the legions under Aetius, supported by such Germans as were already settled in Gaul—Visigoths, Burgundians and Franks. A terrific battle, the battle of Châlons, brought victory to the allies; and Attila retreated into Germany. Next year he sought satisfaction by invading north Italy. Aquileia and Padua were reduced to ashes, the people of the former taking refuge in the lagoons, where their descendants were to build the city of Venice. Verona and Pavia and Milan submitted to escape destruction; and Attila advanced against Rome. There were no legions to defend the city; but bishop Leo came

---

[5] St. Augustine was bishop at Hippo; and the collapse of Roman civilization in Africa moved him to write his great work, *The City of God*.

to the camp of the invader, with rich presents from the emperor and a promise to pay tribute. Attila returned to the north, and next year died at his royal village near the Danube. Hunnish chiefs exhausted themselves in fights for his crown; subject peoples threw off the yoke; and Hunnish power wasted away and disappeared.

So great had been the terror inspired by Attila in Italy, and so astonishing the deliverance, that legend attributed it to a miracle. The heavens had opened above bishop Leo, and SS. Peter and Paul had appeared on either side, with flaming swords to defend the holy man.

Italy now became the sport of the German mercenaries in the legions, who set up and pulled down puppet emperors at will, until Odoacer, commander of the mercenaries, deposed Romulus, last of these puppets, in 476. Still in awe of the ancient Empire, whose magnificent monuments were everywhere, Odoacer continued the Roman administration, content to rule as representative of the emperor at Constantinople, though he seized for his soldiers a third of the lands of Italy.

But when Odoacer was deposing the last of the emperors of the West, a truly great man had just succeeded to the kingship of the Ostrogoths. This was Theodoric, of the family of the Amals. Born in the year when Attila died, Theodoric grew to manhood just when his nation was freed from the yoke of the Huns. He grew up, too, at Constantinople, whither he was taken as a hostage in childhood, and where he became attached to the Emperor Zeno. Theodoric was a Christian as well, though of the heretical Arian party, so numerous in the East.

Theodoric was authorized by the emperor to descend upon Italy, which he did in the spring of 489, taking with him his whole nation, some two hundred thousand. By 493 all Italy had submitted, Odoacer was dead, and Theodoric was king. He had been assisted in the conquest by Visigoths from Spain, and for a brief period was their king as well. He was united by family ties with most of the German kings of the West, having married the sister of Clovis, king of the Franks; having given his own sister to the king of the Vandals, and his daughters to the kings of the Visigoths and the Burgundians. Theodoric was the glory of the new nations of the West, and the best heir to the Caesars. He gave Italy a generation of order, built a splendid new capital at Ravenna, and encouraged litera-

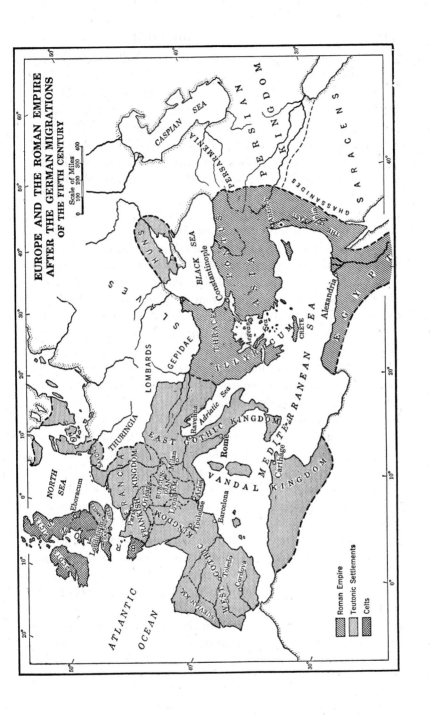

EUROPE AND THE ROMAN EMPIRE
AFTER THE GERMAN MIGRATIONS
OF THE FIFTH CENTURY

Scale of Miles
0   100   200   300   400

ture and the arts, though only for Romans. The Goths were to follow the profession of arms alone.

Theodoric continued the Roman administration. Living himself at Ravenna, he sought the co-operation of the Senate at Rome, and drew into his service distinguished Romans, like the philosopher Boëthius and the historian Cassiodorus. The old theatres and baths, aqueducts and public buildings, were repaired, churches and palaces built. It seemed that a German might bring back the Roman Empire of the West. But Theodoric died in 526, leaving no capable heir; and the influence of his nation over other German peoples disappeared.

The Empire itself was capable of one last struggle for recovery. A year after Theodoric died, Justinian I ascended the throne at Constantinople, to reign nearly forty years, 527–565. He took the offensive against the invaders. His generals recovered Italy from the Ostrogoths, Africa from the Vandals, and a part of Spain from the Visigoths. The Danube frontier was restored, the Persians driven beyond the Euphrates, and protection extended to the persecuted Christians of Asia. But the Empire was exhausted by this last effort. Three years after the death of Justinian, Germans again overran Italy, this time the Lombards; and sixty years later the Arabs, recently converted to Islam, began a steady encroachment in the East that was to bring them, in a single generation, to the limits of Asia Minor, then across North Africa to Spain.

Events were confirming the decision of the Edict of Milan; the life had gone out of the ancient world. Justinian himself had reached the throne by humouring the vices of Constantinople, corrupting the legions, lavishing gold on the public games. His fame is due to no moral excellence.[6] He and his great general Belisarius had been companions in debauchery before they became associates in war. Their victories were made easier, too, by the swift decay of the northern invaders, who were now destroying themselves in the south countries. The drunkenness that had been only coarseness in the forests of Germany became death in the scorching heat of Italy, Spain and Africa. The invaders besides were few in numbers, at war with each other, and hated by the old populations, which unconsciously avenged themselves by communicating to their new masters the vices of civilization.

---

[6] The fame of Justinian rests on his work as a legislator and codifier of Roman law, which he found in great confusion. The study of the *Corpus Juris* of Justinian, revived in the late Middle Ages, has continued into modern times.

The German population of the south, however, could be replenished from the northern forests; and soon after the death of Justinian, as we have seen, the German Lombards were in Italy. They had been milling around, north of the Danube, until invited by Justinian to cross into Roman lands. Within a few years they were through the Julian Alps into Italy, where the imperial control relaxed as soon as Justinian died. Alboin, the Lombard leader, seized the whole valley of the Po without a battle, had himself crowned king in Milan, then captured Pavia and made it his capital.[7] His successor, Klef, carried the Lombard power into parts of central and south Italy.

The Lombards were hated and feared by the Italians. Nominally Arian Christians, they were really barbarians, far harsher and more violent than the Goths. Nor did they themselves hold together. Alboin divided the country into thirty-six duchies, whose dukes were constantly at war with each other, with the king, and with the districts that still remained to the emperor.

This strife was to affect the whole future history of Italy. The unconquered districts could not be governed by the emperor at Constantinople, nor by his representative in Italy, the exarch at Ravenna; and they were separated from each other by Lombard lands. They became independent duchies, like the city-states of ancient Greece, jealous of each other and often at war. Italy was never again to be permanently united until the nineteenth century.

A further result of the Lombard conquest was that the bishop of Rome, isolated from both the emperor and his exarch, began to assume the functions of a political ruler. The duchy of Rome now looked to the bishop for civil government, as did gradually other estates throughout Italy. These were "the patrimony of Peter." The man who did most to bring this about was Pope Gregory the Great (590–604), who had been a statesman before he became bishop of Rome.

The coming of the Lombards was the end of the Roman Empire of the West. Germans were everywhere now in western Europe; though they continued to think of themselves as settlers within an empire that still existed. All around them were monuments of a civilization that excited their wonder, which they had not produced, could not preserve, and would not recover in a thousand years.

[7] North Italy has been "Lombardy" ever since.

The coming of the Lombards was thus the coming also of the Middle Ages, that long, long period between the ancient and modern worlds, when the Germanic nations were tamed by the Catholic Church and educated.

While the ancient world was collapsing, Catholic Christianity itself was changing in various ways, to meet the new situation. Some earnest men and women, despairing of the present world, went into solitude to prepare themselves for the next.

There were excellent precedents for this. The Jews, before the rise of Christianity, had already two orders of ascetics, the Essenes and the Therapeutae, the former dwelling in the desert solitudes that encroached upon Palestine, the latter in Egypt. These had renounced wife and children and home, property and fatherland, hoping through renunciation to find salvation for the soul.

So also in Hellenic society. The Cynics derided marriage, refused property, and lived like beggars. Their zeal for renunciation often extended to cleanliness and good manners. Stoicism, too, commended a life indifferent to physical wants; and Neo-Platonism taught that matter and spirit are antagonistic forms of reality, the body being the enemy of the soul; so that salvation does not begin until physical desires are exterminated.

With such encouragement, some Christians, from the earliest times, leaned to asceticism. St. Paul had difficulty in maintaining the right of the newly baptized to marry, possess property, engage in commerce, assume public office. Enthusiasts were rejecting all these, as impediments to salvation.

Fasting was everywhere a phase of the ascetic life. One reason is found in human psychology; famished persons fall into imaginative ecstasies, regarded in ancient times as supernatural. So fasting was practised in the Church from the beginning; and famished saints were rewarded with the beatific vision. That strange book, the *Shepherd of Hermas,* a book long accepted as Scripture, is a series of revelations granted to Hermas, as the reward of fasting and prayers.

Thus, for reasons that are to be found in human nature and history, asceticism secured a foothold in the Church; and, once established, it was not difficult to find support for it in the words of Jesus. He was reputed to have said: "If any man cometh unto me, and hateth not his own father, and mother, and wife, and children, and brethren, and sisters, yea, and his own life also, he cannot be my disciple." Uncritical Christians did not remember that he was reputed also to have said of his disciples: "I pray not that thou shouldest take them out of the world, but thou shouldest keep them from the evil one." Nor did they remember that his own simple, joyous life had been condemned by Jewish ascetics, as that of "a man gluttonous, and a wine-bibber, a friend of publicans and sinners."

And so before the third century closed, Christian asceticism was becoming a well defined movement. The desire to forsake the world was strong in many minds. It was an ominous time. In seventy years twenty-three emperors had ruled; and all but three had died by assassination. Of the rest, one died in a losing battle with the Goths, another a prisoner of the Persians, another a victim of the plague. And all through the disorder and uncertainty, the Christian Church was living precariously, the victim of recurring persecutions.

So men fled from the cities to live the hermit, or anchorite, life. They lived in lonely huts, or caves, or in the open air, meanly clad, and exposed to all weathers. They abandoned gainful occupations, living by alms or on the produce of little plots of ground around their huts. They fed meagrely, avoiding meats. They wrestled with evil impulses, lashing themselves to subdue the flesh, and spending much time in meditation and prayer. And sometimes they went mad, or rushed back to the city in a fury of reaction, to fling themselves into dissipation.

Best known of these Christian anchorites was Antony, a native of Egypt, who withdrew to the desert in 285, when about thirty years old. Antony was rich; and Christians still took seriously the warning of Jesus against riches, as a peril to the soul. Antony remembered the excellent young man, of whom one reads in the Gospels, who turned sorrowfully away from Jesus because he had great possessions. So Antony gave away his own possessions and went into solitude, first to a hut near his native village, then to one of those rock tombs so numerous in Egypt, then to a ruined castle, whose entrance he blocked with a huge stone. Anywhere for solitude and contemplation and self-discipline! Antony wore a sheepskin, which he never removed, torturing himself with vermin, that he might silence the clamant flesh. And thus, after a full century, he died in Palestine, in a remote spot by the Dead Sea. He was canonized in time, and is now St. Antony.

St. Antony had not found solitude even in flight. The fame of his holiness had soon spread. Great men had come to him for advice, great sinners for spiritual direction, great sufferers for healing. A community of ascetics grew up around the saint, in spite of himself. In the end he left it to the care of his disciple Pachomius, and went into the final solitude.

Pachomius gathered the ascetics into a common building, on Tabennae, an island of the Nile. They called their new home by many names. It was the cloister, the sheepfold, the monastery. Christian monasticism had begun. It spread swiftly over Egypt and the East. The monks submitted to one rule of life. They dressed alike, practised asceticism, observed stated seasons of prayer, and toiled at basket making and weaving. Each monastery had its own abbot (Greek *abbas,* father); but all were under the supervision of the parent monastery at Tabennae.

There were dangers in such a movement. Fanaticism, vanity, sloth, could all get into the monasteries. Men might fly thither, not to find salvation but to escape military service and civil duty. So civil rulers were on their guard; and ecclesiastical rulers sought to bring the movement within the discipline of the Catholic Church, and turn it to her uses.

It had indeed great uses for the Church. In the first three hundred years she had been both buffeted and invigorated by adverse winds; now the soft zephyrs of imperial favour were relaxing her muscles. The world was crowding into the Church, a world nominally Christian but almost as unspiritual as the pagan society to which it had succeeded. So world-renunciation became the antidote to softness; and the ascetic became the athlete, always in training for a better world. Indeed the word ascetic is the Greek *asketikos,* an athlete.

The better ascetics were not lost to society. The fame of great anchorites spread through the world, and gave to decadent civilization an example of simplicity. Bishops and magnates sometimes passed their holidays in retreat with an anchorite, as a moral tonic, quite as modern city-dwellers go to the mountains. Some anchorites were preachers, to whom people flocked as they had to John the Baptist in the wilderness. In later centuries many a monk, disciplined by solitude, was to be called to some high post in the Church, quite as strong men have come to public life in Japan from Zen Buddhism, with its cult of quiet and meditation.

Best known of those who first saw the possibilities of monasticism was Basil, a native of Caesarea in Cappadocia, born in the last years of Constantine the Great. Basil went in his youth to the University of Athens, which was still the great intellectual centre of the world. There he became a brilliant scholar, and the companion of another brilliant youth, the future Emperor Julian.

Returning to Caesarea, to be a rhetorician and sophist, Basil found an ascetic movement under way in that part of Asia Minor. His widowed mother and his sister Macrina had retired to their country estate, to devote themselves to contemplation and labour for the poor. Basil was impressed, and went to Syria and Egypt to observe the monastic movement. Convinced at length, he returned to Cappadocia, gave away his possessions, and settled with a few companions near his mother and sister.

Basil saw the perils of the ascetic life, its tendency to vanity and idiosyncrasy, or to morbid introspection and despair. He therefore set himself to make the monastic movement practical and to turn it to the service of the Church. To that end he promoted the settlement of monks, not in the wilderness but near the cities.

Basil was chosen bishop of Caesarea in 370, at a time when the bishop of Caesarea was *ex officio* the emperor's exarch for the great political diocese of Pontus. As bishop and exarch, Basil continued to live the ascetic life, to establish monasteries and make them educational institutions, supporting the Nicene theology against the active Arianism of the East. When he died in 379, he had become the most influential Christian in all Asia Minor and Syria. His monastic Rule gradually superseded all others, and was authorized for the whole Church by the Oecumenical Council of Chalcedon in 451. Monasteries were put under the supervision of the bishops; and priests were appointed to conduct worship and administer the sacraments in the monasteries, quite as in the parish churches.[8] The monk was no longer to be a premature Free Churchman, out of reach of the bishop, conducting worship in his own way and often attracting people away from both the bishop and the churches.[9]

[8] The Rule of St. Basil is the only monastic rule recognized in the Greek Church today.

[9] Nevertheless extravagances continued to accompany the ascetic movement. The Stylites, or Pillar-hermits, were most extreme of all. Their founder was Simeon, native of a Syrian village, who early became a monk but was expelled from the monastery for

Monasticism spread from the East to the West, slowly and in more moderate forms. The climate of the West discouraged the out-of-doors life of eastern ascetics; and a more practical temper set against their extravagance.

Most influential of the early western ascetics was Jerome (c.340–420). Born in Dalmatia, he was educated at Rome in Rhetoric and the Latin poets. So attached was he to the Latin classics that they became his greatest temptation. Reproached by Christ in a dream, with desiring rather to be a Ciceronian than a Christian, Jerome resolved to devote all his scholarship to the Scriptures, and to this end went east to Antioch, where he lived the hermit life and studied Hebrew, that he might translate the Old Testament into Latin. In time he went also to Constantinople and studied Greek, that he might translate the New Testament.

Called to Rome, the young scholar was set by bishop Damasus to revising existing Latin translations of the Bible; and while engaged in this work, he lived the monastic life and ardently commended it to others. Roman ladies became his disciples; and, finding himself widely criticised, Jerome returned to the East and settled in Bethlehem, surrounded by his women disciples. There Jerome did most of his literary work, notably the translation of the Old Testament, with the aid of Jewish scholars. Out of these labours came the Vulgate, or authorized Latin translation of the Scriptures.

Jerome was the greatest Christian scholar of his age, and was canonized in time. His support of monasticism did much to commend it to the West. Roman ladies began to retire to their country estates, to devote themselves to fasting and prayer, to spinning and weaving for the poor. Roman gentlemen began to retire to the islands off Italy and southern Gaul.

---

his excessive austerities. He then achieved separation from the world by building himself a succession of pillars, higher and higher, until at last he was sixty feet from the earth. There on a platform, railed for security, Simeon lived for thirty years, never descending, and subsisting on whatever food disciples might carry up a ladder to his lofty aerie; and there he died in 459, when nearly seventy years of age.

Simeon was the wonder of the world. Pilgrims came from as far as Spain and Britain, to see the holy man and receive his blessing. Simeon preached to them from his strange pulpit, and conferred there with ecclesiastical leaders, giving counsel about whatever disturbed the Church.

The eccentricity of pillar life did not commend it to the more practical West; but there were many Stylites in Syria and Greece, where they were still to be found as late as the sixteenth century.

The earliest establishment of importance was that of John Cassian, who founded both a monastery and a convent for nuns at Massilia, the modern Marseilles, in 410. Like Jerome, John Cassian had learned the new way in the East, having lived in a monastery at Bethlehem and then for some years with ascetics in the Nile desert.

Cassian was first to provide the West with text-books on monasticism. He wrote a treatise describing the daily life of the monk and its perils, and a volume of dialogues with Egyptian ascetics, on how to avoid these perils.[10]

These writings gave the movement a lasting impetus. Monasteries sprang up in great cities like Rome and Milan; and they became the real centres of spiritual force in the fifth century. Great bishops came from the monasteries, especially from those of Gaul; and in them were to be found such poets, philosophers, historians as the times produced.

The movement was checked for a time by the migrations of the fifth century. Wherever the Goth passed, and the Vandal and Hun, monasteries and convents were likely to be left in ruins. But they rose again in the sixth century, to endure until now. The great name here is that of Benedict of Nursia (c.480–c.542), who may be described as the Basil the Great of the West.

Benedict was an Italian, born at Nursia, in Umbria. The last emperor of the West had recently been deposed; and, under Theodoric the Amal, Italy was having a last chance for recovery. She had not the moral energy to seize it. Sent by his parents to school at Rome, Benedict was appalled at the general licentiousness of Roman youths, and went into retreat in the mountainous district of the Abruzzi. There in a rocky cave on the mountain side, looking across the valley to the ruins of Nero's palace, he took up his lonely abode, secretly supplied with food by his friend Romanus, a monk at a near-by monastery. In a few years the fame of the young hermit spread; and Benedict found himself thronged by disciples. Gradually he established twelve monasteries in the district, with twelve monks in each, and himself over all. Roman senators sent their sons to be brought up as monks; and the fame of the saint became greater and greater. The hostility of a local priest, however, led him in time to leave the twelve monasteries to their own resources, while he went south with a few companions to Cassino, half way between Rome and

---

[10] These two works are the *De Institutione Coenobiorum* and the *Collationes Patrum*.

Naples. There, on a mountain overlooking the town, Benedict established a monastery, destroying a temple of Apollo where pagan worship
still lingered, and winning the rustic population to Christianity. The
monastery on Monte Cassino soon became an important religious centre
for all western Europe, and was to remain so for centuries.

Monastic life in the West had previously shown little uniformity. One
monastery followed the Rule of St. Basil, another the writings of Cassian,
another its own ideas; but now the Rule of St. Benedict began to be the
model for all.[11]

Under the new Rule, admission was to be made difficult. An applicant
was to be left for several days, knocking at the monastery door, to test
his seriousness, and was then to be admitted only to the guest house.
If still desirous of becoming a monk, he must be placed on probation
for a year, under a father confessor, and made completely aware of the
exactions of the monastic life.

After the year's novitiate, one became a monk by taking a three-fold
vow—to remain forever, neither returning to the world nor going from
monastery to monastery; to obey the abbot in all things, and the
deans whom the abbot might appoint; to practise the monk's way of
life.

Everything was done to secure faithfulness to the new way. Such
monks as were sent out on the business of the monastery, were prayed
for at every assembly of the monks for worship; and on their return they
prostrated themselves on the floor of the oratory, asking the prayers of
all. They were forbidden, too, to relate anything they had seen or heard
while out in the world.

Three further obligations of the newly made monk were poverty,
chastity and toil. These were all aspects of that world-renunciation which
was the essence of the monastic life. The monk was to possess nothing at
all, not even his garments. He could not receive a letter, until the abbot
had first read it and given permission; and a gift from home might be
given by the abbot to another monk, if it seemed to him desirable.

The rule of chastity involved that one both abjure home and wife and
children, and preserve one's virginity. And as for toil, the monks all
served their turn in the kitchen and laundry and in the fields of the

---

[11] The Benedictine Rule may be read in Thatcher & McNeal, *Source Book for Mediaeval History*, Scribners, pp. 432–485.

monastery, except the cellarer, or keeper of the stores, and others with special functions.

The daily routine of the monastery included eight services of worship in the oratory. The first was Vigils, soon after midnight, at the close of the first sound sleep; the last was Compline, just before retiring at night. Scripture lessons and psalms and hymns for all services were appointed in the Rule or chosen by the abbot.

The Scriptures were read also at all common meals in the refectory, a brother being appointed each Sunday to perform this service during the ensuing week. Meals were therefore to be eaten in silence, the brothers looking out for each other's wants and making signs when necessary.

There was to be but one meal a day, at noon or in the early afternoon, unless the toil of harvesting, or other special circumstances, seemed to require two. After dinner the monks lay down to rest; though one might read, if he did so in silence. The Collations of John Cassian, the Lives of the Saints, the Rule of St. Basil, the works of the Catholic Fathers in general were approved, in addition to the Scriptures.

The monastery was to be a house of quiet, first because the monk was to listen for the word of instruction and admonition, from the Scriptures and the Church Fathers, or from the abbot and the deans; and also because of the ever-present disposition towards foolish talking and jesting. "Therefore although it (might) be permitted to the tried disciple to indulge in holy and edifying discourse, even this should be done rarely, as it is written: 'In a multitude of words there wanteth not sin.'"

The monks dressed alike, in cowl and robe. No one must be fastidious about the colour and texture of the cloth, which was to be of the stuff commonly used in the region. There were shoes also, and a rough garment for work in the fields. A brother sent out on the road was furnished with trousers and a robe of better material; but these must be returned to the vestiary when the traveller returned.

The brothers slept in one dormitory, though in individual beds; and a candle burned there all night. They slept in their robes, ready for the call to Vigils.

Discipline was strict, and increased according to the degree of the offence. It began with private admonition from the abbot or one of the deans, and advanced to a public reprimand. One might then be excluded from the common meal, and from reading the lessons and leading in the

Psalms and responses in the oratory. No brother might speak to the one thus excommunicated, though all were to pray for his recovery. If the offender would not be corrected, he was to be beaten and even expelled from the monastery, though not thereby released from his vows. Once a monk, always a monk, though a renegade one!

The supreme monkish virtue was humility, which rose through twelve stages to perfection. The first step in the ascent was obedience, without delay, to one's superior, as unto God himself.

The twelfth step of humility is this, that the monk should always be humble and lowly, not only in his heart, but in his bearing as well. Wherever he may be, in the oratory, in the garden, on the road, in the fields, whether sitting, walking, or standing, he should always keep his head bowed and his eyes upon the ground. He should always be meditating upon his sins and thinking of the dread day of judgment, saying to himself as did that publican of whom the Gospel speaks: "Lord, I am not worthy, I a sinner, so much as to lift mine eyes up to heaven."

The defect in all this is clear enough. The sole aim of the monk was the salvation of his own soul, through self-renunciation. In the monasteries of St. Benedict one is very far from Galilee, where men were invited to consider the lily of the field, and to live trustfully before the heavenly Father, who had given it a glory greater than Solomon's; and to love and serve one's fellows, sure that one was thereby doing the will of God.[12]

A further defect of the Benedictine Rule called for repair. There was no provision for elementary education. It was assumed that the monk could read; though there must have been some who could not, and would soon be many more. At the other extreme, men of highly cultivated minds, men like Basil and Jerome and Cassian, were entering the monasteries. They were not likely to renounce the satisfactions of intellectual enlightenment. So a nobleman, Cassiodorus, set himself to turn the monasteries into centres of learning, as Basil had done for the East.

Cassiodorus was born some ten years after Benedict of Nursia, but out-

---

[12] The monks were socially better than their Rule. They were pioneers in agriculture for mediaeval Europe, going where individuals could not go, and establishing model farms in the wilderness. The monasteries, too, were hostels for travellers, and places of refuge for the sick and the oppressed. And, at their best, they were missionary centres, sending out colonies of evangelists to the frontiers of civilization, in Germany and Britain.

lived him by forty years. He was of an illustrious Syrian family, long resident in Italy. His father was an officer of Theodoric the Amal; and he himself became the king's literary secretary, and finally chief of the civil service. When Theodoric died and his kingdom was overrun in a few years by the armies of Justinian, Cassiodorus forsook the world. He founded two monasteries on his own estates, and devoted them to the advancement of knowledge, collecting and editing manuscripts from the past, which his monks copied.

Cassiodorus was a historian as well; but his fame rests chiefly on the *Institutes,* an encyclopaedia of literature and the arts for monks. Cassiodorus saw that if the Christian mind was not itself to lapse into barbarism, theology must receive some illumination from general knowledge. It was what Clement of Alexandria and Origen had seen three hundred years before. So when Cassiodorus died in 585, the monasteries were already becoming schools for the priesthood. It was a fortunate development. Without the Benedictine monasteries, no light would have relieved the intellectual darkness of the early Middle Ages.

Most Christians, of course, continued to live outside the monasteries. Not that they doubted where true Christianity lay! If there was much dissent from monasticism, in principle, we cannot discover it now. It was only that Christians could not abandon society, and especially the family life, for the cloister. Disturbed in mind about this frailty, they nevertheless got along with such assurance of salvation as the prayers of the monks and the ministrations of the parish priests could give them.

The Church had thus to provide a discipline for Christians who followed the vocations of ordinary men. Without that, she could not escape the general decadence; for the world, from the days of Constantine, came crowding into the Church. So she prescribed, first of all, a period of trial, a catechumenate, for those who would enter.

The catechumenate was lengthy, sometimes as much as three years. It began with a solemn ritual, including exorcism and the laying on of hands. The former signified the expulsion of demons, the latter the impartation of Divine grace. Catechumens were required to avoid certain forms of business; and slaves were not received without a recommendation from their masters.

Immediately before baptism the catechumen was required to renounce the devil. Facing the West, with hand upraised, he said, "I renounce thee, Satan, and all thy works and thy power and service." Then, turning to the East, home of the morning light, he confessed the Christian faith, then entered the baptistery, was anointed with oil, over which prayers of exorcism were said, and was further questioned concerning his faith. He was then immersed three times.[13] Other symbolic acts followed—the giving of milk and honey, as to a newborn child; the giving of salt, a symbol of cleansing. The baptized were clothed in white and banded with a fillet. In the East, the loins were girded, as for a hard journey. In the West, a burning taper was placed in the hand.

The ideal set before baptized persons was that expressed in monasticism, superiority to a natural human life. Civil and political occupations were profane. Material possessions were evil. Efforts after culture, all aesthetic adornments of life, were sinful. Marriage was a lower state than virginity. Consecration to God required the centring of one's whole love on heaven. It was a negative conception of morality, born of the despair of regenerating society itself.

It was a conception of morality, too, that could not be made effective. So the shortcomings of Christians required to be made up in several ways. First, if one made gifts to the monasteries, the credit balance of the monks in heaven could be made available for one, who could not himself forsake the world; the merit of the perfect cancelled the demerit of the imperfect. Churchliness, too, was meritorious, zealous observance of ecclesiastical requirements as to prayer and fasting and almsgiving, and especially orthodox opinions. The heat of theological controversy was not all due to argumentativeness; it was due also to belief in the value of orthodoxy for salvation.

Almsgiving, too, was especially meritorious, all the more because of the increasing poverty and distress of the times. And the Church herself had more and more to give.[14] Priests, monks and nuns were expected to present, or at least to bequeath, their possessions to the Church; and

---

[13] There was doubt about the baptism of children; but a mysterious magic was more and more attributed to all Christian rites. The baptism of children therefore became urgent. It was all the more urgent because they were regarded as born in sin, from whose guilt they were to be saved by baptism. So a synod at Carthage in 401 required that all children of Christians, not already baptized, were to be baptized at once.

Any presbyter might baptize; but the laying on of hands was soon separated from baptism and reserved for the bishop, in confirmation.

[14] Public confidence in the bishops made them the best agents of government also, for the distribution of state philanthropy; and they were appointed to that work.

bishops often set an example of voluntary poverty. Laymen, too, were encouraged to bequeath property to the Church. It was thought better that children be left poor in this life than parents in the next.

Alms were beneficial even for those already dead, being sacrifices offered for their sins. "It is not to be doubted," said Augustine, "that the dead are assisted by the prayers of the Church, by the saving sacrifice and by alms, which are offered for their souls, and that the Lord deals more mercifully with them than their sins have deserved."

So the doctrine of purgatory developed gradually, being finally elaborated by Gregory the Great. It was a purifying fire, between death and paradise, where the guilt of one's peccadillos could be burned away. One could achieve that here, and diminish one's discomfort hereafter, by giving alms.

And there were other ways. The Church had a graduated scale of penance, or good works imposed by the priest upon the penitent, for their lapses from goodness. Minor sins sometimes brought exclusion from Holy Communion, "the lesser Ban." The most notorious sins brought expulsion from the Church, "the greater Ban." Between these two extremes were prayers and fasting, alms and pilgrimages and what not. Reconciliation to the Church came only after one had performed whatever penance was imposed.

To administer this discipline, special "priests of repentance" were appointed in the larger churches. This made possible both private confession and the private performance of minor penances, when one's father confessor required no more; and it relieved the bishops of much of the burden of discipline.

Constitutional developments accompanied this elaborate discipline; the Church became more and more clerical. So much so that, if a primitive Christian had returned to earth at any time after the second century, he would not have found anywhere the simple brotherhood of believers that he had known at Jerusalem or Antioch or Ephesus; unless indeed he went off with the Montanists.

We have seen (pp. 137–141) that church organization had been simple and varied until the end of the first century, when leadership by influential Christians and travelling evangelists began to yield everywhere to that of resident officials, locally chosen. These were the presbyters, or elders, and the deacons, the former being the guardians, or superintendents, of the churches, and the latter their business managers. After a further generation of conflict, whose echoes are still heard in the *Letters of Ignatius,* the practice was becoming general of choosing one presbyter to be permanent chairman of the presbyters, and concentrating in him the superintendency, or episcopacy. He was now *episcopos;* and each church had therefore a bishop, somewhat in the modern sense, though he had no diocese, but only a parish, to rule.

And the bishop, two centuries later, had a whole army of clergy to lead. Bishops, presbyters and deacons were now only the *major orders.* There were *minor orders* as well, a dozen of them. Even the *parabolani,* or attendants on the sick, and the *copiatae,* who buried the dead, were now clerics; and men took refuge in the minor orders for dubious reasons, to share the immunities of the clergy and escape from onerous civil duties.

Nevertheless the concentration of authority increased steadily. Circumstances all tended to exalt the bishop. In time of danger the churches of a city sought closer relations; and there came to be one bishop over all. In time of heresy the bishop was the natural judge as to the true apostolic tradition of teaching. In time of schism that party was felt to be the true Church which stood with the bishop. As early as the third century, bishops were everywhere regarded as the successors of the Apostles and heirs to their authority. The bishops had the keys of heaven; and through them the gifts of God were dispensed to men. The true Church, therefore, could only be episcopal; and outside the Church there was no salvation—*extra ecclesiam nulla salus.*

All this contradicted the New Testament idea that men may approach God in their own right. It was a return to the common view of the pagan world, that religion is bound up with a priesthood. But a strong episcopate did secure the unity and catholicity of the Church; without the episcopate, Christianity, as we know it, would not have survived.

Meanwhile the concentration of authority went further still. Rural bishops tended to disappear, their dioceses being attached to those of the nearest city bishops. The bishops in the provinces began to meet at the provincial capitals, under the presidency of the bishop of the capital, the metropolitan. The Council of Nicaea decreed that this should be done twice each year. So there came to be ecclesiastical provinces, like the one hundred and twenty political provinces of the Empire.

When critical questions arose, still more comprehensive assemblies were sometimes needed, which would include the bishops of several provinces. So the bishops of the greatest cities—Rome and Carthage, Alexandria and Antioch—rose to a limited supervision over several ecclesiastical provinces. They were the patriarchs, and remind one of the prefects of the Empire. And, of them all, the bishop of Rome advanced steadily towards primacy in the whole Church.

The Roman bishop had a certain advantage from the beginning. His city was the capital of the world, his church the only one in the West where apostles had been. It came to be generally believed that Peter had been the first bishop at Rome. It was felt therefore that Rome was the place where the true apostolic tradition of teaching and practice could most surely be found. Churches wrote to the Roman bishop for his view of difficult questions; and the Roman bishop voluntarily wrote letters of counsel to other churches, like that *First Epistle of Clement to the Corinthians*. So that, though the churches of the East gave to the Roman bishop only so much honour as they gave the bishops of Constantinople and Antioch, Jerusalem and Alexandria, many churches of the West went further. They called the Roman bishop *pope, papa*. He was *par excellence* the father of Christians everywhere.

Opposition continued, however, for many generations. The Council of Nicaea conceded to the Roman bishop authority over the bishops of Italy only, as the bishop of Alexandria had over Egypt, Libya and the Pentapolis. Even in the West, a council at Carthage, as late as 418, threatened to excommunicate any priest who should appeal from the jurisdiction of his own bishop to that of the bishop of Rome.

There were in the West two well defined parties on the question of the Roman papacy. One thought that all bishops were alike, and the Roman bishop only first among equals. Another thought that the Roman bishop was the heir of St. Peter, to whom Christ had said, "Thou art Peter, and upon this rock I will build my church; and the gates of Hades shall not prevail against it. I will give unto thee the keys of the kingdom of heaven." Thus it was argued, The bishop of Rome is the heir of St. Peter, who was the heir of Christ, who was the vicegerent of

God in the world. It was a new legalism; but it met the conditions of the time.

Indeed the circumstances of the fifth century were all favourable to Roman claims. The churches of Gaul were younger than the rest, and were not jealous for their own rights. Many of them had received the Gospel from Rome, and were predisposed to the church there. They were now oppressed by Germans and Huns; the imperial administration broke down; the churches drew together and drew to Rome. In Italy similar conditions prevailed. Even the churches of Africa, oppressed by the Vandals, looked for guidance to Rome. And the churches of the East, torn by doctrinal disputes, sought the approval of Roman bishops, while denying their authority.

One strong man gathered the fruits for the Roman See. It was Leo I, called "the Great," bishop of Rome, 440–461. All Leo's activity expressed a definite theory of the papal supremacy over Christendom. In his sermons and letters and decisions one reads that the bishop of Rome has "the care of all the churches, and the Lord, who made Peter the prince of the apostles, holds (the Roman bishop) responsible for it"; that the bishop of Constantinople must not presume because he is bishop of the capital —"Constantinople has its own glory and by the mercy of God has become the seat of the empire. But secular matters are based on one thing, ecclesiastical matters on another. Nothing will stand which is not built on the rock which the Lord laid in the foundation. . . . Your city is royal but you cannot make it apostolic." Indeed all other bishops are but assistants of the Roman bishop in the care of souls. They are appointed to "a share in his anxiety, but not to the plenitude of his authority."

Leo the Great is called "the first Pope." The theory that had been gathering strength so long was established in his time. The primacy of the Roman bishop was no longer resisted effectively anywhere in the Church. Outside the Church it was different. The papacy came under control of the German rulers of Italy. Odoacer and Theodoric were both Arian Christians. They would not permit the suppression of Arianism, and controlled the papacy in the interest of public order. When their brief day closed and Justinian brought Italy again within the Empire, the papal authority was overshadowed by that of the Emperor. But that too passed. The papal authority was re-established by Gregory I, called "the Great," bishop of Rome, 590–604.

Gregory was of an ancient and noble Roman family, with a long record of public service. The family had long been Christian also. One grandfather of Gregory was Pope Felix III; a granduncle was Benedict of Nursia. Gregory himself became a monk, spending his wealth on the monasteries. He was thus both trained in public affairs and an exemplar of the contemporary Christian ideal of personal piety.

When Gregory was made Pope against his will, he found Italy oppressed by the Lombards and the emperor at Constantinople powerless to help. Gregory therefore became the sole governor of Rome, treating with the Lombards as a civil ruler, and purchasing safety for Rome with the treasures of the Church. The missionary spirit, too, was not lacking in the great Pope. Colonies of Benedictine monks were sent to the frontiers, including the young nation of the English, carrying the Gospel. When Gregory died, the so-called Petrine Theory of the papacy had a secure place in the thought life of Christendom.

Gregory the Great and the Lombards thus symbolize, in different ways, the same historical fact, the close of an era. A new race was to possess the western world; and the Church, not the Empire, was to direct it. The Roman Empire was now little more than the Balkans, Asia Minor and Egypt. It could more properly be called, as indeed it came to be called, the Greek Empire, or the Byzantine Empire. For it, too, the tide was coming in; it was to be inundated gradually by the sea of Islam. Meanwhile the Germans were masters everywhere in the West. So much as remained, of the native populations that had lived so long under Rome, was either destroyed in the conquest or slowly absorbed by the conquerors. Only here and there, in remote places, communities retained their earlier racial identity—Greeks in South Italy, Gauls at the sea end of Brittany, Britons in Cornwall and Wales.

The Middle Ages had begun, when the new nations would go to school to the Catholic Church. With a vigorous life of their own, that was to colour all their future, they nevertheless needed something of the civilization that had accumulated through three thousand years around the Mediterranean. The Catholic Church was now the custodian of so much of this civilization as she herself approved and was able to communicate.

And first, some light had to be provided against the general intellectual darkness. The decay of literature in Roman society itself had increased steadily since the second century. Poetry, philosophy, law were all neglected; and Latin became barbarous. All circumstances tended to discourage learning; and the dislike of pagan literature by the Church confirmed the general tendency. There seemed no common ground between the Christian spirit and the classical spirit. The ancient culture had magnified balance, clarity, self-control, a life intelligent and free from excess. The Christian spirit rejected all these. To it self-control was not balance or proportion, but the total exclusion of some elements of life; and it renounced happiness, for the pursuit of a "glory to be revealed hereafter." The spread of the ascetic ideal, too, turned potential scientists into monks.

The ruin of literature was completed in the fifth century by the barbarian invasions. The invaders were indifferent to the learning of the race they despised; and the Roman born were encouraged in illiteracy by the example of their new masters. A few Roman Christians, however, set themselves to save something from the past, both classical and Christian. They built a bridge from the ancient to the mediaeval world, and carried over some treasures to endow the future. Foremost among them were Boëthius and Cassiodorus, Gregory the Great and Isidore of Seville.

Boëthius was a native of Rome, a Latin subject of Theodoric, who admired his character and gifts. The king made him consul, then master of the palace, but later cast him into prison, suspecting him of intrigue with the emperor at Constantinople. There, after some years, he was executed in 525, when only forty-three years old.

Boëthius had set himself to provide a translation from Greek into Latin of all the works of Plato and Aristotle; though he succeeded in completing only Aristotle's works on Logic, the *Organon*. These were destined to provide mediaeval schools with their text-books in Logic. Boëthius wrote treatises also on arithmetic, astronomy, geometry and music, which he regarded as the fourfold path to culture, the *quadrivium*. And during the years in prison he wrote *The Consolation of Philosophy,* a reflective work that in later centuries was translated into most European languages, being put into English by Alfred the Great.

Cassiodorus, as we saw (p. 198), was also a subject of Theodoric, who advanced him to the highest post in the Ostrogothic kingdom, that of pretorian prefect. Cassiodorus had forty years, after he forsook the world, to accomplish work that was to be of use to mediaeval society. Within that time he translated from Greek into Latin, and combined into one, the Church Histories of Socrates, Sozomen and Theodoret. *The Tripartite History* that resulted was the mediaeval monk's sole manual of Church History. His *Institutes,* too, were an encyclopaedia of literature and the arts for monks, a preparation in general knowledge for the study of theology.

Gregory the Great set out in simple and understandable form the common beliefs of the Christians of his time, and put behind them the weight of his tremendous influence. His *Dialogues on the Lives and Influence of the Italian Saints,* written to relieve the cares of office, are full of a naïve belief in all kinds of miracles, and became the delight of simple Christians in later centuries. They were thus linked in superstition with the last centuries of the Empire, as the few educated were linked in knowledge by Boëthius and Cassiodorus. Gregory's *Pastoral Rule,* too, was destined to remind mediaeval bishops of the ideals that had motivated their predecessors in bygone days.

Gregory's work was carried forward by his disciple Isidore, bishop of Seville, the foremost bishopric in Spain. He has been called "the first of the Mediaevalists." The designation is just, in that he pretended to no originality whatever, in matters of thought. His treatises are a vast conglomerate of knowledge, drawn from the past, to be transmitted without question to the future.

All this literary bequest to the Middle Ages was in Latin. It was a fortunate circumstance for the young nations. Because Latin was the language of the schools and all educated men perforce could speak it, learning moved freely across national boundaries. There was therefore a certain unity in the intellectual world, that was to continue for centuries, until the European tongues were sufficiently developed for the purposes of literature.

The nations were further cemented as rapidly as they were Christianized. In the churches were one faith, one symbolism, one liturgy of worship. It, too, was in Latin; and if the worshippers did not understand it, nevertheless the impact upon the senses was the same everywhere. An Englishman was at home in the churches of Italy, a German in those of Spain. Indeed one was first a Catholic, then an Englishman, a Frenchman, a German. The daily discipline of the citizen proceeded more from the clergy than from either the feudal lord or the central government. So that life everywhere was lived within a supernational institution, whose higher clergy were often of another nation than those they ruled, and whose theology was impervious to local influences. Indeed theology was the mediaeval equivalent of modern science, in its timelessness and universal application.

In the whole educational sphere the Church was dominant. Some lay schools did survive from ancient days in Italy, but most were clerical. North of the Alps they were almost exclusively clerical. So the intellectual activity of the Church included much more than theology proper. The last will and testament of Roman law, the *Code* and *Institutes* and *Pandects* of Justinian, reached the mediaeval and modern worlds through the clergy.

CHAPTER VIII

THE CATHOLIC MIND

FROM the Council of Nicaea until Gregory the Great, Catholic theology was developing, side by side with the Catholic constitution and discipline. There were many questions that the Nicene Creed did not answer. They were being discussed in schools for the clergy and in the cloisters, and by a few vigorous bishops.

The argument tended in the Greek East to play round the nature of God, and in the Latin West round his scheme for saving men from hell. If the Church of the West had previously received its theology, even as western society had received its cultural ideals, from the East, nevertheless the temper of the Latin world was not Greek. It was more practical and ethical, less aesthetic and speculative. It had a flair for law and government, and made much of the State. So western theologians, long before Nicaea, began to be interested in questions more typically Latin; and doctrinal development took a new direction.

This first became apparent in North Africa. Cut off from its own continent by mountains and desert, and Romanized a century before Christ, it was really an extension of Europe, with this difference, that Greek influence was less there than in Italy and Gaul. So it was in Roman Africa that the Latin spirit first expressed itself in theology. Indeed North Africa became the theological centre of Latin, as Alexandria was of Greek, Christendom.

The first important Latin theologian was Tertullian, son of a military officer of high rank, converted to Christianity in middle life and made a presbyter in the church at Carthage at the close of the second century. Tertullian became a prolific writer, and the founder of western theology, in so far as it was independent of the East. Indeed Christian theology bears his mark to this day.

Tertullian had been a lawyer, and continued to the end legally minded. Man's duties and responsibilities were his central interest, and the relationship to God out of which they sprang.

Nowhere is Tertullian's thought better illustrated than in his idea of God. Where Greek theologians tended to think of God as absolute being, or the all-inclusive, Tertullian thought of Him as personal ruler, to whom all men are subject. It was Tertullian's concern for the omnipotence of God that led him to argue, against the artist Hermogenes, that God created the world out of nothing, not out of matter, which had an existence of its own and was beyond his complete control.[1]

So Tertullian speaks often of God as sovereign of all men, whose proper attitude to Him is humility and fear. Human virtue springs from fear. It is neither the spontaneous expression of one's character as a child of God, nor the fruit of one's love for God. It is not self-realization, or perfection of being. It is obedience to God's law, through fear of the penalty of disobedience; and God's law is to be obeyed, not because it is demonstrably good but because God commands it.

The duty of unquestioning obedience extends to all one's thoughts. The Christian must think within the Rule of Faith, neither stepping outside it nor going beyond it. Truth is not to be found by investigation; it is given by Divine revelation. And as for the human reason, its function is to draw the proper conclusions from what is revealed.

Legalism controlled Tertullian's idea of sin. Sin is not personal corruption, he thinks, but violation of Divine laws. Eternal death, therefore, is not the inevitable result of corruption but the penalty for breaking laws. Nor is this all. One is guilty in more than one's own disobedience; one inherits guilt from Adam, progenitor of all the race, and is punishable for this "original sin," or sin of origin. One's power to do right remains, however, though impaired from the beginning. The good in us "may be obscured because it is not God; it cannot be extinguished because it is from God." So we are free enough to be responsible for our actions.

The doctrine of original sin had appeared in Christian thought before Tertullian, notably in Irenaeus; but the latter had regarded it as an inherited disability, not an inherited guilt. Tertullian regarded men as guilty and therefore punishable, before committing sins of their own.

---

[1] *Adversus Hermogenem,* 14, 16. The same concern for the Divine omnipotence made Tertullian's view the accepted view of the Catholic Church in time—God created the world out of nothing.

The idea became influential, and one permanent difference between East and West.

Tertullian was equally legalistic when he thought of salvation. It was not a new life, as with Irenaeus and the Mysteries and St. Paul. Salvation was escape, in a future life, from the punishment of sin. God is the avenger, who sees that no sin goes unpunished. Only those who repent and are baptized are forgiven; and God is exceeding scrupulous about it. He scrutinizes the repentance we offer Him in return for eternal life. Our happiness hereafter will be exactly proportioned to our merit. "Why are there to be many mansions with the Father, if not because of the difference in men's merits?"

Tertullian pictured the future life in very realistic terms. Its fires were real, its torments physical, and its delights sensuous. Not the least of its pleasures was that the most deserving would have a good seat, from which to view the torments of the damned.

All this was more congenial to western than to eastern minds; but in time it passed muster everywhere. It consorted well with the spread of ascetic ideals, and the general intellectual decline. So Tertullian's influence was enormous, though still greater in the West. There the legal interpretation of Christianity, the doctrine of the sovereignty of God and His avenging wrath, continue in vigour to the present day.

No one did more to advance the influence of Tertullian than did Cyprian, who was a young man at Carthage when Tertullian died. A distinguished teacher of rhetoric, Cyprian was converted to Christianity, closed the books of the ancients, and thenceforth confined his reading to the Bible and the Christian Fathers, especially Tertullian. A man of great force, a powerful preacher, and a rare administrator, Cyprian became the most influential prelate of the third century; and Tertullian's fame advanced with him.[2]

[2] Tertullian and Cyprian were not quite unchallenged. Lactantius, another teacher of rhetoric in North Africa, took a different direction. Called to the East by the Emperor Diocletian, to teach rhetoric in the capital, Nicomedia, Lactantius later enjoyed the patronage of Constantine the Great and in old age was sent to Gaul, to tutor Constantine's son Crispus.

The interest of Lactantius was in ethics. Public-spirited and socially minded, he rejected monasticism and substituted an active goodness for its passive renunciation. Social peace and brotherliness were the things to be sought; Christianity embodied these ideals; and Christ was their perfect exemplar. It was a conception more congenial to the twentieth century than to the fourth, and made little headway against the dominant tendency.

For a century after Cyprian there was little independent thinking in the West; and for much of that time theologians in the East were engrossed with the Arian controversy. Then, in the late fourth century a period of new theological interest opened in the West with Ambrose and Jerome, though the latter was more scholar than theologian.

Ambrose was a Roman nobleman, son of the prefect of Gaul. Educated at Rome for a political career, his talents and integrity were soon recognized; and when about thirty years old he was appointed governor of North Italy, with headquarters at Milan. There, too, Ambrose won an immediate reputation for capacity and uprightness.

The bishop of Milan was Auxentius, who had espoused the Arian cause and who died in 374, soon after the coming of Ambrose. The choice of a new bishop aroused controversy between Arian and Catholic Christians; and when the young governor entered the church to quell the disturbance, he was greeted with shouts, "Ambrose bishop!" Already a Christian, but not yet baptized, Ambrose was elected bishop of Milan. It seemed to him a call from God; and reluctantly he accepted the office. Giving his wealth to the poor and the Church, Ambrose adopted the ascetic life and continued bishop of Milan for more than twenty years, until his death in 397.

Educated in law, Ambrose knew nothing of theology until he became bishop; but thenceforth he gave himself diligently to the subject. Taking most of his theology from the East, he nevertheless followed Tertullian and the West on the question of sin and salvation. Original sin was not simply an inherited disability; it was an inherited guilt. And Ambrose went beyond Tertullian, declaring that man is utterly helpless, until supernatural grace is given him.

Meanwhile there came from Carthage a brilliant young man, Augustine, recently appointed by the prefect of Italy to be professor of rhetoric at Milan. He was to become the most influential theologian of the West, and the father of much that is characteristic of both mediaeval Catholicism and Protestantism.

Augustine (354–430) was a native of Tagaste, in Numidia. His father Patricius was not yet a Christian; but the boy was instructed by his mother Monica in the Catholic faith as she understood it, a rather crass and superstitious kind of faith. In time Augustine was sent to Carthage to study rhetoric; and there, when seventeen, he took a mistress, who next year bore him a son, Adeodatus, whom he loved dearly. At nineteen the study of Cicero's *Hortensius* awoke in Augustine an interest in philosophy, and convinced him that happiness was to be found in the pursuit of wisdom, which required of one contempt for worldly pleasures and control of the passions, a price too great for Augustine. He could only pray, "Grant me chastity and continence, but not yet."

Unable to rest in Catholicism, Augustine attached himself to Manichaeism, an eclectic religious system of Persian origin, combining elements from Zoroastrianism, Buddhism and Judaism, as well as Christianity. Augustine continued a Manichaean for nine years, while still engaged in study and teaching. It was of no use. Still restless and falling into skepticism, Augustine removed to Rome, where Manichaean friends secured his appointment to Milan.

Very fortunately Augustine now came upon the writings of Plotinus, recently translated into Latin by another North African, Victorinus. They were medicine for his skepticism. Augustine grasped the Neoplatonic conception of a world of spiritual beings, outside the world of things, in which alone the soul of man is at home, and the further conception that there is a spiritual sense in man, by which he may know God and the unseen world. Augustine was attracted also to the Neoplatonic idea of evil. It was not, as the Manichaeans thought, an active power or powers, in ceaseless warfare with the good. Evil was nothing at all but the temporary failure or exhaustion of good. Augustine took heart, and was able to resume his search for truth.

Accepting Neoplatonism as confidently as he had once accepted Manichaeism, Augustine was soon back in the Catholic Church. It is not strange. The kinship of Neoplatonism and Christianity had long been recognized by thoughtful men. Augustine now believed that the former was the expression of the latter in philosophic terms. Specifically, the Neoplatonic view of the nature of evil enabled Augustine to return to the Catholic doctrine that God created the universe; and the Neoplatonic method of interpreting ancient writings allegorically enabled him to explain away the difficulties of the Old Testament, which he as a Manichaean had rejected.

It still remained for Augustine to act upon the truth that he had learned from Cicero, and adopt the contemplative life. It was a hard choice. A brilliant career was opening up before him. Could he abandon it? And as for chastity, to which the Catholic ideal summoned him, Augustine had recently sunk lower than ever. Urged by his mother to an advantageous marriage, he had put away the mother of his son and entered into irregular relations with another, who was still too young for marriage. He was filled with shame that simple and unlearned monks could reject what he, a gifted scholar, could not resist. In bitter conflict with himself, he came upon the words of St. Paul in *Romans*: "Not in rioting and drunkenness, not in chambering and wantonness, not in strife and envying; but put ye on the Lord Jesus Christ, and make not provision for the flesh to fulfil the lusts thereof." It seemed to Augustine the voice of God. From that moment moral victory came to him, and the peace he had sought so long.

This was in the late summer of 386; and at the following Easter Augustine was baptized by bishop Ambrose, along with his son Adeodatus and his dearest friend Alypius.

Augustine now left Milan for his African home. On the way Monica died, and Adeodatus also soon after reaching Tagaste. Augustine's second mistress had already been abandoned; and he was now without family ties. He thought to found a monastery and, with that in view, went in 391 to Hippo, on the Mediterranean, some two hundred miles west of Carthage. There, against his will, he was ordained to the priesthood; and four years later he was chosen Bishop of Hippo. During the next thirty years Augustine became the most influential man in western Christendom.

Augustine never lost his philosophic interest, nor ceased to be a Neoplatonist; but his early confidence in the power of reason steadily gave way to reliance on divine revelation for whatever it is important to know. In the authoritative Church and its authoritative Scriptures, especially the Epistles of St. Paul, he found certitude. So his theology is a combination of diverse elements. For example, Augustine sometimes interprets his religious experience in Neoplatonic terms, as oneness with the Absolute,[3] at other times in Catholic terms, as grateful devotion to a

---

[3] Thus, "I could not exist, I could not exist at all, O my God, unless Thou wert in me. Or rather I could not exist unless I were in Thee, from whom are all things, through whom are all things, in whom are all things." *Confessions*, I, 2–3.

Person; [4] and though he himself had come to God directly for salvation, he adopts without question the Catholic doctrine that men may come to God only through Christ, the mediator.[5]

Augustine's system, in fact, is a curious combination of mystical piety, Neoplatonic philosophy, allegorical interpretation of the Scriptures, and Catholic tradition, all handled with rigorous logic, but often inconsistent with each other. The resulting confusion, however, was little noticed then and mattered little. What did matter was that Augustine had a profound sense of having been reborn and a mystical piety, that are of no special time and place. He spoke the language of the twice-born everywhere; and in him this universal quality was linked with a theology that was harmonious with the times. Men were morally enslaved; the Visigoths had sacked Rome; the Vandals were at the gates of Carthage; the minds of men were filled with foreboding. It was no time for a Lactantius, with his confidence in human nature and society. Thoughtful men fixed their hope on God, and the compact and steadfast Church.

To review Augustine's theology, at its centre is naturally a doctrine of God; and this, when Augustine speaks as a philosopher, is Neoplatonic. God is the only reality, absolute, unchangeable, eternal. When Augustine speaks as a theologian, obedient to the Jewish and Christian tradition, God becomes a person, as we have seen, and indeed three persons in one. As time went on, Augustine increasingly stressed this Catholic view.

Consonant with this Catholic view, the universe is an act of God's will, not a part of the all-inclusive Reality, nor an emanation from the Absolute. And since the world was made out of nothing, as Tertullian thought, it will lapse into nothingness, unless constantly sustained by God. He is always creating it, imparting to it afresh his own reality.

This raises the question of evil. Why is there evil in a world created out of nothing, by one who is both good and all-powerful? Augustine

---

[4] "I will love Thee, O Lord, and thank Thee, and confess unto Thy name, because Thou hast put away from me these so wicked and nefarious acts of mine. To Thy grace I attribute it, and to Thy mercy, that Thou hast melted away my sin as it were ice." *Confessions*, II, 7.

[5] Sin "cannot be pardoned and blotted out except through the one mediator between God and man, the man Christ Jesus." *Enchiridion*, 48.

becomes again a Neoplatonist. Evil, he says, is but exhaustion of being. It arises from the tendency of all things to lapse into the nothingness out of which they came. This is as true of men as of all other things. Being created out of nothing, they tend to lapse into nothingness.

Augustine thus did not need the doctrine of original sin to account for the sinfulness of mankind; but he adopted it nevertheless, as being the Catholic tradition. The sin of mankind is the corruption and guilt of Adam, transmitted to his descendants. And death, which on Augustine's philosophical principles is only separation from God and lapse into nothingness, becomes instead punishment for sin. It follows that, since all human beings die, including infants, all must have incurred guilt.

This seems rough justice for infants; and Augustine felt a natural concern about it. He tried to soften the blow, while remaining loyal to Catholic tradition, by arguing that all human beings were implicit in Adam at the beginning and thus sinned with him.

It was a great price to pay for accepting the logic of the Catholic tradition and tracing all sin to Adam, when Augustine's theory of the nature of evil did not require it.

So also in the matter of man's moral responsibility. Both Christian tradition and social health required that a man be held responsible for his deeds, while the doctrine of original sin tended to absolve him. Augustine argued therefore, against the astrologers who attributed man's deeds to fate and the Manichaeans who attributed them to the evil inherent in matter, that the sons of Adam are as capable as he of doing right and growing in virtue, instead of doing wrong and sinking into vice. One thing only man cannot do—he cannot choose God instead of self, without help from above. This help is what Augustine called grace.

Grace had long been regarded in the Church as both the divine kindness that provides a way of salvation and a substantial and enabling something, infused into man. Augustine emphasized the latter. Grace was an indwelling power, supporting men in goodness.

Ambrose had thought this grace given only to those who have themselves faith to believe. Augustine insisted gradually that God gives the faith also.

A logical next step, for one believing in the omnipotence of God, was that anyone to whom God wills to give grace cannot refuse it. Augustine did not hesitate to take the step. "It is not to be doubted that the will of God . . . cannot be resisted by human wills, so that He may not do what He wills."

This reasoning led on to what is known as the doctrine of double predestination, the divine intention that some shall be saved and others damned. Augustine was perhaps reluctant to go so far; for he usually speaks only of some as predestined to salvation, apparently assuming that others are simply left to their deserts; but sometimes he speaks of men as predestined to damnation, for reasons known only to God.

To those whom God predestines to eternal life, He gives the gift of perseverance. They cannot permanently fall from grace and be damned. If people do sometimes abandon the faith, it is because God never predestined them to salvation. They were not of the elect.

Predestination did not seem to Augustine unjust. All men are guilty and deserve damnation. "He who is saved has good ground for gratitude; he who is condemned has no ground for finding fault."

Nor does predestination interfere with true human freedom, which is not freedom from restraint but freedom from evil. He is most truly free who cannot do wrong; and in the future life that will be the happy state of all the elect. It is Augustine's way of saying that in the hereafter the character of the elect will be finally stabilized in goodness; they will no more be able to sin than God is.

The number of the elect is fixed. It is the same as the number of the angels that fell from Paradise. Indeed the elect take the place in heaven of the fallen angels, and thus make up the loss.

It is rather weird; but again Augustine is trying to express, in Neoplatonic terms, his own profound mystical piety and experience of salvation, while being loyal to the Scriptures and Catholic tradition. It was impossible. And as for the doctrine of predestination, it was as yet no part of the Catholic tradition. Augustine's logic led him there.

Augustine was more traditional in his idea of salvation. It was future, rather than present; and Augustine is as vivid as Tertullian when he pictures the joys of eternal life and the torments of the damned. One new note appears, however, struck from Platonism—union with God hereafter is stressed, a union that is occasionally experienced on earth, in mystic contemplation.

As for the method of salvation, Augustine insisted that men are saved wholly by grace, not by any human effort and achievement. It is the grace of God that arouses faith, the primary Christian virtue. It both reveals the God in whom to believe and gives men the will to believe. This is consistent with the Neoplatonic idea that there is no good except from God.

Faith is followed by forgiveness; but forgiveness is only one step towards salvation. One must also be changed gradually into a new person, whose ruling quality is love, and primarily love of God. It manifests itself in good works—those Catholic works, prayer and fasting and almsgiving. These too are the fruits of God's grace.

Augustine made little contribution to ethics. He had the other-worldliness of the Christian Fathers in general. The Christian life is life for heaven; and there is no virtue for virtue's sake, as the classical moralists had thought. Indeed, the pursuit of virtue out of self-respect is pride, the root of all evils.

An inconsistency runs through all Augustine's discussion of salvation. The work of transforming a sinner into a saint, he thinks, is God's work alone; yet he speaks of heaven and hell in the Catholic fashion, as reward and punishment of human effort. And, as we have seen, though Augustine himself had come as directly to God for salvation as Plotinus had come, he speaks of Christ in his later writings as the only way to God. Christ was a part of the system that Augustine had taken over when he returned to the Catholic Church.

Of greater importance, however, was Augustine's theory of the Church. Here he was unhampered by Platonism and his own mystical experience. Moreover his restless mind found rest in the Catholic doctrine of the authority of the Church. He served her unreservedly for forty years. He did not doubt that she was the only ark of safety and the supreme authority on earth; and so he fought untiringly against the Donatists, a heretical Christian church of North Africa, whose heresy was that they regarded clerical acts as invalid when performed by unworthy priests. The church at Rome had long maintained that the personal character of the priest does not affect his official acts. The urgency of the Roman view was this, that if the validity of the sacraments depended on the character of the priest administering them, the laity could have no assurance that they were receiving a true sacrament.

And as saving grace was believed to reach men through the sacraments, uncertainty was intolerable.

Augustine's struggle with Donatists led him to go in greater detail than anyone else into the nature and functions of the Church. He started from the position maintained by Cyprian, and accepted by Catholics and Donatists alike, that the Church was founded by the Apostles, was meant to be ruled by their successors, the bishops, and that outside the Church there is no salvation.

As the controversy developed, both Catholics and Donatists claiming to be the only true Church, Augustine elaborated his doctrine in treatise after treatise. There were, he said, four marks by which the true Church could be known. They were unity, sanctity, catholicity, apostolicity. All were combined in one phrase, familiar ever since—"one holy, catholic, apostolic Church."

By unity Augustine meant that the true Church was united in doctrine and fellowship, free from both heresy and schism. The Donatists were not heretics; but they were schismatics.

The matter of sanctity was more difficult; for the Donatists emphasized sanctity. But Augustine explained, what has been held ever since, that the Church is holy, not in the character of its clergy and members, but in its possession of the holy sacraments. They are God's works, not man's; and no priest can enhance or diminish their efficacy. The Church, in fact, is that kingdom of God, of which the New Testament speaks, though it will not come in full glory until the life hereafter.

The question of catholicity was also difficult, as the Donatists had all the sacraments of Catholicism and a more rigid moral discipline; but Augustine met the difficulty by explaining "catholic" as meaning world-wide. The Catholic Church was everywhere, the Donatists only in North Africa.

This is a rather better argument than appears on the surface. Augustine meant that, in the end, the majority is likely to be right, a conviction that had helped to make him a Catholic and had given him comfort in many controversial situations. Augustine could not be happy in a minority.

By apostolicity Augustine meant that the true Church was founded by the Apostles, possessed their writings, continued their teaching. The Donatist churches failed of catholicity in this at least, that they were not in communion with those churches admittedly founded by Apostles, at Jerusalem and Antioch, Ephesus and Corinth and Rome.

Augustine had much to say about the sacraments. Indeed, since he emphasized the need of divine grace, he was bound to emphasize the sacraments through which grace came to men. But he never reached any consistent theory about them, and often contradicted himself. It could not be otherwise. The emphasis upon the sacraments was inconsistent with Augustine's own experience of direct communion with God, as described in his *Confessions,* and with the doctrine of predestination. How could sacraments be indispensable, for those already predestined for salvation? Augustine tried to meet the objection by saying that God predetermined, not only to save some but to save them through the sacraments.

In all this tradition triumphs over Augustine's deepest instincts and experiences. It is Augustine the Catholic, not Augustine the mystic, who speaks in his doctrine of the Church and the sacraments.

Augustine completed the ecclesiastical edifice built up in his thought, by claiming for the Church the supreme authority on earth. In the moral realm she declares the will of God; in the intellectual realm she declares the truth. Men are answerable to her for what they do and for what they think. And the ground of her infallibility is not that she is guided by infallible Scriptures. Augustine reverses the argument, accepting the infallibility of the Scriptures on the testimony of the Church. It is she who determines what books are canonical, and what is their true interpretation. She made them authoritative.

Augustine could never locate the Church's infallibility, and was in difficulty whenever a crisis arose. Bishops, he knew, could err; and even General Councils. Nevertheless Augustine found in the doctrine an assurance that supported him against skepticism.

The authority of the Catholic Church, Augustine thought, extended beyond the purely moral and intellectual spheres, and included the whole social order. In his greatest work, *The City of God,* he distinguishes between two societies, the city of God and the earthly city, the former sacred, the latter profane. It is the distinction between the Church and the rest of mankind, whom Augustine sometimes identifies with the Roman Empire. The Church is of heavenly origin; the Empire is of the earth. In the Church, therefore, is unity and peace, the worship of one

God and the service of one Lord; in the world are division and war, with the worship of many gods. The State, nevertheless, exists by the will of God, to preserve order among mankind; and in so far as it is good, it is to be supported by the Church. But the State is not an end in itself but a means to that other end, that within it the Church may prosper and the people be educated for the world to come.

So great was Augustine's sense of the glory of the Catholic Church, when contrasted with the decaying Empire, that he believed the millennium had already dawned. Men need not wait for the second coming of Christ; he was already here, reigning through the Church. It was more, therefore, than an institution within the Empire, or an institution side by side with the Empire. It was supreme over the Empire itself, and could rightfully require its obedience.

Augustine had no plan for applying this principle; but it became of tremendous importance later, a foundation of the papal supremacy in the Middle Ages. Nothing, therefore, of all Augustine's teaching has been more influential in European history.

Outside the field of theology, Augustine's views of the physical universe greatly influenced Christian thought. The world, he said, is daily sustained by God; and without his activity it would lapse into the nothingness out of which He created it. In other words, God is always creating the world.

In such a view the distinction between the natural and the supernatural disappears; and miracles require no special explanation. They are no more acts of God than are ordinary phenomena. Augustine is therefore at home with miracles. They are only unusual forms of the divine activity. They are the more to be expected because the world is peopled with invisible beings, angels and demons, to whom God has given the ability to do many things that men cannot do. So Augustine's *City of God* describes contemporary miracles as marvellous as anything now reported from India and Thibet.

This did not preclude the operation of natural forces. God works through the ordinary forces of Nature, as well as independently of them. Augustine, however, did not go far in the investigation of physical phenomena. His vigorous and enquiring mind was restrained by two considerations. First, spiritual affairs were vastly more important. This was the attitude of thinkers, within and without the Church, and had been so since the eclipse of Greece. It was the philosophic temper of a period of social disillusion. Augustine is therefore a child of his age when he deprecates discussion of the form of the heavens and the earth, and their relation to each other. Such discussions are "of no profit to those who are learning the blessed life, and what is worse consume much precious time, which ought to be spent on matters pertaining to salvation." [6]

Again, Augustine was restrained in scientific interest by the belief that the Scriptures contain an infallible account of the world, and that further study is needless. He did write books on creation, as Basil the Great and Ambrose had done; but they were written to exhibit the glory of God. And he appealed to physical phenomena to elucidate the Scriptures. Beyond this he did not go.[7]

Augustine set the fashion for later generations. He was followed by great churchmen like Gregory the Great, and sober scholars like the Venerable Bede. Indeed his view became the Catholic view.

Nothing else, however, in Augustine has wrought so powerfully in Christian history as his religious genius. He himself lived the religious life, as only a minority in all religions ever live it. He was at one with himself, and with the Ultimate Life of the universe. In this he belongs in the great succession of Paul and Bernard, Francis of Assisi and Martin Luther, Thomas à Kempis and John Wesley. And such persons, whenever their religious experience is accompanied by adequate capacity for thought or administration, become the creative forces in progress. Augustine affected the future of Christianity as no one after St. Paul, and this in spite of the fact that much of his theology was at first rejected as a dangerous novelty. The particular quality of his experience and colour of his piety confirmed a tendency already present in St. Paul and Neoplatonism, Tertullian and Ambrose, to shift attention from man and his capacities to God and his grace. In this regard Augustine

---

[6] *De genesi ad litteram,* II, 9.

[7] Men of less intelligence obtained ludicrous results, by using the Bible as a text-book of the natural sciences. Augustine could not quite avoid so using it; and his thinking shows its influence. Thus, in opposition to the general view, he was inclined to believe the earth spherical; but in that case, he said, the antipodes could not be inhabited. The Apostles never preached in the antipodes; they were commanded to preach the Gospel to every creature; disobedience by the Apostles is unthinkable; the antipodes are therefore unhabited.

closed the age of Greek moralists, indeed of all classical antiquity, for the West, and opened the Middle Ages.

The classical spirit, however, was capable of one rearguard action. When Augustine was writing from Hippo, there was living at Rome a British monk of high character, Pelagius, who was labouring to improve the morals of the imperial city. The unsatisfactory state of Christian morals, he thought, was largely due to the diminished sense of personal responsibility, resulting from the doctrine of original sin and man's moral helplessness. Christians were depending too little on their own efforts, too much on God and the Church. In a letter to a woman disciple, Demetrias, Pelagius writes: "Whenever I have to speak concerning moral instruction and holy living, I am accustomed to point out first the force and quality of human nature and what it is able to accomplish. . . . For we are by no means able to tread the way of virtue unless we have hope as a companion."

Pelagius had come by another route than that of Augustine. He had not abandoned hope of society, perhaps because decadence had not advanced so far in Britain when he was growing up and the profound Roman peace was less disturbed there than elsewhere, perhaps also because he had not known Augustine's fierce struggle with passion. In any case, his own mind was better expressed in Cicero and Stoicism than in Plotinus and Neoplatonism.

In theology, therefore, Pelagius wholly rejected the doctrine of original sin. One's sin is voluntary and is one's own; it cannot be transmitted. All human beings are as Adam was at the first. The universality of sin is due to bad example, which one need not follow, and to one's desires, which are innocent when directed and controlled. Men have the power to do right. What they lack is understanding, which can be acquired. And as for physical death, it is not the result of sin. Adam would have died anyway, like all physical beings.

Pelagius spoke often of divine grace, but not in Augustine's sense. Grace was a divine revelation, enlightening men, not a substantial something within them. Indeed Pelagius sometimes spoke of grace even more broadly, as including God's gifts of reason and conscience. These gifts were enough at the beginning, until bad habits and evil example made

revelation necessary. Then God revealed his nature and will, first in the
Mosaic Law, then in the Gospel, and continually thereafter to those
who use the light they have.

Similarly when Pelagius spoke of regeneration, he meant something
different from Augustine. To be regenerated was not to receive a new
nature, but to have the old nature illuminated and the will stimulated, by
revelation and the promises of God.

Pelagius found plenty of support for his positions, in both reason and
the Bible. It was not difficult to quote passages, in which men are
assumed to have free will, are exhorted to virtue, and promised the reward of their efforts. And there were precedents in Christian history for
such views. More than one teacher of the second century, notably Justin
Martyr, had regarded Christianity as a moral system; though it was
generally combined with ideas of another sort, drawn from the mystery
religions.

Pelagianism was not at first a conscious reply to Augustine. It was an
independent system. But soon after the sack of Rome by Alaric and his
Goths, Pelagius left Rome for Carthage, where Augustine's influence
was very great. Controversy was inevitable; and it followed Pelagius to
the East, when he settled soon afterward in Palestine. The activities of
Augustine's disciples, supported by Jerome in Palestine, led to accusations of heresy against Pelagius, before a synod at Jerusalem. He was
acquitted; but that only stimulated the Augustinians to accuse him at
Rome. Under pressure from Carthage, where a council of some two
hundred bishops condemned Pelagius in 418, Pope Zosimus also condemned him and the Emperor Honorius sent him into exile. In the end
the General Council of Ephesus, in 431, condemned Pelagianism.

The condemnation of Pelagianism, however, did not mean the adoption of Augustinianism. Even the Council of Carthage did not commit
itself to all that Augustine taught. Nothing was there said about man's
utter moral incapacity, or predestination, or irresistible grace. Indeed,
most theologians of the day feared one aspect or another of Augustine's
system. Their controlling interest continued to be ethical; and Augustine's doctrine of the divine sovereignty could not be acceptable to anyone who was greatly concerned about human character and conduct.
Pelagianism might well have been approved, had it not been for certain
departures from Catholicism. For example, the idea of grace as simply

illumination tended to make the sacraments appear unnecessary. The Church would suffer if such principles were adopted.

Opposition to parts of Augustine's teaching continued, and was particularly strong in southern Gaul. There the foremost theologians rejected the doctrine that men cannot co-operate with God in their own salvation, while some are predestined to salvation and cannot resist his grace. The protesting movement was called Massilianism, because the chief theological centre was Massilia (Marseilles). It is better known now as Semi-Pelagianism, a misleading name, since it suggests a connection with Pelagius. It was indeed the general belief of the West, earlier than Augustine and Pelagius, and in opposition to both at one point or another. Its great leaders were John Cassian and Vincent of Lerins.

Massilianism was brought to the attention of Augustine; and he attempted to answer it in some of his latest writings. The Massilians agreed with him that all men are sinners because of Adam's fall, and cannot be saved without the aid of divine grace; but they affirmed against him that salvation is offered to all men and all have power to accept or reject it, the exercise of faith being one's own act. They declared, too, that God foreknows, but does not predestine who shall be saved. Augustine's teaching, they thought, was something new and something that made the Church's work ineffective.

Soon after Augustine died, Vincent of Lerins wrote the famous *Commonitorium,* which was meant to rule out all novelties in theology. The standards of Christian truth, he said, are the Bible and the tradition of the Catholic Church. The Bible is infallible and complete, but requires interpreting. The Catholic Church is the only legitimate interpreter. It speaks through the decisions of General Councils and the writings of Catholic Fathers. Even their writings are to be discriminated and what is singular rejected. Only that is orthodox which has been taught everywhere, always and by all. In such a view heresy is more than divergence from the Creed and from the decisions of General Councils; heresy is whatever is new. And progress is limited to the clearer statement of what is already believed.

Vincent's test of orthodoxy was generally accepted. There was little room thenceforth for individual opinion, and no need for General Councils except in great emergencies.

Augustine's doctrine of predestination, being unusual, was regarded in Gaul as heretical, and was officially condemned in 473, by synods at Arles and Lyons. Fifty years later sentiment was changing; and the Second Council of Orange, in 529, under the influence of a great preaching bishop, Caesarius of Arles, committed itself to a moderate Augustianism. Adam's fall, it said, did bring upon the race physical as well as spiritual death; and human nature cannot recover except by supernatural aid. Both the desire for regeneration and the faith to believe are gifts of God.

The Second Council of Orange was small and would have had little influence, had not Caesarius succeeded in securing papal confirmation of its decisions. Augustinianism thus became orthodox, and has so remained, but an Augustinianism somewhat changed. Orange said nothing about irresistible grace, and nothing about predestination, except to anathematize those who said that God predestines anyone to evil.

Pelagianism was also rejected. There is no independent human merit; all depends on grace. Grace, however, was conceived to be given at the moment of baptism; and infant baptism was now almost universal. So that, having recovered free will in infancy through baptism, the adult was able to believe or disbelieve, and accept or reject the grace that was continually offered him through the sacraments. The result was genuinely Catholic. Man was left a responsible being, while being kept humble minded and dependent on the Church.

The real heirs of Augustine, until the Protestant Reformation, were the Christian mystics. Wherever men sought by themselves the knowledge of God, there Augustine was known and revered. The distinction here is fundamental, between those who are directed in the religious life by ecclesiastical discipline and those who "come boldly to the throne of grace." Some, like Augustine and Bernard of Clairvaux, do both; but the combination tends to be in unstable equilibrium. Churchmen and mystics speak a different language, and are ill-at-ease with each other.

One cannot close the history of Augustine without mention of Gregory the Great (c. 540–604), though he lived nearly two centuries later. A man of great force of character and a born leader of men, Pope Gregory was no theologian. That is to say, he had no system of his own. Nevertheless he wrote voluminously on theological questions, and in such a way as to be easily understood. Indeed his influence was all the greater because he was not original, and set out only the common thought of the Church. So much so that his name is still linked with those of Ambrose, Jerome and Augustine, as one of the four great Doctors, or teachers, of the Latin Church.[8]

We have from the pen of Gregory some eight hundred letters and many sermons. And there are *Dialogues,* engrossed with the supernatural experiences and adventures of monks and very credulous. The *Pastoral Rule* is a work on the duties of bishops, that was used for centuries; and the *Moralia* is an extensive work on theology and morals, cast in the form of an interpretation of the *Book of Job.* The allegorical method enabled Gregory to make *Job* say anything that he himself thought important. So the *Moralia* has no value whatever as an interpretation of *Job,* but was extremely influential as a record of Gregory's views on all sorts of things. It was, in fact, for centuries the chief text-book of theology for the Latin Church.

But our present interest in Gregory is this, that it is chiefly through him that the teaching of Augustine was passed on to the Middle Ages. Gregory was a devout disciple of Augustine, and did his best to commend him to Catholicism. He was ill equipped to do so. He knew nothing of Neoplatonism, nothing of the Latin classics, in which Augustine had been educated. Gregory grew up believing that a Christian should scrupulously avoid the ancient literature. When he heard that bishop Desiderius of Vienne was teaching grammar, he wrote: "This conduct in a bishop is so execrable, that the matter should be seriously explained. If the investigation shows that this rumour is false, and that you are not studying the frivolous literature of the age, we shall thank God that He has not let your soul be polluted."

Nevertheless, without the kind of intellectual interest and education to understand Augustine, Gregory made his ideas popular to an extraordinary degree, combining them with the common thought of Latin Christendom. In the process Gregory repeats the inconsistencies of Augustine, without knowing that they are inconsistencies, and adds others

---

[8] Tertullian missed his laurels because his Catholicism was compromised by his adhesion to the Montanists.

of his own. Indeed he thought it dangerous pride, the cause of all heresy, to attempt to resolve theological difficulties. Humility, the willingness to be ignorant, is the truly Christian virtue.

Gregory made great use of the fear of damnation. Anxiety was the only safe attitude, until life was over and temptation past. One would therefore do penance again and again, to make it unnecessary for God to punish; and for those who had not done enough, purgatory was provided for further penance.

This belief in purgatory was very ancient, indeed pre-Christian, being found in Orphism and other cults; and, as we saw, it was common among the Christians of North Africa in Tertullian's day. Augustine was doubtful about it. Gregory had no doubts. He developed the doctrine, and did much to give it a permanent place in Catholicism.

Gregory laid great stress also upon the work of Christ. Through him God had provided a way for men to escape the divine wrath. The whole race had, by Adam's fall, become the property of the devil and were doomed to death. But if Satan claimed too much, he could properly be deprived of everything. If, for example, he should seize Christ, the Son of God, he would forfeit his claim to mankind. So Christ appeared in human form, deceived Satan into thinking him a man, and was crucified. Thus Satan was put in the wrong, and lost his right to humanity. God could therefore forgive sinners without a breach of justice. This grotesque idea was quite congenial to contemporary Christians.

More important still for Catholicism was Gregory's view of the Lord's Supper. It was, as Cyprian had suggested, a daily repetition of Christ's sacrifice for the sins of men. Gregory worked out this suggestion in detail; and his influence made it a Catholic doctrine. Whenever the priest administers the eucharist, he repeats Christ's sacrifice for the sins of men. It has the same effect as penance, which the living would otherwise require to undergo here and the dead in purgatory. Its value for the dead had often been proven, Gregory said. The dead had appeared in dreams and visions to the living, to assure them that their discomfort in purgatory was immediately alleviated when the eucharist was performed for them. Many a "dead monk was by the holy sacrifice delivered from his pains." The doctrine was prominent in Latin Christianity from Gregory's day, and helped to give to mediaeval piety its special colour.

Gregory thought often, too, about the angels; and his conclusions as to their respective places in the government of the world have helped to determine their functions ever since. So also Satan and the demons and their cunning tricks, especially against monks and nuns, often enliven Gregory's *Dialogues*. His stories are such as are current among simple people, of all religions. Here, too, Gregory did not so much create the absurd angelology and demonology of his time as support it by his authority, and raise it to the dignity of Catholic doctrine.

So also with the custom of appealing to the saints and martyrs, to use their influence with Christ on men's behalf. Gregory did not originate the custom; but he lent it his support, and set forth its advantages earnestly and often. "If you had a case to be tried on the morrow before some great magistrate, you would surely spend the whole of today planning for it; you would seek a patron and beg him to become your defender. Behold the severe judge Jesus is about to come; the terror of that mighty council of angels and archangels is at hand. . . . Our holy martyrs are ready to be your advocates; they desire to be asked. . . . Seek them as helpers of your prayers; . . . the judge himself wishes to be importuned, that he may not be obliged to punish sinners." [9]

This is, of course, not new. Christ had always been regarded as both saviour and judge. What is new is that the crude form in which ordinary Christians understood the doctrine is now elaborately set down, by the highest authority in the Church, and becomes Catholic doctrine.

The tremendous importance of Gregory for western Catholicism is thus that he formulated the common faith of the day, and handed it on, in compact and understandable form, to the Middle Ages. Here were the decisions of Councils and the teachings of the Fathers, combined in one system with the ideas of common men, very crude and superstitious, often pagan. All this Gregory's great influence confirmed; and mediaeval Christianity cannot be understood apart from him.

By this time, too, the essential distinction between Greek and Latin Christianity, already visible in Tertullian's day, was finally confirmed. They had many doctrines and practices in common; but in the East Christianity was commonly regarded as a mystical religion, uniting man with God, and so transforming him from a corrupt and mortal being into a holy and immortal one. Its spirit was that of St. Paul and St. John and the Mysteries. In the West Christianity was regarded as a legal religion,

[9] *Homilia in evangelia*, XXXII, 8.

requiring obedience to law and providing an escape from the penalties of disobedience, by a system of sacraments and good works. Its spirit was that of late Judaism and of St. James. It was the religion of Tertullian and Gregory the Great, touched by the philosophy and mysticism of Augustine.

CHAPTER IX

GERMANIC EUROPE

Gregory the Great exemplifies better than anyone else the true character of ancient Catholicism. It was a composite of everything dear to the Mediterranean world, that seemed in any way consistent with the Messianic movement that had sprung up in Galilee six centuries before. Indeed some Christians thought the Church too hospitable to the ideas and modes of the world. When bishop Callistus of Rome decided that even a Christian fornicator and adulterer need not be cast out, that he might be put to penance and absolved, there was a great outcry. And when the worship of images became prevalent, some said that the worship of one God was now left to Jews and Moslems. But the Catholic Fathers were bent on making of the Church, not an exclusive company of men and women exhibiting a better way of life and a better hope, but an all-embracing institution, standing foursquare against disorder and subduing men to a higher law than that of Rome. Asking of men obedience, they accepted from them whatever the Church could use. The reward to the Church was not sanctity, but strength and influence.

There were advantages in such a change of character. We have seen how Augustine of Hippo, the springs of whose piety were not in the Catholic Church, nevertheless drew comfort from her cohesion and strength. Here was at least one lighthouse in the growing storm.

The influence of the Christian clergy, too, was rather increased than otherwise by the Germanization of society. Where there was no lay education, the education of the clergy became conspicuous. And since the imperial service no longer offered a career to gifted men, the Church drew them into her service. The bishops of Gaul, in the sixth and seventh centuries, often came from ancient and distinguished families. And the new German rulers had need of them. German kings were strong in war and in the chase, weak in law and government. The work of government was new, having been thrust upon them by their occupation of Roman lands. They could not govern without the aid of the clergy. So when a road needed repair, or an aqueduct to be built, or flood and pestilence to be subdued, it was often a bishop who provided the initiative and administered the funds. And when a lawless ruler required to be rebuked and overawed, sometimes a bishop had the moral authority for that also.

It was as a recent historian has said: "The chaos of the Empire was the opportunity of the Church, the childish ignorance of the barbarian prepared the triumph of the priest. In an age when books were rare, everything depended on the voice and example of the teacher. The simple and superstitious barbarian was ready to tolerate a degree of interference in his private life which the cultivated Roman lady or gentleman would have resented as a vulgar intrusion. As the task of educating the barbarian world in the rudiments of the Christian faith unfolded itself in all its vast and desperate proportions, the clergy became of necessity . . . a well-marked and influential profession." [1] It was the more influential because of the widespread belief in a secret body of ultimate truth, communicated only by word of mouth and to the initiated, of which the priest was now the admitted custodian.

Distinguished in education and function, Christian priests became distinguished in appearance as well. By the sixth century the clergy of the West were required to wear a distinctive dress. So in Germanic lands the priest, with the long robe and short hair of the ancient Roman, was distinct from the German with his short tunic and long hair. He was to the new peoples the survivor of an ancient civilization, as well as the dispenser of salvation.

Two of the German peoples have been unnoticed thus far, because their migrations did not bring them into the Mediterranean world. These are the English and the Franks.

The English were three German peoples—the Jutes, Angles and Saxons—who lived in what is now Denmark and along the Elbe. Barred from the Rhineland and Gaul by the Franks, they took the sea for their domain and became pirates. When the Roman legions withdrew from Britain that land became the natural prey of the English pirates. There

[1] H. A. L. Fisher, *A History of Europe*, Edward Arnold & Co., p. 175.

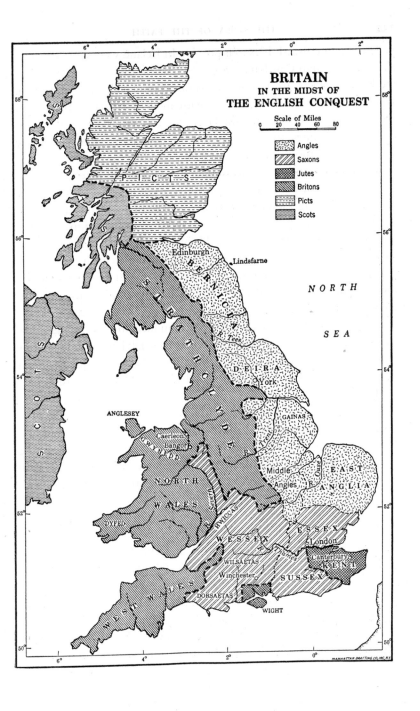

BRITAIN
IN THE MIDST OF
THE ENGLISH CONQUEST

Scale of Miles
0   20   40   60   80

Angles
Saxons
Jutes
Britons
Picts
Scots

P I C T S

Edinburgh
Lindsfarne

B E R N I C I A

R. Tees

D E I R A
York

GAINAS

S C O T S

ANGLESEY

Caerleon
Bangor

GWYNEDD

S T R A T H C L Y D E

Middle
Angles

R. Ouse

E A S T
A N G L I A

N O R T H

W A L E S

R. Severn

HWICCAS

DYFED

W E S S E X

E S S E X

London

T H E

Thames

Canterbury

K E N T

WILSAETAS

Winchester

S U S S E X

W E S T   W A L E S

DORSAETAS

WIGHT

N O R T H

S E A

MANHATTAN DRAFTING CO., INC., N.Y.

had been in the British Isles four peoples. In Ireland were the Scots, who also extended into Caledonia, "Scotland," where they divided the country with the Picts. Ireland and Caledonia lay outside Roman Britain, which was generally co-terminous with modern England. In Roman Britain were the Britons and the Gaels, the former occupying the main body of the country, the latter the Cornish peninsula and Wales. These four peoples of the British Isles were all Celts, like the Gauls.

When the legions withdrew, Roman Britain was left defenceless. The native population had not been permitted to bear arms. Helpless now against marauding Picts and Scots, and unable to get help from Aëtius, the Roman commander in Gaul, they appealed to the English pirates. Two Saxon chiefs, Henghist and Horsa, expelled the marauders and were rewarded with the island of Thanet, off the Kentish coast. They changed quickly from protectors to masters. Henghist took possession of the mainland, from the Channel to the Thames, called his kingdom Kent, and established his capital at Kentburgh, "Canterbury."

The success of Henghist and Horsa was an incitement to all the pirate chiefs; and within a century there were seven small barbarian kingdoms in Roman Britain, "the heptarchy." Britain was becoming England; and the Britons were being destroyed, absorbed, or driven westward among the Gaels.

Christianity had reached Roman Britain late in the second century, probably through Christian soldiers in the legions. There are romantic stories that it came in apostolic times, having been brought by St. Paul himself, or by Joseph of Arimathaea; but these are legends of the Middle Ages.

Christianity was never very vigorous in Roman Britain, being largely confined to the legionary centres. It produced no writers of note except Pelagius, who lived and wrote abroad. It seems to have sent no missionaries to its neighbours. Ninian, a British Christian studying at Rome, went from there to the Picts of Caledonia in 390 (?), where he preached for a short time, but with little effect. Palladius, a British Christian living at Rome, was sent by Pope Celestine in 431 (?), to be bishop of Scots already converted in Ireland. Patrick, a British Christian of Roman education, went to Ireland in 432 (?); but the mission was original with himself. When a captive in Ireland in his youth, he had seen its spiritual destitution and violence; and in Armorica (Brittany) later he was persuaded by a dream to return with the Gospel. As for Roman Britain itself, Christianity there virtually disappeared in the terrible fifth century, before raids of the Picts and Scots and the permanent settlement of Anglo-Saxons. Of the abundant Roman antiquities in England now, almost none are certainly Christian.

A Celtic Christianity did survive, however, among the Gaels of Cornwall and Wales, and lived in fellowship with the Christians of Ireland. Isolated from the continent by the disorders there and the steady encroachment of the English in Britain, the Celtic Christians produced a type of Christianity different from Catholicism. Christianity here spread by the formation of monastic groups, each regarded as a new tribe, "the tribe of the saint." Each monastery had a bishop, to ordain men to the priesthood; but it was the abbot who ruled. The Celtic Churches used an antiquated calendar, the Pre-Dionysian, which made Easter earlier than in the Catholic Church. Priests married, where clerical celibacy was becoming the rule in Catholicism. The tonsure of the monks was not the shaven crown, the *corona,* of Catholics. The Celtic monks shaved half the head, from ear to ear. Most important of all these differences was rule by abbots instead of bishops. There were no dioceses; and monasteries, not parish churches, were the centres of life and activity.

The Celtic Christians were full of missionary zeal. Finnian went in the sixth century from Wales to Ireland, induced thereto by Gildas, historian of British Christianity, and Bishop David, who was to become patron saint of Wales. In Ireland Finnian established a monastery at Clonard, that was soon to have three thousand monks and lay brothers.

From Ireland the Gospel was carried by Columba to the Picts of Caledonia. The story is dramatic. Columba (521–597) was an Irish chieftain, as well as a monk. In a moment of anger he led his tribesmen against the neighbouring clan; and when the deadly deed was done, three thousand men of Meath lay dead among the heather. In an agony of repentance, Columba knelt before his father confessor, who imposed the penance of exile. Columba must leave his native land, and save as many souls as the bodies he had destroyed. He set out in 563, with the customary twelve companions, crossed the northern sea in coracles, little boats made of the hides of cattle, and established a monastery on the island of Iona, off the south-west coast of Scotland. Having christianized the community and created a haven to which his monks could always retire, Columba took them across the highlands to Inverness, capital of king Brude, who soon submitted to the new faith. Within a generation the highlands were won; and the Irish monks then carried the Gospel down the east coast of Scotland and into north England, where they established a monastery on the island of Lindisfarne, off the Northumbrian coast.

All this time, more than a century, the English had remained pagan. Christian Britons, embittered by the long conquest, made no attempt to convert the English; nor did the Gaels of the West. But the monks of Iona now undertook the evangelization of north England; and a mission from Rome was already at work in the South.

Gregory the Great, attracted by English boys, being sold in the market at Rome, determined to go himself to the English. Prevented by his election to the papacy, he sent instead his friend Augustine, abbot of one of his monasteries. The latter set out for England in 596, accompanied by forty Benedictines. On the way evil news of the English filled them with fear; and only letters from Gregory, persuasive and stern, kept them to their mission. Augustine and his party landed in Kent early in 597, and were permitted to establish a monastery at Canterbury. Kent was already densely populated and had advanced in civilization; and King Ethelbert had established his authority as far north as the Humber. His queen Bertha was a princess of the Franks and a Catholic Christian, who had her own chaplain, Bishop Liuhard. King Ethelbert had, therefore, some knowledge of Christianity. He was now baptized into the Catholic faith, on June 1, 597, as were ten thousand of his men on Christmas Day. That year Pope Gregory made Augustine archbishop, with a seat at Canterbury and with jurisdiction over all England. Four years later the Church of the English was recognized as no longer a mission. It was now a national church, the *Ecclesia Anglorum*.[2]

Gregory was aware, when planning the mission to England, that there were British Christians there, and churches in Wales and Ireland that were not in communion with Rome. So Augustine, before he sent his monks westward, enquired of the Pope how he was to deal with

[2] Bede, *Ecclesiastical History*, I, xxii, xxiii, xxix. Everyman's Library.

native bishops. Gregory commited them to Augustine's care, "that the unlearned (might) be taught, the weak reassured, . . . and the perverse corrected." [3]

Augustine tried to fulfil the Pope's commission. Assuming that bishops ruled the British Church, he wrote the monasteries, summoning the bishops to a conference. A few came,[4] and were exhorted to unite with Augustine for the conversion of the English. They asked for a further conference, when more might attend. It met at some place, now unknown; and there were present "seven bishops, and many wise men or monks." The conference failed because of Augustine's assumption of authority.[5] British Christians, during the time of the Roman occupation, had known nothing of the supremacy of bishops of Rome. It did not yet exist. And since the abandonment of Britain by the Empire, Christians there had developed an ecclesiastical system of their own, as dear to them as was Catholicism on the continent.

The sentiment of the Irish Church was the same. So Ireland and Wales drew together, indifferent alike to England and to Catholicism.[6]

With the Church of Iona it was different. The monks there were voluntary exiles. Their loyalty was to Iona, not to the fatherland; and they were active in the conversion of North England. Indeed King Oswald of Northumbria, who had once been a fugitive at Iona, asked for the Gospel; and Aidan was sent from Iona in 635, with a company of monks. The king granted them the island of Lindisfarne, "Holy Isle," for a monastery, as we have seen. It became the centre of an eager mission to North England. Indeed the Irish-Scottish monks penetrated England almost as far south as London.

The Celtic missionaries obedient to Iona and the Catholic missionaries from Canterbury were soon carrying forward parallel missions in the Midlands and the North. Differences in usage made conflict inevitable. It was very confusing that King Oswy of Northumberland should be fasting in preparation for Easter when his queen, a convert of Iona, was

3 Bede, *ibid.,* I, xxvii.

4 Tradition fixes the place of meeting at "Augustine's Oak," near Cricklade, on the border of Gloucester and Wilts.

5 Bede, *ibid.,* II, ii, xx.

6 The independence of British Christianity continued for five centuries longer, until West Wales—or the Cornish peninsula—and Wales itself were brought by conquest within the political dominion of England. As gradually as Britain failed the British Church also diminished, until it became Catholic, obedient to Canterbury and Rome.

celebrating that holy day. King Oswy therefore summoned representatives of both churches to a conference at Whitby in 664. Was it to be Columba or St. Peter in the North? Colman of Lindisfarne and Wilfrid of York were the opposing advocates. Had Christ said to Columba, "I will give unto thee the keys of the kingdom of heaven"? He had not, Colman admitted. Then said the king, I will obey St. Peter, lest when I come to the gate of heaven, I find him my enemy.[7]

Thus was the matter settled. Colman retired to Iona; and Tuda, a Scot trained in Catholic usages, took his place. The victory of the Roman ecclesiastical system over all England was completed within a generation. The Anglo-Saxon monasteries, thenceforth Benedictine, became the centres of civilization and culture and peace in England, as the Scottish-Irish monasteries had been. The poet Caedmon, who died in 680, was a lay brother in the monastery at Whitby. A late contemporary, the Venerable Bede, the most learned man in western Europe, was a monk at Jarrow, near modern Newcastle. Many of the noblest products of Christianity in England in the future were to spring from the continual mingling of the imaginative and eager Celtic temper with the more stolid English genius.

More important than the English for the history of Catholicism were the Franks. When other German nations were spreading consternation through the Mediterranean world, the Franks were a confederation of tribes along the lower Rhine. They had themselves encroached upon Roman Gaul, as far as the Somme; but their king Merovius gave valiant support to Aëtius and the legions, when they turned back the Huns at Châlons (p. 185). Merovius founded a dynasty, the Merovingians; and his son Childeric led the Franks beyond the Somme to the Loire, where they were to remain forever. South of the Loire was the Visigothic Kingdom, extending also through Spain; and along the Rhone were the Burgundians. These three nations now dominated Roman Gaul; and when in 486 King Clovis, son of Childeric, defeated Syagrius, "King of the Romans," near Soissons, nothing whatever remained of the Roman Empire in Gaul.

King Clovis is important for Catholicism. His wife, Clotilda, a princess of Burgundy, was a Catholic Christian; and at the supreme crisis of his

[7] Bede, *Ecclesiastical History*, III, xxv, xxvi.

career Clovis, like Constantine the Great, called upon the God of Clotilda, and swore to become a Christian if given the victory. Clovis triumphed over his enemies, the German Alemanni, east of the Rhine, in a great battle near Strassburg, in 496. True to his vow, he became a Christian, as did three thousand of his chieftains.

Though such a conversion made but a poor Christian of Clovis and left his people pagan, it did make the Frankish king the defender of the Gallic bishops of his kingdom and the Gallic population, who were also Catholic Christians. And as the neighbouring Burgundians and Visigoths were Arian Christians and therefore heretics, the conversion of Clovis was to make the Frankish kings the defenders of Catholicism everywhere in western Europe. In return the Catholic Church helped the Frankish kings against German rivals.

Clovis soon made the Burgundians tributary and drove the Visigoths to the Pyrenees, thus becoming master of almost all Gaul. He combined also the elements out of which the new Europe was to rise—the barbarians, the Catholic Church that was to educate and discipline them and the Roman civilization, to which Clovis showed deference by accepting from the eastern emperor Anastasius the titles Consul and Patrician. A pope wrote him: "The Lord has provided for the needs of the Church by giving her for defender a prince armed with the helmet of salvation; be thou always for her a crown of iron, and she will give thee victory over thine enemies."

The four sons of Clovis, following the German custom, divided his kingdom among themselves; and for fifty years there was little united action among the Franks. One result was that the east Franks, or Austrasians, and the west Franks, or Neustrians, tended towards separation. The tendency was to increase as rapidly as the Franks and Gauls of Neustria combined into one population, with a distinctive character, not German.[8]

Meanwhile the sons of Clovis were leading military expeditions in all directions. Two of them combined to conquer Burgundy, which they compelled to turn from Arian to Catholic Christianity. The Franks thus stood on the frontier of Italy, in what is now Switzerland and south-east France. In Italy that other German, Theodoric the Great, was giving peace to the land. The Franks were thus barred from Italy. They had to

---

[8] The Franks and Gauls of Neustria gradually became the French.

wait two hundred years for that prize; though the Lombards did plant Germanic institutions there, as we saw, soon after the death of Theodoric.

There was little unity among the Franks throughout the whole sixth century. More than once the Austrasians and Neustrians were at war with each other. In Neustria Roman traditions were still strong; for Neustria had been part of Roman Gaul, and the population was still largely Gallic. Neustrians were, therefore, more civilized than Austrasians. In Neustria, too, there was a tendency to support the royal power against the chiefs, just as citizens had once been directly subject to the emperors. In Austrasia the Germanic tradition persisted, of a free association of the chiefs, the *leudes,* with their freely-chosen king. It was the difference between a centralized state and a feudal society.

Nevertheless a century after Clovis all Franks were under one king, Dagobert I (628-638). The power of the Merovingian dynasty was at its height, and the Frankish power preponderant in all western Europe. A change came, however, in the administration of the state. Dagobert himself was engrossed with travels throughout the kingdom, hearing the complaints of great and small, restraining violent nobles, improving and unifying the laws. So he entrusted the central administration to the Mayor of the Palace (*Major domus*) and the bishops of Cologne and Metz. This transfer of authority was to lead in time to a change of dynasty.

Meanwhile the Merovingian kings continued for another century; though it was the Mayors of the Palace who ruled, usually one for Austrasia, another for Neustria. And in 687 Pippin of Heristal, Mayor for Austrasia, with vast estates on the Rhine, led the nobles of Austrasia to victory over the royal power in Neustria, at the battle of Testry. He was soon master of Burgundy as well. After his death the mayoralty was taken over by his son Charles, or Karl, Martel (714-741); though it required several battles to establish his authority.

The triumph of Charles Martel established also the supremacy of Austrasia within the Frankish kingdom, and was the beginning of a new era for the Franks. They had been loosely held together and imperfectly organized. Relations between Neustria and Austrasia were strained by the difference between Romanic and Germanic ideas. The tributary states on the frontiers, too, were in uncertain allegiance. Only

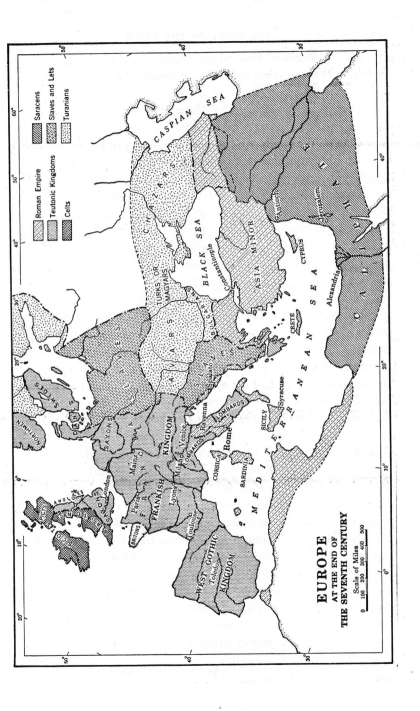

EUROPE
AT THE END OF
THE SEVENTH CENTURY

Scale of Miles

0   100   200   300   400   500

Legend:
- Roman Empire
- Teutonic Kingdoms
- Celts
- Saracens
- Slaves and Lets
- Turanians

CASPIAN SEA

CHAZARS

TURKS OR MAGYARS

BLACK SEA

A V A R S

S L A V E S

BULGARS

Constantinople

ASIA MINOR

Antioch

Jerusalem

CYPRUS

Alexandria

C A L I P H A T E

CRETE

MEDITERRANEAN SEA

ANGLES

London

SAXONS

Mainz

Paris

FRANKISH KINGDOM

Lyon   Milan

LOMBARDS   Venice

Ravenna

Spoleto

Rome

LOMBARDS

CORSICA

SARDINIA

SICILY

Syracuse

Toulouse

BRITONS

WEST GOTHIC KINGDOM

Toledo

the family of Pippin of Heristal and Charles Martel had the riches and the talents, the reputation and authority, to impose order upon this semi-barbarous world.

Swift expeditions of Charles Martel brought back to allegiance Bavaria, Frisia and Saxony on the East, Burgundy and Provence and Aquitaine on the South. And in 732 the infantry of Charles overcame the Moorish cavalry of the Emir Abderrahman, between Poitiers and Tours, and thrust them back into Spain. Western Europe was saved that day from Islam, a new religion, which had been carried swiftly by the horsemen of Arabia across North Africa to the Atlantic.

The work of Charles Martel was carried further by his son, Pippin the Short, who, as we shall see, became king of all the Franks. It was completed by Pippin's son, Charles the Great, or Charlemagne, greatest of all the new dynasty, the Carolingians.[9]

The story of Catholic Christianity among the Franks, in the two hundred years from Clovis to Pippin the Short, is confused. The Austrasians had not inherited Roman civilization. They were not likely to be greatly changed now, by a conversion like that of Clovis and the chiefs. Clovis himself had not adopted a new way of life; and his successor had heathen worship in the very shadow of the church at Cologne. The army continued to offer human sacrifices in war. The Franks had simply found in Christ a new champion. It was one of the singular rôles the Prince of Peace has been thought to play for barbarous men.

In Neustria, however, most of the inhabitants were still Gauls. Christianity had been among them for three hundred years when the Franks came. So that the Neustrian Franks, in the days of Clovis, were already familiar with churches and monasteries, bishops and priests and monks. The bishops there continued the functions they had acquired in late Roman days. The breakdown of the imperial administration had left them to be virtually civil rulers in their communities. They continued so among the Franks. They were thus custodians of the old Roman civilization, as well as of a new religion, with mysterious gifts to dispense.

Frankish princes therefore enriched the Church with gifts. Great landed estates, with armies of slaves, accrued to the bishops and abbots.

---

[9] The word is a derivative of the Latin *Carolus*, Charles. The Carolingians are so named for Charles Martel and Charlemagne.

And as these lands were regarded as given to God and could not be sold, they were always growing.

Spiritual impoverishment kept pace with the material enrichment of the Church. In a semi-barbarous society, bishops could hardly be chosen freely by the Christian population. They were sometimes hereditary, sometimes nominated by the kings, and tended to become their tools. Bishops of Roman descent were gradually displaced by Franks, who were barely literate. They were often devoted to the chase, led armies in the field, enriched themselves from the revenues of their dioceses, and sometimes returned openly to secular life.

Priests inevitably became like their bishops. Frankish nobles worked their sons into the ranks of the clergy, without regard to their fitness. The priesthood sank into semi-barbarism and violence.

In the monasteries there were many holy men, but no established Rule. The writ of St. Benedict did not run in the Frankish kingdom; and the writings of John Cassian and Cassiodorus were unknown or forgotten. The monasteries tended to lapse into barbarism; and the monks were esteemed by the populace chiefly because their prayers would relieve the torments of the damned.

The Frankish Church sat loose to the papacy, like the Celtic churches. The bishops of Rome had been supreme over the churches of Gaul; but the Frankish kings and mayors curtailed their powers. Indeed for a century after Gregory the Great there was no papal representative, or vicar, in the Frankish kingdom. Already among the Franks there was hostility to "Ultramontanism," or control from Italy, and an insistence on "Gallican Liberties," as they were later to be called.

As for the people, there was among them a superstitious awe of God, a pride in Christ as champion of the Franks, great credulity as to all sorts of miracles and portents, a profound sense of sin; but forgiveness was sought, not by repentance and amendment, but by gifts to the Church, the intercessions of holy men, the purchase of Masses, and occasionally by retirement into solitude. Everywhere there was violence, treachery, crime.

Some mitigation of the general violence came through the labours of monks from Ireland. Soon after Columba went to Iona, Columbanus, a monk of Bangor, set out with twelve companions for the Franks. King Gunthram of Burgundy gave him lands for a monastery on the western slope of the Vosges mountains; and soon daughter monasteries arose nearby. But the customs introduced were those of Celtic Christianity; and controversy resulted with the Frankish bishops. Columbanus, therefore, after ten years of successful work, moved to the Rhine, where he established Christian centres on Lake Zurich and Lake Constance. Still later he crossed the Alps into Italy, adopting the hermit life at Bobbio, on the little river Trebbia. There he died in 615. His hermitage is still one of the sacred places of Italy.

One of those who accompanied Columbanus from Ireland was Gallus, who continued his work on the Rhine, establishing on Mt. Steinach a monastery that was ever afterward to be known as St. Gall. As Gallus worked in harmony with the Catholic bishops, he avoided the contro-versy that pursued Columbanus and died at his post in 645(?).

Another disciple of Columbanus carried the Gospel to the eastern neighbours of the Franks, in Frisia. This was Wilfrid, an Englishman. He had studied in his youth in Ireland, and loved the Celtic Church; but he believed in the Catholic Church and its claims. He had cham-pioned Catholicism at the Synod of Whitby, and immediately there-after became abbot of a monastery of Irish foundation at Ripon, and then bishop of York. It was as bishop of York that Wilfrid went to Frisia, where he worked with little effect among the savage fishermen of what is now Holland.

A disciple of Wilfrid, one of his monks at Ripon, continued his work among the Frisians. This was Willibrord, who had gone from Ripon to Ireland for study and, after twelve years, went from Ireland to Frisia with twelve companions. On the way he was careful to secure both a commission from the Pope and the approval of Pippin the Short. Thus supported, he laboured for more than forty years, trained a native clergy, made missionary journeys into Denmark, and died in 739 bishop of Utrecht. Willibrord left in Frisia a flourishing church, in the midst of the prevailing heathenism.

Nevertheless in the early eighth century Christianity among the Franks themselves was sinking in a sea of barbarism. The Irish monasteries were on the frontiers. The gentle lives of the monks, and their cultivated lands, could not compose the general disorder of the Franks. Disorder was aggravated by political instability. It was the time when the Merovingian line was in decay, the conquered provinces renouncing their allegiance, and the Mohammedan Arabs overrunning Spain and Aquitaine.

In this critical situation two great men saved the West for Christianity and the German nations. One of them, as we have seen (p. 242), was Charles Martel, who subdued the rebellious provinces and drove the Arabs back into Spain. The other was Winfrid, an English monk, better known by the Latin name, given him perhaps by the Pope, Boniface, the well-doer.

Winfrid had grown up on the south-west frontier of England, being educated in a monastery at Exeter. He thus knew both the virtues and the defects of the Celtic Christianity of the near-by Britons. Winfrid was sure that the welfare of the churches everywhere depended on obedience to the bishops of Rome. He was doubtless right. Until the nations should emerge into civilization and public order, religious independence was premature.

So thinking, Winfrid went to Rome in 718, and offered himself for missionary work. He was sent to eastern Germany, to combat Celtic influence and bring the clergy into obedience to the Pope. Returning to Rome in 722, he himself took a special oath of obedience to the Pope and was then consecrated "bishop of Germany."

Details of the work of Boniface thereafter are not known. There was no Venerable Bede in the forests of Germany, to assemble and sift monastic annals, and preserve the essential facts for posterity. But we know enough to discern that Boniface is the true apostle of Germany. Working always as the representative of the Pope, he converted the Germans of Hesse and Thuringia, and organized the church in Bavaria.

From all this Charles Martel held aloof. Boniface was a foreigner; and his strictures upon the Frankish bishops, if deserved, were nevertheless resented by them and the mayor. But when Martel died, a new era began. The sons of Martel, Karlmann and Pippin, who now became mayors of Austrasia and Neustria, had been reared in Christianity and were sympathetic with Boniface and reform.

Karlmann summoned an assembly for Austrasia in 742. It is called the First German Council, being justly regarded politically as the first of the German Diets, and ecclesiastically as the first German Synod. Thenceforth in Austrasia Church and State were to go hand in hand.

The Council decreed that there should be a Synod each year, under the supervision of Karlmann, that all clergy not observing Catholic usages should be removed and deprived of their revenues, and that all monasteries must adopt the Rule of St. Benedict. The clergy were forbidden to go to war, or to indulge in the chase and in heathen practices. Bishops were appointed to the cities; and Boniface was set over all as archbishop.

A Synod at Soissons in 744, under direction of Pippin, adopted a similar programme for Neustria; and a general Frankish Synod at Cologne, under the joint presidency of Karlmann and Pippin, attempted to give effect to the decrees. Three bishops were deposed, one for warlike activity, one for adhering to Celtic customs, one for living the hermit life and performing miracles, instead of administering his diocese.

Next year Karlmann himself founded a monastery near Rome, went into retirement there, and in the end died at Monte Cassino. Other princes, repenting their murderous deeds, began to do likewise. Christianity was getting hold on the conscience of the Franks.

The next fifty years were a period of genuine progress. New monasteries, famed ever since, became advance centres of Christian civilization. In one of them, Fulda, Boniface lies buried.

Boniface best symbolizes the recovery for the papacy of the spiritual leadership of the West. Through him the Catholic ideal triumphed among the Franks.

Two things Boniface and the Frankish kings could not do for Catholicism. They could not overcome that new rival, Islam; they could not stop the growing alienation of the Greek East and the Latin-German West within the Catholic Church.

Islam, the new faith of the Arabs, arose within twenty years of the death of Gregory the Great. It captured North Africa, the home of Tertullian and Cyprian and Augustine, within a century. That land, already devastated by the Vandals, was in time withdrawn almost as completely from the Catholic Church as from the Empire.

The Roman Empire had taken little account of the Arabs. Their vast desert home in Arabia was a land of mystery, doing a little trade with the Empire in Syria and Egypt, and contributing a few mercenary soldiers to the legions in the East. Their most important cities, Mecca, some fifty miles from the Red Sea, and Yathrib, two hundred miles to the north, seemed but remote country towns. Six hundred years after Christ, there was yet no Arabian nation, only Bedouin tribes, forever massacring each other. The Arabs were dreamers, fighters, traders, curious figures in the bazaars of Alexandria and Damascus and Antioch, not a conquering race, disputing the earth with Rome. Then almost overnight all this was changed. Indeed, so great was the change that the Arabs themselves call earlier centuries "the time of ignorance." To them the new religion brought a new world; nothing earlier matters.

The founder of the new religion was Mahomet (570–632), camel driver for a rich woman merchant, the widow Khadija, whom Mahomet married. His work required caravan journeys across the deserts, and brought him into contact with Judaism and Christianity. There were synagogues in many places throughout Arabia, and Christian hermits here and there. Mahomet was made to think. Indeed monotheism was emerging among the Arabs themselves before Mahomet. To a few of the purer spirits it seemed that, above the gods, or *allahs,* of the respective tribes, there must be one *Allah* of all the tribes. He dwelt in heaven, not by the spring, or in the stone, or on the hill. He had created the earth. He ordered men's lives by irrevocable decrees.

So there had arisen Arab hermits, the *Hanyfs,* who sought a better religion and escape from the blood feuds that filled the land with slaughter.

Mahomet became a Hanyf, going apart for long periods of meditation. Ignorant and crafty and cruel, with a passionate animal nature, he had the ardour of the religious mystic and the zeal of the reformer; and through meditation he became possessed of certain large religious and ethical ideas. He went into trances and had visions of the one God, of a judgment to come, of the material torments of hell and the sensuous delights of paradise.

A decisive experience came to Mahomet at forty. He was wandering alone at night on Mt. Hira, not far from Mecca, and there fell asleep. In sleep an angel held before him a scroll and bade him read. Mahomet had not learned to read; but the angel insisted, and he read:

Truly man walketh in delusion when he deemeth that he sufficeth for himself; to thy Lord they must all return.[10]

---

[10] Rodwell, *The Koran,* Sura 96. In Everyman's Library.

This is the first revelation that Mahomet preached to his countrymen, that all men must give account before the judgment seat of Allah.

No further vision came for two or three years; and Mahomet was in great distress. He thought himself possessed by a jinn, or evil spirit. Then a second vision came:

Rise up and warn, and thy Lord magnify, and thy garments purify, and abomination shun, and grant not favours to gain increase; and wait for thy Lord.[11]

Thenceforth visions came rapidly; and Mahomet never again doubted his inspiration. Gradually he preached publicly, that men should put away their heathen vices and submit to Allah, that they should observe stated seasons of prayer, give alms, and avoid intoxicants.

Mahomet had no thought of founding a new religion. He was recalling men, he thought, to the pure religion of Abraham, the "Religion of the Book." [12] Nevertheless he attacked the popular religion at Mecca, declared it abhorrent to Allah, and that the fathers who had practised it were now in hell. Naturally there was popular resistance; but after two years pilgrims from Yathrib to the central shrine at Mecca, the *Kaaba*, accepted the doctrine of the prophet and besought him to come to Yathrib. That city had many Jews and a synagogue, was familiar with monotheistic ideas, and was therefore more favourable soil.

Mahomet preached a year in Yathrib, made many converts, and then, returning to Mecca only to find there a plot to assassinate him, fled with his Meccan disciples to Yathrib to remain. The flight, the *Hegira*, is the beginning of the Mohammedan era, June 16, 622.

Mahomet set up a theocracy at Yathrib. It was to be directed by revelations from Allah, communicated through the prophet. The city was now *Medinat en Nabi*, the city of the prophet. Mahomet's judicial decisions, later incorporated in *Al-Koran*, the Book, became the basis of a new jurisprudence. The controlling principle was *islam*, submission, to Allah. Islam became the name of the new faith. It exacted of its converts a confession of faith—"There is no God but Allah, and Mahomet is the prophet of Allah."

[11] *Ibid.*, Sura 74.
[12] Mahomet believed that there is a book in heaven, in which all knowledge is inscribed. The inspirations that come to the prophet in vision and dream are extracts from the heavenly book, sent down by Allah. The heavenly book is thus the source of all inspired literature. It is the "mother of the Book," whether Bible or Koran.

Mahomet built at Medina a mosque, where the faithful assembled for worship and instruction. It was modelled apparently on the synagogue; and its services were like synagogue services. Doctrines and practices were taught with great precision. The people thus acquired the rigid discipline, the *esprit de corps* of later Moslem armies. Intoxicants were forbidden and the cultivation of art, whatever made men soft; and women were required to conceal their charms behind the veil.

The new religion constructed a strong commonwealth, becoming a stronger bond than the old blood tie. Moslems were brothers everywhere. It was their duty to war upon unbelieving Arabs. They fought their own kinsmen. "Islam," they cried, "has rent all bonds asunder; Islam has blotted out all treaties." And those who fell in battle were promised paradise.

Mahomet at first regarded his revelations as a supplement to the Jewish and Christian Scriptures. Moslems prayed towards Jerusalem. But the Jews of Medina did not warm to the crude prophet. So Mahomet received a revelation requiring Moslems to pray towards Mecca. The new *Kiblah,* or orientation in prayer, proclaimed Islam to be distinct from Judaism, with an Arabian centre. The idea was made effective by the capture of Mecca in 630, the destruction of the idols there, and the exclusion from the Kaaba of all but the worship of Allah. The rest of Arabia soon submitted; and Islam became a national faith.

Having completed the conquest of Arabia, Islam looked abroad. There was no true religion anywhere else. Mahomet sent embassies to the Byzantine Emperor Heraclius and to King Chosroes of Persia, demanding submission to Allah and his prophet. The Arab empire was to be a universal, theocratic state. Mahomet was preparing armies to enforce his claims when he died, on June 8, 632.

Islam, in spite of the crudity of its founder, did have the requisite elements for a universal faith. It taught the unity and omnipotence of God, and the responsibility of every human being to Him. The stern requirement of submission was tempered by the doctrine that God sympathises with the efforts and aspirations of all. The Suras of the Koran all begin with the ascription, "In the name of God, the Compassionate, the Merciful."

The first Caliph, or successor, of the prophet was his friend Abu Bekr, who had the oracles of Mahomet collected to form the Koran, whose one hundred and fourteen Suras still contain all the precepts of Moslem morality. The second Caliph, Omar (634-643), became the founder of the Arab Empire. His Bedouin horsemen made raids into Palestine and Irak, found victory easy and plunder rich, and learned how weak the dying Roman Empire was. In 636 they defeated the last army of Heraclius in the East at the river Yarmuk and conquered Syria. In the following year they overran Mesopotamia, and two years later Egypt.

Religion gave the horsemen of Arabia an inspiration and cohesion that made their work permanent. The new religion, too, commended itself to the conquered nations. It seemed not inferior, and not too different, from Christianity, in the form in which these lands now held it. Indeed Islam seemed less compromising to the unity of God than did Trinitarian Christianity, and less open to the suspicion of idolatry than Christians who venerated images.

When Heraclius died in 641 nothing remained of the Roman Empire in Asia except Asia Minor. Fifty years later the Arab dominion extended all the way from the border of India, through Egypt and North Africa, to the Atlantic. In 711 an Arab chief led his horsemen across the Strait of Hercules into Spain. The mountain overshadowing the strait still bears his name. It is Djebel-Tarik, or Gibraltar, the Mount of Tarik.

The Christian Gothic kingdom in Spain was subdued in eight years. Then the Arabs crossed the Pyrenees into Gaul, where they held much of the south until 732, when thrown back into Spain by Charles Martel (p. 242). Germanic Europe was thus saved for Christianity, as was the truncated Byzantine Empire by a greater man, the Emperor Leo the Isaurian (717-741). Of him we know less, because he was a heretic and ecclesiastical historians have done him scant justice. Leo's repulse of formidable Saracen [13] attacks upon Constantinople in 717 and 718 meant more for Christianity than did Martel's victory at Poitiers. Constantinople was nearer the centres of Moslem [14] power; the peoples of the Balkans were but slightly Christianized and were in political disorder. Islam might well have spread like a prairie fire through all southeastern Europe.

The vast Arab empire soon fell apart. In Spain was the Caliphate of

---

[13] "Saracen" is a word of doubtful origin, applied in the Middle Ages to Mohammedans, of whatever race.

[14] A Moslem, or Muslim (Arabic, *muslim,* "a believer in Islam") is a Mohammedan.

the West, sometimes called the Emirate of Cordova; in Africa the Caliphate of Egypt, whose capital was Cairo; in Asia the Caliphate of the East, or the Caliphate of Bagdad, whose most famous Caliph was Haroun-al-Rashid, a contemporary of Charlemagne and the hero of many stories of the *Arabian Nights*.

Political disruption, however, did not stop the development of Islam. It ceased to be a crude faith of the Arabian deserts, gathering new substance and colour from the ancient cities it conquered, quite as Christianity had from Greece and Rome. Indeed, as we saw, the closing of the University of Athens, by the Emperor Justinian, made Islam the latest heir of Greek thought. Culture became more advanced in Islam than in Europe in the Middle Ages. Her capitals—Bagdad and Cairo and Cordova—were all great intellectual centres. Other Arab cities— Samarcand and Damascus, Fez and Granäda—were centres of literature and art, science and industry, while Europe was passing through the Dark Ages. Europe was thus flanked by an aggressive Islam, while the Catholic Church was educating her German converts in both Christianity and civilization.

CHAPTER X

CHARLEMAGNE ATTEMPTS AND FAILS TO
RESUSCITATE THE ROMAN EMPIRE

THE menace of Islam, the disorders of Europe, and the diminished estate of the Roman, or Byzantine, Empire, inclined the popes to rely more and more on the kings of the Franks. The theory at Constantinople still was that the West was part of the Empire. Only Justinian had been able to make the theory effective; but the emperors still had an exarch at Ravenna. Of more consequence, however, to the bishops of Rome were the Lombard kings. If they became masters of Italy, the papacy was likely to be reduced to a Lombard bishopric. In times of danger, therefore, the popes, unable to get help from Constantinople, depended on themselves or looked to the Franks.

A series of events completed the breach between Rome and Constantinople. A party in the East, influenced, among other things, by the example of Islam, demanded the abolition of image worship in the churches and indulged in some image breaking, iconoclasm. The Emperor Leo the Isaurian, in a decree of 726, supported the Iconoclasts and forbade the worship of images anywhere in the Empire. Riots followed throughout the East and revolt in Italy, where images of the saints were dear to the populace. Pope Gregory II sent a stern letter to the Isaurian: "Hearken to us, emperor; abandon your present course and accept the holy church as you found her, for matters of faith and practice concern not the emperor, but the pope. . . . You persecute us and vex us tyrannically with violent and carnal hands. We, unarmed and defenseless, possessing no earthly armies, call now upon the prince of all the armies of creation, Christ seated in the heavens, commanding all the hosts of celestial beings, to send a demon upon you, as the apostle says: 'To deliver such an one unto Satan for the destruction of the flesh, that the spirit may be saved.' . . . Now, therefore, we exhort you to do penance; be converted and turn to the truth; obey the truth as you found and received it." [1]

Meanwhile the people of Rome expelled the imperial prefect; and King Liutprand of Lombardy overran the Exarchate. He was soon on his way to Rome. This was too perilous for the papacy. So Gregory tried conciliation with the Emperor, and used his moral authority to turn the Lombards back to the north.

The controversy with Constantinople, however, soon revived. Iconoclasm persisted; and Pope Gregory III, in an Italian Synod of 731, excommunicated all Iconoclasts. This included the Emperor; and peace was never re-established between the throne and the papacy. Pope Gregory thenceforth looked for protection to the Franks. In 739 he sent to Charles Martel the keys to St. Peter's tomb, conferred upon him the titles Consul and Patrician, and invited him to Rome, to assume the imperial insignia. Martel was too busy to come; and two years later the Isaurian, Pope Gregory and Martel were all dead.

The papal policy continued, however, as before. When Martel died and his sons, Karlmann and Pippin the Short, became mayors of Austrasia and Neustria, they co-operated, as we saw, with the English Boniface, to reform the Frankish church and bring it into obedience to the papacy. When Karlmann renounced the world, leaving Pippin to govern alone, the latter soon received the reward of his piety. The Merovingian line was now hopelessly decadent. The time was ripe for a change of dynasty. The chiefs of the nation were persuaded to offer Pippin the kingship. He made a show of leaving the decision to the papacy; and Pope Zacharias ruled that he who had the power of kingship should have the name as well. A national assembly at Soissons deposed the feeble Childeric III, who was then shut up in a monastery. The assembly proclaimed Pippin king of the Franks. In the cathedral at Soissons Archbishop Boniface anointed him. Two years later Pope Stephen came himself, to anoint the new king and his sons with holy oil, and announce excommunication for any who would choose a king from another family.

Pippin soon rewarded Pope Stephen, who was hard pressed once more by the Lombards. Crossing the Alps into Italy, Pippin was proclaimed

[1] Translated in Thatcher & McNeal, *Source Book for Mediaeval History*, Scribner, pp. 95–100.

by the Pope Patrician of Rome, the highest honour in the gift of the
Emperor himself. As Patrician Pippin subdued Lombardy, occupied the
exarchate of Ravenna and whatever cities the Lombards had taken from
the Emperor, and transferred these, not to their lawful master, but to
St. Peter. The Emperor protested without effect. The popes were now
to be political, as well as ecclesiastical, rulers and were to continue so for
a thousand years.

Whatever scruples Christians may have had, about such an acquisition
by the Vicar of Christ of a political domain, were allayed by a pious
fraud. It was discovered that Constantine the Great, on his conversion,
had made over to the papacy all Italy and the West. Indeed it was to
avoid infringement of papal rights that he had transferred his own seat
to the East. The documentary evidence, the forged *Donation of Constantine,* was not questioned. Five centuries later Dante, an imperialist,
consigned Constantine to hell in poetic measures, for this supposed sin
against civil authority.

Pippin died in 768, leaving his sons Charles and Karlmann a kingdom
greatly extended and a royal authority reinforced by spiritual sanctions.
Fortunately Karlmann also died soon. The political unity of the Franks
was thus saved; and the stage was cleared for the action of Charles, soon
to be called Charles the Great (Charlemagne), whose mighty physical
frame, so dear to his people, was matched by great genius. A thorough
Frank in body and habits, Charlemagne (768–814) was reverent to both
the ancient Roman culture and the Catholic faith.

Before long Charlemagne was in Italy with an army. Didier, king of
Lombardy, had made another incursion into papal lands; and Pope
Hadrian had appealed to the northern Patrician. Charlemagne quickly
crushed the Lombard forces, took the crown for himself, and sent one
more king to the monastery. Received at Rome with grateful submission, the young hero saw for the first time its marvels, the great churches,
with their perfect ritual, their appealing music and wonder-working
relics. Here were, he did not doubt, the Hebrew ark of the covenant, the
table at which Christ ate the Holy Supper, the robe he wore to Calvary,
phials of blood from his pierced side. Who could measure their
miraculous powers? And where in his own rude country could anything
approach this perfection in the science of pleasing God? Charlemagne
determined to bring such things to his Franks.

In the next few years many letters went from the king to his clergy, calling attention to the decay of learning and the crudity of public worship. To the abbot of Fulda he wrote in 787: "Karl, by the grace of God king of the Franks and the Lombards and patrician of the Romans, sends loving greeting in the name of omnipotent God to abbot Baugulf, and to the household of monks committed to his charge. Know that we, with the advice of our faithful subjects, have regarded it as important that in the bishoprics and monasteries of our realm those who show themselves apt in learning should devote themselves to study, in addition to their regular duties as monks. . . . We have frequently received letters from monks in which they make known to us what they are praying for, and in these letters we have recognized correct sentiments, but an uncouth style and language. . . . Therefore we have begun to fear lest, just as the monks appear to have lost the art of writing, so also they may have lost the ability to understand the Holy Scriptures. . . . Therefore we urge you to be diligent in the pursuit of learning, and to strive with humble and devout minds to understand more fully the mysteries of the Holy Scriptures." [2]

Three years later a royal instruction went to the clergy everywhere. "Since we are very desirous that the condition of our churches should constantly improve, we are endeavouring by diligent study to restore the knowledge of letters which has been almost lost through the negligence of our ancestors, and by our example we are encouraging those who are able to do so to engage in the study of the liberal arts. In this undertaking we have already, with the aid of God, corrected all the books of the Old and New Testament, whose texts have been corrupted by the ignorance of copyists. Moreover, inspired by the example of our father Pippin, of blessed memory, who introduced the Roman chants into the churches of his realm, we are now trying to supply the churches with good reading lessons. . . . Accordingly we have commanded Paul the Deacon,[3] our beloved subject, to undertake this work. And he, wishing to obey us, has read through the treatises and sermons of the various catholic fathers and has picked out the best things. These selections he has copied clearly without mistakes and has arranged in two volumes,

[2] Thatcher & McNeal, p. 55.

[3] Paul the Deacon was a scholarly priest of Lombardy, who after the fall of that kingdom was invited to the Frankish court. He is the author of the only important history of the Lombards.

providing readings suitable for every feast day throughout the whole year. We . . . now authorize these volumes and commend them to all of you to be read in the churches of Christ." [4]

Not content with an educated clergy and an improved public worship, Charlemagne planned the education of the populace itself. He knew that the countries of his kingdom, except Germany, had once been literate. He would recover for his people the enlightenment of Roman Gaul. He himself set the example by establishing a small academy, the School of the Palace, which followed him about, and where he and his children and the members of the court went to school. At the head of the academy was placed an Englishman, Alcuin, a scholarly monk of York who was also of noble lineage. The lamp of knowledge still burned in the monasteries of the British Isles. In Ireland Armagh, in Scotland Iona, in England Jarrow and York, were important centres of learning. York had probably the most extensive library north of the Alps. So Alcuin was brought from York to the continent, to be head of the palace school and Charlemagne's minister of education. The Carolingian scholars whose names have survived were his pupils—Rabanus Maurus, archbishop of Mainz; Theodulf, bishop of Orleans; Benedict of Aniane, who reformed monasticism in Aquitaine; Einhard, secretary to Charlemagne, who wrote his life and the annals of the time. These and other pupils of Alcuin founded schools, attached to the monasteries and cathedrals at Fulda and Tours and elsewhere.

The aim of this educational effort was not what is called scientific. The men drawn from everywhere to Charlemagne's court were not research scholars, but competent translators and copyists. The Christian Scriptures contained the truth by which men were to live. It was the work of scholars to see, first, that the text of Scripture was uncorrupted, that copies were available, that men could read; second, that such other literature as would supplement revelation was similarly preserved. So the characteristic contribution of the so-called Carolingian Renaissance to the future is this, that it initiated that long-continued occupation of copying and correcting, preserving and illuminating, ancient manuscripts. A few men, however, were true scholars; and their love of knowledge strayed outside their proper field. The earliest copies of a

[4] Thatcher & McNeal, p. 56.

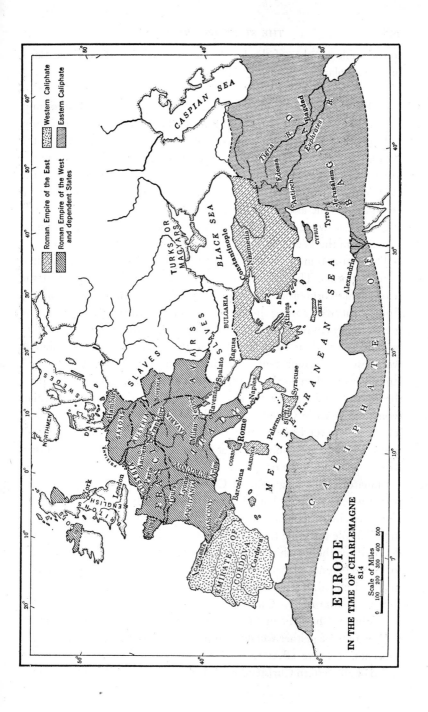

EUROPE
IN THE TIME OF CHARLEMAGNE
814

Scale of Miles
0   100   200   300   400   500

Western Caliphate
Eastern Caliphate
Roman Empire of the East
Roman Empire of the West
and dependent States

CASPIAN SEA

BLACK SEA

MEDITERRANEAN SEA

CALIPHATE OF

TURKS OR MAGYARS

SLAVES

AVARS

SLAVES

BULGARIA

Ragusa
Spalato

SWEDES

NORTHMEN

DANES

London
York
ENGLISH

FRISIANS

SAXONY

BAVARIA

AUSTRIA

THURINGIA

LOMBARDY

Milan
Ravenna
Rome
Naples

CORSICA
SARDINIA
SICILY
Palermo
Syracuse

CRETE
Athens

Constantinople
Nikomedia

Antioch
Edessa
Bagdad

Euphrates R.
Tigris R.

Jerusalem
Tyre
CYPRUS

Alexandria

EMIRATE OF
CORDOVA
Cordova
CANTABRIA

Barcelona

Aachen
Paris
Lyons
Arles
AQUITANIA
GASCONY
FRIULI

considerable number of the Latin classics are the work of these Carolingian scholars.

In the year 800, twenty-six years after Charlemagne's first visit to Italy,
he was there again, to restore order in the Papal States and, unhappily,
to hear charges against the character of Pope Leo III. At a synod in the
Basilica of St. Peter, Pope Leo was acquitted; and two days later, in the
same place, as Charlemagne was kneeling before the great altar at the
close of the Christmas Mass, the Pope placed upon his head an imperial
crown, while the assembled Romans shouted: "To Charles, most pious
Augustus, crowned of God, life and victory!" There was again a Roman
Emperor in the West.

This restoration of an institution so long dead is less amazing than
at first appears. The belief that the Roman Empire was a part of the
permanent world-order still persisted; and many monuments of the
Empire survived among the Germans, to excite their wonder still. The
greatest German princes felt the superiority of Rome, and were proud to
be called Consul, or Patrician. Besides, the emperors at Constantinople
were usually incompetent, sometimes debased; and they and their
Empire were alien to the West, the population being Greek in spirit,
the prevailing language Greek. To crown all, a beautiful Athenian
woman now sat in Caesar's seat, and a wicked one, the Empress Irene.
There had never been women Caesars. The throne was vacant, men
would say, and election as valid at Rome as at Constantinople. So they
tried to bring back the past.

Einhard, in his biography of Charlemagne, says the latter was surprised when crowned that Christmas Day. Possibly, as to the moment
and the circumstances; but Charlemagne had been assuming the
imperial rôle for some time. When a General Council at Nicaea in 787
declared for the worship of images, and Pope Hadrian sent its decrees
to Charlemagne, to be announced in the German churches, Charlemagne declined. Instead he announced a decision of his own, in the so-
called *Caroline Books*. Quite in the manner of Constantine the Great
or Justinian, Charlemagne set aside both Pope and Council. Images, he
said, were to be neither worshipped nor destroyed, but used to adorn the
churches. To give effect to this decision, Charlemagne summoned a
synod of all western Christendom to Frankfort, as Constantine had done

to Nicaea. He himself presided, stated the issue, then announced his decision, which the Synod accepted. In the *Caroline Books* the Emperor at Constantinople is called "king of Byzantium," and Charlemagne asserts his own prerogatives as "ruler of Germany, Gaul, Italy, and the surrounding provinces." It was a Roman, not a German description of the West.

Three years later Pope Leo crowned the *de facto* Emperor. It was worth the risk, he thought; though he must have anticipated some difficulty with the masterful Emperor.

Charlemagne had a plan for the Empire. It was to be a universal theocracy, a state ordained of God and ruled by one chosen of God. It was to be the Roman Empire, but this time a Holy Roman Empire. In his own circle of intimates Charlemagne had been calling himself David, in imitation of that ancient king who had also been called of God. Alcuin of York called his master "priest," and "deputy of Peter." Theodulf of Orleans called him "vicar of Christ," and "vicar of God."

For thirty years before his coronation, Charlemagne was preparing a worthy territorial basis for the universal state. By absorption or annihilation of neighbouring nations, he brought into one kingdom the whole Germanic world. He subdued the Bavarians, most powerful of the tributary peoples, whose duke Tassilo belonged to the ancient family of Agilolfings and regarded the Carolingians as upstarts. Charlemagne reduced the country in 788, divided it into counties under his own officers, and consigned Tassilo to monastic confinement. It took longer to subdue the Saxons. They were stoutly resisting Catholic missionaries and, when threatened with the sword of Charlemagne, destroyed the church at Deventer and slew the converts there. Charlemagne overcame them after many expeditions, destroyed their national idol, the Irmensaüle, set garrisons throughout the country, forced Christian baptism upon the population, and at a national assembly exacted an oath to pay tribute and offer no resistance to the spread of Christianity. The land "was divided among bishops, abbots and priests, on condition of their preaching and baptizing among them." The more stubborn of the Saxons took refuge among the Danes and Slavs; but in the end even their national hero Widukind, deserted and hopeless, submitted and was baptized.

When Charlemagne's campaigns were over, the work begun by

Martel and Pippin was complete. The whole Germanic race was united in one kingdom, except the English in their island home and the Norsemen in the remote Danish peninsula. Francia, the new Roman Empire, now embraced modern France and the Low Countries, Germany and Switzerland, and Italy as far south as Rome. In all that dominion men were required to take an oath of allegiance to the Emperor, which was also a vow to serve God and defend the Catholic Church. To be a sinner was thenceforth to be a criminal also, as in the Mosaic Law.

Charlemagne was able to give some reality to his ideal. National assemblies were deprived of their legislative functions and became only advisers of the sovereign. Listening to the assembly, he gave his own decisions, then promulgated them in the form of Capitularies, many of which still exist. Personal representatives of the sovereign, the *missi dominici,* went everywhere in pairs, a count and a bishop, publishing the Capitularies, hearing the appeals of individuals from the decisions of local officials, righting wrongs, reporting to the Emperor.

But Charlemagne died in 814; and the union of the Germanic nations proved transient. The Empire was too divergent. There was no unity of language. Italians and Gauls spoke dialects of the Roman language, the Germanic nations their German dialects. There was a similar diversity of law. Charlemagne was careful to preserve the customary law of each nation. His Capitularies were supplementary to existing systems. So that law was not the same for Lombards as for Saxons, for Bavarians as for Alemanni. True there was one religion and one government for all; and so long as government remained strong, union continued possible. But government was not strong after Charlemagne; and only one of the constituent nations of the empire, the Austrasians, from whom the Carolingians had sprung, stood firmly for unity.

Disintegration was retarded for a single generation by the memory of the great emperor and the prestige of the Carolingian name; but everyone knew that the master hand was gone. Charlemagne's successor was his son Louis the Pious (814–840), a high-minded man, devoted to duty, but of too mild a temper for the turbulent nobles and so morbidly conscientious as to be unduly susceptible to priestly counsels. Once he confessed his faults in an assembly of the empire, and asked to be put to penance. It was a manner of confession ill-suited to kingship. Once Louis' rebellious sons, having defeated him in battle, compelled him to

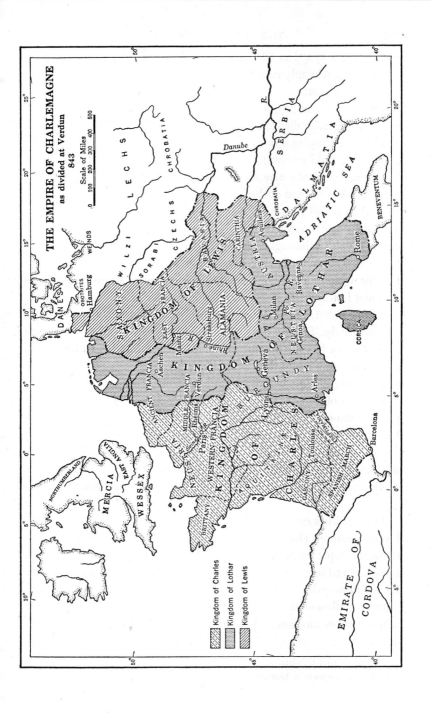

THE EMPIRE OF CHARLEMAGNE
as divided at Verdun
843

Scale of Miles
0 100 200 300 400 500

Kingdom of Charles
Kingdom of Lothar
Kingdom of Lewis

read before a synod at Soissons a recital of his faults. The assembled bishops then solemnly removed his military belt and dressed him in the garb of a penitent.

Dynastic quarrels disturbed all Louis' reign, and broke out with new violence when he died. After three years of civil war, his three sons divided the Empire among them. By the Treaty of Verdun, in 843, Charles the Bald received Neustria and Aquitaine, the West Frankish Kingdom, which we may now suitably call France. Lewis the German received the lands east of the Rhine, the East Frankish Kingdom, which we may now call Germany.[5] Lothair, the eldest son, received a narrow territory, running from the North Sea to Rome, which received his own name. It was Lotharingia, the Kingdom of Lothair.[6] It was weakest of the three kingdoms, having neither racial nor geographical unity. Yet Lothair was nominally emperor of the Holy Roman Empire.

When Lothair died in 855, Lotharingia was divided among his three sons. The eldest, Louis II, was nominally emperor but practically king of North Italy. Thus in forty years from the death of Charlemagne the Holy Roman Empire became a vague, unreal thing. It had been exotic from the first, alien to the German spirit; and only genius could maintain it. The necessary genius was lacking when Charlemagne died.

The ruin of his educational establishment was swift, though less complete. It too was exotic; and the only approach was through the Latin language. When education was no longer a road to the favour of the emperor, Germans threw away their books. The improvement in public worship, however, proved permanent; and in many monasteries earnest scribes continued to copy and beautify ancient manuscripts.

Two institutions of the Middle Ages arose on the ruins of the Carolingian empire. These were the mediaeval papacy and feudalism. Of these, the papacy was the one effective instrument of unity. The empire had dissolved into nations. The nations were dissolving into numberless feudal principalities, ruled by dukes and counts, bishops and abbots, with virtually sovereign rights. It was fortunate that the churches were still one in constitution and creed and ritual, with the Pope at the centre of all.

[5] Germany dates its national existence from 843 and the Treaty of Verdun.
[6] The modern form is Lorraine.

Seven centuries had prepared the papal supremacy. As early as the third century the bishops of Rome were asserting a certain primacy among all bishops; and the claim was supported by an honourable record in doctrine and discipline and missionary activity. So that the primacy of the Pope, if denied in the East, was sympathetically regarded in the West. By the fifth century the Petrine Theory was accepted through all the West, the theory that, by divine appointment, the Pope had the authority over all bishops that Peter was thought to have had over the other apostles. A rising tide of papal influence reached its crest in Gregory the Great. He was influential with the barbarians in defence of law and order, influential through all the Church for uniformity and discipline, and the greatest single force for the extension of Christianity. Then at length the Frankish kings gave protection to the papacy; and they and Boniface bound the Frankish Church to Rome.

The Frankish royal power would almost certainly have limited the papacy to purely spiritual functions, had not that power declined. The papal view of the Holy Roman Empire was that the papacy had brought it into being. The imperial view was that the emperor was successor to the ancient Roman emperors, to whom the bishops of Rome had been subject like all other men. And the imperial view was now reinforced by theocratic ideas; the emperor was as surely called of God as was either pope or bishop.

The imperial view prevailed while Charlemagne lived; and, though slightly challenged, with Louis the Pious also. Nevertheless things were different as soon as Charlemagne died. The papacy ventured to mix in quarrels between Louis and his sons; and, as we have seen, the emperor was even put to penance in the presence of the princes. It was an omen.

The papacy was now to embark upon a career not entirely spiritual; and an adequate legal basis for its pretensions was necessary. So far the Petrine Theory had served; and, since about the year 500, there had been as well a body of documents, "the apostolic canons of Dionysius Exiguus," which provided a definite legal basis. The "canons" were a collection of Bible precepts, quotations from Catholic Fathers, decisions of Church Councils, letters of early Roman bishops, together designed to show what prerogatives popes were meant to exercise. But the canons covered the period only from Constantine, whereas the papacy claimed to have been empowered by Christ himself. To complete the legal basis, documents were needed that would show the papacy exercising its prerogatives before it won the favour of the state. Some monk, or monks, of France performed this pious service. They created a body of documents, the "Decretals of the Pseudo-Isidore," which showed that the papacy, from the days of St. Peter, had exercised the powers that now it claimed.

Five centuries later, when the Renaissance began to restore education to Europe, all scholars knew that the Decretals were fraudulent. There were mistakes as to the names of popes, the order of events, and what not; and the Decretals were written in the corrupt Latin of the Middle Ages. Meanwhile they had served their purpose; and apologists could say that the rightful powers of the papacy were not affected by the misdirected zeal of monks.

With the acceptance of the Decretals a new theory of Church Law came into being, the Decretal Theory. It is that decretals, or decisions, of the bishops of Rome are of equal authority, as ecclesiastical law, with the New Testament, the writings of early Church Fathers, and the decrees of General Councils.

The first to apply the Decretal Theory with vigour and consistency was Pope Nicholas I (858–867). Like Charlemagne, he was a really great man; and the idea governing all his activity was that the papacy is a divine, not a human, institution. It was appointed of God, to be the defender of right and truth everywhere. There was no question it was not competent to decide, and no person whom it might not judge. When Ignatius, Patriarch of Constantinople, was removed for condemning the immorality of the imperial court, Pope Nicholas intervened and was given a respectful hearing. He did not succeed in restoring the Patriarch; but he raised effectively the question of papal authority in the Greek half of the Church.[7]

Similarly in the West, when King Lothair II of Lorraine tired of his wife and put her away to marry his paramour, Pope Nicholas intervened for the injured queen. The real issue was the old one, Were there to be national churches, or "one holy Catholic Apostolic Church," under the bishop of Rome? Lothair had received ecclesiastical approval from a

[7] The Ignatian question outlived both Nicholas and Ignatius, disturbed relations between East and West for two centuries, and finally divided the Church into the Greek Orthodox and Roman Catholic.

synod at Aachen, representing all three Frankish kingdoms. Even the papal legate to the synod had been induced to approve. But Nicholas, wielding the sword of excommunication, forced the restoration of the queen. Heaven seemed to the populace to confirm the papal action. King Lothair, to get release from the papal ban, went to Rome, swore falsely on holy relics, and on the way home was smitten with the Italian fever and died. It was, men said, a judgment of God.

Nicholas intervened with equal success in France, this time to maintain the right of all ecclesiastics to appeal from other courts to the papacy. Bishop Rothad of Soissons had removed a guilty priest, and was overruled by his archbishop. The bishop appealed to the pope; and the archbishop had him arrested. Pope Nicholas demanded of both the archbishop and king Charles the Bald that Rothad be sent to him for trial. The king submitted. Rothad appeared before the pope, was acquitted and sent back to his diocese in charge of a papal legate. It was the first case, so far as we know, in which the papacy cited the forged Decretals of the Pseudo-Isidore.

When Pope Nicholas died his theory of the papacy was generally accepted. All Christendom was a church state, whose emperor was the pope, to whom both princes and bishops were vassals. It was a theory that only resolute and capable popes could enforce; but the theory itself was now Catholic truth.

Like the mediaeval papacy, the order of society known as feudalism rose on the ruins of the Carolingian Empire. True, it existed as early as Merovingian times; but it was confirmed by the disorders of the ninth century. News of the decay of the Carolingian power spread everywhere; and internal disorders were aggravated by attacks from without. The last three years of Charlemagne had been darkened by the knowledge that, although he had subdued so many German and Slavic foes, the Norsemen were now prowling around his coasts. After his death they entered the rivers, followed them inland, and established themselves in bands of five or six hundred. From these inland stations they pillaged the countryside. Before the ninth century closed, most cities of western Europe had suffered their depredations; and the churches and abbeys suffered most, because it was in them the people took refuge. The devastations did not cease until the early tenth century, when the

Norsemen, finding less and less to steal, settled down in the familiar surroundings of earlier raids. Charles the Bald went so far as to give to a dreaded chief Rollo and his men a part of northern France. It was agreed that Rollo should be made a duke, do homage to Charles, and adopt Christianity for himself and his people. He was therefore baptised in 912, settled with his men a part of Neustria, and brought "Normandy" into being.

What the Norsemen were doing in the north, the Saracens did in the south. Like two of their predecessors in North Africa, the Phoenicians and the Vandals, the Saracens became pirates. They devastated Malta and Sicily, Corsica and Sardinia, burned the seaport of Rome and the abbey of Monte Cassino. From the east, too, came invaders of the Hunnish race, descendants of Attila's Huns and the Turks, and called by the Greeks and Latins Hungarians.

In the general disorder of western Europe, neither kings nor counts could protect the people, who had to rely on themselves. Gradually men associated themselves together for defence; and fortified castles dotted the land. These castles became centres of a new system of relationships, cutting across the allegiance of citizens to the king. This was feudalism.

One aspect of feudalism, however, was the holding of land from the king, while giving him services instead of rent. Kings placed their lands, lands acquired by inheritance and conquest and confiscation, in the hands of trusty men, and received in return a vow of perpetual fidelity and soldiers for the royal armies. Lands so granted were a "feud," or "fief," and tended to pass from father to son, in quite the ordinary way, so long as there was a male heir to perform the feudal duties. And these feudal holders were not farmers, but knights fighting for the king. Their occupation was regarded as higher than farming, because it made men intimates of the king.

A further development came with the granting to trusted vassals of sovereign rights. They were empowered to impose taxes, administer justice, levy soldiers, on their fiefs; and were not visited by state officials, so long as they fulfilled their feudal obligations. Such exemption from state control was called an *immunity;* and immunities were most frequently granted to monastic lands and those of great ecclesiastics.

In a society that was undergoverned, as the Frankish kingdom was, immunities were often valuable supplements to the central government;

but they did convert vassals into independent sovereigns, and lessen the sentiment of citizens for the state. The tendency was increased by *subinfeudation,* the granting by vassals to others of lands they themselves held from the king. Vassals of the king thus had their own vassals; and lands nominally belonging to the king were often separated from his control by several intermediate persons. So the country was filled with petty sovereigns, each bound by a feudal oath to someone above or below him. Theoretically the authority of the king reached everywhere; practically men were bound to their immediate feudal superior.

The disorder of the ninth century inevitably encouraged feudalism. Life and property were precarious. Such private owners as remained tended to surrender their lands to more powerful neighbours, and receive them back as fiefs.

Feudalism thus displaced the great establishment of Charlemagne. That establishment was Romanic and alien; feudalism was Germanic. It naturally came to provide the framework within which mediaeval society grew up. Indeed the Middle Ages are sometimes regarded as having begun with the death of Charlemagne. In feudalism, as in education, the Germans returned then to the old paths.

The social relationships of the Middle Ages, idealized in romantic literature, are all feudal—the devotion of the vassal to his lord, the paternal duty of the lord to his vassal, the code of knightly honour that is called chivalry.

CHAPTER XI

A SECOND ATTEMPT AT A HOLY ROMAN EMPIRE

IN THE closing years of the ninth century the dismemberment of the Carolingian empire was finally confirmed. In France the Carolingian family had died out. In Germany a great-grandson of Charlemagne still reigned. This was Charles the Fat, only surviving son of Lewis the German. The magnates of France offered him the crown there as well; and for three brief years the Frankish kingdom was again under one head. But no glamour of the Carolingian name could conceal the dullness and incompetence of Charles the Fat. So at length the exasperated nobles and ecclesiastics deposed him, in a Diet at Tribur in 887. Soon seven kingdoms stood where the Frankish kingdom had been. They were Germany, Lorraine and Italy, France [1] and Navarre, Provence and Burgundy. There were also Brittany and Aquitaine, kingdoms in fact, though not in law. And in Italy petty princes warred with each other, to determine who should be emperor.

Everywhere there was anarchy, in the etymological sense, that is, the absence of any effective central power. Kings were insecure even within their little kingdoms. When a French king rebuked the Count of Champagne, the latter replied: "I am hereditary Count by the grace of God; this is my rank. As to my fief, it comes to me by inheritance from my ancestors, and is in no way connected with your domain. Do not oblige me to do, in defence of my honour, things which will be displeasing to you." Western Europe had scores of petty sovereigns, the feudal lords.

Within each principality the feudal lord administered justice; but no civil power could enforce justice between the feudal lords themselves. Doughty knights never thought of referring their differences to the

---

[1] The lands between the Seine and the Loire, which Charles the Bald had given to Robert the Strong, founder of the Capet dynasty and the only noble who had stood effectively against the invading Norsemen. His territory was known as the Duchy of France, and became a kingdom, slowly absorbing the rest of what is now France.

king. Their appeal was to the sword; and God was thought to give judgment for the victor. Might tended therefore to be right, except when the Church threatened ecclesiastical penalties.

Fortunately the Church did deal with many breaches of public order. She put violent men to penance; and if they resisted, recourse was had to excommunication, exclusion from the Church and the sacraments. The excommunicated one was to be avoided by all other persons and, if he died, was buried in unconsecrated ground. That meant eternal death, since outside the Church there was no salvation. Indeed eternal death was sometimes directly imposed upon the stubborn. The Church washed its hands of them. This was the greater excommunication, or anathema.

The whole edifice of discipline was completed in the papal interdict. The pope, to force peace upon a troublesome knight or submission to papal authority upon some wilful king, cut off the whole county or nation from the Church. The altars were stripped, crosses and images removed from the churches. The Mass was said in silence behind closed doors, but only for infants and transients and the clergy. The community was required to fast and pray and go unshaven, until the ban should be removed. The community was, for the period of the ban, forsaken by God and the Church.

The effectiveness of ecclesiastical discipline was increased in the tenth century by a monastic revival. Monks were normally more respected than the "secular clergy." The "seculars," having remained in society, had not quite forsaken all to follow Christ. The monks were the saints of the people.

Sometimes of course the defects of the monastic ideal overcame its good intentions; [2] but no one doubted the validity of the ideal itself. And as often as monasticism declined, earnest men recalled it to the lost ideal.

Revival came just as the tenth century opened. Count Berno of Burgundy, who was also an abbot, undertook to restore discipline in the monasteries of his county. His feudal superior, Duke William of Aquitaine, co-operated by giving him lands for a new monastery at Cluny, near the French border. There the famous monastery of Cluny was

---

[2] Personal poverty could be made to mean little, where monks shared an extensive property, splendidly equipped and worked by tenants; and obedience to one's superior meant little unless he was superior.

founded in 910; and Abbot Berno made certain additions to the Benedictine Rule, as safeguards against future decline. All monasteries adopting the new Rule were to form a Congregation of Cluny, an association
of monasteries, under the supervision of the parent monastery. Benedictine monasteries would thus surrender their autonomy. Learning, too,
was to be discouraged. The disordered world was more and more manifestly the enemy of the soul. It was more and more futile therefore to
labour for any adornment of the present life. Men must fix their eyes on
heaven.

Learning declined greatly in the tenth century, because of Cluny. The
love of literature survived only in those Benedictine monasteries that
remained outside the Congregation, and especially those of Carolingian
foundation. They kept the impress of Charlemagne.[3]

The Congregation of Cluny spread through all Europe in the tenth
century. The abbot was second only to the pope in influence. Indeed the
Abbot Odo, who died in 942, quite surpassed the pope. The Senator
Alberic, who had set up a republic at Rome, brought Odo into the
diocese of the pope himself, to reform the monasteries and replace unworthy monks with others from Cluny.

Cluny rendered great services for two hundred years, before it also
fell a victim to the inherent defects of monasticism. A great institution,
the Truce of God, was a contribution of Cluny to public order.

The example of monks, however, and ecclesiastical discipline, could
not alone overcome the general disorder of the tenth century. Too many
bishops and abbots were involved in the evils they condemned; and
discipline was hard to administer. Even the anathema, if it damned too
many, might encourage a doubt that it did in fact damn any. So political
action was necessary.

Twenty years after the deposition of Charles the Fat a movement back
to unity began in Germany. The dukes of four great duchies—Franconia
and Saxony, Bavaria and Swabia—chose Conrad, duke of Franconia, to
be king of all Germany, perhaps because he was descended in the female
line from Charlemagne. A National Assembly ratified the choice, the
archbishop of Mainz crowned and anointed the new king; and he be-

---

[3] Notably Hersfeld, Corvey and Hildesheim. Out of such monasteries came Widukind,
historian of Saxony, and Paul the Deacon. The annals of Hersfeld and Hildesheim are
still valuable sources of historical knowledge.

came Conrad I (911–918). Conrad reduced the other duchies to submission, wielding the sword, while the Church aided him with the sword of excommunication.

Coercion roused so many hatreds that on his deathbed Conrad advised that Henry, duke of Saxony, should succeed him. Only Saxony and Franconia agreed; but Henry subdued Swabia and Bavaria with the sword, then conquered Lorraine. There was thus a united German nation once more, under Henry I, "the Fowler" (919–936).

Henry I built a strong military system and dealt successfully with the latest menace to Europe, the Magyars, a Mongolian people, who had moved westward into Europe and settled the Pannonian plain. From Pannonia their mounted archers raided Germany, and at times penetrated to the plains of Italy and France. King Henry developed a mobile cavalry defence, operating from well garrisoned forts, that finally brought the Magyars to battle at the Unstrut river and decisively defeated them, bringing glory to his house and putting heart into all the German peoples. Within Germany, too, Henry concealed an iron hand beneath a silken glove, dealt firmly with separatist tendencies, and in the end secured the consent of all the duchies to the succession of his son Otto, who was to prove strong enough to repeat the experiment of Charlemagne and restore the Holy Roman Empire.

The circumstances that first took Otto the Great (936–973) into Italy were like those that had drawn Pippin and Charlemagne. Civil war in Italy had become chronic; and Rome itself was suddenly thrown into confusion by the death of the Senator Alberic in 954. The papacy became the plaything of Roman factions, that secured the chair of St. Peter for their favourites. Infamous men were put in the supreme place in the Catholic Church; and western Christendom looked to Otto for deliverance from this shame. He marched into Italy in 962, was crowned emperor by the disreputable Pope John XII. Otto took an oath to protect the Holy See. Pope John acknowledged himself a subject of the emperor and swore allegiance. The people of Rome swore to elect no pope without the emperor's consent.

The Holy Roman Empire was once more in being. It was never again to include France, only Germany and Italy; but the underlying ideas were the same. And Otto was able to give them some effect. True, neither he nor his successors could maintain order in Italy. The emperors were foreigners, men said. What right had they in Italy? Otto did, however, control the papacy. When John XII, a dissipated youth of twenty-five, forgot his oath of allegiance, the emperor returned, held a synod in St. Peter's basilica, heard accusations against the pope and declared him deposed. The synod chose, with the emperor's consent, a reputable layman, chief secretary of the papal court. He was ordained a priest, advanced through all the clerical orders in a single day, and at night became Pope Leo VIII. As pope he yielded to the emperor greater powers than even Charlemagne had exercised. Thenceforth the emperor was to choose the pope, and invest all bishops with the symbols of their office.

The Holy Roman Empire reached the height of its power some seventy years later, when a duke of Franconia became Henry III (1039–1056). Henry was highly educated, and of necessity by monks. He was also devoutly religious, and adopted the plan of enforcing public order with religious weapons. France had already been doing so. The Church there, envigorated by the Cluny revival, was using its spiritual authority to mitigate the ceaseless warfare of the feudal lords. It instituted what was called a Peace of God, a covenant of armed knights to submit their differences to the civil courts. The covenant proved too exacting for men who did not farm their own lands, had no intellectual interests and little occupation except fighting. So the Peace was reduced to a Truce of God, enforced by penance. Knights pledged themselves to keep the peace each week from Wednesday night to Monday morning, and during the sacred feasts of the Church. Churches and cemeteries were to be inviolate at all times. Women also and the clergy, merchants and labourers, were to have "peace every day." The Truce was thus a covenant, enforced by the Church, to secure that at least religion and industry and commerce would not be disrupted by violence. The Truce became part of the public law of France.

Henry III acquired the Truce of God from France, and tried with some success to establish a religious basis for public order in Germany. At synods of the duchies he publicly forgave his enemies, asked the princes to do the same, and placed them under oath to settle their differences without recourse to arms. Henry set himself at the same time to reform the Church at large, with the aid of Cluny.

An earlier emperor and pope had co-operated to secure a celibate

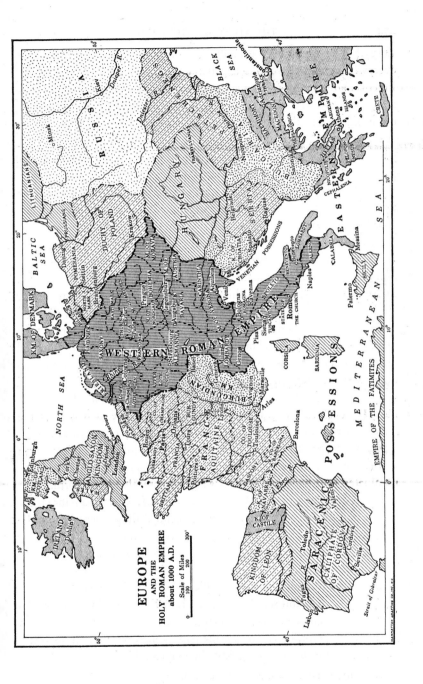

EUROPE
AND THE
HOLY ROMAN EMPIRE
about 1000 A.D.

Scale of Miles
0   100   200   300

clergy.[4] The philosophy of monasticism commanded the conscience everywhere; and there was a general sentiment for clerical celibacy. Practice, however, differed widely. In Lombardy all clerical orders married, their children received the legal status of the mother, and were often endowed by their father out of the property of the Church. A synod at Pavia in 1022, under pressure from the papacy, required all clergy to put away their wives and withdrew from the children their special legal privileges. A similar decree was forced through a synod of Saxony.

Now, twenty years later, Cluny was bending its efforts to secure an unworldly clergy. This was thought to require first of all that bishops and abbots should be elected in harmony with Canon Law, the former by the clergy and people of the diocese, the latter by the members of their order. All outside interference was described as simony; and the nomination of ecclesiastics by emperor or king or feudal lord was so regarded. Henry III assisted Cluny to this extent, that he alone would nominate the higher ecclesiastics within the Empire, and that he would do it on merit. Ecclesiastics were no longer to be warriors or politicians or sportsmen. At a National Synod of the German clergy in 1044, Henry charged the whole German episcopate with simony, and proposed excommunication for future irregularities.

A dramatic climax to all the imperial effort after reform came in 1046. Party politics in Italy had brought it about that three men were at the same time claiming to be pope. Henry entered Italy once more with an army, summoned a synod to Sutri, and there secured the condemnation and removal of all three. In the remaining years of his reign, Henry nominated four popes, all Germans and all committed to reform.

The most notable of these German popes was Leo IX (1049–1054). He had been a disciple of Cluny. He now declined the emperor's nomination, until it should be confirmed by free election in the diocese of Rome. He took with him to Rome, to be his confidential adviser, a monk of Cluny, Hildebrand.

Leo proved himself a worthy disciple of Nicholas I. He went wherever evil was reported, and set it right. Synods in France and Germany submitted to his censures. The Christian masses and the monks were with him. The emperor, by reforming the papacy, had restored an authority that was soon to be turned against the emperor himself.

---

[4] Henry II (1002–1024) and Pope Benedict VIII.

It was Leo IX who quite unconsciously strengthened the papacy by separating Latin from Greek Christendom. Relations had long been strained. Not the least of the reasons were the differences in race and temperament. Mediaeval Italians, for example, were a mixture of Latin and German stocks. Mediaeval Greeks were a mixture of Greek and Asiatic stocks, especially Slavs and Armenians. They were temperamentally unlike. So ecclesiastical controversies in the East still tended to be doctrinal, those in the West disciplinary. Rome wearied of the ceaseless doctrinal discussions of the East.

The formal cause, however, of separation of East from West was that Latin Christendom changed an oecumenical Creed. The Nicene Creed, in its original form, speaks of the Holy Spirit, "who proceedeth from the Father." Western churches began to say, "who proceedeth from the Father and the Son."

The ancient Fathers had differed about the "procession of the Holy Spirit"; but for three hundred years no one tampered with the Nicene Creed. Then synods in the West began to add the second phrase, affirming the "double procession" of the Holy Spirit; and the Caroline Books vigorously supported the change. At last a council at Arles, fairly representative of the whole West, formally admitted the "double procession" to the Nicene Creed. No pope was present; but the papacy did accept the new form. So doing, it violated the Catholic doctrine that a General Council is infallible, and threw doubt upon the first and most famous of all the Councils, that had been predominantly Greek.

Formal division between Greek and Latin Christians did not come, however, for another two hundred years, until Leo IX. Then the Patriarch Michael, seeking support in the West, wrote certain bishops of south Italy in 1054, charging the Latins with heresy in the matter of the double procession, and adjuring the bishops to enter into fellowship with the East.[5] Pope Leo sent the patriarch a bitter, arrogant letter; and a papal legate laid an anathema upon the altar of St. Sophia at Constantinople. The patriarch and other eastern patriarchs replied with an anathema; and the breach was complete. "The Holy Orthodox Church" and "The Catholic Church" went their separate ways forever.

The schism worked to the advantage of the popes. Their constituency

[5] Geographically and commercially connected with Greece, south Italy and Sicily remained somewhat Hellenic in race and character.

was now precisely defined, and that part of the Christian world excluded where their claims were least likely to be admitted. They were the more free to cultivate their own garden.

The victory of the papacy over the German imperial power was not long delayed. An emperor was no match for a pope, when the latter was not hampered by misfortune or misconduct. The Empire was of yesterday, the papacy an ancient institution, whose authority was thought to extend beyond the grave.

When Leo IX died, Hildebrand was papal legate at the German royal court; and he secured the nomination of three more reforming popes. The last of them, Nicholas II, made Hildebrand archdeacon of Rome and the real head of affairs. Nicholas also held a synod at Rome in 1059, which decreed that thenceforth popes should be elected only by the Cardinal Clergy [6] of the diocese of Rome. It was a departure from both recent practice and Canon Law, but was well calculated to deliver the papacy from both local politics and imperial control.

There was marching and counter-marching of papal and imperial supporters for some twelve years, until Hildebrand himself was elected pope in 1073. The Roman populace had raised a shout for him at the funeral of his predecessor. The Cardinal College aquiesced; and Hildebrand became Pope Gregory VII (1073–1085), without consultation with the young emperor Henry IV. The thirteen years of the new papacy were an unresting struggle for supremacy between the *Sacerdotium* and the *Imperium*.

A document survives from the time of Gregory, that is known only by its Latin name, *Dictatus Papae*.[7] It was long believed to be the work of Gregory himself, but is only demonstrably a document emanating from the Cardinal College. It is someone's formulation of the papal prerogatives; but it does embody the guiding principles of Gregory VII. The Church, it says, was founded by God himself; and the pope is its universal bishop. All other bishops are his suffragans, whom he may de-

[6] "Cardinal Clergy," or hinge clergy, are clergy appointed by the pope to permanent positions in the churches of the diocese of Rome. Seven are suburban bishops; the rest are deacons and presbyters of Roman churches. Cardinals throughout the world become so by virtue of their appointment to be deacons or presbyters of churches at Rome. Since Nicholas II only these cardinal clergy participate in the election of a pope.

[7] Translated in Thatcher & McNeal, p. 136.

pose and reinstate. Emperors, too, are his representatives, whom he may depose. He may annul the decrees of any earthly power; and none may annul his or judge his acts. All men everywhere may appeal to the pope from the judgment of any earthly tribunal.

Such ideas were not new; but this squat, ill-favoured pope, of peasant origin, had the conviction and the courage to attempt their enforcement. A Lateran Synod in 1075 was the first great public demonstration of Gregory's programme. It opened the "Conflict of the Investiture," which convulsed Europe.

The synod received a papal proclamation, forbidding the investiture of ecclesiastics by laymen. Investiture was the ceremony in which recently elected bishops and abbots received the ring and staff, the symbols of their new authority. And since they now administered lands and were members of the feudal system, it seemed necessary that they take the usual oath of fidelity and assume feudal obligations. Feudal superiors, therefore, wished to invest such ecclesiastics as held land within their territories. Pope Gregory, however, perceived that the feudal oath strengthened local loyalties, against the universal authority of the papacy. He therefore interpreted the investiture of ecclesiastics by laymen as a form of simony and forbade it.

Submission by the emperor would make effective government in Germany impossible; for bishops and abbots held very extensive lands from the crown, and had their own fortresses and armed retainers. So Henry IV continued to invest ecclesiastics, and was supported in so doing by the National Assembly. Stern letters passed between emperor and pope, the former declaring Gregory deposed, the latter excommunicating Henry.[8]

Within eight months the morale of the German nation was broken. The bishops had been going over, one by one, to the papal side. The king had never been popular. Rebellion threatened in both Saxony and Swabia. The government wavered between national sentiment and fear of the Church, and finally decided for the papacy. The government declared in October, 1076, that Henry must make his peace with the papacy or be deposed, and invited Gregory to come to Germany to judge the king.

The result is not surprising. Europe believed salvation to be by a legal

[8] These letters may be read in Thatcher & McNeal, pp. 146–157.

arrangement, and accepted the Petrine Theory as to the place of the pope in the scheme. Christ had been the legal representative of God in the world. He had bequeathed his authority to St. Peter. That authority had then passed to the bishop of Rome. Inevitably, therefore, the papal authority was supreme over all civil authority.

Henry sent his submission, and proposed to go to Rome for absolution. He would avoid at all costs a public humiliation within Germany, and hurried across the Alps. But Pope Gregory had already set out for the north, determined to carry the demonstration of his authority into Germany. Pope and emperor met at Canossa in Tuscany; and there the emperor, in the poor dress of a pilgrim, waited three days barefoot in the snow, before the castle gate of the Countess Matilda, until granted a reluctant absolution. In letters to the German princes Gregory made the most of the royal humiliation. The *Imperium* could never again sustain the claim to be the first power on earth.

The Conflict of the Investiture did not close for another fifty years, when another pope, of royal blood and broader views than Gregory, found it possible to maintain papal prerogatives, while taking thought for the dignity and difficulties of kings. Pope Calixtus II, of the royal house of Burgundy, entered into a covenant with Henry V in 1122. On the plain of Worms, in the open air and before a vast assemblage, Henry and a papal legate signed the Concordat of Worms and sealed it with an oath. Ecclesiastics were thenceforth to be elected and invested without interference from the civil power. Only ecclesiastical processes should make one an ecclesiastic. But within the Empire the emperor might be represented at both election and investiture, in acknowledgment that his interests were involved. And the new ecclesiastic, before getting legal possession of his lands, must take the feudal oath and receive the feudal sceptre.

This became the legal basis for the determination of all cases. Thenceforth the ecclesiastic, as such, required only the sanction of the pope. And, indeed, so much authority as the Concordat left to emperors was voluntarily surrendered by Henry's successor.

The results of the Conflict of the Investiture were far-reaching, and accrued slowly through four centuries. The imperial power was permanently diminished, the allegiance of many of the richest and most powerful subjects of the emperor being divided. The pope was no longer an ally but a menace. So the universal, theocratic state of Charlemagne, Otto the Great, and Henry III became an empty dream.

Naturally, there began a gradual alienation of the German people from the papacy. Bishops and abbots stood with the popes; the nobles were divided; the burghers stood with the emperors. And as Germany changed slowly from an agricultural to an industrial and commercial community, as culture settled gradually in the cities and rich burghers crowded the feudal lords, German patriotism became a synonym for resistance to the papacy.[9] The process, however, was slow.

Another line of emperors thought the lost imperial prerogatives worth one more struggle. The royal line changed twice within a decade after Henry V, so tenacious were the German princes of the right of election. The kingship passed to the duchy of Swabia. The reigning house there was the Hohenstaufen, whose representatives proved to be men of quite exceptional capacity. Greatest of the Hohenstaufen kings was Frederick I, called Barbarossa, or Red Beard. His reign of nearly forty years (1152–1190) was the most brilliant in the history of Germany; and he remains a great national hero still, whose statue appears in many public places in the Reich.

Secure at home, Frederick Barbarossa turned to recover the imperial authority in Italy and with the papacy. Circumstances were against him. Social development had been increasingly industrial and commercial. Great cities had arisen in Lombardy—Pisa and Genoa, Pavia and Milan, Verona and Venice—and a new set of interests. Feudalism provided no framework for an industrial and commercial community; and the Lombard cities had struggled through to independence of the ruling nobles and bishops. The cities became republics, learned to defend their rights by appeal to ancient Roman law, raised their own militia, entered into leagues for common defence.

The democratic impulse reached Rome itself. The senate was revived, a militia organized, and the pope driven out. Arnold, a priest of Brescia, who had acquired republican ideas in the Lombard cities and in the

---

[9] One sees here a reason why in the sixteenth century the Protestant revolt broke out first in Germany, setting the pace for revolt elsewhere.

lecture hall of Abelard at Paris, was preaching a new phase of ecclesiastical reform in the streets of Rome. The Church, he said, should surrender its vast estate and return to the simplicity of Christ.

The movement of events conflicted with imperial interests; and Frederick Barbarossa was soon across the Alps with an army. He frightened some of the cities into submission, fought his way into Rome, restored the government of the pope, and handed Arnold over to the papal prefect, to be burned for heresy. Returning to Lombardy, Frederick summoned a Diet to the Plain of Roncaglia, that he might settle accounts with both the cities and the papacy. A commission of lawyers decided that all the rights that once belonged to the kings of Lombardy now belonged to the emperor. The decision would reverse the movement of a century, destroying republican forms and reviving obligations long obsolete.

Frederick's claim to the old royal rights affected papal lands as well, and embroiled him with the papacy. There resulted another papal schism, lasting this time nearly twenty years, cardinals of imperial sympathies refusing to acknowledge the choice of the majority.

In the end both republicanism and the papacy won. Events in Lombardy raised a league of Lombard cities, which defeated Frederick at Legnano in 1176. Pope Alexander III had entered into alliance with the league, and profited by its triumph. The Peace of Venice in the following year granted the league a long truce, restored the papal lands, and acknowledged Alexander to be the rightful pope. In Germany itself most of the clergy had supported him, and hundreds of monks had gone into exile to France for their loyalty.[10]

Frederick Barbarossa was drowned in 1190, while leading a crusade to recover Jerusalem, and left the papacy at the height of its power. The fruit of one hundred and twenty-five years of struggle was now gathered. The Golden Age of the papacy began.

[10] Events in England also strengthened the papal position. The Norman kings had kept the clergy there submissive to the crown; and Henry II was trying to keep them so for the Plantagenet house. To this end he made his friend Thomas à Becket archbishop of Canterbury, only to see him turn into an obstinate defender of ecclesiastical independence. In the long quarrel that ensued, Archbishop Becket was murdered in his cathedral. The kingdom was horrified; and Henry, to avoid excommunication, made humble submission to the pope. Four years before the defeat of Frederick Barbarossa at Legnano, England saw its king abase himself before the papal legate. In May, 1172, Henry took an oath of obedience to the papacy, and did penance at the tomb of Becket, being publicly scourged by the monks of Canterbury. St. Thomas of Canterbury had done more for the papacy in death than in life.

CHAPTER XII

THE GOLDEN AGE OF THE CATHOLIC CHURCH

THE twelfth and thirteenth centuries are the Golden Age of Roman Catholicism. The pope, as vicar of God, was now supreme. Chivalry, which was knighthood in the service of religion, was busy with crusades. Monasticism flourished in new forms, better suited to the age. Ecclesiastical discipline was effective, the cultus elaborate and impressive. Art produced a new architecture, the Gothic, conceived especially for the worship of God. Mediaeval science, under the name of Scholasticism, was enlisted in the service of religion, discovering rational foundations for the dogmas of the Church. All the ideals and institutions of mediaeval society came to full flower; and in the midst was the resplendent figure of Pope Innocent III (1198–1216).

Ascending the papal throne soon after the death of Frederick Barbarossa, Innocent III exercised an authority unmatched before or since. Romantic lovers of Catholicism look back to him, as do German imperialists to Frederick Barbarossa.

In Germany papal action was restrained, by reason of recent events and the party feeling aroused. In Italy, however, Innocent championed the independence of the cities, and restored the Papal State. In France he had to deal with a nation, united under Philip Augustus and advanced in national sentiment; but the great pope subjected both king and nation to ecclesiastical discipline. Philip had tired of his wife Ingeborg, consigned her to a convent, and been granted by a French synod the dissolution of his marriage, that he might wed another. Ingeborg appealed to Rome; and Innocent required the king to submit the case to him, under pain of national excommunication. Philip rallied the nation for resistance; and Innocent suspended religious services in France, until after seven months the waning loyalty of the people foreshadowed re-

Multitudes enlisted, women and children, old men and boys, robbers and prostitutes, all stirred about the holy places, anxious also to ensure their own souls against the torments of the hereafter. Christians had long been taught that martyrdom is especially meritorious. So wise a man as Origen had thought martyrdom a sort of second baptism, by which those who had sinned after the first baptism might again find forgiveness.

So a vast and motley crowd set out in the spring of 1096, led by Peter the Hermit and Walter the Penniless. There was no military organization, no commissariat; and beyond Germany were six hundred miles of wilderness. The crusaders could only live off the country; and were slaughtered by the enraged inhabitants. The emperor Alexius sent a force to rescue them, then hurried them across the Bosphorus into Asia Minor, where three hundred thousand are said to have fallen in hopeless battle. A regular army followed in the autumn, under Robert of Normandy and Tancred and Godfrey of Lorraine, all figures of romance. Nicaea was captured; and the crusading army crossed the deserts and defiles of Asia Minor, took Antioch and Edessa, and entered Jerusalem, July 15, 1099. A certain William of Tyre describes the moving scene, as the crusaders went in procession to the Holy Sepulchre, recovered part of the cross and bore it to the Temple. "All the people went after, which wept for pitie, as much as if they had seen the Saviour Jesus Christ still hanging on the cross."

A tiny Christian kingdom was established at Jerusalem, and garrisons left at Edessa and Antioch. They were islands in a sea of Mohammedanism.

After fifty years Edessa fell to the Saracens. It had been a Christian centre from the very earliest times, and was second only to Jerusalem in the affection of the Church. Besides it was a military outpost of Jerusalem; and its fall threatened the new Christian kingdom. So Bernard of Clairvaux roused Europe to another crusade. Two great armies set out in the summer of 1147. They did not co-operate; nor did the kingdom of Jerusalem co-operate with them. In the end the crusaders returned with nothing but the glory of devotees.

Forty years later Saladin, governor of Syria and Egypt for the Sultan, exasperated by the conduct of the kingdom of Jerusalem, led a Moslem crusade for its recovery. Jerusalem was taken. All Europe was stirred again. Frederick Barbarossa, Philip II of France, and Richard Coeur-de-

Lion of England, all raised armies in 1189. There followed the most romantic of the Crusades, made famous by Sir Walter Scott in *The Talisman*, with many brave deeds, but with jealousy and strife and terrible losses. Frederick Barbarossa, after defeating Saladin at Iconium, lost his own life by drowning; and his army was destroyed. Richard was given command of the English and French. A great knight, but neither general nor statesman, and hampered by jealousies, Richard won minor successes; but Jerusalem remained to Saladin.

When, less than ten years later, Innocent III became pope, Europe still remembered the unfinished task in Palestine; and Innocent despatched a fourth crusade, only to see it turned against Constantinople, for the commercial advantage of Venice. There were shocking scenes in the streets of Constantinople, and even in holy St. Sophia itself.[4] This was the outcome of an undertaking to recover

> Those holy fields
> Over whose acres walked those blessed feet
> Which, fourteen hundred years ago, were nailed,
> For our advantage, on the bitter cross.[5]

The great pope, however, did not yet despair. One purpose in calling the Fourth Lateran Synod (p. 283) was to rouse Europe to one more crusade. This time it was to be thoroughly prepared, and to be unsullied by the irregularities and excesses of earlier crusades. Innocent did not live to see the Fifth Crusade set forth, and was therefore spared a prolonged spectacle of dallying and doublemindedness, involving the honour of the papacy itself.

The period of the general crusade soon closed.[6] The populace, unable to distinguish mass excitement from divine inspiration and believing that laudable ends justify all means, could still be roused to such adventures; but responsible leaders found the ends dubious, the cost too great.

The Crusades, however, had permanent and quite unexpected results. The commercial empires of Genoa and Pisa and Venice were founded.

---

[4] The story is told by Villehardouin, a French knight, in one of those superb French memoirs, that have so little counterpart in English. Villehardouin's account of events has been translated by Sir Frank Marzials, in *Memoirs of the Crusades*, by Villehardouin and Joinville, in *Everyman's Library*.

[5] Shakespeare, *King Henry IV*, Act I.

[6] Local crusades were to continue for a long time.

The wares of the Levant flowed into Italian cities, and thence to the north, giving new wealth and colour and importance to the towns. The new arts and crafts, Arabic chemistry and medicine, meant much to European society. As for the knights-errant that remained at Jerusalem, they found Syrian society more refined and dignified than their own; and their fanaticism was tempered. Frankish and Arab gentlemen became friends. Some of the former would be astonished to find that cultivated gentlemen knew nothing of popes, and were only faintly amused by the anathema. Such things, little perceived at the time, would work silently in Christian minds, preparing change.

Monasticism flowered again in the Golden Age. The Cluny movement had succumbed to those twin enemies of monasticism, riches and sloth, aggravated by the illiteracy that followed upon the exclusion of the classics. The Cistercians, another revival within the Benedictines, then flourished briefly. Robert of Arbrissel, abbot of a Benedictine monastery in Brittany, despairing of restoring there the strict Rule of St. Benedict, founded a new house at Cîteaux in 1098; and Bernard of Clairvaux (1091–1153) entered there in 1113, with his brothers and several friends. Cîteaux itself speedily became a popular centre, too lax for Bernard. So he plunged with a few disciples into the forest, and in a sunny valley founded the house of Clairvaux.[7] Bernard of Clairvaux became the ideal religious hero of the Middle Ages, representing in his person all the religious ideals of the time. Himself an ascetic monk, and exhibiting the mystical piety that Catholicism has always revered, Bernard was also an ardent churchman. A sober scholar, he was a stern represser of individualism in thought.

The personality of Bernard gave the Cistercians [8] great influence for more than a century. The white cowl of the Cistercian monks was the symbol of purity everywhere.

When Bernard died in 1153 there were five hundred Cistercian abbeys; and it was resolved to have no more. Yet there were soon two thousand abbeys. By the time of Innocent III the Cistercians were returning to the old paths.

New orders, however, sprang up in the thirteenth century. There were

[7] Clairvaux is from the Latin *clara vallis,* sunny valley.
[8] The name is from *Cistercium,* the Latinized form of Cîteaux.

hospital orders, the Hospitallers, for the care of the sick;[9] and spiritual orders of knights.[10] These were both by-products of the Crusades. More important, however, were two orders of begging Friars, the Franciscans and Dominicans. These associations of mendicants both arose during the papacy of Innocent III; though that great man seems to have been almost unaware of them, and they were not officially recognized until after he died. Both orders were new departures. That is to say, they were not revivals within the Benedictines, but attempts to adapt monasticism to the needs of the time. The Benedictines had begun in a flight from the world, a world too violent and chaotic to be redeemed. The Benedictine Rule, therefore, permitted indifference to society; but the Mendicants would live among men, preaching the Gospel and, if necessary, begging their bread. The Franciscans arose in Italy, to lead the neglected peasantry back to religion. The Dominicans arose in Spain, to overcome heresy and restore doctrinal purity. The former were, therefore, evangelical preachers, the latter doctrinal preachers.

The Franciscans were founded by Giovanni Bernadone (1182–1226), son of a rich merchant of Assisi in Umbria. The boy was nicknamed Francesco because of his proficiency in French. In his early twenties he was arrested, like St. Antony of old, by the command of Christ to the apostles to go forth and preach, without money or food or change of raiment. Giovanni felt called to restore apostolic Christianity; and set out to travel the world, with bare head and bare feet, begging his bread and preaching repentance. The result was amazing. There was in Giovanni a singular simplicity and purity, coupled with a love for all living things. Disciples sprang up everywhere, who became missionaries to their own neighbourhoods. They met once a year at Assisi, for confession and counsel, and called themselves little brothers, *fratres minores*. Soon an organization became necessary; and after fifteen years they were constituted by the papacy the order of *Fratres Minores,* and commissioned to be preachers and pastors at large. The brothers were popularly known as Minorites, or Franciscans.

The Friars[11] went barefoot, in brown cape and a girdle of rope. Their

[9] Best known are the Crucifers in Italy, the Hospitallers of the Holy Spirit in southern France, and the Brothers of St. Antony.

[10] Like the Knights of St. John, with their black mantle and eight-pointed white cross, devoted to the care of sick and poor pilgrims to Jerusalem. The Knights Templars, with a similar purpose, wore a white mantle, with an eight-pointed red cross.

[11] Friar is from the Latin *frater*, brother, through the French *frère*.

ideal was poverty in the service of mankind. Some travelled preaching; some did menial work for the poor in their own communities. They had no monasteries. Even the cells to which they retired were not their own. When the inevitable gifts of land and monasteries came, the Franciscans simply used the property, while transferring title to the nearest town.

The order soon outgrew its simple founder; and the purity of his ideal was smudged before he died. Begging was continued, toil often forgotten.[12] The Friars declined money; but their agents accepted it. Education became a hobby, not a handmaid. Franciscans became teachers in the young Universities.[13] Many of the Chapter-General, as the annual assembly was called, demanded some relaxation of the Rule; and a new Rule was adopted in 1221, from which Christ's commission to the apostles was eliminated. Francis, therefore, resigned the leadership to an ambitious disciple, Elias of Cortona; and he himself went with a few disciples into solitude, where he died five years later, blind and broken-hearted.

On his deathbed Francis dictated a *Testament* to the Friars. It was a plea for return to the first ideals of the order. Five years later, in 1226, Francis was canonized; but his *Testament* was declared invalid. It was a truly Catholic action. Men here below could not reach his ideal; but they were authorized to pray to him, and St. Francis in heaven would importune the Father on their behalf.

The dissension in the order was never healed. There continued to be *Conventuali*, who would conform to common monastic usages, and *Spirituali*, or *Observants*, who clung to the ways of St. Francis.[14] Nevertheless the Franciscans were a great force for two hundred years. They were the true evangelists and preachers of repentance, where the parish priests were absorbed with the Mass. Their world renunciation and contemplation broke forth in hymns of repentance and love, a few of which appear in modern hymnologies.[15] But the most far-reaching work of the

[12] Francis himself spoke mordantly of "the friar fly, who plies his jaw more than his hands."

[13] It is said, "Paris destroyed Assisi."

[14] Pope Leo X in 1517, on the eve of the Protestant Reformation, divided the Franciscans formally into two orders, the *Spirituali* and the *Conventuali*.

[15] The Franciscan hymn best known to English-speaking Christians is probably that of Thomas of Celano, translated by Dean Stanley:

"Day of wrath, O dreadful day!
When this world shall pass away."

Franciscans was the cure of souls. They were authorized by the papacy to hear confession and became the spiritual advisers of the people, coming thus into conflict with the parish priests. They soon gained a firm footing, too, in the Universities. Paris admitted them before St. Francis died, in return for their prayers for the dead of the University's teachers.[16]

The second mendicant order was founded by Dominic (1170–1221), a learned Spanish priest of noble birth and a contemporary of St. Francis. Stirred by the persecution of the Albigenses in France, Dominic urged that heresy should be overcome by preaching the Gospel, and by setting an example of poverty and self-denial. He and his disciples visited the Albigenses in prison, while Innocent III was waging a holy war upon them. When Innocent died, his successor promptly instituted the Order of Preaching Brothers,[17] popularly known as the Dominicans. Like the Franciscans, they were empowered to preach and hear confession everywhere, but with a special view to the conversion of heretics. They cultivated liberal studies from the first, sought chairs in the Universities, and were zealous missionaries to Judaism and Islam. Dominic and a few companions were given quarters in the papal household.[18] And a few years after the death of Dominic, the papacy established the Holy Tribunal of the Inquisition, and placed it in the hands of the Dominicans (p. 283).

The Franciscans and Dominicans were organized alike. Each had a General at Rome, a Provincial over the monasteries of each nation, and a Guardian or Prior over each monastery. Their histories were to be different as their aims were different, the Franciscans being more loved by the people, the Dominicans more powerful in the Church.

Most Catholic Christians, of course, were neither absent on crusades nor in the monasteries. They were playing the normal rôle of householders and citizens. What appearance would their religion present to an observer? In other words, what was Catholicism after a thousand years of growth and accommodation?

It was a very elaborate religious system indeed, and included many things that had been unknown to Cyprian and Ambrose and Augustine, some that would have seemed strange to Gregory the Great. In spirit,

[16] The first at Paris was Alexander of Hales, the famous Scholastic.
[17] The official title is still The Order of Preaching Brothers, *Ordo fratrum praedicatorum*.
[18] The Master of the Sacred Palace has ever since been a Dominican.

however, it had not changed; it was thoroughly otherworldly still.

Nothing better illustrates this than does the new architecture, the Gothic, created then for the worship of God. Churches had been basilicas in the ancient manner, like other buildings, symmetrical perhaps and richly adorned, but frankly grounded in the steadfast earth. Change began in the eleventh century, with the appearance of Romance architecture. It was basilican still, but discarded the earlier flat roof for the vaulted, which heightened the interior. Towers were added also, fingers pointing to the sky.

Side by side with the Romance, and perfected in the thirteenth century, was the new Gothic architecture. The basilica was rejected, the ground plan of churches becoming cruciform, with pointed arches towering to airy heights. Great pillars symbolized the heavenward striving of the soul. Church walls became supporting pillars, a framework for great windows, through whose painted glass rich colours filled the depths within. A rose window was placed above the portal, a symbol of silence; no worldly voice was to be heard within the sanctuary. And victory over the powers of evil was depicted in demonic forms and repulsive reptiles, that were made to bear the pillars of the church.

Quite suitably it was the Benedictine monks that first achieved this wonder. Their pupils, however, became autonomous corporations, unhampered by monastic rules and episcopal control. *Free Masons* they called themselves, and built for themselves *Lodges,* where they met for consultation and discussion. The lodges became training schools of architecture, and artistic laymen were not excluded; but all was in the Catholic spirit.

From the labours of these artists came the great structures of the thirteenth century, like Cologne cathedral and the Strassburg minister, to remind posterity what great things men will undertake, for whatever supports the belief that life is both significant and safe.

As for the cultus, it appealed less to the intellect, more to the senses, since the populace was generally illiterate. An occasional bishop or priest expounded the Scriptures, but only to scholars. An occasional bishop preached, when on circuit through his diocese; but contemporary writers record it as an act of rare devotion.

In public worship the central feature was the office of the Mass, with an imposing liturgy; but the office was in Latin, as were the hymns. All was in Latin, and incomprehensible to the worshippers. It was regarded as a work of magic, in which the people had no part. Their presence therefore, though a commendable act of piety, was not necessary.

Masses were normally daily sacrifices, offered to God for the daily sins of the people; but they came to be performed for all sorts of purposes— to secure good weather, good crops, husbands, children, and peace for dead men's souls. It is a sorry reminder of the ceaseless drag of society on Catholic Christianity that Masses were sometimes performed to secure the death of an enemy. A Spanish synod found it necessary to forbid such things.

And as the uses of the Mass increased, so did the number of priests and altars. The larger churches came to have many altars, privately endowed, that Masses might be said there for private ends.

Increasingly prominent, too, was the worship of images, and of relics of the apostles and martyrs and saints. Officially the Church said images might be worshipped, but not adored; practically they were both wor-shipped and adored. And every church coveted relics, sometimes going to great lengths to get them, that the church might be a centre of pilgrimage and the scene of miraculous events. When St. Romuald thought to leave Catalonia, he only succeeded in doing so by feigning madness. There was a scheme afoot to kill him, that his bones might be kept as relics.

Most effective for education in right conduct was the discipline of penance. The parish priests imposed the penances for peccadillos, the bishop for notorious offences. On his itineraries the bishop held court in the presence of the count or his deputy; and there he judged as sins the things the civil court had dealt with as crimes. Reputable men were chosen by the bishop to be witnesses; and the accused were sworn on relics, as they now are on the Bible.

Penances were of many sorts. Men were scourged, imprisoned, sent on pilgrimages, sometimes in chains. Theoretically penance was public proof of one's repentance; practically it was satisfaction given to the Church for breaches of her teaching and discipline.

The penitential system was often compromised by what were called redemptions of penance, methods of shortening the period of penance or escaping it altogether. Offenders might say more prayers, repeat more psalms, make larger gifts to pious purposes, or grant a serf his freedom for performing his master's penance. Such compromises were long opposed by good men; but by the end of the ninth century they were generally accepted.

The greatest of all redemptions of penance was the indulgence, which was the remission of penances. Occasionally the indulgence was made plenary, remitting all penances in a community or for those everywhere who met the required conditions. This was to celebrate some great event like the dedication of a church, or to move the people to some great undertaking like a crusade. Always it was assumed that those receiving an indulgence had first confessed their sins and promised to amend; but practically the indulgence was a substitute for confession and amendment, as well as for penances.

As with Catholic discipline, so with Catholic doctrine, almost all that is now described as "Catholic truth" was already defined in the days of Innocent III. It was generally agreed, for example, that the divinely appointed sacraments were seven in number. That had been an open question. One had said they were but two, baptism and the Lord's Supper. Another had said they were numberless, that every act of consecration was a sacrament. The dedication of churches, kneeling in prayer, making the sign of the cross, were therefore sacraments. Peter the Lombard, in the twelfth century, taught that the sacraments were seven—baptism, confirmation and the Lord's Supper, penance and extreme unction, marriage and ordination. That was the prevailing view by the time of Innocent III, though not officially adopted for another two centuries.[19]

Of all the sacraments, the Lord's Supper continued to be central; though it was no longer a supper but a sacrifice, on an altar, not at a table, and was now known as the Mass.[20]

Thought had been fluid as to the nature of the mystery concealed within the Mass. Ancient Catholic Fathers, when the Mass was still the Supper, had spoken of a mystical presence of Christ in the bread and

[19] By a Council at Florence in 1439.
[20] The concluding words of the Mass are *Ite, Missa est*, "Go, the congregation is dismissed." The populace, catching the sound without the meaning, called the service the Mass.

wine, mystically received by the participants through faith. An unbeliever would receive only bread and wine. But some Fathers had leaned to another and miraculous view; and mediaeval society loved a miracle. So the popular belief came to be that the bread and wine were changed into something else, when the priest spoke the words of consecration.

Legends confirmed the popular belief. Worshippers, at the moment when the priest consecrated the elements, had seen a lamb appear on the altar, or Christ himself, in the form of a child. Clearly here was a miracle; and it came to be the general belief that bread and wine were, by the words of the priest, transformed into the flesh and blood of Christ.

The first man to develop at length this doctrine of transubstantiation was Peter the Lombard. Scholars soon gave it scientific support; and Innocent III, at the Fourth Lateran Council, declared it Catholic truth. "Jesus Christ," he said, "is at once priest and sacrifice, whose body and blood are truly received in the sacrament of the altar under the form of bread and wine, inasmuch as the elements are transubstantiated by the divine power into body and blood, . . . a sacrament which only the duly appointed priest can perform."

Logically, therefore, the laity were no longer given the wine at communion. Since it was now the blood of Christ, devout minds would shudder at the thought that it might be spilt. So the priest alone consumed the wine, except on rare occasions, like the coronation or death of a king.

This practice also receives scientific support. Christ in his entirety, men said, was present in each of the consecrated elements. Miracles proved it. The consecrated bread, the Host,[21] was seen to bleed, thus proving that both flesh and blood were there.

The doctrine of transubstantiation led naturally to other changes in Catholic practice concerning the Mass. It brought, for example, the adoration of the Host, which was also general by the time of Innocent III. At that moment in the office of the Mass when the priest was about to elevate and bless the Host, a small bell was rung and the people prostrated themselves.[22] In the streets, when the Host was carried to the

---

[21] Latin *hostia,* victim. The consecrated bread, transformed into the body of Christ, is now a sacrifice to God.

[22] The elevation of the Host was common in the Greek Church from the seventh century, and in the Latin Church from the eleventh; but it was then regarded only as a symbolic act, not the announcement of a miracle.

sick, a bell-ringer preceded the priest; and the people along the route prostrated themselves while the Host passed.

Transubstantiation led also to the appointment of a day for the special celebration of the Mass, a Feast of Corpus Christi. The festival commended itself immediately to Christian sentiment, and was ordained for the whole Church in 1264, by Pope Urban IV.

Gradually, too, people at the Mass ceased to receive the bread. That is to say, Mass was not followed by Holy Communion. So general did the practice become that Innocent III decreed that all must receive the bread once a year. It was not, however, because the Mass was incomplete without Holy Communion, but that men were required to come to confession at least once a year, and Holy Communion seemed to follow suitably upon confession and the shriving of the guilty soul.[23]

From all this it follows that, at the height of the Middle Ages, the chief function of the priest was to produce each day the body of Christ, and offer it as a sacrifice to God for the sins of the people. The Christian presbyters of primitive days were now back in the office of the Jewish and pagan priests.

One advance in the cultus resulted from the crusades to the Holy Land; there was a great increase in the veneration of relics. Syrian merchants did a thriving trade in relics with Christian pilgrims and crusaders. There was no very critical judgment as to their authenticity. Europe venerated several robes, all accepted as the seamless coat of Christ. There were enough pieces of the true cross to make several crosses. There were even two heads of John the Baptist.

There were stern protests against the abuse of Christian credulity, but no rejection of the principle that material objects, once associated with the saints, were charged with supernatural potency. The superstition was to be checked in time by the Renaissance, but still survives.

The worship of the saints, too, was now a part of Catholic practice. It had begun simply as reverence for the great dead. Churches were built over the graves of martyrs, or dedicated to martyrs; and the dates of their martyrdom were observed as holy days. As early as the fifth century, however, prayers for the saints, in Christian liturgies, had become prayers to the saints; and the worship of the saints was well under

---

[23] There is a widespread tendency now in Catholic countries to consummate the Mass by Communion.

way. Officially the Church distinguished, as it did in the matter of relics, between adoration and worship, the former being reserved for God alone. The distinction was probably kept alive in popular thought by the special use to which the saints were put. They were men's advocates with God. It was as Gregory the Great had said: "Our holy martyrs are ready to be your advocates; they desire to be asked. . . . Seek them as helpers of your prayers."

The Virgin Mary now stood securely at the head of the whole company of saints. If Christians might worship, but must not adore, the saints, there was nevertheless given to the Virgin a sort of super-worship, hard to distinguish from the adoration reserved for God. It was the profound reverence due to "the Mother of God," who was also man's supreme advocate. Bernard of Clairvaux placed the Virgin at the top of the ladder by which man reaches God: "Christ is indeed given as mediator to sinful man, recoiling in terror before God the Father; but the divine majesty of Christ also awes the sinner, who therefore seeks an intercessor with Him. Flee to Mary, whose pure humanity the Son also honours. The Son hears the Mother, the Father the Son. This ladder for the sinner is my whole hope."

The salutation of the angel to Mary,[24] the *Ave Maria*, became the foundation of every prayer. It was the duty of the parish priests to teach the people the *Ave Maria*, in addition to the Creed and the Lord's Prayer, or *Pater Noster*. And soon the rosary came into use, that the faithful might count the Aves and Pater Nosters they repeated in prayer. The use of the rosary was already common among Buddhists and Moslems. It was introduced into the Church by the Dominicans.[25]

Naturally the priest advanced with the cultus. Not only could he produce the body of Christ and thus provide the saving sacrifice, he had also the "power of the keys," was a sort of lesser pope. That is to say, the function of the priest in the confessional had been to intercede with God for the one confessing; but by the thirteenth century it was Catholic doctrine that God forgave only those whom the priest forgave. And so, as we have seen, Innocent III required all Christians to confess at least once a year.

[24] "Hail, thou that art highly favoured, the Lord is with thee." *Luke* 1: 28.
[25] The Common Rosary is a string of five decades of beads, separated by five large beads, to which is appended a cross. Each small bead represents an *Ave Maria*, each large one a *Pater Noster*, and the cross the Creed.

It is not to be thought that Catholicism raised no doubts in Christian minds; but doubt was not widespread in the Middle Ages. There was little theology and philosophy outside the monasteries; and, sharply as learned monks differed there, all parties found a way to reconcile their doctrines with Catholic truth. Indeed Catholic truth was the premiss from which their thought proceeded, and logic the road from truth to further truth, not philosophy, not the sciences. This is what is called Scholasticism.[26]

First of the Scholastics in importance was Anselm (1033-1109). When a young nobleman of Lombardy, he made his way to the monastery of Le Bec in Normandy, to study with the prior, his countryman Lanfranc, who was the most famous teacher of the day. Anselm became abbot in time, and left Le Bec to succeed Lanfranc as Archbishop of Canterbury.

Though a devout man, deeply concerned for the spiritual welfare of his clergy and people, Archbishop Anselm is better known as a theologian. Utterly orthodox, he accepted without question all Catholic truth. "No Christian," Anselm said, "ought in any way to dispute the truth of what the Catholic Church believes in its heart and confesses with its mouth. But always holding the same faith unquestioningly, loving it and living by it, he ought himself as far as possible to seek the reason for it." [27]

So much mediaeval thinkers in general could have said; but Anselm went beyond others, labouring to prove that Catholicism is, in fact, both rational and demonstrable. To preach the truth to believers is not enough; one must prove it to unbelievers.

So Anselm's earliest theological treatise, the *Monologium*, or *Soliloquy*, was devoted to proving the existence of God, on the basis of reason alone. He followed it with another treatise, the *Proslogion*, or *Address*,

---

[26] Scholasticism came slowly, and did not entirely dominate scholarship until the eleventh and twelfth centuries. The best example of a brilliant mind, still working freely in the Middle Ages, is John Scotus Erigena, a native of Ireland, who made his way to France and there enjoyed the patronage of Charles the Bald. In Ireland Erigena had acquired a knowledge of the Greek language and philosophy, not possessed by scholars on the continent, and developed a system peculiar to himself. Its ruling principle was the immanence of God, his oneness with the Universe itself. Erigena had no patience with the western idea of God, as outside the world and ruling it as a sovereign rules his people.

This was foreign to Christian thought; but, being a Catholic Christian, Erigena found ways of reconciling his system with Catholicism. He was not, however, a Scholastic. Catholic doctrine was not the premiss from which his thought proceeded.

[27] *De fide trinitatis,* 2.

in which he sought to find one proof, which alone would remove all doubt. The result was the famous ontological argument, which fairly withstood attack for seven hundred years, until Immanuel Kant. A third treatise,[28] most famous of all, was devoted to proving that the incarnation and death of the Son of God were necessary, being grounded in the very nature of things.

Anselm's ontological argument and his theory of the atonement are justly famous; but more important then was his claim that Catholic truth can be demonstrated by the reason alone, without appeal to revelation. Time was to prove him wrong in this and in his other main postulate, that the mind must submit to the Catholic Church. Honest minds could not forever keep within the limits fixed by authority; nor was all Catholic doctrine demonstrable. One very notable dissenter appeared immediately. This was Abelard.

Abelard (1079-1142), a young nobleman of Brittany, was some thirty years old when Anselm died. He had refused the career of a feudal lord, for the study of philosophy and theology, and gained great fame at Paris. A tragic love affair with Heloise drove him into a monastery, but did not diminish his fame. Believing in the rationality of Catholicism, Abelard nevertheless could not subscribe to the dictum of Anselm, that "No Christian ought in any way to dispute the truth of what the Catholic Church believes in its heart and confesses with its mouth." Without going so far as to affirm that one must always understand a doctrine before accepting it, Abelard did maintain that one must have some perception of its meaning and be convinced that it is not irrational. Abelard was aware that an undue reticence can shelter more than truth, that no error lives so long as that about which it is wicked to enquire. So he resisted all compulsion in matters of religious faith.

Nor did Abelard share Anselm's confidence that all Catholic truth is demonstrable. He had no difficulty about the divine inspiration of the Bible; though he deprecated allegorical fancies about it, and thought some philosophers and sages outside the Bible were also inspired. But Abelard did reject the orthodox attitude to the Catholic Fathers. His famous work *Sic et non, So and not so,* was a selection of quotations from the Fathers, set side by side without comment, to show that the

[28] The treatise, dealing particularly with the atonement, is known only by its Latin name, *Cur Deus-homo.*

Fathers had often disagreed and that the alleged unity of Catholic tradition was a myth. Abelard was a mediaeval liberal, genuinely concerned to make Christianity more acceptable to thoughtful men.

Scholasticism was little disturbed for a century after Abelard. Several of his disciples wrote compends of Catholic teaching, which found a place for his ideas; but none broke bounds, as Abelard had done in the matter of Catholic tradition. Indeed the most famous of them, Peter Lombard, made a compend that became the chief text-book for theological instruction, and remained so to the end of the Middle Ages. Peter was a native of Lombardy, who became a student and teacher of theology at Paris and finally its bishop. His *Four Books of Sentences* is a sort of enlarged *Sic et non,* quoting the Creeds and decisions of Councils, in addition to the Bible and the Fathers; but where Abelard had left quotations to speak for themselves, Peter set himself to reconcile inconsistencies and explain away contradictions. So that, unlike Abelard, who had raised doubts about the infallibility of the Fathers, Lombard tended to restore confidence in them.

Soon, however, a new problem confronted Scholasticism. Aristotle returned to Europe by way of Spain, where he was being diligently studied by Arabian scholars, notably Averroes. The West had known Aristotle's works on Logic, the *Organon,* through translation by Boëthius. Now his metaphysical and scientific works were being translated into Latin; and soon there was a great stir in the monasteries.

The first reaction to Aristotle was hostile; and his physics and metaphysics were excluded from the University of Paris in 1210. But some orthodox scholars became convinced that Aristotle could not be ignored. The foremost of these was Thomas, son of Landulf, count of Aquino, a town midway between Rome and Naples.

Thomas Aquinas (1225?-1274) received his early education at Monte Cassino, which was near his home, then became a member of the recently formed Order of Preaching Brothers, or Dominicans. Later he made his way to Paris, to study with Albertus Magnus, a Dominican scholar and student of Aristotle.

Thomas set himself to achieve a combination of the Catholic faith and Aristotelian philosophy, that would leave the former intact, while adopting the principles and method of the latter. Christian theology in the West, since Augustine, had been profoundly influenced by Platonism, especially in the Neo-Platonic form; and Platonism had assumed that man has an intuitive perception of God and the spiritual world, independent of anything he may learn through the senses. Aristotle, on the other hand, had maintained that all human knowledge comes through the senses. Thomas Aquinas now brought Aristotelianism and Christian theology together in one system, by distinguishing between natural and revealed theology.

Natural theology, Thomas says, consists of all the truths concerning God and His relation to mankind that can be deduced from sense-experience, without the aid of divine revelation. What these truths are, Thomas sets forth in the first three volumes of his great work *Summa contra gentiles.* They are God's existence, His eternity and perfection, His method in creation, human immortality, the angels. The fourth book of the *Summa contra gentiles* treats of revealed theology, which is inaccessible to reason. Here are included the doctrine of the Trinity, the incarnation of the Son, the resurrection of the body, the last judgment.

The significance of the *Summa contra gentiles* is in the first three books, in which Thomas was commending Christianity to philosophers, especially unbelievers. Indeed, his creation of a natural theology, on the basis of Aristotle's philosophy, was his greatest achievement. In his revealed theology he was hampered by Christian tradition. Here he shows himself a good Catholic, in that he treats impartially many things that have little significance for him, because they belong to the Catholic faith. He shows himself also a good Scholastic, in that he is never content to leave theology without such support as the reason can bring. It was the duty of the theologian, Thomas thought, to justify the ways of God to men.

In another work, the *Summa theologiae,* Thomas addresses himself to Christian scholars. Here he proceeds scholastically. That is to say, he assumes the truth of Catholic thought, though excluding the Fathers.[29]

It is unnecessary to describe the system elaborated in the *Summa theologiae;* but the second part of the work is the most complete treatment of Christian ethics that had yet appeared. Thomas distinguishes between the natural and the theological virtues. The former are the decencies of which mankind itself is capable—justice, fortitude, temper-

---

[29] I. 1: 8. Thomas respected the Fathers as teachers, but did not regard them as divinely inspired.

ance, prudence, the virtues traditional in Christian thought ever since Ambrose, and acquired by him from Stoicism. The Stoic interpretation of the natural virtues, however, is strained, as indeed it had been with Ambrose, to accommodate Catholic ideals, like humility, virginity, fasting, otherworldliness in general.

Only theological virtues, however, received from the Holy Spirit through faith in Christ, lead one to eternal blessedness. They crown the natural virtues, as revealed theology crowns natural theology. The theological virtues are faith, hope and charity. Faith is the first; but charity is the greatest. It is primarily love of God, and secondarily love of one's neighbour, for God's sake.

Thomas' treatment of ethics, confused by its varied origins, is nevertheless sane and practical, and admirably adapted to a great institution like the Catholic Church, which included people of all degrees of culture.

Thomas Aquinas was a modernist in the thirteenth century, and was regarded with suspicion by the conservatives of his day. Opposition soon died, however; and Thomas was canonized by Pope John XXII in 1323, some fifty years after his death. His synthesis of Aristotelian philosophy and Christian theology brought new support to the Catholic system, support that was regarded then as scientific.

There were a few scholarly men who kept out of the scholastic argument. They were Scholastics in this sense, that they assumed the truth of Catholic doctrine; but they asked, Why discuss it? Why labour to demonstrate Christianity, or reconcile it with other systems? Christian doctrine will prove itself to him who walks with God in contemplation and good deeds.

Those who so thought were the Mystics, who sought direct communion with God and inner illumination. There had always been such men in the Christian Church. One need only recall how the first Christians expected the "gift of the Holy Spirit" to accompany their baptism, and sought divine guidance through prayer. Catholicism itself was a compromise with this religion of individual experience, to secure uniformity and continuity in the Church.

In the Golden Age of Catholicism there was enough active Mysticism to constitute a defined movement. The founder was a certain William of

Champeaux, a Scholastic whom Abelard had beaten in public debate and humiliated. William withdrew to the monastery of St. Victor at Paris, to give himself to prayer and contemplation; and his disciples there became known as the Victorines.

But the great name in mediaeval Mysticism is Bernard of Clairvaux (*See* p. 286), a younger contemporary of both William and Abelard. Great Catholic and churchman as he was, like Augustine of Hippo, the real springs of Bernard's life, like those of Augustine, were in Bible study and prayer and ecstatic communion. Bernard thought the Church, its doctrines and sacraments, necessary to salvation. He believed, too, that all doubts concerning them would vanish, if one lived a holy life, contemplative and loving.

So Bernard rebelled against the dialectics of Scholasticism. It was his influence that crushed Abelard and consigned him to monastic retirement. His influence also delayed for two centuries a movement in philosophy called Nominalism (*See* p. 307), that was to shake Scholasticism and open the door to modern intellectual freedom.

Many sermons and tracts of Bernard are preserved; but his greatest work is the *De consideratione, Giving Thought,* a treatise on the duties and dangers of the papacy. And since the great hymns of the Church come chiefly from the Mystics, it is not strange that Bernard wrote many hymns, some of which have been translated successfully.[30]

Mysticism is of the intuitive, spontaneous type of religion, that may break forth anywhere, and of which no connected history is possible. The great lights of the thirteenth century were the Victorines. The next century, however, was the flowering time of Christian Mysticism, its great exemplars being from the Mendicant Orders, notably Meister Eckhart and his disciple John Tauler.

[30] The hymns of St. Bernard best known to English-speaking Christians are "Jesus, the very thought of thee," translated by Edward Caswell, and "Jesus, thou joy of loving hearts!" translated by Ray Palmer.

CHAPTER XIII

PREMONITIONS OF CHANGE

When in 1215 Pope Innocent III dissolved the Fourth Lateran Council and the prelates went home, it must have been with the pleasant feeling that Catholicism was now complete and immovable. Yet it is clear that there were already forewarnings of change. Mediaevalism was slowly, very slowly, passing away; and with the Middle Ages would pass the conditions that had produced Catholicism and given it supremacy in Europe.

Already in the twelfth century there were various dissenting religious movements. We have spoken of those Albigenses in southern France, for whose suppression Innocent III called the faithful to a crusade. They were but one of a number of sects, that went by the general name Catharists. They were to be found in Spain and Italy, Germany and Belgium and England. The phase of their teaching most abhorred by Catholics was their doctrine of Jesus. He had not been a man, they said, but a spiritual being with the appearance of a man. Such teaching undermined the whole doctrinal system of Christianity, and was naturally feared. So the Inquisition was active against Catharists for a century; and they were stamped out.

Dissent from Catholicism in the twelfth century, however, was chiefly on moral grounds. Popular education was not sufficiently advanced to cause much doctrinal dissent; but there were many who were aware of the contradiction between prelacy and the simplicity of Christ. The aspiration after Christlikeness had never ceased in Catholicism. Sometimes it created reform movements within the Church; sometimes it led reformers out.

Most extensive of the latter movements were the Waldenses, who originated like the Albigenses in southern France. A certain Waldus, a rich usurer of Lyons, was convicted by the word of Jesus, "If thou wouldest be perfect, go, sell that which thou hast, and give to the poor, and thou shalt have treasure in heaven: and come, follow me." Waldus therefore gave away his possessions, and founded in 1177 a society for preaching the Gospel, the *Poor Men of Lyons*. They went out two by two, a generation before the Franciscans, without money or change of raiment and wearing wooden sandals, to recall men to the simplicity and purity of Christ. Women were soon admitted to the order. The members called themselves brothers and sisters. They were itinerant preachers, who had adopted the celibate life and the rule of poverty, strove to obey the Sermon on the Mount and, in the manner of modern Quakers, declined to take an oath.

The Waldenses of France made no attack upon the doctrines and rites of Catholicism. Their chief offence was unauthorized preaching. They were forbidden by the Archbishop of Lyons to preach, persisted in doing so, and were excommunicated. Innocent III attempted to change them into an order of Poor Catholics, who should preach and expound the Scriptures, but under control of the bishops. It was too late. The Waldenses had had a generation of freedom, and both disliked and feared episcopal control. So Pope Innocent banned them at the Fourth Lateran Council.

A similar organization sprang up in Italy, and was popularly known as the Waldenses. A mission from there spread the movement to Germany, where it went further in ecclesiastical reform than in France. The German Waldenses acted on the principle that everything in Catholic Christianity was to be rejected, that had not been expressly taught by Christ and the Apostles. So they rejected pilgrimages and ecclesiastical processions, the worship of images and the wearing of clerical vestments. They suffered frequently at the hands of the Dominican inquisitors, but were to survive into the sixteenth century, to be largely absorbed into various Protestant bodies.

These devout sectaries, both Catharists and Waldenses, appealed to the Scriptures in defence of their principles and practices, and to show how far Catholicism had departed from the New Testament. So the Church found it necessary to restrict the use of the Scriptures. Innocent III pronounced it commendable that the faithful desire to know the Scriptures, but dangerous to read them, except under clerical supervision. Later generations were sometimes forbidden to possess the

Scriptures. It was a new departure. Jerome had translated the Bible into Latin, that Christians of the West might read. It was then assumed that the Scriptures and the Church were always in agreement. Now that the former were being quoted against the latter, there seemed no alternative but to keep the Scriptures out of the hands of the people.

There was a noticeable intellectual movement, too, outside theology. The Dark Ages were now far in the past. There had been a definite advance in general enlightenment in the eleventh century; and progress was rapid in the twelfth, especially in Italy. Indeed one may properly speak of a twelfth-century Renaissance there.

In Italy culture had never become a monopoly of the clergy. An intellectual interest, especially in law and medicine, survived among the laity from ancient Graeco-Roman days. In less degree there was now some intellectual interest among Catholic laymen everywhere. Paris and Oxford were *Studia Generalia,* or cosmopolitan centres of study, in the twelfth century, as well as Salerno and Bologna. Wandering students, boys and grey-haired men together, might be seen on the roads of Europe, making their way to these, and other less famous, centres of study.

But, to return to Italy, the *Studium* of Salerno had long been famous. There in the sunny south four cultures met—Greek and Latin, Arabic and Jewish. Thought was therefore not in subjection to Catholic theology. Besides the *Studium* was for medicine only. In north Italy studies took another direction. Attention to the Latin classics stimulated interest in Roman law. Ravenna had been the chief centre of instruction in law through all the Dark Ages. Bologna superseded it in the eleventh century; and in the twelfth a legal Renaissance came to Bologna. It was connected with the arrival from Ravenna of a copy of the ancient Roman Code, the *Corpus Juris.* With such resources the great teacher Irnerius initiated the scientific study of civil law. Almost simultaneously Gratian, a monk of Bologna, undertook the codification of Canon Law, made up of the opinions of Church Fathers, papal decretals, and the decisions of Church Councils.[1]

Canon Law became as important at Bologna as Civil Law; but our

---

[1] Beginnings of codification had already been made by others, like Anselm of Lucca and Cardinal Deusdedit; but the *Decretum* of Gratian now superseded all others.

present concern is with the latter, and the authority it gave to lay scholars. The jurists of Bologna, in the twelfth century, attracted hosts of students from all Europe, and did not hesitate to take the side of emperors against popes, attributing to the former the prerogatives that had been exercised by the ancient Roman emperors. There was hardly a sovereign in Europe who did not, at some time or other, appeal to the lay jurists of Bologna against the pretensions of popes.

As for Paris, the fame of Abelard first made it a *Studium;* and it became the most influential centre of study north of the Alps. The *Studium* grew out of the Cathedral School. Masters obtained licenses from the Chancellor of the Cathedral School, then opened schools of their own. They must first have studied for some years under a licensed master, and received his consent to teach. One of the charges against Abelard was that he had begun to teach theology at Paris without the consent of his master, Anselm of Laon.

The twelfth-century Renaissance cast a shadow across imperial-papal relations. Frederick Barbarossa had married his son Henry to Constance, heiress of the kingdom of Sicily. That rich and powerful island state, which Barbarossa had hoped to conquer, thus passed to the Hohenstaufen family by a marriage contract. When Barbarossa died in 1190, Henry VI found himself undisputed king of Germany, with a warlike feudal nobility at his service, and king of Sicily as well, with a powerful fleet, a well-trained army of Saracen mercenaries and a full treasury. His heirs would be in a position to deal with both the papacy and the Lombard League. This was a matter of grave concern to the papacy.

When Henry VI died in 1197, his son Frederick was but an infant, Italian born and destined to be more familiar with the orange groves of Palermo, the Sicilian capital, then with the less benignant climate of Aachen or Cologne. His mother Constance made him a ward of Innocent III; and the great pope did his duty by the child. Frederick reached manhood well educated, fluent in six languages, a patron of literature and the arts, a lyric poet of repute. Without the aid of his guardian, he became as well a skilful soldier and a statesman of great subtilty.

While Frederick was growing up in Sicily and at Rome, two kings ruled in Germany, Frederick's uncle, Philip of Swabia, and Otto IV, of the great Brunswick family of Guelf. The unpopularity of the latter brought an embassy of German princes to Frederick, with an offer of the German crown. Frederick entered Germany with an army in 1212, backed by Pope Innocent and King Philip Augustus of France, and steadily won the whole kingdom. At eighteen years of age he was king of Germany and Sicily, and emperor of the Holy Roman Empire. He was to reign for nearly forty years (1212–1250).

There was peace with the papacy so long as Innocent III lived. Then Frederick II proved himself the craftiest, most talented, most dangerous enemy the papacy had ever encountered. It is difficult to know the facts; for to contemporary writers Frederick was an enigma, even to those who admired and loved him. Religious ideas that were axiomatic to others had no place in Frederick's mind. Perhaps it was more difficult at Rome than in Germany to think of the pope as Vicar of God. Certainly it was difficult at Salerno, in friendly concourse with cultured Saracens and Jews, to think of Christianity as the only permissible religion. Besides Frederick II was a Renaissance man and not intellectually submissive. He was as well a reformer of the Church, and not in the manner of other reformers. Frederick was a critic of Catholicism as such; and he was fearless of the anathema, because he disbelieved the underlying claims.

All this is illustrated in Frederick's career as a crusader. He consented quite early in his reign to lead a crusade; but was busy establishing good government in Germany and Sicily, subduing the Lombard cities and making Italy the real centre of the Empire. Twice the crusade was postponed; and when in 1227 the crusaders were assembled in Apulia and Frederick still delayed, he was excommunicated by Pope Gregory IX. Soon thereafter he set out for Palestine, without having the ban removed. Christendom thus witnessed the extraordinary spectacle of a holy war, led by a man excommunicate. Frederick won Jerusalem for Christianity by a treaty with his friend the Sultan, without bloodshed and waste of treasure, and was anathematized by the Patriarch of Jerusalem for treating with the infidel.

In the end Frederick died excommunicate; and with him died the Holy Roman Empire. His son Conrad IV, though king of Germany, never received the imperial crown at Rome. Another son, Manfred, the brilliant king of Sicily, warred with the Papal States and, like his father, was excommunicated in vain. At length Pope Urban IV offered the crown of Sicily to Charles of Anjou, brother of Louis IX of France, and secured from the clergy of France a tithe for a crusade against Manfred. Pope Clement IV pressed the crusade, and crowned Charles king of Sicily at Rome. Manfred fell in battle with Charles at Benevento. The papacy had triumphed for the moment; but Frederick II was still a disquieting portent.[2]

Heretical sects and Renaissance men were not the only ill omens at the height of the Middle Ages. There was disturbance in the scientific department of the Church. Thomas Aquinas, Duns Scotus, and their schools, the Thomists and Scotists, were endeavouring to harmonize Christianity with other assured truth; and they were, some thought, too ready to believe this other truth complete in Aristotle. A few men thought more was to be discovered in Nature than Aristotle had found. Roger Bacon, an English Franciscan, ventured to suggest that Aristotle, admittedly very wise, had only planted the tree of knowledge, and that it had "not as yet put forth all its branches nor produced all its fruits." "If we could continue to live for endless centuries," said Bacon, "we mortals could never hope to reach full and complete knowledge of all the things that are to be known. No one knows enough of Nature completely to describe the peculiarities of a single fly." Bacon thought the truth was discoverable by experiment with real things, better than by poring over Aristotle. "If I had my way," he said, "I should burn all the books of Aristotle."

A new philosophy, called Nominalism, was at hand to defend this interest in Nature. Nor was it wholly new. Aristotle himself had insisted that all knowledge comes through the senses; and Aquinas had felt constrained to make room for that teaching in his system.[3] But now some

---

[2] The Holy Roman Empire continued in name for more than five hundred years. Germany, however, was ruined. Her kings had been busy beyond her borders, and had granted the German princes virtually independent sovereignty in return for their support of imperial enterprises. Seven magnates became a college of "Electors," for the choice of emperors. They chose men rich but impotent, and not always Germans. The farcical empire ceased in 1806, when Francis II abdicated, to save the imperial crown from Napoleon. The German states were reunited in 1871, under the kings of Prussia, the Hohenzollerns, only to drench the world in blood, struggling to recover for Germany the "place in the sun" she had lost.

[3] By distinguishing, as we saw, between natural and revealed theology. Natural theology, or philosophy, includes whatever may be known through sense-experience about God and his relation to the world.

disciples of Duns Scotus (1265?–1308) were going right over to Nominalism, which means, for our present purpose, that they believed the reality of things to lie in individuals, not in classes or species. There was no such thing as horse, or tree, or house; there were only individual horses, trees and houses. There was no abstract truth and justice, only true men, just men. The general concepts were but names, *nomina,* with no reality outside the mind. In other words, general concepts, or "Universals," were conclusions of our own, drawn from our observation of individuals.[4] In this Nominalists followed the ancient Stoics.

Scholastics in general, however, were Realists. Some of them adopted Plato's doctrine of ideas. Truth and justice and beauty, he had said, were realities and models for the world before it began. The Universals thus exist before the individual things. They are archetypes, or norms; and things are but visible images of these patterns.[5] And man has an intuitive knowledge of Universals before he meets individual things through the senses. So that, to a Platonic Realist, one's knowledge of things is first reached through ideas already latent in the mind.

Other Scholastics were Aristotelian Realists. They believed in the reality of Universals, but thought the Universals were in the individual things, and entered the human mind through experience.[6]

This is much more than a question of words. Philosophical principles affect one's attitude to theological doctrines. Before Thomas Aquinas and Duns Scotus were born, Berengar, an early Nominalist, head of the Cathedral School at Tours, was already in difficulty, on philosophical grounds, about transubstantiation. Berengar could not believe the bread and wine of the Eucharist to be other than they seemed. Roscellinus, another Nominalist, teacher of Abelard at Paris, got into difficulty about the doctrine of the Trinity. The reality of God, he said, was in the individual persons of the Trinity; the word Godhead was but an abstraction.

So also with mediaeval doctrines of Church and State. A Realist believed the Church to have an existence of its own, in the Divine Mind. It was therefore a sacred entity, independent of the individuals within it, and beyond their control or criticism. The Nominalist rejoined that Christians are the Church, and apart from them it is but a name. As for

---

[4] Universals follow from individual things. *Universalia post res.*

[5] *Universalia ante res.*

[6] *Universalia in rebus.*

the State, Nominalists thought the citizens the State. Arnold of Brescia was a republican, with ideas of individual rights based on Nominalism.

These early Nominalists, with their attention to the particular thing and the individual man, are the real heralds of both modern science and social democracy. Meanwhile they were under suspicion for two hundred years. Thomists and Scotists were both Realists. Nevertheless Nominalism gradually became irresistible.

The man most influential in bringing this about was an English Franciscan, William of Occam (1280–1349), a teacher at Oxford. Occam was of the stricter party of Franciscans, the Observants; and his championship of the ideal of poverty, both individual and corporate, brought him into conflict with Pope John XXII, who was supporting the Conventual Franciscans. Occam was summoned to the papal court, tried for heresy, condemned and imprisoned, but escaped and spent the later years of his life at Munich. There he wrote several treatises against Pope John, declaring him in error and appealing from him to the Scriptures. He denied, too, the political authority of the papacy, maintaining the independence of the State.

It was Occam who completed and systematized the Nominalistic philosophy, so that it became a recognized system. One result, for Nominalists, was the separation of philosophy from theology, and the grounding of theology on revelation alone. Occam had found himself in a dilemma. He was a devout and orthodox Catholic; and Catholic theology presupposed a philosophical Realism that his mind rejected. What should he do? He must either abandon some Catholic doctrines, or admit that Catholic doctrine is not always rational. So deeply was Catholicism rooted in his mind and will, that Occam chose the latter alternative. Catholic Christianity, he said, was to be accepted on the authority of divine revelation; but it could not be said to be rational. Reason could not even lead one towards faith, as Aquinas had thought.

This principle of the double truth, as it is called, was not at all the dishonourable thing that it sounds. Occam and his school meant only that the divine reason and the human reason are not the same, that what is true for man is not necessarily true for God, and that Christianity is of God, miraculous throughout. Christianity, therefore, is to be accepted on divine authority, the authority of the Catholic Church. Occam in his controversy with the papacy had not appealed from the Church, but from the pope, to the Scriptures. He still believed that Bible and Church spoke with one voice. Pope John had departed from both.

Nominalism was to have one result that William of Occam did not foresee and would have deplored. His principle of the double truth was a makeshift. No devotion to Catholicism could lead men forever to accept on authority what they believed to be irrational. Some Nominalists after Occam re-examined Catholicism itself. What they found led them to reject it.[7]

The Universities, too, were becoming forces for change. They were a by-product of the twelfth-century Renaissance. During the Dark Ages the centres of enlightenment had been the schools of the monasteries, and those attached to cathedrals, under the authority of the bishops. The monastery schools were the more important. So much so that the Dark Ages are often described educationally as the Benedictine Age. The twelfth-century Renaissance, however, transferred intellectual supremacy from the monasteries to the Cathedral Schools, though scholarly monks often taught in them.

The Universities, except in Italy, were an outgrowth of the Cathedral Schools. These had been directed, sometimes by the archdeacon of the diocese, sometimes by a special master, the *Scholasticus,* sometimes by a Chancellor. He was at first the only teacher; but as the popular thirst for knowledge grew, the Chancellor granted licenses to other masters. And the growing respect for scholarship made even bishops and cardinals ambitious to acquire a licence to teach. To be Master, or Doctor, or Professor,[8] gave added dignity to even the cardinalate.

As the masters grew in number there arose in educational centres guilds of licensed masters.[9] The University of Paris was a guild of mas-

---

[7] Such men were John Wyclif, who died in 1384, and his disciple, John Huss, both of whom turned back to Augustine and the Bible for their doctrine of salvation and who were forerunners of the Protestant Reformation, on the doctrinal side.

[8] These titles were then synonymous.

[9] The masters at Bologna formed a number of faculty-guilds; but a student-guild formed the University and made the masters their servants. The masters lived by the fees of the students, took an oath of obedience to student-rectors and student-statutes, were fined for being late, for closing a lecture late, for evading a difficulty, for failing to complete the course. The instability of such a system, and the rivalry between city-republics for the best masters, led the city governments to secure control over appointments and to pay salaries. This is the beginning of the professoriate proper. In time almost every Italian city-state had its civic University.

ters who, having obtained licences from the Chancellor of the Cathedral School, opened schools of their own. The University consisted of those initiated into the masters' guild.

Universities soon received recognition and protection from the State. The first formal recognition of the University of Paris was a charter granted by King Philip Augustus in 1200, to compensate the masters for violence done them by rioting townsmen, led by the Provost of Paris. Future Provosts were to take an oath to respect the privileges of the masters.

The University of Paris, however, made its independence and privileges secure only after a long struggle. There were conflicts with the Provost and his police, for control of the students. There were conflicts with both Dominicans and Franciscans, against attempts to secure University chairs, without submitting to University regulations.

In these conflicts the chief weapons of the University were "dispersion," or moving to another place, and "dissolution," the temporary suspension of its existence. As the University had at first no buildings or endowments, but met in churches and the chapter-house of the cathedral and hired lecture rooms, dispersion and dissolution were simple. Secessions and migrations from early Universities were common anyway.

Paris influenced the other Universities of northern Europe. The city of Oxford seems to have become a *Studium Generale* by a migration from Paris in 1167, when John of Salisbury and other English teachers were expelled from France; and as a University constitution developed at Oxford, it followed the Paris model. Cambridge resulted similarly by migration from Oxford.

The curriculum of studies in the Universities outside Italy was practically the same everywhere. In the Dark Ages schools had tried to continue the classical tradition. They taught the *Trivium* and the *Quadrivium,* the former comprising grammar, rhetoric and logic, the latter arithmetic, geometry, music and astronomy. The text-books were the remnants of the classics preserved in compends like that of Boëthius. Of all this, Aristotle's Logic was the chief intellectual stimulus; and the recovery of the other works of Aristotle resulted in the eclipse of classical studies in general.[10] Subservience to Aristotle was confirmed when Al-

[10] This delayed the Renaissance proper, that of the fourteenth and fifteenth centuries, which was, on the literary side, a return to the ancient poetry and art.

bert the Great and Thomas Aquinas incorporated him into Catholic theology. By the thirteenth century the substance of education in the Faculty of Arts was Aristotle; though the *Trivium* and *Quadrivium* were still formally recognized. An "Arts Course" was compulsory for students going forward to medicine or theology. In the Faculty of Theology the text-books were the Bible and the "Sentences" of Peter Lombard.

The Universities were very influential in the late Middle Ages. The revived study of Roman Law in Italy influenced the whole development of jurisprudence in France and Germany.[11] In particular, the jurists of Bologna, as we have seen, tended to bring Roman Law to the support of the civil power everywhere, as against ecclesiastical pretensions and Canon Law.

The Universities were influential, too, in that they provided highly educated men, for the direction of both private and public affairs. Through the Universities poor boys of exceptional ability had opened to them a road to civil office, such as the Church had long provided for poor clerics. Popular education still lagged; but the number of students receiving University education was probably as great proportionately as it is to-day in Europe. The existence of the Universities is itself evidence of an intellectual enthusiasm in the late Middle Ages, that is often overlooked.

What of the papacy amidst the new currents? Pope Clement IV, as we saw, performed the funeral rites of the Hohenstaufen family and the Holy Roman Empire. When Manfred fell at Benevento, Clement may well have thought to bring back the great days of Innocent III. It was not to be. Charles of Anjou proved as little amenable as the Hohenstaufen; and the papacy was coming under the dominance of France.

After thirty troubled years, Pope Boniface VIII (1294–1303) determined to recover papal independence. He was a daring and crafty man, as staunch for papal prerogatives as Hildebrand had been; and there were issues between popes and kings that could always be revived. Was church property to be exempt from taxation? Could offending priests be

---

[11] In England practising lawyers were taught, not at the Universities but at professional schools, the Inns of Court; and the Common Law of England was thus better preserved than that of France and Germany.

tried in the civil courts? How far might the Vicar of God intervene in the affairs of the nations?

The clash came over the question of taxation. King Philip IV of France and Edward I of England were both in financial straits. They could not squeeze from the Jews and the cities and the feudal lords enough money to carry on the government; and exemption was claimed for the estates of the Church, as belonging to God. King Edward nevertheless exacted one-fifth of the personal property of the clergy; and Philip one-fiftieth of all property, lay and clerical. Pope Boniface replied in 1290 with the famous Bull, *Clericis Laicos,* forbidding churchmen to pay any part of the Church's revenue to the civil authorities, without papal permission. The Bull also forbade kings and princes to exact such payment, under pain of excommunication.

Unfortunately for the pope, King Philip had just stopped the export of gold and silver from France; and an important source of papal revenue was thus shut off. The pope felt it necessary, therefore, to explain that he had not meant to forbid the clergy to pay the customary feudal dues, or to make loans to the king.

Boniface resumed the attack five years later. He summoned the French prelates to Rome, that he might dictate a settlement of the disorders of France. King Philip thereupon consulted his lay lawyers, who declared the civil power supreme over the ecclesiastical and advised the king to punish the insolent pope. A warning was sent to Boniface who, undaunted, berated the royal envoys.

There followed the famous Bull *Unam Sanctam,* which is both an excellent example of the allegorical method of interpreting the Scriptures and the classic statement of the papal claim to universal sovereignty. The Bull runs, in part, as follows:

The true faith compels us to believe that there is one holy catholic apostolic church, and this we firmly believe and plainly confess. And outside of her there is no salvation or remission of sins, as the Bridegroom says in the Song of Solomon: "My dove, my undefiled is but one"; . . . In this church there is "one Lord, one faith, one baptism" (*Eph.* 4: 5). For in the time of the flood there was only one ark, that of Noah, prefiguring the one church, and it was "finished above in one cubit" (*Gen.* 6: 16), and had but one helmsman and master, namely, Noah. And we read that all things on the earth outside this ark were destroyed. . . . Therefore there is one body of the one and only church, and one head, not two heads, as if the church were a monster. And this head is Christ and his vicar, Peter and his successor; . . . By the words of the gospel we are taught that the two swords, namely, the spiritual authority and the temporal, are in the power of the church. For when the apostle said, "Here are two swords" (*Luke* 22: 38)—that is, in the church, since it was the apostles who were speaking—the Lord did not answer, "It is too much," but "It is enough." . . . Both swords, therefore, the spiritual and the temporal, are in the power of the church. The former is to be used by the church, the latter for the church; the one by the hand of the priest, the other by the hand of kings and knights, but at the command and permission of the priest. . . . For the truth itself declares that the spiritual power must establish the temporal power and pass judgment on it if it is not good. . . . Therefore if the temporal power errs, it will be judged by the spiritual power; and if the lower spiritual power errs, it will be judged by its superior. But if the highest spiritual power errs, it cannot be judged by men, but by God alone. . . . We therefore declare, say, and affirm that submission on the part of every man to the bishop of Rome is altogether necessary for his salvation.[12]

Philip now summoned the States-General, including the prelates of France, and was there assured of the support of the nation. He appealed to a General Council of Christendom; and he and all France were put under an interdict. The king sent to Italy his chancellor, Nogaret, who there collected a band of soldiers and forced his way into the presence of the pope, in the papal palace at Anagni. The envoy heaped insults upon the defiant old man, who died broken-hearted soon after at Rome.

The successor of Boniface dropped all measures against France, and himself died in a few months.[13] Then the influence of France secured the election of the Archbishop of Bordeaux, who became Pope Clement V (1305-1314). Helpless without the support of France, he remained there, moving from one abbey to another throughout his pontificate. Under compulsion of the king, he brought the dead Boniface to trial, and heard him accused by the king's lawyers of abominable crimes. Under the same compulsion he brought the Knights Templars to trial, condemned them without a hearing, and declared the order abolished. Its vast wealth was confiscated to the crown.

The successors of Clement V took up residence at Avignon, on the

---

[12] Thatcher & McNeal, pp. 314-317.
[13] Benedict XI, 1303-1305.

Rhone. There they built a sumptuous palace, that is still a marvel to travellers. For more than seventy years, 1305–1377, the bishops of Rome were absent from their own diocese. It was the "Babylonian Captivity" of the papacy. The blow to papal prestige was very great. Good men were indignant that the Vicar of God should be subservient to the kings of France. They were affronted, too, by the luxury of the papal court, and the increased demands on the rest of Christendom, by reason of the loss of Italian revenues. There was a tendency to disregard papal claims. The Petrine Theory seemed far-fetched at Avignon. No scenes of Peter's ministry were there, no tomb of the apostle beneath the great altar. Paul had not died at Avignon, nor any of the early martyrs of the faith. And the present successors of the apostles seemed more likely to die of self-indulgence.

The effect was felt everywhere in western Europe. In Italy the city-states consolidated their independence. Rome itself became once more a republic, under Cola di Rienzi.[14] In Germany many people lived without the Church. In England Edward III discontinued the tribute that had been paid most of the time since king John.

Another result of the papal exile was the growth of anti-papal theories, especially in France. When the papacy was supreme over the civil power, Thomas Aquinas had believed that to be the divine plan and had provided for it a theoretical basis. Now that the civil power was supreme, men were disposed to see that as the plan of God. The secular power, said John of Paris, is as directly from God as the ecclesiastical. The pope has no secular jurisdiction, said Pierre Dubois. Many treatises set forth the new views.

Of all this literature, the most important single document is the *Defensor Pacis,* by Marsiglio,[15] an Italian priest, teaching at Paris. It is an exposition of political theory, based on the *Politics* of Aristotle and anti-papal in tendency. The State, Marsiglio says, exists for the good of the people, whose right it is to make the laws and choose the form of government. The State has spiritual, as well as temporal functions, being charged with the duty of promoting the welfare of men in both this world and the next. In discharge of this duty, the State is guided by the

---

[14] See Bulwer-Lytton, *Rienzi, Last of the Tribunes,* Everyman's.

[15] Latin *Marsilius,* a canon of the church at Padua. A translation of the *Defensor Pacis* may be had in Thatcher & McNeal, pp. 317-323.

Scriptures. Doubtful passages are to be interpreted by General Councils of Christendom. They will say which are to be regarded as articles of faith. Christians, through their chosen rulers, provide the necessities of life for the clergy; but they decide what these necessities are. They do not pay tithes, or other excessive church levies. Indeed they may turn the existing estates of the Church to other uses, if these are greater than are needed.

Within the Church, Marsiglio thinks, the supreme authority is not the pope, but a General Council. All bishops are of equal spiritual authority, and receive their commission direct from Christ. Neither pope nor bishop nor priest can excommunicate a Christian. Only the Church, the society of all who believe in Christ, can do that. Nor can the pope place a community under the interdict; for Christian people, through their chosen ruler, may compel the clergy they support to continue divine services and administer the sacraments.

Similar doctrines were heard everywhere. In Italy Dante declared the State to be of God as truly as the Church, and profane history to exhibit his work as surely as sacred history. In England William of Occam and his disciple John Wyclif took up the theme. Occam affirmed that the papacy must adopt the principle of Christ, "My kingdom is not of this world." John Wyclif, Master of Balliol College at Oxford, set forth in many treatises the principles that were later adopted by the Protestant reformers.

Wyclif (c. 1324–1384) requires more than passing notice, because his dissent took shape in a movement that was to prove permanent. There were such movements already, the Beghards in Germany, the Vaudois in the valleys of the Alps, the Catharists in Corsica. These were alike in their rejection of the sacraments and ceremonies of Catholicism. They were Puritans three hundred years before the rise of Puritanism. And they had vigour, too, and great tenacity; so much so that the Inquisition could not subdue them. But they were scattered and illiterate movements. The Wyclifite movement was different. It was a protest against the whole Catholic system, made by a great Oxford scholar and divine, who had at first the support of Oxford, and who applied his scholarship to bring the Gospel to simple folk and provide for them an alternative to Catholicism. Wyclif set himself to turn the Scriptures into English, so that they might be available to the common people; and his order of poor preachers, the Lollards, carried the Gospel through the land.

Wyclif was first drawn into national affairs as the expert adviser of John of Gaunt, Duke of Lancaster, third son of Edward III. John of Gaunt was one of many notable men, who desired to see the Church in England disendowed and the drain upon English resources by the papacy brought to an end. Wyclif sympathized with such aims and, as his thought developed, was led further and further, until virtually the whole Catholic system came under his censure. In treatise after treatise, he affirmed that the king had such jurisdiction over the Church as he had over all other institutions within the nation, that the bishops were neglecting their legitimate duties for politics, that monasticism was useless, that the preaching of the Friars was claptrap. In the end he rejected the Catholic doctrine of the Mass, condemned prelacy, called for a democratic Church, and appealed from the authority of the Church to that of the Scriptures.

Before Wyclif died he was expelled from the University; and soon his preachers, too, were refused admission. Educated leadership thus died out of Lollardy. Nevertheless it survived, though banned by law, hunted and driven under ground, until educated leadership came again, through the Renaissance and the Reformation. Lollards were among the earliest recruits for Protestantism in England; and many who were not Lollards abandoned Catholicism more readily because they had learned from Lollardy that one may be cut off from Catholicism without being thereby cut off from Christ.

On the continent Lollardy had important results in the Kingdom of Bohemia. Its Slavic population had first received Christianity from the Greek Church; and it was only by German coercion that they were brought into the Roman Church. The Czechs retained the mystical temper and excitability of the Slav, and his dislike for the German. The pomp of Catholicism, too, continued uncongenial to the Czech peasantry. Puritan heresy was already widespread in Bohemia in the twelfth century; and in the late fourteenth century protests against ecclesiastical abuses were stimulated by the writings of Wyclif. There began then a great national movement for the reformation of Christianity.

Bohemia had recently received a foreign dynasty, of the house of Luxemburg. They were members of that brilliant French-speaking aristocracy, introduced to the modern world in the sprightly *Chronicles*

could not look to popes to end the papal schism. But reforming spirits continued to agitate, especially Gerson, who was a Nominalist and thought General Councils supreme in the Church. Gerson was deeply moved, too, at the shame of the Church. He wrote: "The court of Rome has created a thousand offices by which to make money, but hardly one for the propagation of virtue. From morning to night there is talk of nothing but armies, lands, towns, and money; rarely, or rather never, do they speak of chastity, charity, justice, fidelity, and a pure life." At last the Cardinal College summoned the Church to a General Council at Pisa in 1409.

The Council of Pisa immediately found itself divided in judgment, one party favouring reform by action of the Council itself, another party favouring the election of a pope, under whose direction reform would proceed. The latter opinion prevailed. After exacting from each cardinal an oath that he would, if elected pope, continue the Council until a thorough reform of the Church was effected, the Council declared the rival popes deposed and elected Alexander V. Christendom now found itself with three popes, anathematizing each other.

Alexander V hastily dissolved the Council of Pisa and, dying soon, was succeeded by John XXIII. But the demand for reform could not be silenced. Gerson and the University of Paris continued to agitate. The Emperor Sigismund visited Rome, to press the case; and Pope John yielded. He would summon a Council to Italy, to one of the Lombard cities. Sigismund insisted upon a Council in Germany; and one was called to meet at Constance in 1414.

The Council of Constance proved to be the greatest assemblage in the history of the Church. Indeed it had the appearance rather of a congress of statesmen and politicians, to settle the affairs of Europe, than a General Council of the Church. Pope John and the Emperor were present, with some eighteen thousand ecclesiastics and numberless princes and knights. The Council began by declaring itself the supreme authority in the Church: "This holy synod of Constance, being a general council, and legally assembled in the Holy Spirit . . . declares that this synod, legally assembled, is a general council, and represents the catholic church militant and has its authority direct from Christ; and everybody, of whatever rank or dignity, including also the pope, is bound to obey this council in those things which pertain to the faith, to the ending of the schism, and to a general reformation of the church in its head and members." [19]

Thus fortified, the Council heard accusations against Pope John, who thereupon fled and commanded the Council to dissolve. The authority of the Emperor, however, and the eloquence of Gerson held it together. Pope John was imprisoned. Pope Gregory XII sent his resignation. Pope Benedict XIII was declared a heretic and deserted by his own party. The schism was thus ended. But reform proved exceedingly difficult. There were vested interests, long established, everywhere. Most cardinals were opposed to reformatory action, except by the Cardinal College and the papal court, or Curia. So it seemed necessary to look for leadership to the pope about to be elected. The Council tried to commit him in advance by decreeing that, before the Council should be dissolved, "the future pope, by the grace of God soon to be elected," must reform the Church, with the aid of the Council, in certain particulars. First, the question of the number of cardinals, and their distribution among the nations, was to be reviewed. And those "papal reservations" were to be reconsidered, by which popes reserved to themselves the right to appoint clergymen to the richest livings everywhere and made them pay well for appointment. The matter of Annates, too, was to be reviewed. Annates were the income of a bishopric during the first year of the new bishop, and the income from every living, or benefice, made vacant by the death of a cleric. These were now claimed for the papacy, a new form of extortion, resented everywhere. Then there was the sale of "expectancies," i.e. the chance of succeeding to the benefices of those still living. And there were the appeals from national courts to the papal court. Such appeals were a source of revenue to the Curia, but delayed and confused judicial processes everywhere.

Other reforms were listed. Simony was to cease, and the sale of indulgences. A method was to be devised for disciplining a pope, and even for deposing him when necessary. And finally it was decreed that there should be frequent General Councils.[20]

With such safeguards the Council chose as pope Odo Colonna, of an ancient and distinguished Roman family, who assumed the name Martin

[19] Thatcher & McNeal, p. 328.
[20] Thatcher & McNeal, pp. 329–332.

V. He was an astute Italian politician, sympathetic with papal autocracy, and bound to frustrate constitutional change. His interest was in the Papal State and the Curia; and he did restore order and alleviate somewhat the poverty and shame of Rome. As for reforms elsewhere, he preferred to enter into separate concordats with the respective governments of Europe, rather than work through a rival authority, the General Council.

One thing the Council of Constance did achieve, as we have seen. It burned as a heretic John Huss. It also commanded that the bones of Wyclif be exhumed from holy ground, burned and scattered to the winds. The Council that worked in vain for moral reform, would not endure doctrinal change.

The demand for a General Council, however, persisted. The University of Paris still agitated. The Hussites were gathering strength and boldness. The English government threatened to undertake its own reform of the Church in England. Pope Martin yielded at length, summoned a Council to meet at Basel in 1431, and on the eve of the Council died. He had already strengthened the papacy for resistance, and destroyed the hope of reform.

Martin, the Roman noble, was succeeded by Eugenius IV, a gentleman of Venice. A General Council, setting itself above the pope and presuming to improve his ways, was as abhorrent to Eugenius as to Martin. The Council of Basel had to contend throughout with the hostility of the papacy. The nations, too, could not agree. Spanish sentiment was as hostile to change in the Church as German and English sentiment was insistent for it. Most Frenchmen cared chiefly that the papacy should be a perquisite of France. The Council struggled on intermittently for eighteen years, then died of inanition in 1449.

The papacy had won. Having been so long Vicars of God, popes could not now be controlled, as if they were but men. After another ten years Pope Pius II, in the Bull *Execrabilis,* condemned and prohibited all appeals to a General Council. "The execrable and hitherto unknown abuse has grown up in our day, that certain persons, imbued with the spirit of rebellion, and not from a desire to secure a better judgment, . . . presume to appeal from the pope to a future council, in spite of the fact that the pope is the vicar of Jesus Christ. . . . Wishing therefore to expel this pestiferous poison from the church of Christ and to care for the salvation of the flock entrusted to us, and to remove every cause of offence from the fold of the Saviour, with the advice and consent of our brothers, the cardinals of the holy Roman Church, and of all the prelates, and of those who have been trained in the canon and civil law, who are at our court, and with our own sure knowledge, we condemn all such appeals and prohibit them as erroneous and detestable." [21]

The clerical leaders of reform lost heart, and one by one went over to the papal party; [22] but forces were gathering that no reaction could withstand. Having evaded reformation in the fifteenth century, the leaders of reaction brought on a revolution in the sixteenth.

[21] Thatcher & McNeal, p. 332.

[22] The nations were able to gather some fruit of the struggle. A French National Assembly at Bourges, in 1438, adopted for France the reforms decreed at Basel, and embodied them in the *Pragmatic Sanction of Bourges*. A German Diet at Frankfort, in 1439, adopted them in the *Charter of Acceptation*. These mitigated, without removing, the evils against which the Christian conscience had cried out.

CHAPTER XIV

THE ADOLESCENCE OF EUROPE

WHEN the Conciliar Movement was ending in frustration, another movement was under way, which neither indifference nor reaction could stay. It was a steady growth of individualism. The ideal man of the Middle Ages had effaced himself for the monastery, the Church, the Empire. The traditions of institutions, therefore, regulated the lives and thoughts of men. Now men were becoming intolerant of control, and anxious to secure for themselves free scope in spheres outside the regulation of authority. There was a certain joy of exploration in the air.

The resulting movement is called the Renaissance, or re-birth. It took many forms. In politics it ran to nationalism. In jurisprudence it meant a return to Roman Civil Law, as a foil to the omnipresent Canon Law. In literature and painting and sculpture the Renaissance was a return to classical models, in which men had freely depicted the beauty of Nature and the human frame, before Catholicism taught men to disparage the present life. And because there was a new interest in Nature, science and invention and geographical discovery accompanied the Renaissance.

The word Renaissance, however, is commonly used in a narrower sense, to describe the revival of literature and art; and as this aspect is of special significance for religion, we shall consider it alone. The Renaissance, in this narrower sense, was at first a return to the past. The young languages of the West were, or were thought to be, inadequate instruments of literature. Greek and Latin were the better vehicles of ideas; and classical writers supplied the models. We have seen that Latin Classics did survive through all the Middle Ages, especially in the Benedictine monasteries. Even the Greek Classics never quite disappeared. The Greek tongue could still be heard in South Italy and Sicily. The University of Salerno was a centre of Greek culture. But the present-worldliness of the Classics set against the other-worldliness of Catholic Christianity; and the Classics could not flourish where the enjoyment of the Classics was a sin.

As early as the thirteenth century there were signs of a new attitude. Humanism returned, the eagerness of men to know themselves, their history and achievements. The scientific spirit, too, appeared, study and observation for the sake of new knowledge. All this is well seen in the Emperor Frederick II.

This early Humanism was largely confined to Italy, and was not hostile to the Church. The hierarchy gradually recovered from its first distrust. Cardinals became the patrons of Humanism. Knowledge of the Classics became a road to preferment, within the Church itself. The implications of "the New Learning" for mediaeval Christianity were not yet seen. And anyway religious indifference was not uncommon among the prelates, who felt secure in the vast edifice of Catholicism.

By the fourteenth century, therefore, Humanism was an influential movement. Its chief exponents then are famous still. They were Dante, Petrarch and Boccaccio, all associated with Florence, which was becoming the spiritual capital of Italy.

Dante Alighieri, who died just as the fourteenth century was well begun, shows that strange mingling of the old and the new that appears in all times of transition. He is scholastic in thought, steeped in the philosophy of Aristotle and Aquinas, and enthusiastic for the Catholic Church. Nevertheless, taking Virgil for his master, Dante is delicate and minute in his observations of Nature. The *Divina Commedia,* the religious epic which Dante, because of its literary pattern, calls a comedy, shows a striking fusion of the spirit of Virgil with mediaeval ideas, and a capacity for independent judgment of the most sacred things. Dante thought the Church corrupted by wealth and power, and consigned several popes to hell, only one to heaven.

In Francesco Petrarca (1304–1374) Humanism advanced a step further. Petrarch, as we call him, grew up at Avignon, where his father, a political exile from Florence, was employed at the papal court. Necessity made Petrarch a copyist, teacher, lawyer, librarian and what not; but his interest was in Nature and life, and the description of them in literature. Disparaging "the vulgar tongues," he tried at first to write in Latin; but his laborious epic, the *Africa,* written in imitation of Virgil's

when Lorenzo de'Medici was master of Florence and the leading city-states were at peace among themselves, arts and letters advanced swiftly. In the city of Dante, Petrarch and Boccaccio, there appeared in one generation Michael Angelo and Donatello, Filippo Lippi and Botticelli, Luca della Robbia and Leonardo da Vinci, and other artists of almost equal repute.

These artists were Catholic Christians. The Church was their patron. Most of their subjects were chosen from the Bible. Three distinguished painters—Angelico and Filippo Lippi and Bartolomeo—were Friars. Nevertheless art became less and less ascetic, more and more humane. Artists, too, became less imitative. The severe simplicity of classical art, especially in architecture, gave place to something softer and more luxuriant, expressing the Italian passion for decoration.

In literature there was a notable diminution in scholastic and theological interest. Authors disclosed the beauty and meaning of the ancient world, recovered Plato for mankind, and introduced scientific historical criticism. The pioneer in criticism was Lorenzo Valla, teacher in various Italian Universities, then literary attaché at the court of King Alfonso of Naples. Valla's examination and rejection of the so-called *Donation of Constantine* introduced a new epoch in criticism. The document was the legal title of the papacy to its lands, and had long been unquestioned. Dante, Marsiglio of Padua, John Wyclif, the reforming Councils, had assumed its genuineness. Valla examined it in 1440, and showed that it was much later than Constantine and therefore a forgery.

The Italian Renaissance was stimulated by the fall of Constantinople to the Turks in 1453, and the flight of Greek scholars to the West. Some of them—Chrysoloras, Theodore Gaza, George of Trebizond—became famous as schoolmasters of great men from other lands, like Reuchlin and Erasmus, John Colet and Sir Thomas More.

The Vatican shared the enthusiasm for the new culture. A little of the prestige, lost by the papacy during the Babylonian Captivity and the papal schism, was recovered by its patronage of literature and the arts. Rome itself, long in decay, was restored and adorned by a succession of popes. Paul II restored the arches of Septimius Severus and Titus, and collected gems and bronzes for the Vatican. Nicholas V founded the Vatican Library. Leo X, a Medici, brought both Renaissance architecture and papal munificence to their summit when he completed the magnificent new St. Peter's, whose cost spread consternation through the Catholic world.

The invention of printing came just in time to serve the Italian Renaissance. Printing from movable types seems to have originated in Germany, at Mainz, in or about 1455, when Johann Gutenberg set up a press there. From Mainz the new art spread swiftly to other lands. In Italy it was employed to further classical studies. Aldus Minutius established the Aldine Press at Venice, and devoted himself to improve education in Italy, by providing good and cheap literature. Classic after classic came from the Aldine Press, in editions beautiful and inexpensive, that could be carried on the person. The vast folios of the past were no longer necessary to literary studies, and were now buried in the depths of great libraries and museums.

The Italian Renaissance continued in full flower just long enough to communicate its tastes and activities to the northern nations. Until the close of the fifteenth century aristocrats in France and Germany and England were still without intellectual interests, addicted to little but arms and the chase. Then Charles VIII of France, finding his kingdom sufficiently recovered from the Hundred Years' War and his mettlesome knights dull for lack of adventure, resolved to revive the old Angevin claim to the Kingdom of Naples. Italian political discords encouraged foreign adventures in Italy. So King Charles descended upon that country in 1494.

The aggression of Charles whetted the appetite of Spain, which had recently become a great European power through the marriage of King Ferdinand of Aragon with Isabella of Castile and the political union of their countries. Isabella was a bigoted Catholic. The first exploit, therefore, of united Spain was the conquest of the little Moslem state of Granada, a state more highly civilized than any other part of the Iberian peninsula. And the conquest was the prelude to Franco-Spanish contests for possession of Italy. Joanna, daughter of Ferdinand and Isabella, married Philip of Flanders. Their son, Ferdinand the Catholic, therefore inherited both Spain and the Netherlands. In time he was elected emperor of the Holy Roman Empire, and bethought him that the emperors had once ruled Italy.

The march of Charles VIII into Italy thus opened a sixty-years' struggle between French kings and Spanish king-emperors. When the struggle ended, both Lombardy and Naples were in the power of the solemn and bigoted Spaniards. And the Italian Renaissance, so brilliant in the fifteenth century, was smothered in a blanket of Spanish and clerical tyranny in the sixteenth. The Jesuits, the Inquisition, the Index of Prohibited Books, destroyed the eager, vivid academies. The Renaissance, therefore, aristocratic and exclusive from the beginning, was stopped before it reached the Italian masses.

But if the march of Charles VIII into Italy led to repression there, it led towards freedom in the North. It was not until the invasion of Italy that the French became aware of its splendours and were prepared for a Renaissance at home. The lands that are now France had just been united by a fortunate series of accidents. The death of Duke Charles the Bold of Burgundy in 1477, without a male heir, brought Burgundy, Picardy and Artois back to the French crown. The death in similar circumstances of René, King of Aix, in 1480 brought Maine, Anjou and Provence. When Francis, Duke of Brittany, died, no son was left to carry on the ancient quarrel of Brittany with France. And in England the long-drawn-out war of the Yorkists and Lancastrians precluded effective activity abroad. So mediaeval feudalism in France was displaced by a national monarchy.

France was open now to intellectual currents from Italy, at a time when they were flowing in from Flanders as well. The county of Flanders had been under the dukes of Burgundy. These had held court at Brussels and made it a brilliant city. They had fostered the fine arts throughout all Flanders, as well as trade and commerce, and made Antwerp a great commercial city. When Burgundy reverted to France, the art of Flemish painters[1] and sculptors spread westward through Burgundy into France. By the late fifteenth century North Germany also, in matters of art, was a colony of Flanders.

In general education, too, Germany was advancing. As early as the fourteenth century there was a notable movement, one aspect of which

---

[1] This art of the Netherlands was not an abrupt change from the mediaeval and Gothic, and a reversion to antiquity, as in Italy. It came as a natural development. The Netherlands had an affluent, vivid city life. Here was the second great town system of Europe, as that of Italy was the first. And the Flemish painters were original, painting from the life. To please rich patrons, proud of their homes, the artists reproduced interiors.

was the rise of the great Universities.[2] These Universities were still
mediaeval. That is to say, the teachers were monks and the substance of
study Scholasticism. There was more of Aristotle than of Jesus, and
more of Logic than of either Nature or life. The Universities did, however, stimulate some broader intellectual interest, as Universities usually
do. Besides, there were in Germany organizations of Christian mystics,
of more liberal mind than the Universities. Most important of these
educationally were the Brethren of the Common Lot, founded by Gerard
Groot, a wealthy burgher, won to piety by the example of a Flemish
mystic, Ruysbroeck. The aim of the Brethren was to improve the religious education of youth. The houses of the order had excellent
libraries. The brothers translated Christian authors into German, distributed tracts, and supported themselves by copying and selling manuscripts. They had schools everywhere, the most important being that at
Deventer, from which came Erasmus and other famous men.

By the middle of the fifteenth century humanist associations existed
in German cities, companies of rich youths, to study Latin and Greek, to
paint and to write poetry. They had been educated in the schools of the
Brethren of the Common Lot, had then gone to Italy, and returned to
Germany to become patrons of learning. Art also began to put on the
humanistic dress, as the influence of Italy was added to that of the
Netherlands.

Humanism entered the Universities more slowly; but classical
scholars were admitted at length, and chairs founded in poetry and
oratory. Erfurt was the first; and an association of Humanists was soon
formed among its alumni. The leader was Conrad Mut, who had been
at Deventer before coming to Erfurt, and who went from Erfurt to
study Canon Law at Bologna. Mut became the friend of Italian Humanists, and returned to Germany to be Canon of the cathedral at Gotha and
centre of the humanist circle at Erfurt.

German Humanists were loyal Catholics. They aimed to make the
new learning serve the best interests of religion; but they were critical
of abuses. "We cozen money," said Mut, "we consecrate God, we shake
hell, and we work miracles; whether we be heavenly minded or earthly
minded makes no matter."

[2] Prague was founded in 1348, Vienna in 1365, Heidelberg in 1386, Cologne in 1388,
Erfurt in 1392, Leipzig just after the century closed.

So German Humanists occasionally got into difficulties with the Church. John Reuchlin was once a storm-centre for all Germany. Reuchlin (1455–1522) was a scholar, not only in Latin and Greek but in Hebrew as well, a thing then unknown. He found a certain Pfefferkorn, a dubious convert from Judaism to Christianity, advocating the destruction of Hebrew literature. That policy was approved by the Dominicans. They appealed for support in the pious work to the Emperor Maximilian, who turned for advice to Reuchlin and the Universities. Was it safe for Christians, he asked, that Hebrew writings, except the Bible, should be permitted to exist? Only Reuchlin advised against the proposed vandalism. He favoured a fearless investigation of all literature in the search for truth, reminded his public that there were known to be errors in the authorized translation of the Bible, the Vulgate, and urged toleration.

Reuchlin immediately found himself in furious controversy with Pfefferkorn and the Dominicans of Cologne. The Humanists of Germany rallied to his support; and he published certain *Letters from Distinguished Men*.[3] They were followed by anonymous letters, satirizing in brilliant fashion scholastic interests and methods of reasoning. The satires, which sprang into immediate fame, were called *Letters of Obscure Men*,[4] and seem to have proceeded from the humanist circle of Erfurt, and especially from Ulric von Hutten, a nobleman of Swabia, recently crowned Poet Laureate by Maximilian.

The controversy continued six years, and ended in defeat for obscurantism. No cause could survive the ridicule poured upon it in the *Letters of Obscure Men*. Reuchlin had been summoned to Mainz, for trial before the Grand Inquisitor, but appealed to Rome, where the trial was quashed.

Of greater fame than Reuchlin, most famous indeed of all Humanists, was Reuchlin's younger contemporary, Erasmus of Rotterdam. In him the humanistic tendency was developed into a system. As Albert the Great and Thomas Aquinas had attempted so to interpret Catholicism as to show it harmonious with the Aristotelian philosophy, as Ficino and Giovanni Pico, of the Academy at Florence, attempted to combine Catholic Christianity with Platonism, in a philosophy-religion for all

---

[3] *Epistolae Clarorum Virorum.*

[4] *Epistolae Obscurorum Virorum.* These may be had, in both Latin and English, in F. Griffin Stokes, *Epistolae Obscurorum Virorum,* Chatto & Windus.

mankind, so Erasmus now attempted to interpret Catholicism as funda-
mentally humane, and the natural faith of enlightened men.

Desiderius Erasmus (1467–1536), a native of the Netherlands, was
the natural son of a priest,[5] orphaned in childhood and placed in the
school of the Brethren of the Common Lot at Deventer. Religion there
was mystical and practical, devoted to the imitation of Christ, and little
concerned with rites and ceremonies. The most famous son of the school,
Thomas à Kempis, was still living when Erasmus was a child, and his
Imitation of Christ was being carried abroad by the new race of printers.

Leaving Deventer while still in his teens, Erasmus was persuaded by
his guardian to enter a monastery. He chafed at the restrictions of the
new life and, having already a reputation as a scholar, he was able after
a few years to secure a papal dispensation, permitting him to lay aside the
monastic garb and live where he would. Erasmus now became a wandering scholar and citizen of the world, teaching briefly at Cambridge, then
at Louvain, living at Venice, to be near the Aldine Press, and at Basel,
near the famous publisher Froben.

Erasmus was a scholar in both Latin and Greek, writing all his books
and pamphlets, and even his letters, in Latin. It became more familiar
to him than his native Dutch. And his Latin was that of the Augustan
Age, not the corrupt Latin of the Middle Ages. Erasmus was the acknowledged stylist of his time.

He was also a deeply religious man, profoundly concerned about the
religious conditions of his time. There was abundant reason for concern. The papacy itself, though admonished by the reforming Councils,
was as debased in fifty years as it had ever been. When Erasmus was
twenty-five, a wealthy Spaniard, Rodrigo Borgia, bribed the Cardinal
College to make him pope. He was worldly, sensual, treacherous, a match
for the fierce Roman families with which he had to cope. His brilliant
son, Caesare Borgia, brought every resource of violence and fraud to
the aid of his father, and is immortalized by Machiavelli in *The Prince*.
Machiavelli saw in Caesare Borgia the model for a new and better state-
craft, superior to pity, unhampered by morality or religious faith.

There was much genuine religious life in Europe; and the Rome of
the Borgias was distressing to good men. "The scandal," said Savonarola,

[5] He is the Gerard of Charles Reade's great historical novel, *The Cloister and the Hearth,*
Everyman's Library.

"begins in Rome and runs through the whole clergy; they are worse than Turks and Moors. . . . They buy preferments and bestow them on their children or brothers, who take possession of them by violence and all sorts of sinful means. Their greed is insatiable, they do all things for gold. . . . They sell their benefices, sell the sacraments, traffic in masses. . . . If a priest or canon leads an ordinary life, he is mocked and called a hypocrite."

This was the scene that met the eyes of Erasmus when he wrote his famous satire, *The Praise of Folly*. A good Catholic, he nevertheless mocked at pilgrimages, rites, ceremonies, the tiresome disputes of the Scholastics, the personal character of many of the monks. His own idea of the Christian life, Erasmus set forth in a charming little *Handbook of a Christian Soldier,* better known by the first word of the Latin title, the *Enchiridion*. It was written, he said, to correct the error of those who thought religion a matter of external observances. "Most Christians," he said, "are superstitious instead of pious and, except for the name of Christ, are not far from the superstition of the heathen." True piety is following Christ.

The piety inculcated by Jesus is described by Erasmus, in humanistic fashion, as the philosophy of Christ. Its controlling principle is charity. "For this cause chiefly Christ was born and died, that he might teach us not to do as the Jews do but to love. . . . Paul, when writing to the Corinthians, put charity before miracles and prophecy and the tongues of angels. And do not tell me that charity consists in going often to church, in bowing before the images of the saints, in lighting candles, in repeating the prescribed prayers. God has no need of these things. Paul means by charity to edify your neighbours, to count all men members of the same body, to think of them all as one in Christ; . . . in short to employ all your wealth, all your effort, all your care, for this end, that in Christ you may be as useful as possible."

Such piety, Erasmus thought, was beyond the power of man unaided to achieve. Being a Humanist, he did stress the dignity and worth of man; but man was of worth by reason of what God had done for him, in creating him, redeeming him, making his physical frame a temple of the Holy Spirit, and his mind a habitation of God. To continue worthy of so great a heritage, one must be aided by both prayer and knowledge. And while self-respect alone requires one to live the Christian life, one is urged to it also by the prospect of a world to come, where God rewards the good and punishes the evil. Thus for Erasmus, as for Christian Humanists in general, the doctrine of a future life of rewards and punishments remained as fundamental as in mediaeval and in ancient Christianity.

The *Enchiridion* was widely read; and, though many monks and Schoolmen were outraged, it was warmly approved by others. It was unusual, without being heretical; and its presentation of a simple, ethical Christianity met a widespread need.

More important, however, than any other single achievement of Erasmus was his publication of the New Testament in Greek. Keenly aware of the general ignorance as to Christ's teaching, Erasmus wished to see the New Testament translated into modern languages and made available to the public. To this end he went straight to the Greek original of the New Testament, ignoring the Latin Vulgate, in order that scholars translating the sacred writings might have a dependable Greek text from which to work.

The popularity of Erasmus' writings was immense; and they were supplemented by a few contemporaries in other lands. From England John Colet, son of a Lord Mayor of London, went for humanistic studies to Italy, then returned to lecture at Oxford on the Epistles of St. Paul. Colet applied to the Epistles a scientific method, treating them as communications from a living man to living people, not as an "arsenal of texts to defend the dogmas of the Church." The Scriptures had never been so interpreted in England; and Colet's lecture-hall was thronged. Called to London, to be Dean of St. Paul's Cathedral, he preached an ethical Christianity there and denounced publicly the sins of the clergy.

So also with Sir Thomas More, son of a London barrister and a brilliant student of the Classics at Oxford. More became a distinguished lawyer, and Lord Chancellor of England for Henry VIII. He died at last a martyr for the Catholicism he loved; but in life he had joined Erasmus in satirizing its faults. His *Utopia* is a brilliant satire on Catholic society in England, and a picture of the ideal Christian State.

The century of the Renaissance was a century, too, when men's ideas of the world were enlarged. Erasmus was twenty-five, Luther nine, years of age when Columbus discovered America. It was the crowning event in a period of discovery, begun two centuries before, when the Polo brothers, Nicolo and Maffee, merchants of Venice, went overland to China and were welcomed by the Mongol emperor at Peking, Kubla, the great khan. On a second visit, the brothers took with them young Marco, son of Nicolo. The party traversed Persia, went on and on to the plateau of Pamir, and thence descended upon Kashgar, Yarkand and Khotan. Crossing the desert of Gobi, they came again to Peking in 1275. Young Marco acquired the language of the country, entered the public service, travelled as an imperial commissioner to the borders of Tibet and into India, and *en route* made note of such things as might interest Kubla Khan.

After seventeen years the three Polos, having grown rich in the East, returned by sea to Persia, thence overland to Venice, which they reached in 1295. There Marco Polo commanded a galley for the Doge Dandolo, in battle with the Genoese. He was taken prisoner to Genoa, and there dictated to Rusticiano of Pisa an account of his travels. Europe thus learned of regions that were not again to be described until the nineteenth century. Before Marco died the earliest *Portolani,* or scientific coast-charts for mariners and merchants, were being published. They were an attempt to represent the known world on the basis of observed fact, without appeal to ancient books and theological views.

Marco Polo's *Book* precipitated an intellectual revolution among the geographically minded. The Mediterranean was not, as its name suggested, the centre of the world. Seven thousand miles to the east was a land, no longer legendary, of vast population, with a culture equal to that of Italy and an opulence much greater. To acquire its silks and spices, without paying exorbitant tolls on the way home, to Abyssinians and Arabs and the Mamelukes of Egypt, it seemed worthwhile to avoid the Red Sea route and explore other ways to the East. So the sailors of Genoa and Portugal took to the Atlantic. For a century they crept along the west coast of Africa, establishing settlements. Then in 1428 Don Pedro of Portugal procured a copy of Marco Polo's *Book* and presented it to his brother, Prince Henry the Navigator. The prince began, and Vasco da Gama continued, the organization of maritime trade and discovery. They circumnavigated Africa, and founded the Portuguese empire in India.

These events led on to the attempt of Columbus to reach the East by sailing westward across the Atlantic, an attempt that brought to light a great new continent in the western sea.

The discovery of America, just when printed books were first diffusing knowledge everywhere, stirred the mind of Europe. The geography taught by learned monks, confirmed by the Scriptures, and accepted in the Universities, was now proven wrong. The world was much larger than had been thought. The Mediterranean ceased to be the centre of civilization. Commercial supremacy passed from the city-states of Italy to the nations fronting on the Atlantic, to Portugal first, then in succession to Spain, to the Netherlands, to France and England. A new era opened, an era of colonies and empires beyond the seas, and the spread of European ideas and institutions everywhere.

Catholic piety had a part in all this early maritime adventure. At the Vatican, and especially among the Franciscans, it was hoped that the enterprises of Spain and Portugal overseas would lead to the conversion of heathen peoples, and to another attempt to conquer Islam, this time from the East. For was not the Negus of Abyssinia a Christian? And did not a Christian state survive in India, from the very days of the apostles, St. Thomas having preached there when St. Paul was evangelizing Europe? It was believed that Catholic Europe, supported by these Christian states, might triumph in one last crusade against the infidel. This was "the plan of the Indies," published by Pope Nicholas V as early as 1454, in a papal bull to the king of Portugal. And it was with such pious hopes that Columbus himself set out to find the Indies in the West.

Nevertheless the effect of geographical discovery on the Catholic mind was to be very great. Authority could no longer go unchallenged, nor the past remain forever supreme. What the times invited was not renaissance but discovery, less from ancient books, given by revelation, than from observation and experiment. And when Pope Alexander VI, a Spaniard and a Borgia, awarded to Spain and Portugal all the lands "in the West, towards the Indies or the Ocean Seas," events proved that his writ no longer ran with sea-captains and merchant princes, in France and Holland and England.

The reader will naturally infer, from this long recital of disturbing movements and events, that Catholicism, when the sixteenth century opened, was near collapse. Doctrinal dissent and defection on moral grounds, the scientific interest created by the twelfth-century Renaissance and encouraged by the Nominalistic philosophy, the Universities that resulted and their restlessness, the Babylonian Captivity of the papacy and the anti-papal theories it encouraged, the reforming Councils, with their acrimonius debates and near-futility! How could the fabric of the great Church be intact, after such shaking events, so long continued? And at length the ardent individualism of Renaissance men, and their Humanism! Not all Humanists felt the concern for Mother Church that Reuchlin felt, and Erasmus, Dean Colet and Sir Thomas More. Many Humanists, persuaded that "This world's no blot or blank," and finding Catholic piety too preoccupied with the next world, abandoned Catholicism, and with it all religion. This was especially true in Italy, and under the very shadow of St. Peter's. Even in northern lands, where most Humanists remained Catholic Christians, they were now assailing Mother Church with satire, making sport of familiar Catholic assumptions and practices.

Yet the Catholic Church had kept disparate tendencies within her ample embrace for a thousand years. There had always been men, chiefly ecclesiastics, who sought in her, not religion but a career. There were others who followed the mystic way, seeking satisfaction for the soul in contemplation and communion and ecstasy. They were doctrinally obedient, chiefly because uninterested in doctrine and incurious about it. There were others who, like the Christian Humanists but without their educational equipment, sought to recover the simplicity of Christ and his moral beauty, loving their enemies, returning blessing for a curse, and serving all mankind. If some of them, like the Waldenses, had thought it necessary to leave the Catholic Church, others, like the Franciscans, had stayed within. Thus in one great fellowship of the Catholic Church many men had many minds; and she endured them all and turned them to her uses, if only they did not too openly resist her authority and disturb her peace. And outside all parties were the common people, the rank and file of Catholics, who had no mind of their own about religious questions. In infancy they awoke to consciousness within the Church; in childhood they were indoctrinated into the rudiments of her teaching; through life they came to her mysterious rites, submitted to her discipline, and looked less timidly on that account to the dread hereafter. At the end Mother Church would lay their bodies away in consecrated ground, and interest herself in the post-mortem discipline still requisite to the final shriving of their souls.

The masses of western Europe, in the time of Erasmus, were just such obedient Catholics, illiterate still and untroubled by the conflicts of ideas among the literate. They thought of Mother Church, not as herself in error, but as betrayed sometimes by faithless leaders. They asked of her, when they asked anything, not change but revival. Then a German monk, shocked by a specific abuse of Christian credulity, brought the matter to the attention of his bishop and archbishop, only to find himself reprimanded as a disturber and reported for discipline to the bishop of Rome. Luther was thus driven to defend himself and, in developing his defence, arrived at what has ever since been called Protestantism. His example encouraged others; and in Germany and Switzerland, France and Italy and England, there were soon movements, no longer protesting single abuses, but rejecting Catholicism as such.

CHAPTER XV

GERMANS REVOLT AGAINST MOTHER CHURCH

MARTIN LUTHER was a native of Saxony, born at Eisleben, November 10, 1483. His father, John Luther, was of honest, rugged, thrifty peasant stock; his mother, Margaretha, of somewhat higher station and more refined. During the infancy of Martin, his parents left Eisleben for Mansfeld, a few miles away, in a district of copper-mines; and there John Luther advanced slowly to be a mine-owner, a member of the town council, and armourer to the Counts of Mansfeld.

John and Margaretha Luther were devout. They taught their child to pray, and nourished him on legends of the saints and the superstitions of the German peasantry. Having learned from Mother Church that God dealt strictly with their sins, they dealt strictly with their children's. Martin tells long afterward, though quite without bitterness, of discipline so severe that he was completely cowed. Sent early to school, more discipline awaited him, which also he remembered to the end.

Happier days dawned for Martin, when at fourteen he was sent to the city of Magdeburg, to a school of the Brethren of the Common Lot, and soon thereafter to Eisenach, the city of his mother's family. As John Luther had not yet reached affluence, Martin sang for alms at the windows of the rich, a practice made respectable by the example of the Friars. His sweet voice and open countenance attracted the attention of Madame Ursula Cotta, wife of a prominent citizen, who took him into her home. There Martin was in a peaceful, cultivated Christian household. And in the school, to which he went daily, was a master learned and courteous, a certain John Trebonius.

Under John Trebonius, Martin's progress was rapid; and after four years he entered the University of Erfurt, "the German Bologna," of which it was commonly said, "He who would study well, must go to Erfurt." The professors at Erfurt were still Scholastics, but of the later Nominalistic sort; and Humanism had found a footing. Luther was introduced to philosophy and the physical sciences, and to the Greek and Latin classics. The classics opened for him a window upon another world, not Catholic. He pored over the Bible too, which he had known only from the lessons in the Missal and Breviary. He had now, for the first time, the whole Latin Bible in his hands. Nor did he neglect prayer, taking as his motto "to pray well is to study well." Erfurt regarded him as the ideal student, brilliant but devout; and at nineteen he became a Bachelor of Arts, and at twenty-two a Master.

A religious crisis now developed. Luther's father had prepared him for the practice of law; but the sudden death of a companion, and his own narrow escape from death, determined him to obey a higher law. In the forest amidst a violent storm, with trees crashing around him, Luther called upon St. Anna, patroness of the Saxon miners, vowing if spared to become a monk. A fortnight later, after a last evening with his friends in music and song, Luther said farewell to them at the gate of the Augustinian monastery at Erfurt, and donned the monastic habit.

A recent attempt to reform the Augustinian Hermits had led to the formation within the order of a "congregation" of monasteries, as with ancient Cluny. The Augustinians of Saxony belonged to the "congregation"; and John Staupitz was their Vicar-General. Staupitz was to become the devoted friend of Martin Luther. Meanwhile the young novice was subjected to a stern discipline. Sweeping, scrubbing, begging from door to door, subdued whatever pride still lurked within. He who had sniffed the free air of Humanism, was now taught how to stand properly, to walk, to sit, to kneel, how to hold his hands, to eat and drink, to bear himself before his superiors, to analyze every thought and word, in search of sin.

With such a round of duties there was little time for study; and indeed Luther's new associates reminded him that his duty was not to study but to beg. Observing, too, his devotion to the Scriptures, the monks admonished him that the marrow of the Scriptures was in the Scholastics, and that to think one could find truth for oneself was dangerous spiritual pride. At length the University intervened, and secured for its distinguished alumnus some mitigation of discipline and some freedom.

At the end of the year Luther was admitted to full membership in the Augustinian Hermits; and a year later, in 1508, he was ordained also to

the priesthood. Celebrating his first Mass, he broke into a cold perspira-
tion and shook with fear, lest he should stumble in the ritual, fail to perform the miracle of transubstantiation, and thus imperil the souls of the
people.

Meanwhile circumstances were preparing the transition of the young
priest-monk to the permanent scene of his labours. The residence of the
Electoral Prince of Saxony was at the little city of Wittenberg, some sixty
miles south-west of Berlin. There the Elector Frederick the Wise had
recently founded a University, and made Staupitz Dean of Theology.
Staupitz brought promising young scholars from the Augustinian
cloisters, to be instructors at Wittenberg. Luther came in the year of his
ordination to the priesthood.

At Wittenberg Luther lived in the local monastery, lectured at the
University, continued his studies, and became in time Doctor of Divinity.
At twenty-nine he was Professor of Theology, had rejected Scholasticism
and was teaching directly from the Scriptures. Like John Colet at Oxford, he had no thought of breaking with Mother Church. Luther was
another devout Catholic Humanist, going direct to the Scriptures that
Catholicism declared authoritative, but in danger of drawing therefrom
conclusions that Catholicism had not drawn. Before long he became
known as a reformer, liberating theology from the dominance of Aristotle and returning to the Scriptures, and to St. Augustine as their best
interpreter. Young theologians were adopting his views; and at Wittenberg, Erfurt and elsewhere Augustinianism was being revived. Luther
was becoming famous also as a preacher, and in 1515, when thirty-two
years old, was made a Vicar of the Augustinian Hermits, with authority
over eleven monasteries.

Next year it was announced that Pope Leo X, an urbane Renaissance
man, of the Florentine Medici, would offer indulgences to Christendom.
Leo's habits were extravagant, his schemes grandiose; and there was the
vast new St. Peter's, not yet complete, and the decisive war with the
Turks still to be fought. The money of the faithful was needed; and the
faithful needed what indulgences could buy. There were always sins un-
confessed, for which the Church had therefore imposed no penance. Such
sins must be expiated in purgatory. There was no escape, except by the
superfluous merit of the saints, husbanded from the beginning in a

spiritual treasury, upon which the Church could draw for the benefit of the less meritorious. Such drafts were now to be made.

One of the papal commissioners, to superintend the sale of indulgences in Germany, was Albert, Archbishop of Magdeburg and Mainz, Margrave of Brandenburg, an Electoral Prince, Imperial Chancellor, and quite the most influential man in Germany. A cultivated scholar of twenty-seven, a friend of Erasmus, recently celebrated in verse by Ulrich von Hutten, Archbishop Albert was nevertheless heavily in debt to the Augsburg bankers, the Fuggers, through whose good offices he had paid Pope Leo an immense sum for the *pallium* of an archbishop. Albert would now receive half the proceeds of the sale of indulgences in his own territory, and get out of the clutches of the Fuggers.

To sell the indulgences throughout Saxony, the archbishop engaged a popular orator of the Dominicans, John Tetzel, who was soon riding through the land, preceded by a red cross, emblazoned with the papal coat of arms. Bells announced his approach to every town and hamlet. Civic officials and the children went in procession to the church. There Tetzel placed the papal cross before the great altar, the indulgence chest beside it, and preached a lurid sermon on the purgatorial torments of the people's dead. The orator did not keep within the limits of Catholic theory; and he had no time to test the penitence of his hearers. Money was required; and letters of pardon were to be sold. There was nothing therefore that letters of pardon could not do for the people, just as they were, and for their dead.

In the annual visitation of his monasteries in 1516, Luther heard what was going on, and began to preach, not against indulgences but against the abuse of indulgences. People, he said, were being taught to dread, not sin but the punishment of sin. Unaware of the archbishop's connection with the traffic, Luther also wrote him and, receiving no reply, wrote them to his bishop, who warned him against opposing the Pope.

Complaints about Tetzel continued to reach Luther, and appeals from friends for advice. He determined at length to invite a discussion of indulgences by the theologians of Wittenberg. It was their custom to meet each Friday morning for discussion, the leader posting in advance the propositions he would defend. Luther posted on the door of the Castle Church, the *Schlosskirche*, October 31, 1517, ninety-five propositions, not in German but in Latin. To his dismay they proved to be the opening gun in a religious war, that was to divide the Church forever.

The theses of Luther affirmed that penance and penitence are quite different, the former being a deed, the latter an attitude. As for penances, those imposed by the Pope can be remitted by the Pope; but his writ does not run in purgatory. And as for the penitent, they have from God the remission of their sins, without papal letters of pardon.

Two theses affirmed that the Pope did not know what wrongs were being done in his name. Others warned the clergy that indulgences were stirring lay resentment, and raising keen questions. Why does not the Pope empty purgatory for the love of souls, if he will do it for money? Why does not the Pope return money bequeathed for anniversary masses, for those of the dead who are now being redeemed by letters of pardon? Why does the Pope, to commend fresh indulgences, suspend those granted long ago?

The theses spread over all Germany in a fortnight, reaching a public for which they were not intended. The University was alarmed. The Augustinians foresaw another Savonarola from their order, burning in the market-place. The archbishop forbade Luther to preach, and sent the theses to the Pope. The urbane pontiff was disinclined to act. Luther, he said, was a drunken German, who would sober up. The Dominicans, however, kept up a clamour; and at length Luther was summoned to appear for trial at Rome.

Meanwhile reform sentiment had time to rally; and support began to come from many quarters. The Count of Mansfeld advised Luther against leaving Wittenberg; and the Elector insisted, against both Pope and Emperor, that the trial must take place in Germany. The Emperor yielded, and summoned Luther to appear before an Imperial Diet, then meeting at Augsburg, to be examined by a papal legate, Cardinal Cajetan.

Luther came to Augsburg in October, 1518, under an imperial safe-conduct, and attended by advisers provided by the Elector. The examination effected nothing. Required to recant his errors, Luther quoted Scripture in defence of them, while Cajetan quoted a papal Bull against them. In the end Luther was shouted down; and having appealed "from the Pope ill-informed to the Pope better informed," he left for home.

The papacy, slowly awake to the disaffection in Germany, now tried conciliation. The Elector Frederick was given a papal decoration; and a Saxon nobleman, Carl von Miltitz, who had represented the Elector at Rome for some years, was sent to displace Cajetan. Luther, too, wrote the Holy Father an abject letter, full of distress that words of his, meant only for discussion among experts, had gone abroad, and vainly wishing they might be recalled. It was too late. The dike was breached; the sea was coming in.

Very fortunately for Luther's cause, the international situation gave him a respite of many months, for thought and writing. The Emperor Maximilian died in January, 1519. Until a successor could be elected, Frederick of Saxony was regent for North Germany. Frederick could indeed have been elected to the imperial throne, but declined the honour; and the Electoral Princes chose Charles, grandson of Maximilian, who had recently succeeded to the throne of Spain and the Netherlands, at the age of eighteen. Elected Emperor in June, it was not until October that this grave, unimaginative Hapsburg youth could come to Germany, to be crowned at Aix-la-Chapelle, at the tomb of Charlemagne.

The chief fruits of Luther's respite were three treatises, that are still known as "The Three Great Reformation Treatises."[1] They contain the essentials of Luther's theological system, and indeed of early Protestantism everywhere.

The first of the Treatises, an address *To the Christian Nobility of the German Nation*, is a discussion of the responsibility of laymen in ecclesiastical affairs, and has been called "the trumpet call to battle." In it Luther attacks the "three walls," by which "Romanists" have protected their prerogatives. "Firstly, if pressed by the temporal power, they have affirmed that the temporal power has no jurisdiction over them, . . . that the spiritual power is above the temporal. Secondly, if it were proposed to admonish them with the Scriptures, they have objected that no one may interpret the Scriptures but the Pope. Thirdly, if they are threatened with a council, they pretend that no one may call a council but the Pope."

Luther deals summarily with these claims. "It has been devised that

---

[1] The three treatises, together with Luther's letter to his archbishop and the ninety-five theses, may be read in English in Wace & Buchheim, *Luther's Primary Works*, Hodder & Stoughton.

the Pope, bishops, priests and monks are called the *spiritual estate;* princes, lords, artificers and peasants are the *temporal estate.* This is an artful lie. . . . All Christians are truly of the spiritual estate, and there is no difference among them, save of office only. . . . We are all consecrated as priests by baptism, as St. Peter says: 'Ye are a royal priesthood, a holy nation.' To put the matter even more plainly, if a little company of pious Christian laymen were taken prisoners and carried away to a desert, and had not among them a priest consecrated by a bishop, and were there to agree to elect one of them, . . . this man would as truly be a priest, as if all the bishops and all the popes had consecrated him. . . . In this way the Christians used to choose their bishops and priests, . . . without the pomp that now prevails."

So also with the claim that no one may interpret the Scriptures but the Pope. Luther rejoins: "We will quote the Scriptures. . . . Christ himself says, 'And they shall all be taught of God.' . . . It is a wickedly devised fable—and they cannot quote a single letter to confirm it—that it is for the Pope alone to interpret the Scriptures. . . . They must needs acknowledge that there are pious Christians among us, that have the true faith, spirit, understanding, word, and mind of Christ: why then should we reject their word and understanding?"

So also with the papal claim to the exclusive right to call General Councils. "They can show nothing in the Scriptures, giving the Pope sole power to call and confirm councils; they have nothing but their own laws. . . . Thus we read (*Acts* xv) that the council of the Apostles was not called by St. Peter, but by all the Apostles and the elders. . . . Moreover, the most celebrated council of all—that of Nicaea—was neither called nor confirmed by the Bishop of Rome, but by the Emperor Constantine. . . . Therefore when need requires, and the Pope is a cause of offence to Christendom, in these cases whoever can best do so, as a faithful member of the whole body, must do what he can to procure a true, free council."

Having thus encouraged the civil authorities to believe in their right to reform the Church, Luther proceeds, in twenty-seven articles, to a scathing denunciation of papal abuses and a plan for reform.

The second of the Reformation Treatises, *The Babylonish Captivity of the Church,* is a critical examination of the Roman sacramental system, written in Latin for theologians. Luther begins by rejecting four of the seven Catholic sacraments—confirmation, marriage, ordination and extreme unction. Indeed he virtually excludes a fifth, penance, or repentance, on the ground that it is less a sacrament than a returning to one's baptism, when one has fallen from it into sin. So there remain only two Christian sacraments, the Lord's Supper and baptism; and to understand them, one must inquire, not of the Church but of the Scriptures.

For a doctrine of the Lord's Supper, then, Luther examines the words of Jesus when He instituted the Supper, and the account later given by St. Paul.[2] On their authority Luther rejects transubstantiation. The priest cannot turn bread and wine into the flesh and blood of Christ. The sacramental bread and wine are already flesh and blood also,[3] by the promise of Christ.

The chief effect of Luther's doctrine is to break the power of the priest over men, by denying that he can perform miracles on their behalf; but there is more than this. Luther, having appealed to the Scriptures, as the ultimate authority in religion, will not himself refuse what he finds there; and in the Scriptures it is written, "The Lord Jesus, in the night in which he was betrayed, took bread; and when he had given thanks, he brake it, and said, 'This *is* my body, which is for you.'" Luther submits. "What if philosophy does not understand these things? . . . Greater is the authority of the Word of God than the capacity of our intellect."

Luther rejects also that other aspect of the Catholic doctrine of the Supper, the doctrine that the Mass is a daily sacrifice offered to God for the sins of the people. We must "put aside all that has been added by the zeal or the notions of men to the primitive and simple institution, . . . and must set nothing else before us but those very words of Christ, with which He instituted and perfected that Sacrament and committed it to us. In that word, and absolutely in nothing else, lies the whole force, nature and substance of the mass.

"Now the words in which Christ instituted this sacrament are as follows: 'While they were at supper Jesus took bread, and blessed it, and brake it, and gave it to his disciples, and said, Take, eat; this is My body

---

[2] I *Cor.* 11: 23–26.

[3] Not "transubstantiation," but "consubstantiation." "Fire and iron, two different substances, are so mingled in red-hot iron that every part of it is both fire and iron. Why may not the glorious body of Christ be in every part of the substance of the bread?"

which is given for you. And He took the cup, and gave thanks, and gave it to them, saying, Drink ye all of this; this cup is the new testament in My blood, which is shed for you and for many, for the remission of sins.'" So that "the mass or Sacrament of the altar is the testament of Christ, which He left behind Him at His death, to be distributed to those who believe in Him.

"If then we inquire what a testament is, we shall also learn what the mass is. . . . A testament is certainly a promise made by a man about to die, by which he assigns his inheritance and appoints heirs." "Christ testifies of His own death when He says, 'This is My body which is given, this is My blood which is shed'; He assigns and points out the inheritance when He says, 'For the remission of sins'; and He appoints heirs when He says, 'For you and for many,' that is, for those who accept and believe the promise of the Testator, for it is faith which makes us heirs." "Life and salvation are freely promised in plain words, and are bestowed on those who believe the promise." "Nothing else is required for a worthy reception of the mass than faith, resting with confidence on this promise." And "on this faith a spontaneous and most sweet affection of the heart will speedily follow, . . . How can one fail to love such a Benefactor, who of His own accord offers, promises, and gives the greatest riches and an eternal inheritance to an unworthy sinner, who has deserved very different treatment."

All this, Luther declares, is undone by the Catholic doctrine that the Mass is a sacrifice to God. "Where we ought to be grateful for blessing bestowed on us, we come in our pride to give what we ought to receive. . . . We thus make the Testator no longer the Bestower of His good gifts on us, but the Receiver of ours. Alas for such impiety!"

Luther explains similarly the second Christian sacrament, baptism. "The first thing we have to notice in baptism is the Divine promise which says, 'He who believes and is baptised shall be saved.' . . . On this promise depends our whole salvation, and we must take heed to exercise faith in it, not doubting at all that we are saved, since we have been baptised. Unless this faith exists and is applied, baptism profits us nothing." [4]

---

[4] Luther recognized the difficulty of applying his doctrine to the baptism of infants. "An argument will perhaps be drawn from the baptism of infants, who cannot receive the promise of God, or have faith in their baptism; and it will be said that therefore either faith is not requisite, or infants are baptised in vain." Luther, too humane to ex-

All this is not to deny the value of good works. "Thy faith will be followed by these very works."

The third Reformation Treatise, *The Freedom of a Christian Man,* is the fruit, not of theological controversy, but of religious contemplation. Its sense is this, that the Christian, set free by his faith, becomes the willing servant of all men, through the love that is now born within. Faith has done for him what consecrated vestments, consecrated buildings, and works ecclesiastically imposed, could never do; it has made him a voluntary doer of good deeds.

Three principles, then, underlie the Reformation Treatises; and they are the foundation principles of the Reformation everywhere. Reformers in the various nations differed as to the application of these principles, and several churches resulted; but the principles governing all were the sole authority of the Scriptures as the standard of Christian truth, salvation by faith, and the universal priesthood of believers.

First, then, the Christian life was to be lived under the direction of "the Word of God," the Scriptures. Those, therefore, who exalted the Church above the Scriptures, and those who exalted individual inspiration, were equally wrong. The Scriptures are both the guide and the creative force in the Christian life.

Second, salvation is by faith in God. Circumstances had made of the mediaeval Church a stern school of discipline. Its special mission had been to subdue the barbarian world to the will of God, as the Church conceived it.[5] And Luther was at first a typical mediaevalist, overwhelmed by the demands of a righteous God and his own inability to meet them; but before he broke with Mother Church he had already found deliverance, in the belief that salvation is by faith in God. "At length by the mercy of God, meditating days and nights, I observed the connection of the words, 'Therein is the righteousness of God revealed from faith to faith, as it is written, The just shall live by faith.' "

---

clude infants, replies: "Through the prayers of the Church which brings the child in faith, to which prayers all things are possible, the infant is changed, cleansed, and renewed by faith infused into it." Luther thus fell back upon magical ideas implicit in Catholic usage. Other reformers were to deal in different fashion with the problem of infant baptism; and it was to become an occasion of controversy and division.

[5] The sort of man it produced is best seen in Anselm of Canterbury, whose dominant characteristic was an intense perception of the justice of God and his inexorable demands. It is what Dante expresses in poetry, the mediaeval man's sense of the inexorable justice of God.

It became, therefore, a Protestant principle that, just as there can be no true fellowship between persons without mutual trust, so fellowship with God requires that one trust Him. This is not to say that He will then remit the penalty of one's sin; but Luther knew that personal forgiveness is more needful to all true hearts than remission of penalties, that if only one were restored to God's favour, one could welcome penalties, as the discipline imposed by divine love.

This was the centre of Luther's theology. God had descended into the world in Jesus Christ, had promised man forgiveness here and security hereafter, if man would but trust Him. Such a promise surpassed all other gifts, and deserved man's faith. That faith God would Himself bestow. The Word of God and its promises create the faith that believes.

Here was an immense deliverance from the spiritual terror of the Middle Ages. Luther had known that terror; and they still knew it to whom he preached. He offered them peace.

The third principle of Protestantism is the spiritual priesthood of all believers. Christian laymen, Luther said, have spiritual faculties and powers of the same sort as the clergy. They may feel, in all natural relationships, a spiritual dignity like that of the priest. It is not only at the altar and in the cloister that the work of God is done; it is in toil, in government, in marriage and parenthood.

The general effect of these Protestant principles was to restore to men their spiritual autonomy. It was a work the Renaissance had already been doing, and that Protestantism confirmed by solemnizing it. The result was to be an enlargement of life, expressed through literature and science, national quickening and social change, wherever Protestantism was adopted.

The papal Bull excommunicating Luther reached Germany in October, 1520. It commanded all clergy and ecclesiastical institutions to reject the Lutheran doctrines, and all civil officials to search out Lutheran writings and burn them publicly. Any place harbouring the heretic was threatened with the interdict. It was the duty of a Christian to arrest Luther and send him to Rome for punishment. Whoever failed in this duty would "incur the indignation of Almighty God and of the blessed Apostles Peter and Paul."

The Bull was received generally with contempt. The University of Wittenberg suppressed it. The students of Erfurt and Leipzig tore up the Bull and assaulted the bearer. Luther himself publicly burned the Bull, and with it a copy of the Canon Law, inviting "all friends of evangelical truth" to witness the act.

The new Emperor was in Germany when the Bull arrived, having come to be crowned. Charles V was a loyal Catholic; and the papal party urged upon him the view that Luther had already been judged by the proper authority, and had only to be delivered to the curia at Rome. But Charles was indebted to the Elector Frederick for his crown, was uneasy about those German knights who were befriending Luther, and had sworn at his coronation not to condemn a German without a hearing. Charles therefore instructed the Elector to bring Luther to his first Imperial Diet, which was to assemble at Worms in the spring.

Luther set out for Worms in April, conducted by an imperial herald, protected by an imperial safe-conduct, and accompanied by several colleagues. He preached to great crowds as he advanced, and entered Worms on April 16, to be greeted by the whole population. Summoned next day to the Diet, in the bishop's palace, he found himself required to answer, without argument, two questions. Had he written the books attributed to him? Would he now recant? Luther acknowledged the books, but asked to be judged by the Scriptures. He was ready, he said, if proven unscriptural, to recall every error and to cast his books into the fire. It was of no avail. Being required still to answer without discussion, he exclaimed, "I am convinced by the passages of Scripture which I have cited, and my conscience is bound in the Word of God. I cannot and will not recant anything."

The Diet fell into disorder; and Luther was dismissed, the Emperor declaring his intention, as defender of the Catholic faith, to arrest him so soon as his safe-conduct should expire. Meanwhile the Emperor entered into a covenant with the Pope to stamp out Lutheranism and, to that end, issued the Edict of Worms, threatening death to all who should support Luther.

The Edict of Worms was the end of the road for devout Humanists, like Reuchlin and Erasmus, Dean Colet and Sir Thomas More, who hoped to keep the Church intact, while returning to the simplicity of Christ. It was impossible. St. Francis had tried that long before, and had died brokenhearted. Most Humanists of the sixteenth century would not even attempt it. Their Humanism came out of ancient Italy, not out of Galilee, and was tinctured by its origin in paganism. They were not disposed, either to repent of their sins or to exchange their emoluments for the simplicity of Christ. It is significant that the supreme pontiff and the erring archbishop, both set against reform, were distinguished Humanists.

Meanwhile Luther was on his way back to Wittenberg, preaching everywhere to great crowds, until, deep in the Thuringian Forest, he was seized by a body of armed knights and carried off for safe keeping to the home of one of them, the Castle of the Wartburg. The Elector imposed silence upon him; and for seven months he was popularly believed to have been done to death. Then the Archbishop of Magdeburg and Mainz again advertised the sale of indulgences. He had forty million years of relief from purgatory to dispense. Luther broke silence, writing the archbishop and threatening to expose him. This time His Grace sent a humble apology, acknowledging his sin, and promising to suppress the sale.

Luther had used this second respite to good effect. From the Wartburg came the New Testament in German. There had been earlier translations; but all were from the Latin Vulgate, were stilted in form and costly. Luther went back to the Greek text of the New Testament, and provided a version in idiomatic German, so vigorous and lucid that it did much to give the German language a permanent literary form and has remained the standard version of the New Testament in Germany.

The reform movement grew during the enforced silence of Luther. Other leaders came forward at Wittenberg. Chief of them was a certain Philip Schwartzerd, some fourteen years younger than Luther. Schwartzerd's mother, Barbara Reuter, was a niece of Reuchlin; and that great man took an interest in her boy. After the fashion of the early Humanists, Reuchlin turned Schwartzerd's name into Greek, Melancthon; and by this name he is known to history.

Melancthon became a student at Heidelberg and, on graduation, was called thence by the Elector of Saxony, to be Professor of Greek at Wittenberg. He came shortly after the ninety-five theses were posted, became a leading spirit among the Humanists, stimulated Luther's Greek

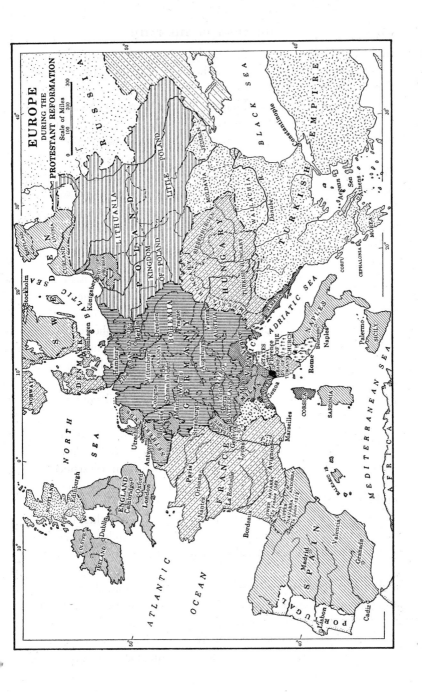

EUROPE
DURING THE
PROTESTANT REFORMATION

Scale of Miles
0   100   200   300

studies, and edited his translation of the New Testament. As he was a layman and married, Melancthon's home at Wittenberg became the first domestic centre of the Reformation.

While Luther was busy with his pen in the Wartburg, Melancthon too was writing, and his *Loci communes* was the earliest systematic statement of the new theology. It was but the first of Melancthon's many services to the cause. He became known as "the scribe of the Reformation." Most official documents of the movement in Germany were to be penned by him. As Melancthon was less polemic and more conciliatory than Luther, it was through him also that negotiations for peace tended to be carried on, with other Protestant bodies and with Rome. Luther acknowledged gratefully that Melancthon "trod more softly" than he.

The younger generation of Reformation leaders was already in training. The students of Wittenberg were reading the Scriptures and preaching through the countryside. The University was now the theological seminary for the new movement.

But there was much uncertainty and confusion in the reform movement. It was very difficult indeed to apply the new principle, that the Scriptures are the sole authority in religion. It was equally difficult, after many centuries of clerical control, to apply the principle of the universal priesthood of believers and the authority of the civil power over the Church.

So Luther came from retirement, to unify and stabilize the forces he had released. The Reformation was spreading rapidly. The Augustinian monasteries were propagating centres. Students from Wittenberg were teaching and preaching. Before 1523 closed, the civil authorities in most of the North German States had asked for the Gospel from Wittenberg, the kings of Denmark and Sweden had welcomed it to their dominions, and disciples of Luther were ranging the Netherlands, where the first Lutheran martyrs were burned at Brussels in that year.[6]

Luther travelled widely during 1522 and 1523, advising magistrates and princes about the reorganization of congregations, about the choice and support of pastors, about new forms of public worship. In the matter of worship, Luther was guided by the principle that nothing was to be changed unless it contradicted the Word of God. Two changes, however, seemed necessary. Luther placed the sermon at the centre of public

[6] Henry Voes and John von Esch.

worship, as being instruction in the Word of God; and he translated mediaeval chants and hymns into German, that the people might participate more actively in public worship. He himself wrote many hymns as well, some of them among the great hymns of the Christian Church.

Disorder, however, continued. It was inevitable. Society was only beginning to emerge from the long illiteracy of the Middle Ages. The Bible was a new book; and it was not what the Church had so long believed it to be, a book of one view concerning God and salvation and history. Only allegorical interpretations had ever enabled the Catholic Church to maintain the unity of the Bible; and, in their new loyalty, the reformers were interpreting it literally. So there were differences of opinion and some crudities. Carlstadt, a colleague of Luther at the University, abandoned both his professorship and the priesthood, and became a peasant, having read in the Scriptures that things hidden from the wise and prudent were revealed to babes. Becoming a Protestant pastor later, Carlstadt acknowledged only the Bible and, on the authority of the Old Testament, approved polygamy, condemned the taking of interest, and advocated the restoration of purchased lands to the original owners every fifty years, as in the Mosaic Year of Jubilee.

There were other idiosyncrasies. A crude mysticism was abroad. A certain Thomas Münzer, leader of a company of prophets at Zwickau, had been preaching in central Germany, and came with a few followers to Wittenberg. They affected complete receptivity to the Holy Spirit, held conversations in a church tower with God, and preached as divine revelations what came to them there. They were the first of the "Pentecostalists," that were to appear periodically, to plague Protestant churches.

But more difficult than anything else was the question of the social implications of the Gospel. The peasants of South Germany had been in frequent insurrection for fifty years before Luther; and there was still in existence a widespread alliance, the *Bundschuh,* or League of the Shoe. The *Bundschuh* complained of the exactions of feudal lords, the burden of taxation, and the steady substitution of Roman law for German customary law, which was excluding peasants from the forests and streams. Restlessness was increased by the new religious ideas, as the Gospel was carried abroad. Why should men be serfs, when Christ had redeemed all? Why should not men hunt in the forests and fish in the streams, since God had given all men dominion over the works of His hands? So there were demands for the abdication of the nobles, and the demolition of their costly houses. Fanatics, like Thomas Münzer, were ready with inflammatory literature, appealing to the Scriptures in defence of violence; and the peasantry embodied their demands in "Twelve Articles."

The Elector of the Palatinate appealed to Melancthon concerning the Articles; and he condemned the peasants. They appealed to Luther, who in a treatise, *An Exhortation to Peace,* condemned oppression by the nobles and plead for relief, but condemned equally the violence of the peasantry, declared serfdom consistent with Christianity, and proposed arbitration. Münzer, "Champion of the Lord," urged the peasants to violence. "Show them no mercy, as God commanded Moses, . . . To work while the fire is hot; let not the blood cool upon your swords. . . . God is with you; follow Him."

Many thousands rose in rebellion. Luther encouraged the rulers in ruthless suppression. The desolation was terrible, the conditions of the peasants worse than before. Luther was widely blamed, as having encouraged rebellion and then deserted the rebels; and South Germany and its peasantry were lost to Protestantism.

Luther's influence everywhere was shaken; and it was further weakened when he married a nun, Catherine von Bora, in June, 1525. His enemies cavilled; and his friends were distressed. But the future was to vindicate Luther. Catherine was a woman of gentle birth, capable and devoted. The Elector gave them a whole Augustinian monastery for a home. Catherine managed the immense establishment. The friends of reform met at her table. Many principles and plans for the future were there clarified. Meanwhile the Archbishop of Magdeburg and Mainz, who had perhaps got clear of the Fuggers, sent the bride a gift of gold florins.

During these years Luther was reluctantly providing for the reorganization of the churches. He was himself indifferent to questions of organization, and hoped also to avoid great changes. Ten years after his excommunication, he still protested his loyalty to the past, in a confession of faith intended for the Imperial Diet at Augsburg: "Our meaning is not to have rule taken from the bishops; but this one thing only is requested, that they would suffer the Gospel to be purely taught, and that they would relax a few observances, which cannot be held without sin." But changes were forced upon Luther, as hope of amendment by Mother Church receded and disorder in his own movement grew.

Two ideas were fundamental in Luther's organization from the first. They were those he had enunciated in the address *To the Christian Nobility of the German Nation*. First, there is no religious caste, only a universal priesthood of believers. Second, the civil government is as truly ordained of God as the ecclesiastical; and powers claimed by the papacy belong to the civil government. The emphasis shifted, however, as Luther was disillusioned by disorder and violence. He came to distrust democracy and to stress the second of these principles, the authority of the civil government. Magistrates and princes have such authority over the Church as they have over other institutions within their dominions.

In the free cities, reorganization proved comparatively easy. The City Council, or *Rath,* took charge, and appointed one of the clergy to be superintendent of the churches, in place of the bishop and responsible to the *Rath*. Luther and a few associates drew up an order of public worship for all churches, "The German Mass."

The lands of the princes proved more difficult. Here a beginning was naturally made with Electoral Saxony. The Elector Frederick the Wise died in 1525, and was succeeded by his brother John, who had also championed the reform cause. By his authority there was a religious survey of his dominions in 1526–27, to determine what ecclesiastical arrangements were desirable. For purposes of the survey, Electoral Saxony was divided into four "circles," and a commission of clergy and lay lawyers appointed to visit each. These commissions became permanent "consistories," for the supervision of their respective circles.

The visitors questioned the priests, the heads of homes in the country, the *Rath* in each town. They received few complaints about the priests, except that many were too old and too ignorant. Some could hardly repeat the Lord's Prayer and the Apostles' Creed. Most villages had no schools; and those in many towns were poor. The relief of poverty had broken down, endowments for this work having been diverted to other uses.

As a result of the visitation Luther set about the preparation of two catechisms. The "Greater Catechism," for the clergy, was a "short summary and extract of the whole of the Scriptures." The "Small Catechism" was a text-book for the people, setting forth, in the form of question and answer, the Ten Commandments, the Apostles' Creed, the Lord's Prayer, the meaning of baptism and the Lord's Supper, family prayers and grace at meals. The Small Catechism became the most influential of all Luther's works, except the translation of the Scriptures.

The visitors recommended to the Elector that assistants be provided for aged priests. As rapidly as these came from Wittenberg, an educated clergy would be secured. Meanwhile many priests were forbidden to prepare their own sermons, and required to await sermons from Luther.

The visitors recommended, too, that priests, now better called ministers, should act as schoolmasters, until educated laymen could be provided for that work. The ministers would be assisted by the parish clerks; and children were to be excluded from the Lord's Supper, on those Sundays when they could not pass a test in the week's lessons from the Small Catechism.

It was recommended further that ancient endowments for poor relief be restored to their intended purpose; and that monastic lands and endowments, confiscated by the Elector, should be devoted to the support of ministers and schoolmasters. And instead of the old bishop's court, the superintendent minister in each Circle should sit with the magistrates, in ecclesiastical matters.

There were several visitations of Electoral Saxony; and in the end the "Wittenberg Ecclesiastical Consistory" was adopted as the general basis of church organization. It gave legal recognition to Luther's principle that the ruling prince is head of the Church in his dominions. An Ecclesiastical Consistory, appointed by the prince, was to take the place of the bishop's court, of theologians and canon lawyers. There was also to be a General Synod, composed of the Consistory and the Superintendents of the Circles, and a Synod in each Circle, composed of the Superintendent and clergy of the Circle.

Though other Protestant princes did not follow the Saxon model in all respects, this consistorial system became characteristic of Lutheran churches everywhere. It preserves the past where possible. It asserts the supreme authority of the civil power in religion. It gives the people no control. When another Protestant prince, the Landgrave Philip of Hesse, gave his dominions a democratic church constitution, adopting Luther's earlier principle, Luther protested and the Landgrave withdrew the constitution.

In all the work of reorganization, the reformers did not regard themselves as founding a new Church. They were "the associates of the Augsburg Confession," in the Catholic Church. But the breach with Mother Church became wider and wider. Thus, in the matter of the ordination of ministers, Luther had long thought that it need not be by a bishop; and the difficulty of securing episcopal ordination led to its discontinuance after 1525. For ten years ministers were simply given a solemn introduction to office. Then ordination was restored, but ordination without the bishop.

During the first years of the Lutheran movement, similar movements were under way in other parts of the German world. They represented the general recoil of devout and scholarly Catholics against ecclesiastical abuses, stimulated by the new intellectual awareness of Humanism. Of these secondary reform movements, the most important was in German Switzerland.

Switzerland, in the early sixteenth century, was a group of republics, German in the north and east, French in the south and west. Thirteen of these were loosely joined in a "Swiss Confederation." Zurich and Lucerne, Bern and Basel, were within, Geneva without, the Confederation. A Federal Diet dealt with matters of common interest, but with very limited authority. The little republics clung tenaciously to their autonomy. Only in the matter of foreign relations was the Diet supreme.

The Swiss were courted by the other governments of Europe, because of their military prowess. To secure Swiss mercenaries, foreign governments, including popes, bribed officials of the little republican cantons. So official corruption was general; and there was little patriotism, Swiss mercenaries often fighting each other in foreign wars. The Diet decreed in 1503, and asked the cantons to enforce the decree, that no one should thenceforth accept any salary or gift from a foreign power. It was of little avail. Switzerland continued to be deluged with foreign gold, subsidies from Austria and France, Rome and Milan. Luxury and dissipation were general. The warlike peasants wore silk jackets and ostrich plumes, drank foreign wines, and gambled recklessly. And many sumptuary laws were passed, with little effect.

The clergy were children of their generation. Ignorance was prevalent, and immorality not uncommon. Bishops Christopher of Basel and Hugo of Constance reported to synods of their dioceses their distress at the conduct of many priests, and charged them sternly against getting drunk at funerals, living in concubinage, walking up and down in church conversing during public worship, and even leaving church in the course of the services, to make purchases in the market. Priestly conduct in Switzerland was more reprehensible than in Germany.

The relations of the Swiss with the papacy were exceptionally friendly, partly because the Swiss were doctrinally obedient, partly because Swiss mercenaries were the mainstay of papal armies. So the papacy dealt gently with early movements for reform in Switzerland.

Education was much as in Germany. There was very little primary education, and only a few High Schools; but there were circles of Humanists in the cities. And the learned Pope Pius II had recently founded the University of Basel, which was already becoming an important centre. Dr. Thomas Wyttenbach, "most learned and holiest of men," was there and teaching that salvation is by faith; and Erasmus was in the city after 1513, to be near the Froben Press. An educational renaissance preceded, and largely caused, the religious reformation. Several notable cities—Basel and Bern, Geneva and Zurich—became reformation centres; and of these Zurich was the pioneer.

There came to Zurich in January, 1519, to be "people's priest" at the "Great Minister," a scholarly priest and distinguished Humanist, Huldreich Zwingli. He had studied at the University of Basel, and had there acquired Protestant principles from Thomas Wyttenbach, ten years before Luther posted the ninety-five Theses; but Zwingli continued zealous for papal interests and, in the early years of his priesthood, received from the Pope a small pension "for the purchase of books." Visiting Italy, however, as chaplain to Swiss mercenaries, Zwingli became doubtful of papal aims and set himself to stamp out mercenary service in Switzerland.

At Zurich Zwingli soon became famous as a "preacher for the times," who denounced luxury and vice and the military spirit, and who went straight to the Scriptures for his doctrines. People crowded in from the country to hear him; and he was soon preaching in the market-place.

Before long there came to Zurich a seller of indulgences, a Franciscan called Samson, whom Zwingli had encountered and silenced in his previous parish. Zwingli now preached against him, encouraged by the bishop and clergy; and the magistrates requested Samson to withdraw. The latter appealed to the Federal Diet, then meeting in Zurich; and the Diet permitted him to remain, but only until it could complain to Rome and receive the Pope's reply. Pope Leo, made tractable perhaps by the turmoil in Germany, granted the request of the Diet and the magistrates of Zurich; and Samson withdrew.

Events followed each other in rapid succession at Zurich, until in 1522 there was a public debate between the Augustinians and a certain Franciscan from France. As a result the priests of Zurich resolved to preach only from the Scriptures; and a revolt against Roman practices and the authority of the bishop spread through the canton and into neighbouring cantons. Next year the Government called a public disputation, to determine what was the Gospel and to regulate preaching thereby. Zwingli published in German sixty-seven Articles, very much like the Theses of Luther; and the debate took place in the City Hall. At its close, the Government approved the Articles, and decreed that priests throughout the canton should "preach nothing but what can be proved by the Holy Gospel and the pure Holy Scriptures." It was the official beginning of the Reformation at Zurich.

Before 1523 closed, Zwingli developed the Articles into *The Exposition and Proof of the Conclusions or Articles,* which became a text-book for the people. It set Zwingli upon his feet, as leader of the Reformation in German Switzerland and South Germany.

Next year Zurich broke completely with the Roman Church. All was deliberate and orderly. The Government called for another public discussion; the defenders of the old order were beaten; and all were required to submit to the new order or leave the canton. There was no more open opposition.

There were, however, excesses within the new order. The peasants, warned by the fate of those in South Germany, did not press their grievances very far; but theological radicals were less reticent. Meeting in private houses, discussing Zwingli's sermons, they devised plans for speedier action and attacked churches, removing pictures and statues. What chiefly distinguished them, however, was their rejection of the baptism of infants. It seemed to follow logically upon the principle that the sacraments are of no avail, except for those who receive them in faith.

Because of this special emphasis, the radicals of Zurich were called "Baptists"; and because they baptised again those who had been baptised in infancy, they were called also "Anabaptists." They entered into correspondence with that Thomas Münzer, whom we found agitating at Wittenberg; but soon a famous theologian and friend of Zwingli espoused their cause and became their leader. This was Balthasar Hübmaier, a priest of Austria, who was to be burned at the stake in Vienna, in 1528.

Meanwhile at Zurich the government held another public discussion in January, 1525, to determine the true doctrine of baptism. At its close further meetings of Baptists were forbidden, Zurichers with unbaptised infants were commanded to have them baptised within a week, and banishment was decreed for any who should refuse. At Zurich, as elsewhere, it had not been expected that an appeal to the Scriptures would eventuate, not in one Reformed Church but in several. The Government would not tolerate schism; and those who breached the Reformed Church might expect the penalty that Mother Church had exacted from similar offenders.

There were further discussions with the Baptists of Zurich, but without effect; and they were subjected to a shameful persecution. They were dispossessed, driven into exile, drowned, as a fate particularly suited to Baptists; and their leaders were burned at the stake. Baptists were virtually wiped out in the Canton of Zurich, though they were to survive elsewhere and to spread, to become the Baptist Churches of the world.

The first Synod of the Reformed Church met at Zurich in 1528, having been called by the Government. It examined the clergy as to their doctrinal correctness and personal rectitude. It settled the order of worship, excluding from it music. Worship was thenceforth to be understandable; existing music was in Latin; the Reformed Church had no hymn writer. So music was omitted. Preaching was given the central place; and, as the chief means of religious education, it was to be frequent. There were to be sermons twice daily, instead of the Mass, and three times on Sundays. Only a few of the holy days of the Catholic Church were to be observed, little more than Christmas, Good Friday and Easter; and an ecclesiastical calendar for the year was published, in which Bible heroes displaced the Catholic saints. The churches, too, were simplified, costly ornaments being removed and melted down, for other purposes. The Government set aside revenue for the support of the clergy, having already, in 1525, established a theological seminary for their education. The Bible was its central text-book. So Hebrew and Greek, the languages of the Bible, were taught. The clergy of the canton attended the seminary, as did many laymen.

The Reformed Church was what was later to be called Congregational. That is, local congregations were independent of each other, each having for its own guidance the Word of God. They were bound together, however, by uniformity in doctrine and organization, and by their common opposition to Rome and Luther and Baptists. There were Synods, too, in the various localities; but regulation of church affairs was chiefly by the magistrates.

Meanwhile the skies were darkening for the reformers everywhere. The Emperor had summoned an Imperial Diet to Speyer as early as 1526, to enforce the Edict of Worms (*See* p. 351) against religious innovations. Suddenly threatened by a hostile alliance of France with the papacy, he had granted the reformers an "Imperial Recess"; but three years later he summoned a second Diet to Speyer. It decreed that dominions in the Empire, still loyal to the Catholic Church, should continue to enforce the Edict of Worms, that all others should cease innovations, and that Zwinglians and Baptists should be destroyed.[7]

The Zwinglians were already in danger, having faced in 1528 a league of the Forest Cantons of Switzerland, in alliance with King Ferdinand of Austria, for the suppression of Zwinglianism. A treaty was achieved without fighting; but everyone knew the peace was unstable.

With the reform movement everywhere imperilled, the evangelical princes of Germany formed a military alliance in secret, and sought to include the evangelical cantons of Switzerland. Luther, however, was

[7] The evangelical minority in the Diet protested, and won for the reformers a new name, Protestants.

opposed to any appeal to force; he would use only spiritual weapons. He was equally opposed to union with the Swiss, because of theological differences. It was not for him, he thought, to compromise the truth so recently acquired from the Scriptures.

In vain the Landgrave Philip of Hesse brought Luther and Zwingli together, in his castle at Marburg. Zwingli was essentially a Humanist and statesman, bent on the reform of abuses; Luther was essentially a man of religion and a preacher of the Word of God, bound by its very letter. Zwingli thought the sacraments human acts, pledges to God of one's fealty. Luther thought them divine acts, promises of God's grace to believers. The difference was sharpest concerning the Lord's Supper, and the nature of the presence in the bread and wine. Facing each other across a table, Luther wrote upon it in chalk, "This *is* my body," and argued for a physical presence. Zwingli reasoned against literal interpretations of the Scriptures. The words of institution, he said, meant only that the bread and wine represented the body and blood of Christ. Discussion was vain. The "Marburg Colloquy" broke down; and the reformers separated, having promised only to "abstain from bitter words and writings."

Six months later, in April, 1530, another Imperial Diet met at Augsburg. Luther, who was dissuaded from attending, prepared a "Confession of Augsburg," that was on sale before the Diet opened; but the profession of faith actually presented to the Diet was written by Melancthon, whose statement was preferred by Luther himself.

The Diet decreed that all must return to the Catholic faith within a year and that nothing controversial was to be published; though it did give assurance that a General Council of the Church would meet, to remedy abuses. The reform leaders in the Diet withdrew to Wittenberg; and the supporting princes formed a military confederacy, the Schmalkald League, which made treaties with Denmark and France, and had the sympathy of Henry VIII of England.

War was averted for a long time. Charles V was engrossed elsewhere, and was not again to set foot among his German subjects for a decade. Affairs in his hereditary dominions were pressing. Those dominions, which included Spain and the Netherlands, Austria and Milan and Naples, were diverse in temperament and tradition. And while Italians were not averse to having the stiff and solemn Spaniard in Italy, protecting the country against the French and the Turks of Tunis and Algiers, there was fierce dislike of Spaniards in the north, among the Flemings and Dutch of the Netherlands. Only in Spain was Charles himself really popular. When he received the imperial crown and proved his orthodoxy by the Edict of Worms, there was a pardonable pride among the people of Aragon and Castile.

The Spanish dominions, too, were being extended beyond the seas. Providence, it seemed, was on the side of the Hapsburgs. Cuba was Spanish. Cortes had subdued the Aztecs of Mexico and seized their land for Spain. Spanish conquistadors were in Florida, along the Mississippi, and in Panama. There Pizarro, greatest and least scrupulous of the conquistadors, heard of Peru, a land on the Pacific coast of South America, inhabited by the Incas. It was rich in gold and silver and precious stones, with roads and canals, temples and palaces, and an opulent population of sun-worshippers. Pizarro explored this wonderful land between 1526 and 1529, and by 1533 had seized it for Spain. Before long Venezuela and Bolivia, Western Chile and Argentina and Paraguay, were annexed to the Spanish crown.

With this scattered empire on his mind, the Emperor was absent from Germany for long periods. So the reformers there had only internal problems and differences with their Catholic neighbours to settle.

The Zwinglian movement, however, had troubles enough. Within a year of the Diet of Augsburg, civil war broke out in Switzerland. Zurich and Bern were pressing the reformed faith upon the five Forest Cantons, whose peasants, in their log cabins high among the Alpine forests and pastures, knew less of ecclesiastical abuses and nothing of movements of thought in the cities, and clung tenaciously to the Virgin and the Catholic saints. The peasants maltreated evangelists from Zurich, which then placed an embargo against their exports. Armed forces from the mountains invaded Zurich, and routed the Zurichers at Cappel. The war was over in six weeks, each party remaining in its own faith and engaging not to molest the other; but Zwingli had fallen in battle, having been present as chaplain to the Zurich forces.

At Zwingli's death, in 1531, six of the Swiss cantons and a few cities of South Germany had adopted his reforms; but the direction of the movement now passed, first to Bern and then to Geneva, where John Calvin was at work within five years of Zwingli's death. Calvin was a greater man. His ecclesiastical organization and theology spread through the Protestant cantons of Switzerland and into South Germany, obscuring the fame of Zwingli. Geneva became the capital city of Protestantism on the continent, outside the North German States, and the chief city of refuge for persecuted minorities everywhere. The Reformed Church came to regard Calvin, not Zwingli, as its founder.

As for Lutheranism, it continued to spread in Germany. Saxony and Hesse, Prussia and Brandenburg, where civilization was youngest, embraced the Lutheran faith. Bavaria, Austria and the Rhineland, which had been within the ancient Roman Empire and whose roots were deeper in the past, remained faithful to the ancient Church. Throughout all Germany a League of Catholic States and the Schmalkald League kept watchful eyes on each other. When the Emperor returned in 1541, the gulf between Lutheran and Roman was too wide to be bridged and Lutheranism too strong to be suppressed. In several Diets Charles worked for reconciliation, perhaps not sincerely and playing for time. In any case, he did not succeed; and Lutheranism seemed likely to become the religion of a united majority in Germany.

The Reformation continued, however, to be dogged by certain defects of its first principles. It was difficult, for example, to submit to the civil power, without impairing the integrity of ecclesiastical leaders. It was equally difficult to apply the principle that the Scriptures are the court of appeal for Christian conduct. The greatest blunder of Luther's career was a reprehensible interpretation of Scripture on the question of marriage. The Landgrave Philip had married, when very young, a daughter of Duke George of Saxony, and had later made her moral and physical infirmities the excuse for frequent infidelity. Adultery was too common a vice among princes to occasion much criticism; but Philip now read in the Bible the divine judgments upon such conduct. Unable or unwilling to return to his wife, he now proposed, with her consent, to follow Old Testament precedents and take a second wife. Luther, anxious to relieve the Landgrave's distress of conscience and help him to a purer life, and reluctant to admit that anything sanctioned in the Old Testament could be sin, declared that the New Testament nowhere abrogates polygamy. Melancthon and certain theologians of Hesse agreed. Dispensations could be granted, they said, but only in very exceptional circumstances; and they must then be kept secret, to avoid disturbing simple minds.

Philip took a second wife in March, 1540, violating a law of the Empire. The transaction soon became public. The Elector was indignant. The public was scandalized, and the confidence of Evangelicals in their leaders shaken. Melancthon nearly died of anxiety; and Luther, who later rejected plural marriages, never quite recovered his authority.

The day of Luther's boisterous popularity was past. He had been a truly national leader, so long as he was resisting Catholic abuses. Now that he was devising a substitute for Catholicism, the difficulty of applying his principles was too great to be overcome in a lifetime. Luther's dependence on princely favour offended moderate Catholics. His failure to discover a way by which the wrongs of the peasantry could be righted, and his approval of savage repression, made him seem to many an enemy of freedom. His determined allegiance to the Scriptures, making him intolerant of dissent, was distasteful to Humanists. Considerate and affable in private life, and free from personal rancour, without any ambition except to be faithful to his divine mission, he nevertheless seemed to many to be self-assertive and severe. Thus whole classes in the nation were alienated.

Throughout 1545 Luther was in ill health, aggravated by forebodings. The General Council, so long desired, was meeting at last in the little city of Trent, in the Austrian Tyrol; but there was now no hope that it would adopt the new principles. It was mending the fences of the Catholic Church, intent on keeping intact what remained of its ancient inheritance. And Luther feared lest his younger colleagues in reform should yield too much of the new, to retain a footing in the old. He was tortured, too, by the defects of his own movement. Evangelical princes were as factious as they had been before the new order. Moral laxity continued in Reformation centres. Things were better than they had been, but still unworthy of the Gospel. Hearing at Leipzig of irregularities among the students at Wittenberg, and the failure of the preachers to correct them, Luther wrote his wife, "Away from such a Sodom! I would sooner wander about and beg my bread than vex my last days with the irregular proceedings at Wittenberg." Suffering constantly in body and mind, he longed for death.

Called to Eisleben, to arbitrate a difference between the Counts of Mansfeld, Luther died there, February 18, 1546. The Counts wished that he be buried there in his native land; but the Elector commanded that he be taken to Wittenberg. And in the Castle Church, the *Schloss-skirche,* on whose door Luther had posted the Theses nearly thirty years before, he was buried beside the pulpit, while Melancthon delivered a tender and moving tribute in Latin to his friend.

The *Schlosskirche* is the Westminster Abbey of the Lutheran Church. There Melancthon lies, and the Elector Frederick the Wise, with almost a hundred instructors of the University, while the ninety-five Theses are cast in the bronze doors.

When Luther lay dying at Eisleben, the last hope of religious unity in Germany was already dead. The Emperor had returned to Germany in 1541 (*See* p. 366), and held a Diet at Regensburg (Ratisbon). The growing menace of the Turks made him anxious for unity; and a conciliatory spirit manifested itself also in the Diet. But Roman and Evangelical views of the Church and the Sacraments were really irreconcilable; and a plan for reunion failed. It was significant, too, of the divided state of the nation that, while the Archbishop of Mainz was at Regensburg, the Reformation was being introduced into his lands with the support of the Elector of Saxony, and against the archbishop's protest.

A Diet at Speyer (Spires) in June, 1544, promised toleration of Protestantism until a General Council should meet. The Pope yielded and summoned a Council to Trent, for March, 1545 (*See* p. 367); but he warned the Emperor that his soul was being imperilled by his toleration of heresy. Charles made no reply; but, at the urgent request of the Elector, Luther reviewed the papal letter in a caustic document, *Against the Papacy at Rome, Instituted by the Devil.* It was a reaffirmation of all that Luther had taught.

When the Council of Trent achieved nothing for religious peace and the Pope found a pretext for transferring it from German to Italian soil, the Emperor defied the Pope, denied the validity of the council, and determined to unite Germany in a National Church. To that end he brought Spanish troops into Germany soon after Luther died. Before 1547 was far advanced, the Elector John Frederick was defeated and in prison, Wittenberg had fallen, and Philip of Hesse had surrendered on terms. Almost all Germany was prostrate at the feet of the Emperor.

Charles now resolved to be a second Justinian and try an experiment in Caesaropapism. Unable to bring the conflicting parties together, he resolved to construct a creed himself and force it upon both. He therefore chose three theologians—a Mediaevalist, a Humanist and a Lutheran— to make a creed. They produced the *Augsburg Interim,* which confessed by its name that it did not expect to survive.

The *Interim* declared the Pope the head of the Church, accepted transubstantiation, the seven sacraments, the adoration of the Virgin and the saints, and retained most mediaeval ceremonies. As a concession to Lutherans, it approved the doctrine of salvation by faith, the marriage of priests, the doctrine that the Mass is a Supper, all with qualifications and reservations. Each proposition was capable of different interpretations. The *Interim* was a layman's settlement of theological questions, artificial, tailor-made. Charles forgot that, though creeds may become lifeless with age, they are born out of the living conviction of those who frame them.

The *Interim* passed the Diet in 1548, with considerable difficulty, and became the law of the Empire. Charles was proud of his creed, and did his best to enforce it. Protestant princes were intimidated, City Councils purged of Protestant burghers, and some four hundred preachers exiled; but the people could not be coerced. They absented themselves from the churches, sang doggerel verse about the *Interim,* heard fugitive preachers rail against it. Catholics, too, resented the presence in Germany of Spanish soldiers; and dislike of the Emperor grew everywhere. At length a revolt flared up under Duke Maurice of Saxony, in 1552; and Charles fled through the Brenner Pass into Italy, in a storm of rain and snow. It was through the Brenner that he had entered Germany in 1530, at the height of his power, confident of suppressing religious innovations.

Charles ventured in time to return to Augsburg, counting on the dissensions among Protestant princes, and once more summoned a Diet; but his authority was gone and his presence all that was needed to unite the opposing forces. Before the Diet gathered at Augsburg, in February, 1555, Charles had left Germany forever, having handed over the direction of affairs there to his brother, Ferdinand of Austria, with the title "king of the Romans." Next year Charles resigned his hereditary king-dom of Spain and the Netherlands to his son Philip, who was to find the Protestants of the Netherlands as intractable as those of Germany. As for Charles V, he retired to a Spanish monastery, worn out with his labours, and there died in 1559.

Ferdinand, wisest of the Hapsburgs, saw that recognition of Lutheran-ism was inevitable. Protestant princes in Germany were now unanimous in support of the Confession of Augsburg; and after months of debate the Diet reached a compromise settlement, that was to be known as the Peace of Augsburg. By its terms Lutheranism was to be acknowledged as a lawful religion anywhere within the Empire; and each prince was to determine what the creed and organization of the Church should be in his own dominion. It was decided, however, that if a prince, who was also a Catholic prelate, should change his religion, he could not take his territory over to Protestantism with him, a decision which the Prot-estant members of the Diet refused to accept. They in turn demanded toleration of Lutheran dissenters in Catholic territories. This the Catholic members of the Diet rejected; but King Ferdinand promised to give it effect.

The Peace of Augsburg was not a great charter of religious freedom. No Swiss confession was to be recognized within the Empire, only the Confession of Augsburg. The Reformed Church and the Baptists were therefore heretics and outlaws. But at least a step towards freedom of conscience had been taken. Catholic hegemony in Western Europe had been successfully challenged. The Pope's writ was to cease to run in more and more of the nations, as it had long since ceased in the East.

CHAPTER XVI

THE REVOLT SPREADS TO OTHER LANDS

WITHIN a year of Luther's death, a masterful and lusty king of England was laid to rest in St. George's Chapel at Windsor. Henry VIII died as he had lived, a Catholic Christian. The smoke of burning heretics continued to the end to rise, if not by the royal command, at least with the royal consent; and only Henry's unwieldy corpulence prevented him from creeping to the cross on his last Good Friday, as he had been wont to do. But if Henry continued Catholic to the end, he had found occasion twenty years before to turn the papacy out of England, and had acted more effectively than Luther and the Schmalkald League.

Henry VIII had succeeded to the throne in 1509, a ruddy, handsome youth of eighteen, an accomplished scholar and linguist and musician, the first English monarch educated under Renaissance influence. That year he married a grave and gentle princess from Spain, Catherine of Aragon, who was six years his senior. Catherine had previously wedded his elder brother Arthur, when Arthur was but fifteen and she sixteen; but in five months Prince Arthur died, and Catherine was then betrothed to Henry. His father, Henry VII, wished to retain the rich dowry of Catherine, to help endow his new Tudor dynasty; and Ferdinand of Aragon wished to have England for a satellite of Spain. When therefore Henry VIII ascended the throne, he consummated by marriage a betrothal made when he was ten years old.

From the moment of the betrothal there had been scruples in many minds about the arrangement. Henry himself had been doubtful, and Catherine too. Pope Julius II had hesitated to grant a dispensation for the marriage of anyone with his deceased brother's widow, but in the end had found it consistent with the Levitical prohibition of such unions.

Eight children were born to Henry and Catherine; but only one lived, the future Queen Mary. It was an ill omen. Heaven was not blessing the union. And the lack of a male heir to the throne meant much to England. The land had suffered a century of recurring strife, to determine whether England was to be ruled by the descendants of John of Gaunt, Duke of Lancaster, or by those of Edmund, Duke of York, both true sons of old Edward III. The Wars of the Roses ended when Henry Tudor, of the Lancastrian line, fought victoriously at Bosworth in 1485, was crowned Henry VII next year at Westminster, and married Elizabeth, eldest daughter and heiress of the Yorkist king Edward IV. What could be more auspicious for England than that the red rose of Lancaster and the white rose of York should now bloom together? Nevertheless there were conspiracies against the crown in the reign of Henry VII; and if now his son should die without male issue, civil war was still possible. England was not yet accustomed to the rule of female sovereigns.

After nearly twenty years of wedlock, Henry VIII sought from Pope Clement VII the dissolution of his marriage. He was confident that a dispensation would be granted. His sister Margaret had been relieved of a husband, to marry James IV of Scotland. His sister Mary had recently married the Duke of Suffolk, whose earlier marriage had been dissolved for that purpose. But when Henry now sought a dispensation, Pope Clement wavered. As often as French arms triumphed in Italy, a dispensation seemed possible. When Spanish arms triumphed and Spanish cavalry was stabled at the Vatican, it seemed impossible; for Catherine of Aragon was aunt to the Emperor Charles V.

So in 1529 King Henry summoned Parliament. He was aware, being an educated man, that distinguished Catholics had thought the royal power derived from God as surely as the papal, and that a king might be head of the Church in his own dominions. He knew also that England, orthodox and Catholic, was nevertheless anti-clerical and anti-papal. There were plenty of complaints against the hierarchy and the Pope, awaiting ventilation in Parliament, and enough devotion to the new dynasty to support such anti-papal action as was necessary.

A lay revolt against clerical control had been gathering momentum for a hundred and fifty years. It echoes humorously in Chaucer's *Canterbury Tales*. It is heard more ominously by the middle of the fifteenth century, in a quaint document [1] of Bishop Pecock of Chichester, complaining of

---

[1] *The Repressor of overmuch Wyting of the Clergy.*

the anti-clerical temper of "the lay party." It persisted into the reign of Henry VIII. Fitzjames, bishop of London, declared in 1516 that any London jury would convict a cleric, "were he innocent as Abel." And indeed the flame of discontent was now being fanned by distinguished Catholic Humanists. Sir Thomas More was writing satires, to goad the hierarchy to reform. Dean Colet was condemning the sins of the clergy in the Convocation of Canterbury, and preaching the Gospel from the pulpit of St. Paul's. Lollards came from secret worship on the moors and fens, to hear from the lips of this great man things they had held in secret, ever since John Wyclif's doctrines had been condemned and his preachers excluded from the Universities, more than a century before. More than one poor Lollard was burned in Colet's day, because he could read the Scriptures and did read in the presence of credible witnesses, and, more suspicious still, had walked all the way from Yorkshire or Devon, to hear Dean Colet preach.

Deprived of education, Lollardy had ceased to be an influential movement soon after Wyclif died; but at least it accustomed Englishmen to the idea that they might be outside the Catholic Church, without being thereby cut off from Christ. And when the Christian Humanists appeared, and then disciples of Luther also, Lollard principles received educated advocacy once more; and Lollards were among the first recruits to the Protestant cause. Indeed when Protestantism began to stir in England, Tunstall, bishop of London, declared, "It is only that new arms are being added to the great band of Wyclifite heretics." And the Protestant ferment came quickly from the continent to England. The Reformation Treatises of Martin Luther were being read at Cambridge almost as soon as written; and men were speaking, under the breath, of a certain quarter of the town as "Germany." [2] The Treatises reached Oxford in 1521.[3]

And so when Henry VIII concluded that his domestic question would not be settled on its merits in the papal court, he shrewdly guessed that there was enough anti-papal sentiment in England to make it safe for

[2] Among the first students of the Bible and Luther at Cambridge were several men who were to become distinguished pioneers of Protestantism in England. There were "little Bilney," the martyr, William Tyndale, translator of the Scriptures, Hugh Latimer, great preacher, bishop and martyr, Thomas Cranmer, first Protestant archbishop of Canterbury, also a martyr.

[3] The facts cited in these paragraphs may be read in *The Letters and Papers, domestic and foreign, of the Reign of Henry VIII.*

him to summon Parliament and appeal to the nation. He was not mistaken. In the balance of forces, public devotion to the dynasty and to
himself turned the scale. Parliament continued to sit intermittently from
1529 to 1536; and anti-clerical legislation advanced step by step. Parliament limited the income of bishops, restrained the holding by clerics of
several benefices and imposed penalties for non-residence. It threatened
the papal income by forbidding payment of Annates to Rome, except
with the king's consent. Henry used this threat to secure papal confirmation of Thomas Cranmer as Archbishop of Canterbury; and Parliament then made the archbishop's court the supreme court for ecclesiastical cases, forbidding appeals to Rome. Cranmer thereupon annulled the
marriage of Henry and Catherine, and validated the marriage of Henry
to Anne Boleyn, a lady-in-waiting to the queen.

Henry now threw off all pretence of devotion to the papacy. He cut
off the papal revenues, was excommunicated, and withdrew his ambassador from Rome. Parliament then enacted that the sovereign "justly and
rightfully is and ought to be supreme head of the Church of England,"
and made it illegal for church courts to meet and legislate without the
royal consent. To crown all, Parliament made dissent treason. It passed
an Act, fixing the succession to the throne and exacting from all civil
and ecclesiastical officials an oath, repudiating the papal supremacy in
the Church.

Opposition was now hopeless; but some did not yield. Bishop Fisher,
the most learned prelate in England, recently made a cardinal, and the
saintly Sir Thomas More, now Lord Chancellor, acknowledged the
right of Parliament to fix the succession, but could not swear disbelief in
the papal supremacy. They were executed, as were the heads of the
Carthusian order of monks. An inspection of the monasteries followed.
The report was damaging; and within four years all monasteries, good
and bad, were suppressed, and their property confiscated to the crown.[4]
Charges of treason, with torture and death, brought the submission of
the monks. Many buildings and their treasures were wantonly destroyed.
Most of the wealth went to Henry and the new Chancellor, Thomas

[4] The truth of the report is a matter of controversy; but there was at least great need
of monastic reform. In any case, the monasteries would have remained centres of papal
intrigue. If the nation was to remain united, and the new order to be permanent, the
monasteries had to go.

Cromwell. Some went to found the navy, some to endow new families. Nothing was done for education, and little for religion.

Catherine of Aragon died in January, 1536, while the "Reformation Parliament" was still in session. Four months later Anne Boleyn was dead. She had borne a child, Elizabeth, but no male heir. Henry was already tired of her. She was accused of adultery and executed. Ten days later Henry married Jane Seymour, who gave the king a son but died in doing so. The frail prince Edward, himself to die at fifteen, was the last of the Tudor children.

The closing years of Henry's life were perilous for Protestants. The reaction had set in, that often comes with old age. Henry was very Catholic again. Bishops of Protestant convictions had to resign, until only Cranmer remained to stem the tide of reaction. Protestant in his sympathies, Cranmer did believe in the royal supremacy. The last word in religious matters, he thought, was not his but the king's. Cranmer could therefore submit, where he could not agree.

In spite of reaction, certain changes had been made by Henry's authority, that would make for a Protestant order when he was gone. First, he had authorized the publication of the Bible in English, and ordered it set up in the churches. England had now "the open Bible"; and in the churches groups might be seen clustered about the lecterns, while anyone who could do so read for them the ancient and mysterious book, that had never before been open to the common people. Here was something by which plain men would judge the words and deeds of prelates.

The Litany too, was published in 1545. It was the work of Cranmer, beautiful, devout, plaintive, echoing the conflict of principles in Cranmer's mind, as well as the universal sense of sin. It was substantially as in the present Book of Common Prayer, except that it included invocations of the Virgin, the angels, apostles and martyrs, and a derogatory reference or two to the Pope.

Meanwhile religious change was beginning among the French. In the last year of the Reformation Parliament in England, a brilliant young Frenchman, Jean Cauvin (Calvin),[5] reached Geneva and undertook the

[5] From the Latin form of his name, *Calvinus*.

organization of that city republic into a Protestant and Puritan state. Calvin (1509–1564) was a native of Noyon, a small town of Picardy, some sixty miles northeast of Paris. His father, Gérard Cauvin, was a leading citizen of Noyon, a lawyer; and John was well educated from childhood and at home in polite society. At fourteen he was sent to the University of Paris, which was still the most eminent seat of learning in Europe, though mediaeval in outlook and averse to Humanism. Paris gave Calvin a brilliant Latin style and great skill in debate. Refined, accomplished, and religious, he attracted to himself the best student life.

After graduation, in 1527 or 1528, Calvin went for Law to the University of Orleans, a place of pleasant and leisurely study, sympathetic with Humanism. In a year or two, drawn by the fame of Andrea Alciati, a great teacher of Law, Calvin moved on to the University of Bourges, a young institution, where Law was becoming a science, instead of a mass of facts. And from Bourges he returned in 1531 to Paris, where King Francis I had now appointed "Royal Lecturers," to introduce Humanism into the University. Here Calvin perfected his Latin, studied Greek and Hebrew, and became a notable member of a brilliant circle of lawyers and Humanists.

Up to this time Calvin was more devoted to the Classics than to the Scriptures, and does not appear to have participated in the theological controversies of the day; but in 1532 or 1533 he was converted to Protestant principles, under the influence of the New Testament and the writings of Erasmus and Luther. The change in him was so great that he could not but attribute it to the direct intervention of God. Calvin felt the divine authority of the Scriptures more explicitly than any other of the Protestant Reformers; and through them he was led on and on, in a way that recalls the conversion of Augustine of Hippo.

The University of Paris was now in turmoil over Humanism. The Faculty of Theology had bestirred itself; the *Parlement de Paris* had begun proceedings against heretics; and Francis I had ordered the suppression of "the Lutheran Sect." Calvin fled to Angoulême, some two hundred and fifty miles southwest of Paris, where he found shelter with a wealthy friend, Louis du Tillet, a Canon of the Cathedral. Here Calvin taught Greek, wrote sermons for priests of Protestant views, and began writing the *Institutes,* the ablest handbook of theology of the whole

Protestant movement. Soon, however, life became insecure for reformers everywhere in France; and Calvin went to Switzerland, to Basel, where Erasmus was still living.

At Basel the first edition of the *Institutes* was completed and published. The Introduction, addressed to Francis I, was a courteous, acute defence of Protestantism. Francis was courting the Protestant princes of Germany, as desirable allies for a struggle with Charles V; and, to justify, his persecution of Protestants in France, he charged them with anarchical aims, dangerous to all government. Calvin's reply, in the Introduction to the *Institutes,* made him the recognized leader of French Protestantism. He immediately became adviser to Evangelical Christians far and wide, with a correspondence like that of Erasmus and Melancthon.

Visiting Paris in 1536, to wind up his affairs and take his brother and sister with him to Basel, Calvin returned through Geneva. His presence there was reported to William Farel, the stormy petrel of French Protestantism, who was striving to establish the Reformation at Geneva. Farel adjured him to stay and assume the leadership. Very reluctantly Calvin obeyed. "Farel kept me at Geneva," he said, "not so much by advice and entreaty as by a dreadful adjuration, as if God had stretched forth His hand upon me from on high to arrest me." [6]

Geneva had recently become a republic, having won independence of Savoy by force of arms. In this it had been assisted by its ally Bern, another Swiss republic. Bern had adopted Protestantism in 1528; and in 1532 the citizens of Geneva awoke one morning, to find their public buildings placarded with criticisms of the papacy and with Luther's doctrine of salvation by faith. The Government, annoyed at the breach of order, reaffirmed its allegiance to Catholicism, but made a gesture towards reform by ordering that the clergy preach only "the Gospel and epistle of God according to truth, without mingling with it any fables." And soon William Farel arrived, with letters of introduction from the Government at Bern, to preach the Reformation.

Farel was a native of southern France. He had studied at the University of Paris, had become a Humanist, then a Protestant, and had fled from persecution to Basel, only to fall into controversy there with Eras-

---

[6] For those who can read French and Latin, excerpts from original documents, relating to the years of Farel and Calvin at Geneva, may be had in B. J. Kidd, *Documents Illustrative of the Continental Reformation,* pp. 477–651.

mus. For some years thereafter he was a wandering missionary of Protestantism to the French cantons of Switzerland, and helped to win Bern
to the Reformation.[7] But Farel was a fiery evangelist; and tumult followed him wherever he went. In Geneva he was assaulted in the streets
and violently expelled. Nevertheless gentler advocates took up his work;
and next year, 1533, it was possible to preach in the public square, and a
Protestant congregation was formed. The authorities wavered; and Farel
found it possible to return.

Fostered by Bern, Protestantism grew; and in 1534 Farel and his associates ventured to seize a Franciscan monastery, for a place of worship.
Circumstances were favourable. The bishop was found to be in league
with the Duke of Savoy, against the newly-won freedom of Geneva. So
Protestantism and liberty became identified in the public mind. The
Government declared the office of bishop vacant and, hearing of a plot
to poison the new preachers, took them under its protection.

A prolonged public discussion of the religious question was held in
1535. The bishop forbade the faithful to participate; and the champions
of Protestantism had an easy victory. Confident now, they seized the
churches of the city, including the cathedral of St. Pierre. The Government yielded, and moved for a religious reformation. It suspended the
celebration of the Mass; and the priests left the city. They were ignorant,
inefficient, and not innocent of moral irregularities. The Government assumed control in religion, as at Bern and Zurich. The monasteries were
converted into hospitals and houses of refuge. Decrees made blasphemy
a crime, as well as gambling, drunkenness, and absence from public
worship. Next year, May 21, 1536, the citizens voted full acceptance of
Protestantism. They would "live in this holy, evangelical Law and Word
of God, as it has been announced to us, desiring to abandon all Masses,
images, idols, and all that which may pertain thereto."[8] The same assembly voted that all parents must send their children to school, and
that education be free to the poor.

Here, therefore, was a republic, of Geneva and twenty-eight villages,
committed to Protestantism and to universal education, and inclined to a
state-controlled church; but the church was quite unorganized and had

[7] In 1532 Farel attended a synod of the Waldenses, high in the Cottian Alps; and as a
result a considerable body of Waldenses accepted the Protestant Reformation.
[8] Kidd, p. 518.

no Creed, except the decision to live by "the Word of God." Such was the situation when Calvin called at Geneva, in transit to Basel, and was pressed by Farel into leadership.

Geneva had been an important centre since the days of ancient Rome, and the seat of a bishopric since Constantine the Great. In the two centuries before Calvin, it had been ruled by a bishop, and a deputy for civil affairs, the *vicedominus,* appointed by the duke of neighbouring Savoy. The burghers, however, had had a considerable measure of self-government. They met each year in a General Assembly, and elected four administrative officers, the Syndics. They had also an executive government of twenty-five members, the Little Council. It was composed of the four Syndics and seventeen councillors chosen by them, together with the Syndics of the previous year. And there was a Council of Sixty, appointed by the Little Council, to discuss questions of general policy, not easily debatable in the General Assembly. Finally the growing spirit of Genevan independence led to the establishment in 1527 of a more representative council, the "Two Hundred," chosen by the Little Council and absorbing the business of the Council of Sixty. Before long the office of *vicedominus* was abolished; and in 1534, as we have seen, the office of bishop was declared vacant.

Geneva was a great commercial centre. Situated on the border of Switzerland, near the most frequented passes of the Alps, she traded the wares of Germany, Italy and France. Her merchants were prosperous, her workmen famed for their skill. The city was ecclesiastically famous too. The Benedictines and Dominicans, the Franciscans and Augustinians had monasteries there, and the nuns of the second order of St. Francis, the Clarisses. Unhappily ecclesiasticism improved conduct but little at Geneva. A lively city, a favourite place of residence for the gentry of neighbouring lands, her moral standards were low. The burghers, energetic and independent as they were, were keenly devoted to pleasure. Into their midst in 1536 came John Calvin, chaste, austere and determined. The Little Council made him "Professor of Sacred Letters in the Church of Geneva," and voted him a small salary. In January, 1537, he presented to the Council certain "Articles," embodying a plan for a reformed church.[9]

In the forefront of his plan, Calvin puts the Lord's Supper. Instead

[9] The Articles may be had in Kidd, pp. 560–567.

of the daily Mass, the Supper is to be observed each month; and if it is to be observed worthily, the unworthy must be excluded. This will require discipline, a difficult thing at Geneva. So Calvin asks the Council to appoint "certain persons of upright life and good reputation among all the faithful, who being divided and distributed in all the quarters of the city, shall have an eye to the life and conduct of each one." What they see amiss, they will report to one of the ministers, who will "admonish the one in fault and exhort him fraternally to reform." If he is obstinate, he will be reported to the Church itself. If he will not then confess his sin and reform, he is to be excommunicated by the Church; that is, "rejected from the company of Christians." Beyond this the Church cannot go. If, therefore, the evildoer is defiant still, the civil government must consider whether it will "leave unpunished such contempt, and such mockery of God and of His Gospel."

Thus Calvin moves to recover something of the independence of the Church, which earlier Reformers had sacrificed through the need of State support. His ideal is a Puritan society, of trained and conscientious Christians, needing no moral restraint by the civil authority, except for those who abandon the Church.

With this recommendation went another of almost equal importance, that the whole population be required now to choose between Romanism and Protestantism. The members of the Council were asked to profess publicly the Reformed faith, then appoint representatives, who in cooperation with the ministers would receive a profession of faith from all persons in Geneva, "that it may be understood who of them agree with the Gospel, and who love to be of the kingdom of the Pope rather than the kingdom of Jesus Christ." Calvin does not say what shall be done with those who reject Protestantism. The Government had already declared that they must leave Geneva.

There was thus to be a fresh beginning. Calvin prepared for the adult population a Confession of Faith, and for the children a Catechism. It was an orderly and lucid outline of Christianity, as Calvin understood it, a sort of pocket edition of the *Institutes*. The Council was asked "to order parents to exercise care and diligence that their children learn this outline and present themselves to the ministers" at appointed times, to be examined in it. The future of Protestantism at Geneva would thus be assured.

The Little Council adopted the Articles, but with modifications. The Lord's Supper was to be observed only four times a year. A monthly observance, preceded by rigid scrutiny of their conduct, was too much for the Genevese. They were averse to any strenuous discipline, and preferred the system at Bern, where the Church was under control of the State, as at Zurich. The demand, too, that they subscribe the Confession of Faith was irksome to many, who were Catholic still and had sup-Assembly of 1537 chose Syndics favourable to the Reformation; and ported Protestantism only for political reasons. Nevertheless the General both Little Council and Two Hundred agreed to enforce the Confession. Copies were therefore distributed; and officers were commanded to bring the people to St. Pierre, to subscribe the Confession.

There was enough resistance to necessitate a special meeting of the General Assembly. The session was stormy; and the Government weathered the storm with difficulty. Calvin and Farel were dauntless. It was not their will, but the will of God, for which they strove. They asked the support of the Little Council in excluding from the first communion those who refused the Confession. The Council held back. It voted that "the Supper be refused to no one," thus supporting the Confession of Faith, while thwarting the discipline.

Next year, 1538, political reaction set in. Opponents of the reformers were chosen Syndics. The Two Hundred commanded the preachers to keep out of politics, and voted to "live under the Word of God according to the ordinances of the Lords of Bern." That would be the end of ecclesiastical independence. Almost as serious was the fact that Bern had retained many Catholic usages.

The situation was now impossible, for men whose convictions were those of Calvin and Farel. They were asked by the Little Council to approve the Bernese system, and refused. They were forbidden to preach, and preached in defiance. The Little Council, Two Hundred, and General Assembly thereupon ratified the Bernese system, and commanded the two reformers to leave Geneva, in April, 1538.

Calvin and Farel had no thought of abandoning the work. They betook themselves to Bern, whose Government, alarmed now for Protestantism at Geneva, interceded for them. The Genevan authorities were adamant. Calvin and Farel therefore pushed on to Zurich, to a Synod of the Protestant cantons. The Synod approved the Articles, urging only that in giving them effect more allowance be made for Genevan inexperience of discipline. The Synod requested the Bernese authorities to attempt a reconciliation once again. They did so; but the Little Council refused admission to Geneva, to both the reformers and the Bernese embassy.

Calvin was sharply criticised by both friend and foe. He was deeply wounded. He had been entirely disinterested, seeking nothing for himself, and for Geneva only this, that she might become an orderly Christian community, with a church free to fulfil its mission. He went with Farel to Basel, where they were welcomed to the home of the publisher of the *Institutes,* Johann Oporin. Thence Farel soon went to a pastorate at Neuchatel, while Calvin yielded to a warm invitation from leaders at Strassburg to settle there.

Strassburg proved both a haven and a mission. It was the bulwark of the Reformation in southwestern Germany. Martin Bucer was there, kindly and wise, second only to Luther and Melancthon in influence throughout all Germany. Johann Sturm, too, had established a school system, quite the best as yet in Protestantism anywhere. His brother Jacob was a statesman, talented and tolerant. The city, too, was giving friendly welcome to Protestant refugees, and had a congregation of French exiles, the Church of St. Nicolas. Martin Bucer pressed upon Calvin the needs of this congregation, and adjured him to remember Jonah and his flight from duty at Nineveh. Calvin once more thought himself called of God, and became minister of St. Nicolas.

In Strassburg Calvin was poor, but respected, with time for study and for the perfecting of his theological system. He became acquainted, too, with leaders of the German Reformation,[10] gathered experience, married. And under the supervision of the Strassburg Government, he was able to organize the French community of some five hundred souls, and give effect to his Geneva plan. The Lord's Supper was observed monthly; and, in spite of some opposition, a vigorous discipline was maintained. All who would approach the Holy Table came first to Calvin for questioning. It was his substitute for the Roman confessional. The congregation of St. Nicolas became serious, decorous and influential; and Calvin

[10] Here began a friendship with Melancthon, enduring and beautiful, the rather timid caution of the German scholar complementing the severely logical and courageous quality of the young Frenchman's mind.

won to his principles many Anabaptists, who were numerous in the region.

At St. Nicolas, too, Calvin used a liturgy that was to become the general model for Reformed worship everywhere, as distinguished from Lutheran and Anglican forms. It was a modification and translation into French of a liturgy already provided for Strassburg by Martin Bucer and others. Calvin's most noteworthy addition was the singing of the Psalms in French. The Psalms were to take the place in Reformed worship that hymns did in Lutheran. Calvin and Farel had provided in the Articles for hymns at Geneva; but Calvin's view of the Scriptures was really better expressed by the use of Psalms alone, and Puritanism was later to restrict music to the words of the Bible.[11] Meanwhile Calvin provided for St. Nicolas a brief collection of metrical Psalms. In this he was assisted by Clément Marot; and Calvin's critical taste led him to substitute Marot's translations for his own in later editions of the Psalter. Marot became the great Psalm-translator of French Protestantism.

The educational system at Strassburg, devised by Johann Sturm, began with elementary studies and advanced to courses in Greek, Latin, Hebrew, Mathematics and Law, the whole being crowned by instruction in Theology, given by the ministers. They naturally desired the co-operation of the author of the *Institutes;* and Calvin soon began public instruction in the Bible. His *Commentary on Romans* was published in 1540, the first of a long series of commentaries, that were to make Calvin the foremost interpreter of the Bible in the Reformation era.

Calvin's lectures added to his fame in Strassburg, and drew thither from France many persons of Protestant sentiments. They saw at St. Nicolas the model Christian community, serious, disciplined, well taught, and bound together in worship, whose pastor was influential in the city and beyond its walls. Calvin's influence was further increased by a new and enlarged edition of the *Institutes,* in which his theology was complete; though the *Institutes* continued to be enlarged until the final edition in 1559.

Meanwhile things were not going well at Geneva. The Government, having stopped the Mass, excluded the priests, and converted the monas-

---

11 Calvin anticipated the Puritan prejudice against the use of the organ in worship, as likely to divert the attention of the worshippers from the words of the hymn.

teries to public uses, found both themselves and the ministers incapable of creating a new ecclesiastical order. The Government, too, having come to office through a reaction against discipline, found indiscipline running to license. The morals of Geneva were visibly declining. The Government looked to the ministers, the ministers to the Government, to arrest the decline. And the more religious citizens thought longingly of the informed and steadfast leadership the Church had enjoyed for so short a time. There was a disposition to disown the existing ministers. At the end of the year they sent their resignations to the Little Council, "since we can no longer have fruit such as we desire in this place, matters being in such disorder."

The Council rejected the resignations of the ministers, and proceeded to punish their critics. Calvin wrote from Strassburg a calm and earnest letter, full of solicitude, stressing the sacredness of the pastoral office and deploring dissensions. An assembly of Catholic bishops at Lyons sent, through Cardinal Sadoleto, an appeal to Geneva to return to the ancient faith, and a letter to the Little Council. The Council were asked to consider whether their salvation would be more secure in following what the Catholic Church had approved for fifteen centuries, or "innovations introduced within these twenty-five years, by crafty, or, as they think, acute men." The Council gave little heed to the letter, but sent the appeal to the Government at Bern, which asked Calvin to reply. Calvin's *Reply to Sadoleto,* like the earlier letter to Francis I, was a scholarly and brilliant defence of Protestantism everywhere, and made new friends for him at Geneva.

Politics, too, turned the minds of some to Calvin. The Government of Geneva had sent an embassy to Bern, to negotiate a new treaty. The embassy was thought to have sacrificed the interests of Geneva; and a revolution restored the party of Calvin and Farel. The Little Council, in September, 1540, asked Calvin to return; and the Two Hundred and the General Assembly supported the request.

Calvin clung to the quiet of Strassburg; but the Protestant pastors of French Switzerland urged him to accept the call and Farel went to Strassburg to press it. Calvin yielded. His plan for an ideal Christian commonwealth could be tried more auspiciously in a French republic than in a French church in a German state. At Geneva, too, he could do much more for the Evangelical cause throughout France. So in September, 1541, Calvin was back at his post in Geneva.

On the day of his arrival, he appeared before the Little Council and asked for a committee, to assist in preparing a constitution for the Church. He had, he was now sure, been called of God to Geneva. His banishment was but a brief interruption of his work; and in the pulpit of St. Pierre on the first Sunday, he resumed the interpretation of the Scriptures at the passage reached when he was banished.

The Little Council appointed a committee of six, four from the Council itself and two from the Two Hundred, to co-operate with the ministers. The Council decreed, however, that the constitution when drafted should be submitted for approval to itself, the Two Hundred, and the General Assembly. The work was soon done; and Calvin spent a month explaining it, article by article. It was changed somewhat by the Council and Two Hundred, then adopted by the General Assembly. The Government, even in the first enthusiasm over Calvin's return, clung to its prerogatives. Calvin was to be adviser, not ruler, in giving the Church a constitution.

The *Ordonnances*,[12] as the proposed constitution was called, were an elaboration of the Articles of 1537. The primary purposes still were to reserve to the Church self-government, while maintaining helpful relations with the State, and to provide a discipline that would secure in the Church sound doctrine and right living. Calvin did not get all he thought needful, in either of these matters.

The *Ordonnances* affirmed at the outset that only the offices of pastor, teacher, elder, and deacon, not those of priest and bishop, were instituted by Christ for the Church. As for the first, men were to become pastors, or ministers, only after being examined and elected by those already ministers, the election to be confirmed also by the Little Council. Ministers were to take an oath of fidelity to God in spiritual matters, obedience to the Government in temporal matters. They were to meet each week on Friday, to discuss the Scriptures, and quarterly for confession and self-criticism. The ministers collectively were called the *Vénérable Compagnie;* and their meeting was popularly known as the *Congrégation.*

Teachers were assistants to the ministers, in the same educational task,

[12] Kidd, pp. 589–602.

instructing the people in the Scriptures. Calvin felt that before one can "profit by such lessons he must first be instructed in the languages and human sciences." The teachers were therefore to provide this preparatory instruction. They were regarded as in the ministry, were subjected to the same discipline, and were installed by the ministers. The Little Council insisted, however, that they must first be "presented" to the Council and examined before a committee of its members.

The elders were laymen, twelve in number, chosen by the Little Council, after consultation with the ministers, and with the final approval of the Two Hundred. They were to be chosen, two from the Little Council, four from the Council of Sixty, and six from the Two Hundred. Their duty was "to watch over the life of each individual, to admonish affectionately those who are seen to err and to lead a disorderly life, and, where there shall be need, to make report to the body which shall be appointed to make fraternal correction."

The body so appointed was the *Consistoire,* composed of the elders and ministers together. It met each week, under the presidency of one of the Syndics, and could summon anyone, to be examined as to his beliefs and conduct. The penalties imposed for heresy or misconduct might extend to excommunication; but all was to be so done "that the corrections should be naught but medicines, to bring back sinners to our Lord." Back of the Consistory, however, stood the Government, ready to deal with such as disregarded excommunication and were content to remain outside the Church. Calvin thus secured through the *Ordonnances* the substance of Puritanism.

The Reformed Church, in this reliance on discipline, was more like the Roman Church than was either the Lutheran or the Anglican. And since the Church embraced the whole community, discipline reached everyone, as it had in the Roman Church. What was new was this, that the rule of conduct was now the Bible, not ecclesiastical tradition and Canon Law. God had revealed in the Bible the pattern of right living. It was the duty of both Church and State to see that men conformed to it.

The deacons were chosen like the elders, and filled their ancient rôle, the discharge of church business. At Geneva this included the administration of poor relief and management of the hospital, which was to be both a medical centre and a refuge for widows, orphans and the aged. There was to be no begging in Geneva.

Since all life was to be guided by the "Word of God" and the age of Bible-reading was not yet well begun, there was great emphasis on preaching. There were to be sermons on Sundays at daybreak, at nine o'clock, and again at three, with instruction in the Catechism at noon. Very soon, indeed, there was a sermon every day, in all the churches.

Calvin wished a monthly celebration of the Lord's Supper, but was still unable to carry the Government with him; and communion therefore continued to be observed only quarterly. Children were not to be admitted to the Holy Table until familiar with the Catechism and able to profess the faith set forth therein.

With the adoption of the *Ordonnances,* even in their modified form, Geneva became a theocracy, in the sense that all government, both civil and religious, was to express the will of God, as revealed in the "Word of God." Calvin was its foremost interpreter, and therefore the supreme instructor of the people and adviser of the Government. The Consistory co-operated faithfully. Its Registers show that people were punished for more than those failings that are normally regarded as evils, such as dishonesty, violence, sins of the flesh. They were punished also for criticising the ministers, absenting themselves from preaching, dancing, for family quarrels, for calling the Pope a good man. The magistrates, too, were severe in cases referred to them.

Conflicts were bound to arise. Old Genevan families resented the influence of Calvin and other French refugees. They resented the compulsion to hear sermons, to submit to reprimands, to abstain from Geneva's abundant amusements. Calvin's position was sometimes insecure, so much so that he thought only a supernatural intervention could save his system from collapse. One sure support, however, was the growing community of refugees, people of education and conviction, from France and Italy, England and Scotland and the Netherlands. Calvin had aimed to make Geneva "a firm sanctuary for God . . . and a faithful asylum for the members of Christ." It became so. No other centre in Europe had so many noble and distinguished people, who combined staunch character with wealth and learning; and as rapidly as the refugees became burghers, opposition to Calvin became futile. Geneva became a Puritan city, religious, disciplined.

We have seen that Calvin regarded church and school as complementary agencies. A true faith must be intelligent. So the school was given a prominent place in the *Ordonnances;* but because of both the cost and the difficulty of securing good teachers, the intended school system was delayed nearly twenty years. Calvin himself taught theology; but for general education parents sent their children to other cities. For advanced studies, Lausanne, in the canton of Bern, had the only institution for French Protestants. At length, however, the Little Council was persuaded to authorize the establishment of a college at Geneva; and Calvin himself sought gifts and legacies for its construction and endowment. Troubles at Lausanne provided it with a Faculty. The teachers and ministers at Lausanne believed in Calvin's ecclesiastical system and tried to introduce it there. The Bernese Government would have none of it; and, anticipating the storm, several teachers left for Geneva. Among them was Antoine Chevalier, once tutor in French to the princess Elizabeth in England, now professor of Hebrew. Another was Theodore Beza, professor of Greek, a devoted disciple of Calvin, who was to succeed Calvin in the leadership at Geneva and become his biographer.

The *Vénérable Compagnie* nominated several of the Lausanne teachers to the Little Council, to be the first Faculty of the Academy, as it was called. Beza was made rector; and an educational system was inaugurated like that of Johann Sturm at Strassburg. Children in the lowest grades were taught the vernacular French, and Latin as the accepted basis of culture everywhere. They advanced gradually to Hebrew and Greek, as aids to an understanding of the Scriptures; and logic, philosophy and theology were added. Instruction was free; but students were admitted only after a confession of faith.

Thus Calvin provided for the education of the children of Geneva, and training in theology for candidates for the ministry from everywhere. Geneva became the theological centre for the Reformed churches of all lands.

The Academy was the crown of Calvin's work, the final provision for the Christian commonwealth of which he dreamed. To the preaching of the Gospel, and discipline in the practice of it, there was now added religious education. Christians were to be able to give a reason for their faith, deserving the respect of learned men. In the *Institutes* [13] they had

---

[13] The *Institutes* circulated throughout Europe, as the standard presentation of Calvin's system. They were published repeatedly in French, once in Italian, Dutch and English, while Calvin lived. They appeared in German and Spanish soon after his death.

the sum of theology, and in the *Commentaries* a guide to the Scriptures from which that theology was drawn. The *Commentaries* were the best interpretation of the Bible that the Protestant Reformation produced, resting on an adequate knowledge of the languages of the Bible, applied with reverence and diligence and a sound judgment. There was, of course, no thought of the Bible as a literature, composed by many men, in many circumstances, separated by many centuries; nor was there conceived to be any error in the Bible. The language was the language of men; the thought was all that of the Holy Spirit. Here Calvin and the Reformers in general continued in the teaching of the Catholic Church.

As for Calvin's theology, it was, of all the variants of Protestant theology, the most effective alternative to Romanism. True, Calvin had not an original mind; but originality was not what was then required. The general principles of Protestantism were already fixed, and were firmly held wherever Protestants were found; but many questions had yet to be answered, many inferences to be drawn, and all to be brought together into a system. It was the work of Calvin to systematise what others had begun. He did it so well that he became the foremost Protestant theologian of the age. His *Institutes* are the best statement of Protestantism, as well as the standard for what is distinctively Calvinistic.

Calvin's precise and logical mind led him to begin with a definition of God. He is sovereign over men and events. Everything exists by His will and for His glory. The honour of God is therefore the first concern of the citizen and the first duty of the State. Life is right and laws are good, as they express His will. To know Him is therefore supremely important.

God may be known from the physical world and through the human mind; but the light of reason is as nothing, when compared with the Scriptures, whose authors are "the sure and authentic amanuenses of the Holy Spirit." "The full authority which (the Scriptures) ought to possess with the faithful is not recognized, unless they are believed to have come from heaven, as directly as if God had been heard giving utterance to them." Their dignity and simplicity, their truth and effectiveness, prove this; but better still, the Spirit of God in the enlightened soul recognizes the same Spirit Speaking in Holy Writ. "Those who are inwardly taught by the Holy Spirit acquiesce implicitly in Scripture." The Bible, therefore, does not need the authority of the Church to commend it. "The secret testimony of the Spirit" does that. The Bible is truth, awakening response in the soul; and what it contains is the new law, for the direction of human life.[14]

As for the human race, the first man Adam was created in the image of God; but ambition and pride led him into faithlessness. He fell into sin, and involved all his descendants in "a hereditary corruption and depravity" so complete that "the soul, when plunged into that deadly abyss, not only labours under vice, but is altogether devoid of good."

Luther had not dwelt much on this doctrine of inherited depravity, or "original sin"; and Melancthon, when he did develop the doctrine, affirmed that man is not so fallen that he cannot co-operate with God in his own redemption. Calvin's personal history, however, like that of Augustine of Hippo, had seemed to him a series of decisive supernatural interventions in his life; and he read into the Scriptures what Augustine had read out of experience, "the will is enchained as the slave of sin, it cannot make a movement towards goodness, far less steadily pursue it."

From this hopeless condition God in His mercy rescues some men, quite undeservedly. This He can do, without impairing His justice, because Christ paid Him the penalty due for the sins of those whom He willed to redeem. "Christ, in His death, was offered to the Father as a propitiatory victim" and "He bore in His soul the tortures of condemned and ruined man."

But the work of Christ for men is of no avail, unless they receive him in faith. This faith is not their own achievement; it is wrought in them by the Holy Spirit and is always accompanied by repentance and followed by Christian conduct. Such conduct is not easy; but the Bible, the Law of God, is always at hand, inciting one to holiness. Those, therefore, who are indifferent to the Gospel, can only be so because God did not will to lead them to faith and repentance.

This had been the doctrine of Augustine, the doctrine of the Divine predestination of some to salvation, and was held by the Reformers in general; [15] but Calvin, rigidly logical, went beyond Augustine. God, he

[14] So great is Calvin's pre-occupation with the Scriptures that, having acknowledged reason and nature as sources of a knowledge of God, he virtually dismisses both. It was characteristic of the Reformers in general, except Zwingli, who was essentially a Humanist.

[15] Except that Melancthon thought man could co-operate, or refuse to co-operate, with God in his own redemption. Melancthon finally brought the Lutheran churches to that view.

thought, predestined some to damnation. One must not ask why. "If we cannot assign any reason for His bestowing mercy on His people, but just that it so pleases Him, neither can we have any reason for His reprobating others but His will."

The doctrine of predestination was a reassuring doctrine. If one desired salvation, he knew that grace had been given him, and that he was elected to salvation. Neither adversity nor death could frustrate God's plan. And on the other hand, predestination explained the persecutor and the notoriously wicked. They "were raised up by the just but inscrutable judgment of God, to show forth His glory by their condemnation."

Calvin exalted the Church, as Rome had done. It was the means by which the people were to be nourished in the Christian life. "To those to whom (God) is a Father, the Church must also be a mother." And the Church is "all the elect of God, including in the number even those who have departed this life." So much of it as is on earth, the visible Church, is to be governed by such officers only as are found in the New Testament, having been instituted by Christ. These, as we saw in the *Ordonnances,* are pastors, teachers, elders and deacons.

Calvin's system approaches ecclesiastical democracy more closely than either Lutheranism or Anglicanism. Only one of the four offices is clerical; and the "call" to the ministry, the voice of God in the soul, must be confirmed by "the consent and approbation of the people." Circumstances at Geneva led Calvin to accept approval by the Government as "the consent and approbation of the people," but elsewhere, in lands not officially Calvinistic, the democratic nature of the Church was to be better expressed.

Like all the Reformers, Calvin gave much thought to the Sacraments. It was inevitable, in a generation just emerging from Roman Catholicism, where life turned so much upon the Sacraments, and where powers fairly described as magical were attributed to them. With Protestants in general, and for the same reasons, Calvin rejected five of the seven mediaeval Sacraments, retaining only baptism and the Lord's Supper; and with him too the controversy raged round the Supper, as the Protestant substitute for the Mass. The heart of the discussion everywhere was as to the nature of Christ's presence in the bread and wine. Zwingli had admitted no physical presence in the elements. The Supper was but a commemorative meal, stimulating the faith of men in Christ's death for them. Luther, more bound to the past and to the letter of Scripture, had said that Christ was present in the elements, but not by the action of a priest. Calvin, bound like Luther to the ancient past, yet found it impossible to conceive that Christ's body could be at the same time in heaven and at many places on earth. "Let no property," he said, "be assigned to His body inconsistent with His human nature." Equally Calvin found Zwingli's doctrine too alien to Christian history and too little grounded in Scripture. Calvin contented himself with affirming a real presence in the elements, whose reality was spiritual and could be received only by faith. Only the true disciple receives Christ in the Holy Supper. "To speak with Augustine, I deny that men carry away more from the sacrament than they can collect in the vessel of faith." In all this, Calvin was anticipating better than anyone else the common sentiment of Protestant Christians in later centuries.

Thus the influence of Geneva was felt everywhere in Europe. The *Institutes* were regarded as the best statement of the Gospel, and the best answer to Romanism. Protestants outside Germany reached an essential doctrinal agreement, on the basis of Calvinism. Even Anglicanism was powerfully affected, as we shall see; and its vigorous rival in England, Puritanism, was Calvinism under another name.

It is evident that one element in Calvin's strength was his conservatism. He left intact most of the things that had long been regarded as essential to Christianity. The familiar notes of Augustine and Anselm were heard in his treatment of sin and salvation. The Nicene doctrine of the Trinity and the doctrine of Chalcedon concerning the person of Christ remained. Calvin clung to the past in all those things about which Christians were not yet divided. Indeed when a brilliant Spaniard, Servetus, ventured to question the Nicene doctrine of the Trinity, he died for his temerity at Geneva, with Calvin as prosecuting attorney. Whatever posterity may think of this event, it made Calvin appear to his own age a stern defender of Christianity.

Moreover Calvin's intellectual superiority was unquestioned. Studious and polite, with none of the animal vigour and coarseness of Luther, Calvin was a lawyer by training, an acute dialectician, a master of expression in both Latin and French, with a quite exceptional store of historical and Biblical learning. These things made him the supreme controversialist of a controversial age. His private life, too, was above reproach, simple, austere, controlled. Calvin was a Stoic to the end, believing that virtue should be practised for its own sake, though he expressed the matter in Christian terms. One might be securely elected to salvation, but must nevertheless study to do the will of God, "for the honour of God."

And nowhere in Protestantism was the life of Christians so supervised and directed. Calvin knew that in the first three centuries unworthy Christians had been excluded from the Lord's table. He determined to revive that ancient discipline, and to reserve the Supper for persons of proven godliness. To this end he did not shrink from a minute supervision of the private lives of Christians. Nor did he shrink from enforcing stern penalties for irregular conduct. Adultery, blasphemy, heresy were capital offences at Geneva. It is not to the modern taste; but it gave to Calvinists everywhere a certain vigorous and dauntless quality, and it made Geneva seem to multitudes the ideal Christian commonwealth.

Calvin's maintenance of ecclesiastical independence, too, gave strength to the Reformed Church. It escaped the servility that infected both Lutheranism and Anglicanism. And the stream of leadership never dried up in the Reformed Church, as it did in the Lutheran, because Calvin laid exceptional stress on education and laboured to make theological knowledge the common property of Christians.

To crown all, Calvin was a statesman. Being widely travelled, a scholar, trained in law, he grasped the whole religious situation in Europe. He is quite justly described as "the one international reformer." He was the counsellor and mainstay of the persecuted churches of France. Nearly a hundred churches there were modelled on the Geneva plan, and were receiving their ministers from the Academy at Geneva before Calvin died in 1564. These Huguenot churches met at Paris in 1559, and formed the first national Protestant Church, independent of the State.

Calvin's influence was as great in the Netherlands as in France. That land swung quickly from Lutheranism to Calvinism, which did much to fashion the Dutch Republic. In Poland Calvinism was strong among the educated and highborn, though weakened there by quarrels with Lutheranism; and in Hungary it became widespread and, though often persecuted, continues to be the dominant Protestant faith.

CHAPTER XVII

MOTHER CHURCH AWAKES

When the Reformation was firmly established at Geneva, it must have been clear to many who loved the Catholic Church that something must be done, by way of confession and amendment, or she would not survive. Most of Germany was lost. England retained Catholicism, but a Catholicism distorted and unnatural without the Pope. In Switzerland the city cantons were lost; and Catholicism was becoming the religion of rustics. In France, the Netherlands and the British Isles, the influence of Calvin was spreading.

There was still enough vitality in Mother Church, however, for recovery, and enough love for her among her children. Indeed in Spain the Catholic Church was recovering her pristine virtues before the Lutheran movement began. Shut off from Europe by the Pyrenees and knit closely by her age-long struggle with the Moslem Moors, the Church in Spain was little affected by Humanism and anti-clericalism. She was thoroughly mediaeval still, aspiring only to be obedient to the hierarchy, unquestioning about Scholasticism, stern with heretics, and dependent on the civil power only so far as was necessary to good order in the Church. It is no accident that out of Spain came the great instruments of Catholic recovery—the Dominicans, the Jesuits, and the Inquisition. Sainthood, too, in Spain was of the sort so long esteemed. It was a life of pure asceticism, sustained by mystical experiences.

So the Church in Spain was already being renovated in the last years of the fifteenth century, by authority of the sovereigns, Ferdinand and Isabella. Their agent in the good work was Cardinal Ximenes. Born to poverty, then a Franciscan, then father confessor to Queen Isabella, Ximenes became Archbishop of Toledo in 1495, and primate of the Church in Spain. In his palace at Toledo the archbishop continued to practise the austerities of a Franciscan, and gradually made asceticism the personal ideal of the Spanish clergy. By authority of the crown, he purged the monasteries and convents, and established new schools of theology, for the better education of priests.[1] In them only the pure theology of Thomas Aquinas [2] was taught, the later doctrines of Duns Scotus and William Occam being excluded. The aim of the Spanish reformation was the recovery of mediaeval Catholicism in its purity.

So when Luther cried out against practical abuses in Germany, Spain had already remedied them; and it was the Spanish idea of reformation that Charles V took with him into Germany. He and Luther might have stood together against a degraded papacy, had not Luther moved on to doctrinal reform as well.

Piety was further stimulated in Spain by a revival of mediaeval mysticism. Three great mystics there—Peter of Alcantara, Theresa, and John of the Cross—were late contemporaries of Luther; and all were to be canonized in time. St. Peter of Alcantara, a devout Franciscan, was the pioneer; but most famous was his disciple, St. Theresa de Jesus. Born at Avila, in Old Castile, in 1515, Theresa entered the order of the Carmelites at Avila, when nineteen years old. A spiritual revolution began in her with the reading of *The Confessions of St. Augustine;* and it was completed by the death of her brother, whom she loved dearly. She dedicated herself to the work of reforming the Carmelites, and faced alone the general hostility to change. Of delicate health, her high courage and vivacious, wholesome womanhood overcame all obstacles. St. Theresa leaned to mysticism, and this increased her influence. The fame of her visions and trances spread through Spain. Of her numerous writings, the most famous was the *City of Mansoul,* a work of great beauty, in which she described the progress of the soul to complete union with God. Theresa became an incomparable force for personal piety; [3] and her work was continued after her death by her fellow-labourer, St. John of the Cross, whose *Climbing of Mt. Carmel* was only slightly less famous than the *City of Mansoul.*

The mysticism of St. Theresa and St. John of the Cross made its way gradually into other orders than the Carmelites. In time it won many of the secular clergy as well, and a few knights and ladies of Spain.

[1] The Universities of Alcalá, Seville, Toledo begin with Ximenes; those of Salamanca and Valladolid are older.

[2] So out of Spain came "the New Thomists," that are active once more in the twentieth century.

[3] Theresa was canonized in 1622, and in 1812 was proclaimed patron saint of Spain.

Italy, too, was not quite untouched by revival, though the masses were less affected than in Spain. The peasants of Italy were virtually pagans, whose religion was one of magic; and the rural priests were little better. Only one healing influence remained among the peasants, the memory of St. Francis. In the cities, however, all classes recognized the degradation of the Church. Contemporary writings disclose a certain despair of the Church, hostility to the hierarchy, and especially to the Roman Curia. Italy knew that a corrupt papacy was the poisoned spring of Europe.

And so associations of Christian scholars arose in Italian cities, like those Academies of the Renaissance. The associates were not converts to Lutheranism but Catholic Humanists, bent on a Catholic revival. Foremost of these new Academies was the *Oratory of Divine Love* at Rome; and it gave impetus to similar Academies in other cities. Famous cardinals—Contarini, Caraffa, Reginald Pole—came out of the Academy at Venice. It enjoyed the patronage of noble ladies; and its correspondence covered Italy, as that of Erasmus did Europe. But the members of the Academies were disinclined to ascetic practices, were out of sympathy with the common people, and therefore failed of their purpose. A few of their members, however, helped forward a revival of monasticism, and did something to elevate the tone of clerical life.

The most influential movement among the monks of Italy was a revival within the Franciscans. A widespread longing to return to the ideals of the founder came to a head when Matteo de Grassis, a Franciscan of Umbria, determined to obey St. Francis to the letter, even to wearing the hood with the pointed peak, the *capuze,* that the saint had worn. The *capuze* became the symbol of those who wished for reform; and in 1528 Pope Clement VII made them an independent congregation of monasteries, the Order of the Capuchins. The Capuchins lived close to the people, restored the simple preaching of St. Francis, and did most to win the masses back to Catholicism. They were seconded in the good work by a similar reorganization within the Benedictines.

All sentiments for reform in Italy were quickened when Pope Paul III (1534–1550) appointed reformers to the Cardinal College,[4] and named a commission to report on the state of the papal Curia itself. The members of the commission were chiefly from the *Oratory of Divine*

[4] Contarini, Caraffa, Sadoleto, Pole.

Love; and their report was a scathing indictment.[5] Pope Paul went further and, in the face of fierce opposition, permitted Cardinal Contarini to go to Germany, to attempt reconciliation with Protestant leaders. Charles V still hoped to include Protestants in a reunited Christendom; and Pope Paul would not forbid the attempt.

At the Diet of Regensburg, therefore, in 1541 (*See* p. 368), a conference was held. It revealed a surprising measure of agreement; and there were great expectations among liberal Catholics in Italy. The irreconcilability of Protestantism and Romanism became clear, however, when the conference reached the question of the Lord's Supper. The Protestants insisted on the spiritual priesthood of all believers, the Romanists on a mediating priesthood, that performed the miracle of transubstantiation and, by refusing to do so, could withhold divine grace. So the conference split, as the Marburg Colloquy had done, on the doctrine of the Supper.

Contarini and the liberal leaders in Italy lost influence after Regensburg; and the men of the Academies, despairing of reunion through reform, turned to the work of a Catholic revival. A few, however, broke with Mother Church and saved their lives by flight, to do honourable service to the Protestant cause in other lands.[6]

Nothing else, however, wrought so powerfully for a Catholic revival everywhere as the Jesuits. They originated in the ambitious mind of a young Spanish noble, of the mountainous Basque country, Inigo Lopez de Recalde, born at the castle of Loyola in 1491. Inigo became a page at the court of Ferdinand and Isabella, then turned to the career of arms. Wounded in battle with the French at Pampeluna, the capital of Navarre, he was debarred from arms and determined to seek fame as a saint. But sainthood could not be reached in Spain, except by asceticism and the mystic way. So Inigo determined to be a hermit, and to go in time to Palestine. To this end, he went as a pilgrim to the Benedictine

[5] The report is the *Consilium delectorum cardinalium et aliorum praelatorum de emendenda ecclesia.*

[6] Bernardino Ochino, General of the Capuchins, fled to Geneva, worked later at Basel and Augsburg, Strassburg and London, and died in Moravia. Peter Martyr, an Augustinian monk, became professor at Strassburg, then at Oxford, and died at Zurich. Peter Paul Vergerius, bishop of Capo d'Istria, read Luther's writings to refute him, but was converted to Lutheranism and died a professor at Tübingen.

abbey of Montserrato, and made his confession, gave his costly clothes to a beggar, and dedicated his knightly service to the Virgin. Laying his sword upon the Lady altar, he spent the night before it in prayer, and in the morning, having received the Holy Eucharist, he left for a cave near Manresa. Thenceforth he was known by the Latin name Ignatius.

At Manresa Ignatius passed through spiritual conflicts like those of Luther at Erfurt, using vainly all the prescribed aids to perfection—fastings and flagellations, frequent confession and prayer. At length he found peace by throwing himself upon the mercy of God. It was the experience of salvation by faith; but Ignatius did not pursue the theological implications of his conversion. Instead he gave himself, with the renewed energy of a mind at peace, to mystical practices. By prayer and contemplation he fell into ecstasies and visions, in which he saw into the Catholic mysteries, like transubstantiation, the incarnation, and the Trinity.

All this was common enough among the mystics of Spain, where it was accepted that he who attains to mystical union with God is divinely illuminated; but Ignatius went on to analyse his moods, learned how to induce vision and ecstasy at will, and in the *Spiritual Exercises* committed to writing what he learned. The *Exercises* systematised mysticism. They became in time as important a text-book for Catholic revival as was Luther's *Liberty of the Christian Man* for Protestantism.

Going on a pilgrimage to Palestine in 1523, Ignatius' ardour endangered the relations of Christians there with the ruling Turks; and the Franciscans in charge of the holy places induced the pilgrim to return home. He then studied Latin at Barcelona, philosophy at Alcalá, theology at Salamanca, and in 1528 was at the University of Paris. The strife between Catholics and Protestants was then at its height; and Noel Beda, head of the Faculty of Theology, the *Sorbonne,* was leading the fight against innovations. Calvin was there, and others whom time was to make famous. Ignatius Loyola mingled, observed, and was silent.

By the end of 1529 the silent man had drawn to himself those who were to be the first Jesuits. There was Pierre Lefèvre of Savoy, known to the English-speaking as Faber, and Francis Xavier from Navarre, then teaching philosophy at Paris. There was a young Castilian, Diego Lainez, who had heard of Ignatius at Alcalá and now sought him out at Paris. Three others of less note soon came; and the company of seven cemented their union with special vows. On the Feast of the Assumption in 1534, they assembled in the crypt of the church of St. Mary on Montmartre; and Faber, the only priest among them, said Mass. They took vows of poverty and chastity; and pledged themselves to the Pope, for whatever service he might choose. The essence of religion, they thought, was utter submission to "the true spouse of Christ and our Holy Mother, which is the orthodox, catholic, and hierarchical Church." To her it was their duty to surrender the mind as well as the will. "If the Church pronounces a thing which seems to us to be white to be black, we must immediately say that it is black."

Gathering to Venice in 1537, the associates were ordained to the priesthood; and Ignatius decided that they should thenceforth bear the name, The Company of Jesus. They took possession of a deserted convent, and gave themselves to the work of preaching to those outside the Church and to teaching the young. After a year, in which they failed to find a way to Palestine, some went to Rome, where Pope Paul III appointed Faber to teach the Scriptures and Lainez to teach theology, in the University of the Sapienza, while Ignatius continued his work for the indifferent and the young. The work was so strenuous that he called the other associates to Rome; and in 1540 a papal Bull of Paul III constituted them The Society [7] of Jesus. Ignatius was chosen first General of the Society.

The Society of Jesus applied to the service of the Church things Ignatius had learned in military service. The Society was a band of soldiers, living under martial law, whose weapons were spiritual. At their head was a General, whose king was the Pope. Ever since Luther raised the standard of revolt, the Church had been at war. No cloistered virtue would stop the spreading conflict. Education, firmness of character, a taste for affairs, placed at the command of a superior, were the necessary things. In his famous *Letter on Obedience* Ignatius declares that the General, standing in the place of God, is to be obeyed, making his will one's own, thinking what he thinks. This "sacrifice of the intellect" is the crown of obedience, well pleasing to God.[8]

---

[7] "Society" is not a very good translation of the Latin *societas*, which is nearer the Spanish *Compania*, the name adopted by Ignatius. It meant, among other things, an alliance, or confederacy.

[8] It did not preclude that the inferior might make representations to his superior in all causes.

It was in this spirit a Jesuit undertook the special duty assumed by Ignatius and confirmed by the Pope, the propagation of the Catholic Faith, especially by the education of highborn youths. Ignatius was aware that dependable changes in the spiritual direction of mankind can come from the school alone, through gifted men. He knew also that the ignorance and profligacy of the Catholic clergy encouraged the Protestant movement. He saw that Humanism was establishing a new standard of values, that culture was crowding theology and freedom endangering dogma. So Ignatius focussed attention upon the potential leaders of the future and gave them the culture of Humanism, while subjecting them to an iron rule of spiritual discipline. The vow to be taken by every novice, at the close of his novitiate, ran thus, "I promise to Almighty God, before His Virgin Mother and the heavenly host, and to all standing by; and to thee, Reverend Father General of the Society of Jesus, holding the place of God, and to thy successors, Perpetual Poverty, Chastity and Obedience; and a peculiar care in the education of boys according to the form of life contained in the Apostolic Letters of the Society of Jesus and in its Constitution."

There were other solemn promises. The initiate would not accept election to any position outside the Society, except by command of his superior. If made a bishop, he would still turn for advice to the General, though not sworn to adopt it.

The "Spanish priests," as the Jesuits were called, soon became influential in Italy. Their schools were good, their educational methods the best then known. In their schools incipient Protestantism in Italy was stopped and held.

Portugal capitulated to the Jesuits immediately. Spain hesitated, all the more because Charles V was suspicious of men bound by a special oath to the Pope; but gradually Jesuit devotion and impeccability [9] won their way. Progress in France and Germany was slow; but the Jesuits founded colleges, formed associations of students, and rallied Catholic sentiment. South Germany might still be held for the Catholic Church;

---

[9] The principles that were later to give the Jesuits an evil reputation were two. The doctrine of "probabilism," by which a Jesuit might choose the worse course, if he could quote authorities for it, seemed to undermine his integrity. So did the Jesuit doctrine of "mental reservation," which excused a Jesuit under oath from telling the whole truth, or even giving a correct impression.

and Vienna was its centre. There Ignatius sent an ardent and scholarly Dutchman, Peter Canisius, whose zeal and ability had already saved Cologne for the ancient Faith. Canisius procured for the Jesuits an ascendancy over education in Austria, that was to be permanent. Elsewhere in Germany educational centres were established at Cologne and Munich, and all along the Rhine and the Main.

The greatest Jesuit conquest, however, was in Poland, the largest state in Europe west of Russia. Sparsely populated, professing Greek Christianity, Poland had opened its arms to immigrants of brawn and brains, without regard to their religion. Jews in flight from the Catholic west, Hussites from Bohemia, Lutherans, Calvinists and Unitarians, all lived in peace in Poland and propagated their beliefs. Religious toleration and Protestant divisions gave the Jesuits their opportunity. Before long they were in control of higher education in Poland. Within a century it became one of the most Catholic countries in Europe.

The work of the Jesuits was supplemented by other agencies, coercing where the Jesuits persuaded those wandering from the Catholic way. When Cardinal Contarini returned from the conference at Regensburg, to report to Pope Paul III that the differences between Catholicism and Protestantism were irreconcilable, Cardinal Caraffa was ready with other plans. As keen for reformation as Contarini himself, Caraffa had not believed it could come through the reunion of Christendom and had advised against a conference. Nor did he think Jesuit education swift enough to meet the immediate danger. "The whole of Italy (was) infected with the Lutheran heresy, which (had been) extensively embraced by both statesmen and ecclesiastics." Caraffa therefore proposed the Inquisition. Ignatius supported him; and the Holy Father was convinced. Hardly were the delegates to Regensburg back in their several homes, when Pope Paul established the *Congregation of the Holy Office*.

Inquisition was not new. Mediaeval bishops had been expected to enquire into the thinking of their people, and to deliver to the civil authorities such as were stubbornly heretical; but bishops' courts had not been very effective. Too many bishops had been indisposed to condemn, too many magistrates tardy in punishing, vagrant thoughts. So that doughty man, Pope Innocent III, had taken direct action in 1203, and established the *Apostolic Tribunal for the suppression of heresy*. This was the beginning of *The Inquisition* proper, which was soon placed in the keeping of the Dominicans. It was sometimes awake, sometimes somnolent, in the next three centuries.

When Martin Luther was a boy and Cardinal Ximenes was renovating the priesthood in Spain, the Inquisition had already been at work there. Ferdinand and Isabella were as keen for doctrinal purity as for clerical celibacy throughout their dominions; and an excuse for coercion was provided by the *Conversos,* rich and influential converts from Judaism. Spanish Catholics shared the general dislike of prosperous Jews, and were not mollified by their adoption of Christianity. Their conversion was suspect anyway. So Torquemada, who preceded Ximenes as father confessor to Queen Isabella, persuaded her and her consort to establish a unique sort of Inquisition, the *Holy Office,* an institution of the State. Torquemada was made Inquisitor-General for Spain, with a Council of inquisitors under his direction. Inquisitors went everywhere. Civil officials were sworn to assist them; and the sentence of the inquisitor was carried out by the State. The *Holy Office* became the most powerful instrument of the Catholic reformation in Spain. Ten thousand were burned, a hundred thousand imprisoned, during the presidency of Torquemada; and inquisition was extended to the Netherlands. All this activity prepared the soil for the gentler tillage of Cardinal Ximenes and the Spanish mystics.

So when the Protestants of Germany would not return to the fold, and "the whole of Italy was infected with the Lutheran heresy," Caraffa could cite the excellent example of Spain; and Pope Paul III was persuaded to create the *Congregation of the Holy Office*. Six cardinals were named Inquisitors-General, with Caraffa at their head. Their authority was to extend to all Catholic Christendom.

Caraffa immediately appointed an Inquisitor-General for each country, and himself hired a house, equipped it with a dungeon and instruments of torture, and bent himself to enforce the true faith. It was a fearful expedient, when thought was changing and wise men differed. The obscurantist had now a weapon against the enlightened. Men accused their enemies. The Christian Academies separated. Weak men submitted; strong men died. Some, like Ochino and Peter Martyr, fled, to fulfil their mission in other lands. The communities of refugees grew steadily in Swiss and German cities.

Caraffa promulgated a decree that no book might be printed without permission from the Holy Office, that booksellers must submit catalogues of their stocks, that customs officers must not deliver books until they were examined and approved. And a growing list of prohibited books, the *Index*, was set up in the cities. In time a special *Congregation of the Index* was established, to censor publications; and those condemned were publicly burned.

The success of these repressive measures varied, according to the degree of support given by the civil authorities; but the decisions of inquisitors were generally enforced.

One other means to Catholic convalescence remained, a General Council, and very reluctantly Pope Paul III used that one too. The papacy had had experience of General Councils in the fifteenth century, and regarded them as evils to be avoided. One could not now be sure that they would faithfully echo the papal voice, as in the great days of Innocent III. But a Council was earnestly desired by Charles V and the Spanish Church; and popes could not ignore either the Emperor or Spain. Paul therefore summoned a Council to Mantua in 1537. It was delayed by war between the Emperor and France. The Pope then chose Ferrara; but Charles would have the Council outside Italy, where it would be less easily controlled from Rome. At long last the Council met in 1545 at Trent, a small city of mixed population, in the Austrian Tyrol (*See* p. 367). It sat intermittently until 1563, being interrupted nearly ten years by the revolt of Duke Maurice of Saxony and the abdication of Charles V. It was during the long recess of the Council that Charles' brother Ferdinand granted the Peace of Augsburg, making Lutheranism a lawful religion within the Holy Roman Empire (*See* p. 370).

The long-drawn-out Council of Trent was torn between the demand of Italian prelates for a rigid definition of Catholic doctrines and the demand of Spanish prelates for the reform of abuses. In the end doctrines and reforms were discussed alternately; but Italians were always in the majority, and papal approval always necessary. There was much intrigue, and many stormy scenes, faithfully described for us by Paolo Sarpi, a scholarly Augustinian of Venice. The man who did most to carry the papal cause to victory was Lainez, second General of the Jesuits, an eloquent and invincible advocate of autocracy. He and Peter Canisius fanned the anti-Protestant flame at Trent.

In the matter of doctrine there was room for discussion; for doctrine had been measureably fluid in the Middle Ages. There were differences yet to be settled between Thomists and Scotists, and about Mysticism and Humanism. But discussion at Trent was confined to the questions that Protestantism had raised; and here the Council was adamant. The Rule of Faith, it said, the body of revealed truth for Christians, was not the Scriptures alone, as Protestants affirmed, but the unwritten tradition also of Christ's teaching, preserved by the Church from the beginning, under the guidance of the Holy Spirit. The Council did not say who might declare the tradition; but gradually it became accepted later that popes, when they speak *ex cathedra,* have equal authority with the Scriptures.[10]

As for the Scriptures, Protestants were acknowledging as the Old Testament only the books of the Hebrew Canon. The Catholic Church had acknowledged all books of the Septuagint, which includes the Apocrypha. Trent reaffirmed the canonicity of all the Septuagint; and Jerome's translation into Latin, the Vulgate, was declared to be the authoritative one. Catholics and Protestants did not differ as to the New Testament; though Protestants rejected Jerome's translation.

Concerning the doctrine of salvation, it was found that many members of the Council held the Protestant view, that the sinner gets right with God by faith in the merits of Christ, and that good conduct is the fruit of one's faith. The Council could not debate calmly such doctrine; and a few men of Protestant inclinations went home, under one pretext or another, lest they draw the fire of the Inquisition. The decision of the Council was that the sinner is justified by the merits of Christ, if they produce merits in him; that is, "if he walks by the commandments of God and the Church." So ecclesiastical discipline was to be maintained.

[10] This was formally declared to be Catholic dogma when the Vatican Council, in 1870, under the leadership of Pope Pius IX, declared that "The Roman Pontiff, when he speaks *ex cathedra,* that is, when in the discharge of the office of pastor and teacher of all Christians, by virtue of his supreme apostolic authority, he defines a doctrine regarding faith or morals to be held by the universal church, by the divine assistance promised to him in blessed Peter, is possessed of that infallibility with which the divine Redeemer willed that His Church should be endowed." It was the final rejection of the doctrine of the supremacy of a General Council, that has advocates still.

The decision concerning the sacraments followed logically upon this view of salvation. The seven sacraments of the mediaeval Church, all said to have been instituted by Christ, are necessary to salvation. It is through them one's salvation begins, continues, and is recovered when lost; and they are effective of themselves, apart from the faith of the recipient.

Thus the sum of the doctrinal decisions of Trent was this, that ecclesiastical tradition was to be as authoritative as the Scriptures, both having been inspired by the Holy Spirit; that the Bible of Catholics was the Vulgate, which had been kept free from error by the inspired Church; that saving grace is imparted to men, step by step, by the Church, through the sacraments; and that outside the Church, therefore, there can be no truly religious life.

The ablest defence of these doctrines was published just as the Council of Trent dissolved. It was the work [11] of a Spanish theologian, Melchior Cano, who was influential at Trent. All theology, he says, rests on authority, the authority of the Church. It is the Church that sifted the ancient writings, and determined which were Scripture. And it is the Church that preserves the true tradition of such ancient Christian doctrines as were never committed to writing.

The practical reforms effected at Trent were considerable. Provision was made for the better supervision of clerical morals, and the better education of priests. Priests must reside in their parishes, bishops in their dioceses, and perform the duties of their office. The Scriptures were to be expounded in the larger towns; and the people everywhere were to be taught plainly what is necessary to salvation.

Popes were thenceforth chosen with more scruple, and themselves set an example of better things. The popes of Renaissance days had been highborn, cultivated, patrons of literature and the arts, but worldly and of dubious morals. All this was now changed. Paul IV, elected in 1559, was a devout Milanese of lowly birth, devoted to reform; and his nephew, Carlo Borromeo, was one of the saintliest figures in the Church. Pope Pius V, elected in 1565, was also of humble birth, a devout ascetic, who as pope rose daily with the sun, dispensed with the Roman siesta, walked barefoot in the streets of Rome, and ruthlessly simplified the papal court. As fanatical as he was austere, Pope Pius called upon the

[11] The *De Locis Theologicis Libri XII.*

French government to crush the Huguenots in France, and gloried in the ruthlessness of Spanish soldiery in the Netherlands. In this, too, he was a symbol. Catholicism was now to be more narrow, more intense.

A new devotion gradually stirred everywhere in Mother Church, encouraged by the example of the Holy Father and feeling the contagion of Spain. It received direction and unity from the decisions of the Council of Trent. And everywhere there were the Jesuits! Catholicism was militant once more; and barriers were raised against the further spread of Protestantism in Europe. It had already captured North Germany, and was seeping into the Rhineland from all sides, from Saxony and Holland and Switzerland. Indeed in the lovely Palatinate, a succession of Electors had made the capital, Heidelberg, a centre of Calvinism and worked in league with their co-religionists in Switzerland and France. And at the eastern extremity of Germany, in the ancient kingdom of Bohemia, the Czechs still clung to the principles of John Huss and were now being confirmed in their old hostility to Rome by Lutheran preachers from neighbouring Saxony.

But Germany was at once the stronghold and the Achilles' heel of Protestantism in Europe. It was the stronghold, because Protestantism was oldest there and no strong central government existed, to support the Inquisition and compel obedience. It was the Achilles' heel, because the Church there tended to be subservient to the State, and states to differ on the religious question. Bohemia and the Palatinate were as far apart religiously as geographically, the Lutheran theologians of the former being indisposed to fraternise with the Calvinists of the latter. When at length the Lutherans throughout Germany settled their own differences,[12] they still excluded the Calvinists.

Moreover the original fervour of Lutheranism did not long survive the reformer's death. The lowered tone that follows revolutionary changes came to Germany. The old German profligacy continued; German literature was ignoble, and the Church servile. Only the piety of humble people and Christian hymns, a gift from Luther, kept the churches alive for a century, until a new afflatus came and great leaders arose once more.

Meanwhile Catholicism, rejuvenated, concentrated first upon Germany, though omitting the Inquisition. A Hapsburg emperor burning

[12] In the *Formula of Concord*, of 1580.

Germans would have spoiled everything. The Dukes of Bavaria, however, fostered the Catholic revival; and the Jesuits trained gifted and privileged youths, to lead the re-formed legions of the Church.

Against this renewed zeal, Protestantism made no territorial gains on the continent. Indeed its hold on the Rhineland and southern Germany was weakened; and in Switzerland the lands contiguous to Geneva itself were recovered for the Catholic Church. Francis of Sales, nominally bishop of Geneva, who combined a rare mystical piety with devotion to the Church, recovered for Catholicism those parts of Savoy near Geneva. *St. Francois de Sales* is one of the many Catholic saints, canonized for their services to the revival.

The rejuvenation of Catholicism did not mean, however, that Europe could ever again be united in the old Church. Principles were abroad that, as Luther had found, could not be recalled. They were not of sudden birth. They had been incubating through all the Babylonian Captivity of the Church. They had now come alive, in a religious alternative to Catholicism. In the new religion men were saved by their faith, not by penance; priests were just Christians set apart for special duties, not another order of beings supernaturally endowed at ordination; and the Scriptures were construed in a new way.

Nor was the issue entirely between Catholic Christianity and Protestant. Humanism had come to stay. It was at present a handmaid, not a member of the Christian family. It would one day assert its rights, recalling that Christ himself had seen in the lilies of the field an authentic revelation of God and in man a certain capacity for the redeemed life. There would then be a third Christianity, different from both Romanism and Protestantism.

CHAPTER XVIII

PROTESTANTISM ESTABLISHED BY LAW
IN BRITAIN

WHILE a reformed Catholicism and a well-reasoned Protestantism thus faced each other on the continent, religion was following a devious course in England. Henry VIII died when Calvin was at the height of his influence and the Council of Trent just getting under way. Henry had used his great authority and the prestige of the dynasty to fix the royal succession for some time to come. He bequeathed the crown to his son Edward, who, in certain eventualities, was to be followed by Edward's half-sisters, Mary and Elizabeth. And since Edward was but a child of nine years, King Henry named a body of executors, to administer the kingdom during the new king's minority.

Thus in January, 1547, a child ascended the English throne, and became "supreme head of the Church of England." In such circumstances Government and Parliament would determine the course of religion. The Government consisted of a Protector, who was the Duke of Somerset, uncle to the king, and with him, as Privy Council, the executors named by Henry VIII.

The secular power immediately took control, displacing the usual Convocations of the Church. Existing bishops were required to secure new licenses; and new bishops were to be appointed by the Government, not by Cathedral Chapters. Such elements of Roman Catholicism as still survived were almost all eliminated from the faith. Parliament repealed the Act of Six Articles, by which Henry VIII had sought to enforce a moderate Catholicism. Images were ordered removed from the churches, and the marriage of priests made legal. The confiscation of church lands was completed by dissolving the chantries, or endowed chapels where Masses were said for the souls of the donors.

A delicate question remained to be answered. Was it to be Mass or

Holy Supper in the Church of England? Archbishop Cranmer, who had published the Litany for Henry VIII, had moved slowly in the matter of the Lord's Supper, because he was anxious to carry with him the old bishops; but now in 1548 a new Communion Service was published by royal proclamation. It described the sacrament as "The Supper of the Lord, and the Holy Communion, commonly called the Mass." All phrases describing the consecrated bread and wine as a sacrifice were eliminated; and the elevation of the Host, for worship by the people, was forbidden.

Next year, 1549, a book of worship, including the Litany and the new Communion Service, was complete; and Parliament passed an Act of Uniformity, making its use compulsory. It was the first English Prayer Book, and was chiefly the work of Cranmer, who probably consulted whom he chose from time to time. It was submitted by the Protector Somerset to the bishops, who approved it with reservations. Convocation seems not to have been consulted; nor was the House of Commons. And the consent of the House of Lords was probably assumed from the signature by the bishops.[1]

The *First Prayer Book of Edward VI,* as it is called, was not popular. Men of Roman convictions disliked the changes it introduced. Men of Protestant convictions disliked the Catholic features it retained— prayers for the dead, the anointing of the sick, exorcism at baptism. Protestant opposition was strengthened by the presence in England of theologians from the continent, in flight from Charles V and the *Augsburg Interim.* Most influential of them was Martin Bucer of Strassburg, who was now for a brief time Regius Professor of Divinity at Cambridge. Peter Martyr, too, an Italian of extreme Protestant views, was Regius Professor at Oxford. And there was constant correspondence with Calvin and other Swiss leaders. So a revision of the Prayer Book was soon under way.

Meanwhile religion was caught in another political whirlpool. There was considerable agrarian discontent in England. The Protector Somerset was a man of humane and liberal mind; and his sympathy with the landless peasants aroused the bitter hostility of the new nobility, who saw

[1] The early history of the book is obscure, because records were destroyed in the fire of London, in 1666. Surviving documents, from the reign of Edward VI, may be read in Gee & Hardy, *Documents Illustrative of English Church History,* pp. 322–376.

their profits from the sale of church lands imperilled. Peasant discontent broke out in several armed risings in 1549. They were suppressed largely by the vigour of a certain Earl of Warwick, who became the champion of the great landowners. A conspiracy against the Duke of Somerset succeeded. He was imprisoned in the Tower of London; and Warwick, soon to become the Duke of Northumberland, came to the head of affairs.

Northumberland was irreligious and unscrupulous, but thought his own interests likely to be served by supporting the party of extreme Protestantism. The Prayer Book was therefore revised, with the aid of Bucer and Martyr, Calvin and Bullinger; and a second Act of Uniformity in 1552 imposed it upon the nation. It was so framed as to prevent lovers of the old order from interpreting it in the Catholic sense. The word "altar" was eliminated from the Communion Service, and all suggestions of a physical presence in the elements. The Protestantism of the Church of England reached its highest point in this *Second Prayer Book of Edward VI.*

Cranmer had been engaged also on a Creed; and in the same year, 1552, the Privy Council ordered it submitted for examination to six theologians, of whom a certain Scot was one, John Knox, then a minister in England. When finished, in forty-two Articles, the Creed received the royal signature, in July, 1553. Though moderate in tone, it was Calvinistic in theology and more thoroughly Protestant than the Prayer Book.

The boy king was near death when he authorised the Creed. Northumberland was both determined to maintain his own power and fearful for his life, if Mary should ascend the throne. So Edward was persuaded to bequeath the crown to Lady Jane Grey, wife of Northumberland's son and granddaughter of Mary, that sister of Henry VIII who had married the Duke of Suffolk. It was a wild plan to which Archbishop Cranmer gave a reluctant consent.

The nation was aroused. Northumberland was already generally detested; and he had now affronted English sentiment for hereditary succession to the throne. All England, Catholic and Protestant, rallied to Mary. She was soon on the throne, and Northumberland on the scaffold.

Mary was a woman of thirty-seven, half Spanish, and not only a loyal

Catholic but a bigot, soured by neglect in her youth and the wrong done her mother Catherine. Her supreme duty, she thought, was to return England to the Catholic faith. She was cautious at first, guided by the advice of her cousin, the Emperor Charles V. Nevertheless Protestant bishops and other higher clergy were removed; and men active in the Protestant cause fled to the continent, to the hospitality of Calvin and Geneva. Catholics were restored to office throughout the country; and Mary's first Parliament repealed all the ecclesiastical legislation of Edward's reign. Religion was again in law, as at the death of Henry VIII.

Mary now married her cousin Philip, son of the Emperor Charles V and soon to be King Philip II of Spain. The marriage was unpopular. Philip was disliked in England, as was his Spanish *entourage;* and there was widespread disquiet, lest England be made a satellite of Spain.

Reconciliation with the papacy had thus far been delayed; but the balance of parties in England made anything possible. The authority of the crown was thrown upon the side of a complete Catholicism; and Parliament, as soon as it was assured that no attempt would be made to recover church lands, voted the restoration of the papal authority in England. Then, in an excess of submission, Parliament knelt and received absolution from Cardinal Pole, the Pope's legate, on November 30, 1554. It proceeded next to repeal the ecclesiastical legislation of Henry's reign, and to re-enact the ancient laws against heresy.

Persecution began immediately. In 1555 nearly a hundred persons were burned at the stake in various parts of England. They included three bishops of Protestant convictions—Latimer, Ridley and Hooper. The queen would be satisfied, however, with nothing less than the death of the archbishop who had declared the marriage of her mother invalid and put another in her place. Cranmer was excommunicated at Rome in November 1555, and Cardinal Pole made Archbishop of Canterbury. Cranmer's position was hopeless. He had believed in the royal supremacy over the Church. The sovereign had now secured his excommunication and removal from office. He submitted; but submission did not save his life. He was burned at Oxford in 1556, withdrawing in the hour of death an earlier recantation of his Protestant principles, and holding in the flame, until it was consumed, the hand that had signed his submission.

Cranmer was not a heroic figure. He was a refined and learned Cambridge divine, of deep religious feeling and blameless life, whose genuine concern for the reformation of the Catholic Church made him useful to a wilful king and precipitated him into affairs for which he was not suited. High office, however, gave him one opportunity to render an immortal service to the Church. In the Prayer Book his sensitive and aesthetic nature produced quite the best Protestant substitute for the noble Latin ritual of the mediaeval Church. It was to be the chief support of the religious spirit in the Church of England for many generations.

Persecution continued while Mary lived, fanned by her conviction that she could not do enough to remove from herself the stern judgment of God. She was childless and unloved, alike by her people and her husband, who left England in 1555, never to return. What could it be but a judgment of heaven? Mary would expiate her sins by destroying the enemies of the true faith. When she died execrated in 1558, nearly three hundred had been martyred. These martyrdoms rekindled a flame of anti-Roman feeling in England, that has never quite died out. It was not that the burning of heretics was unusual in England. It was only that Mary did it more thoroughly, and chose for her victims men of learning and piety and of unimpeachable character, who were national figures.

Martyrdom purged Protestantism in England, and gave it dignity in its own eyes. Beginning when all issues were confused, compromised by its association with base interests, it had now produced martyrs. The record of their sufferings, preserved by John Foxe in a Martyrology, was to be second in esteem only to the Bible and the Prayer Book, among future generations of Protestants. They, too, had had fathers of unyielding spirit who, believing the faith sacred, had made it sacred to posterity.

Elizabeth, who was now to direct the destinies of England for forty-five years, 1558–1603, was in sharp contrast to her sister Mary. She was *not* a religious woman; and she *was* a statesman. Reaching the throne at twenty-five, skilled in dissimulation by the perils of her youth, she had the guile of her grandfather Henry VII, the masterful will of her father, and the uncanny Tudor understanding of Englishmen. If she had also the vanity and coquetry of her mother Anne Boleyn, these qualities were balanced by pride and high spirit, and by great practical wisdom. They never dampened the enthusiasm of most Englishmen for their queen.

Nevertheless the first years of the new reign were perilous. England was religiously divided, and Catholicism aggressive everywhere in Europe. In the British Isles themselves, the north of England, the Scottish Highlands and the Irish were Catholic; and in the Scottish Lowlands a French army was supporting the Catholic cause against an incipient Scottish Protestantism.

Catholics regarded Elizabeth as illegitimate. In that case her cousin Mary Stuart, Queen of Scots, was lawful queen of England. A daughter of James V of Scotland and a French princess, Mary of Guise, she was nevertheless granddaughter of that Margaret, sister of Henry VIII, who had married James IV of Scotland. Mary grew up in France, while her widowed French mother ruled Scotland as regent, with the aid of French forces. In France Mary married the heir to the throne, who became King Francis II within a few months of Elizabeth's accession in England. If Elizabeth was not a legitimate daughter of Henry VIII, Mary might well wear the crowns of both Scotland and England, while being queen consort of France. Catholics everywhere wished it so.

Fortunately Philip II of Spain, Catholic as he was, had no desire to see the crowns of England, Scotland and France united. Nor did he wish an unfriendly England athwart his communications with the Netherlands. Antwerp was one of the wealthiest trading cities of the world; and Amsterdam was fast rising into prominence. The Netherlands were the financial heart of the Spanish dominions. So Philip for a time supported Elizabeth. He would change when English mariners, in search of Cathay, the fabled earthly Paradise, and of the Spice Islands in the East Indies, challenged the trade monopoly of Spain and Portugal in the South Seas.

For the present, however, Philip was friendly; and, very fortunately for Elizabeth, she had as adviser at home William Cecil, Lord Burghley, one of the most far-sighted statesmen in English history.

The settlement of the religious question was the most immediate and difficult problem for statesmanship. Catholics wished the Church continued as under Mary, moderate Protestants as under Edward and Somerset. Extreme Protestants, returning from exile on the continent, desired a more thoroughgoing Protestantism, as at Geneva. They would rid the Church of England of "the rags of popery."

Elizabeth determined, with the concurrence of Lord Burghley, to be

Protestant. She was predisposed to Protestantism anyway. The Boleyns had been among the early sympathisers with Protestantism in England; Elizabeth had been educated under the supervision of Archbishop Cranmer; Catholics thought her illegitimate. She would be Protestant. Moreover Protestantism would clash less with her Tudor ideas of kingship. She was resolved to be "over all causes and over all persons, ecclesiastical as well as civil, throughout (her) dominions supreme."

A royal proclamation, immediately after Elizabeth's accession, suspended preaching in the churches. She would not have men advocating changes, until she and Parliament could determine what changes. Meanwhile the existing order of public worship, which included the Mass, was to continue.

The religious settlement was largely effected during Elizabeth's first Parliament, in the spring of 1559. It was a laymen's settlement, opposed by Convocation, and forced upon an unwilling clergy, in the interest of national unity. There was no party in the Church whose convictions it really expressed; and it affected the integrity of the clergy of all parties. The public, being neither educated nor theologically minded, was more at ease.

The "Elizabethan Settlement" was embodied in two Acts of Parliament, the Act of Supremacy and the Act of Uniformity. The former, passed only after a stern fight, declared the sovereign to be "the only supreme governor of this realm, . . . as well in all spiritual or ecclesiastical things or causes as temporal." The objectionable title "Head of the Church" was omitted; but with characteristic guile, Elizabeth secured the re-enactment of certain laws of Henry VIII, in which the sovereign was described as "the only and undoubted Supreme Head of the Church of England." If, therefore, controversy should arise and "supreme governor" require to be defined, it would be defined in the old sense.

The Act of Uniformity was designed to compel all Englishmen to unite in one form of public worship, the form provided in the Second Prayer-Book of Edward VI. The Book, however, as appended to the new Act, omitted offensive references to the Bishop of Rome.[2] It also changed to their present form the words used in the administration of

[2] Notably a prayer in the Litany, for deliverance from "the tyranny of the Bishop of Rome and all his detestable enormities."

Holy Communion. The Prayer-Book of Edward had made the Lord's Supper appear a memorial only, in the Zwinglian sense. The new Book, spoke of the bread as "The Body of our Lord Jesus Christ," and of the wine as "The Blood of our Lord Jesus Christ." It thus suggested a presence in the elements, without defining its nature. The Supper could be understood in the Roman, Lutheran, Zwinglian, or Calvinistic sense.[3]

Most of the clergy found it possible to accept the new order in the Church; but the bishops refused to take the oath required of them by the Act of Supremacy.[4] Having acknowledged the papal supremacy when Mary reigned, they felt it impossible to acknowledge the royal supremacy because Elizabeth reigned. They were therefore deprived of office; and the Church of England found itself without bishops.

All other Protestant churches had dispensed with bishops, finding in the New Testament no warrant for a governing episcopate. That consideration would not weigh with Elizabeth. What concerned her was the unity of the nation. The Church must therefore be comprehensive, giving standing room to Catholics. These had already seen the Pope rejected, the Mass revised, the liturgy turned into English, and the Bible given to the people. What would remain of Catholicism if bishops disappeared? There must be bishops.

In this situation Matthew Parker, once chaplain to Henry VIII and now Master of Corpus Christi College, Cambridge, was chosen Archbishop of Canterbury. He was a scholar, of liberal mind and statesmanlike.

To consecrate the new archbishop, in the Catholic manner, was difficult. It must be done by four bishops. These were secured by restoring to office those who survived from the reign of Edward VI, and who had then been deprived for refusing to acquiesce in extreme Protestantism. The archbishop was thus consecrated by bishops, who had themselves been consecrated by bishops, in unbroken succession from the apostles. This at least was to be the claim of Anglican divines in the future.[5]

---

[3] There were other changes, of less importance. One was an "ornaments rubric," prefixed to the Order of Morning and Evening Prayer, which required officiating ministers to wear more elaborate vestments than Protestants in general thought right. The rubric required cassock, surplice and cope. Most clergymen ignored it, wearing only the surplice.

[4] So also did many of the Deans and other members of Cathedral Chapters.

[5] The "Apostolic Succession" of the English episcopate has always been denied by Roman theologians, on various grounds, and was formally rejected by Pope Leo XIII in

Thus some of the magical elements that had accumulated in the mediaeval Church were to be preserved for the Church of England. If she had no pope, made holy by the merits of St. Peter, and no priest who could perform a miracle in the Mass, at least her bishops were to possess some supernatural efficacy, acquired through an ancient rite, thought to be of divine appointment.

The election of new bishops was left, nominally, to the Deans and Chapters of the Cathedrals; but a royal "permission to elect" (*congé d'élire*) told them whom they might choose. This was thought more persuasive than a direct nomination by the crown.

The Elizabethan Settlement was put into effect by means of a Royal Visitation. That is to say, England was divided into districts and representatives of the crown appointed to visit each. The visitors were instructed to be conciliatory. They administered the oath of supremacy to the clergy and other ecclesiastical officers. They saw that the Prayer Book was used, encouraged preaching and the reading of the Scriptures, and replaced the stone altars by communion tables. Soon the Prayer Book was in general use.

The making of a Creed was purposely delayed. There was none at first, except what was to be inferred from the Prayer Book. But in 1563 Convocation adopted the "Thirty-Nine Articles of the Anglican Church." They were a revision of the Forty-Two Articles adopted in the last year of Edward VI, and embody the Calvinistic (Reformed) theology, rather than the Lutheran (Evangelical).

The Thirty-Nine Articles were confirmed by Parliament itself in 1571, and were placed in the Prayer Book, as a rejoinder to the action of Pope Pius V, in excommunicating Elizabeth.

Most Englishmen were prepared to accept on patriotic grounds whatever kind of Church the queen and her advisers chose.[6] National feeling was strong, religious feeling weak. Neither the vigorous Protestantism, nor the revived Catholicism, of the continent had yet touched the

---

1896. The Church of England therefore recognizes the validity of Roman orders; the Church of Rome denies the validity of Anglican orders.

[6] Dissenting congregations did, however begin as early as 1566. Two heads of Oxford Colleges had been brought to trial, for failing to wear the surplice. They defended themselves by quoting the Scriptures against the Prayer Book. Elizabeth determined that the regulation should be enforced; and as a result thirty-seven clergymen in London alone resigned their parishes. That year secret congregations, with a thoroughly Protestant form of worship, began here and there.

English masses. The Settlement itself was a political device, not the expression of a faith. If the religious spirit should revive in England, the Settlement could neither express it nor restrain it. And religion did begin soon to revive, partly as a breath of life from the continent, partly as a concomitant of the increased national consciousness and devotion. Then it became clear that there were still in England two types of religion, Catholic and Protestant, and that within each there were parties.

When the queen was excommunicated in 1570, Catholics had finally to determine where their ultimate allegiance lay. A minority of them renounced the Elizabethan Settlement. They were again Romanists, or "Papists," to Englishmen; and Recusancy Laws, as they were called, placed them under certain disabilities. Most Catholics, however, continued to recognize the Settlement, and were thenceforth Anglicans, as distinct from Roman Catholics. How far they were Catholic at all was to be a disputed question forever.

True Protestants in the Church of England were now called Puritans, a term of contempt. They sought from the first to change the Settlement in various ways, in order to "purify" the Church from such "Romish errors" as remained. The Puritans soon included most of the genuinely religious people of the nation. They were disturbed at the low temperature of the parish clergy, who seldom preached and who tended to read the Church service as a civil duty. The few churches where preaching was heard were soon drawing the people.

In these circumstances some of the more earnest clergy, Puritan in outlook, began in 1573 to meet together, to discuss religious questions and help each other to acquire the art of preaching. These meetings, called prophesyings, spread rapidly through the country; and the queen in alarm issued a letter to the bishops, commanding that the prophesyings be suppressed. Archbishop Grindal, who had been appointed on the death of Matthew Parker, refused to send to the bishops the royal letter. He saw that, in suppressing religious controversy, the Government was in danger of suppressing religion itself. He was suspended from office; and when he died six years later, a vigorous disciplinarian, Whitgift, was appointed to succeed him.

Whitgift established a High Commission Court, to enquire into breaches of the Settlement, to remove clergymen whose teaching did not conform to the Thirty-Nine Articles, and to punish persons absenting themselves from the churches.[7] Before long he had driven to Holland many unyielding Puritans, who were later to cross to America in the *Mayflower* and found the New England colonies.

A wiser defence of Anglicanism was made by Richard Hooker of London, minister of the famous Temple Church. Disturbed at the growth of Puritanism and the threat to Anglicanism, Hooker retired to the country and worked for years on a literary defence of the latter. In his *Laws of Ecclesiastical Polity* Hooker rejects the Puritan doctrine that all questions about ecclesiastical government are to be answered from the Bible, and that the Church is not Christian unless built on the New Testament model. God, he says, reveals His will in man's mind and conscience, as well as in the Scriptures. The State is a divine institution, as well as the Church, both being aspects of the same Divine Commonwealth. And both the episcopate and the royal supremacy are justified, because through them the unity of Church and State is best maintained.

Nevertheless the vigour of the Church was in Puritanism; and its vitality was drawn from the new Bible study. The founders of Anglicanism had no perception that, in adopting Protestant principles to the extent of commending the study of the Scriptures, they were making uniformity in religion impossible. The Puritan, alone with the Bible at his own fireside, was searching out the will of God for himself and establishing a standard by which to judge religious things. His imagination was kindled and his mind set free by this private study. It opened the door to intellectual liberty in England, and to a hundred religious sects.

Puritans themselves were of different sorts. Some accepted bishops, objecting only to the kind of man appointed. Some rejected all bishops on scriptural grounds, and the royal appointment of bishops, as destroying the independence of the Church. Such Puritans desired the Geneva system, and were soon called Presbyterians. Still others rejected, on scriptural grounds, the idea of a centrally-controlled Church, and asked freedom for each congregation to worship as it should decide. These

---

[7] It was the Inquisition, without power to impose the death penalty, and was disapproved by Lord Burghley himself. It expressed the policy that, fifty years later, was to recoil upon King Charles I and Archbishop Laud, bringing both to the scaffold.

were known as Independents, and are the forerunners of Nonconformists in general.

The Church of England was thus an uneasy alliance, that would not
long outlive Elizabeth. What were now parties within the Church
would one day become independent churches, each providing out of its
own resources new places of worship and education, and leaving to the
Church of England the whole surviving estate of the mediaeval Church.
These dissenting bodies would be united in their rejection of mediaeval
Christianity, as an apostasy from Christ; they would be divided by their
inability to agree as to what Christ actually required of them.

Meanwhile Puritanism, while still within the Church of England, was
establishing certain new, and very fruitful, traditions in English life,
notably the family Bible, family prayers, and the "English Sunday." The
last is often represented only as a kill-joy institution. Puritans rejected
Sunday work as well as Sunday play, when Elizabeth's government was
encouraging trade and industry on that day. The "Day of Rest" is a
Puritan gift to England. So also is the idea of faithful self-examination,
the Puritan substitute for the Catholic practice of confession to a priest.
In the century after Elizabeth, it was to produce the greatest allegory in
all literature. John Bunyan, a Puritan imprisoned for unauthorised
preaching, devoted the years in prison to a study of the Bible and Foxe's
Book of Martyrs, then described his own spiritual struggles in the immortal *Pilgrim's Progress.*

As the years of Elizabeth lengthened, English hostility to Spain and
the Papacy remained constant. Whatever might happen in the Church
of England, it would not return to the Church of Rome.

This was confirmed by international events. Francis II of France had
died in 1560, some two years after the accession of Elizabeth; and Mary,
Queen of Scots, a beautiful and gifted widow of eighteen, returned to
Scotland to take over the government. An ardent Catholic, Mary
matched her wits six years against Protestant leaders in Scotland, then
lost all by misdemeanours in her domestic life. By 1567 she was a prisoner
in Lochleven Castle, where she abdicated the throne in favour of her
infant son, who was now to be James VI of Scotland and would one day
be James I of England. Mary herself escaped from Lochleven, fled across
the border into England, and threw herself upon the mercy of Eliza-

beth. She was to be a prisoner of Elizabeth for nearly twenty years.

Mary in prison speedily became a rallying point for all Catholic designs against England. Within the country there were still Roman Catholics everywhere. If they were few in the populous south and east, they were numerous in Wales and North England. Nobles of the north tended to regard Protestantism as an odious innovation, imposed upon the country by upstart families of the south, who had gained control of the throne. So when Mary had been in prison but a year, northern nobles rose in revolt, destroyed the Bibles and Prayer Books in Durham Cathedral, and looked to Spain and Scotland for help that never came.

The rebels were crushed; but Catholic plots against Elizabeth continued, encouraged by English Catholics abroad, by the king of Spain and the Pope, who helped the evil cause by excommunicating Elizabeth and declaring her subjects freed from their allegiance. At last there was clear proof of Mary's complicity in a plot to destroy the queen. Both Houses of Parliament petitioned for the execution of "the monstrous and huge dragon, the Queen of Scots." Very reluctantly and with painful misgivings, Elizabeth signed the death warrant in February, 1587.

The execution of Mary was a gauntlet thrown down to the Pope and to Spain. Mary had come to be regarded by the Catholic world as a saint and martyr. The sins of her youth were now far in the past. And had she not been, even in youth, the champion of the faith? Her death called for vengeance. And who but the king of Spain should execute the judgment of heaven? So the Catholic world reasoned.

Philip of Spain was now both better disposed and better placed to settle accounts with England. The death of King Sebastian of Portugal in 1580, without direct heirs, had brought that kingdom under the Spanish crown. Spaniards would never be liked in Portugal; and the union of the two countries would soon be dissolved. Meanwhile the fine Atlantic seaboard of Portugal, the Azores, the mines of Brazil, the factories of the Spice Islands, the varied resources of the East Indies, were at the command of Philip II. And the mariners of England, more reckless than their queen and determined to establish the freedom of the seas, had been "singeing the king of Spain's beard" in every part of the world for thirty years. When at last Sir Francis Drake burned the shipping in Cadiz harbour itself, there was nothing for Philip to do but prepare a vast armada for the conquest of England. He would both do his duty as a Catholic prince and vindicate the honour of Spain.

The story of the Spanish Armada, 1588, is familiar everywhere. The armada was to proceed up the English Channel to Dunkirk, convoy the army of the Duke of Parma across to England, depose Elizabeth, and set a Spanish princess in her place. It was a mad scheme. Those English Catholics on the continent, who kept the Pope and Philip informed about the situation in England, had little idea how far a generation of peace and prosperity had united the nation in loyalty to the throne. Nor did they realize that English abhorrence of the holocaust fed by the Inquisition in Spain and the Netherlands was deepening into a settled loathing of all things Spanish. Though there were still plotters in England, no party would now support a Spanish invasion or tolerate a Spanish queen.

The armada, prepared at staggering cost and with elaborate care, blessed by the Pope and the Spanish clergy, and followed by the prayers of the Spanish people, foundered on the rock of Spanish incompetence at sea. It was the beginning of the end of Spanish dominance; though the war continued for another sixteen years, outlasting both Philip and Elizabeth. Within that time Spain, in league with English Jesuits and Irish rebels, landed troops in Ireland, to help O'Donnell and Tyrone against the English overlord. Spanish hopes there were dashed at the battle of Kinsale. Elizabeth's savage suppression of the rebellion, and the transfer of county Munster to English landlords, were an incident in the melancholy struggle between Catholic and Protestant in Europe.

Spain was meeting reverses also on the continent. A series of defeats in France destroyed her foothold there, and left King Henry IV the undisputed master of the country. Reverses in the Netherlands forced Spanish acknowledgement of the independence of the Dutch in 1609.

The consequences for religion were considerable. In England the Spanish attack completed the process of making the land a Protestant nation, a process begun when Spanish Mary set up the Inquisition. In Spain the continued reverses led to fresh intolerance. The clergy interpreted Spain's humiliation as a judgment of heaven, upon a land not sufficiently set against heresy. The Government expiated its sin upon the one considerable non-Catholic community in the country, the Moriscoes, a community of some half-million survivors of the Moorish power. They must now profess the Catholic faith or leave the country. They left, taking with them much of the skill of Spain, in scientific agriculture and craftsmanship. Spain was less able than ever to sustain the burden of empire; and her decline was confirmed.

While the Reformation was thus pursuing its devious way in Tudor England, a parallel movement was advancing in Scotland. When Henry VIII died, a young priest, recently converted to Protestantism, was preaching the Gospel in Scotland, moving quickly from place to place, one step ahead of the Inquisition. Soon he was persuaded to take refuge in the Castle of St. Andrews, then held by a band of armed men, who had avenged the death of a saintly heretic by assassinating Cardinal Beaton, primate of Scotland. From that time, through the reigns of Edward and Mary Tudor, and well into that of Elizabeth, the young priest, John Knox, was to have as stormy a career as William Farel in Switzerland.

Scotland had always sat loose to the papacy. The land had been won to Christianity by the Irish monks of Iona. Its great names were Columba and Aidan. It continued until the eleventh century to be evangelized from the monasteries and governed ecclesiastically by the abbots. Then the decay of this Celtic Church made Scotland a mission of the Roman Church in neighbouring England. The land became Catholic. But the Celtic spirit of independence remained, and obedience to Rome was always doubtful. When, in the opening years of the fourteenth century, Edward I of England and his son attempted the conquest of Scotland and were blessed by Pope Boniface VIII, the Scots braved excommunication in support of their national heroes, William Wallace and Robert Bruce. At the close of that century, Scottish students returning from Oxford were preaching the doctrines of John Wyclif. The University of St. Andrews was founded by Bishop Wardlaw, as a barrier against the spread of Lollardy. Nevertheless the doctrines of Wyclif continued to be taught in Scotland. When Martin Luther was a child of ten, thirty persons stood before King and Privy Council in Edinburgh, charged with Lollardy. They defended their principles, and were discharged without penalty. So uncertain was Catholic authority in Scotland.

Luther's writings were found to be circulating in Scotland in 1525, and the English Bible in 1527. In that year Patrick Hamilton, once a student of Lutheranism at Paris, was burned at St. Andrews, the city of the Roman primate, for preaching Lutheranism in the streets. John Knox was a student then at St. Andrews and was probably affected; for "the reek of Patrick Hamilton infected as many as it blew upon." Nevertheless Knox was ordained a priest of the Church of Rome in 1540.

James V died in December, 1542; and the Earl of Arran became regent for his infant daughter, Mary Stuart. Arran was sympathetic with the Protestant movement on the continent; and the Parliament of 1543 made modest advances towards religious liberty. It legalized the possession of the Scriptures in English; and some preaching of evangelical doctrines began.

A decisive moment came when a certain George Wishart returned from exile on the continent and at Cambridge. Wishart had been an early teacher of Greek in Scotland, had read the New Testament in Greek with his pupils, and had fled abroad from a charge of heresy. He was now back in Scotland preaching widely, in the churches, in the streets, in the fields, wherever men would hear. John Knox, the priest, found Wishart "a man of such graces as before were never heard of in this realm," and was one of a little band of men, who carried swords to protect the itinerant preacher. Nevertheless Wishart was arrested, tried before Cardinal Beaton, and burned at the state.

Before long Wishart's death was avenged by the assassination of Beaton himself; and the conspirators fortified themselves in the Castle of St. Andrews. There, as we have seen, John Knox came in 1547, when his activities as an evangelist put his life also in jeopardy.

Knox soon became minister of the Castle congregation, a strange aggregation of godly reformers and corrupt adventurers. He grew famous as an interpreter of the Scriptures and a controversialist; and Archbishop Hamilton, who had succeeded Beaton, found Protestantism being defended openly in his metropolitan city. There were many converts; and Knox began the Lord's Supper in Scotland, rejecting the Mass. Soon, however, he was a refugee on the continent, where he became confirmed in the Calvinism he had already imbided from Wishart.

From the continent Knox was speedily invited to England, where Archbishop Cranmer and the Protector Somerset were working for a genuine Protestantism. Knox was appointed minister at Berwick, on the Scottish border; and his brief ministry there, 1549–1551, was one of the important beginnings of Puritanism in England. Advanced by the Government to Newcastle, Knox ignored the Prayer Book and followed his own Calvinistic principles. Nevertheless he was offered the bishopric of Rochester, which he declined, holding himself for the service of Scotland.

The accession of Mary Tudor made Knox again a refugee on the continent. He became minister of a congregation of English refugees at Geneva, and so continued for three years. Calvin was then at the height of his influence. Knox was perfected in Calvinism, and impressed by its religious discipline. Geneva, he thought, was "the most perfect school of Christ that ever was in the earth since the days of the Apostles."

When Mary Tudor died in 1558, Knox prepared to return to Scotland. Protestantism there had grown. Mary of Guise, the new regent, had been tolerant and Archbishop Hamilton averse to persecution, knowing the need for reforms. So congregations of Protestants began to form, meeting apart for the Lord's Supper.

This open secession of many from the Church aroused both Mary of Guise and the archbishop. Persecution was renewed; and reform leaders in Edinburgh formed a league for united action, in December, 1557. They drew up a "Common Band," the first Scottish "Covenant," pledging both life and property to "establish the most blessed Word of God and His congregation" and "to have faithful ministers purely and truly to minister Christ's evangel and Sacraments." [8]

The Covenant was signed by certain nobles of Protestant mind, including the Earls of Argyle, Glencairn and Morton. The subscribers became known as the "Lords of the Congregation," and formed a sort of Protestant national council. They petitioned the regent, in the spring of 1558, for liberty of preaching and public worship, including the Lord's Supper in the Protestant manner, and rigid ecclesiastical discipline, "that the wicked, scandalous, and detestable life of prelates and of the State Ecclesiastical may be so reformed that the people have not occasion to contemn their ministers." They wished "the grave and godly face of the primitive Church restored." [9]

The regent's reply was conciliatory, but only because she was playing for time. Her daughter Mary would soon marry the Dauphin of France.

[8] Knox, *History of the Reformation*, i., 273.
[9] *Ibid.*, i., 302–306.

Her son-in-law and her daughter would be king and queen of France and Scotland, with the latter country a satellite of the former. The Roman Church could then be maintained in Scotland, with help from France.

Mary married the Dauphin in April; and the regent soon entered into an open alliance with the hierarchy for the suppression of Protestantism. She was forewarned, by the death of Mary Tudor and the accession of Elizabeth in the neighbouring kingdom, that Protestantism must be suppressed now, if ever, in Scotland. Before the storm broke, Knox returned from the continent. At St. Andrews he preached on "Cleansing the Temple" and swept the city. The magistrates removed "all monuments of idolatry" from the Cathedral and the parish churches.

The religious war was on. Armed forces soon faced each other at St. Andrews, Perth and Edinburgh, while Knox travelled far and wide, informing the masses of the questions at issue. Very fortunately for the reformers, a league was secured with the English Government, for joint resistance to Romanism and France. At a critical moment an English fleet appeared in the Forth and an English army crossed the border. In that situation Mary of Guise, now in her last illness, urged that both foreign armies be dismissed from Scotland. Her plea was heeded. England and France signed a treaty, agreeing to leave the government of Scotland to a Council of Twelve, five to be chosen by Parliament, seven by the young queen. The religious question was left open.

Parliament assembled in August, 1560. As neither the queen nor a royal commissioner was present, it was constitutionally a Convention rather than a Parliament. But the attendance was very large; and it was immediately clear that Parliament was strongly Protestant. A popular petition, largely signed, recounted the false claims of the papacy, the "idolatrous" administration of the sacraments, the immorality, greed and tyranny of the Scottish hierarchy, and plead for deliverance from a "burden intolerable upon the Kirk of God within the realm."

Parliament asked for a statement of principles; and Knox and other ministers drew up a "Confession of Faith professed and believed by the Protestants within the Realm of Scotland." It was not substantially different from the other Protestant Confessions of the day.

There was little discussion of the Confession in Parliament, and little open dissent. The Earl Marischal said, "Since the pillars of the Pope's

Church here present speak nothing to the contrary of the doctrine proposed, I cannot but hold it to be the very truth of God"; and Lord Lindsay, "as grave and goodly a man as ever I saw," uttered a *Nunc Dimittis*. So the English ambassador, Randolph, reported to Lord Burghley. Astonished at the near-unanimity of Parliament, he wrote, "I never heard matters of so great importance neither sooner dispatched nor with better will agreed to." [10]

Parliament proceeded to forbid religious usages contrary to the Confession, to deny the authority of the Pope in Scotland, and to make the celebration of Mass a crime. Thus a year after the English Parliament, under the guidance of Elizabeth, made Protestantism the national faith of England, the Scottish Parliament, in the absence of Mary, made Protestantism the national faith of Scotland.

The work of protestantising the Scottish people had yet to be done. Protestant congregations were still few and unrelated. There was no authorised ritual of worship, no system of church government. So the organization of the Reformed Church of Scotland was undertaken immediately.

A beginning was made when the Lords of the Congregation asked the authors of the Confession to prepare a *Book of Discipline*. It was done in consultation with Calvin and other Swiss reformers, and submitted to the Government and then to Parliament in 1561. Parliament rejected the Book. The objection was not to the proposed form of organization, or worship, or discipline, but to the assumption that the Reformed Church was to inherit the whole estate of the Catholic Church. Many Catholics, to whom it mattered little that there was to be a new Confession of Faith, were firmly bound in sentiment to the visible estate of Mother Church, her churches and lands, chapels and monasteries. Men urged, too, with justice that, if Masses were not to continue in Scotland, endowed chapels for the saying of Masses ought to be restored to the families of the founders. Still others, venal landowners, hoped to grow rich on lands of the Church, as men had done in England.

The *Book of Discipline,* therefore, was given effect only in so far as was possible without civil support. It followed the familiar lines of Geneva, in rejecting bishops, creating lay elders, or presbyters, and admitting the laity to a share in church government.

[10] Laing, *Works of Knox*, vi., 116, 117.

Five offices were recognized as valid in the Church, those of minister, elder, deacon, reader and superintendent. Readers and superintendents were, perhaps, not meant to continue, when ecclesiastical organization should have been completed. In any case they soon disappeared.

Scotland succeeded beyond Geneva in building what is called the Presbyterian system. Its aim is democratic self-government within the Church, giving logical expression to Luther's principle of "the spiritual priesthood of all believers." That principle had been compromised in both Germany and Switzerland, by varying degrees of subservience to the civil power. In Scotland it found classic expression, though it had a long struggle for survival with the Stuart kings.

At the base of this Presbyterian organization is the parish Congregation, which appoints the minister and elects a company of elders, the Kirk-session, to supervise his conduct and teaching, and to co-operate with him in guarding the spiritual interests of the Congregation. Above the Kirk-session is the Presbytery,[11] corresponding to the Catholic Diocese, and composed of the ministers of the area and an equal number of elders, elected by the Congregations. Above the Presbytery is the Synod, of ministers and elders, corresponding to the earlier ecclesiastical Province; and over all is the General Assembly, of ministers and elders, the Parliament of the Church.

Here then was the most democratic of the Reformed Churches, one in which all leadership was recruited by the people, appointed by them, kept amenable to them. It tended to breed a people pedantic, argumentative, a little unlovely, but forthright and inflexible as their Scottish hills.

To equip the Christian population for its responsibilities, the *Book of Discipline* stressed the necessity for "virtuous education and godly upbringing of the youth of this realm." There was to be a school in each parish and an academy, or secondary school, in the larger centres. Education was to be compulsory, and free to the poor. Bursaries were planned, to encourage promising students to proceed to the Universities. The authors of the book wrote the Government: "If God shall move your hearts to establish and execute this order, . . . your whole realm, within few years, will serve itself of true preachers, and of other officers necessary for your Commonwealth."

---

[11] The Presbytery is later in origin than the *Book of Discipline*, and grew out of weekly meetings of local ministers and elders, for the study of the Bible.

For the financial support of the ministry, the *Book of Discipline* assumed that legitimate sources of income in the Catholic Church would now descend to the Reformed Church. It was not contemplated that ministers would receive those funeral fees, Easter gifts, and other emoluments of the priesthood, such as the best piece of cloth in the draper's stock. Catholic practice at its best, however, was to continue; the Church would support its ministers, encourage education, relieve poverty and distress. There was, however, to be no begging in Scotland.

The *Book of Discipline,* as we saw, was rejected by Parliament, its financial plan being unsatisfactory. So bishops and abbots continued to receive two-thirds of their previous revenues and to sit in Parliament as the Spiritual Estate, though having no ecclesiastical status. It was a situation that could not continue indefinitely.

The year 1560 was an anxious one for the Reformers. The young Queen of Scots and her French consort did not confirm the legislation establishing the Reformed Church. There was dread of a French invasion. The sudden death of King Francis was hailed as a "wonderful deliverance"; but there was still danger. Queen Mary would soon be in Scotland. A clash was inevitable. The Reformers felt called of God to establish the Reformed Church; Mary felt called to restore Romanism.

Mary landed in August, 1561, amidst general foreboding. "The mist was thick and dark. . . . The sun was not seen to shine two days before, nor two days after." There followed, for two years, a succession of royal interviews with Knox, who was now minister of St. Giles Cathedral, Edinburgh, not far from the Castle and Holyrood Palace. Mary stormed, asserted the royal prerogative, wept, tried womanly wiles, hoping to win an acknowledgement of the royal authority in religion. It was of no use. Knox maintained, unlike Luther and Zwingli and Cranmer, the duty of Christians to resist an evil ruler. "I perceive," said Mary, "that my subjects shall obey you and not me." "My travail," Knox replied, "is that both princes and subjects obey God."

The antagonism of Queen Mary to Knox was intensified by his marriage, in 1564, to her cousin, Margaret Stuart, daughter of Lord Ochiltree. It was insupportable that the reformer should ally himself, even remotely, with the royal family. "The Queen," wrote the English ambassador, "stormeth wonderfully."

Meanwhile differences of long standing, between Knox and the nobles of Protestant sympathies, were disturbing the reform movement, as similar differences had disturbed all other Protestant movements. Knox was incapable of compromise. He was not doing his own will, but the will of God. He would not "traffic with Satan." He would not connive at "idolatry." He would enforce the law against the Mass, even upon the queen and in the Royal Chapel at Holyrood. Protestant statesmen, on the other hand, hoped to establish the Reformation by peaceful means. They sought also the entrance of Scotland into union with England on the most favourable terms. Mary could not be recognized as Elizabeth's successor unless she became Protestant. The Lords of the Congregation would trust to her good sense.

There were differences, too, concerning the General Assembly. Some Protestant statesmen, familiar with the situation in Tudor England and fearful of a break between the sovereign and the Church, denied that the Assembly could meet and legislate, except at the call of the queen. Knox said: "Take from us the freedom of Assemblies and you take from us the Evangel. Without Assemblies how shall good order and unity in doctrine be kept?"

A crisis came in Mary's first Parliament, that of 1563. Knox and men of his views expected to see the *Book of Discipline* legalized and financial provision made for a Protestant ministry. The Lords of the Congregation would not press the queen; and Knox, from the pulpit of St. Giles, charged them with "betraying God's cause." The General Assembly could not compose these differences; and thereafter "precise" ministers "were held of all courtiers as monsters."

Dark years followed for Scottish Protestantism. Indeed the winter of 1565–66 was dark for Protestantism everywhere. The ferment of the recent Council of Trent was working in Catholic minds. The Catholic forces of Europe were massing to crush Protestantism, and expected much from Mary Stuart. The Catholics of North England were thought to be ready to co-operate with those of Scotland. Catholic nobles thronged the court, and went openly to Mass in the Royal Chapel. "The faithful in the realm were in great fear, looking for nothing but great trouble and persecution to be shortly."

Knox held Scotland for the Reformation. From the pulpit and with his pen he kept Protestant convictions alive. The folly of the queen helped his crusade. She had married her cousin, Lord Darnley, in May, 1565. He too was a grandchild of Margaret, sister of Henry VIII, and heir, after Mary, to the English crown; but he was dissolute and worthless. Mary was soon estranged and openly infatuated with the dashing Earl of Bothwell, whose feats of horsemanship were the envy of the young bloods of Edinburgh. In February, 1567, Darnley was murdered on the outskirts of Edinburgh; and Mary married the supposed murderer in May. It was too much. An army of both Catholics and Protestants rose against misgovernment and this crowning outrage. Bothwell fled; and Mary, as we saw (p. 419), was imprisoned in Lochleven Castle. The General Assembly convened. It was the only medium for the expression of the national will, since Parliament was unconstitutional without the queen.

Opinion in the Assembly was divided. Some would restore the queen, if she would promise amendment. Knox, who was master of the Assembly, took the side of the "Confederate Lords," the league that had imprisoned the queen. Her restoration, he knew, would be dangerous to both Church and State. Mary must either abdicate or be brought to trial, for complicity in her husband's murder. The former alternative seemed preferable.

The Assembly adjourned for a month, after appointing a Sunday for national fasting. During the adjournment Knox continued to denounce from the pulpit the conduct of the queen, to prepare the public mind for her abdication, the policy the Confederate Lords meant to pursue.

When the Assembly met again, a conference was arranged between certain ministers of the Assembly, some sixty nobles, and representatives of the boroughs. The conference pledged itself to bring to trial the murderers of the king and to protect his infant son James, against whose life Bothwell was known to have designs. The signatories of the pledge engaged also to complete the establishment of the Reformed Kirk as soon as Parliament should meet, to make provision for the support of the ministers, and to "root out" all remaining "monuments of idolatry." [12]

While the Assembly was still sitting, Mary was constrained to abdicate in favour of her son and to appoint the Earl of Moray regent. Soon the child was crowned James VI, in the Greyfriars Church at Stirling.

---

[12] Calderwood, *True History of the Church of Scotland*, ii., 378–383.

Two lords took an oath on his behalf, to maintain the Protestant faith; and the Bishop of Orkney, who had embraced Protestantism, anointed him in the ancient manner.

Most of the nation acquiesced in the new situation. Parliament, in December, 1567, approved the action of the Confederate Lords and gave effect to the agreement with the General Assembly. It legalized the Reformed Church by ratifying the acts of the Convention of 1560. It made the support of the ministry a first charge upon the ecclesiastical revenues of Scotland. It enacted that all teachers in schools, colleges and universities must profess the Protestant faith, and that "all kings, princes, or magistrates, occupying their place, shall at the time of their coronation, take their great oath, in the presence of God, that they shall maintain the true religion now received, and shall abolish and withstand all false religion contrary to the same." [13]

Knox thought his work complete, and planned to return to his congregation in Geneva; but fresh dangers to the Reformation kept him in Scotland. Mary escaped from Lochleven in May, 1568; and the magic of royalty worked again. Many nobles, Catholic and Protestant, rallied to her standard. She was defeated, but escaped to England, leaving several garrisons in Scotland, a constant menace to the Regent Moray. There were many secessions to the "Queen's Party." Those seceding disclaimed any intention to change the existing religious situation; but Knox knew that the restoration of Mary would revive Catholic ambitions.

Harder to be endured was the venality of some Protestant nobles. They sought personal enrichment out of ecclesiastical lands. They used their influence to get unworthy men into parishes, having secured from them pledges concerning the revenues. Knox said bitterly, "If they can have the Kirk lands annexed to their houses, they appear to take no more care of the instruction of the ignorant, and of the feeding of the flock of Christ, than ever did the Papists." [14]

General Assemblies, in 1570 and 1571, protested to Parliament against the "presentation" of unqualified ministers to livings and the assigning of ecclesiastical revenues to laymen. Parliament treated the protests with

[13] Calderwood, ii., 388–90.
[14] Laing, vi., 603; Calderwood, iii., 113, 114.

indifference and soon, partly for constitutional and political reasons, partly in simple venality, restored episcopacy in the Reformed Church of Scotland.

The constitutional argument was that the validity of parliamentary proceedings was being imperilled. Bishops and abbots in Parliament were dying off. Legislation was as invalid without the "Spiritual Estate" as without the sovereign. So, at least, men might argue in the future, if they desired a counter-revolution. And there was the political argument, that since the union of Scotland with England was expected to follow the death of Elizabeth and the Church of England was episcopal, the Church of Scotland might well be so.

A less defensible motive was that the Government needed money, feared to seize the revenues of the bishoprics, but might venture to appoint as bishops such men as would agree to the retention by the Government of part of the revenues. And there were nobles in Parliament, who had been rewarded for past services with episcopal and abbey lands, and who might by such agreements assure themselves of permanent possession.

Most Church leaders acquiesced in the proposed appointment of bishops. The Reformed Church was not yet committed to the doctrine of Zwingli and Calvin, that episcopacy is unscriptural; and the substitution of bishops for superintendents would both overcome the financial difficulties of the Reformed Church and restore to her direct representation in Parliament. It seemed better to reinstate the episcopate, in a modified form.

In these circumstances, representatives of Church and State met at Leith early in 1572, and drew up the *Concordat of Leith,* which was ratified by Parliament and the General Assembly. By its terms the old offices, dioceses and revenues of the bishops and archbishops were restored, with the important proviso that all prelates were to be subordinate to the General Assembly. The Reformed Church regarded the episcopate as expedient, "until further and more perfect order be obtained." [15]

Knox, now in ill health and in semi-retirement at St. Andrews, did not participate in the negotiations and regarded the Concordat with

[15] Calderwood, iii., 168–172.

misgiving. He seems, however, to have thought episcopacy permissible, so long as supreme authority was vested in the General Assembly, which, since it included laymen, was not a hierarchy.

The General Assembly adopted certain "reasonable and godly" safeguards, to prevent long vacancies in parishes, the appointment of unqualified persons to bishoprics, and discreditable financial arrangements by bishops.[16] Nevertheless the results of the Concordat were as Knox feared. Men were made bishops who had privately agreed that much of the revenues should go to the lay patrons securing their appointment. They were conduits, through whom the wealth of the Catholic Church passed to the Scottish nobles.

Bishops were brought to trial before the General Assembly for this "simoniacal paction" and "dilapidation of patrimony";[17] but the evils persisted. The Presbyterian episcopate was thus morally compromised at the outset. It was unsuitable on other grounds as well. The new bishops were too manifestly an artifice. They had none of the merit thought to attach to unbroken succession from the Apostles, and were without the authority of mediaeval bishops, being subject to an Assembly of ministers and laymen. Indeed the episcopate could not be grafted upon the democratic Presbyterian system, without ceasing to be recognizable as an episcopate.

The restoration of episcopacy was to disturb the Church of Scotland for a hundred years, all the more because the Stuart kings, ruling from Westminster as well as Holyrood, were to show as little comprehension of Scotsmen as of English. Episcopacy in Scotland would fall with the Stuart kings.

Meanwhile Knox was back in Edinburgh. In August, 1572, the month in which the General Assembly ratified the Concordat of Leith, Knox came at the call of his old congregation at St. Giles. He came knowing that a garrison of the Queen's Party still held the castle, not far away; and he stipulated that he should not be expected "in any sort to temper his tongue, or cease to speak against the treasonable dealings of the Castle." Though not yet an old man, being but fifty-nine, Knox was now worn out with his labours and anxieties. The English ambassador re-

[16] Laing, vi., 620, 621.
[17] Calderwood, iii., 330, 347, 361.

ported, "(he is) now so feeble as scarce can he stand alone, yet doth he every Sunday cause himself to be carried (to the church), and preacheth with the same vehemence and zeal that ever he did." [18]

The "Chief Priest of Puritanism" lived only three months after the return to Edinburgh, dying in November, 1572.

The period of the Protestant Reformation may suitably be regarded as closing with the death of Knox. More than fifty years had now passed since Luther posted his Ninety-Five Theses on the door of the Castle Church at Wittenberg, and some twenty-six since he was laid to rest within its walls. In those twenty-six years the creators of Protestantism had all passed away—Melancthon and Martin Bucer, the Sturm brothers of Strassburg, Calvin at Geneva, Cranmer in England, and many others of less fame.

The field, too, was now finally delimited. What were Catholic and Protestant lands in Europe in 1572 were to remain so until modern times. Only in other lands were further conquests to be made. In Europe the work of Catholic and Protestant alike was to cultivate their own domain, and learn to tolerate each other.

For the era about to open, Protestant Christianity was the better equipped. Society was on the march. The Renaissance was broadening into a new world of science and invention and discovery, in which individual enlightenment and initiative would play a decisive part. Here Protestantism was more at home. Inviting men to find for themselves the will of God, and spreading education that they might do so, it developed individualism and became identified with progress. Catholic lands, schooled in obedience, became the backward lands. The seventeenth and eighteenth centuries in the western world, and most of the nineteenth, are the Protestant era.

[18] Laing, vi., 633.

CHAPTER XIX

THE AFTERMATH OF RELIGIOUS REVOLUTION:
EUROPE

THE century of the Reformation closed in bloody violence. The rivalry of France and Spain had given the Reformation a chance to spread, and had facilitated the makeshift Peace of Augsburg in 1555, dividing Germany between Lutherans and Catholics. Then the political scene changed. Spanish victories over France at St. Quentin and Gravelines made Spain supreme and Catholicism throughout Europe more politically united and confident, under the leadership of Philip II.

Catholic France now turned to domestic questions; and her wars of religion were disastrous to the country. City was set against city, village against village, family against family. Only the little humanist group stood aloof, finding salvation in an enlightened skepticism. The essays of Montaigne were published during the wars of religion.

When King Henry II died in 1559, the Genevan, or Huguenot, movement had many devout adherents in the towns of France. That year they were strong enough to hold their first General Synod in Paris, and adopted the Presbyterian constitution and a Calvinistic creed. A body of Protestant conviction, inflamed by the recent martyrdom of Protestant bishops in England and the nameless cruelties of Spain in the Netherlands, thus confronted the weak and impoverished Government of France.

A wise and tolerant king might have preserved the peace; but Henry II was succeeded by three of the feeblest kings in French history, his own sons. Francis II was an invalid, Charles IX a near-madman, Henry III a degenerate. The real power lay with their mother Catherine, an Italian woman, of the Florentine de' Medici. Catherine was cultivated and capable, but unprincipled and vindictive. The last of her sons described her as *Madame La Serpente*. The controlling ambition of Catherine de' Medici was to preserve the monarchy for her sons and control for herself. To do this, she tried to balance the fanatical parties of France in a general toleration.

The Italian queen and her sons had to deal with three aristocratic parties in France, the Guises, the Bourbons, and the *Politiques*. All three were opposed to the centralization of power in the hands of the king. They represented the interests of the old feudal nobility.

The Guises, a family of Lorraine, were strongly Catholic. They were led by two brothers, Francis, Duke of Guise, a capable and popular soldier, and Charles, Cardinal Archbishop of Rheims, the first prelate of France. Their sister was Mary of Guise, recently queen of Scotland, their niece Mary Stuart, consort of Francis II. Fifteen Guises were bishops. The Catholic world expected much of the Guises.

The Bourbons were influential in Normandy and the west of France. Two princes of the family, Antoine, King of Navarre, and his brother Louis, Duke of Condé, were the political leaders of the Huguenots.

The third party, the *Politiques,* was strong in central France. Its leaders were generally Catholic; but they disliked the Guises and thought their foreign connections dangerous to France. The *Politiques* changed colour somewhat religiously when three leaders espoused the Protestant faith. One of them, Gaspard de Coligny, Admiral of France, became the political hope of the Huguenots, and therefore the special object of Catholic animosity. Coligny was a man of profound religious convictions and dauntless courage.

Catherine de' Medici, to further the reconciliation of parties, permitted a public discussion between Catholic and Protestant theologians at Poissy in 1561. A royal edict also granted the Huguenots freedom of worship in France, except in fortified towns.

The Guises determined to fight; and three brief but savage wars between Catholics and Huguenots raged between 1562 and 1570. The Huguenots were helped somewhat by French resentment against Spain and Spanish influence. They were able in 1570 to secure the Peace of St. Germain, which at last acknowledged the Huguenots as a lawful part of French life. Huguenot nobles were to be permitted to continue Protestant worship in their castles, for all who wished to attend; and there were to be two places of worship for the common people in each civil department of France. As a guarantee of the treaty, four cities of military importance were to be under Huguenot control for two years.

In the struggle Duke Francis of Guise had been assassinated; and, of the Huguenot leaders, Antoine of Navarre and his brother Condé had died of wounds. Coligny was left to defend the Protestant cause.

Many persons in France were now ready to work with the Huguenots for the recovery of French independence of Spanish influence. To signalise the reconciliation, they arranged a marriage between Henry of Navarre, son of Antoine, and Margaret of Valois, sister of the king.

This was too much for Catherine de'Medici, who feared the influence of Coligny with the king. She plotted with the Guises for the assassination of Coligny. The plot failed; and Catherine fell into panic. She had alienated the Huguenots, without depriving them of leadership. She determined upon a general massacre of Huguenots on St. Bartholomew's Day, August 24, 1572. Several thousands fell in Paris, many thousands throughout France. Coligny was among the slain. Henry of Navarre saved his life by renouncing Protestantism.

There was great rejoicing at Rome and Madrid. The head of Coligny was sent to the Pope, who returned a golden rose to Charles IX and ordered a medal struck, commemorating the extermination of so many heretics. Philip of Spain ordered a *Te Deum* in all the churches. The Huguenots, however, were not crushed. Further wars ravaged the land; and when Charles IX died in 1573 and was succeeded by his vicious brother, Henry III, the Huguenots were still vigorous. The *Politiques*, too, were strengthened, by the support of Catholics who saw that repeated wars were ruining France and that a basis of peace with the Huguenots must be found.

The *Politiques* were answered by a Catholic union in 1576, "the League," with Philip of Spain and the Pope as patrons, to stiffen Catholic resistance in France. Their existence drove the *Politiques* more and more into alliance with the Huguenots, under the leadership of Henry of Navarre, who had recovered his Protestantism.

The childlessness of Henry III made Henry of Navarre, as head of the Bourbon family, prospective heir to the throne. To prevent his accession the Catholic League in 1585 entered into a compact with Philip of Spain; and Pope Sixtus V co-operated, issuing a bull that pronounced Henry of Navarre debarred from the throne. The result was an eighth Huguenot war. The feeble king was declared by the League deposed. He would treat with those whom he ought to exterminate; he could no longer be endured. Henry was driven from Paris in May, 1585, and was assassinated by a fanatical monk in 1589. So died "the worst ruler of the worst dynasty that ever governed."

The minds of Frenchmen had been turning more and more to Henry of Navarre. He was shrewd, good humoured, with exceptional military gifts. Though a Protestant, he was a man, in striking contrast to the last Valois kings. So reasoned many a Catholic Frenchman. When the Valois dynasty came to an end with the assassination of Henry III, Henry of Navarre became King Henry IV. He had to fight three years to establish his authority. He defeated the Catholic League at Ivry in 1590. He was resisted in Paris and Rouen until 1592, by the Duke of Parma and Spanish troops, called in from the Netherlands. Then Parma died; and Henry was master.

For political reasons Henry IV became a Catholic. It was a wise decision. Henry was not a man of deep religious convictions; and his return to Mother Church gave peace to France. For Henry did not betray his earlier Huguenot associates. An *Edict of Nantes,* in April, 1598, declared Huguenots eligible for public office, granted them the right of public worship, except in Paris and four other fanatically Catholic cities,[1] and placed certain fortified towns in Huguenot hands as guarantees.

That year Philip of Spain died, convinced to the end that what he had done was for the glory of God, but defeated in his efforts to overthrow Protestantism. Things had not gone well with any of his crusades for the Catholic faith, whether in England or France or the Netherlands. Even in Spain, unimpeachably orthodox, men must have reflected sombrely upon the dubious rewards of a violent piety.

The Huguenots were now a State within a State, and were secure for a generation. They completed their national organization, and built excellent schools throughout France. Then their semi-independence clashed with the centralizing policy of Cardinal Richelieu, great minister of Louis XIII. He terminated their political independence, but guaranteed their religious privileges. They came under increasing attack, however, especially by the Jesuits, and in the closing years of the seventeenth century were again a martyr people,[2] seeking safety in exile, to the great benefit of England and Holland and America.

---

[1] Rheims, Toulouse, Lyons and Dijon.
[2] Louis XIV revoked the *Edict of Nantes* in 1685.

Meanwhile the troubles in France under the last Valois kings, and the folly of Philip II of Spain, were helping the Protestant cause in the Netherlands. The struggle there for political independence of Spain went on through all Philip's reign. The seventeen provinces were tenacious of their local rights; Philip was determined to have centralized control, as in Spain. The provinces resented interference with commerce; Philip was determined to control it to the advantage of Spain. The provinces tolerated religious differences; Philip determined that all Netherlanders should be Catholic. The decrees of the Council of Trent were to be enforced and heresy suppressed.

The religious situation in the Netherlands had been relatively stable. The earlier Lutheranism was now largely displaced by Anabaptism among the peasants and workmen, and by Calvinism in the middle classes. The nobles were still Catholic, and most of the people in the southern provinces.

In pursuit of his aims Philip appointed as regent his sister, Margaret of Parma, and gave her an advisory council that virtually displaced the Parliament, or States General.

The effort to curb heresy drove skilled craftsmen to emigrate, and hurt trade. Three noblemen therefore, all Catholics, founded a party of freedom. They were William of Nassau, Prince of Orange, and the Counts of Egmont and Hoorn. A petition, largely signed, was presented to the regent in 1566. Its signatories were nicknamed "Beggars"; and that became the name of the party of freedom. In the excitement Calvinistic mobs wrecked Catholic churches, in spite of their leaders.

Philip replied by sending to the Netherlands in 1567 the Duke of Alva, with a picked force of Italian and Spanish mercenaries. Alva was particularly charged to entrap and execute the three leaders. They were the very men whom a wise monarch would have made the mainstay of his Government. William of Orange withdrew to Germany. Egmont and Hoorn were taken by treachery, given a mock trial, and executed in the public square in Brussels. It was a political crime, from which Spanish authority in the Netherlands never recovered.

For six terrible years Alva harried the populace of the Netherlands. It was in vain. Orange organized resistance from abroad. His sea-rovers preyed on Spanish commerce and hid in English harbours. Their activities prolonged the campaign, and compelled Alva to levy a heavy sales tax to pay his troops. The tax crippled trade, and roused Catholic merchants as well as Protestant to white heat. Encouraged by the successes of the "Sea-Beggars," the men of the northern provinces determined to be independent of Spain, and called William of Orange to lead them. Unable to meet the forces of Alva in the field, they fought behind city walls and made the defence of Haarlem and Alkmaar and Leyden memorable forever.

Events in the south brought unexpected help to the rebels. The Spanish forces there, ill-paid, broke into mutiny and pillage. Their terrible sack of Antwerp, "the Spanish fury," swept away all indecision in the Catholic states of Flanders and Brabant. Catholic south and Protestant north united in 1576 to expel the foreigner.

That decision was reversed when the Duke of Parma, statesman as well as general, came to lead the Spanish forces. A great victory at Gembloux in 1578 recovered the southern provinces for Spain. Then Parma turned to good purpose the jealousy of Catholic south and Calvinistic north. The south was induced to form the *League of Arras* in 1579, for the protection of Catholicism. Calvinists rejoined immediately with the *Union of Utrecht*. Very reluctantly William of Orange, who had himself become a Protestant, approved the Union and abandoned hope of a united Netherlands. Many thousands of Protestants migrated to the north, many Catholics to the south. Ultimately Parma saved the ten southern provinces for Spain, and became the founder of modern Belgium.

In 1581 representatives of the seven northern provinces met at the Hague and signed an *Act of Abjuration,* renouncing allegiance to the king of Spain. The king had recently declared William of Orange an enemy of the human race, and set a great price on his head. He was assassinated in 1584. It was too late. The permanence of the Dutch Republic was already assured.

It was during the years of the Spanish terror that the Calvinistic churches of the Netherlands completed their organization. The First National Synod met in 1571, though it had to meet outside the country at Emden. It gave the Reformed Church of the Netherlands a Presbyterian constitution, like that of the Reformed Church of France. The degree of its independence of the State varied from province to province, and was long a matter of controversy.

In one thing the Reformed Church of the Netherlands was distinguished from all other churches of the time, its toleration. Having struggled bitterly for its own existence, needing the aid of all possible friends, and interested beyond others in avoiding obstacles to trade, the Reformed Church made the Dutch Republic a refuge for the religiously oppressed, and so added strength to the nation. Anabaptists received legal recognition first in Holland in 1577. Such recognition was withheld from Catholics only. They were denied the privilege of public worship and debarred from public office, though they might live and work without molestation in Holland.

Twenty-five years of warfare followed the death of William of Orange. The federated provinces had found a truly great statesman in John van Oldenbarnveldt, and an accomplished soldier in Maurice of Nassau, son of William of Orange. Maurice built an army that could overcome the Spaniards in the open field, liberated the soil of the federated provinces, and proved himself the first soldier of the period. And on the sea the Spaniards, beaten by English seamanship in 1588, were decisively beaten again by the Dutch at Gibraltar nineteen years later, in 1607.

Spanish pride would not yet stoop to a peace with Dutch rebels, who prohibited the celebration of Catholic rites and insisted on trading in lands reserved to Spain by the Pope; but Spain found it necessary to sign a truce of twelve years at Antwerp in 1609. Religion was not mentioned; but the independence of the Dutch Republic was acknowledged, and its right to trade in Spanish waters.

It must not be inferred from the sanguine events in France and the Netherlands that persecution and war engaged the whole attention of the Catholic Church in the late sixteenth century. The ranks of the faithful were engaged in the whole multifarious piety of Mother Church. The late sixteenth century, and all of the seventeenth, were a flowering time in Roman Christianity. The decrees of the Council of Trent were in force, and the clergy living a more decent and orderly life. The faithful were not distracted and disillusioned by shame for the Church. Education of the young of the upper classes was spreading enlightenment; though it was no substitute for the vigorous popular education being spread by the Reformed Churches and, in the skilful hands of the Jesuits, concentrated upon such studies as would not encourage inde-

the *Spiritual Guide;* and Molinos dutifully recanted and went into retirement in a Dominican monastery.

Quietism, however, had found distinguished adherents in France. Madame de Guyon, a widow of noble birth, adopted the contemplative life. Coming at length to Paris, she made disciples at the royal court. Her ecstatic fervour found expression in forms thought heretical; and, largely through the influence of Bossuet, she was imprisoned in a convent. She left a very distinguished disciple, however, in Fénelon, Archbishop of Cambray, who published a book in 1697, *Maxims of the Saints concerning the Inner Life,* to prove that Madame de Guyon's doctrine was in accord with principles held by the saints of all ages.

This defence of Quietism precipitated further controversy; and Pope Innocent XII appointed a commission of theologians, who examined the *Maxims* and condemned the work. Receiving the news as he was entering the pulpit of his cathedral, Fénelon preached on the duty of the Christian to submit to his superior. Fénelon himself submitted.

Mysticism, like sainthood in general, is not a product of the normal ecclesiastical routine of piety. It springs out of personal experience and insight. It tends, therefore, to be regarded by ecclesiastical leadership as an idiosyncrasy, greatly to be admired in the simple minded, greatly to be feared in men and women of original minds. Its prevalence, nevertheless, is one evidence of the vitality of the religious life wherever it appears.

The new life in the Roman Church found expression also in increased missionary activity. The Jesuits and the Mendicants were equally active. The Mendicants had long been at work in Moslem lands; and Jesuit activity began as soon as the Order was founded. The first great name is Francis Xavier, whom Ignatius Loyola sent to India, at the request of King John III of Portugal, in 1542. Xavier preached seven years throughout southern India, then entered Japan, and after three years set out for China, where he soon died. His work in the Orient was too widespread to be thorough, and was rather in the nature of missionary exploration.

The example of Xavier was contagious, as it was meant to be. His work was continued in India by an Italian Jesuit, Roberto de'Nobili, and in China by the Jesuit Matteo Ricci. A Board of prelates and other learned men was set up at Rome in 1622, to direct missions everywhere.

This is the "Propaganda," [4] which established a college for the training of missionaries and a press for the printing of books in all languages. To the College of the Propaganda capable youths were sent from all lands, to be educated for work in their own countries. A native priest-hood, thoroughly indoctrinated in Roman ideas, has since then been the mainstay of Roman missions to non-Christian lands.

The methods of Jesuit missionaries raised doubts at home. Father Nobili was permitted by his superiors in the Order to adopt the dress of a Brahman and avoid contact with low-caste people in India. So unchristian a device for making Christians was sternly opposed by the Dominicans; and after a century the "Malabar Usages" were condemned at Rome. So also in China, Ricci used his extensive knowledge of science to win the respect of Mandarins, then adopted their silk dress and worked exclusively among them. His successors permitted converts to continue the worship of ancestors, as the Chinese equivalent of Catholic prayers for the dead and invocation of the saints. These "Chinese Usages" were also forbidden at length. But the work of the early Jesuits, hampered by these controversies, nevertheless proved permanent.

Jesuit missions appeared at their best in America. In the West Indies and South America the cruelties practised by Spaniards upon the natives had made the word Christian hateful. The Spanish Jesuit, Las Casas, crossed the Atlantic seven times, to wring from the Spanish Government an edict protecting the natives, and particularly forbidding that they be made slaves. A Portuguese Jesuit, Antonio Vieira, did a similar work in Brazil, teaching the natives arts and crafts, as well as the Catholic faith, and fighting their enslavement by Europeans. In Paraguay, too, the Jesuits found their work so hampered by the evil example of European Christians that they persuaded the Spanish Government in 1610 to transfer to them the entire administration of Paraguay. They excluded other Europeans, converted the natives, treated them as children, taught them to be farmers and shepherds, and excluded all forms of knowledge thought harmful. Paraguay became a peaceful and happy community of children, until the system collapsed with the expulsion of the Jesuits, a century and a half later.

In Canada French Jesuits began work in 1611, and some suffered

4 *Congregatio de Propaganda Fide.*

martyrdom at the hands of the Iroquois Indians; but men were never lacking to fill their places, and in 1675 Louis XIV established the first bishopric at Quebec.

While bloody events were transpiring in France and the Netherlands, and Mother Church was mending the frayed garment of her righteousness, the situation was confused in lands no longer Catholic. In Germany there was prolonged and devastating strife. Germany, like her neighbours, had enemies abroad; and in addition was hopelessly divided within her own borders. Germany was a land of many scores of principalities, each jealous for its own rights, and all loosely bound together in the Holy Roman Empire by the uncertain authority of an elected emperor. So a disunited Germany was forfeiting its "place in the sun," a place it would one day embroil the whole world to recover.

Between the German principalities, and within them, the antagonism between Catholic and Protestant was as sharp as in France, with this further aggravation, that Protestantism was itself divided. Luther's attempt at purity of doctrine, through loyalty to the Scriptures, had not worked out as he expected. Men read out of the Scriptures conflicting doctrines, and into the Scriptures doctrines they had really learned elsewhere. So Lutheranism was not the only form of Protestantism in the German States. Of its rivals, Calvinism was most widespread and vigorous.

By the Peace of Augsburg only Lutheran Protestants had been given legal rights in Germany. This conflicted with another provision of the Peace, that the religion of a prince was to be the religion of his principality. It eventuated that some Protestant princes were not Lutherans.

More disappointing still, Lutheranism was itself divided. Luther's experience of salvation by faith in God was not repeated in the Lutheran rank and file; and when Luther died, faith tended to be interpreted as belief in what the great reformer had taught. So a Protestant scholasticism arose, as complete as ever ruled in the Catholic Church. Reasoning about religious things began by assuming the truth of the Augsburg Confession and other Lutheran standards.

Even so, men would differ, as mediaeval scholastics had differed. Loyal to the same standards, they did not draw from them the same inferences. Philip Melancthon, influenced by Humanism, did not think mankind so helpless as Luther had believed, and taught that a man must co-operate with God in his own salvation. Melanchton did not stress Christ's physical presence in the bread and wine of the Supper, tending rather to the doctrine of a spiritual presence. Christ was given, "not in the bread, but with the bread," a doctrine more Calvinistic than Lutheran.

Thus Melancthon and those who thought with him found themselves bitterly attacked by conservative Lutherans; and when Melancthon lay dying in 1560, he was willing to go, that he might escape "the rage of the theologians."

Tension in Protestant Germany grew with the steady advance of Calvinism into the southwest. Frederick III, Elector of the Palatinate, was led by his studies to adopt Calvin's doctrine of the Supper. Theologians, having been appointed by him to draw up a creed, prepared the *Heidelberg Catechism,* quite the gentlest and most attractive exposition of Calvinism then known. The Elector adopted it for the Palatinate in 1563; and, since Calvinism had no legal standing in Germany, both Lutherans and Catholics protested.

As the fiftieth anniversary of the Augsburg Confession approached, a number of Lutheran theologians of various States, troubled by the dissensions, framed a creed they thought all Lutherans could accept. It was the *Formula of Concord,* the last great Lutheran creed, and was published in 1580. Fifty-one princes, thirty-five cities, and more than eight thousand ministers approved it; but a few princes and cities refused. The new creed was too technical, too scholastic; and disciples of Melancthon, or "Philippists," thereafter turned increasingly to Calvinism, which made great advances in Germany. Most influential of those adopting Calvinism was the electoral house of Brandenburg, the Hohenzollerns.

Revived Catholicism, led by the Jesuits and supported by Catholic princes like the Dukes of Bavaria, had a great advantage over a Protestantism so divided. Duke Albert V of Bavaria used the Peace of Augsburg to oust his Protestant nobles and people. In Austria and Bohemia the position of Protestants became steadily worse. And in 1608, in the Reichstag for all Germany, Catholics demanded the restoration of all church property confiscated since 1555. They were strictly within the Peace of Augsburg in so doing; but such restitution would involve districts which a half-century had made solidly Protestant.

In these circumstances a number of Protestant princes formed a "Union" for common defence; and Catholic princes, led by Duke Maximilian of Bavaria, countered with a "League." It needed only a spark to set the land aflame. The conflagration began in Bohemia.

The Protestants of Bohemia were sufficiently numerous and influential to extract from their king in 1609 a Charter of Toleration, the *Majestätsbrief.* Three years later King Rudolf was succeeded by his feeble and childless brother Matthias, who was emperor also and absent from Bohemia for long periods. The Protestants there soon found their cherished charter being administered against their interests by Catholic regents. When at length a decree denied to Protestants the right of assembly, there was a heated interview of Bohemian nobles with two Catholic regents in the *Hradshin,* the great fortress-palace that looks down upon Prague. This was in May, 1618. In the altercation the two regents and a private secretary were thrown from a window into the castle moat.[5] Soon afterward the Emperor Matthias died; and his cousin, the Hapsburg Ferdinand of Styria, became both king of Bohemia and emperor.

Ferdinand of Styria, the Emperor Ferdinand II, was the first pupil of a Jesuit college to become emperor. His mind had been narrowed and directed by Jesuit teaching. He hated Protestants, and was determined to exterminate them wherever he ruled. As early as 1598 he had begun persecution in Styria, and gradually carried it through all his Austrian dominions. The Protestant movement there was crushed, and the intellectual and religious life brought under the iron rule of the Jesuits.

Protestant nobles of Bohemia were already in revolt, at the prospect of Ferdinand's accession. They were defeated in November, 1620, by imperial forces under Baron Tilly, a Walloon general brought in from the Netherlands. Their lands were confiscated, chiefly to the advantage of the Jesuits, and the Catholic revival enforced through all Bohemia.

The ensuing war spread to the Palatinate, and then to the Protestant north, raging with varying fortunes until 1648. Motives were always mixed; and political lines crossed religious. King Gustavus Adolphus of Sweden, who intervened on the Protestant side, was an honest

[5] This is the famous "Defenestration of Prague," literally the "out-the-windowing."

champion of Protestantism, but was also bent on turning the Baltic into a Swedish lake and making Swedish trade secure. Cardinal Richelieu, who took France into alliance with Gustavus Adolphus, was presumably a convinced Catholic; but he was less concerned about Bohemian heretics than for the glory of the French crown. Richelieu was simply resuming the ancient quarrel of France with the Hapsburgs of Austria and Spain, by assisting their enemies. In the end all religious idealism vanished; and the war degenerated into a struggle on German soil, between Bourbon and Hapsburg interests, for ascendancy in Europe.

By the Peace of Westphalia, 1648, Ferdinand [6] was acknowledged to be rightful king of Bohemia, and the crown to be hereditary in his family. The Hapsburg dominions in Germany were thus to be Austria and Bohemia. Sweden secured the German shore of the Baltic, and France most of Alsace, a doubtful gain, since it provoked German resentment and sowed the seeds of future strife. The Palatinate, conquered by the armies of Tilly and Maximilian of Bavaria, was transferred by the emperor, on his own authority, to Maximilian.

The religious results were important. It was not to be expected that Catholic and Protestant would learn in the violence of war to love each other, but out of hard necessity the Peace of Augsburg was now changed. Though the rule remained that the religion of the prince was to be the religion of his principality, it was modified to this extent, that minorities existing in any principality in 1624 were to be permitted to continue. This did not apply to Austria and Bohemia, where the emperor would concede no privileges to Protestants. The Hapsburg dominions were delivered over to the Jesuits; and there no heretic should preach or worship. In the Palatinate, too, the stronghold of Calvinism in western Germany, Protestantism was banned. Elsewhere, however, Calvinists were now recognized as one party with Lutherans, having legal rights in Germany, as against Catholics.

The social effects of the Thirty Years' War were disastrous for Germany. For a generation lawless, plundering armies had crossed and recrossed her soil. Fields were laid waste, commerce and industry destroyed. Intellectual life stagnated, morals were corrupted, religion depressed. Germany, which in the sixteenth century stood in the forefront of European civilization, sank in the seventeenth to a near-

[6] Now Ferdinand III, son of Ferdinand of Styria.

barbarism. Yet in this desolate time lived Jacob Böhme, great Protestant mystic, a shoemaker of Görlitz, whose life distilled a fragrance that time has not dissipated. Here, too, belongs Paul Gerhardt, greatest of Lutheran hymn writers, who sang amidst the carnage about faith and courage:

> Give to the winds thy fears;
> Hope, and be undismayed;
> God hears thy sighs, and counts thy tears;
> God shall lift up thy head.

CHAPTER XX

THE AFTERMATH OF RELIGIOUS REVOLUTION: GREAT BRITAIN

WHILE the wars of religion raged on the continent, and Catholic princes and the Jesuits struggled to subject men again to the Catholic Church, events in England were making it clear that such an attempt was hopeless in the island kingdom. When Elizabeth was declared excommunicate and deposed in 1570, and a foreign plot against her life was uncovered, Parliament replied by making it high treason to question the orthodoxy of the queen or her title to the throne. And when the Jesuits began a mission to England in 1580, led by two English exiles, Edmund Campion and Robert Parsons, Campion was seized and executed. Parsons escaped to the continent and intrigued for a Spanish invasion of England and a Catholic rising there. Very unfortunately he won to his plans William Allen, a Catholic exile, who had established at Douai a seminary to educate young English priests. His students were crossing to England in considerable numbers, and seem to have been without treasonable designs. Nevertheless their presence was resented; and when Parsons' plot was discovered, these priests were hunted down and executed.

But the main issues in all Britain were between parties that agreed in their rejection of Rome, but differed about other things. In England were Anglicans and Puritans and Congregationalists, in Scotland Episcopalians and Presbyterians.

As we have seen (p. 417), Puritan clergymen in the Church of England began to meet apart as early as 1573, to discuss religious questions and learn the art of preaching; and soon these "prophesyings" spread through the country. Archbishop Grindal was suspended for refusing to suppress them; and Archbishop Whitgift made many Puritans exiles by enforcing conformity to the Elizabethan Settlement.

The foremost leader of the Puritan party was Thomas Cartwright, Lady Margaret Professor of Divinity at Cambridge. Another Cambridge scholar, Walter Travers, published in 1574 the *Declaration of Ecclesiastical Discipline,* which became the standard for Puritans. Most had no thought, however, of separating from the Church of England. They thought to introduce as much of Puritan practice as possible, and await changes by Parliament.

There were some, however, who thought delay sinful. They would establish at once what they believed the Scriptures to require. They were the Separatists, the first Congregationalists. As early as 1567 the authorities in London imprisoned a congregation of Separatists, who had left the Church of England and chosen for themselves a minister and a deacon. The congregation seems to have been extinguished. Another Puritan, however, Robert Browne, adopted Separatist principles in 1580 and founded a Congregational Church at Norwich. He was imprisoned, and on release sought refuge in Holland, with most of his congregation. Here he published *A Treatise of Reformation without Tarrying for Any,* and another, *A Book which showeth the Life and Manners of all true Christians*, which set forth the principles of Congregationalism.

According to Browne, the only true Church is the local company of believers in Christ, bound to him and to each other by a voluntary covenant. Christ is its head; and it is ruled by such laws and officers as he appointed at the first—pastor, teacher, elders and deacons. Each church is self-governing, and chooses for itself these officers. No church has authority over any other; but each owes all others a brotherly interest.

Congregationalism reappeared in England in 1587, when John Greenwood, a clergyman, and Henry Barrowes, a lawyer, were arrested for holding Separatist meetings in London. From prison they smuggled treatises, to be printed in Holland, attacking both Anglicans and Puritans and explaining Congregational principles. Some converts were made; and a Congregational Church was formed in London in 1592. Next year Greenwood and Barrowes were hanged for denying the royal supremacy in the Church; and Parliament passed a statute, banishing all who should challenge the queen's authority or attend worship in unauthorised conventicles.

The Separatist movement survived, however, to plague the aged queen. A few months before her death John Smyth, a Puritan clergyman, adopted Separatist principles and established a church at Gainsborough. Its influence spread; and another congregation was formed in the home of William Brewster at Scrooby, which soon received as minister a learned and lovable clergyman of the Church of England, John Robinson. In a few years both congregations took refuge in Holland, the former at Amsterdam, the latter at Leyden.

At Amsterdam the Separatists came into contact with a Protestant sect of the continent, the Mennonites, who, like those Anabaptists we met at Zurich, rejected the baptism of infants as unscriptural. A reexamination of the New Testament convinced the Separatists. Smyth re-baptised himself, and then his parishioners; and when part of the congregation returned to England, in 1611 or 1612, it became the first Baptist Church on English soil. Congregationalism, too, was permanently replanted in England in 1616, when a part of John Robinson's congregation at Leyden returned and established a church at Southwark.[1]

From all this it is clear that the Elizabethan Settlement did not settle all religious questions in England, and that the civil power could not coerce the consciences of all. In Elizabeth's last years, Puritans were still active within the Church of England, looking forward to changes in the Church by law, while other Puritans had become Separatists, who were being separated from each other also, by their loyalty to one principle or another, drawn from the New Testament.

When Elizabeth died in 1603, and James VI of Scotland became James I of England also, the Puritans looked to him hopefully. James had been brought up in Presbyterianism, and might be expected to understand. The Puritans forgot that James had struggled long and hard to turn the nominal bishops of Scotland into genuine governing bishops, under the royal control, and thus put an end to the Presbyterian system. In this he had been sternly opposed by the Church, under the leadership of

---

[1] The most memorable event, however, in the history of the Leyden Congregational Church was the decision to send a mission to America. John Robinson reluctantly stayed with the Leyden Congregation; but its elder, William Brewster, led the mission across the Atlantic in the *Mayflower* in 1620. These "Pilgrim Fathers" founded the colony of Plymouth and planted Congregationalism in New England.

Andrew Melville, who had succeeded to something of the moral authority of Knox. Melville had been a teacher under Theodore Beza, in the Academy at Geneva. He was firmly rooted in Calvinism, and bound in conscience to the independence of the Church. "I must tell you," he said to King James, "there are two kings and two kingdoms in Scotland; there is King James the Head of this Commonwealth; and there is Christ Jesus the King of the Church, whose subject James the Sixth is, and of whose kingdom he is not a king nor a lord nor a head, but a member."

James did not think so. His religion was the Divine Right of Kings; and he perceived, as he said, that "a Scots presbytery agreeth as well with a monarchy as God with the devil." And James Stuart was a very determined person. By 1597 he was strong enough in Scotland to enforce the view that General Assemblies could meet only by his command. Now he was king at Westminster also.

James I (1603–1625) was the strange offspring of that sad *mesalliance* of Mary Stuart and Darnley. He was clever, learned and humorous, but conceited and without political acumen. He had a wrong theory of Parliament, and a certain witlessness in proclaiming it. Parliament, he said, had no legislative function of its own, only such as he conferred. The shaping of national policy and the directing of the national church were his affair.

The ancient tradition of English rule was parliamentary. The Tudor despotism had been an interlude, tolerable only as a relief from the Wars of the Roses, and commended by the personal popularity of Henry VIII and Elizabeth. When the peril of the Spanish Armada was safely passed, Elizabeth herself had more than once to bow before the reviving spirit of independence in Parliament. James I, with none of her grace and no understanding of England, had no chance for a successful despotism.

On James' arrival in England several hundreds of the Puritan clergy presented to him the "Millenary Petition," [2] asking that the wearing of the surplice be made optional and that clergymen be permitted to use the Prayer-Book, without declaring their belief in all it contained. King James summoned a conference to Hampton Court to consider the petition, and there denied the Puritan request. "I will make them con-

[2] "Millenary" because it professed to express the views of a thousand clergymen.

form," he said, "or I will harry them out of the land." Only one important concession was made; there was to be a new translation of the Scriptures. The Authorised, or King James, Version of the Bible was completed in some seven years, and in so admirable a manner that it retains its hold on English-speaking Christians still, in the face of a Revised Version, made by British and American scholars.

For the rest, Puritans were ordered to conform; and Convocation followed up the Hampton Court Conference by making compulsory many practices that offended the Puritan conscience. As a result, some three hundred clergymen resigned their livings; and the Separatist movement gathered force, as we have seen, with some emigration to Holland and America.

Puritanism became stronger and stronger politically through all the reign of James I. His arbitrary treatment of Parliament, and the identification of Anglicanism with his policies, made the House of Commons sympathetic with Puritanism.

The situation was even more strained in Scotland. In 1610, with Melville and others already in exile, James established two courts of High Commission, each under an archbishop, and both usurping the authority of Presbyteries and the General Assembly. In 1612 a Parliament, packed with the king's minions, restored to the bishops their ancient diocesan authority, diminishing further the authority of Presbyteries. In 1621 James forced through both Assembly and Parliament enactments requiring the confirmation of baptised persons by bishops, kneeling at Communion, the observing of Catholic Christian festivals. Scotland was seething with religious discontent when James died in 1625.

Charles I (1625–1649) was a man of more dignity than his father, of exemplary family life, and sincerely religious; but he too was a Stuart and ill suited to England. A modern biographer describes him as "part woman, part priest, and part the bewildered delicate boy who had never quite grown up." [3] From the beginning he had the collaboration of an ecclesiastic who had quite grown up, in the authoritarian school. William Laud was an Oxford don, of strong but narrow mind, morbidly conscientious and a martinet, bent on uniformity in the Church. James I on his accession had found Laud an ardent young Anglican, hostile to

[3] John Buchan, *Oliver Cromwell*, p. 120.

Calvinism, and outspoken in the conviction that "there could be no true church without bishops."

In 1628 Charles made Laud bishop of the strongly Puritan diocese of London, and in 1633 Archbishop of Canterbury. At sixty years of age he was therefore the foremost prelate of England. He was as well the king's chief political adviser.

Under the guidance of Laud, King Charles was soon at odds with Parliament. The House of Commons was Calvinistic in sympathy. Charles tried to stop Calvinistic interpretations of the Thirty-Nine Articles by decreeing that no man should "put his own sense" on any Article, but should "take it in the literal and grammatical sense." The House of Commons was jealous for its control of taxation. Charles imposed taxes by his own authority and imprisoned some who refused to pay, while a royal chaplain, Roger Manwaring, preached that the king ruled as representing God and that those who refused to pay taxes thereby risked damnation. Relations between king and Parliament became so strained that Charles dismissed the House in 1629, and ruled without it eleven years.

During these years Laud enforced religious uniformity with a heavy hand; and many Puritans despaired of England. Emigration to Massachusetts had already begun; and in 1630 John Winthrop went thither with a considerable band. Churches sprang up around Massachusetts Bay, under clergymen like John Cotton and Richard Mathers, who had no wish to leave the Church of England but could not find freedom of conscience within it. At least twenty thousand Puritans migrated to New England in ten years. The colony of Connecticut was established in 1636, that of New Haven in 1638.

The colonists were united in the principle that the Bible is the sole authority for Church organization, and that it requires independent local churches. Those of New England began therefore as Congregational churches.

The first great achievement of Archbishop Laud was thus, quite unexpectedly, the foundation of the New England colonies. The second, equally unexpected, was an armed rising in Scotland against the Prayer-Book. James I had not ventured to abolish the Presbyterian form of worship in Scotland. King Charles, encouraged by Laud in a fatuous desire for uniformity, imposed upon the Scottish churches in 1637 the Anglican liturgy. There was disorder in St. Giles and other churches. A National Covenant to defend true religion was widely signed. The General Assembly deposed the bishops, and repudiated the whole ecclesiastical structure established by James and Charles.

By 1640 King Charles determined to reduce Scotland to order, and found it necessary to summon the English Parliament to secure supplies. When Parliament renewed its old complaints, it was promptly dissolved; but a Scottish army was soon on English soil, and Charles was compelled to recall Parliament. It proved to be the "Long Parliament," and is justly famous as that in which the country gentlemen of England, led by Pym and Hampden, set final limits to the royal authority, with far-reaching consequences for political liberty throughout the world. This Parliament of angry men abolished those special courts, like the Star Chamber and the High Commission Court, through which the sovereign could bring citizens to trial, outside the ordinary Judiciary; and it declared illegal the raising of money by the sovereign, except through Parliament. Thenceforth the civil rights of a citizen were not to be infringed by the sovereign; and Parliament would direct public policy, through control of public finance.

A rising of Irish Catholics, and a great massacre of Protestants, raised in Parliament the question of the army. Pym determined that Parliament, not the king, should officer the army for Ireland. Parliament would then control the army, as well as finance and the Church.

To all this Charles would not assent. He determined to impeach Pym, Hampden and three others, and came with royal officers to the House in January, 1642, to arrest them. "The birds were flown"; and six days later Charles himself fled from the hostile London crowds. Very soon England was in civil war, in which the South and East stood with Parliament, the North and West with the king.

Parliament, with the support of the city of London, drove forward with measures to change the character of the State. It abolished episcopacy in the Church of England in January, 1643. A Puritan Church seemed preferable to an Episcopal one, directed by bishops who were nominees of the king, and who were disposed to autocracy in government and ritual in worship.

In July of the same year Parliament, stepping into the place of the sovereign, summoned an assembly of clergy and laymen to meet at

Westminster, to advise Parliament about arrangements for the Church. This "Westminster Assembly" was dominated by Presbyterian Puritans; though it did include a few Anglicans and Congregationalists, or Independents. The Presbyterian preponderance was all the greater because representatives from Scotland soon entered the Assembly. Pym had not hesitated to turn to Scotland for military aid, when the war did not at first go well with the Parliamentary forces. The Scottish and English Parliaments, too, had entered into a Solemn League and Covenant to oppose "prelacy" and achieve the greatest possible uniformity in religion in England, Scotland and Ireland, on Calvinistic lines. Quite suitably therefore Scots sat in the Westminster Assembly.

The Assembly presented to Parliament in 1644 a Presbyterian plan of church organization and a *Directory of Worship,* embodying a Presbyterian ritual; and Parliament, in January, 1645, abolished the Prayer-Book and adopted the Directory. In the same month Archbishop Laud, who had been four years in prison, was executed; and in June, 1646, Parliament, with considerable misgiving, adopted the Presbyterian form of church government.

The Assembly now prepared the famous *Westminster Confession,* which it submitted to Parliament before the end of the year. Parliament withheld approval until June, 1647, and even then made some changes. The Confession had meanwhile been adopted by the General Assembly in Scotland. It is a notable exposition of Calvinism, and is still the nominal standard of doctrine for Scottish and American Presbyterians.

Meanwhile the civil war had run its course. Early successes of the royalist cause, led by Prince Rupert, nephew of the king, were soon reversed when a great cavalry leader, Oliver Cromwell, emerged from among the members of Parliament. Cromwell and his "Ironsides", a picked troop of "religious men," dashing but disciplined, overcame the royalist forces at Marston Moor, near York, in 1645, and again at Naseby in 1646. King Charles gave himself up to the Scots, who surrendered him to the English Parliament.

Cromwell's army was a body of religious enthusiasts, including Baptists, Congregationalists, Puritans, all who were agreed in opposition to Rome and "prelacy." It disliked a compulsory Presbyterianism as much as rule by bishops; and its dislike prevented the establishment of that full Presbyterianism, proposed by the Westminster Assembly and approved by Parliament.

The attitude of the army displeased the Scots. It was not for this, they thought, that they had entered into a Solemn League and Covenant with England, and had sent Scots to fight beside Yorkshiremen at Marston Moor. King Charles was quick to turn their displeasure to account. He intrigued with Scottish leaders to invade England, intimating that he would support Presbyterianism. A Scottish army came in August, 1648, only to be scattered by Cromwell's men at Preston; and Cromwell returned from the North determined to deal finally with "the man of blood," who seemed to think little of England and less of good faith. Parliament was purged of all members opposed to the army's policy; and Charles was then brought to trial for his alleged treasons and perfidies, condemned to death, and beheaded before his palace at Whitehall, in January, 1649. Charles the Martyr died like an English gentleman and saint, and erased from many minds his grave and numerous faults.

That year Cromwell subjugated Ireland, the next year Scotland; and in 1651 the remnants of the royalist forces in England were defeated at Worcester. Opposition was at an end, and Cromwell "Protector" of the British Isles. He was himself an Independent, and predisposed to religious toleration, except for "Papists." The pope was still the "man of sin"; and Cromwell wrote his name in blood in the history of Ireland, in a swift and cruel campaign to make the island English and Protestant.

As for the Scots, though they had resisted Charles and Laud and had refused the Prayer-Book, they did not warm to English sects that executed a Stuart king. They welcomed his son to Scotland, and crowned him Charles II at Scone, in September, 1650. He was least Scottish of all the Stuarts, a gay and sprightly youth, of no religion, who was probably diverted by the Solemn League and Covenant he was required to sign. Not unsuitably, therefore, hopes of the restoration of the Stuarts, through Scottish Presbyterianism, were shattered by Cromwell within a year, with victories at Dunbar and Worcester. The Parliament at Edinburgh was suppressed, as was that at Dublin; and for the first time, and only briefly, one Parliament legislated at Westminster for the British Isles, under the Protector.

Oliver Cromwell died in 1658, with genuine achievements to his credit. He had advanced the toleration that would yet become a substantial element in English liberty. He had established briefly the supremacy of moral considerations in public policy. Abroad he had entered into the long Anglo-Portuguese alliance, that opened to the English fleet the splendid harbour of Lisbon, and made it possible for her, before the age of steam, to become a Mediterranean power. He had waged the first of three Anglo-Dutch wars, that brought England to maritime supremacy in the world. Nevertheless his brief rule was but an interlude in the domestic history of England. Against his own nature, he was compelled by circumstances to rule by force. His position in the public mind was further compromised by the men who shared with him administrative responsibility. England was divided into eleven districts, each administered by a quasi-military officer, whose duty it was to give effect to the ancient theocratic idea of government. Keeping the public peace, he was expected also to suppress vice and promote virtue. Most of those appointed were low-born men, of rigid views. England was better disposed toward men high-born, though lax. And, being pleasure loving, the English people were irked by the compulsory godliness of Puritan rule.

Oliver Cromwell was succeeded as Protector by his son Richard, a man without force; and in less than two years Presbyterians combined with Royalists to bring back the monarchy.

Charles II (1660–1685) profited by the national recoil from Puritanism. His own lightness and irreligion mattered less on that account. His first Parliament was fiercely Royalist and Anglican. The first Convocations of Canterbury and York made many changes in the Prayer-Book, but none in the direction of Puritanism. One more Act of Uniformity required all clergymen to use the revised Prayer-Book, and each must swear "unfeigned assent and consent to all and everything contained and prescribed" therein. He must swear also "that it is not lawful, upon any pretense whatever, to take arms against the King."

These provisions were meant to banish Puritanism from the Church of England, and were effective. Nearly two thousand clergymen refused the oath and gave up their parishes. The Puritan party was thenceforth outside the Church. Puritans had become "Dissenters"; and oppressive Acts of Parliament sought to make it impossible for them to form congregations for preaching and public worship.

In Scotland Parliament did not dare to restore the Anglican liturgy of public worship, but it did restore episcopacy; and church officials were required to renounce the Covenants of 1638 and 1643.

Many Presbyterian ministers were now removed from their parishes. A High Commission Court was recreated, to enforce religious obedience. In consequence "Covenanters," or supporters of the Covenants, rose in rebellion in 1666. The rebellion was crushed, the rebels treated with great cruelty, and James, brother of the king, put in charge of Scottish affairs. He was a Roman Catholic, of sterner stuff than his royal brother and of less perception. Under him "Cameronians," as uncompromising Presbyterians were called,[4] became hunted outlaws.

The intentions of the shifty king were suspect in both Scotland and England. He probably favoured Catholicism, as being ancient, the religion of his fathers and of France, for which he had the Stuart predilection. In any case, when, on his own authority, he issued a Declaration of Indulgence for England in 1672, Parliament forced its withdrawal. While granting Dissenters the right of public worship, the Declaration also remitted the penal laws against Catholics. This was thought to be its real intention; and Parliament balked. The position of Catholics was already fixed. Only the status of Protestants was still debatable. In place of the Declaration of Indulgence, Parliament passed a Test Act, requiring civil and military officers, within thirty miles of Protestant London, to participate in the rites of the Church of England. The Act was aimed at Catholics, but bore heavily on Dissenters as well.

Charles II died in 1685, and was succeeded by his brother James, Duke of York.

James II (1685-1688) was a man of conviction and courage, who cared nothing for constitutional history and much for the Divine Right of Kings. He was as well an ardent Catholic, whose chief aim was the restoration of Catholicism in Britain. From the outset he ignored the Test Act and appointed Catholics to office. He encouraged the monks to return, after an absence from England of nearly two centuries, and brought in the Jesuits. He packed the Court of King's Bench, secured

---

[4] From one of their leaders, Richard Cameron.

from it a judgment that the sovereign might "dispense with all penal laws in particular cases," then re-established the High Commission Court. On his own authority James issued a Declaration of Indulgence, granting religious freedom to everyone.

Parliament was aroused by this usurpation of its functions. Protestants were alarmed at the prospect for religion. Everyone knew that the ultimate aim of the Declaration of Indulgence was to make England again a Roman Catholic country. Dissenters, though relieved of their own disabilities by the Indulgence, united with Anglicans against it. When in April, 1688, James ordered the Declaration read in all the churches, seven bishops protested, were brought to trial and acquitted, amidst public demonstrations of joy. James had gone too far.

The direction of events was similar in Scotland, where James filled his Privy Council with Catholics, issued Letters of Indulgence for all faiths, and raised both Episcopalians and Presbyterians against him.

It must have been plain to all informed men, except bigots, that wherever England and Scotland might go in religion, they would not return to Rome. Though a hundred years had elapsed since the battered hulls of Spanish ships strewed British shores from the Channel to the Orkneys, the horror of the Spanish Inquisition and the nameless cruelties of Spain in the Netherlands still lived in English hearts. Persecution had even now broken out again in France. In the very year when James II came to the English throne, Louis XIV and his fanatical wife, Madame de Maintenon, renewed the attack upon the Huguenots. The protection given them by the Edict of Nantes was withdrawn in 1685. They were first persecuted, then expelled. Their knowledge and industry and skill were transferred to Protestant lands, to enrich the rivals of France and remind them that the danger of a Catholic reconquest was not quite past. The vivid dread of Catholic tyranny somewhat palliates, though it cannot excuse, the violence of Protestant repressive measures in the British Isles. Britain was the spearhead of Protestant resistance to Louis XIV.

And so in 1688, when James II thought to undo the work of nearly two hundred years, English leaders called in William of Orange, Stadholder of the Dutch Republic and great-grandson of that William the Silent who had saved Holland from Spain. William was a Protestant above suspicion, and was as well the husband of the Princess Mary, daughter of James himself but a Protestant.

William landed with an army at Torbay, on November 5, 1588; and the "glorious revolution" followed, glorious for England in that it was effected without bloodshed.[5] The Protestantism of London, the eastern counties and the fleet secured that neither lord nor bishop would raise a banner for King James. The Catholic Counter-Reformation was defeated, so far as England was concerned, and Protestantism secure enough at last to be tolerant. There were no outrages upon the vanquished party.

The steadfast Protestant mind of William III (1688–1702) did great things for Britain. Bred in the republican tradition of Holland and the House of Orange, William succeeded in making Britain a united country, under parliamentary control. Louis XIV, observing from the continent, thought it would not be so, that the transfer of authority from the crown to Parliament would mean divided counsels, venality and instability. There was plenty of all these things in Britain; but free discussion in Parliament, by the landed gentry, proved a safer road to public order and financial stability than did the autocracy of France, working through personal servants of the king, "Intendants," in the provinces. Europe was to learn also, from the victories of Marlborough at Blenheim and Ramillies, that a parliamentary government could conduct a successful war, while permitting no standing armies in times of peace. The general admiration of English institutions, felt throughout Europe in the eighteenth century, began with the reign of William III.

As for the religious settlement, William stamped resolutely upon the fires of vengeance, and happily had the co-operation in so doing of Lord Halifax and other parliamentary leaders. Some of the clergy had themselves made their continuance in the National Church impossible. They had maintained the Divine Right of Kings during the Stuart tyranny; and, to their eternal credit, did not now recognize the Revolution. Seven bishops and some four hundred clergymen were on that account removed, and bore themselves with commendable courage and dignity.[6]

As for those outside the Church of England, a Toleration Act in 1689 declared that all who would take the oath of allegiance to the sovereigns

---

[5] Most of the fighting was in Ireland; and here the victory of William at the Boyne, and the surrender of Limerick, subjected Catholic Ireland for two hundred and forty-two years to the political dominion of Protestant England.

[6] They are the "Nonjurors," who died out in time.

and renounce the Pope, the Mass, the worship of the Virgin and the saints, might have freedom of worship, within the doctrinal limits of the Thirty-Nine Articles. Diverse forms of Protestantism could therefore exist side by side.

It was only a partial liberation. Protestant Dissenters—Baptists and Congregationalists, Presbyterians and a strange new sect, the Quakers— were required to pay tithes to the National Church and endured other disabilities. They had the substance, without all the appurtenances, of religious liberty. As for those Protestants who denied the doctrine of the Trinity, they were held not to be Christians, and had no legal recognition. Nor had Roman Catholics, who were to regain liberty only after another hundred years and more.

The Revolution raised some special difficulties in Scotland. Presbyterians there approved the Calvinism of "Dutch William"; but Episcopalians liked it as little as the Catholicism of James. Parliament, however, in 1689, recognized William and Mary as sovereigns, and in 1690 restored all Presbyterian ministers who had been deprived under Charles II and James II, and declared Presbyterianism the national religion of Scotland.

Cameronians and Episcopalians were equally disappointed. The former disapproved of all control of the Church by the State, and thought, too, that the Covenants ought to be renewed. Episcopalians, who were numerous in northern Scotland, yearned for bishops and a ritual.[7]

Great Britain was now as securely Protestant as law could make her; and, to assure that no future sovereign should try to undo what had been done, the English Parliament in 1700 passed an Act of Settlement, fixing the succession to the throne and decreeing that whoever, by the provisions of the Act, should in future receive the crown must "join in communion with the Church of England, as by law established." King William "ratified and confirmed" the Act; and for two hundred years a Catholic in religion was thereby debarred from the throne of Great Britain and Ireland.

One portent, little understood, appeared in England in this Stuart period, foreshadowing that Protestantism itself would not endure for-

---

[7] One more Act of Toleration, in 1712, permitted them to use the English Prayer-Book in public worship.

ever. George Fox, a shoemaker's apprentice, some twenty-five years old, interrupted the clergyman in an Anglican church at Nottingham, and was charged and imprisoned under the Blasphemy Act. It was in the year when Charles I died for insisting on the divine authority of kings; and the Nottingham clergyman, a man of Puritan principles, was proclaiming the divine authority of the Bible. Fox was moved to rise in his seat and interject that not the Scriptures but the inner illumination, by which prophets and apostles had spoken in the Scriptures, was the authoritative thing. That "inner light," Fox said, is given to believers still.

Three years before, in 1646, George Fox had had a transforming religious experience, and in 1647 had begun a stormy preaching mission throughout the land. His doctrines were neither Catholic nor Protestant. Fox would have no consecrated churches, only "meeting-houses," since one building is as sacred as another. He would have neither priest nor minister to lead the people, but all men and women to whom God gave the inner light. He rejected sacraments, since every deed a Christian does is to be a sacrament, or means of grace. He would not take an oath, since every word a Christian speaks must be as sacred as an oath. He would not acknowledge titles or social grades, since all men are brothers. He would not go to war, since lawful ends cannot be attained by violence and hatred.

Fox found many disciples. A "Society of Friends," he called them; "Quakers," the public said in derision. By 1661 more than three thousand were imprisoned. Their radical departure from Protestantism was the denial that divine revelation is complete in the Scriptures. The Protestant Reformers had conceded formally that Reason and Nature are sources of a knowledge of God. It was but a bow in passing to the mind of man and the physical world; they concentrated their attention upon the Bible. Its writers were "the sure and authentic amanuenses of the Holy Spirit." No one like them had appeared before, or would appear again. So Protestantism preserved the ancient distinction between Reason and Revelation.

The distinction could be maintained in the Middle Ages, when there was no popular interest in such questions. It wore thin in the late Scholastics and the early Humanists; but they, too, were a numerically insignificant minority. Now, however, Protestantism was setting itself to educate the masses, that they might read for themselves the revealed

Word of God. They would read, finding what the Reformers had found, but much else besides. They would stray as well into other fields, satisfying both intellectual curiosity and the deep needs of the human spirit through observation and experiment. And so there was to arise a science and philosophy and religion, one field of experience, in which revelation would be an aspect of the mental life.

George Fox, all unwitting, belongs in the early stages of this evolution; though Protestantism was not to be seriously shaken for another two hundred years. So firmly do men hold their sacred things.

CHAPTER XXI

NEW FORMS OF PROTESTANTISM; NEW LIFE
IN SCIENCE AND PHILOSOPHY

WE HAVE seen that the Protestant Reformers retained most of the theology they inherited from Mother Church. They were far from being Modernists. But an individual here and there was led by the new freedom to re-examine beliefs that had been unquestioned from ancient times. The Spanish physician and thinker, Miguel Serveto (Latin *Servetus*) died at Geneva, at Calvin's instigation, for denying, among other things, the doctrine of the Trinity.

Servetus left no disciples and founded no school; but two Italians of Siena, contemporaries of Servetus, were more influential. These were Lelio Sozzini (Latin *Socinus*) and his nephew Fausto. Lelio lived briefly at Wittenberg, where he had the friendship of Melancthon, and went thence to several Swiss cities, including Zurich, where he died. His mind had been turned, by the martyrdom of Servetus, to the doctrine of the Trinity; but Lelio Socinus died without making public his conclusions. Fausto, however, already a theological radical, and influenced by his uncle's notes and papers, broke at length with the Roman Church. Having done so, he left Italy to find security at Basel, and finally made his way to Poland, where he lived for twenty-five years, until his death in 1604.

It was in Poland that "Socinianism" was systematized and became a movement. Fausto Socinus and his disciples, "the Polish Brethren," published at Rakow the *Racovian Catechism,* in which Christianity was simplified. Man, it said, cannot by his own efforts find the way to eternal life. So God gave him the Scriptures and the great example Christ, who, for his complete submission to God, was granted resurrection from the dead and a certain delegated divinity. Believers, therefore, may rightly pray to him; but he is not God. As for man, he has some moral capacity and moral freedom. The doctrines of total depravity and unconditional predestination are therefore false.

Socinianism was Protestant in that it was founded on the Scriptures; but its use of Scripture was freer than that of the Reformers. And the most influential of its doctrines was that concerning the atonement. The Reformers had agreed with the Catholic past in regarding the death of Christ as the central fact in redemption. Their view of it was controlled by the same pre-occupation with the justice of God, that had marked Catholic Christianity. An even-handed justice in all His dealings, they said, was necessary to God by His very nature. No overflowing mercy, without regard to justice, was possible to Him, whatever men themselves might do. If then God was to forgive the sins of men, the penalty for their infringement of His laws must nevertheless be exacted. This was done through the death of Christ. As Son of God he exhibited the love of God by going willingly to death; as man he offered for men a sacrifice to God for their sins.

There is here both a contradiction of the teaching of Christ and a confusion of ideas as old as Anselm. Christ had taught that men ought to forgive penitent offenders freely, and so become sons of God, who himself freely forgives.

This is to say, not that justice is unimportant, but that it is not for Himself God demands it. Being more than just Himself, God nevertheless imposes justice upon others, as a sort of minimum morality, without which society is impossible. A retributive justice is written into the constitution of social life. It is God's rules of the game, which remain applicable even to those who have been reconciled to Him through repentance.

It was something like this the Socinians said. The nature of God does not require satisfaction for sins. Forgiveness and the demand for satisfaction are mutually exclusive. Nor is justice vindicated if the sins of the guilty are punished in the innocent. Christ's "obedience unto death" was but the great example of what every Christian owes to truth and right.

Socinianism was suppressed in Poland. Its breach with the past was too great; and the Jesuits were particularly active against it. It found some support, however, in the Netherlands and in England. In England it was the anti-Trinitarian aspect of Socinianism that was most

influential. The last Englishmen burned for their faith were Bartholomew Legate and Edward Wightman, two Unitarians, who died under
James I in 1612. A century later, when what is called *Rationalism* was
growing in England, Unitarian tendencies were also quickened. Samuel
Clarke, rector of St. James Church, Westminster, the most philosophical
of the Anglican clergy, published in 1712 the *Scripture Doctrine of the
Trinity,* in which he championed Unitarian views of Christ. As the
eighteenth century advanced, Unitarianism became a movement in
England.

Meanwhile Protestantism in Holland was flowering in one more
system, destined to be more important than Socinianism. Humanism,
with its liberal-mindedness, had survived in the homes of the Dutch
burghers; and there was more distaste in Holland than elsewhere for
the harsher aspects of Calvinism. Foremost in dissent was Jacobus Arminius (1560–1609). Made an orphan in childhood by the wars with Spain,
he was sent by friends to the University of Leyden, then by the Merchants' Guild of Amsterdam to the University of Geneva. Arminius returned in 1588, to be minister of a Reformed church in Amsterdam and
to become noted for his liberal and conciliatory spirit. In 1603 he was
appointed Professor of Theology in the University of Leyden, where he
died in 1609.

His studies at Leyden had led Arminius to reject the whole doctrine
of unconditional predestination, and to ascribe to man a degree of moral
freedom that had no place in Calvinism. A bitter controversy had con-
sequently flared up, between Arminius and his colleague Gomarus.

After the death of Arminius his views were systematized by others.
The resulting "Arminianism" gave little place to dogma, regarding
Christianity rather as a moral force than as a doctrinal system. Its advocates, encouraged by the patriot and statesman Oldenbarnveldt (*See*
p. 441), drew up a demurrer to Calvinism, called the "Remonstrance." It
was Calvinistic in denying the ability of men to be and do good, except
by the aid of divine grace; but it declared that Christ died for all, not for
the elect only. It expressed doubt, too, of Calvin's doctrine of the perseverance of the saints, thinking it possible for men once "in grace" to
fall from it.

The Netherlands were soon torn by religious controversy, the ablest defender of the "Remonstrants" being the historian and jurist, Hugo Grotius, founder of the Science of International Law. At length a National Synod was called by the States-General. It met at Dort in 1618, and continued in session six months. Delegates were present from England and Switzerland, and from several German States.

The Synod of Dort condemned Arminianism. Its conclusions, the Canons of Dort, were aggressively Calvinistic and were thereafter linked with the Heidelberg Catechism and the Belgic Confession, as the doctrinal standards of the Dutch Church.

The Remonstrants were banished from the Dutch Republic, but were soon permitted to return; though they did not receive legal recognition for nearly two hundred years. In England Arminianism was more influential, being adopted by a considerable number of clergymen of the Church of England, chief of whom was John Wesley.

One is not to think of the tortured seventeenth century, however, as a time of war alone and religious controversy. We have already seen that it was a flowering time in Catholic Christianity; and if Protestants fought each other, one reason was that they felt keenly about religion. The century that produced in England *Pilgrim's Progress, Paradise Lost,* and the *Journal of George Fox,* and in Germany the visions of Boëhme and the hymns of Gerhardt, was not without religious feeling. And one movement in Germany, Pietism, deserves more than passing notice.

Pietism was a reaction against the scholasticism into which Lutheranism had fallen. Lutheranism was now a rigid dogmatic system, demanding intellectual assent. Purity of doctrine and the observance of the sacraments constituted the religious life, quite as in the Roman Church, but more narrowly. For Catholicism emphasized good works, while the vital faith in God, which Luther had trusted to produce good works, had now become faith in the dogmas, which produced instead assent. Some Lutherans yearned for a religion of greater inwardness.

Pietism was an assertion of the primacy of feeling in religion. It stressed, too, the responsibility of the laity, as Luther had done, and recalled Christians to the world-renunciation that the Church had exalted for a thousand years and more. The most effective single cause of all this was Spener, a German of Alsace.

Philipp Jakob Spener (1635–1705) studied in youth at Strassburg and then at Geneva. In both centres he found a more direct approach to the Scriptures, a more careful instruction of youth, and a better church discipline than were then common in Lutheranism. He read, too, devotional writings by English Puritans; but what finally roused him to decision was the book of a recent German ascetic and mystic, Johann Arndt. Arndt, too, had studied at Strassburg and Basel; and then as a Lutheran minister had laboured to bring Lutherans to personal piety. Dying in 1621, Arndt left behind him the memory of a pure and unselfish life and a book, *True Christianity,* whose influence was felt over all Germany. Its purpose was to win students and preachers from a formal piety and the controversial spirit to faith that "works by love." This miracle would happen in those who lived in mystical union with Christ.

Spener returned from Switzerland in 1666, to become superintendent minister of the churches of Frankfort. He tried to give effect to what he had seen at Strassburg and Geneva, but found himself hampered by the subordination of the Church to the civil authority. One notable change, however, began when in 1670 he established in his own home an association for the deepening of the religious life, by Bible reading and conference and prayer. Five years later Spener published a book, the *Pia Desideria,* setting forth his aims. There was need, he said, of a new spirit in the ministry. To defend the dogmas, while caring little about one's own spiritual life, could not awaken spiritual life in one's hearers. Candidates for the ministry should be educated in piety, as well as dogma. Piety, too, was required in the laity, who were forgetting that all Christians are priests, as Luther taught.

Spener's work caused considerable excitement. Many ministers adopted his views and tried to give them effect. Prayer-meetings began in many places. *Collegia pietatis,* they were called, brotherhoods in piety.

Spener's influence grew; and he was called to Dresden in 1686, to be chaplain to the court of the Elector of Saxony. He set himself immediately to reform teaching in the Saxon Universities, Wittenberg and Leipzig. At Leipzig theological students were receiving no education in the Bible, only in dogma and philosophy, dialectic and rhetoric. Leipzig had reverted to the mediaeval tradition. Spener secured from the Elector an order for the restoration of Bible teaching, with a view rather to the quickening of religion than to scholarship; and three young pro-fessors undertook this work, one of whom was a certain August Her-mann Francke. Their classes were soon being attended by townsmen, as well as students, and were resented by the older instructors and ministers. The feeling against the young masters became so strong that they had to leave Leipzig in 1691; and almost simultaneously Spener accepted an invitation to Berlin, having offended the Elector by rebuking his man-ner of life.

A defender of Spener at Leipzig, Christian Thomasius, had already removed to Berlin and had persuaded the Elector of Brandenburg to found a University at Halle. It was the more readily done because candi-dates for the ministry in Calvinistic Brandenburg were being educated at Leipzig and Wittenberg, and were there being prejudiced against Calvinism and the Reformed Church. At Halle the chairs were now filled by nominees of Spener, foremost of whom was Francke; and Halle be-came the centre of Pietism for Germany.

Francke (1663–1727) became a sort of second founder of Pietism. From Halle his preaching and spiritual conferences and works of benevo-lence spread far and wide, while his writings were read everywhere. Schools for the poor were founded, and an orphanage. They were under-taken almost without financial resources and were maintained by prayer, gifts flowing in from all Germany.

Halle also became the Protestant centre for the propagation of the Gospel in non-Christian lands, when as yet Protestants in general recog-nized no missionary obligation. When in 1706 King Frederick IV of Denmark wished to send missionaries to Danish possessions in India, he procured them from Halle; and during the eighteenth century sixty missionaries went from there to foreign lands.

Pietists continued to increase in Germany after the death of Francke. Their numbers can only be guessed, as they did not separate from the Lutheran churches. Piety within Lutheranism, however, became more vital, the tone of the ministry being elevated and its preaching quickened, while the Christian education of youth became more as Luther had in-tended. Devotional study of the Scriptures and a sense of duty spread among the laity, who became more conscious of their spiritual priest-hood. A Puritan note, too, entered Lutheran ethics, with some disposi-tion to a more Spartan simplicity and renunciation of the world.

Meanwhile an intellectual movement was gathering force in Europe, that was independent of both Protestantism and Catholicism. Never since the days of ancient Greece and Rome had men, in any considerable number, speculated freely about Nature and the human mind, guided only by observation and experiment and reflection. The Catholic Church, for rather good reasons, had imposed upon men a different approach to truth. Taking over the leadership of the Mediterranean world when Greece was dead and Rome declining, the Church soon had to deal with a population with little taste for speculation and great need to be reduced to order. In the long struggle for order, the Church acquired a coherent philosophy of life and history, preserved in a closed body of doctrine. It was the premiss from which reasoning now began.

Protestantism was mediaeval in many things. It too thought of doctrine as imposed by an authority outside the human mind, of human nature as depraved and helpless, of the authority of God in the world as direct and arbitrary. In such things Protestantism was as little affected by Humanism as Catholicism had been.

In the seventeenth century a new spirit was abroad. Intellectual freedom followed the wars of religion. Wherever the battle went against Mother Church, the power to impose her beliefs collapsed. Wherever Protestantism split and the right to dissent was conceded, the right to think freely advanced. So there began a very slow permeation of society by new ideas and attitudes.

The Italian Renaissance had long since heralded the approach of the physical sciences. A few men had begun then to speculate whether certain of the ancient Greeks had not been right in fancying the sun to be the centre of the Universe. This heliocentric theory was not elaborated, however, until Nicolaus Copernicus of Poland, a contemporary of Luther. Even then it attracted little attention, and that unfavourable; so much were Catholic minds distracted by the Lutheran affair, and so thoroughly were the Reformers themselves grounded in the Ptolemaic theory. Man was still the centre of the Universe, the world created to be his habitation and the heavenly bodies to illumine it.

Almost a century passed. Then Johann Kepler (1571–1630), a sober Lutheran, developed the Copernican theory but confused the astronomical question by mixing in controversy about the Lord's Supper and getting himself debarred from a professorship at Würtemberg. Simul-

taneously in Italy, Galileo Galilei (1564-1642) of Pisa developed mechanical physics by experimentation, applied the telescope to the study of the
heavens, and finally demonstrated the truth of the Copernican theory.
The publication of his observations in 1632 roused bitter opposition; and
next year Galileo submitted to the Inquisition.

English air was more salubrious; and it was there modern science and
philosophy took root. The reasons are not far to seek. The Catholic
Revival failed to affect England; and the Roman Church had no power
of repression there. England was more secure, and therefore less disposed to persecute, than most lands. The conflicts within Protestantism
were never so bitter and so dangerous as those between Catholic and
Protestant on the continent. Comparatively free, therefore, "the English people received its education from Humanism, the Bible and the
sea. What was lost in the mechanical dislocation of schools throughout
the Reformation was regained by the fresh tides of inspiration, which
passed into the life of the people through these very different sources. In
the Elizabethan age the English, though still rustic, had become a poetry-
loving, music-loving, Bible-loving, and sea-loving people. . . . The romance of geography seized hold of the people, as if anything were possible to an age which had thus enlarged the boundaries of hope and
knowledge." [1]

When the great queen died in 1603, the stage was set for a scientific
movement in England; and Sir Francis Bacon (1561-1626), a contemporary of Kepler and Galileo, had a more responsive audience than
they. The movement began with Bacon's announcement that new knowledge was to be reached by the inductive study of Nature, not by deduc-
tion from Aristotle and the Scholastics. The movement advanced
through all the Stuart tyranny, the Commonwealth and the Revolution.
It reached a sort of consummation just when William and Mary in
Holland were weighing the invitation to England. Sir Isaac Newton
(1642-1727) published the *Principia* in 1687. It submitted a precise
demonstration that the Universe is one vast mechanism, and made a
sensation in Europe. It seemed indisputable now that the motions of the
heavenly bodies were all explicable by gravitation, that mechanical cause
and effect were everywhere, and that the conception of the world as a
field of arbitrary divine action must be abandoned. The world, too, that

[1] H. A. L. Fisher, *A History of Europe*, pp. 639, 640.

had so long been thought the exclusive object of God's concern, was but one of numberless bodies, many of them immeasurably greater.

While men's ideas of the physical world were thus being revolutionized, philosophical speculation began afresh in Europe, under new auspices. The philosophers of the Middle Ages had been ecclesiastics; the new philosophers were laymen. Sir Francis Bacon, who may suitably be regarded as the herald of modern philosophy, was a lawyer and statesman. Interested in science, Bacon became a philosopher also because he saw that the new-methods in science must be carried through to some satisfactory view of human life as a whole. But it was of no use to begin with theological dogmas. Philosophy was already at a standstill, by reason of the dead weight of dogma it carried.

A generation after Bacon modern philosophy was well begun, the effective pioneer being a native of France and a Catholic, René Descartes (1596–1650). Having a passion for knowledge, educated in a famous Jesuit school at La Flèche, Descartes found himself full of doubts. He determined to seek light through the study of himself and the world. "So soon as I was old enough to be no longer subject to the control of my teachers, I abandoned literary pursuits altogether, and, being resolved to seek no other knowledge than that which I was able to find within myself, or in the great book of the world, I spent the remainder of my youth in travelling, . . . and reflecting on all occasions on whatever might present itself. . . . I gradually became emancipated from many errors which tend to obscure the natural light within us, and make us less capable of listening to reason. But after I had spent some years thus in studying the book of the world, and trying to gain some experience, I formed one day the resolution to study within myself.[2]

"I was then in Germany, whither the wars, which were not yet ended there, had summoned me; and when I was returning to the army, from the coronation of the emperor, the coming on of winter detained me in a quarter where, finding no one whom I wished to talk with, and fortunately having no cares nor passions to trouble me, I spent the whole day shut up in a room heated by a stove, where I had all the leisure I desired to hold converse with my own thoughts. . . . As for all the opinions which I had accepted up to that time, I was persuaded that I

[2] *Discourse upon Method*, Part I. Torrey's translation. Henry Holt & Co.

could do no better than get rid of them at once, in order to replace them afterward with better ones, or, perhaps, with the same, if I should succeed in making them square with reason." [3]

Nothing could better illustrate the spirit and method of seventeenth-century philosophy. It was individualistic, rather contemptuous of the past, confident of the power of reason. Emboldened by the achievements of the human mind in the physical sciences, men applied the scientific method to metaphysics, to discover the ultimate meaning of the Universe and of human life. They were suspicious of all that has to do with the emotional life of man, his feelings and aspirations and enthusiasms. They were "rationalistic."

It is unnecessary for our present purpose to describe Descartes' philosophical system. We need only note his significance for the history of religion. The beginning of knowledge, he said, is not faith but doubt. "I have long cherished the belief that there is a God who can do everything, and by whom I was made and created such as I am. But how do I know that he has not caused that there should be no earth, no heavens, no extended body, no figure, no size, no place, and that, nevertheless, I should have perceptions of all these things? . . . I shall suppose, not that God, who is very good and the sovereign source of truth, but that a certain evil genius, no less wily and deceitful than powerful, has employed all his ingenuity to deceive me. I shall think that the heavens, the air, the earth, colours, figures, sounds, and all other external things, are nothing but illusions and idle fancies, which he employs to impose upon my credulity. [4]

"I make the supposition, then, that all things which I see are false. . . . Myself, then! at the very least am I not something?

"But I have already denied that I have any senses or any body; . . . I have persuaded myself that there is nothing at all in the world, that there are no heavens, no earth, no minds, no bodies; am I then also persuaded that I am not? Far from it! Without doubt I exist, if I am persuaded, or if I have thought anything whatever." [5]

The foundation of Descartes' philosophy is therefore the existence of

[3] *Discourse upon Method*, Part II.
[4] *Meditations*, I.
[5] *Meditations*, II.

the self. *I think; therefore I am.* With this point of departure, he takes the road back to certainty.

Following that road, Descartes reaches the certainty that God exists. For to examine one's thinking is to come upon thoughts greater than one could oneself originate. One, therefore, infers a cause great enough for the effect, and is led to believe in God, who implants them in the mind. But it is reason that has brought one to belief.

For the Christian Church of the seventeenth century the sensational things in the Cartesian philosophy, as it is called, were the rejection of Scholasticism and the substitution of two principles—that all conceptions are to be doubted until proved, and that no proof is adequate that has not the certainty of mathematical demonstration.

The influence of Descartes was very great. Enthusiastic Cartesians sprang up everywhere, especially in Holland and France. The most brilliant was a late contemporary of Descartes, Baruch Spinoza.

Spinoza (1632–1677) was a Portuguese Jew, living in Amsterdam, where his parents had fled from persecution. Excommunicated by the synagogue for his heretical opinions, which were equally distasteful to Christians, Spinoza became a recluse, living very simply and supporting himself by grinding lenses. His brilliant mind and the beauty of his character attracted a few disciples; and as his fame grew he was offered the Chair of Philosophy at Heidelberg, which he declined, preferring freedom to think his own thoughts in seclusion.

Spinoza's system is difficult to understand and is variously interpreted. It interests us here as showing in what various directions the appeal to reason could lead. Descartes had thought the world divided into three parts—two distinct substances, mind and matter, and an ultimate reality, God, who is separate from both. After Descartes, the Rationalism that sprang from him tended generally to remove God farther and farther from the world, until God became superfluous and the world of things without a unifying explanation. Spinoza, on the other hand, became a Pantheist. To him God and Nature were one. All existence is one substance, known in two attributes, thought and extension.

Of another mind was the German Leibnitz (1646–1716), a mathematician and philosopher, who spent his last forty years as a librarian at Hanover. Starting with the Cartesian test of truth, Leibnitz thought the

Universe not one substance, but an infinite number of substances. Each substance is a monad, or indivisible centre of force; and each is a mirror of the Universe itself. All ideas are innate in each monad, requiring only to be drawn out to clearness. God is the original monad. All things are clear to Him.

Leibnitz thought that monads, as indivisible and independent centres of force, do not influence each other. What seems like mutual influence is really the pre-established harmony of monads, that all mirror the same Universe. Men come to knowledge by the elucidation of their innate ideas.

By this time it was clear that, whatever Rationalism might produce, it could not produce agreement. It was time to examine afresh its first principles, and reach some sure theory of knowledge. An Englishman, John Locke, undertook the task. In an *Epistle to the Reader,* attached to his *Essay on the Human Understanding,* Locke says: "Were it fit to trouble thee with the history of this essay, I should tell thee that five or six friends meeting at my chamber, and discoursing on a subject very remote from this, found themselves quickly at a stand by the difficulties that arose on every side. After we had awhile puzzled ourselves, without coming any nearer a resolution of those doubts which perplexed us, it came into my thoughts that we took a wrong course, and that before we set ourselves upon inquiries of that nature, it was necessary to examine our own abilities, and see what objects our understanding were or were not fitted to deal with. This I proposed to the company, who all readily assented." There were many meetings, continued through twenty years and interrupted by exile, before Locke gave his *Essay* to the world.

John Locke (1632–1704), a sober Oxford scholar, was the most influential thinker of the late seventeenth century. A life-long friend of the Earl of Shaftesbury, a statesman of the reign of Charles II, Locke was early drawn into politics and, on the fall of his friend, was compelled to take refuge in Holland, where he remained five years. On the accession of William of Orange, he returned to England and became the oracle of the so-called "Whig" philosophy, that underlay the opposition to the Stuarts and their doctrine of the divine right of kings.

Locke's attention was first drawn to philosophy by the incident we have cited; and his *Essay on the Human Understanding* was published in 1690. Its general purpose is that of all Locke's writings, to advance the cause of liberty by showing the necessity for humble observation and enquiry, instead of either acquiescence in traditional opinions or high-sounding speech. To observe and to think modestly will bring society to an enlightened freedom. Neither the current science nor the current philosophy, Locke thought, was blameless in this matter. So in the *Essay* he attempts a philosophical defence of freedom, by examining the powers of the human mind. "If by this inquiry into the nature of the understanding, I can discover the powers thereof, how far they reach, to what things they are in any degree proportionate, and where they fail us, I suppose it may be of use to prevail with the mind of man to be more cautious in meddling with things exceeding its comprehension; to stop at the utmost extent of its tether; and to sit down in a quiet ignorance of those things which, upon examination, are found to be beyond the reach of our capacities." Men ought not to complain of this limitation. "They have light enough to lead them to the knowledge of their Maker, and the sight of their own duties. Men may find matter sufficient to busy their heads, and employ their hands with variety, delight, and satisfaction, if they will not boldly quarrel with their own constitution and throw away the blessings their hands are filled with, because they are not big enough to grasp everything." [6]

So Locke undertakes an enquiry into the origin of such knowledge as men may have; and, like Sir Francis Bacon, decides that it is wholly empirical. That is to say, all that we can know comes through experience. Those innate and universal ideas, on which Rationalists tend to rely, have no existence. Take, for example, the two ideas " 'whatever is, is' and 'it is impossible for the same thing to be and not to be'; which, of all others, I think have the most allowed title to innate." "These propositions are so far from having a universal assent, that there are a great part of mankind to whom they are not so much as known." In children, savages, the illiterate, "being of all others the least corrupted by custom or borrowed opinions, . . . one might reasonably imagine that in their minds these innate notions should lie open fairly to everyone's view." [7] They do not.

[6] *Essay*, Bk. I, Chap. I, 4, 5.

[7] *Essay*, Bk. I, Chap. II, 27. Leibnitz, in a work first published some fifty years after his death, defended his doctrine of innate ideas against Locke. In the *New Essays on the Human Understanding*, Leibnitz concedes that universal truths do not exist consciously in the mind at birth; but they are there implicitly, as *petites perceptions*, else we should

For innate ideas Locke substitutes sensation and reflection, as the sources of all knowledge. "Let us then suppose the mind to be white paper, void of all characters, without any ideas; how comes it to be furnished? . . . To this I answer in one word, from experience; in that all our knowledge is founded, and from it ultimately derives itself. Our observation, employed either about *external* sensible objects, or about the *internal* operations of our minds, perceived and reflected on by ourselves, is that which supplies our understanding with all the materials of thinking. These two are the fountains of knowledge, from whence all the ideas we have, or can naturally have, do spring." [8]

This, then, is Locke's theory of knowledge. The mind is as a sheet of white paper, on which are written hourly the things received through sensation. The mind, by reflection, combines sensations into simple ideas, and the simple ideas into more complex ones.

The rationalistic philosophy was to expire at length in intellectual skepticism, a result reached in David Hume, the foremost British philosopher of the eighteenth century. Its place would be taken by a new philosophical movement, of which Rousseau was the precursor, and which would find a place for aspects of life that Rationalism neglected, and especially for feeling.

The seventeenth-century thinkers we have mentioned, and others of less note, were generally religious men; but their real interest was in science and philosophy. With the exception of Locke, they made little attempt to harmonize the new ideas and the old faith. Adjustment would require to be made; and in England men tried to make it, quite as Albert the Great and Thomas Aquinas had tried to adjust mediaeval Christianity and Aristotle. It cannot be said that the English adjusters did their work very well; but they must be judged by contemporary standards. What is common knowledge now, about the history of religions and the psychology of the religious life, was quite unknown then. At least the adjusters attempted to keep reason and religion harmonious; though the attempt was distasteful alike to the conventional and to those firmly

---

never have them at all. Universal and necessary truth cannot possibly come through the senses. "The senses never give anything but instances, that is to say, particular or individual truths. Now all the instances which confirm a general truth, however numerous they be, are not sufficient to establish the universal necessity of this same truth."

[8] *Essay,* Bk. II, Chap. I, 1, 2.

grounded in religious experience. To both of these "Rationalism" appeared an intrusion.

Rationalism is always present in religion; but in England it became an aggressive movement in the early eighteenth century, all the more because the new trade and commerce with the East acquainted Englishmen with other civilizations, much older than their own, and with cultures not Christian.

Theological Rationalism tended to the type of thought known as Deism. It regarded God as far away from human life. He had contrived and set in motion a mechanical world, which now ran of itself. He had established rules of morality and principles of religion, which constituted the primitive, rational and universal religion of mankind, before it was cluttered up with superstitions and spoiled by priests. Its principles were five—that there is a God, that He is to be worshipped, that virtue is the true service of God, that men ought to repent and forsake their sins, that there are rewards and punishments after death.

The forerunner of the Deistic movement was a certain Baron Herbert of Cherbury, a pioneer in what was later to be called Comparative Religion. As early as 1645, Herbert published a volume [9] designed to show that religion is the essential characteristic of mankind and that the five truths mentioned are everywhere recognized, that they constitute the universal religion. These truths came to be acknowledged by Deists in general; and many men elaborated the theme in many books.[10]

Deism, and Rationalism in general, brought many replies. Indeed in the early eighteenth century attempts at refutation of the new ideas were quite the vogue among orthodox clergymen. The essayist Addison, too, wrote much banter in the *London Spectator;* and the immortal Dr. Johnson, the leading man of letters of his day, turned his vigorous conversation to the support of Christian orthodoxy. It was not difficult to show that the Deist's knowledge of Christian history was inadequate, just as it is common knowledge now that his primitive, universal religion was a figment of the imagination. The refutation, however, was more

---

[9] *De Religione Gentilium.*

[10] Notably *Christianity not Mysterious,* by John Toland, and *Discourses of Free-thinking,* by Anthony Collins, a disciple of Locke. More important still was *Christianity as Old as the Creation,* by Matthew Tindal, ablest of the Deists. Thomas Paine, most aggressive of them, published in 1795 the *Age of Reason.* His earlier works, *Common Sense* and the *Rights of Man,* did great service to the American and French Revolutions respectively.

effective as a counter-attack than as a final defence of Christian orthodoxy itself.

The Deists in England were overborne by their able opponents; and little is heard of them after the middle of the eighteenth century, all the more because the Wesleyan revival provided a diversion that was to continue effective for more than a century. The Deists did, however, kindle a fire that burned fiercely and long in France; and they were not without influence in Germany and America.[11]

As for England, the re-thinking of religion could wait. What could not wait was moral regeneration. The labouring masses were spiritually destitute and generally neglected. Illiteracy was widespread, drunkenness more general than ever before or since. The penal laws were savage, the jails cesspools of iniquity and disease. And England was approaching the Industrial Revolution, that was to transform her swiftly from an agricultural to an industrial society, and put great strain upon the social structure.

Life in the Church of England was at a low ebb. To maintain the Elizabethan Settlement, the Puritans had been expelled after the Stuart Restoration, the Non-jurors after the Revolution of 1688. These were among the most earnest and distinguished leaders of the National Church, which was impoverished by their expulsion. Bishop Butler is said to have declined the Archbishopric of Canterbury in 1747, because it "was too late for him to try to support a falling Church."

Earnest men were naturally disturbed; and from 1729 to 1735 there existed at Oxford a little society of dons and undergraduates, of whom Bishop Butler heartily disapproved as "enthusiasts." They were dedicated to the deepening of their own religious life, and the quickening of the National Church. The roystering, wine-drinking University called them the "Holy Club," and "the Methodists," for the methodical way in which they planned their devotions and duties. Their leader was a young Anglican clergyman and Fellow of Lincoln College, John Wesley. Their inspiration was a recent book, the *Serious Call to a Devout and Holy Life,* by one of the Non-juring clergymen, William Law.

Throughout the country, too, there were "Societies," for the cultiva-

[11] Frederick the Great of Prussia was a Deist, as was Joseph II of Austria, Holy Roman Emperor. In America Benjamin Franklin and Thomas Jefferson were Deists.

tion of the religious life, by prayer, the reading of the Scriptures, and frequent celebration of the Lord's Supper. They busied themselves also with the poor and with prisoners, with soldiers and sailors. Many of the clergy, however, regarded the Societies as fanatical; and they were continued with difficulty.

The Holy Club at Oxford was but one of the Societies; but it included among its members three remarkable men—George Whitefield, and John and Charles Wesley.

Whitefield was the son of an innkeeper of Gloucester, was reared in poverty, but managed to reach Oxford University in 1733. There a serious illness brought on a religious crisis, from which Whitefield emerged with a joyous sense of salvation and peace with God. Ordained a clergyman of the Church of England, he was nevertheless without any denominational sentiment, and preached with extraordinary power wherever opportunity was given him, and especially in the open air. He made several visits to the American Colonies; and a preaching mission to New England in 1740 was followed by the greatest spiritual revolution ever witnessed there, "the Great Awakening."

John and Charles Wesley were the fifteenth and eighteenth of a family of nineteen children, born to the Reverend Samuel Wesley, Rector of the country parish of Epworth, and his wife Susanna, a woman of remarkable ability and strength of character, daughter of a great Puritan and Non-juring divine, Dr. Annesley. John and Charles Wesley were gifted boys, reached Oxford in time, and won distinction as scholars. Both, as we saw, were members of the Holy Club; and both became great preachers. John founded a denomination; and Charles, his collaborator, became one of the great hymn-writers of the Christian Church.

John Wesley (1703–1791) became a Fellow of Lincoln College in 1726, a priest of the Church of England in 1728, and leader of the Holy Club in 1729. The Club had little influence in Oxford; and its members did not long remain there. John and Charles Wesley went as missionaries to America in 1735, to the colony of Georgia, recently founded by General Oglethorpe. Crossing the Atlantic they were fellow travellers with a party of Moravians, whose cheerful courage in a violent storm convinced John Wesley that they had what he lacked, faith in God. Reaching Savannah, John Wesley fell in with the Moravian Spangenberg, who asked him: "Do you know Jesus Christ?" "I know," said Wesley, "that He is the Saviour of the world." "True," said Spangenberg, "but do you know that He has saved you?" Wesley did not know.

The work of the Wesleys in Georgia was disappointing; and Charles returned almost immediately to England. John continued, a zealous, punctilious clergyman, of great gifts, but ill-suited to the mixed and turbulent society of Savannah. In little more than two years, he was back in England, bitterly disappointed.

Fortunately the Wesley brothers now came upon Moravians in London. The Moravians were a remnant of the ancient Hussites, that had recently found refuge at Berthelsdorf, Saxony, on the estate of young Count von Zinzendorf, a man of Pietistic leanings, educated in a school of Francke at Halle. The Moravians at Berthelsdorf became a village community, with an organization of its own, calling itself *Herrnhut,* Lord's guard. The Brotherhood spread beyond Saxony, to Prussia and Denmark, Switzerland and Russia. Wherever the Brethren went, they were witnesses for a heartfelt piety, amidst the general Rationalism and indifference. They had also the missionary spirit, in which Protestantism was still deficient. They began work in America in 1735, and in London in 1738. There John Wesley, within a week of his return from America met the Moravian, Peter Böhler, who was on his way to labours in Georgia. Böhler was teaching complete surrender to Christ, sudden conversion, and joy through believing. He formed a Society in London, of which John Wesley was one of the original members, and which became known as the Fetter-Lane Society.

Neither of the Wesleys had yet found peace. That experience now came to Charles, on May 21, 1738, in the midst of a critical illness. A like experience overtook John three days later. In the evening, he tells us in his *Journal,* he went, troubled and reluctant, to a Society in Aldersgate Street, London, and there heard one read Luther's Preface to his *Commentary on Romans.* "About a quarter before nine, while (Luther) was describing the change which God works in the heart through faith in Christ, I felt my heart strangely warmed. I felt I did trust in Christ, Christ alone, for salvation; and an assurance was given me, that He had taken away my sins, even mine, and saved me from the law of sin and death."

It was Luther's experience of salvation by faith. John Wesley quite properly called it "conversion." It was a shift in the centre of consciousness, from anxious striving after salvation to quiet trust in the ultimate Being, or Reality, of the Universe. It is an experience not confined to any one religion, or religious philosophy; and wherever it happens, it is transforming.

The manner of Wesley's conversion determined his view as to the normal entrance upon the Christian life. He was to bring many thousands to Christ by the same way. Their Christian life was to be, as Luther intended, not an anxious ecclesiastical discipline, but the joyful expression of a changed nature, changed by faith.

John and Charles now preached as opportunity offered, but chiefly in the Societies around London, pulpits tending to shut against their "enthusiasm." Whitefield was then preaching at Kingswood, a colliery district outside Bristol, to immense crowds of miners. They were virtually savages, unchurched and unschooled, against whose plundering raids the Government protected Bristol with troops; but now tears were "making white gutters down their black cheeks," as Whitefield recounted their sins and offered salvation. Converts were many; and Whitefield called John Wesley to share in the work. That scholar, gentleman, Anglican priest, hesitated but took the plunge, and became the great open-air preacher of English history. Charles, still more reluctant, soon followed his brother's example.

Less imaginative than Whitefield, John Wesley was earnest, precise, lucid, more practical than Whitefield, more self-controlled, and entirely fearless. And he was tireless. A dapper, diminutive gentleman, he had an iron constitution, sustained by regular habits, great common sense and a quiet mind. For more than fifty years he travelled the British Isles on horseback, averaging five thousand miles a year and fifteen sermons a week. It is all set down in his *Journal,* which Augustine Birrell thought "the most amazing record of human exertion ever penned by man."

Wesley continued to the end an Anglican clergyman; but circumstances compelled him, step by step, to create a separate organization, to build churches, and to ordain ministers. Even so, he called his congregations "societies," his churches "chapels," and thought his ordination of ministers consistent with Anglicanism.

The first truly Methodist Society was founded, the first chapel built, at Bristol, in the spring of 1739. In London Methodists still met with the Fetter-Lane Society; but Wesley's cool reason rejected some features of Moravian piety, especially a certain vision-seeking. So in the autumn of 1739 the Methodists withdrew from the Fetter-Lane Society, to an old foundery in the Moorfields, which was converted into a chapel and hostel. There Susanna Wesley, now widowed, took up her abode and gave sound counsel to her sons in critical moments.

John Wesley preferred that all preaching be done by clergymen; but in the stress of circumstances there was a little lay preaching from the beginning. In 1742, however, returning from a visit to Bristol, Wesley rode up to the Foundery, an outraged and angry priest. Susanna Wesley, herself an orderly Anglican, enquired the cause of her son's disquiet. "Thomas Maxfield," he said, "has turned preacher." Maxfield, a trophy of Wesley's open-air preaching at Bristol, had himself begun preaching there daily. Susanna said: "John, . . . take care what you do with respect to that young man, for he is as surely called of God to preach as ever you are." Soon Thomas Maxfield preached at the Foundery; and as John Wesley sat on the hard benches listening, he recalled his mother's words, "as surely called of God to preach as ever you are." It was true; and lay preachers were soon sharing Wesley's growing work throughout England.

For six years Wesley himself visited all Methodist Societies, which as yet were about Bristol and London. Then personal supervision became impossible. So Wesley summoned the preachers to meet him in London in 1744. It was the first "Conference," became an annual affair and a permanent feature of Methodism. Two years later the whole territory then covered was divided into "Circuits," with preachers for each; and soon thereafter an "Assistant" to Wesley, later called the "Superintendent," was placed in charge of each Circuit.

Wesley's work required a literature. There were his preachers to be educated, and a constantly-growing public, to be fed on more than preaching. So, with no literary ambition, Wesley nevertheless wrote ceaselessly. He opened the age of "tracts," anticipating by fifty years the Religious Tract Society. He anticipated also the age of cheap books, publishing for his people the *Christian Library,* an abridgement of fifty famous works. He published many sermons, that had an immense sale, and left for posterity the *Journal of John Wesley*,[12] a diary as interesting and more significant than two other self-portraits of the time—the *Letters* of Horace Walpole and Boswell's *Johnson*.

The Methodist movement was disturbed quite early by doctrinal differences. Wesley did not believe in predestination and election. He was Arminian, as were most Anglican clergymen of the time. Whitefield, however, was a convinced Calvinist, and found an influential supporter in Selina, Countess of Huntingdon, a convert to Methodism but as masterful as John Wesley himself. As years passed and the theological division was not overcome, the Countess began in 1761 to establish Societies of her own and to build chapels, gradually founding what was to be known as "Lady Huntingdon's Connexion." Very fortunately, those who thus separated from Methodism were not embittered and hostile. They carried on a parallel movement for the evangelization of England.

After a few years of itinerating between London and Bristol, Wesley carried the Gospel to the north, establishing a third base at Newcastle-on-Tyne. The centres of population between these three bases were his particular parish. His itinerary took him through the new industrial centres, where villages were growing into busy cities and smoking chimneys darkened the sky. It was here that life was most crowded, disordered, neglected.

Wesley's labours as a preacher are without parallel in Christian history. He preached almost daily for fifty years, usually in the open air, and sometimes to as many as thirty thousand persons. In the early years he and his helpers were often in danger from English mobs, then sodden and brutal. Gradually all this changed; and Wesley became the most venerated figure in England. Crowds assembled spontaneously and listened reverently wherever he went. A whisper of his coming would run through a community; and he was often awakened by crowds assembling in the grey dawn, sometimes singing the Wesleyan hymns as they came, in readiness for the preaching service that he held regularly at five.

[12] The *Journal* may be had in *Everyman's Library*, E. P. Dutton & Co. The definitive edition, for scholars, is in eight volumes, edited by Nehemiah Curnock and published by Robert Culley, London.

So it went on until Methodist Societies dotted England, and the work was going forward in Scotland and Ireland as well. Then it spread to the American Colonies. A lay preacher, Philip Embury, began work in New York in 1766; and another, Robert Strawbridge, in Maryland at about the same time. The response was encouraging; and in 1771 Wesley sent out Francis Asbury, wisest and best of the early workers in America. The first Conference met at Philadelphia in 1773.

The War of American Independence came swiftly; but Methodism grew during the struggle. When it closed, however, dependence on England was no longer desirable. The question of the sacraments, too, was more pressing in the United States. In England Methodists had continued to go to the Church of England for baptism and the Lord's Supper. In the United States there was often no Episcopal Church in their community. And Wesley had never permitted the administration of the sacraments by unordained men; nor had he succeeded in finding bishops willing to ordain his preachers, few of whom were clergymen.

In these circumstances Wesley acted on a conviction he had long held. He was aware that in the early Church bishops and presbyters (or priests) had been one ecclesiastical order, bishops being simply presbyters, to whom was assigned the special duty of superintendence. So, while anxious to conform to Anglican usage, Wesley thought ordination by a presbyter as valid, in principle, as ordination by a bishop. At Bristol, therefore, he and Thomas Coke, both presbyters of the Church of England, ordained two preachers, Richard Whatcoat and Thomas Vasey, to be presbyters in the United States; and next day Coke was set apart to be "superintendent" there.

Here, then, was a definite breach with the Church of England; though Wesley did not regard it as such and, not being ejected, continued until his death a clergyman of the Established Church.

On September 10, 1784, Wesley notified American Methodism that he had appointed Coke and Asbury to be "superintendents" in America; and at a Conference in Baltimore in December the presbyters ordained Asbury a presbyter, then consecrated him superintendent. The same Conference decided that Methodism in the United States should be an independent church, the Methodist Episcopal Church. Four years later, in 1788, the Conference designated Coke and Asbury "bishops"; and the title "superintendent" disappeared.

Having made a beginning for America, Wesley accepted the logic of his action. During the next few years he ordained men for Scotland, then for Newfoundland, and finally for England.

In 1784 Wesley wrote in the *Journal*: "I have entered into the eighty-third year of my life. I am a wonder to myself. I am never tired, either with preaching, writing or travelling." He went forward with his incredible labours another seven years. Then, returning to London in 1791 from a preaching visit to Surrey, Wesley descended heavily from the coach and climbed with difficulty the narrow stairs of the house he had built, adjoining "Wesley's Chapel," in the City Road. He was visibly dying; though he spoke cheerfully to his anxious attendants. The stupor of death quickly enveloped him. He roused himself sufficiently to say: "Give my sermon on the love of God to everyone," then sank again. Once more he returned, to say in an ecstasy: "The best of all is God is with us," then died.

After Wesley's death it was impossible to continue the fiction that Methodism was within the Church of England. Most Methodists now knew no religious life except that of the Societies. They were now educating and ordaining their own ministers. Such Methodists, therefore, as were also in the Established Church were under the hard necessity of choosing between it and Methodism. Most elected to remain in Methodism, which developed swiftly into one more Protestant denomination, the Methodist Church. Some Methodists elected to remain in the Establishment and became a well-defined party there, the Evangelicals. Their emphasis was on the Gospel, the Evangel. Soon they were known also as the Low Church Party, as distinct from High Churchmen, whose pre-occupation was with the ecclesiastical institution, its continuity with the ancient past, and the supernatural benefits thought to depend on the manner of ordaining clergymen and on the sacraments.

The influence of Methodism, however, within and without the Established Church, was very great. Much of the religious energy of the ensuing century, in England and America, was generated in Methodism. Cambridge University, even before Wesley died, was producing the new kind of clergymen, the Evangelical. The chief agents in this transformation were two devout priests of the Establishment, Isaac Milner and Charles Simeon. Milner was a professor at Cambridge. Simeon was a Fellow of King's College and vicar of Holy Trinity Church.

Laymen of the Establishment devoted themselves to the dissemination of Evangelical ideas. Such were William Cowper, foremost English poet of the late eighteenth century, and Hannah More, prominent in artistic and literary circles. Better known, however, are William Wilberforce and John Howard. Wilberforce was a member of Parliament, popular and rich, who was converted in 1784, through the influence of Isaac Milner. Three years later he began a long struggle against slavery, which resulted in its abolition throughout the British Empire. Howard visited the jails of England, laid his horrible discoveries before Parliament, and became the "father of prison reform." Howard carried his work to the continent and died in south Russia, studying methods to prevent the spread of the plague.

Notable, too, was Robert Raikes, an Evangelical layman of Gloucester, who sought to bring education within reach of the children of the poor. He established schools, to which the children came each Sunday, the only day when they were not working in the mills or the mines. In these schools, the originals of the present *Sunday Schools,* children were taught "the three R's" and the elements of Christianity, studies being suspended for attendance also at Church. The movement spread rapidly through the country; and from England it passed to the continent and to America.

CHAPTER XXII

BACKGROUNDS OF RELIGIOUS CHANGE:
HUME AND VOLTAIRE, ROUSSEAU AND KANT

WHILE Methodism was bringing religion to the masses in Britain and Evangelicalism was infusing vitality into the Established Church, Rationalism, as an alternative to orthodox Christianity, was ending in frustration. It had served a purpose in clearing the ground of credulity and superstition, and turning upon religion something of the scrutiny devoted to contemporary science; but it had been too disdainful of the past and too indifferent to the feelings and aspirations of the human spirit. Rationalism tended to strip life of its graces and its hopes, until wise men wearied of the endless negation and questioned the competence of the human mind. Locke and the Empiricists intimated that those innate and universal ideas, on which Rationalists relied, had no existence, that knowledge is limited to what comes within experience. There might be many things, therefore, that men could not know. And so in Britain Rationalism faded out at length into intellectual skepticism, exemplified in David Hume. On the continent it called forth a rejoinder, Romanticism, whose greatest exponent was Rousseau.

David Hume (1711–1776) was a Scotsman, a native of Edinburgh, a shrewd and tolerant philosopher and man of letters. His significance for philosophy is that he carried to its conclusion the Empiricism of Locke. All human knowledge, he says, is traceable to either impressions or ideas, impressions being "all our sensations, passions and emotions, as they make their first appearance in the soul," ideas being "the faint images of these in thinking and reasoning." [1]

In the light of this principle, Hume examines those relations that bind our ideas together into knowledge, the most important being that of cause and effect. Can the idea of cause be carried back to any impression?

[1] *Treatise of Human Nature*, Bk. I, Pt. I, 1.

Hume thinks not. It is due only to two relations between objects—contiguity and succession. We have seen certain phenomena follow others in the past; and it is their "constant conjunction" that leads us to infer that they are cause and effect. In reality "objects have no discoverable connection together."

And so reliance on reason, so confidently urged by Descartes, led in a hundred years to where the fabric of the physical world dissolved, a conclusion in which the mind could not rest. Instinctive beliefs may yield to reason in an argument; but when argument ceases, the mind returns to its beliefs. Of this Hume himself was well aware. "My intention, then, . . . is only to make the reader sensible of the truth of my hypothesis, that all our *reasonings* concerning causes and effects are derived from nothing but custom; and that belief is more properly an act of the sensitive, than of the cogitative part of our natures."

So the effect of Hume's argument is to destroy, not beliefs, but the assumption that beliefs can be proven. Our beliefs are due to instinct and custom, not to reason; and we must expect to fall into skepticism about them.

Again and again Hume declares his intellectual skepticism. "The understanding, when it acts alone and according to its most general principles, entirely subverts itself and leaves, not the lowest degree of evidence in any proposition, in either philosophy or common life." "Most fortunately (however), it happens that, since reason is incapable of dispelling these clouds, nature herself suffices to that purpose, and cures me of this philosophical melancholy and delirium, . . . I dine, I play a game of backgammon, I converse and am merry with my friends; and when, after three or four hours' amusement, I return to these speculations, they appear so cold, and strained, and ridiculous, that I cannot find it in my heart to enter into them further."

The intellectual skepticism illustrated in Hume was as disturbing as Rationalism. If Rationalism endangered religion, skepticism threatened science, which was offering some compensation for the diminishing faith of the times; for in science at least the mind of man demonstrated its power to reach some forms of assured truth. But if cause and effect in Nature were but man's expectation that things would continue to happen as they had happened in the past, what became of science, its dependability, its light on the nature of things?

Intellectual skepticism would not do; and men were soon at work, examining Hume's premises, to correct the assumptions that had led, through strict logic, to a conclusion so unsatisfactory. The Scotsman Thomas Reid, Professor of Moral Philosophy at Glasgow, rejected skepticism. In an *Enquiry into the Human Mind on the Principles of Common Sense,* he denied that impressions and ideas are the only sources of knowledge, adding to them an intuitive knowledge of the external world.

Reid became founder of the so-called *Scottish School* of philosophers; but his fame was obscured by the brilliance of a great German contemporary, Immanuel Kant, who caught from Hume an idea that was to revolutionize philosophy. Before we speak of Kant, however, we must trace the development of an intellectual movement on the continent, leading up to Kant. It paralleled the scientific and philosophical movement in Britain, and drew its early inspiration from there.

The bloodless revolution of 1688 in England, the establishment there of parliamentary government and freedom of the press, of intellectual and religious liberty, made a profound impression in Europe. None of the evils, believed in France to follow inevitably upon popular government, had ensued. England was stronger than before, and the spearhead of resistance to the imperial designs of Louis XIV. A wave of rationalizing thought crossed the Channel and broke upon the shores of France. Royal autocracy and Catholic repression came to appear shabby and outworn, and British skies even rosier than they were.

The man who did most to popularize English ideas in France was Francois Marie Arouet, who called himself Voltaire, a writer so brilliant that he became the foremost figure in Europe. Voltaire (1694- 1778) had known what it was to be thrown into the Bastille without trial. He resented bitterly the tyranny and inequality of his native land. Living in England from 1726 to 1729, where arbitrary imprisonment was unlawful, where religious sects flourished and a man might speak and publish what he thought, Voltaire was enchanted. Returning to France, he told his countrymen of the happy island people. Another great Frenchman, Montesquieu, came and, returning, reported with equal enthusiasm; [2] and soon an intellectual movement was under way in France, that was less concerned with philosophical speculation than with the reformation of society. Men applied themselves, dispassionately and without theological assumptions, to the removal of what remained of mediaevalism. There grew up a whole literature, of philosophy and sociology and history, of tragedies and comedies, culminating in the famous *Encyclopedia,* in thirty-four volumes, attacking all that was thought obsolete and unjust. Some writers, like Voltaire himself, were Deists; some were frankly irreligious.

What was thought in France was felt everywhere; for the French language had now supplanted Latin as the language of culture. It was the *lingua franca* of Europe. So the spirit of Voltaire entered royal courts, as an incentive, not to democracy, but to a more paternal despotism. Voltaire himself was no democrat. To him it mattered little who made laws and administered government, so long as freedom existed, to think, to speak, to write. All necessary reforms would follow upon freedom.

The movement was thus a true Rationalism, in its confidence in reason. The triumph of reason would mean the triumph of right. In religion it would mean the end of priestcraft and superstition, the return of that natural, universal religion, so long obscured. This confidence imbued the literature of the "Enlightenment." Having lost faith in the doctrines of the churches, Voltaire and the Encyclopedists had acquired faith in the dignity of man and his perfectibility.

The Enlightenment inevitably affected the German churches. There Pietism had weakened orthodoxy, without producing intellectual leaders to take the place of the Lutheran scholastics. English and French Deism thus found the intellectual field in Germany vacant; and the new ideas advanced rapidly.

The "road-breaker of the Enlightenment" (the *Aufklärung,* as the Germans call it) was that Thomasius, of whom we have spoken (p. 472); but its great protagonist was Christian Wolff, a lecturer in mathematics at Halle, where the works of Leibnitz turned his mind to philosophy. Wolff's views were quite inconsistent with the Pietism of Halle; and he was expelled from the University by King Frederick

---

[2] Voltaire in *Lettres sur Anglais,* Montesquieu in *Travel Notes.*

William I of Prussia in 1723. He was restored to Halle, however, in 1740 by Frederick the Great, a prince of the Enlightenment and patron of Voltaire. The influence of Wolff put an end to the reign of Pietism at Halle, and made Rationalism its rival throughout Germany.

Influential, too, in spreading the Enlightenment was Mosheim, professor at Göttingen, who has been called "the father of modern church history," being the first church historian to labour, without any apologetic purpose, to describe events and movements just as they happened. Reimarus, too, professor of Oriental languages at Hamburg, spread the Enlightenment. He had travelled in England, had become a Deist, and believed that all that was true in religion was what reason could ascertain—a wise Creator, an elementary morality, and personal immortality. The world itself was the only revelation of God.

The writings of Reimarus were put into circulation by Lessing, an eminent author and dramatist, art critic and *littérateur,* who also wrote the *Education of the Human Race,* setting forth a theory of his own. The human race, he said, like the individual, passes through the successive stages of childhood, youth and manhood. For each stage God has given a revelation, suited to its aptitudes and capacities. Childhood is moved by immediate rewards and punishments; and for the childhood of the race God gave the Old Testament, with its promises of material blessings. Youth is ready to forego present benefits for future success; and for the youth of the race God provided the New Testament, with its call to present self-sacrifice and its promise of eternal reward. Manhood is ruled by duty; and for manhood God gave reason, and may send yet more revelations to aid it.

The *Education of the Human Race* was a typical product of German Rationalism; and the fame of Lessing helped to spread throughout Germany the view that historic Christianity had gone into the past, having been appropriate only to an earlier stage of human development. Among Christian scholars in general, however, Rationalism took another direction, characteristically German. It turned to a methodical and constructive investigation of the books of the Bible, which was to lead on to the "Higher Criticism" in the nineteenth century. Bengel, head of a theological seminary at Würtemberg, was the first to recognize that the books of the New Testament can be classified, according to their origin and purpose. Reimarus subjected the records of the life of Christ to the

rigid scrutiny applied in other historical studies. Semler, professor at
Halle, taught that, while there is divine revelation in the Scriptures, not
all Scripture is revelation.

The "Higher Criticism," however, was still in the future. Of greater
importance in the eighteenth century was a philosophical reaction
against Rationalism and Skepticism, associated particularly with Rousseau in France and with Kant in Germany (See p. 493).

Jean Jacques Rousseau (1712–1778), a native of Geneva and an almost
exact contemporary of Hume, was in sharp contrast to the Scottish
philosopher. Where Hume was a rigid logician, Rousseau had an extraordinary sensitiveness and capacity for feeling, so much so that Hume
likened him to a "man stripped, not only of his clothes but of his skin."
Rousseau, a child of the Enlightenment, came gradually to reject its
ideal—a civilization of intellectual culture, advanced in the arts and
sciences, replete with mechanical inventions. He rejected, too, the idea
that man is primarily intellect, and his life a play of ideas. Man, he said,
is primarily feeling.

It was here that Rousseau made his distinctive contribution to
philosophy and social theory. He saw in the emotional outgoing of
man to other men and to Nature a revelation of man's essential kinship
with the world. He saw, too, that feeling is the incentive to both self-
realization and social reform.

This new insight coloured all Rousseau's later philosophy. A Deist,
his Deism was so touched with emotion, that he thought himself the
only man of his generation who really believed in God. Religion was an
affair of the heart, not of the head. If it could not rest on tradition, no
more could it rest on cold reason. Conscience and feeling were as
integral parts of a human being as were his intellectual processes. "I
believe in God," said Rousseau, "as fully as I believe in any other truth,
because to believe or not to believe are the things in the world that are
least under my control." And as for revelations of God, they were as
possible now as at any time in the past. God had not "gone in search of
Moses to speak to Jean Jacques Rousseau."

As for his social theory, Rousseau was the apostle of the common
man, treating of those fundamental human traits that underlie all

external and artificial differences; and his writings [3] on this theme were among the most effective causes of the French Revolution. In Germany, however, their total significance was more clearly seen and their influence more benignly felt. Germany had as yet a meagre literature, and no great philosopher except Leibnitz. Now there burst upon the land a great literature and a great philosophy, both stressing the significance of the inner life, and together ushering in one of the most illustrious eras in human thought. The authoritarianism of the Middle Ages and the cold intellectualism of the Enlightenment were both rejected, while the new freedom, encouraged by the Enlightenment, was devoted to the art of living itself. A new way of looking at things began, a new sympathy, that included an appreciation of the past, increased by the study of Greek art, recently introduced into Germany by the archeologist Winckelmann and the dramatist Lessing.

On the religious side, the pioneer was Lessing (*See* p. 495), whose *Education of the Human Race* broke unconsciously with Rationalism and opened the way to a better appreciation of both religion and history. It introduced, too, a new idea of God, which was also a very old one. God was not to be reached by logic, as in Deism. He was present in Nature, in history, and in individual experience.

The foremost philosopher of the new movement, however, was Immanuel Kant (1724–1804), a native of the ancient Baltic seaport of Königsberg, in East Prussia, son of a saddler and grandson of a Scottish immigrant. Königsberg was a stronghold of Pietism; and Kant grew up under its influence. In 1770 he became Professor of Logic and Metaphysics in the University of Königsberg. For another decade he remained comparatively obscure. Even to his neighbours he was but a quiet, methodical, diminutive man and a bachelor, who walked every day in an avenue of lime trees nearby, eight times up, eight times down, followed in rough weather by his old servant Lampe, bearing an umbrella. Then in 1781 Kant published his *Critique of Pure Reason,* and swiftly became the foremost of living philosophers. The *Critique* was expounded in the Universities of Germany, and invaded the schools of the Roman Church. Young men flocked to Königsberg as to a shrine. More than a thinker, Kant was well versed in history and the sciences,

[3] Notably the *Discours sur les arts et sciences*, the *Contrat Social*, and the *Emile*.

in *belles lettres* and works of travel, in Voltaire and Rousseau, in English philosophy and literature. He became a sort of oracle, to be consulted on all questions of fact and in all moments of difficulty.

Kant's system, *Ethical Idealism,* is a fresh beginning in both philosophy and ethical theory. Earlier philosophies had assumed that religion is grounded in certain metaphysical principles, notably this, that God is the ultimate cause and the sustaining power of the Universe. Correct ideas about God are therefore the beginning of religion and the guide to morals. Kant believed the beginning of religion to be, not metaphysical principles but devotion to duty, and knowledge of God to be derived from man's moral insight.

This was not quite new. One or two prophets of ancient Israel had unconsciously affirmed it when, as their insight grew, they transformed Jehovah from a jealous tribal deity into the father of all men. An occasional Christian teacher did likewise; but Kant was the first to declare explicitly that the right to reinterpret God, in the light of man's growing insight, is the controlling principle in creed-making. How he reached this position, we shall now see.

The oracle of Königsberg had been disturbed at the intellectual skepticism that threatened. Impressed by the new scientific discoveries and their testimony to the competence of the human mind, Kant could not rest in skepticism. Nor could he acquiesce in the growing estrangement between science and religion. Religion and science, he knew, were major concerns of mankind; and his philosophy was an attempt at their reconciliation.

But why had the mediaeval unity of science and religion been broken? It was because in the new science, as in empirical philosophy, the test of truth was verifiability by the senses; and the truths of religion seemed incapable of such verification. Empiricism, therefore, led to religious, as well as intellectual, skepticism.

Kant could not reject the empirical test of truth. He knew that science was building up an exact and verifiable knowledge of the world, that would be universally valid. Perception by the senses was the way, by which reality was commonly to reach the mind. But what really happened in perception? What was the true theory of knowledge?

Kant thought the Rationalists right in regarding the mind as more than a passive recipient of impressions from without. There are innate ideas, at least in the sense that mind has a constitution of its own, that is always affecting the character of knowledge. On the other hand, Kant thought the Empiricists right in this, that there can be no knowledge quite independent of sense-perception. It is the senses that fetch the raw materials for knowledge. So that knowledge is a joint product, of things perceived through the senses and of the mind, at work upon them.

Examining the structure of mind then, Kant finds three faculties—*sensibility, understanding,* and *reason*—that are always active in the process of knowing.

Concerning *sensibility,* it is sufficient to note that nothing can be sensed, that is, become an object in consciousness, unless it can be placed by the mind in time and space. For example, one could not sense blackness in a world where all is black. One senses it only in contrast to other things or states, before, or after, or around. Similarly, one sees one's friend only at home, or on the street, or in his office, and at some time, in summer or winter; and if in his absence one try to imagine him, one must still place him in space and time.

As for the faculty of *understanding,* it cannot work on the raw materials of sensation, but only on these materials when arranged by the mind in space and time. For example, causal connection between two events cannot be deduced by the *understanding,* unless one succeeds the other in time. And causality, though the most important, is but one of twelve forms of apprehension, which Kant calls categories [4] and which the faculty of *understanding* adds to the space-time arrangement, already made by the faculty of *sensibility.*

As for the faculty of *reason,* it can deal with sense materials, only when arranged in space and time, and constructed in harmony with the twelve categories. To these the faculty of *reason* adds three ideas—the world, the soul, and God—, to which we shall return later.

This theory of knowledge is developed in the *Critique of Pure Reason;* and the question of religion and science is involved in that part of it which deals with *"synthetic judgments à priori."* A synthetic judgment is one whose predicate adds something to the subject, as when I say,

---

[4] Kant's categories are, in general, those given by Aristotle and accepted without question for centuries. Kant's twelve, corresponding to twelve possible forms of judgment, are as follows: Unity, Plurality, Totality; Reality, Negation, Limitation; Substantiality, Causality, Reciprocity; Possibility and Impossibility, Existence and Non-existence, Necessity and Contingency.

"This man is six feet tall." A judgment is also *à priori,* when it is made in advance of experience, as when I say, "The next man I shall see will be six feet tall."

An analytic judgment, one in which the predicate is already contained in the subject and simply unfolds its meaning, presents no serious difficulty; nor does a judgment *à posteriori,* one that rests on previous experience of the object concerned. But how are *"synthetic judgments à priori"* possible? Such judgments are actually made in the pursuit of knowledge, and not in metaphysics alone but in the most dependable of the sciences, like mathematics and physics. Consider, for example, the judgment that every event will have a cause. It is a synthetic judgment and one that is *à priori,* since experience can only show that events so far observed have had causes. And here the exact sciences are not unlike religion, whose basic assumptions—God, the soul, and immortality— are all synthetic *à priori.*

Synthetic *à priori* judgments, then, are possible; and Kant asks why they do not seem to have the same validity in metaphysics and religion as in mathematics and the physical sciences. It is, he says, because objective knowledge is limited to what is capable of conforming to the structure of space and time.

Concerning space, Kant says, its essential structure is expressed in the axioms of geometry; and the synthetic *à priori* judgments used in demonstrating geometry are unquestioned by normal minds, because the pattern of order presented in geometry is the pattern existing in the mind itself. So also with time, Kant tries to show the same identity between its structure and the principles of arithmetic. The outcome of his discussion, therefore, is this, that those synthetic *à priori* judgments in which the mathematical sciences consist are a dependable foundation for our knowledge of the world, because they conform to the nature of mind itself; and, whatever may be true of such reality as lies outside experience, so much of reality as comes within experience must conform to the structure of the mind. What does not so conform does not come within experience.

If, then, objective knowledge is limited to the data presented in experience, what does this signify for those three ideas—the world, the soul, and God—that *reason* adds to the categories? The categories of the *understanding* are not applicable to them. The category of causality, for example, is no longer valid if we try to apply it to the whole world at once, searching for its cause. For we cannot experience the whole world at once, but only so much of it as comes within the space-and-time field of our personal experience. Moreover the sequence that suggests causality occurs only in processes that happen in time, not in processes between the whole temporal world and something that may lie beyond it. Are, then, the synthetic *à priori* judgments valid, by which we reach the ideas of the world, the soul and God? And what is *reason* reason trying to do in using them?

They are an attempt to systematize the whole of human experience. The world is the unity of all objects external to the mind; the soul is the unity of all processes within the mind; and God is the necessary condition of both. The mind requires these ideas. It cannot stop with the causal connections between particular objects and events. It seeks to combine all particulars into one system. These ideas, then,—the world, the soul, and God—symbolize that unity of truth, which the mind demands and hopes some day to demonstrate.

Kant admits that we cannot *know* that these ideas correspond to objective realities. Granted, for example, that the mind requires the idea of God, as creator, preserver, and disposer of the whole realm of external phenomena and inner experience, nevertheless one cannot bring Him into space and time, so as to make Him an object of knowledge. God remains for the enquirer a regulative ideal only, though a necessary one.

Here, then, is Kant's solution of the problem presented by synthetic *à priori* judgments. Those made in the sciences conform to the essential structure of the mind itself and respect the limitations of human thinking; those made in metaphysics and religion disregard these limitations. They are permissible only as guides towards the goal of unity of knowledge. Kant, like Hume, is not trying to prove the unreality of the world, the soul, and God, but only to show them beyond the reach of knowledge, which is limited to data given in experience.

In his theory of knowledge, then, Kant emphasizes the limitation of knowledge to things received through the senses. In his moral philosophy, set forth in the *Critique of Practical Reason,* he emphasizes an idea of right, felt by all men everywhere. The objective facts here are the wants and desires, that psychology discovers within us and that we are disposed to satisfy. We are restrained, however, by considerations of right and wrong. To gratify desires indiscriminately, we know, is to subordinate *reason* to *sensibility,* the higher to the lower. The important thing, therefore, in deciding questions of conduct, is to see clearly the rational law that ought to govern desire.

We may do this by analysing reason once more, this time to discover what it requires of us in the matter of conduct. We shall find it demanding that we obey, in all situations, what we should wish to be a universal law for such situations. In other words, we must not ask for ourselves special privileges; we must govern our conduct by the rule we should wish others to follow. So that the principle, by which wants and desires are to be tested before they issue in conduct, is a philosophical formulation of the Golden Rule.

We reach the same conclusion, if we adopt another method of enquiry, observing our moral judgments, to discover what tests they actually apply to conduct. So doing, we find that if we do not lie and steal, loaf and defame, it is because we should thus violate the Golden Rule, doing to others what we do not wish them to do to us.

The moral law, Kant says, is a "categorical imperative"; it admits no exception or qualification. It requires that the desire for happiness be subordinated to duty. It is a law more frequently broken than observed. Nevertheless we feel that it ought to be observed always and unconditionally. So that here is an *à priori* judgment, independent of experience, proceeding from the rational nature of mind.

This moral philosophy provides Kant with a new foundation for religion. Our sense of moral obligation involves certain assumptions about the Universe and our place in it. These assumptions are personal freedom, personal immortality, and God. Freedom means that we are not caught in the causal determinism of events. Since duty commands us to obey the moral law, it is a necessary inference that we can obey, in spite of circumstances and desires. We cannot *know* this; but we are morally sure of it.

So also with the other two postulates of the practical reason, personal immortality and the existence of God.

With these postulates, however, we go beyond the field of knowledge. We cannot *know* God and freedom and immortality; but they are necessary to a reasonable moral faith.

What, then, are we to do, when moral considerations lead to beliefs, which the nature of knowledge deprives of objective proof? We must follow the *practical reason,* reason dealing with matters of conduct, even though it lead us beyond *pure reason,* which operates only in cognition. In other words, a belief founded on the moral law is valid; though it is not capable of objective demonstration.

This conclusion is not so strange as may at first appear. It is in the *practical reason,* not the *pure reason,* that the total rational nature of man is expressed. The whole cannot be subordinated to one of its parts.

This, then, is the status of those beliefs, or "postulates of practical reason," which are not knowledge but are yet necessary inferences from our devotion to the moral law. Their status is that of a faith, founded in the *practical reason.* They are rational, in that they are inferences from that loyalty to the moral law, which is the supreme expression of our rational nature. They are faith, however, not knowledge. Their function is, not to add to scientific knowledge, but to clarify our moral life and the nature of the cosmos in which that life is placed.

Kant's great contribution is this reconciliation of science and religion, and the transformation of theology from a metaphysical system into a morally grounded faith. Where Spinoza had seen science as itself a religious quest, Kant saw science and religion as having separate functions, which need never conflict. To science belongs the pursuit of knowledge, to religion the illumination and support of duty. Religion is the recognition of duties as divine commands, in the sense that to understand our sense of duty is to infer a Supreme Being, whose will is revealed in the moral law. Morality, for Kant, is primary, and religion derived from morality.

This ethical approach to religion was to be very influential in the nineteenth century. Two young contemporaries of Kant carried forward his work. These were Fichte and Schleiermacher. A generation later Hermann Lotze developed the implications of Kant's system for philosophy in general. Still later came a reconstruction of Protestant theology by Albrecht Ritschl, influenced by Kant and Lotze. To-day Kant's Ethical Idealism influences religious philosophy, in what are called Modernism and Religious Humanism, and in the Ethical Culture Movement.

Meanwhile Kant himself, in old age, ran into foul weather in Prussia. Lutheran orthodoxy had been uneasy about him from the first. No one could reconcile the Lutheran view of the Bible as the standard of morals with Kant's doctrine that the Bible itself must be brought to the test of man's moral judgment. No one could reconcile the doctrine of the total depravity of all men by nature, with Kant's belief in the moral competence of man. Kant felt the tension but little, while Frederick the Great lived. That ardent and unscrupulous monarch, who gloried in the French Enlightenment and brought Voltaire to live in the royal circle at Potsdam, was not likely to concern himself with the digressions of others from Lutheranism. But Frederick died in 1786 and was succeeded by Frederick William II, who regarded his predecessor as somewhat less than a good Prussian. The new monarch was not likely to be indifferent that the supreme philosopher of his kingdom wept for joy, while monarchy shivered, at the news of the French Revolution. Moreover Kant now crowned his earlier offences by writing the most daring of his books, and one which plain men could read, an essay on *Religion within the Limits of Pure Reason*. In it he proclaimed that religion reached its nadir when Church and clergy became the instruments of political oppression and intellectual obscurantism. This is just what was happening under Frederick William II. He had made Wöllner, a reactionary cleric, his Minister of Education; and Wöllner issued a decree in 1788, forbidding teachings that deviated from Lutheranism and establishing a censorship of publications.

Kant acted with great vigour for a man of seventy. He sent the essay on religion outside Prussia to Jena, a university town within the jurisdiction of the liberal Duke of Weimar. There the essay was published by the university press. So that when in 1794 Kant received a stern warning from the Prussian king, he replied that scholars ought to be free to think their own thoughts and to make them known, but that he would be silent while the present king reigned. It was an undertaking not too difficult for an old man, who had already spoken and was now approaching the great silence. Kant withered slowly, and died in 1804, at seventy-nine.

The disquiet of Protestant orthodoxy about Kant is not strange. If there were in his system new foundations for religion, there were none for the special forms of historic Christianity, whether Roman or Protestant. Kant would have been more at home at Athens than at either Rome or Wittenberg; though he would not have been a stranger to Galilee. Kant could well have said to contemporary Lutheranism, that if ever the Church should return to Galilee it would find him there, engaged with the Sermon on the Mount and the parables of the Lord.

CHAPTER XXIII

BACKGROUNDS OF RELIGIOUS CHANGE:
THE INDUSTRIAL REVOLUTION;
THE FRENCH REVOLUTION

The balance of power in Europe changed greatly in the century of Hume and Wesley, Voltaire and Rousseau and Kant, through a succession of violent conflicts. At first it seemed that it might be otherwise. There was at London and Paris a steadfast will to peace, nourished by the intellectual and dispassionate Cardinal Fleury, Prime Minister of France, and by that coarse Norfolk squire, Horace Walpole, who was Prime Minister of England and the best financier and parliamentarian of the age. A political alliance between France and England tended to stabilize all Europe. A peace worthy of the Age of Reason seemed at hand. Then suddenly there irrupted into European affairs the Prussia of Frederick II, "the Great" (1740–1786).

The house of Hohenzollern had ruled for nearly three hundred years in that part of Prussia known as Brandenburg, before producing a remarkable man in Frederick William, "the Great Elector." So great was the advance then made in the art of government, and in military and financial strength, that Frederick William's successor, Frederick I (1685–1713), was not satisfied with the title Elector. He asked and was granted by the Emperor the right to be crowned King of Prussia, then characteristically placed the crown upon his own head, in the cathedral at Königsberg.

Prussians were not liked elsewhere in Germany. The more refined Saxons, Franconians and Rhinelanders thought them uncouth. Before the eighteenth century was far advanced, however, everyone knew that the Prussians were a formidable problem for European statesmanship. They were not politically minded; but they were sturdy and frugal, obedient to the word of command and disposed to aggression.

In 1740 the Emperor Charles VI, of the Austrian Hapsburgs, dying without male issue, bequeathed to his daughter Maria Theresa his hereditary dominions and a promise from the crowned heads of Europe to acknowledge her right. Before the year was out Frederick the Great, without any provocation, fell upon her province of Silesia. Frederick wanted its linen industry, its iron mines and commercial waterways, and *lebensraum* for Prussia. His objects were achieved; but all Europe was involved in the War of the Austrian Succession.

Meanwhile the mariners of England had been quarrelling on the seven seas with their commercial rivals, the men of France and Spain. There was strife in Newfoundland and Acadia, on the St. Lawrence and the Ohio, in Bengal and the Carnatic. At last popular clamour against the search of English ships, trading in the Spanish Main, forced Walpole into war in 1739. The conflict raged at intervals until the Peace of Paris in 1763. By that time the balance of power in the western world was changed. The victories of Wolfe in Canada and of Clive in India had transferred the sceptre of colonial dominion to England.

Of all the nations, England alone was not impoverished by the wars. Even Prussia paid a terrible price for Silesia, while England, her commerce vastly increased, bore without distress the long and costly struggle.

Trouble in North America came swiftly, however. Relieved now of danger from Spaniards in Florida and the French in Canada, the English colonists along the Atlantic seaboard paid taxes unwillingly for a standing army, and regarded as oppressive certain regulations governing imperial trade. Colonials, moreover, could advance a good English principle, that people ought not to be taxed who were not represented in the taxing body.

Men took both sides, at home and in America. In England the three foremost statesmen—Chatham, Burke and Fox—all opposed coercion of the colonies; but George III, making a last stand for personal rule, knew only one way of dealing with mutinous subjects, the way of force. In the end representatives of twelve colonies met in Congress at Philadelphia in 1774, and concerted resistance to Britain. France and Spain, smarting from recent wounds, entered the war on the side of the colonies. In 1783 the independence of the American Republic was acknowledged.

Other things were happening, of vast import for the future. Monarchic France, in helping to establish a republic in America, had given a last push to the crazy edifice of French finance and raised the mirage of a republic in France, just when responsible government was saved in Britain and economic changes were making her the workshop of the world.

In this the aristocracy had an active part. Unlike the aristocracy of France, it was interested in commerce. The Nonconformists, too, excluded from political careers until 1828, turned a grave and disciplined energy to the pursuit of wealth. Science contributed. Its influence had been growing ever since Francis Bacon; and the intellectual curiosity it awakened was now applied to the chief preoccupation of the British people, which was no longer religion but industry and commerce. So inventions multiplied the output of workers, while the substitution of steam for water power drew them from village and riverside, to populate large towns. Soon England was no longer an agricultural and commercial, but an industrial, society.

With the change the era of Capitalism began. Master and men no longer worked together, their labour humanized by personal contact; and even wise men watched without understanding, and therefore without foreboding, the swift, unregulated growth of towns, with mean houses, from which little children went forth to toil in factory and mine, and grow up dwarfed and semi-barbarous.

Protestantism itself saw little that was wrong in the structure of the new society. For if a knowledge of the Scriptures fostered personal purity and sobriety among Protestants, it did not greatly clarify their social theory. Here the Scriptures were not consistent. Men read in the Gospels the word of the Lord, "It is easier for a camel to go through the eye of a needle, than for a rich man to enter into the kingdom of God"; they read in *Proverbs,* "Honour the Lord with thy substance, and with the first-fruits of all thine increase: So shall thy barns be filled with plenty, and thy presses shall burst out with new wine." Being thus offered a choice, it was more congenial to regard one's riches as the reward of piety, another's poverty as a defect of will or an inscrutable purpose of God. So Wilberforce, an Evangelical, crusading against the enslavement of blacks in the tropics, saw nothing wrong in the enslavement of whites in the factories of England. Wilberforce was thoroughly otherworldly, as preoccupied as a mediaeval saint with the future destiny of the human soul. If he was aware at all that factory life stunted soul as well as body, he doubtless believed that the hereafter would redress that.[1]

There was more understanding in Methodism, which flourished in the new industrial towns, and whose chapels gave to the poor the one outlet for their emotions and their idealism. But Methodism, too, was otherworldly, teaching the poor that, for this brief life, "they should learn resignation amid the painful chaos of a world so made, for good reasons of His own, by God." [2] So it was rather unconsciously than consciously that Methodism trained the early leaders of the Labour Movement. Educated in Methodist Sunday Schools, taught to manage chapel affairs and to speak in chapel committees, men became equipped to lead also in the later fight for economic freedom.

Meanwhile what of France? We have seen (p. 493) how that land was affected by "the Glorious Revolution" of 1688, that terminated the Stuart tyranny in England. A body of rationalizing thought crossed to France, to be popularized by Voltaire and the Encyclopedists, and to produce an extensive literature. It was generally anti-clerical, because the French philosophers regarded the hierarchy as the real enemy of progress. They did not so regard the monarchy as yet. The benevolent despot was highly regarded in France.

After fifty years of the *Enlightenment,* however, the monarchy was engulfed in the revolutionary current released by the opening sentence of Rousseau's *Contrat Social,* "Man is born free but is everywhere in chains." The current had been quickened by the triumph of republicanism in America. It had reached the growing body of industrial workers in the cities of France. It had reached the peasants, whose food supply had long been insecure, by reason of antiquated methods of agriculture and the inequities created by privilege. For there was privilege everywhere in France, impoverishing government, balking justice, and excluding talent from the service of the State. Privilege transferred the main burden of taxation to the shoulders of the poor. The higher clergy, in disesteem already by reason of their wealth and their vices, paid no

---

[1] A change for the better began when Evangelicalism produced a champion of the poor in Lord Shaftesbury, who, against fierce opposition from the mill owners, carried through Parliament the Factory Act of 1847.

[2] J. L. & B. Hammond, *The Town Labourer*, p. 283.

taxes. The nobles were chiefly non-resident, collecting the ancient rents and feudal dues, but performing no social function.

When therefore Louis XVI ascended the throne in 1774, he took over a land where bread riots were chronic and sections of the population embittered, but where a benevolent despot would still be received with enthusiasm. For such a rôle the young king was quite unfitted. With every private virtue, he had little capacity for government. His beautiful queen, the Austrian princess Marie Antoinette, was of tougher fibre but unpopular. So when the king assembled the States-General in 1789, the Commons, or Third Estate, seized control, declared itself a National Assembly, and proceeded to give France a new Constitution, that was intended to be a model for the world. A National Guard was created, including many violent men and criminals, commanded by Lafayette, co-liberator of America. Anarchy was rife, nobles fled the country, to become hateful centres of danger to the new State, the *émigrés*. The king and his ministers could not control the Assembly. The Assembly could not govern. The populace was uneducated for freedom. Control passed to the political clubs, of which the most important was the Jacobins.

Nothing could better illustrate the political incompetence of the Assembly than the Civil Constitution it gave the Church. Talleyrand, Bishop of Autun, a friend of the Revolution, had advised the Assembly that the clergy were but trustees of ecclesiastical lands, which really belonged to the State. The State could rightly reclaim its property, devote part to the maintenance of religion, the rest to paying the national debt. The Assembly therefore confiscated the estates of the Church and a few months later, in July, 1790, gave it a Civil Constitution. Each of the departments, into which France was now divided, was also to be a diocese. The bishoprics of France were thus automatically reduced from 136 to 83. Both bishops and parish priests were to be chosen by popular election. Protestants, Jews and atheists might therefore participate in the election of Catholic bishops and *curés,* whose salaries would be paid by the State. Monastic vows, regarded now as incompatible with the rights of man, were no longer to be recognized by law.

Naturally the Catholic conscience everywhere was wounded; and the Pope condemned the Civil Constitution. This made it still more difficult for conscientious priests to accept it; and the Assembly attempted to coerce them, by requiring of all an oath of allegiance to the nation, the law, the king and the new Civil Constitution. Many would not take the oath, yet refused to give up their office, and denounced those appointed to succeed them. The clergy were thus divided, the majority becoming enemies of the Revolution, many of them taking refuge in foreign lands. They were followed by the loyal devotion of their flocks, and became centres of resistance to the new order.

Meanwhile, in an excess of democracy, the National Assembly, having completed the Constitution, voted itself out of existence and left the working of the Constitution to new and untried men. It was succeeded by a Legislative Assembly, and the Legislative Assembly by a National Convention; but from the autumn of 1791 to the spring of 1795 the chief authority in France was the Paris mob.

As for the Church, the Legislative Assembly voted that priests who refused the oath should be excluded from the churches and their salaries withdrawn. The king withheld his assent and was brought to the guillotine. Religious skepticism, long fashionable among philosophers and the nobility, spread in coarse forms to the populace. The calendar was reformed, to obliterate all traces of Christian influence. A new epoch was to begin with the foundation of the Republic in 1792, "the first year of Liberty." Marriage was made a civil contract and dissoluble; and in two years five thousand marriages were dissolved in Paris alone. The ornaments and sacred vessels of the churches were declared national property and sold. The Goddess of Reason, in the person of a ballet-girl, was enthroned on the high altar of Notre Dame. The Convention substituted worship of Reason for Christianity; and the churches were closed or converted into temples of Reason. The existence of God was denied, and the immortality of the soul. Over the entrance to cemeteries was inscribed, "Death is an everlasting sleep."

This would not do. Leaders of the Revolution feared that the collapse of religious belief would drag down with it civic virtue. Robespierre, a lawyer of Arras, persuaded the Convention to declare that France believed in the immortality of the soul and recognized a Supreme Being, who was best served by the faithful discharge of one's duty. A national festival was held, with absurd theatrical pomp, in honour of the Supreme Being.

During these disordered years the military spirit of the French people revived, expressions of peace and universal brotherhood died away; and the National Guard proceeded to take Belgium from Austria and carry the French frontier to the Rhine. That imperilled Holland as well, and brought Britain into the war. Her entry rallied opposition to the Revolution. Russia, Prussia and Austria made common cause against the French Republic.

In this crisis the National Convention formed a small, secret cabinet, the Committee of Public Safety, which saved the Republic but disgraced France. For a brief year, 1793–1794, the Committee, led by Robespierre, carried on a Jacobin Terror, brought many distinguished men to the guillotine, and began to organize the armies with which Napoleon was to overrun Europe.

Sickening soon of terrorism, France nevertheless remained revolutionary. Incapable, however, of working the new Constitution, she came under a Directory of five men; and when in 1795 reaction set in, and cries of *Vive le Roi* were again heard in the streets of Paris, the Directory entrusted the pacification of France to a young Italian of Corsica, a General of France, Napoleon Bonaparte. Next year he was given command of French forces in Italy. Napoleon established himself in the palace of Mombello, near Milan; and, without reference to Paris and the Directory, waged war, imposed treaties, created states, and extorted from the papacy money and lands. France was made supreme in Italy.

By the end of 1799 the French Revolution had run its course. France wanted peace and ordered liberty. To whom could she look but to Napoleon, who by this time had made her armies feared in Europe and Egypt and Syria? A *coup d'état* in November, 1799, brought to an end the Directory and gave France still another Constitution, which made Napoleon Consul for ten years, with plenary powers.

Napoleon himself was the living embodiment of the forces that had been at work in France for fifty years. The literature of the Enlightenment had formed his mind; the Revolution had given him his opportunity. One side of the Revolution he was resolved to preserve, its social democracy. Political liberty might go, social equality must remain, and a free career for talent. New talent had been the mainstay of the Revolution and the strength of the armies of the Republic. So the First Consul called to his aid the best brains of France. Men of science were taken into the Council of State; Marshals in the army rose from the ranks.

Supreme over all parties, Napoleon applied his detached judgment to the appeasement of French society. Tyrannical laws were repealed, taxation made equitable, the Bank of France established and financial stability secured. Freedom of worship was granted, and a Concordat made with the Pope. Napoleon's generals cavilled; but he knew that religious freedom was a prerequisite to domestic peace. As for the papacy, Napoleon thought its days were numbered anyway. Meanwhile it would help him regiment the Catholics of Europe.

By the terms of the Concordat of 1801, Roman Catholicism was recognized as the religion of most Frenchmen, and was granted freedom, within the law of the land. Archbishops and bishops were to be nominated to the Pope by the First Consul, and before entering on office must take an oath of fidelity to the Head of the State. The Government would provide stipends for the clergy, and permit laymen to endow religious services; and the Pope would make no claim against the new holders of Church lands from the Government.

The Pope implemented the Concordat by asking the old legitimate bishops of France to resign their sees, for the sake of Catholic unity; and most did so. Both Pope and Government required the new constitutional bishops to resign; and they chose to submit their resignations to the Government.

To allay criticism of the Concordat among his lieutenants, Napoleon published seventy-seven "Organic Articles," explaining and somewhat modifying the Concordat. They declared that no pronouncement of the Pope should be published in France without permission from the Government, that offending bishops must be tried by the Council of State, that teachers in theological seminaries must subscribe the four articles of "the Gallican Liberties," [3] that no catechism might be used in schools without the sanction of the State, that priests might not perform the marriage ceremony, except for those already united in civil marriage.

The Pope [4] repudiated the Organic Articles and sought their recall, but

[3] The "Gallican Liberties" were embodied in four propositions, adopted by a National Assembly of French bishops, summoned by Louis XIV in 1682, at a time of controversy with Pope Innocent XI. The propositions are that (1) kings are not subject to ecclesiastical power in temporal affairs; (2) the Pope's power is limited by the decisions of General Councils, and (3) by the canons of the Universal Church and the customs of the French kingdom and Church; (4) the Pope's judgment in matters of faith is not final until confirmed by the Universal Church.

[4] Pope Pius VII, 1800–1823.

in vain; and indeed when Napoleon became master of all Italy, he made new demands, which the Holy Father steadily refused, continuing resistance in such ways as were open to him. He would not institute to office the clerics nominated to vacant bishoprics in France. In time twenty-seven were unoccupied and there was great discontent among French Roman Catholics.

Thus after the Concordat the Catholic Church in France was no longer that of the *ancien régime*. The lands and tithes, the princely establishments and great social influence of the prelates, were gone. The bishop was now a modestly paid officer of State, who kept to his diocese and could neither summon a synod nor consult the Pope. The parish priest, too, was an officer of State. He read from the pulpit the army bulletins, urged men to the colours, and taught obedience to the Head of the State. Worship, however, was as before, the Sunday rest restored; and the Angelus again called men to prayer.

The codification of French law was to be Napoleon's most enduring achievement. The reform of the Civil Code had been one of the aims of the Revolution. Napoleon fulfilled it. His Civil Code fixed in clear outlines the structure of a society, grounded in social equality and religious freedom, with private property secure and a coherent family life. Civil marriage and divorce opened lawful domestic relations to those who did not regard marriage as a sacrament. For the first time since the fourth century, when the Roman Empire adopted Christianity, a western nation legalized a completely secular life.

The pacification of Europe was more difficult; for Britain stood in the way. Hostility to the Revolution had been created there at the outset, by a brilliant political pamphlet of Edmund Burke, *Reflections on the Revolution in France*. Moreover British security and sea room were endangered, if the frontiers of France were on the North Sea and the Rhine and satellite republics existed in Italy and elsewhere. William Pitt would not accept such a Europe; and Napoleon answered with a continental blockade against British trade.

To exclude British wares from Italy, Napoleon refused to recognize the neutrality of the Vatican. In May, 1809, the Pope was removed to Savona, on the Gulf of Genoa, and the Papal States were annexed to France. It was a cardinal blunder. Italians were not profoundly religious;

but the papacy was a part of the ancient glory of Italy, and Italians resented its degradation, as did Catholics elsewhere.[5]

Simultaneously Napoleon launched an attack upon Spain. That, too was a cardinal blunder. Spain, aloof behind the Pyrenees, was the most Catholic country in Europe. Spaniards cared little for the rights of man, everything for the Catholic faith and their ancient customs. They now carried on a guerrilla warfare, baffling to the best generals of France, and gave Britain space to deploy a land army on the continent. By 1813 almost all Europe was leagued against France. At Fontainebleau in 1814, with foreign armies in Paris, Napoleon's Marshals, war-weary themselves and sensing the weariness of France, exacted of him abdication. Napoleon sought asylum on Elba.

The peace terms imposed upon France by the Treaty of Paris, in May, 1814, were moderate, but included the restoration of the Bourbon kings. So there came from exile a fat old gentleman, Louis XVIII, who had little to contribute except a link with the past. The detailed settlement of all Europe was left to a Congress, to meet in Vienna in November. The map of Europe there drawn, against revolutionary dangers from France, made Prussia dominant in the Rhineland and Austria in north and central Italy.

The Congress of Vienna was inspired by no respect for either nationality or the rights of populations. The well-being of Europe was to be secured by submission to legitimate authority, the legitimacy that had brought back the Bourbons to France.

While the Congress was still in session, Napoleon landed once more on the soil of France. He struck swiftly for the recovery of Belgium, the one prize that might rally his people; for Belgium and the estuary of the Rhine had a certain symbolic significance for Frenchmen. But Napoleon was stopped at Waterloo, in June, 1815. The "Hundred Days" were over. Napoleon went to St. Helena, a prisoner of the British, whose moderation secured to France her ancient frontiers and steadied the Bourbon régime. It was a temporary expedient. No Bourbon could prevent the

---

[5] In the summer of 1812 Pope Pius was brought to France, to Fontainebleau, where he remained virtually a prisoner until the fall of Napoleon, protesting always that he was under duress, was deprived of his lawful advisers, the cardinals and papal secretaries, and could perform no official act.

revival of Bonapartist ideas and the rise of a Second Empire. Meanwhile the settlement gave Europe forty years of comparative peace.

The Revolution and the Napoleonic wars produced an emotional reaction in Europe. A decade of disorder in France, in the name of Reason, followed by a decade of French aggrandisement everywhere, seemed more than enough. Men thought better now of the past, and of the institutions that time had tested. Among the *émigrés* who returned to France, when Napoleon granted religious freedom, was Chateaubriand, a nobleman of Brittany, who in exile had lived in a garret among the London poor, and in the United States had known the friendship of certain heroes of American independence. Returning to France, Chateaubriand devoted his great talents to showing, not that Catholicism is reasonable, but that it is beautiful and comforting, impressive in its doctrines, lofty in its morality, the effective cause of all that is best in civilization. A contemporary, Madame de Staël, eulogized with great skill and charm the Christian faith and in the novel *Delphine* displayed the Divine activity in the world. Chateaubriand and Madame de Staël were but the most distinguished of many in France, who dwelt lovingly on the past and the ancestral faith.

In Germany, too, a new patriotism and devotion to duty were aroused. Saved at great cost from an alien tyranny, Germans came to dislike foreign influence, especially French. German youths, particularly students, tried to return to the old Teutonic ways, imitating the fathers in speech and dress. Coincidently the religious indifference of the eighteenth century vanished. Romans and Protestants alike recognized that Rationalism could not satisfy the human soul. Unable to breathe the rarefied air of Immanuel Kant and return to religion by way of philosophy, they returned by the road of patriotism and romance. The Middle Ages were idealized. Aristocrats in particular, and students of Constitutional Law, found a new attractiveness in mediaeval society, where classes had been distinctly marked and there was none of the promiscuity of a Paris rabble.

One aspect of this Romanticism was a certain tendency among distinguished Protestants to return to the Church of Rome. Religious differences, they said, had cost Germans their place in the expanding world. They forgot that, for a thousand years before the Protestant revolt, separatist tendencies had kept Germans politically disunited, and that an earlier Romanticism, the dream of a Holy Roman Empire ruled by Germans, had delivered Germany herself over to neglect and misgovernment. This misreading of history was stimulated, however, by a certain weariness of speculation and a longing for rest in the infallible Church. So the Romanticist poet, Frederick von Schlegel, and the scholarly and distinguished Count Frederick von Stolberg, with others of less note, returned to the Roman Church.

This religious Romanticism and cult of the antique were ephemeral. Rationalism and its political manifestations had permanently diminished the Catholic Church. In France the Concordat continued to govern the relations of Church and State. Its effect was to make the clergy regard the Pope as their one security against the State. French Catholicism, therefore, became Ultramontane in spirit, and to that extent foreign to France.

In Germany, too, Napoleon's arrangements lowered Catholic prestige. The Archbishops of Mainz, Treves and Cologne had been princes of the Holy Roman Empire and members of the Electoral College. In 1803 their ecclesiastical principalities ceased to exist, being divided among the surrounding secular states. In 1806 Francis II of Austria resigned the title Roman Emperor. The venerable Holy Roman Empire therefore went out of existence, dissipating forever the dream of a universal Church and a universal State, together directing the life of mankind, in the name of God.

There was to be some slight compensation in the New World. In South and Central America, where immigration was Spanish and a single type of civilization was imposed upon the natives everywhere, Roman Catholicism was to be dominant, until overtaken by the secularism that had diminished it in France. In North America, too, Quebec was already an enduring monument to Jesuit devotion, a rural France successfully transplanted, while urban France was being fertilized to new forms by the ideas of Voltaire and Rousseau. North America, however, was in general an outpost of European Protestantism. Many stocks contributed to the new population, some driven by the urge for religious freedom. American society was an agglomeration of individualists, having a high degree of initiative, but compelled by conditions in the new world to a mutual toleration. Roman Catholicism was at a disadvantage here, its exclusive pretensions unreal. The immigration that was to augment enormously the Catholic Church was delayed until the United States was already Protestant, as was Canada also, outside Quebec.

In the background, however, for Catholicism and Protestantism everywhere, obscured by the absorbing pursuit of wealth, were those unspent forces of the eighteenth century, that would confront Christianity again. Rationalism, arrested rather by its own crudities than by the Christian rejoinder, still lived and was altering the balance between Reason and Religion, the two sources of truth that Christianity itself acknowledged. Science was pressing for a place among the things surely spoken of God to the race. Secularism advanced everywhere, as the material world offered greater and greater rewards to intelligence and industry. Industrialism opened the way to new forms of oppression and a new social cleavage, in whose presence organized Christianity was to be confused in thought and uncertain in action. In all this conflict of forces, Ethical Idealism and related philosophies brought support to religion, but not more for a Christian than for a Buddhist mendicant or a Muslim Sufi.

CHAPTER XXIV

THE NINETEENTH CENTURY

THE dominant idea of the sovereigns of Europe and their ministers, in the early nineteenth century, was that there must be no more Napoleons and no recurrence of revolution. There was grim reaction throughout the continent. It was different in Britain. No invading armies had carried devastation through her countryside; and she had emerged from the Napoleonic wars with a new industrial system and an enlarged empire. So there was no thought in Britain of suppressing civil liberties and the parliamentary system. The most reactionary government was liberal, when compared with those of Russia, Austria and Prussia.

Before long a "Holy Alliance" of these three continental autocracies was formed, to resist Liberalism. It muzzled the intellectuals of Germany, suppressed a constitutional movement in Italy, restored autocracy in Spain, and refused recognition to certain new South American States. It had some slight justification as an instrument of peace and order, but ran counter to the popular aspirations of the age. It was not to be expected that lands sown with the ideas of Voltaire and Rousseau, and stimulated by the example of British freedom, would forever buy peace at the price of liberty. Belgians chafed under the yoke of Holland, Poles under Russia and Prussia, Italians under Austria; and great minds in Germany wondered whether, after all the blood and tears of the Napoleonic struggle, Germany was to continue forever disunited, a loose confederacy of thirty-nine states, each directing its own foreign policy and most of them governed by unenlightened despotisms.

Meanwhile ecclesiastical leaders in Europe, encouraged by the example of political despotism, sought to recover for the Catholic Church the position she had held before the French Revolution. In 1814 Pope Pius VII returned to Rome from virtual imprisonment in France; and the Congress of Vienna restored to him the States of the Church. The populace preferred lay to clerical rule. So there were insurrections in the States of the Church; and a secret society, the *Carbonari,* sworn to resist despotism, grew steadily. Patriots throughout Italy tended to regard the temporal power of the papacy as the chief obstacle to Italian unification.

The first important act of Pope Pius on returning to Rome was the restoration of the Jesuits.[1] He went in solemn procession to the Church of the Jesuits, said Mass at the altar of St. Ignatius, and caused to be read a papal Bull. His Holiness, it said, would commit a grievous sin if, amidst the storms that raged round the barque of St. Peter, he failed to bring back the experienced oarsmen, who were capable of bringing it through the menacing waves. That day the Jesuits received back their three palaces in Rome; and in the following year they were given sub-stantial grants for the establishment of colleges throughout the Papal State.

There was anger throughout Europe at the restoration of the Jesuits; but anger dies, while the deed that caused it remains. The revived Com-pany of Jesus worked for control of Catholic education everywhere. The claim of civil governments to regulate primary and secondary education was answered by the Jesuit watchword, "freedom of Catholic instruc-tion." The sons of the privileged classes entered Jesuit boarding-schools, to be imbued with ultramontane principles, while sisterhoods, under Jesuit inspiration, did a similar work for girls. Few persons of original genius were to come from these schools, but many distinguished in the sciences, especially astronomy, where ability was less hampered by au-thority.

The Jesuits sought influence with the governing classes. Jesuit preachers conducted missions in fashionable quarters. Rival Orders ceased from rivalry, in face of the common difficulties of Catholicism. The history of Romanism was thenceforth to be the history of the Jesuits, whose General would always be at the elbow of the Holy Father.

When Pius VII died in 1823, his successor, Leo XII, entrusted to the Jesuits the *Collegium Romanum,* a sort of graduate school at Rome for

---

[1] Their political machinations, their commercial adventures in Spanish and Portuguese colonies, the intellectual radicalism that stemmed from Voltaire, had been their undoing in the generation before Napoleon. The Jesuits were expelled from Portuguese territory in 1759, suppressed in France in 1764, expelled from Spain and Naples in 1767. The rulers of these lands at length exacted from Pope Clement XIV the abolition of the order itself in 1773.

young priests from everywhere. It gave the Jesuits immense influence with the worldwide priesthood. Pope Leo entered into Concordats with Catholic German states, rebuked the French Government for allowing public worship to Protestants, condemned philosophers who taught religious toleration, condemned Bible Societies, and enforced religious observances in the Papal State by the aid of the police.

The next two popes pursued the same policy. Popular insurrections resulted in the Papal State. They were suppressed with the aid of Austrian troops, while the *Carbonari* filled the minds of Italian youths with equal hatred of Austrian rule and the political rule of the papacy. So there were two thousand political prisoners in papal prisons.

The accession of Pius IX in 1846 was greeted with popular enthusiasm. A genial, handsome man, of courtly manners, he had adequate strength of character and was thought to be sympathetic with progress. Pope Pius was to sit in Peter's chair more than thirty years,[2] a period longer than that of any other pope. He proved to be as great a pope as the modern world permits, a sort of reduced copy of the great Innocent III.

Pope Pius speedily issued an amnesty to political prisoners. Conservatives thought the action dangerous; but the Pope persisted. He simplified the papal court, granted greater freedom to the Press, opened the higher offices of state to laymen, reformed and liberalized the municipal constitution of Rome, and moved for a confederacy of the Italian states.

The policy was doomed to failure. It went too far for papal theory, not far enough for Italian patriots. The leader of the patriots was Mazzini, the anti-clerical son of a Genoese doctor, who all his life had laboured for a free, united nation of Italians. Their example was King Victor Emmanuel II, of the little Kingdom of Piedmont, whose reforms there satisfied the aspirations of Italian patriots everywhere. The King, in 1848, expelled the Jesuits from Piedmont, made clerics amenable to the civil courts, then sent the Archbishop of Turin into exile, for condemning the reforms and refusing to appear before a civil tribunal. Victor Emmanuel proceeded to establish civil marriage, withdrew from ecclesiastical institutions their special exemptions, and abolished all Orders that did not justify their existence by preaching, or education, or the care of the sick. It was a miniature French Revolution. When the Pope pronounced an anathema and priests disturbed the public peace,

[2] From June 16, 1846, until February 7, 1878.

Piedmont annulled its Concordats with the papacy, on the ground that they were not treaties between sovereign powers but concessions by the State to the Church, which could be withdrawn.

Piedmont found support in the little Kingdom of Sardinia, whose very able Prime Minister, Count Cavour, declared himself for constitutional government and against Austrian rule. By 1870 the Austrian forces in Italy had been defeated with the aid of the French, the French troops themselves were withdrawn to meet the perils of the Franco-Prussian War, and Victor Emmanuel was in Rome, king of a united Italy.

A civil law of the following year guaranteed to the Pope an adequate income and independent rule in the Vatican and its gardens, the cathedral church of St. John Lateran, and a summer estate, the *Castel Gandolfo*. In spiritual affairs the Pope was to exercise his authority without interference by the State, except that in Italy bishops might not assume office without the royal assent.

The Pope rejected this arrangement, and immured himself in the Vatican. The contributions of the faithful throughout the world, however, the so-called Peter's Pence, provided him an ample income; and crowds of pilgrims brought him rich gifts. His Holiness continued to the end to protest the seizure of the States of the Church, but died in 1878, still the "prisoner of the Vatican." Nevertheless the papal institution had gained in moral authority. It was no longer compromised by wretched misgovernment in the States of the Church, and by the dubious things done in its name in international politics.

Meanwhile Pope Pius had made solid advances of another sort. Certain events of his reign were the final consummation of the policy adopted by the Council of Trent (*See* pp. 403–405) three centuries before. Faced then with Humanism and the Protestant revolt, the Council had set its face against change. The Church of Rome, it determined, would follow the old paths. She would not change either ritual or creed. She would define them, that none need misunderstand, and enforce them by a more faithful discipline. The decision was now reaffirmed in three spectacular events of the reign of Pius IX—the promulgation of the doctrine of the Immaculate Conception of the Virgin Mary, the publication of a "Syllabus of Errors," and the declaration by a Vatican Council that popes are infallible.

In the Middle Ages Franciscan and Dominican scholars had hotly debated whether the Virgin Mary was, from the moment when she was conceived in her mother's womb, miraculously preserved from the taint of original sin. By the nineteenth century it had long been a pious opinion, especially in Spain and Italy, that the Virgin had been so preserved. It was now a widely accepted part of Catholic tradition; and in St. Peter's Church in 1854, in the presence of many cardinals and bishops, gathered to the Festival of the Conception of the Virgin, Pope Pius declared the Immaculate Conception a part of Catholic dogma. Thus the Virgin Mary, so long venerated as the ideal of a maiden's purity and a mother's compassion, was confirmed in her place at the head of the hierarchy of semi-divine powers, that could confidently be engaged by the sinful to plead their case with God.

Ten years later, in 1864, Pope Pius summarized all the pronouncements he had made against the errors of the age, in a "Syllabus of Errors." It cited eighty, which a good Catholic must abjure for the safety of his soul. Among them were Rationalism, the belief in religious liberty and the freedom of the Press, the doctrine that all men, lay and clerical, are equal before the law, Bible Societies and all secret societies. Above all His Holiness condemned the idea that a pope could approve what modern society had come to regard as progress.

Some four years later Pope Pius summoned all bishops of the Roman Church to assemble in General Council at the Vatican in December 1870. Soon there appeared in *Civiltà Cattolica,* the official organ of the Jesuits at Rome, a forecast that the Council would be brief, as it would only confirm the Syllabus and proclaim the infallibility of the Pope. There was alarm among Catholic laymen, which bishops in France and Germany sought to allay. It was unthinkable, they said, that a General Council should announce as dogma what could not be drawn from either the Scriptures or apostolic tradition.

When the Council assembled, it devoted three months to a summary of accepted Catholic doctrines, then turned to the proposed doctrine of papal infallibility. Four German prelates led the opposition within the Council, while Catholic laymen wrote letters to the Press of Europe, the most remarkable, attributed to Lord Acton, being published later under the name "Quirinus." Opponents of the doctrine had no difficulty in showing that it had been unknown in the ancient Church. The infallibilists rejoined that history must yield to divine revelation, that if His Holiness was the Vicar of Christ, he must have been granted the infallibility of Christ.

The discussion continued into the hot Roman summer. In the end fifty-six bishops signed an address to Pope Pius, that they still could not concur and that they would rather return to their homes than oppose His Holiness further. In July the vote was taken, only two bishops dissenting; [3] and amidst a violent thunder storm the Pope announced the result and confirmed the decree. Infallibilists thought the storm a supernatural reminder of that great day, three thousand years before, when God gave to Moses the Law on Mt. Sinai.

The newly-defined dogma does not mean that in Catholic theory all papal utterances are infallible. It means rather that when a pope declares officially (*ex cathedra*) what was the teaching of the apostles concerning anything now found in Catholic faith and practice, he speaks "by the divine assistance promised him in blessed Peter." The dogma thus completes the Petrine Theory (*See* pp. 203–205), that was already taking form in the second century.

The truth of the dogma of Papal Infallibility can hardly be maintained; its practical value cannot be doubted. The one possible source of unity for the Catholic Church was now the papacy. Developments in the modern world were undermining national churches, in working alliance with national governments, while yet within the universal Catholic Church. Ultramontanism was therefore growing steadily. The Vatican decree confirmed the tendency of the times.

Besides it had been abundantly demonstrated that General Councils do not necessarily advance unity. Discussion, by clarifying issues, confirms differences as frequently as it produces agreement, and publishes the differences to the world. It is both logical and wise that truth, conceived as supernaturally revealed and supernaturally preserved, should be kept outside democratic procedures. Catholic theory requires an ecclesiastical autocracy.

Catholic bishops throughout the world proceeded to exact of their priests and teachers of theology assent to the new dogma, under pain of excommunication. Many educated laymen disliked the dogma, but thought it their duty to submit. The Catholic masses were probably but little interested. They knew nothing of historical evidence, were

---

[3] The Italian Ricci and the American Fitzgerald, of Little Rock, Arkansas.

satisfied to accept what the Church taught, and had long regarded the Holy Father with a reverence that would easily pass into a belief in his infallibility.

Some German theologians, however, were in difficulty. They were aware that the doctrine of Papal Infallibility was new. They denied that a General Council had authority to invent doctrines, and disliked the methods employed at the Vatican Council. The Catholic Church, they thought, had now become another Church. Those who loved true catholicism must adhere to the ancient traditions.

Those who so believed were soon called "Old Catholics." Five hundred of them met at Munich in 1871, in the first Old-Catholic Congress. It included some of the foremost Catholic scholars of Germany.[4] Three years later there was a small but distinguished Old-Catholic Church, of some one hundred congregations, consoled in their loneliness by the hope of union with the Greek and Anglican churches. In time the Old-Catholic Church saw many of its members pass over into various Protestant bodies.

How little the main currents of life were affected by the Vatican Council was soon manifest. It was only two months after the Council dissolved, that the States of the Church were seized and incorporated within the Kingdom of Italy (See p. 522). A few years later, in 1888, champions of intellectual freedom, from all over the world, held an anti-papal demonstration in Rome, where they unveiled a statue to Giordano Bruno, burned in 1600 for teaching that God reveals Himself in and through the universe.

Meanwhile in France the restoration of the Bourbon monarchy had brought little change. The *ancien régime* was gone forever. The great gains of the Revolution—the new judicial system, equality before the law, the National Guard, the Concordat—remained; and when in 1824 Louis XVIII was succeeded by his brother, Charles X, an elderly bigot, of clerical principles, it was soon clear that the revolutionary spirit still lived. Charles chose as Prime Minister one of the émigrés, Jules de Polignac, a Catholic reactionary, who thought himself under the direct guidance of the Virgin Mary. With such an adviser, the king soon fanned into flame the old controversy between crown and people, priest and lay-

---

4 Notably the canonist J. F. von Schulte and the historian Ignaz von Döllinger.

man. Royal decrees, in July, 1830, limited the freedom of the Press and dissolved Parliament. It was clear that the king and his ministers meant to tear up the Constitution. Paris responded with street fighting, in which the palace of the Archbishop was levelled, the Church of St. Germain sacked, and the monarchy once more overthrown.

Strangely the "July Revolution" produced neither a republic nor an empire, but another monarchy, under Louis Philippe of Orleans, head of the younger branch of the Bourbons. Louis had fought in the revolutionary armies, was a man of the new order, and seemed to Liberals a sort of French William of Orange, who would give France the blessings of constitutional rule. They were not wholly mistaken. Louis Philippe gave the land eighteen years of economic progress and peace. The religious situation, however, continued disturbed.

In the general unrest a certain Abbé Chatel succeeded in setting up an Anti-Roman French Catholic Church. Its resistance to the papacy gave it a brief vogue; but it was a manufactured thing, and in little more than a decade it disappeared. Other Catholic reformers adopted other plans. The Abbé Lamennais, an eloquent preacher and vigorous writer, had long believed that the Church got more harm than good from her connection with the State. Let her abondon her privileged position, reconcile herself to apostolic poverty, and depend for support on the love of the faithful. Lamennais dreamed that the Catholic Church might then, under the headship of the Pope himself, lead in the struggle for intellectual and political freedom.

Warmed by such dreams, Lamennais, soon after the July Revolution, founded the journal L'Avenir, to be the organ of "New-Catholics," who would fight for "God and Liberty, for Pope and People." A few illustrious men were drawn to the movement, notably the Count of Montalembert, a devout man, of literary gifts, and the priest Lacordaire, soon to become the greatest preacher in France. The publication of L'Avenir was suspended, however, in 1831, and the movement censured by the French bishops. Lamennais, Montalembert and Lacordaire set out hopefully for Rome, to plead their cause with the Pope himself. They were coldly received; L'Avenir was condemned. Lacordaire and Montalembert submitted humbly to the Holy Father,[5] and set themselves to revive Catholic feeling in France and to restore respect for mediaeval theology

---

[5] Lamennais, embittered, became a free lance, of the rationalistic type.

and philosophy. They and their disciples, "Sons of the Crusaders," believed that the Catholic past was consistent with the contemporary scientific movement and that general enlightenment would advance Catholic principles. They were soon disillusioned. Refined, devout and tolerant, the "Sons of the Crusaders" had little influence with the masses. Most of rural France was indifferent to science, most of urban France to the Middle Ages.

Political change was to trouble France through all the nineteenth century. The House of Orleans was overthrown and the monarchy ended by another revolution in 1848, which set up a Republic, under the Presidency of Louis Napoleon, nephew of the first Napoleon. After three years a *coup d'état* made the President an autocrat, and in the following year, 1852, he assumed the imperial title, as Napoleon III. Most of the clergy, fearing disorders, heartily approved; but Catholic intellectuals opposed the new tyranny. Montalembert and Lacordaire preached that political servitude corrupts the souls of men and debases the Church, producing time-serving bishops, who infect the clergy with timidity and self-interest. Liberal Catholics adopted the watchword, "A free Church in a free State."

Events confirmed the judgment of Catholic Liberals. The Government maintained itself by gross corruption. Materialism was rampant. Public taste and morals declined. All that had been gained by the Catholic Revival was being lost. Then suddenly Napoleon III was toppled from his throne in 1870, by the shock of the Franco-Prussian War and another insurrection in Paris. Once more the people looked for help to supernatural powers. The Virgin Mary became the special protectress of France. She would deliver Rome from Italian nationalists, and France from the Prussian.

A National Assembly in 1871 restored the Republic; and the new Government sought to rally the nation by winning the support of the clergy and making France appear the defender of Roman Catholicism throughout the world. It was an unnatural rôle for France; and the old uncertain equilibrium continued. Society was divided between Ultramontanism and Liberal Catholicism, with Rationalism and Materialism interpenetrating all, and small groups of Protestants, both Reformed and Lutheran, maintaining a sturdy but inconspicuous existence.

In 1880 began a series of legislative acts, that were to make France a permanently secular State, on the Napoleonic model. That year Jules Ferry, Minister of Education, introduced a Bill, removing the representatives of the bishops from the Council of Higher Education and forbidding members of unauthorised ecclesiastical Orders to teach in schools. This included the greatest of the Orders, like the Benedictines and Franciscans, the Dominicans and Jesuits, which had continued since the days of Napoleon I, without asking authorisation by the State.

Ferry's Bill passed the Chamber of Deputies in 1880; but the clause excluding unauthorised Orders was rejected by the Senate. Grévy, President of the Republic, replied in two decrees, applying statutes regarded as obsolete, requiring the Jesuits to dissolve within three months and giving all other unauthorised Orders six months, in which to apply for governmental recognition or dissolve.

The police were resisted when they tried to enforce the decrees; and two thousand advocates pronounced them unconstitutional. The Government then proceeded to make ordinary courts incapable of trying such cases, abolished chaplaincies in the army, made students for the priesthood liable for military service, and established boarding-schools for girls, to offset the convent schools.

The severest blow to religious instruction was dealt in 1882, when an Education Bill, introduced by Paul Bert, was carried. It required all children in France to attend elementary schools, supported by the State, excluded the clergy from such schools, and relegated religious education to the home and the Church. Crucifixes and other religious symbols were ordered removed from the walls of class-rooms. When the Pope addressed to President Grévy a solemn remonstrance, Grévy treated it as a private letter, which he did not communicate to his Ministers.

The final breach came in 1904. President Loubet visited the King of Italy at Rome. The visit was resented by French Ultramontanes and protested by the Pope, a protest which the French Government resented. Tension grew when two French bishops, in favour with the Government, were summoned by the Pope, to answer charges of irregular conduct. The Government declared it a violation of the Concordat and severed diplomatic relations with the papacy.

In the following year, 1905, a Bill separated Church and State in France. The new law began with a proclamation of liberty of conscience and of worship for all, with government support for none. The property of the churches was to be transferred to *Associations Cultuelles,* associations for the support of public worship. Churches and chapels were to be left to the Associations; but theological seminaries, bishops' palaces and parsonages were to remain with them for only two years, after which they must be secured by fresh negotiations with the civil authorities. Elderly priests and ministers, who had been receiving State salaries, were granted small pensions. The Associations might raise funds for religious work by such subscriptions, collections and fees as the faithful would provide.

"Gallicanism" was now at an end. The French Government had withdrawn from the religious field. Popes could thenceforth exercise such authority over the clergy as they could enforce by purely spiritual penalties.

What of Spain? When the armies of Napoleon invaded that country, Spain was still a world power, with extensive dominions beyond the seas. The "Spanish Indies" included most of South and Central America, a group of states, Creole and Indian and Negro in population, with an infiltration of Spaniards, ruled by colonial governors appointed by the Spanish crown. Upon the mixed native population, Spanish civilization and the Catholic faith were imposed from the beginning.

Christianity in Spanish America was two hundred years old when North America, west of the Atlantic seaboard, was still a wilderness; for the monastic Orders came early to the Spanish Indies. Hardly was Christopher Columbus laid to rest in the Carthusian monastery of *Santa Maria de las Cuevas* at Seville, when Franciscans reached what was later called Venezuela. Within a generation they were established in Peru and the Argentine, Brazil and Mexico. Within a century they were in New Mexico, then in Texas. In Napoleon's time they were evangelizing California. The Dominicans followed the Franciscans; and gradually both were overshadowed everywhere by the Jesuits.

Revolt among the Spanish American colonies followed the Napoleonic wars. It was not, as in North America, a blow struck for constitutional government. The colonies had been kept at peace and bound in sentiment to each other by a common religious faith and a common loyalty to the Spanish crown, tirelessly inculcated by the Jesuits. When in 1768 the Jesuit Order was expelled by the home Government, the loyalty of the Spanish Indies to the crown was undermined. When a generation later the autocrat Ferdinand VII was excluded by Napoleon from the throne of Spain, the crown became identified in colonial minds with democratic innovations from France.

The destiny of the Spanish dominions in America was settled when Spain submitted to alliance with Napoleon. An English fleet then crippled the Spanish navy at Trafalgar, while another swept Spanish ships from the Pacific. In these circumstances, and fired by the example of a great soldier-statesman, Simon Bolivar, the Spanish American States one by one established their independence. Bolivar, a Spanish aristocrat, born in Venezuela, became the liberator of what are now Venezuela, Columbia and Ecuador, Panama, Peru and Bolivia,[6] whose Congresses all conferred upon him the title *Libertador*.[7]

Bolivar derived much comfort from those ancient enemies of Spain, the Anglo-Saxons, who concluded in South America the quarrel that had begun with the Spanish Armada and the Inquisition. English seamen screened the coasts. English adventurers formed the nucleus of Bolivar's first armies. An English Foreign Minister, George Canning, was the first statesman in Europe to give recognition to the new republics. The United States had already done so and was to confirm the exclusion of Spain from the Americas in 1898, by annexing Puerto Rico and helping Cuba to establish her independence.

Spanish America continues in the Roman faith, whose antiquity, authoritarianism and mysteries all suit the romantic Spanish and native genius. Opposition comes less from Protestantism, or contemporary currents of thought, or a demand for democratic freedom, than from the perception by patriots that Catholic control of education tends to a low level of general enlightenment and diminishes the place of the Spanish states among the nations. So events have followed the French pattern, tending to advance by revolutions, initiated by patriots or adventurers and followed by the familiar anti-clerical legislation, expulsion of the Jesuits, separation of Church and State, legalizing of the secular life, to all of which the masses are largely indifferent.

Spain herself has not recovered the lost prestige. It is not that her

[6] Bolivar became the first Dictator-President of Bolivia, which during his lifetime adopted his name for the State.

[7] Bolivar's letters, addresses and proclamations provide students of history with their clearest picture of the Spanish colonies.

people are decadent; it is rather that the Spanish temper is ill-adjusted to the modern world. Spain is romantic, devoted to the past, submissive to authority, if only it is ancient authority. So she has always been. It is not strange that St. Dominic, who restored the authority of Catholic doctrine in mediaeval Europe, came out of Spain, as did Ignatius Loyola, who arrested the spread of Protestantism. The Catholic Counter-Reformation, when every Catholic virtue flowered again, had its spearhead in Spain. The nineteenth century found Spain still legitimist, authoritarian. Revolutions brought parliamentary institutions, which quickly died, for want of an electorate to sustain them. When the twentieth century dawned, Spain was still romantic, still unready for democratic action, half her populace illiterate, education controlled and public opinion dominated by the Catholic Church. Liberals were under suspicion as dangerous radicals, imitators of the French. Not until the Bourbon monarchy was overthrown and the Second Republic established in 1931 did a Spanish government attempt to apply the only remedy for Spanish ills, the education of the populace, in preparation for democratic procedures. The attempt failed, by reason of Catholic sentiment in Spain, supported by anti-Catholic dictators abroad.

In England Christianity, differently conceived, had begun the education of the masses a century before.[8] In 1812, when as yet religious zeal alone could move men to educate the poor, two Christian organizations undertook the work. These were the Anglican National Society and the British and Foreign School Society. When a few years later public men began to realize that popular education is necessary to a sound national life, the State adjusted itself to the Christian institutions already established, assisting them from public funds, providing for the training of teachers and appointing inspectors. Other social services followed. So that, when the continent was being shaken by revolution, in 1830 and again in 1848, Parliament had already laid the foundation of a system of social services, that opened the way to a tranquil enlargement of liberty and social health.

This was the fruit chiefly of the Methodist revival and the related Evangelical, or Low Church, movement in the Church of England,

---

[8] Just as it had done in Scotland, two centuries earlier still, with Knox and his fellow reformers.

which were in full vigour in the early nineteenth century. Their most notable figure was Antony Ashley Cooper, Earl of Shaftesbury, who gave himself with patience and great courage to philanthropic work, and the springs of whose piety were the Bible and a vivid sense of the presence of Christ.

The defect of Evangelicalism was that it provided little help for minds caught in the tide of new ideas, about politics and social theory, science and philosophy, theology and Biblical interpretation. This was the special contribution of another party, the Liberals, called in the Church of England the Broad-Church Party. Liberals differed among themselves, as men who think freely are likely to do; but they were one in acknowledging the unity of truth. Nothing that science and history disproved could be true for religion. Christian Liberals were confident that Christianity would survive this test of truth; but they usually meant by Christianity a few essential things, like the love of God and his self-disclosure in Christ. Liberals did not expect to find in science corroboration of orthodox views of creation, redemption, the nature of the Church, the infallibility of the Scriptures. And when they enquired into the nature of God and his relation to the Universe, they tended, like scientists to look first to Nature.

Earliest of distinguished Christian Liberals of the nineteenth century was the poet Samuel Taylor Coleridge (1772–1834), who thought orthodox theology "a science of shadows under the name of theology," and who tirelessly affirmed, in the manner of Kant, that "the moral nature is the beginning and the end of religion." Wordsworth, too (1770–1850), taught men in verse to bring within the compass of religion all the physical world. Greater than either, the greatest English poet since Shakespeare, was Robert Browning (1812–1889), who devoted his comprehensive knowledge and great gifts to showing that Christianity provides the one adequate philosophy of life. Of like mind were the dour philosopher, Thomas Carlyle, and a great preacher of the Establishment, Frederick Denison Maurice.

Liberalism was bound to affect contemporary interpretations of the Bible. A new method had already been adopted by Thomas Arnold, headmaster of Rugby, who applied to the Scriptures the method by which he interpreted for his pupils the Greek classics, though still finding in the Scriptures oracles of God. His pupil, Dean Stanley of St.

Paul's, and his friend Benjamin Jowett, Professor of Greek at Oxford, applied his method to the Epistles of St. Paul, and were fiercely attacked for so doing. The agitation increased when there appeared in 1860 a volume, *Essays and Reviews,* by seven scholars. The volume was meant to encourage free discussion of those religious questions, about which men were known to differ but where differences were concealed. The book was condemned by the bishops; and two of the essayists were tried and condemned by ecclesiastical courts. The sentences were reversed, however, by the Judicial Committee of the Privy Council. Two years later John William Colenso, a brilliant mathematician, who had gone to South Africa and become Bishop of Natal, published a book, *The Pentateuch and the Book of Joshua critically examined,* in which he showed that the first five books of the Old Testament, described in the Bible as "Books of Moses," were compiled from different, often contradictory, sources and that very little of their contents could have come from Mosaic times.

Churchmen at home called upon Colenso to resign; and Bishop Gray, Metropolitan of South Africa, deposed him. The Judicial Committee again reversed the judgment; and Colenso continued in his position until death, though regarded by Churchmen generally as deposed.[9]

A new political Liberalism, too, was applying to English institutions the ideas of the French Revolution, though with more caution. It had won two early victories, in the Catholic Relief Bill of 1829, which permitted Catholics to enter Parliament, and in the Reform Bill of 1832, which extended the vote in parliamentary elections to great sections of the population. Liberalism had then proceeded to require of the Church an accounting, for the great power and wealth that the nation had left in its hands. The Government in 1835 appointed an Ecclesiastical Commission, to investigate the uses of Church property. As a result the incomes of the richer bishops were reduced, and a better distribution of the wealth of the Church effected.

[9] Out of these agitations arose a Cambridge School of Liberals, whose leaders were three Professors at the University, Lightfoot, Westcott and Hort. The first two became bishops; and the union in them of true piety and great scholarship began a transformation of the episcopate. Until Lightfoot and Westcott the record of the Anglican bishops had been rather inglorious. They had been amiable, respectable men, appointed by the Prime Minister, who enjoyed their considerable emoluments and were willing that so many of the clergy as were their special friends should experience a similar enjoyment. The bishops were the natural enemies of the new political Liberalism.

Acts of Parliament, however, though they may remove abuses, cannot revive religion. This was done through the Low Church and Broad Church leaders, and those of another party, of which we have yet to speak. The zeal of good men, differing from each other and from the main body of the Church, but ready to endure opposition and some obloquy for their convictions, communicated itself measurably to the whole Church.

The third of the parties was the High Church, or Anglo-Catholic, the English equivalent of that Romanticism, which in France is associated with Chateaubriand and Madame de Staël. There were still in the Church of England a few who regretted the Protestant Reformation, and whose thoughts turned back to mediaeval Christianity and the imperial days of the Church. Such men had been given standing room by the Elizabethan Settlement, which had contemplated the continuance of Catholics in the Established Church, so long as they would repudiate the Pope and one or two "errors."

This latent Anglo-Catholicism became a movement almost immediately after the Reform Bill of 1832. The first Parliament elected under the enlarged franchise was strongly Liberal; and one of its earliest achievements was the Church Temporalities (Ireland) Act, by which two archbishoprics and eight bishoprics in Ireland were discontinued, ecclesiastical incomes reduced, and a commission appointed to administer the revenues thus saved. Men who held lofty views of the Church were shocked at the annihilation of ten bishoprics, by action of the State; and a clergyman, John Keble, Fellow of Oriel College, Oxford, preached there a sermon on "National Apostasy." That day, July 14, 1833, was to be regarded as the birthday of "The Oxford Movement." A few days later a little party of friends met at a rectory in Suffolk, to devise plans for the defence of the Church; and soon there went to the Archbishop of Canterbury an address, signed by seven thousand clergymen and more than two hundred thousand heads of families. Churchmen were stronger than their critics thought, and were heartened by the discovery of their strength. It was necessary, however, to inform the public as to the issues involved; and to this end three men, all Fellows of Oriel, began the publication of *Tracts for the Times*. These men were Keble himself, his pupil Richard Hurrell Froude, and John Henry Newman.

John Keble (1792–1866), son of a devout and scholarly country vicar, had been a brilliant youth, of singular simplicity and purity, who at nineteen was already a Fellow of Oriel. Growing quickly into a poet and theologian, he continued void of personal ambition, reverenced for the sweetness of his disposition. He seemed the ideal Anglican, inclined to neither Romanism nor Puritanism, and at thirty-five published *The Christian Year,* a running commentary in poetry on the Prayer Book, a poem being provided for each Sunday and Saint's Day. The book was to have a permanent influence on the character of Anglican piety. So that Keble was already reverently regarded, when at forty-one he preached the sermon on "National Apostasy."

Froude, as brilliant as his master, was an impetuous and aggressive anti-Protestant, who had "never heard any good" of the first Protestant Archbishop of Canterbury "except that he burnt well."

John Henry Newman (1801–1890) was a remarkable man, brought up an Evangelical, converted vividly and decisively at fifteen, and controlled to the end by the Evangelical (and Catholic) view of man as naturally depraved and helpless and in need of supernatural aid. Newman was supremely conscious of the spiritual world and believed in divine guidance, through an inner light and by visible signs and tokens. As Fellow of Oriel, he came speedily to regard the Church as of divine origin and authority, endowed with rights of its own, independent of the State. Imaginative and poetic, he was another, but blameless, Rousseau, distrustful of reason, his convictions springing from imagination and affection. He disliked public discussion of sacred beliefs and encouraged "economy" in self-disclosures before unsympathetic persons, so much so that ardent Evangelicals, like Kingsley, accused him in later life of being too little devoted to truth for its own sake. The charge brought a reply from Newman, in the form of a history of his religious beliefs, the *Apologia,* which is still a classic among autobiographies.

Meanwhile the *Tracts for the Times* were coming from the Press, and were reinforced in sermons by Newman, quiet, simple, appealing, from the pulpit of St. Mary's, Oxford. They recalled things once believed in England, but long forgotten; and both Evangelicals and Liberals were surprised and indignant.

In 1834 the Oxford Movement won a distinguished recruit in Dr. Edward Bouverie Pusey, Professor of Hebrew at Oxford, saintly and learned and soundly Anglican. The prestige of his position, his patience and self-possession, added stability to the movement; and he came to be regarded by the public as its head. Soon the Oxford Movement had grown sufficiently to seem to its opponents formidable; and by 1840 the tendency of some of its leaders back to the Roman Church was unmistakable. "Tractarianism" had at first been content to defend the rights of the Church of England. Keble and Pusey continued to do so; but others were now asking whether the Church of England was an adequate expression of Catholicism. Newman, in particular, was more and more impressed by the Church of Rome, and more and more doubtful that a true Church could exist outside it. In Tract 90, published in 1841, he reasoned that the Thirty-Nine Articles of the Church of England could be understood in the Roman sense.

This seemed dishonest; and most bishops condemned Tract 90. In 1845 secession to the Church of Rome began, Newman himself going over that year. Fresh controversies brought fresh secessions, among the most notable being that of Henry Manning, an archdeacon of the Church of England, who was in time to be made a Roman cardinal, as was Newman himself.

Keble and Pusey stood firm in their allegiance to the Church of England; and the movement was but slightly arrested by the secessions. It spread through the land in the latter half of the century, broadening its activities. Men now concerned themselves to restore something of the ancient ritual. Surpliced choirs appeared in parish churches, and surplices in the pulpit, instead of the customary black gown. Efforts were made to adorn the Lord's Supper. The crucifix appeared on the Holy Table, and the Credence Table beside it, to hold the bread and wine until consecrated. The celebrant stood in front of the Holy Table, his face to the East, clad in Eucharistic vestments. All this signified more than the "enrichment" of the liturgy; it meant that the Holy Table was again an altar, the Supper a sacrifice, the clergyman a priest, as in pre-Reformation days.

There was resentment, and in some places disorder; and complaints were carried to the law courts, and from them to the Judicial Committee of the Privy Council. The Committee decided most cases against the new Ritualists; but little attention was paid to its decisions.

Clerical relations in the Church of England have ever since been in unstable equilibrium; for the most aggressive party is the Anglo-Catholic, while the nation and Parliament are Protestant. Catholicism, whether Roman or Anglican, is not strong in Britain; nor is it likely to become so. The popular dislike of priestly religion, echoed in mediaeval days in Chaucer's Canterbury Tales, fostered by Wyclif and the Lollards, capitalized by Henry VIII when he wished to turn the Pope out of England, long ago became the dominant temper. This was indicated once more in 1928, when the bishops and the Church Assembly decided to approve certain changes in public worship, and submitted to Parliament an Alternative Prayer Book, only to have it rejected. The Book would have passed the Commons without difficulty, except the service of Holy Communion, which had been changed in the direction of mediaevalism. The prayer to be used in consecrating the bread and wine suggested that the substance of the elements is changed by consecration, and included a petition that the Holy Spirit might be communicated to the elements themselves, not simply to the communicants. Parliament would have none of it; and it became clear that if the Church of England wished to return to mediaevalism, it would be required first to surrender its position and emoluments as the National Church.

Popular religious life, however, in the Church of England is less confused by party differences than might be thought. Laymen are only occasionally theologians; and the distinctions between Anglo-Catholicism, Evangelicalism and Liberalism are probably but little sensed. The faithful come together to Holy Communion, without enquiring whether the saving grace of God reaches them in the consecrated bread and wine, or through the faith with which they receive the bread and wine, or through the Christian culture which the Church is called to disseminate. Indeed between clergymen themselves party lines are somewhat blurred. For both Anglo-Catholicism and Evangelicalism are found consistent with a measure of Liberalism; and Liberalism, in varying degrees, is the prevailing intellectual tone of clerical life.

The Church is spared, too, the conflict of parties that would accompany the election of bishops. For the growth of political democracy has brought it about that bishops, long chosen by the sovereign, are now chosen by the Prime Minister; and he, of whatever religious faith himself, usually regards the quality of the episcopate as a matter of real national concern. Good men of all parties are made bishops.

As for Roman Catholicism, it had never died out in Britain. In the Highlands of Scotland and in North England, far from the great centres of population and the scrutiny of the law, devout Romanists had continued to go to Mass and to receive an occasional message of consolation from the Holy Father at Rome. Their lot was hard, and too little consistent with British tolerance. More than one statesman had desired to remedy the evil; but national feeling was too readily excited to permit of substantial relief. There was reason for this unreason. There was the English dislike of adherence by Englishmen to any foreign authority; the sympathy of Roman Catholics with the impossible Stuarts; the plots, or rumours of plots, against the reigning sovereigns; the belief, general throughout Europe, that the Jesuits were a scheming, dangerous lot. So for two centuries after Henry VIII Roman Catholics were denied many of the rights of Englishmen. It was illegal to celebrate the Mass; and though the law was not enforced, except in times and places of popular excitement, Roman chapels were kept unobtrusive and priests avoided distinctive dress. At length in 1778 leading Roman Catholics presented to King George III an Address, reminding him that their conduct had long been irreproachable and that they held no views inconsistent with their duties as citizens. A Bill was introduced almost immediately by Sir George Savile, supported by the Attorney General, and was passed by both Houses of Parliament, making legal the celebration of the Mass and removing restrictions on the acquisition of landed property by Roman Catholics. The Act did not apply to Scotland. There was to be a second Bill, extending similar rights to Roman Christians there.

There was an outcry in Scotland. Pulpit and Press denounced the proposed Bill. Protestant Associations were formed in Scottish cities, to defend religious principles thought to be imperilled; and the ferment spread to England. There was no further enlargement of liberty for Catholics for nearly fifty years. Then in 1829 Parliament, yielding to the eloquence of an Irish member, Daniel O'Connell, and fearing civil war in Ireland, passed a Catholic Relief Bill, granting to Roman Catholics the ordinary civil and political rights.

"Catholic Emancipation" brought swift changes. Stately churches rose again; and the old ceremonial reappeared. In 1840 Pope Gregory XVI ventured to divide England into eight ecclesiastical districts, to each of which he appointed a bishop "in partibus." [10] There was little popular excitement; and ten years later the papacy, encouraged no doubt by the Oxford Movement and recent accessions to Rome, ventured to establish twelve dioceses in England, with bishops bearing the old territorial titles. A shout of anger rose everywhere; and Parliament proceeded to pass an Ecclesiastical Titles Act, forbidding Roman bishops to assume diocesan titles.

Many Anglicans disapproved the Act, believing, with William Ewart Gladstone, that "all attempts to meet the spiritual dangers of the Church" by penal legislation are unwise. There was little disposition to enforce the Act; and in 1872 it was repealed.

Outside both the Established Church and the Church of Rome were those Protestant Churches, once minorities within the Establishment, whose right to secede was sooner or later acknowledged. They were the Dissenters, or Nonconformists, now better called the Free Churches, because bound by no ties to the State. They descended in the main from three bodies—the extreme Puritans of Elizabeth's reign, the main body of Puritans, who left the Established Church after the restoration of the Stuarts, and the disciples of John Wesley. They were themselves divided in time, by conflicting beliefs, into the Protestant Churches of to-day; and to their number were added in the nineteenth century the Catholic Apostolic Church, popularly called "Irvingites"; the Plymouth Brethren, or "Darbyites"; and the Salvation Army, an offshoot of Methodism. These three, like the older Free Churches, have spread through the Christian world.

Free Churchmen in England and Wales are of about the same numbers as Anglicans. Throughout the English-speaking world they are four times as numerous. They are all firmly Protestant; there is among them nothing corresponding to the Oxford Movement. That is to say, their attention has been fixed upon the Bible and its teaching, rather than the Church and its prerogatives. They are alike, too, in retaining Luther's principle, the priesthood of all believers; their ministers are fellow-

---

[10] A bishop *in partibus infidelium,* "in the lands of unbelievers," is one appointed to a See where there are not Catholics to be supervised and who can therefore be sent by the pope anywhere, when a bishop's functions are needed.

workers, trained for special tasks, not priests, endowed at ordination with supernatural powers. In all this they are akin to the Evangelical Party in the Church of England, differing from it rather on the question of Church and State.

The first real freedom for Nonconformists came with William III and the Toleration Act of 1689. Thenceforth they were at least free to worship in their own way; but in the early nineteenth century they were still disqualified for public office, for studies at Oxford and Cambridge, and for performing the rites of marriage and burial. These might only be performed by clergymen of the Establishment, to the maintenance of whose churches Nonconformists were still required to pay "rates." These disabilities were removed one by one in the nineteenth century, by Acts of Parliament. Meanwhile Free Churchmen were providing themselves with dignified churches, instead of the shabby chapels of earlier days, and with an educated ministry.

There is in all the Free Churches a tradition of strong conviction and vigorous action, the persistence of the spirit that led their fathers to endure the odium and deprivation of exiles for conscience's sake. Politically they have been associated with the Liberal Party, as the Established Church has tended to be with the Conservatives; and their fight for freedom has predisposed them to assist others in their struggles. They supported the move for Catholic Emancipation, and that for the abolition of slavery throughout the British Empire. They were the soul of the agitation for the Reform Bill of 1832, which extended the parliamentary franchise to "the lower-middle classes." The "Nonconformist conscience" has been a great force in English public life. Lord Palmerston said: "In the long run English politics will follow the consciences of the Dissenters."

Thus far we have been concerned almost exclusively with the religious history of Europe; but the weightiest event of the nineteenth century was the rise of the United States of America. With it began a shift in the balance of the Christian forces of the world, and a certain new colour and emphasis within Christianity itself. Religious conviction had been one of the forces creating the English colonies in America, though less in the South than in New England. The earliest colony, Virginia, planted in 1607, was given the Church of England at the outset; and it remained the Established Church until the American Revolution. It was poorly provided with clergy by the Bishop of London, and failed to create an adequate native ministry. The attempt, supported by the English Government, to collect its dues was among the causes of the Revolution.

Virginia's northern neighbour, Maryland, chartered to Lord Baltimore in 1632, began with complete religious toleration. Baltimore was a Roman Catholic and granted toleration in the interest of Catholic freedom; but when Maryland became a royal colony in 1691, the Church of England was made the Established Church. It too was poorly provided with clergy; and long before the Revolution both Roman Catholics and Anglicans were outnumbered by Methodists, Presbyterians and Quakers.

In North and South Carolina the Church of England was established; but the establishment was made ineffective by the preponderance of Baptists, Huguenots, Quakers and Scots-Irish Presbyterians. In Georgia there was religious freedom for all but Roman Catholics.

In general religion was lukewarm in the southern colonies; and the existence of an Established Church did not greatly help matters, though the formation in England, in 1701, of a Society for the Propagation of the Gospel in Foreign Parts was a noble exception, which perpetuates in America the name of a certain Thomas Bray, a commissioner of the Bishop of London.

The planting of Congregationalism in New England by the "Pilgrim Fathers" in 1620, and the erection there of the Congregational colonies of Plymouth, Massachusetts, Connecticut and New Haven, made New England a Puritan community, founded in religious enthusiasm and creating its own ministry. Harvard College was founded for this purpose in 1636, Yale in 1701. Congregationalism was established by law in these colonies; and there was some suppression of other religious bodies.

The settlement of Rhode Island was begun in 1636 by Roger Williams, a Baptist under sentence of banishment from Massachusetts; and Rhode Island became a haven for those seeking freedom of worship. New York, founded as a Dutch trading post in 1624, had the Dutch Reformed Church from the beginning, but soon had Lutherans and Mennonites as well, and English-speaking Puritans and Roman Catholics. New York passed to England in 1664; and the Church of England was established there, but with little effect.

Pennsylvania was granted by royal charter to William Penn in 1681, and was settled by Quakers. Quaker tolerance soon made it more varied religiously than any other colony. There were Baptists from Wales and Ireland, Mennonites from Germany and Holland, German Lutherans, German Reformed and Moravians, with the Church of England an inconspicuous minority.

In similar ways Presbyterians, Scots from Northern Ireland, settled much of Maine and New Hampshire, spread thence to New York, then to Pennsylvania, where they wrested political control from the Quakers. These vigorous Scots-Irish sought the frontiers too, settling West Virginia, Kentucky and Tennessee, and forming in time a considerable part of the population of most southern colonies.

Thus when the colonies became independent of England, Protestantism in many forms was the dominant faith, with no single religious body dominant everywhere. In these circumstances the American Constitution, adopted in 1787, excluded all religious tests, as a qualification for public office in the United States of America; and the first Congress, in 1789, adopted as a governing principle that "Congress shall make no law respecting an establishment of religion, or prohibiting the free exercise thereof, or abridging the freedom of speech or of the press, or the rights of the people peaceably to assemble, and to petition the government for the redress of grievances."

The rise of the Republic was one cause of a new outlook, that was to be characteristic of religious thought in America. So many ties with the past were now severed, that the authority of antiquity was undermined, that of the present and future strengthened.

In nothing is this more clearly seen than in the history of the Church of England under the Republic. At a conference in Maryland in 1780, it changed its name to "Protestant Episcopal." The First General Convention of the Protestant Episcopal Church, at Philadelphia in 1785, framed a new constitution; and that of 1789 adopted an American Book of Common Prayer. Later Conventions affirmed their allegiance to the Apostles' and Nicene Creeds, but rejected the Athanasian. Its place in Catholic tradition did not avail to save a creed, that admonishes all men that "Whosoever would be saved, before all things it is necessary that he hold the Catholic Faith, which Faith, except everyone do keep whole and undefiled, without doubt he shall perish everlastingly."

Methodists and Baptists received most accessions from the revivals, and attained the numerical superiority they have held ever since. Not only was conversion a part of their tradition; they were more ready than others to employ such human instrumentalities as were available. Like John Wesley, they welcomed the aid of converted men, often uncouth, who spoke, in the language of ordinary men, things ordinary men wished desperately to hear. Congregationalists and Presbyterians, on the other hand, clung to the tradition of an educated ministry, to which Methodists and Baptists also came in time.

From the life generated in the great revivals sprang the characteristic Christian institutions of America. The Sunday School, first introduced from England to Philadelphia in 1791, appeared everywhere, and the mid-week prayer-meeting. Church schools and colleges dotted the land, anticipating the State universities. Missionary organizations provided, first "circuit-riders," then settled ministers, for the population moving westward across the continent. Foreign missions were inaugurated when the Congregationalists established the "American Board of Commissioners for Foreign Missions" in 1810, the Baptists a "General Missionary Convention" in 1814, and the Methodists a "Missionary Society" in 1819. Other churches followed; and by the middle of the century all American Protestantism was engaged in Christian work abroad.

This foreign service was enlarged in the latter half of the century by the formation of women's missionary organizations, for work among women and children; and to help the churches secure missionaries, the Student Volunteer Movement for Foreign Missions was formed in 1886, crossing all denominational lines in America and tending to obliterate them in foreign lands. A similar influence was exerted at home by the Young Men's Christian Association and the Young Women's Christian Association. Founded in England in 1844 and 1855 respectively, they soon crossed to America, to reach in the new world their greatest development, and from there to spread as missionary agencies everywhere.

The period of great revivals passed; but vast organizational development has continued, a natural expression of the unlimited resources of the country, the energy of the population, and the unprecedented increase in material riches. These things have tended even to encourage what is called "activism," the readiness for great enterprises, prepared too little in theory and attended too little by thought.

CHAPTER XXV

THE BIRTH OF MODERNISM

WE MUST think now of certain currents of thought since the French Revolution, that have profoundly affected the outlook of the modern man, whether in America or in Europe. Society is more or less aware of the impact upon life of Napoleon; but few have weighed the verdict of Heine, that the philosophy of Immanuel Kant was as influential in the world of thought as the French Revolution in the world of affairs. Both affected historic Christianity. The Revolution tended to deprive it of the political support it had received since Constantine the Great; Kant removed those rational supports, on which Anselm and the Scholastics had relied so confidently. Since then both Church and theology have had to depend more and more on their intrinsic worth. The drift in thought about religion has been towards what is called Immanentism.

By the immanentist tendency in theology one means that the case for religion is built on religious experience, not on revelation, or the Church, or the rationality of religious ideas. In Immanentism, too, the traditional preoccupation with the life to come gives place to the search for religious values in the life that now is.

Philosophy, science and Biblical studies in the nineteenth century all led towards Immanentism. In philosophy Kant's drastic criticism of traditional arguments for the existence of God and the immortality of the soul, and his substitution of arguments drawn from man's sense of moral obligation, instituted the new tendency. Kant's successors did not find him satisfactory at all points; but there was less disposition thereafter to justify religious faith by anything but religious experience.

Greatest among the successors of Kant was Friedrich Daniel Schleiermacher (1768-1834), a man of extraordinary vigour of mind and sensitiveness of religious feeling. Brought up under the influence of the Moravians, he was taught a strict orthodoxy but found repugnant the doctrines of the total depravity of human nature, everlasting punishment, and the salvation of men through the vicarious sufferings of Christ. Escaping at length from Moravian influence, Schleiermacher plunged into the study of art and literature, philosophy and history, was deeply affected by Plato and Spinoza, and in 1810 found an adequate field for his knowledge and eagerness in a theological professorship in the young University of Berlin.

Schleiermacher was interested in everything; but his central interest continued to be religion. He thought religion necessary to life, and that it could not be fed on historical evidences or the word of authority. Religion is the sense of dependence on God. Theology, therefore, is to be drawn from the life of the soul with God. If theology is thus grounded in experience, it will not be shaken by every school of thought, every new system of philosophy.

This did not mean for Schleiermacher that one's own consciousness is an adequate religious guide. Religious persons naturally form churches, fellowships for the nurture of the higher life; and Christian theology is to be founded on the consciousness of the fellowship.

Schleiermacher thus applied the empirical method, in his search for a philosophy of religion. Strangely it had not occurred to Hume and other skeptical Empiricists that this might be done. They examined the arguments for religion advanced by Rationalism and Supernaturalism, found them incapable of demonstration, and became agnostic. Such a procedure, if adopted in the laboratory, would make scientists agnostic about everything, whose earlier definition was disproved by later evidence.

This, then, is Schleiermacher's chief contribution to religious thought, that religion has as much right as science to reconstruct its theology, by constant reference to religious experience. It is a principle that has ever since been fundamental to what is called theological Modernism.

The disciples of Schleiermacher in the nineteenth century were many. Most of those who strove to reconcile science and religion were more or less consciously his pupils. The greatest perhaps was his young contemporary, David Mendel, a Jew, who was converted to Christianity by Schleiermacher's famous *Addresses on Religion,* and changed his name to Neander, new man. Applying Schleiermacher's principle, Neander wrote a luminous history of the Church, as the fellowship through whose experience Christian theology had taken form.

Next in importance to Neander is probably Albrecht Ritschl (1822–1889), who devoted his life to the study of theology, in the spirit of Schleiermacher. Ritschl strove to keep theology separate from metaphysical speculation, religion from dogma. Christ, he said, had been appointed to preach on earth the love of God for mankind and to establish the kingdom of God. The earthly society in which God's love is regnant is the kingdom, the community of the reconciled; and conversion is normally the slow transformation of the individual, through membership in the reconciled community. Its consciousness of redemption becomes his consciousness. His relation to God thus follows upon his relation to the Church.[1]

While the new method was being applied to theology, a re-examination of Biblical literature was going forward. There had been a forewarning of change as early as the seventeenth century, when Spinoza published in 1670 his famous *Tractate*. In it he discussed, among other things, the authorship of several books of the Bible and suggested that they were compilations from earlier works. Most of the problems that were to be posed by critics in later centuries were foreshadowed in the *Tractate*.

Spinoza, however, was a Jew and therefore not likely to be heeded by Christians. In the eighteenth century the position was changed. Rationalism was prevalent everywhere; and in Germany, as we have seen (p. 495), it turned to a methodical investigation of the books of the Bible. Bengel, though a Pietist and head of a theological seminary, classified the books of the New Testament in "families," according to their origin and purpose; and Reimarus, professor of Hebrew in the Hamburg gymnasium, deplored the depreciation of reason then fashionable in the pulpit, cast doubt upon the miracles reported in the Bible, described the work of Jesus as essentially that of a moral reformer, and attributed his tremendous influence upon the future to the belief that he had risen from the dead.

Reimarus (1694–1768) gave expression to his ideas in a work, the *Defence of Reasonable Worshippers of God,* which he continued to revise for some twenty years but died without making public. Lessing, however, in the years between 1774 and 1778, published parts of the *Defence*

---

[1] Ritschl did not deny that conversion is sometimes by an individual spiritual conflict, as with St. Augustine and Luther; but he thought such conversions abnormal.

under the title *Fragments of an Anonymous Writer,* which he described as having been found in the library at Wolfenbüttel. They became known as the *Wolfenbüttel Fragments* and made a great stir. When Rationalism lost influence, however, the *Wolfenbüttel Fragments* were forgotten, except in academic circles and among literary men.

It remained for the nineteenth century to produce a critical movement in Biblical studies, that was to be permanent. The movement was due in some measure to Romanticism. We have seen how in France the outrages done by the Revolution to mediaeval society and the Church stirred in Chateaubriand an imaginative devotion to mediaevalism, and led to a rebirth of Catholicism, associated especially with the name of Lamennais. Romanticism was uncritical in France, less so in Germany and Britain. In Germany it captured especially the poets and philosophers; and their influence was transmitted to Britain by such men as Coleridge and Thomas Carlyle. In these lands Romanticism stimulated what is called the "historical sense." That is to say, men searched the writings of antiquity, not in search of facts alone, or for models for our time, but to understand the ancients for their own sake. And thus in Germany and Britain Romanticism combined with the scientific spirit to encourage the critical study of the Scriptures.

Such study was an almost inevitable concomitant of the spread of knowledge. It is a singular testimony to both the vitality of the Bible and the strength of traditional views of its character that, in the early nineteenth century, after three hundred years of Protestantism, during which the public had been encouraged to "search the Scriptures," they were still regarded very much as they had been in Luther's day and Calvin's. To most theologians they were an "arsenal of texts," to defend the dogmas of the churches; to the Christian masses they were an authoritative guide to the conduct of life; to the devout they were "precious promises," "letters from home," on which their souls were stayed. In all these attitudes, Christian minds were now to be affected by what is called the "higher criticism," or "historical criticism."

Examination of the Scriptures had traditionally proceeded on the assumption of their verbal inspiration and freedom from error, and had aimed only at securing that the text was dependable, free from mistakes by copyists and translators. If the text was pure, truth was sure. But students of other ancient writings were aware that what purported to be a continuous document, by a single author, sometimes showed such contradictions of fact and variety in style as to indicate that it must be a composite work. Students of the Old Testament now discovered that this was true here also. *Genesis* contained conflicting accounts of creation, *Kings* and *Chronicles* conflicting history, *Leviticus* and *Deuteronomy* different stages in the development of ritual. It was no longer possible to maintain that the "Books of Moses," the Pentateuch, were actually the work of Moses.[2]

To the old supernaturalist view of the history and religion of early Israel there was now added the evolutionist view. According to the former, the religion of early Israel was the system described in the Pentateuch, which had been communicated to Moses in a series of divine revelations. According to the latter, the religion of early Israel was nature worship, upon which Moses grafted a special devotion to Yahweh, the whole being elaborated gradually into the Pentateuchal system.

Controversy followed the publication of the new ideas, the most serious incidents in England being associated with the *Essays and Reviews,* published in 1860, and the volume, *The Pentateuch and the Book of Joshua critically examined,* published two years later by Bishop Colenso (*See* p. 533). Broad Churchmen were generally hospitable to the new views, High Churchmen and Evangelicals opposed, Dr. Pusey and the Earl of Shaftesbury joining hands to withstand them. Free Churchmen, too, were opposed; but gradually most educated Christians saw that some revision of the traditional view of inspiration was inevitable.

Revision was less disturbing because the Church from the earliest times had recognized that the divine inspiration of the Old Testament could be maintained only on the supposition that many things in it were not to be understood literally. The Church had resorted to allegory, to interpret the Old Testament. It had not thought it necessary to do so in interpreting the New Testament; and the application of historical criticism here aroused graver fears.

A beginning had been made in Germany, when in 1835 David Friedrich Strauss, a brilliant young scholar of twenty-seven at the University of Tübingen, published a *Life of Jesus,* in which he treated the four

---

[2] There were difficulties, of course, with other books than those of the Pentateuch. For example, it was impossible to maintain any longer that *Isaiah* was all the work of that prophet, or that all the "Psalms of David" were his.

Gospels as little more than collections of myths, which subsequent generations had spun around the life of a great man. And as myths come into existence only after the lapse of time, when the facts are obscured, Strauss concluded that no one of the Gospels could have been written by immediate disciples of Jesus.

This was accommodating fact to theory, as more sober criticism was to show; but Strauss' book was vivid and daring, and made an immense impression among the uncritical. Its vogue encouraged an equally brilliant Frenchman, Ernst Renan, to publish a *Life of Jesus* in 1863. The new *Life* was theatrical and sentimental; but it was written with great skill and charm, and had an enduring popularity in France.

Meanwhile a more scrupulous examination of the New Testament was being made by a German scholar, Ferdinand Christian Baur (1792–1860). Baur, an instructor of Strauss at the University of Tübingen, was familiar with the philosophy of Hegel, who had also been educated at Tübingen and was now a teacher at the University of Berlin and the foremost philosopher of Germany. Hegel's system, an episode in the "romantic movement," was to be very influential for a time in England, and later in America.

Georg Wilhelm Friedrich Hegel (1770–1833) was the most distinguished of those philosophers who, while clinging to the religious view of the world, championed an evolutionary view of human history. Customs, beliefs, institutions become what they are, and will pass slowly into other forms, not by divine decrees but by a long process of development. This process corresponds to that in the individual mind, where thought advances through thesis to antithesis to synthesis. That is to say, the mind reaches a position, the thesis, only to find itself confronted by opposing or limiting considerations, the antithesis, which is at length combined with the thesis in a higher unity, the synthesis.

Baur found this principle exemplified, when he investigated the origins of the Gospels and the rise of Christianity. Christianity began, Bauer concluded, as a messianic movement in Judaism. It is thus it was regarded by the original twelve apostles. This was the thesis. It ran into a contrary view, the antithesis, when the Gospel was preached to Gentiles at Antioch and was found applicable to all men. There was conflict between thesis and antithesis, between the Judaizing party, represented by Peter, and the Pauline party, a conflict clearly indicated in the

Epistles of St. Paul. *Acts* was written to promote a reconciliation of the Petrine and Pauline parties; and a synthesis, the Catholic Church and Catholic theology, was reached in the second century.

Bauer proved to be the first of a considerable company of Biblical critics, the "Tübingen School," who adopted his method and concurred in general in his conclusions. We shall not examine them at length. Later studies have not left Baur's positions intact; but he gave a permanent impetus and direction to New Testament research, which before the end of the century reached certain generally accepted results. For example, *Mark* was accepted as earlier than *Matthew* and *Luke,* whose authors used *Mark* and another document, containing discourses of Jesus and called by scholars *Q* (German *Quelle,* "Source"). The date and authorship of *John* remained in doubt; but it was generally admitted that *John* was later than the three "Synoptic Gospels," further removed from the facts and different in intention, and might not be quoted as a record of the words and deeds of Jesus, of equal value with the others.

When the nineteenth century closed, Protestant churches had not yet adjusted themselves to the new views of Scripture. It was partly that the clergy were reluctant to disturb a faith so ancient as that in infallible Scriptures. It was partly that Protestant scholars adopted a theory that absorbed some of the shock of change, the theory of progressive revelation. The Bible, they said, was divinely inspired, as Christians had always believed; but in it God revealed Himself by slow degrees, as men were able to comprehend, the revelation culminating at length in Jesus Christ.

This was the evolutionary view of history, applied to the Scriptures, and was a manifest makeshift. *Leviticus* is not an advance on *Deuteronomy,* though it is later; nor are *Habbakuk* and *Zephaniah* an advance on *Amos* and *Hosea, Micah* and *Isaiah*. Indeed, judged by all tests, there is a certain decadence in later books of the Old Testament, when set beside the great prophets of early Israel. In the New Testament, too, *Revelation,* though later, is more Jewish, less Christian, than the Epistles of St. Paul, a fatal objection in Christian minds to the theory of progressive revelation.

Nor did the theory overcome the moral difficulties involved in the older theory. Why did God require of Israel non-moral religious rites and immoral deeds against neighbouring peoples? The difficulty is not overcome by saying that revelation is progressive and Israel was very young. If God says less to children than to men, it is to be assumed that so much as He does say will be both true and right.

Meanwhile, quite outside the field of religion, there had appeared in the middle years of the nineteenth century a portent, that added greatly to the difficulties of religious thinkers. More than two hundred years had elapsed since Kepler and Galileo demonstrated the truth of the Copernican theory and Sir Francis Bacon announced that new knowledge was to be reached by the inductive study of Nature. Then Sir Isaac Newton published the *Principia,* demonstrating that the Universe is a vast mechanism, that the motions of the heavenly bodies are explicable by gravitation, and that the conception of the Universe as a field of special divine interventions must be abandoned. All these things had made sensations in Europe; but scientists were few and popular education not far advanced. So excitement died away; and the course of religion was but little affected.

Thereafter, until the middle of the nineteenth century, the impact of scientific thought upon religious thought was but slightly felt. Scientists were seldom hostile to Christianity, and were not always awake to the religious significance of their discoveries. Then in 1859, a year before the appearance of *Essays and Reviews* (*See* p. 533), there appeared also in England a scientific treatise, that conflicted so sharply with contemporary religious ideas, that it seemed a direct challenge to faith. The treatise was Darwin's *Origin of Species by means of Natural Selection.*

Charles Robert Darwin (1809–1882) was an English naturalist, of frail body but patient and indomitable spirit, who had in early manhood spent five years voyaging, as naturalist with the surveying ship *Beagle.* What he then observed laid the foundations of his scientific knowledge. After twenty years he published the *Origin of Species.* It created a sensation like that of Newton's *Principia* or Rousseau's *Contrat Social,* and gave to the study of biology an impetus that has not yet exhausted itself.

Darwin's theory that species "undergo modifications, and that the existing forms are the descendants by true generation of pre-existing forms," had been one of the cosmic theories of the ancient Greeks. In the modern world it had received philosophical credentials from Immanuel Kant, but continued to attract little attention. In 1831, however, Patrick land, the shift from transcendence to immanence in the philosopher's thought of God and from the objective to the subjective in men's thought of religion, new views of the Bible and the origin of man! What must these things have meant to Protestant Christians! Very little, except when agitation in the clerical mind became acute, or the fever of public controversy spread. For popular education was not far advanced; and education itself is not synonymous with thoughtfulness. There was little time or taste for theory, except among the few who lived by thought and the many who were excluded from the general prosperity and whose thoughts were not about theology.

Besides, institutions outlive the ideas that create them. It is enough, when they grow old, that they are a part of the familiar scene and that they render useful service of some sort. They are the more stable if their service is of the sort that kindles emotion and engages the conscience. The ill omen of the nineteenth century was not that Christian people ceased to love the churches, but that more and more intellectuals looked doubtfully at what had so long commanded the minds of men, the Christian faith. And because the clergy were among the better educated of their communities and were committed to the work of teaching, they were themselves exposed to doubt. The most serious fact for organized religion, when the nineteenth century closed, was the spreading uncertainty in the clerical mind. "If the trumpet give an uncertain voice, who shall prepare himself for war?"

The Catholic clergy were comparatively immune. It is impossible to say what passes in the mind of an enlightened priest, when fact and dogma seem to clash; but so much is clear, that where the Protestant minister feels the compulsion of the truth, the Catholic priest feels the duty of submission. The problem of the truth is not his but the Church's. He speaks, not with his voice but with hers. Occasionally, as with Lamennais, the compulsion of the truth is too great; usually, as with Montalembert and Lacordaire (*See* p. 526), the duty of submission is supreme. Submission at the close of the nineteenth century was easier, too, because discussion within the Catholic Church was no longer public. The era of Oecumenical Councils had closed. The successor of Peter could now speak for the Catholic Church, on all disputed questions of faith. So Pope Pius IX and the Vatican Council had declared in 1870, in the dogma of papal infallibility.

The faithful were firmly reminded of this dogma as the twentieth century opened. Modernism, the effort to reconcile religion and the new discoveries in philosophy and science and Biblical studies, was spreading. Ultramontanism had not quite succeeded in excluding it from the Catholic Church. Pope Pius X set his face against the movement, as Pius IX had done. In a *Syllabus* and *Encyclical* in 1907 he condemned Modernism and set in motion plans for its suppression, which brought outward submission. Alone in the Christian world the papacy would stand like a rock in the swirling current of new ideas. What erosion would do, only the distant future could reveal.

The result of this long disintegration is religious confusion. In all the major denominations there are many shades of opinion. Some insist that there is no occasion for change, that Christian truth is still what the historic creeds declare it to be. Those who so believe, the "Fundamentalists," are found more and more, as we have said, in lay conventicles, in uneasy relations with the churches. They are usually Millennialists, living in expectation of a catastrophic intervention of God in the world and the return of Christ.

In sharp contrast to the flux of contemporary Protestantism is the fixity and antique air of the Roman Church; and it would not be strange if Protestants in considerable numbers, alarmed at the cost of progress and the chaos that accompanies it, should turn again to Mother Church. Indeed it is alleged that this is taking place. In a volume, *Through Hundred Gates*,[1] one of the *Religion and Culture Series* of the Roman Church, it is said that converts to the Catholic Faith in the United States number about 50,000 annually. The editors add (p. 7): "The fact that not only well-educated people of all walks of life, but also many Protestant ministers of various denominations are returning to the Church is symptomatic of the failure of Protestantism." England, too, "has an average of from eleven to twelve thousand converts each year"; and in the fifty years since the death of Cardinal Newman "more than nine hundred Protestant clergymen returned to the Mother Church, and in the whole world no less than 3,000 Protestant ministers resigned their pastorates and became laymen." "The qualitative gain of the Church, however, does not numerically outweigh her quantitative loss during the trying postwar years. . . . The unwholesome influence of Rationalism and Materialism, the decline of spiritual values after the World War, the social insecurity of the masses, the satanic propaganda of Communism and National Socialism greatly augmented the number of renegades from the Church."

These statements are illuminating. First, the gains of Catholicism are "qualitative," not "quantitative." This is confirmed by civil records. In the United States the growth of the Catholic Church is slightly less than that in population. Second, Catholic gains are most notable in England,

---

[1] Edited by Fathers Severin and Stephen Lamping, O.F.M., and published by Bruce, Milwaukee, 1939.

where the character of the Established Church was determined as much by political as by religious considerations, and where an approximate Romanism, the Anglo-Catholic party, has existed for a hundred years.

Significant, too, is the nature of the testimony borne by the forty-one "notable converts from twenty-two lands," who in this book describe their spiritual pilgrimage. Not truth, but circumstances and personal preferences, seem to have determined their course. An American football coach, in a Catholic College, observing how his players fortify themselves by going to Mass before the game, becomes himself a Roman Catholic. If the players had been Quakers and had gone into silence, the coach would presumably have turned to religion in that form. An English authoress has already for twelve years thought herself a Catholic. By becoming one openly she is relieved of the responsibility of self-examination in religious matters. "I have been given a faith which is objective, and I am delivered from that uneasiness which accompanies most subjective ventures." An English journalist has been in the company of those who feel the urge to Catholic Christianity, and interprets this as a general condition. "The world has become conscious that it is not Catholic. . . . That sort of pressure of the Church I believe to be universal and ubiquitous today." An Anglo-Catholic clergyman, beginning with the assumption that a clergyman must be a priest and that the Church of England believes in the Mass, comes to the conclusion that he is not a priest and that the Church of England does not believe in the Mass. He therefore enters the Church of Rome.

It is clear that in *Through Hundred Gates* one is not confronting the question of truth and its verification. One is in the presence of the Romanticism that followed the French Revolution. Weary of the trial and error of history and impatient at the cost of progress, a progress whose benefits they do not lack, privileged persons turn back to the great Church that has outridden the storms of centuries. Whatever continuity history has seems to be in her; her temples are houses of quiet in a noisy world; her ritual of worship is one through all the divided earth; and what she asks is what a child can give, not understanding of her mysteries but submission to her discipline. The distinguished converts probably do not hold the Catholic Faith in detail. They may be doubtful about the Immaculate Conception of the Virgin and the Infallibility of the Pope; and their idea of God and of prayer is perhaps not quite the

Catholic view; [2] but in all these things they are prepared to observe a dutiful silence, which is all that Mother Church requires.

The return of distinguished people to the Church of Rome is heartening, as indicating the unquenchable thirst of the human spirit for religious satisfaction; but it will not serve to rejuvenate the ancient Church. It is counterbalanced already by the disquiet of enlightened Catholics who, having grown up in Mother Church and being better acquainted with all aspects of Catholicism, are in uneasy allegiance. Catholic Liberals know that the Protestant doctrine of the infallibility of the Scriptures is that of the Catholic Church, and that the reasons for abandoning it are unanswerable. Some Catholic scholars ever since Abelard have been aware that the alleged unity of Catholic tradition is a myth. Some gave no more than a dutiful submission to the new dogmas of the Immaculate Conception of the Virgin and the Infallibility of the Pope; and some do still. There are "Old Catholics" and "New Catholics" within the Church, torn between love of her and love of truth. There are Catholic patriots who are aware that, as once in France and Italy, wherever Mother Church controls education the general enlightenment is lower and illiteracy more widespread than elsewhere, that a Catholic nation is a backward nation. They may, like Montalembert and Lacordaire, submit; but they cannot but be unhappy that the papacy will not come to terms with progress. All this is more significant for the distant future of Catholicism than the accession of privileged persons who, having gathered elsewhere the fruits of freedom, retire to enjoy them in an authoritarian Church.

Confronting a Christianity thus confused, both Protestant and Catholic, are those ancient rivals, philosophy and science. The menace of philosophy is somewhat less than formerly, [3] partly because philosophy

[2] The Catholic view is implicit in the appeal of a Cardinal to the faithful in 1940. On the approach of the Feast of the Immaculate Conception, the dean of the Roman hierarchy in the United States sent his blessing to priests and people, then said: "Let us all unite in beseeching the Queen of Peace to intercede with her Divine Son that He may send His peace to the distracted world."

[3] Catholicism, of course, has still a philosophy of its own, the philosophy that first flowered with Thomas Aquinas in the thirteenth century. It proceeds still from the assumption of the divine authority of Catholic dogma, and brings all innovations in philosophy to the test of dogma.

is not a major intellectual interest of mankind, partly because Christian Liberalism has already adjusted itself to philosophical trends. In other words, the immanentist tendency in theology since Kant and Schleiermacher, the disposition to rest the case for religion on experience, has obligated philosophy to take account of religion. For philosophy is a generalization from facts; and among the most ancient and widespread of facts is religious experience.

With science the case is somewhat different; for it impinges upon life everywhere and has become a popular pre-occupation. One is not in the mode unless one speaks the language of science; and it is indisputable that science tends to depreciate the spiritual. In physics, on which the other sciences build, one hears only of space-time, of electrons and protons within the atom, of neutrons and positrons, of energy and negative energy. Building on such foundations, some have arrived at a naturalistic view of man, in terms of carbon and hydrogen, oxygen and nitrogen, in combination under colloidal conditions. Mind, consciousness, life itself, are, in their view, the resultant of physical processes.

Men of religious faith need not be timid in the presence of such doctrine. Scientists are specialists; and specialists are not philosophers. Within their own restricted fields, too, they change their minds as frequently as others.

The limitations of science are becoming manifest to scientists. It has no philosophy, no theory of knowledge, no unifying creed. Its reputation rests on its technique; and to its technique religion can be deferential. All that liberal religion now asks of science seems likely to be conceded, the soul and immortality.

Concerning the soul, whose name psychology does not like, it is an easy concession to call it instead the self, or consciousness. By whatever name, it is that something that must be more than any combination of carbon and hydrogen, oxygen and nitrogen, since it will die for its country, its faith, its honour, for what it thinks the truth. It is that of which Heraclitus said: "You will not find its boundaries by travelling in any direction, so deep is the measure of it." And it is here that psychology interposes the most serious obstacle to religion. For there are psychologists who deny the existence of the soul, who have developed a science of the self without the self. The founder of the school was that

David Hume (*See* pp. 491 f), who could find no link between cause and effect. So also he could not find the self.[4]

There are better arguments against the existence of the self, to be drawn from the phenomena of alternation or dissociation of personality and from the gaps in consciousness during sleep or trance; but here one enters the little-explored territory of the relation of the subconscious to consciousness.[5] Meanwhile psychology has not succeeded in dislodging the soul. There is no substitute. Reason cannot conceive, nor the imagination picture, the advent of consciousness in a purely material world, the coming of age of electrons and protons, oxygen and hydrogen and nitrogen. There is something in us that Nature has not given, the ever-present representative of some necessary principle of the Universe, a constituent of reality. And however long we may have to await the demonstration of this truth, man's intuition seems likely to be proof against material interpretations of his being. Here he will trust the poets, and perhaps the men of religion.

And what of immortality? To look around is to observe a universal will-to-live. When it fails, as once it did with Tolstoy, it is not in life but in the conditions of life the reason lies. Tolstoy had assumed that death ends all, and that we know enough of the present life to estimate its value. With such premises, the conclusion is inevitable. If there be no life beyond the present, the world condemns itself and religion receives a mortal wound. Here indeed is a double sorrow of our time, that in so many minds belief in progress and the expectation of immortality have died together.

To deny the future life is to deny the rationality of the world. It is not reasonable that his art should survive the artist, his poetry the poet, that the edifice should endure, the builder turn to dust. Death is frustration, and unreason at the heart of things, if dying one ceases to exist. Men are not disposed so to believe. The belief in immortality is among the most widespread and ancient of beliefs. That does not prove it true, but does

[4] In this case, however, as in the other, Hume became doubtful of his reasoning and took refuge in backgammon with his friends. He says, in the *Treatise of Human Nature,* "Upon a more strict review of the section concerning personal identity, I find myself involved in such a labyrinth, that I must confess that I neither know how to correct my former opinions, nor how to render them consistent. . . . All my hopes vanish when I come to explain the principles that unite our successive perceptions in our thought or consciousness."

[5] See Gustave Geley, *From the Unconscious to the Conscious,* Harper.

invite enquiry. Are there any "intimations of immortality" in Nature or human nature? That some men find it incredible is not a serious difficulty. Bacon died without believing that the earth revolves around the sun. The evidence of his senses was too strong for such a fancy. And the evidence of the senses that death is the end for men, as for all living things, is not conclusive. Indeed immortality is less incredible than life itself, to survive less incredible than to have emerged out of the darkness and the silence. In life one is in the presence of marvels, and not least in the unexplored resources of the mind. What do we know of premonitions and apparitions, of alternating personalities, of telepathy, of hypnosis?

Science is now at work on psychic phenomena, long known but dismissed as demonic, or fraudulent, or what not, and already it is guessed that we have other relations with Nature than those through the senses, relations of which we have been quite unconscious. When extra-sensory perception is established, it will precipitate a scientific revolution. Already men who add to their science a philosophy begin to say, with F. H. Bradley: [6] "I should certainly be willing to agree to the possibility of selves which after death would be perceptible by, and recognizable by one another, and would so far have something in the way of a body." It is again what Heraclitus hinted two thousand years ago.

Our lives are part of the Universe; and our final harmony with it is the goal of existence. Science and philosophy have told us little yet, of what we are and what we may become. Meanwhile psychical research is on the way to demonstrating immortality. It means, after all, only the permanence of that which gives the physical world whatever of beauty and of worth it has. All the goodness, truth and beauty of the world are in persons. Science has been slow to see this, in spite of Aristotle and Immanuel Kant. It has assumed, ever since the Renaissance, an objective world, quite outside ourselves and unconditioned by our presence. At long last it is recognized that there is but one door to the external world, the door of human consciousness; and, entering it, the observer carries with him all the powers and prepossessions of the mind. The things we see and touch and taste are what they are for us alone, not in themselves. In themselves they are, as A. N. Whitehead says, "nothing but an average stability of certain events in a set of agitations."

[6] In *Appearance and Reality*, Macmillan.

Christianity has other rivals, however, more recent but more violent. During most of the period when philosophy and Biblical Criticism and science were infiltrating Christian theology, the ethical front remained unbroken. Men might deny that some Biblical narratives, some dogmas, were consistent with the teachings of Christ, or that contemporary Christian conduct conformed to his example; but it was generally agreed that a right ethical code was that of the Sermon on the Mount and the parables of Jesus. As the nineteenth century drew to a close there were signs of another attitude. In particular the German philosopher Nietzsche directly impugned distinctive features of Christian morality, especially patience, humility and compassion.

It is not altogether strange that Nietzsche concentrated upon the passive Christian virtues. Christian theology had made much of the uncomplaining sufferings of Christ; and Christian art had followed theology. Little was made of the dauntlessness of Christ, who had "set his face steadfastly to go to Jerusalem," to confront his enemies in their stronghold, and who had driven mercenary men from the temple precincts. There was a positive righteousness from the beginning of Christianity; but it had been obscured. Now Nietzsche rejected the passive virtues, for "the will to power."

Nietzsche has had a motley company of disciples in Germany. At one extreme have been neo-pagans, at the other certain Protestants, who intend to remain Christian but wish to see Christianity Germanized. Midway has been the German Faith Movement, whose acknowledged leader was Professor Wilhelm Hauer of Tübingen. Hauer, once a Protestant minister and missionary, was convinced that Christianity is alien to the German nature. He undertook to justify a religious nationalism for Germany, superior to Christianity.

The German Faith Movement stood firmly on the modernist principle that experience is the test of religion, but interpreted religion so inclusively as to admit almost any mass enthusiasm. It thought it quite valid to regard National Socialism, with its enthusiasm for German destiny, as a religious movement. Every nation might find religion in its own way, and Germans who so chose ought to be free to find religion in the Christian way; but they must be tolerant of those who found religion in the great events and personalities of German history. "We desire," said Hauer, "to injure no man's sanctities; but we have a right to call our own history sacred. Thus the German Revolution is for us an event born of the nation's primal will, an event in which eternal powers are revealing themselves by the accomplishment of newer and greater things. . . . We know of nothing which so challenges our devotion as this divine movement. We can see God advancing over German soil, seeking his instruments in spite of all opposition, molding events according to his purpose. That is why German history is our sacred history, why Germany is our holy land." [7]

The German Faith Movement illustrates very well the religious confusion of the twentieth century, and how it was aggravated by the first World War, 1914-18. The Movement sprang out of the profound humiliation of a vigorous and somewhat arrogant people, who had had a great history and confidently expected a greater. Defeat brought bewilderment and despair; and the German Faith Movement was but one of the devices by which ardent patriots fed the national vanity, in the interest of national recovery.

Hauer thought himself a monotheist, but identified the activity of God with the dubious political activities of an aggressive people. It was, for a monotheist, the negation of religion itself. The German Faith Movement was logically a revived polytheism, whose new German Yahweh was quite suitably to be toppled soon from his throne by the gods of wiser nations.

Other systems, of like spirit with Nietzsche, rose out of the ashes of the first World War. Established by violence, they did not, like the German Faith Movement, clothe violence in the garb of religion but did win the allegiance of multitudes who were brought up in religion. These are Russian Communism and Italian Fascism, the latter emulated in a German Fascism, the National Socialism to which Hauer looked so reverently.

The prophet of Communism was Karl Marx, a German Jew of the Rhineland, who died a generation before the first World War. It was said of him that he combined "the righteous fury of the great seers of his race with the cold analytical powers of a Spinoza." After a revolutionary youth on the Continent, Marx settled in London, where for thirty years his home was a garret, his study the reading room of the British Museum.

[7] *Germany's New Religion,* trans. T. S. K. Scott-Craig, Abingdon Press, p. 55.

On the Continent he had issued the flaming *Communist Manifesto;* in London he wrote *Capital,* which was to become the Bible of the proletariat everywhere. Marx, an outcast of an outcast race, hated nationalism. The natural association of humanity, he thought, was not in nations but in classes. The workers of the world belonged together. "Let the governing classes tremble before the communist revolution," said the *Manifesto,* "The proletarians have nothing to lose in it but their chains. They have the whole world to gain. Proletarians of all countries, unite!" Having united, the workers would proceed to create a classless society, in which all citizens would be workers and the State the only employer.

The First International, established in 1864 to unite the workers of the world, foundered on the rock of the Franco-Prussian War and the national sentiment it inflamed. The Second International, which was rich in political talent,[8] was destroyed by the war of 1914–18. It was clear that national sentiment was still stronger than class interest. Nevertheless in France and Italy, and still more in Russia, the doctrines of Marx continued to stir the imagination of many intellectuals; and in Russia, where the general well-being was low and labourers unprotected by Trade Unions, they captured the factories.

Revolution had in fact reached Russia before the first World War closed. The Russian armies had been poorly armed, poorly fed, poorly led; and there had been four million casualties. All classes were alienated from the Tzar, who abdicated in March, 1917. A Committee of the Duma attempted to govern, but with little success. Soviets, or councils of workers and soldiers, formed throughout the country. In April they gathered in a central congress in Petrograd; and there extremists, the Bolsheviks, swiftly mastered the assembly of simple and hungry men. The Bolsheviks promised immediate peace, bread for all, the land for the peasants and a dictatorship of the proletariat, then set themselves to corrupt discipline in the army. In July the Russian front collapsed; in November revolutionaries swarmed round the Winter Palace and the provisional government fell.

The chief organizer of the revolution was Ulianoff, who called himself Lenin, a Russian conspirator whom the German General Staff

---

[8] It included Bernard Shaw and Ramsay MacDonald in Britain, Briand in France, Vandervelde in Belgium, Pilsudski in Poland, Lenin and Mussolini.

caused to be conveyed home from Switzerland. Lenin, a man of powerful intellect, rare gift of lucid speech and great physical vigour, had long preached secretly in Russia the doctrines of Marx, and had reached an ascendancy among Russian revolutionaries. Years in Siberian prisons, and in cheap lodgings in London and Switzerland, had not overcome Lenin's conviction that he was destined to overthrow the old régime in Russia and establish a dictatorship of the proletariat. He was aided now by the Jew Braunstein, who called himself Trotsky. Together they took Russia out of the war in three months, dispersed a representative assembly convoked to frame a republican constitution for Russia, then signed with Germany the Treaty of Brest-Litovsk.

Lenin organized the Communist party and the Red army, and inherited a secret police from the Tzarist régime. He and his ministers, the Commissars, were ruthless and without scruple in suppressing opposition; but they were cosmopolitan and humanitarian, and of apostolic fervour in their central purpose, the establishment of a classless society of workers through all the world. And they lived simply, practising the asceticism they commended to others. So Communism became a new religion in Russia, the Communist party a Church. The Russian Orthodox Church, too other-worldly and too long associated with Tzarist repression, itself now suffered repression. Religion, Lenin said, was the opium of the people.

Lenin was not without statesmanship. The first stage in the world revolution, he thought, was the consolidation of the new order in Russia itself. He would first see every peasant there literate and comfortably housed. He therefore resisted a wild scheme of Trotsky and others for an immediate propaganda throughout the world.

Lenin ruled Russia six years, transformed the life and institutions of the country, and died with semi-divine honours, his brutality forgiven by most Russians, only his loyalty to the people's cause remembered.

In Italy the shade of Lenin aroused misgiving. Italians had suffered much and gained little from the first World War; and there was general lassitude and disillusion. Lenin was popular in the factories of Lombardy, strikes were frequent, old soldiers derided as dupes. And in Rome a Parliament of many parties wasted time in endless debate.

As so often in Italian history, paralysis of government opened the door to the tyrant. Benito Mussolini, once editor of a Socialist paper, had observed that German Socialists, pacifist in peace time, had supported the nation in war as ardently as other parties. Mussolini guessed that national sentiment was still stronger than internationalism. What talkative Italy required was not Communism but a dictator.

Mussolini therefore formed in Lombardy a party of action, the *Fascisti,* disciplined, virile, Spartan, to rule the State, themselves obedient to a leader, *Il Duce.*

The *Fascisti,* organized in Milan in 1919, soon controlled the streets, attacked their opponents, sacked the houses of Liberals, formed disgruntled veterans into a militia. In 1922 they marched on Rome and took over the Government, with the tacit consent of the feeble king. The Press was converted into an instrument of the State; imprisonment and exile silenced the *litterati.*

The Fascist party, authoritarian, Catholic, anti-feminist, now displaced the Liberalism that had informed Italian parliamentary life for two generations, since Cavour and the unification of Italy. It extended control to industry, making it part of a national system, in which workers and business were alike protected.

The energy of *Il Duce* communicated itself to the nation; a new efficiency stirred in the Public Service; great public works were undertaken, and archeological exploration. Fascism gradually won general admiration in Italy. The loss of freedom seemed not too great a price to pay for the new enthusiasm. The ancient Empire lived again under a new Augustus, vain, corrupt, but vigorous.

Germany might, in normal times, have been immune to the Italian fever. Enlightenment and well-being, pride in German institutions and German power were general. The first World War changed all that. Germany was prostrate and revolution in the air. Everything was as it ought not to be, in the opinion of an Austrian house painter, Adolf Hitler, who had been a lance corporal in the World War. Hitler was a fanatical racialist, patriotic, arrogant, hating Communists, Liberals, Jews, everything that was not in the German mode. What Germany required, he thought, was to recover the "will to power"; and he proclaimed his creed in a certain violent and hysterical oratory. By 1920 he had a small following, compounded equally of idealists and ruffians, who called themselves National Socialists and were called by the public Nazis. They demanded the union of all Germans in Europe in one German State. Wherever Germans were numerous, the territory belonged to the Reich. The Treaty of Versailles must be renounced, the German colonies recovered, German Jews disfranchised. These things Hitler set forth in an autobiography, *Mein Kampf*.

The new German Republic, that had emerged from the first World War, was vulnerable to attack by fanatics. It had been born of frustration and defeat. Its first Parliament, the Weimar Assembly of 1919, had had the hard duty of ratifying the Treaty of Versailles which, the Nazis said, had been imposed upon Germany by the treachery of Jews and the deceit of the Allied Governments. And the Republic had rivals, Communist and Royalist parties.

Germany entered the League of Nations in 1926 in the face of opposition. It had been a stipulation of the Treaty of Versailles that she should become a permanent member of the Council of the League, on an equality with the recent victors, and that, having disarmed Germany, they would themselves disarm. Yet when Stresemann, foremost statesman and champion of peace in Germany, died in 1929, there was still no considerable disarmament elsewhere; and German youth was demanding passionately that the Reich should not continue unarmed amidst the armed nations of Europe.

Economic disaster now overtook the Reich. There had been five years of artificial prosperity, when there was an orgy of expansion, financed with foreign loans. A financial collapse in New York in 1929 caused the withdrawal of American credit from Germany. German banks closed; factories curtailed production; six million Germans became unemployed. The plaint of the workless was heard everywhere; the red flag of Communism appeared in the streets; and the Nazis conducted a campaign of propaganda, to stamp out Communism, rid Germany of Jews, and revive the military glory of the Fatherland.

By 1933 the Nazis were bold enough to organize terror and control the streets. With German thoroughness the brown-shirted storm troopers were more brutal than the blackshirts of Italy. The Government was not strong enough to enforce order. The President of the Republic, the illustrious but now senile Von Hindenburg, was convinced and appointed Hitler Chancellor of the Reich. That year Hitler took Germany

out of the League of Nations. In the following year many Nazi leaders
were suddenly murdered and their bodies burned, for reasons unknown
outside the leadership of the party. Then President Von Hindenburg
died; and the German people by an overwhelming vote, though under
heavy governmental pressure, accorded to Adolf Hitler, *Der Fuehrer,*
autocratic powers. Within a few months *Der Fuehrer* restored military
conscription in Germany, in violation of the Treaty of Versailles. The
nation was thrilled. Everything was forgiven in the wild hero, who had
rejuvenated the nation and now shouted defiance to the world.

The rearmament of Germany had already begun secretly, and was
now pressed with great vigour. Outside Germany fear and incredulity,
hope of appeasement, common lethargy, delayed effective measures
against the threatening conflagration, until neighbouring states were
overrun and incredible horrors perpetrated upon the conquered peoples.
The Nazis would clear the ground of central Europe for an enlarged
Germany, by any method thought necessary.

When victory for the new tyranny seemed assured *Il Duce* cast his
lot with *Der Fuehrer,* to secure for Italy some of the spoils; and before
long free men everywhere were fighting desperately to preserve their
heritage of freedom.

Tyranny devoured itself at length. *Il Duce,* after twenty years of
strutting and declamation on the Italian stage, died meanly, leaving
Italy impoverished, degraded, without respect in the world. *Der Fuehrer,*
after little more than ten years of strutting and declamation, disappeared
in the flames of his Chancellory, leaving Germany divided and devastated. Of the major tyrannies, only Bolshevism survived, redeemed by
the benefits it conferred upon the Russian poor and the humaneness
of its distant ideal; by the accident, too, that Nazi duplicity had driven
Bolshevism into the camp of the democracies.

That the recent tyrannies are significant for the Christian Church is
manifest. The methods by which they were established, in nations where
the Church had existed for many centuries, would not have been endured by a Christian population. The pride of the churches in their
history and achievements ought therefore to be tempered by the discovery that the society they had been thought to refine is still semi-
barbarous. The future may reveal, too, that the Roman Church has been

further compromised by papal policy. The Vatican signed Concordats with Mussolini in 1929, Hitler in 1933, and with Franco, dictator of Spain, in 1943. In 1943, too, as the victory of the Allies, including Russia, became certain, the Vatican changed from denunciation to conciliation, in its attitude to the Bolshevik régime.

This need not occasion surprise, as the papacy is a world power, demanding a voice in world affairs, influenced therefore by considerations of statesmanship. Its conduct in the recent crisis does serve, however, to remind all men that it is not a purely religious institution, above mundane considerations, speaking for God in the world.

Events in Italy have been particularly damaging to papal authority. The papacy thought to live at peace with Fascism. Church and State were now both authoritarian, and equally hostile to Liberalism and the democratic process. By the Concordat of 1929, between Pope Pius XI and the Fascist régime, the papacy was conceded autonomous rule in a tiny principality and an enormous grant of money. The grant made the Holy See financially independent of Anglo-Saxon Catholics, who had been the almost exclusive support of the papal budget since the first World War and whose contributions were accompanied by firm pressure for greater representation in the Cardinal College. The grant made it likely that popes would continue to be, as they had been for four centuries, exclusively Italian. The Curia felt no need for new blood in the Catholic Church.[8a]

Pope Pius soon had bitter reason to regret the Concordat. Within a few weeks Mussolini, in an address to Parliament, spoke scornfully of the Christian Church. It had been, he said, a paltry sect, until it established itself in Rome; and as for the present, the State was "Fascist, exclusively Fascist, essentially Fascist"; if the Catholic Church dared to oppose it, Italy would be a desert.

Pope Benedict XV, predecessor of Pius XI, believing the effects of liberty to be religiously beneficial, had granted Catholic laymen virtual autonomy in the social and political fields. In Italy therefore the Popular Party had risen, led by the priest Don Sturzo, to associate the Church with social progress. The party was now dissolved; lay religious organiza-

---

[8a] Later events indicate that the Curia has at last been awakened by the eclipse of Italy and her poverty. The Vatican, in December, 1945, announced the appointment by Pope Pius XII of thirty-two new Cardinals, only four of them Italians. The new College, of seventy Cardinals, would contain only twenty-eight Italians.

tions lost their vitality; and the papacy, denuded of its natural defenders, had to face Fascism alone, to endure one humiliation after another.[9]

The policy of Pius XI did not, of course, involve ecclesiastical approval of Fascist violence. The Pope himself wept that he had signed "Treaties with 'people without faith and without God,' like Hitler and Mussolini"; and it may safely be assumed that many a faithful priest, in the confessional, admonished Fascists against violence, that many a gentle Franciscan wept for the new paganism and prayed that the scourge might pass. Nevertheless Church and State did unite in Italy, if in a somewhat shamefaced alliance.

Outside Italy, in the lands overrun by Germany, the moral situation was equally confused. There were many who collaborated with the invaders; but not all were traitors. There was room at first for an honest judgment that peace and stability would not come to Europe, except under German authoritarian leadership. As Nazi brutality and corruption became everywhere naked and unashamed, it became possible to distinguish between the traitorous and the misguided. There were few traitors, but many confused persons, in the churches. In Protestant bodies the contemporary fluidity and lack of conviction now plagued the congregations; but the greater personal responsibility among Protestants brought it about that most Christians who suffered notably were Protestants. Civil officials, in particular, retired from office to concentration camps, rather than give effect to anti-Christian instructions from Nazi superiors.

There were evidences everywhere of spiritual resources available still in Protestantism. The sale of Bibles in Germany doubled in the decade of Nazi rule, though Hitler forbade its sale in ordinary bookstores; in France the sale increased fourfold. In Norway, when bishops were required to report regularly to the police, they were accompanied through the streets of Oslo by crowds, who sang outside the police station Luther's great hymn, "A mighty fortress is our God."

Prelates, Roman and Protestant, everywhere revealed heartening reserves of moral energy. The German Evangelical Church, in June, 1936, sent Chancellor Hitler a letter, which discloses that already in Prussia, breeding ground of German militarism, seven hundred pastors had been

[9] On all this see Count Carlo Sforza, *Contemporary Italy,* E. P. Dutton, 1944, pp. 336–341.

arrested for reading from their pulpits a proclamation of the Old Prussian Synod against modern paganism. The letter reminded Hitler that:
"When blood, race, nationality, and honour are raised to the rank of
qualities that guarantee eternity, the Evangelical Christian is bound, by
the first commandment, to reject the assumption. When the 'Aryan'
human being is glorified, God's Word bears witness to the sinfulness of
all men. When, within the compass of the National Socialist view of life,
an anti-Semitism is forced on the Christian that binds him to hatred of
the Jew, the Christian injunction to love one's neighbour still stands for
him opposed to it." [10]

The churches in the devastated countries of Europe have probably
gained from the resurgence of paganism and their comparative stead-
fastness. The only open and sustained resistance, proceeding from principles publicly stated, came from the churches. In Holland, where they
never ceased to protest against Nazi misdoing, and Catholic and Protestant bodies sometimes united in protest, attendance at public worship was
greatly increased and a new respect manifested. This did not necessarily,
of course, signify a return to religion. "There were those who in time
of need learnt to ask for God's Word. There were also those who did
not so much wish to hear the Word of God, but came because they ap-
preciated the Church as the 'only place where one could really hear a
plain Dutch word.' " [11]

No similar movement is noticeable in lands where the hoof of the
Nazi has not fallen; and any quickened interest in religion in desecrated
lands will prove to have been one more brief Romanticism after tragedy,
unless religious leadership proves capable of a religious reconstruction,
that was already overdue when the recent neo-paganism was let loose
upon the world.

The brutalities that accompanied the rise of Communism, Fascism
and Nazism are the judgment of history upon progress. Progress has
been inadequately moralized, knowledge and wisdom have not advanced
together. In particular, the increased knowledge of the physical world,
through the study of physics and chemistry, has been applied to the

[10] The letter may be had in *International Conciliation*, Nov., 1936, published by the
Carnegie Endowment for International Peace, Division of Intercourse and Education.
[11] Visser 't Hooft, *The Struggle of the Dutch Church*, London, S.C.M. Press, 1944,
p. 10.

mechanization of life by such methods and to such ends that man has tended to become "a mere parasite of machinery." This mechanization will become more and more terrifying, unless those who create machines, those who direct them, and the very motives back of them are made good.

This is a work of religion, which has to do with the totality of life, its meaning and destiny; and religion as a guide to progress is hampered by conservatism. Men are reluctant to change what is holy. It is not entirely unfortunate; for the sanctities stabilize our life. Nevertheless religion in an age of change tends to be outrun.

Roman Catholicism is especially unfitted to play an important rôle. To serve progress in any large way, one must be sympathetic with progress; and Rome has decided otherwise. It is too late to reverse the decision. There is already, as we have seen (pp. 560–2), something archaic in the Roman Church. In nothing is this more manifest than in its view of the present world. With all the evil men have done to life, and all their profanations of Nature, wise men are present-worldly still. They know that, whatever supplementary revelations God may give to men, the primary revelation is in life and Nature. If there are no grounds for religious faith here, there are none anywhere. Good men receive no heavenly admonitions now against the love of life, as did the Abbot Odo who, falling asleep over Virgil, was warned in a dream against that poet's love of Nature. It was a needed warning to one committed to the Catholic view, though it came, not from heaven but from the recesses of Odo's Catholic mind. It is a needed warning still, for those like-minded. Nevertheless the modern wise are more at home with Virgil than with Dante, or Augustine, or Gregory the Great.

It would seem therefore that the Roman Church can minister to humanity only in a way out-moded. That it is old will commend it to the romantic. That it has withstood the shock of centuries will commend it to the timid. That it is authoritarian will commend it to those to whom individual responsibility is a burden and progress an illusion. That its divorce from life may be complete a hundred years from now does not derogate too much from its present worth.

As for Protestant Fundamentalism, its eclipse will come much more swiftly. True to the Protestant tradition, Fundamentalism invites all men to "search the Scriptures," but insists that they find nothing there to invalidate traditional views. It has thus the weakness of Protestantism without its strength, the weakness that it is divided among many sects, without the strength of freedom, a freedom that makes it possible to keep abreast of truth.

Within the limits of Protestant tradition, Fundamentalism has its own special emphasis, devoting much attention to ancient prophecies and expecting a catastrophic end of the existing world order, through an intervention of God. It thus rejects both the evolutionary view of history and the immanentist tendency in theology. It tends indeed to a certain idiosyncrasy, best exhibited perhaps in the belief of some Fundamentalists that the "lost ten tribes" of Israel, to whom are applicable the promises of God through the prophets, are the British people. They, and not the Jews, are therefore the true heirs of ancient Israel, and may expect the destiny of a divinely-chosen people. "British Israel" is the English equivalent of the German Faith Movement, but more urbane.

Fundamentalism, it would appear, is an arrested development within Protestantism, that is not likely to arouse more than a certain curious interest in the modern mind.

Some things in the modern mind are, of course, unassimilable to Christianity in any form. Tolstoy's choice must still be made. "I gave up," he says, "the life of the conventional world, recognizing it to be no life, but a parody on life, which its superfluities simply keep us from comprehending." Tolstoy forsook the Russian aristocracy, became a peasant, and was at peace, finding the eternal verities more open to the mind that dwells with Nature. That, however, is an issue as old as civilization, and is only sharpened by the contemporary mechanization of life. The characteristic issue at present is that between knowledge and religion. Is Christianity made obsolete by the advance of knowledge?

The answer lies with Christian Liberalism, which is present in varying degrees in all the major Protestant churches and is the prevailing tone of clerical life. Liberalism is, for the present, at a disadvantage. It admits the need of religious change, but is of many minds as to the nature of the change. It has made, however, the essential concessions to the modern mind. Liberals know that what is discoverable from human nature and history is the real revelation of God in the world. They know, with Amiel, that "The eternal life is not the future life; it is life in harmony with the true order of things—life in God." They know that Christianity is not the absolute religion. They think Christianity superior to all other religions, and regard Jesus as the central figure in history; but there is little disposition to deny that an authentic religious experience is known, an authentic religious life lived, outside Christianity. God answers to the loyalties of men, not to their creeds. For a conscious communion with Him this is a sufficient creed: "He that cometh to God must believe that he is, and that he is a rewarder of them that seek after him."

Efforts after recovery are being made in Protestantism. There is, for example, a general tendency to improve the forms of worship, and to strengthen ties with the past by using ancient hymns and prayers and creeds. This liturgical renaissance, however, is at best a temporary expedient, at worst an evasion. It is an expedient because a religion that has no longer anything vital to say about life and destiny will not be appreciably strengthened by recourse to forms. It is an evasion because antiquated beliefs, excluded from the sermon, are embalmed in the ritual; and theological reconstruction, so long delayed, is further delayed. More serious still, the return to ancient forms encourages the insincerity and unreality that are the bane of religion.

Another Protestant attempt at recovery is seen in a number of movements for the reunion of the churches. These have included certain approaches to the Greek and Roman churches, which, however, have not accomplished much. The Roman Church replies to such advances that other churches need only return to Mother Church, to effect the desired union. It does not admit that Protestant clergymen, even those of the Church of England, have been validly ordained to the ministry, the Apostolic Succession of bishops having been broken at the Protestant Reformation. The Church of England admits the validity of Roman ordinations, but rejects the primacy of the Pope. The Greek and Anglican churches admit the validity of each other's ordinations, but are too widely separated geographically and historically to gather much fruit of the admission. In any case, it is unlikely that the question of ordinations will be generally regarded in future as important for the salvation of either individuals or society. It is a question only of ecclesiastical law and order, and of continuity with the past, and is more seriously regarded in episcopal than in other churches.

Efforts after the reunion of Protestantism itself continue; and there is much talk of the Church as the "Body of Christ" and of the "sin of schism." The presence of all the members does not make a living body, however, nor the absence of some destroy it. The well-being of a body is normally conditioned by the health of nerves and glands and cells; and the health of Christendom depends in the first instance on conditions within, not among, the member churches. It is therefore not surprising that such reunions as have been achieved have been disappointing. There was in the uniting denominations enough vitality to survive, not enough for transplanting. In other words, sentiment for their own denominational past was still strong, religious beliefs too little explicit and vigorous to thrive in a new environment. It would seem that the reunion of Christendom would not effect much for religion, unless the basic conditions of religious revival were first met.[12]

The first of these conditions would seem to be an honest and courageous re-examination of the true source of Christianity, such a re-examination as Schleiermacher undertook a century ago and the Church has never carried through. The process ought now to be completed; for the times are critical and Protestantism approaches exhaustion. Why this is so, and what must be done, will perhaps become clearer if we now review this "story of the faith."

Protestantism approaches exhaustion for reasons implicit in the process by which a religion,·originally simple, becomes complex and comprehensive. Great religions spring from the solitary experience of a unique person. Very few repeat that experience; but many admire it, desire it, associate themselves with it, and build a religion around it. The religion is as much theirs as his, being tinctured by their preconceptions and environment. When the simple, but profound, faith of Jesus went out into the Mediterranean world, it drew to itself Syrians and Egyptians, Greeks and Romans, and adopted so many of their previous ideas and practices as seemed assimilable. The primitive Church drew upon certain Oriental cults for its ritual of worship, upon Roman law for its doctrine of salvation, upon the Jewish synagogue and then the Roman Empire for its constitution.

---

[12] Meanwhile much more fruitful are the co-operative efforts of churches for common ends. These sometimes take the form of national organizations, such as the Federal Council of the Churches of Christ in America, sometimes of international organizations, such as the World Missionary Conference, first held at Edinburgh in 1910, and the Conference on Life and Work, at Stockholm in 1925.

After four hundred years, when the Church seemed to have reached the saturation point, St. Vincent of Lerins thought it time to rule out further novelties, at least in theology. Only that was to be regarded as Catholic truth which had been believed everywhere, always and by all. This became the Catholic mind. Nevertheless further adjustments required to be made. For example, when the writings of Aristotle came back to Europe, by way of the Arabs of Spain, a few Catholic scholars saw that they could not be ignored; and within fifty years Albert the Great and Thomas Aquinas succeeded in incorporating Aristotle into the Catholic system.

It was believed that all this vast system, Catholicism, was implicit in certain writings, adopted by the Church quite early as authoritative, or canonical. Catholicism, it was thought, was simply these Scriptures, the Bible, made explicit.

Catholicism was, by the twelfth century, a very comprehensive and impressive system; and Catholic Christians were just the population itself, participating in mysteries they did not understand, and submitting to a discipline that made them somewhat better here and much safer hereafter.

Catholicism stood intact for three centuries, and might have continued so indefinitely, except for certain practical abuses. Earnest men tried in the fifteenth century, through three General Councils, to effect reforms, and found vested interests too strong for them. Others renewed the attack with literary weapons, having been equipped for it by a renaissance of Greek and Latin learning. They, too, made little headway. Then a German monk, shocked by a specific abuse of Christian credulity, brought the matter to the attention of his bishop and archbishop, only to find himself reprimanded as a disturber and reported for discipline to the Bishop of Rome. Luther was thus driven to defend himself and, in developing his defence, arrived at what has since been called Protestantism. His example encouraged others; and in Germany and Switzerland, France and England and Italy, there were soon movements, no longer protesting single abuses, but rejecting Catholicism as such.

Protestantism was a simplification. Like certain Jewish and Moslem sects, that rejected the endless discussions of the theological schools and went straight back to the Mosaic Law and the Koran, Protestants went to the Scriptures themselves. And, on the authority of the Scriptures, they declared all the mediatorial mechanism of Catholicism unnecessary to salvation. One need only believe certain promises of God, recorded in the Bible, and show one's gratitude by good deeds.

The relief to the human spirit was very great indeed; but catholicity, in the sense of comprehensiveness, was lost. The Scriptures were sometimes silent, sometimes inaudible, sometimes capable of different interpretations. Christians had regarded the Bible as divine legislation. They were now differing sharply as to what the law-book prescribed for the baptism of converts, the creation of a ministry, and the general organization of a church. In course of time there were scores of Protestant sects, where once there had been "one holy, catholic, apostolic Church." Nevertheless the liberation of spirit remained; and within the individual sects there was a vigorous life, made more vigorous by the confidence that, having the Bible, they walked, not by faith alone but by sight.

Protestants continued vigorous for three hundred years. Then a fresh examination of the Bible disclosed that it is not a book, but a library of books; that it is not law, but a record of ancient experiences and beliefs; that in its pages men differ on the most serious religious questions. It is strange that this was generally overlooked for three centuries; but no error persists so long as that about which it is wicked to enquire. And it was wicked to doubt what was in the Bible. Besides devout Bible-readers had read selectively; and there are plenty of eternal verities there to feed the soul.

The new view of the Bible is now the common property of Protestant ministers, having been taught them in most Theological Seminaries. The result was inevitable, and is devastating. Quite ordinary men could preach extraordinarily, so long as they could say "thus saith the Lord." They spoke, not out of their own wisdom but out of a divine revelation, whose custodians and reporters they were. Now they must range the fields of human knowledge, in search of preachable truth. And where the scientist confines himself to one field and has no necessary moral concern about what he finds, the minister gleans in all fields, seeking food for the soul. Sometimes he is a poor gleaner; sometimes there is little to glean.

The change in preaching is very great; and the churches are correspondingly less distinctive and vigorous, more comprehensive, than formerly. People are received into membership on what are virtually

their own terms, if only they will support their church and live decorously. Protestant Christians are therefore just a vertical section of the
population itself. The comprehensiveness that Catholicism won by assimilation and Protestantism lost through wrong views of the Bible, it is
now recovering by the fluidity and indefiniteness of its beliefs. But Protestantism, like Catholicism in the twelfth century, has reached the saturation point.

A great simplification of Christianity is once more indicated by events.
Having turned back long ago from Canon Law and Scholasticism to
the Bible, Protestantism ought now to go behind the Bible to Christ
himself. So doing, it would be confronted again by that distinction
between the Gospel and the teachings, that is so clear in the Epistles of
St. Paul. The Gospel is the primitive Church's interpretation of the mission of Christ, and was later to be compressed into the Rule of Faith and
the Apostles' Creed. The teachings are the precepts of Christ, preserved
in the parables of the Lord and the Sermon on the Mount.

The primitive Church put the Gospel first; though it did not forget
to inculcate the precepts (*See* pp. 97–101). "Put on therefore, as God's
elect, holy and beloved, a heart of compassion, kindness, humility, meekness, longsuffering; forbearing one another, and forgiving each other, if
any man have a complaint against any; even as the Lord forgave you, so
also do ye . . . let the peace of Christ rule in your hearts. . . . Let the
word of Christ dwell in you richly in all wisdom!"

The Gospel was modified somewhat, even in apostolic times, as we
have seen (p. 98), particularly in the matter of the second coming of
Christ. As the period of waiting lengthened, the more spiritually-sensitive
Christians found compensation, as they have continued to do, in the
experience of a mystical presence of Christ, forever among them. The
advent hope persisted; but meanwhile there was a presence of Christ in
the Church. It was a surer support to right living than was the hope of
catastrophic events to come.

Very slowly the preaching of the Gospel ceased. The Middle Ages
substituted for the Gospel a group of saving mysteries, the sacraments,
and a discipline. Not all the efforts of eager men—Waldenses, Franciscans, Lollards—could keep the Gospel in its ancient place.

Protestantism was a return to the primacy of the Gospel, and so continued for three hundred years. Once more, however, the Gospel is losing

its ancient place. This time the teachings are supplanting it, without any clear perception that this is so.

To make this tendency explicit is the only road to one more invigoration of the faith; for that road leads back to the parables of the Lord and the Sermon on the Mount, where one is again among elemental and universal things, as one is not when engaged with the sacrificial ideas and Messianic hopes of Judaism, that were incorporated into the Gospel.

It is from the parables and the Sermon on the Mount, made alive by the example of Jesus, that Christianity sprang. It is not because he was virgin born that a religion began with Christ. Other men in history had been thought virgin born, without creating a religion. Nor did Christianity grow out of the miracles of Christ. The wonder-worker was not unfamiliar then, and is not unfamiliar now, in the East. Christianity grew out of the ineffable goodness of Jesus. It was born on that day when men first said of him, "Never man so spake," and were drawn to his knees in tears for their sins. Some Jews then said, He is Messiah. Some Greeks then said, He is the Saviour-God.

The conviction was sound; though the language was contemporary. For if God is personal, He is supremely good; and the one demand of the human mind concerning Him is that He shall be so, that He can neither do nor countenance an evil thing.

The parables and the Sermon on the Mount are the experience of Jesus, set out in story form. He was no Sophist, playing with ideas. In the teachings was a philosophy of life, in pursuit of which he had found the sense of unity with God and a moral strength unshakable. The spiritual resources of the Universe were all available to him.

If that experience can be repeated in human life, Christianity is capable of still further renewal. Here the immanentist tendency in theology is at home, the empirical test relevant, and Christ once more the great contemporary.

A return to Christ is indicated by events; but the way to Christ is very strait and very narrow. It leads towards love for one's enemies, prayers for the persecutor, a preference for giving before receiving. It leads away from both contemporary nationalism and contemporary economics. The churches are not likely to take it, unless—which is not impossible—the ghastly confusion of world politics and economics should work in the churches the grace of a sudden conversion.

Until then one cannot wisely expect too much of the churches. They have neither unanimity nor great striking power. There is no such thing as "the church view" of any great question, except certain sins of the flesh, like drunkenness and vice. For the rest, Protestants hold the views of their nation or their class. A saving exception is that, haunted by the memory of Christ, they are often disposed to permit individuals among them to take more advanced positions.

All this involves that great souls, deeply religious, may require at present to fend for themselves. There are excellent and very ancient precedents for doing so. The prophet Amos, finding the sanctuaries unsatisfactory, admonished the devout to "seek not Bethel, nor enter into Gilgal, and pass not to Beersheba: . . . seek him that maketh the Pleiades and Orion, and turneth the shadow of death into the morning." A modern Amos would probably add, however, that those who have immediate access to "him that maketh the Pleiades and Orion" cannot wisely ignore the churches. Original religious experiences and prophetic ideas require a fellowship, through which to propagate themselves; and the churches are available everywhere. Moreover the paucity of sensitive and enlightened souls within them helps to make these indispensable institutions as pedestrian as they are.

The churches *are* indispensable. They are fellowships in pursuit of the ideal, in the name of Christ. They cross social lines, in a community of good works, better than any other institution. They tend to elevate the tone of society, are the custodians of the decencies. They solemnize birth and marriage and death, things that greatly need to be solemnized, against the horrible cheapening of life. They are worth what they cost, and are often priceless. And on some distant day their strength may be restored by individuals, whose presence just now tends to disarrange the churches. In *Collegia Pietatis* or Holy Clubs, in ashrams or in solitude, or with the toilers in the city or by the sea, they are gathering spiritual energy and wisdom against the day of change. Neither Catholic nor Protestant, they are still Christians.

THE ANCIENT MEDITERRANEAN NATIONS

IN THE Oriental world that compassed the eastern Mediterranean, and on whose soil Christianity grew up, highly developed civilizations had already existed for three thousand years. Indeed in the valley of the Nile, where the story of human life runs longest without interruption, that story goes back to 4241 B.C., the earliest fixed date in history, the date when the astronomical calendar was first introduced into Lower Egypt. One is therefore to think of Christianity as a recent phenomenon in the life of mankind.

One is to think of it also as owing something to the past and to contemporary civilization. Like Judaism, it drew from the common store of the Mediterranean world; and a student must therefore know something of that world, and will inevitably begin with Egypt.

Under the militant kings of the eighteenth dynasty, 1580–1350 B.C., Egypt was the dominant power of the Mediterranean world, her dominion sometimes extending to the Euphrates, thus including Syria and Canaan, later called Palestine. It was not until Egypt declined that other peoples had their opportunity. The kings of western Asia then shook off the rule of the Pharaohs. Syria fell to the Hittites, who moved in from Asia Minor; and Canaan was overrun by the Hebrews, coming in from the deserts of Arabia.

Long before this, however, when Egypt was rising to power, another civilization, the Sumerian, had grown up farther east, on the fertile Plain of Shinar, between the Tigris and the Euphrates. The Sumerians were a hardy race from the mountains; but they were soon in conflict with a hardier still, the Akkadians, who were nomad Semites from the desert. A long struggle on the Plain of Shinar ended in victory for the Akkadians. Under Sargon, the first great Semitic leader in history, 2750 B.C., they subdued the city-states of Sumer down to the rivers' mouth. They acquired the Sumerian civilization. They adopted the calendar of Sumer, the calendar still used in the East by both Jews and Moslems. They learned to write their own language with the cuneiform, or wedge-shaped, characters of Sumer. Thus a Semitic language was first committed to writing.

The men of Sumer and Akkad brooded on the mysteries of life and death, and reached conclusions that are faintly echoed in the Old Testament. They wrote and sang of the fisherman Adapa, who was offered by the sky-god the bread and water of life, but refused and so lost immortality for himself and mankind. They told of a deluge, and of a solitary hero and his wife, who were saved in a great ship. There is manifest kinship between these stories and the *Genesis* stories of the fall of man and the flood.

In time the kings of Sumer and Akkad were overcome by a new tribe of Semites, the Amorites of Syria. They made their way down the Euphrates, developed the village of Babylon into a city, and after 2100 B.C. gave the name *Babylonia* to the whole land of Sumer and Akkad. Their king Hammurabi combined the laws of his Amorites with those of Sumer and Akkad; and the *Code of Hammurabi,* engraved on a shaft of stone and set up in the Temple of Marduk, was accepted as having come from the sun-god, even as long afterwards the Ten Commandments were believed by the Hebrews to have been given by Jehovah to Moses.

The beliefs of Babylonia passed in time to the West. Ishtar, goddess of love, became the Aphrodite of Greek religion. Babylonian star-reading developed into Greek astronomy. Babylonian arches and temple-towers developed into the Roman arch and the church spire. Babylonian ideas became a part of the permanent inheritance of mankind.

While Babylonia was rising to power, another Semitic tribe of nomads settled at Assur, a highland north of the Plain of Shinar, along the upper Tigris, and took possession of the little cities already existing in its fertile valleys. Soon Assur gave its name to the new inhabitants and to the whole kingdom they won. They became known as *Assyrians* and it as *Assyria.* The Assyrians spoke a Semitic dialect, like that of their kinsmen of Babylonia. They too adopted the Sumerian calendar and much of the Sumerian civilization. They learned the use of horses in war, and by 1300 B.C. had overawed Babylonia and pushed back the Hittites of Asia Minor, who were crowding down to the Euphrates.

The Assyrians next sought access to the Mediterranean, where they met obstinate resistance from Phoenician cities along the coast and from another Semitic people, the Syrians, or Aramaeans. A group of flourishing Aramaean kingdoms had arisen, of which the greatest was Damascus; and Aramaean merchants were capturing the commerce of western Asia. Their caravans spread their language as well. Gradually the Assyrians learned to speak Aramaic; and in the end it became the language of all Semitic peoples, displacing even Hebrew in Palestine.

Assyria, however, continued her political expansion. Damascus fell to her in 732, after three centuries of resistance. The neighbouring Hebrews of Palestine were now in danger, all the more because they themselves were politically divided. The ten northern tribes, forming the Kingdom of Israel, whose capital was Samaria, were overcome by Assyria in 722. A few years later Sennacherib of Assyria led an army down the Mediterranean coast to the very borders of Egypt. Stopped by a pest in the delta marshes, he turned homeward. So the southern Hebrew kingdom of Judah, and its capital

Jerusalem, survived for another century. Sennacherib turned his wrath against Babylon instead, which he laid in the dust, and built for himself a new capital, Nineveh, greater than Asia had seen.

A mistaken imperialism undermined the Assyrian power at length. Citizens of vassal states were drafted into the army, which thus ceased to be Assyrian. Tillers of the soil were conscripted from the fields, and the agricultural community failed. The commerce of the land passed to Aramaean traders, whose language had already become the language of the cities. Pressure increased from without as Assyria weakened within. Semitic Aramaeans drifted in from the desert; Semitic Chaldeans crept up the shore of the Persian Gulf; Indo-European tribes, led by the Medes and Persians, moved westward through the mountains of northern Assyria. At length the Chaldeans wrested from Assyria her Babylonian province in the south, and combined with the Medes against Nineveh itself. The great city fell in 612 B.C.

The period of Assyrian supremacy, however, profoundly affected the future. The palaces of Nineveh were the first great structures, as her libraries were the first libraries, of western Asia.[1] And the rise of Assyria familiarized the nations with the idea of a world-state. Its conquerors continued its organization and prepared the way for the Roman Empire. The effect on religion was also great. The resistless power of Assyria compelled the prophets of Israel and Judah to find a more adequate religious faith. No tribal god could avail them against Assyria. So the prophets began to think of one God, who "made heaven and earth," and who was God "of all the kingdoms of the earth." The Hebrews began to be monotheists.

Judah attempted to profit by the fall of Assyria and struck for freedom; but the Chaldeans, the new masters of Babylonia, soon turned their eyes to the west. Nebuchadnezzar, greatest of the Chaldean emperors, descended upon Judah, carried the leaders of the nation to Babylonia, and destroyed Jerusalem in 586.

The Chaldeans now made their contribution to the future of mankind. They carried forward the whole civilization of ancient Babylonia. In particular, the ancient astrology was zealously pursued. The heavens were mapped, the twelve signs of the zodiac determined; and the five great Babylonian deities were identified with the five planets then known. These became the great gods of Rome as well, and enter European history under Latin names, as Jupiter, Mercury, Venus, Saturn and Mars.

With the death of Nebuchadnezzar and the early decline of Chaldean civilization, the age of Semitic leadership drew to a close, to be followed by that of new peoples. The grasslands of what are now southern Russia and west-central Asia had in ancient times a population of shepherd nomads, the

[1] Many thousand clay tablets, the imperial library of Nineveh, now rest in the British Museum.

Indo-Europeans, who are the ancestors of modern Europe. The Indo-Europeans advanced until they spread from India across Asia and Europe to the Atlantic, facing a similar line of Semitic peoples to the south. The most easterly tribes were the Aryans, or Iranians, some of whom moved southeast into India, to develop a tongue of their own, the Sanskrit, and a religion of their own, preserved in the Vedas. The most powerful of the Aryans, however, were the Medes and Persians. Before 600 b.c. the Medes established a strong kingdom in the mountains east of the Tigris, made the Persians their vassals, and laid proud Nineveh low. Soon they were disturbing the sleep of Nebuchadnezzar and his Chaldeans in Babylonia.

The Aryans professed a lofty religion in Zoroastrianism, which included some beliefs that reappear in Judaism and Christianity. Mazda, or Ahuramazda, the Lord Wisdom, was the Zoroastrian counterpart of God, the All-Wise, in Jewish and Christian thought. With Him stood angelic beings, one of whom was Mithras, the Light. Opposed to Ahuramazda was Ahriman, spirit of evil, who became the Satan of Jewish and Christian thought, and whose agents were the "principalities and powers" described in the Epistles of St. Paul.

Sixty years after the fall of Nineveh there arose among the Persians a man of destiny. Cyrus, petty king of a single tribe, united all Persians into one nation and speedily reduced the Median king to submission. All nations watched his rise with alarm. Within five years Cyrus had swept across Asia to the Mediterranean, crushed the Chaldean army of Belshazzar, and taken Babylon in 539. Religious leaders among the Hebrew exiles there were excited. Cyrus appeared as one raised up by Jehovah, to punish Babylon and release the exiles. Their hopes were partially realized; for Cyrus did encourage the return of the exiles and the re-establishment of a Hebrew state in Palestine.

The rise of Cyrus marked the final eclipse of the Semitic peoples. His son Cambyses added Egypt to the Persian dominions; and the vast empire was organized and consolidated by a son of Cambyses, the just and enlightened Darius the Great. The Persians absorbed the civilization of their predecessors in Babylonia and on the Nile; and for two hundred years the Oriental world prospered under Persian direction. "Ahuramazda brought me help," says an inscription of Darius, "because I have ruled according to righteousness." The influence of Persia carried Zoroastrianism into Asia Minor, to lands that were to be evangelized by St. Paul. From there Mithraism, the cult of the Persian divinity, passed into Europe and spread throughout the Roman Empire, to become a rival of Christianity; but that was long afterwards.

While empires were rising and falling in western Asia, an European civilization, the Aegean, had arisen in what was later to be called Greece and in the islands of the Aegean Sea. The island of Crete was its centre; and there the Aegean civilization was already flourishing twenty centuries before Christ. But into the Aegean world came very early the Greeks, a group of Indo-European tribes from the Danube, kinsmen of the Medes and Persians. They gradually conquered the Aegean world, including the coast of Asia Minor. It was the pressure of the Greeks in the twelfth century that drove Aegeans of Crete, the Philistines, to southern Canaan, where they disputed the occupation of that land by the Hebrews.[2]

Greek civilization advanced until, in the Greek city-states of the Aegean world, it attained the highest development of ancient times. From the Hittites the Greeks learned the use of iron. From the Phoenicians they learned the multiform decorative art of the Orient. From the Phoenicians they acquired also an alphabet and paper (papyrus) on which to write. All these things were used to better advantage by the Greeks than by any other ancient people; but they were especially superior in science and philosophy. This affected religion. Some Greeks abandoned the gods. The world, they said, was governed by law, not by gods. Thales taught that an eclipse was not an outburst of divine wrath; it could be predicted if one knew the laws of celestial bodies. Pythagoras developed the principles governing mathematics. Others discovered from the rocks the history of life on the earth. The era of science began. So that when Greek arms triumphed over Persian at Marathon and Thermopylae, their success meant the survival of science as well as the immediate freedom of Greece.

Greek freedom, however, was short-lived. The rivalry between two Greek city-states, Athens and Sparta, led to the destruction of the Athenian power, and soon to that of Sparta and Thebes. No strong Greek state remained; and the Hellenic Age might well have closed, had not the kings of semi-barbarous Macedonia begun to cultivate Greek literature and art, and to assume the championship of Greek culture.

It was worthy of their advocacy. Greek architecture and sculpture had come nearer perfection than ever before or since. Greek painting had reached new heights, by the discovery of the use of light and shade and perspective. Greek religion had achieved the doctrine of immortality. A good life would bring one at last to the Elysian Fields; or one might achieve immortality by studying the Book of Orpheus, or by witnessing a mysterious religious drama, the life of Demeter and Dionysius, presented by the priests in the temple at Eleusis.

For those who were above all this, learning from the Sophists and the tragedies of Euripides to be skeptical, there was the teaching of Socrates that by faithful questioning one might learn to discover reality and through knowledge might attain to virtue. And there had grown up a body of knowl-

[2] Canaan was later to be known by their name. It became Palestine, or Philistine-land, a name first used in literature by Herodotus, so far as we know.
Some scholars incline to the view that the Philistines were Carians from Asia Minor.

edge about the natural world, set forth in treatises on astronomy and mathematics, botany and zoology, history and geography, the science of government and the nature of freedom.

Here were great gifts for the world; and the kings of Macedon were great men. Their Macedonian mountaineers, too, were vigorous in physique and character. King Philip, who had been educated in Greece, saw the weakness of that country and determined to make himself its master. An anti-Macedonian party at Athens tried to unite the Greek states for resistance, but even the "Philippics" of Demosthenes could not achieve this; and a long struggle closed with the victory of Philip over a Greek army at Chaeronea in 338 B.C.

Philip now put himself at the head of a league of Greek states, and began a campaign to liberate the Greek cities of Asia Minor from the overlordship of Persia. He fell by the hand of an assassin; but his son Alexander, a brilliant youth of twenty years, assumed the leadership of the Hellenic world against Asia. Alexander had been educated by the Greek Aristotle, and was enthusiastic for Greek culture.

Alexander carried an army of Greeks and Macedonians into Asia Minor and scattered a Persian army at the river Granicus in 334. In less than three years he had freed the Greek cities and carried his conquests to the Euphrates. He then pressed on to complete the conquest of the Persian Empire. Crossing the Tigris Alexander overwhelmed Darius III at Arbela and established himself in the royal palace at Babylon, then led an army into India. Seven years later he was back in Babylon, having established Greek kingdoms on the borders of India and carried Greek civilization far and wide.

Alexander's plan was nothing less than the Hellenization of the world. It was a more-than-human undertaking; and to achieve it Alexander made himself divine. That was not impossible. The idea of the divine man was familiar to the Orient. In Egypt the king had been divine, the offspring of the sun-god. In Greek thought there was no sharp distinction between gods and men; great men had been deified. So Alexander went to the shrine of Egyptian Amon, far out in the Sahara, and after a secret initiation came forth a son of the god Zeus-Amon. A royal message to the Greek cities commanded that Alexander be enrolled among the gods.

Alexander's vast schemes alienated the friends of his youth and provoked treason; and the disloyalty of friends embittered his soul. He died at thirty-seven, while planning the conquest of the Mediterranean world westward to the Atlantic.

The untimely death of Alexander prevented the political unification of the world under Greek leadership. A long struggle among his generals for control of the new empire resulted in its division into three parts. In Europe Macedonia fell at length to Antigonus. In Africa Ptolemy held Egypt, where he made himself king and founded a dynasty, choosing for his capital Alexandria, recently created by Alexander himself. In Asia Seleucus established himself and built a new capital, Antioch, on the river Orontes, which became the commercial rival of Alexandria.

Seleucus and his successors adopted the plan of Alexander. They planted Greek colonies, founding scores of Greek cities, as far east as Persia and India. Each city was given self-government, on the Greek model. The Seleucid Kingdom, often called Syria, was thus dotted with Greek city-states, each paying tribute and divine honours to the king. So Greek life took root throughout western Asia; and Palestine exchanged her Persian masters for the Greek Seleucids.

The three centuries after Alexander the Great, the last three before Christ, are known as the Hellenistic Age. The conquests of Alexander had placed Egypt and western Asia in the hands of men who spoke Greek. Government was carried on and business transacted in Greek. The new cities were laid out on Greek models, with streets at right angles and fine public buildings at the centre. There was a great market square, colonnaded, with a large audience room, where both the local Council and the Assembly of citizens could meet.

Alexandria, with the noble marble palace of the Ptolemies and the royal gardens, became the greatest city of the ancient world. The scientists of Alexandria, living together at the Museum on the bounty of the Ptolemies, began the earliest systematic scientific research, and acquired that body of scientific knowledge which served mankind until the beginning of modern times. Indeed Archimedes made discoveries in higher mathematics that were lost and had to be recovered for the modern world; and Euclid prepared a work on geometry that is still used as a text-book. The Ptolemies built an astronomical observatory, and there Aristarchus of Samos discovered that the earth revolves around the sun; though his conclusion was rejected then. An astronomer, Eratosthenes, computed the size of the earth; and another, Pytheas, sailed northward from Gibraltar, penetrated the North Sea, mapped the coast of Britain, and brought back word of mysterious *Thule,* Iceland, and the frozen sea beyond. The Ptolemies provided a laboratory for the study of anatomy, and the criminals upon whom vivisection was practised. They built a library, the greatest of the ancient world, containing a half-million rolls and Callimachus, the librarian, prepared a catalogue of all known works of value. The work of editing began; and Alexandrian editions became the standard for other libraries and copyists.

There was a similar advance in popular education. Elementary schools, supported by the state, began to appear everywhere. Beyond the elementary schools, youths might attend lectures on mathematics and science, philosophy and rhetoric, in the lecture-halls of the local gymnasia. They might find higher learning still, in science at the Museum in Alexandria, in philosophy at Athens. There one could join the disciples of Plato at the Academy, or those of Aristotle at the Lyceum, and later those of the Stoics and Epicureans also. Zeno, a Semite from Cyprus, taught in the Painted Porch, or

Stoa, of the market-place. There is no good thing, he said, except virtue and no evil except wickedness. To choose virtue is to find tranquillity, which makes one superior to both pleasure and pain. This was Stoicism.

Epicurus, an Athenian who set up a school in his own garden, taught a different doctrine. The highest good, he said, is pleasure, but pleasure of the intellect as well as of the body, and pleasure consistent with virtue. This was Epicureanism.

To the highly educated Stoicism and Epicureanism tended to become religions. To the masses, however, losing faith in the ancient gods of Greece, the gods of the Orient became more and more attractive. Thus around the eastern Mediterranean a civilization grew up, at once Greek and Oriental.

By 200 B.C. the Hellenistic-Oriental lands were threatened by a power not Greek, the Roman Republic in Italy, where civilization had been delayed until that of the eastern Mediterranean was growing old. The Greeks, in conquering the Aegean world, had inherited an ancient civilization; the Italic invaders of Italy had conquered a land without civilization. But when a group of Latin tribes became the Roman Republic, they were not above accepting gifts from the Greeks. Rome adopted the Greek alphabet, Greek silver coinage, Greek measures of length and weight. She yielded to Greek religious influences, identifying her gods with those of Greece. She looked for advice to Greek oracles, seeking revelations of the future in the utterances of the prophetess of Apollo at Delphi, preserved in the Sybilline Books.

The Roman genius, however, was for politics and government; and in time Rome developed an invincible state. Her Senate became the greatest governmental body of ancient times; and under its leadership the little Roman Republic moved on to the conquest of Italy, then looked across the sea. In all the West only Carthage in Africa seemed a possible rival. In time the strength of Carthage was broken by the defeat of Hannibal at Zama; and a generation later, in 146 B.C., Roman jealousy led to the destruction of Carthage itself. Her territory became a Roman province, the Province of Africa. Within a century Macedonia and the Seleucid Kingdom were also conquered; and Egypt, unequipped for a struggle, acknowledged herself a vassal of Rome.

The Roman Republic was thus lord of the Mediterranean world. How would she govern so vast a dominion, so swiftly acquired? Most of the conquered lands were made provinces, and required to pay taxes to Rome and obey a governor sent from Rome. He usually held office for only one year, and was often ambitious to get rich ere his brief day closed. Contractors, called Publicans, worked the state lands or collected state taxes, at great profit to themselves. Roman money-lenders grew rich, lending to the natives of the provinces at oppressive interest. The Senate passed laws to abolish these abuses, but could seldom make them effective. Meanwhile in Rome itself the citizens were relieved of taxation by the wealth flowing in from the provinces, and commanders grew rich on the spoils of war.

In civilization Rome and Italy became increasingly Hellenic. Romans abroad felt instinctively the superior culture of the captured Greek cities. They returned home to build Greek houses and fill Rome with Greek sculptures. Greek temples and theatres rose in Latin Italy. Greek literary classics were translated into Latin; and Latin literature copied Greek models. Roman lads had Greek tutors at home, or attended the schools of freed slaves from Greece. Cultivated Romans spoke Greek as well as Latin. High-born youths went for advanced studies to Athens.

The common people, untouched by the new culture, nevertheless elected the rulers; and ambitious men secured their favour by feasts, lewd shows and bloody combats. Laws were passed to check the slow corruption of the people. Roman power, it was seen, could not continue if Roman virtue declined; but decline went on apace. Roman nobles were above trade, and aspired to become great landowners. So the small farms disappeared from Italy, swallowed up by great estates, worked by prisoners of war. The ruin of the small farms was completed by the absence of fathers at the wars. So the sturdy yeomen died out in Italy. In the provinces also business and agriculture began to fail, by reason of official extortion. All the higher civilization of the Hellenic world decayed. The inability of the Roman Senate to provide an efficient government for a vast dominion, as it had for an Italian republic, brought the Mediterranean world to the brink of ruin. The disaster could be averted only if the Roman Republic could transform itself into a true imperial state.

A struggle of sixty years between the Senate and the popular Assembly, for control of the state and reform of abuses, opened the way to power for any military leader whom the people would trust. One of these, Pompey, was elected Consul in 70 b.c., and was then given supreme command of the Mediterranean and its shores. He cleared the sea of pirates, thus setting commerce free. He stamped out resistance in Syria, and subdued the restless Jews. Then, like Alexander the Great, he led an army to the Euphrates. On his return he was supported by two other popular heroes, Julius Caesar and Crassus.

Rome was now in the hands of a triumvirate. Out of their rivalries Caesar rose to supreme authority. It was clear to him that the policy for the Roman world was that of permanent control of the government by a patriotic man, supported by an army. Caesar published the story of his own Gallic wars. It gave him great prestige, and helped him to secure control for himself. By 45 b.c. he was master of the Roman world.

Caesar fell next year beneath the daggers of assassins, who thought him the enemy of Rome; but he had accomplished the transition to one-man rule. His death brought to Rome his grand-nephew and heir Octavian, a youth of eighteen, pursuing his studies in Illyria. Great patience and cunning secured for Octavian command of Caesar's veterans. In fourteen years his victory was complete. He had won the East by a victory over his rival Antony at Actium. He had taken Egypt and made it a Roman province when Cleopatra, last of the Ptolemies, took her life at his approach. One-man power was established.

The rule of Octavian, 30 B.C.—14 A.D., is of special importance. A dissolute youth, Octavian nevertheless grew into a man of wisdom and justice and strength. He was soon given by the Senate the title *Augustus* and brought in the Golden-Age of Rome, brief as it was to be. Augustus scrupulously respected republican forms. He called himself, not King but *Princeps* and *Imperator,* first citizen and commander-in-chief. Republican sentiment was thus conciliated; but the Republic had really become a military monarchy. Oriental influences tended in the same direction. In Egypt Augustus was king in name as well as in fact, successor of the Pharaohs and the Ptolemies.

Augustus set himself to organize and consolidate the empire already won. He fixed its boundaries at the Euphrates in the east, the Sahara and the Atlantic on south and west, the Tyne and Solway in Britain, the Rhine and Danube on the north-east. He maintained a standing army, posted on the frontiers, recruited chiefly from the provinces, and including many men from the subject peoples, who were given Roman citizenship in return for military service.

Within the Empire's distant frontiers was now a world, the Mediterranean world, at peace, with time to recover from its wounds. Government became efficient. The governors of frontier provinces were chosen by the Emperor, and were responsible directly to him. A great census of the people and an assessment determined what taxes were to be paid; and levies were no longer capricious. The Mediterranean nations, united and prosperous, became themselves a nation, except that Jews kept their religious consciousness and restlessness.

In old age Augustus asked the Senate to associate with him in the government his stepson Tiberius. The death of Augustus therefore found an able man, already trained in government. Tiberius abandoned all pretence of republican rule, dispensed with the Assembly, and ruled as an absolute monarch until his death. Four years of the mad Caligula (37–41), thirteen years of the industrious and well-meaning Claudius (41–54), fourteen years of the depraved and cruel Nero (54–68), and the line of Augustus ended; but the good done by Augustus and Tiberius was not all lost. Government continued fairly stable and most of the Roman world at peace for a century longer.

In this same century, however, the history of the Jewish nation in Palestine closed in tragedy. Jerusalem was destroyed and Judaism proscribed by the Roman power, as an episode in the fight for public order. A Messianic movement came to birth, however, in Judaism and grew into the Christian

Church. Jesus of Nazareth was born into a Jewish community, which was also an island, partially inundated, in a sea of Greek life, under the political dominion of Rome. When the inundation became complete, the Church had already learned to swim.

THE HEBREW TRADITION OF THEIR
NATIONAL ORIGIN

THE first six books of the Bible, the Hexateuch, consist of a fascinating narrative, certain cosmogonic speculations of great dignity and beauty, songs, law codes, and what not. The substance of the narrative is as follows:

A very long time ago, so long that creation itself seemed but a few generations away, an old sheik Terah set out with his family from Ur-Kasdim, near where the Euphrates disgorges into the Persian Gulf. His destination was the land of Canaan, eight hundred miles westward across the north Arabian desert. The travellers, however, avoided the desert route, choosing rather to ascend the Euphrates and descend upon Canaan from the northeast. They broke their journey at the ancient city of Haran, on the Belikh, a tributary of the Euphrates, and there Terah died. The family stayed on at Haran and acquired a considerable establishment. The new sheik was Terah's eldest son Abraham; and Abraham's nephew Lot was of the household. Abraham, it seems, was a monotheist. This is strange, as the people of both Ur-Kasdim and Haran were polytheists, specially devoted to the moongod. But Abraham worshipped God; and God now sent him forward to Canaan, promising that he should become the founder of a nation and a benefactor of all mankind.

Abraham and his retinue trekked past the oasis of Palmyra and the orchards of Damascus, and penetrated Canaan as far south as Shechem, a Canaanite sanctuary, where a deity dwelt in a sacred terebinth, or turpentine tree, and gave oracular advice to enquirers. There God renewed his promise to Abraham; and there Abraham built an altar to God. On he went still farther, to the south country, the Negeb, thus traversing the whole land of Canaan.

Thereafter Abraham led the nomad's life, pitching his tent anywhere from Shechem to Egypt and sometimes in Egypt itself. His son Isaac was more settled, living chiefly in the Negeb; but Isaac's son Jacob, or Israel, wandered at will, growing up in Canaan, going east to the ancestral home for his wives, and emigrating in old age to Egypt to escape a famine in Canaan. The family of Jacob remained in Egypt, where his son Joseph had already been living and had risen high in the government of the Pharaoh. Joseph grew old and died in the land of his adoption; but at the end he "said unto his brethren, I die; but God will surely visit you, and bring you up out of this land unto the land which he sware to Abraham, to Isaac, and to Jacob" (*Genesis* 50: 24).

The children of Israel in Egypt, after the death of Joseph, "were fruitful, and increased abundantly, and multiplied, and waxed exceeding mighty; and the land was filled with them" (*Exodus* 1: 7), until some change of dynasty brought to the throne a Pharaoh "which knew not Joseph." He did know that the presence of so many aliens was neither pleasant nor safe. They crowded the pasture and fruit lands, and might become the allies of future invaders. So the Pharaoh reduced the children of Israel to serfdom, and advanced to the terrible expedient of slaying the male infants. During the period of this stern decree a child was born to a "daughter of Levi," who saved his life by a ruse and transferred him to the care of Pharaoh's daughter. The princess adopted the Hebrew babe and called him Moses.

When Moses was grown to manhood a natural sympathy with his suffering people brought him into danger, and he fled to a Midianite settlement across the Red Sea. The Midianites were kinsmen of the Hebrews; and Moses was hospitably received by Reuel, the chief priest of the tribe. Reuel (also called Jethro) gave the stranger his daughter to wife; and Moses lived as a herdsman with his father-in-law. But evil news continually came of the sufferings of the Hebrews in Egypt. One day, in the course of his duties, Moses "led the flock to the back of the wilderness, and came to the mount of God, unto Horeb" (*Exodus* 2; 3: 1). There God called to him out of a burning bush, and commanded that Moses rescue his people. Very reluctantly Moses obeyed. He went to the Pharaoh repeatedly, demanding that the children of Israel be released. The demand was repeatedly refused. Each refusal brought upon Egypt some startling manifestation of God's anger. Disease was sent among the fish of the Nile; frogs infested the land and the houses, the bed chambers and the ovens. Swarms of flies were sent, and a murrain among the cattle, a devastating hail and clouds of locusts. The Nile was turned to blood; and an unnatural darkness overspread the land. At last God's anger rose to the pitch of destroying the firstborn in every Egyptian home. This was too much. The Pharaoh summoned Moses and his brother Aaron in the middle of the night, and besought them to be gone with their people. So the children of Israel departed, having "sojourned in Egypt . . . four hundred and thirty years" (*Exodus* 7–11).

The moving host were miraculously convoyed across the *Yam Suph,* an arm of the Red Sea; they were miraculously given food and drink in the wilderness. By a miracle they overcame the Bedawin that disputed the way; and at "the Mount of God," amidst great convulsions of Nature, they entered into a covenant with God. Soon thereafter an elaborate ritual law, preserved in the *Book of Leviticus,* was divinely communicated. Thus equipped with a national constitution, of divine origin and authority, the people of Israel journeyed on, with frequent complaints and some mutiny, to Kadesh, an oasis near the southern frontier of Canaan (*Numbers* 10–13). An ill-conceived attack upon the Negeb failed; and Israel turned back to the wilderness, condemned of God to live the nomad's life until the whole gen-eration that had been brought out of Egypt should pass away. So Israel wan-dered wearily forty years between Egypt and Canaan, and came at length to the land of Moab, east of the Dead Sea and the Jordan.

Israel lay encamped for some time in the plains of Moab; and there God revealed to Moses that he would never cross the Jordan into the promised land. He would die in the land of Moab, a vicarious sacrifice for the sins of Israel. From the summit of Mount Pisgah, Moses looked upon the land of his dreams; and then in the Arabah, the deep valley of the Dead Sea, he com-municated to Israel the final instructions of God. He told them of a new covenant, into which he had entered with God on their behalf. It may be read still in the *Book of Deuteronomy*. The covenant embodied a code of life and worship suitable for a more developed society than that of the wil-derness. It was to be adopted when Israel should be settled in Canaan.

Moses died in the land of Moab. Farther north, in Gilead, certain tribes of Israel settled down east of the Jordan. Joshua, son of Nun, led the rest across the river, the waters being miraculously divided for them, as the *Yam Suph* had been for their fathers. Scouts soon reported that the Canaanites were everywhere in a panic. The city of Jericho was captured by a miracle, and its people destroyed. The city of Ai fell quickly. A host of Canaanites were routed at Beth-horon. The cities of the whole region were captured and the inhabitants without exception put to the sword, a "devotion" to God. So Joshua moved through Canaan, until the whole land lay open for partition and occupation.

Such is the tradition of early Hebrew history preserved in the Hexateuch; but it is impossible to regard it as dependable. Canaan in the time of Abraham was thickly settled, the inhabitants living in fortified towns, frequently at war with each other. So we learn from the cuneiform tablets, discovered in our own time at El-Amarna in Egypt. An immigrant clan, moving across the land building altars, would be in straits in Canaan. As for Egypt, modern Egyptologists can find on the monuments no evidence for a Hebrew occupa-tion of that land; and the writers of *Genesis* and *Exodus* are equally ignorant of Egypt. We should expect to hear something in these books of the gods of Egypt, of Mnevis and Apis, of the crocodiles of Ombos and the ram of Mendes; but there are no echoes whatever of religion in Egypt, as there are of religion in Babylonia and Assyria, Chaldea and Persia, in other Old Testa-ment books.

As for the conquest of Canaan, can it have been as short and sharp as the *Book of Joshua* recounts? And did the conqueror exterminate the inhabit-ants, devoting them to his god? Statements in *Joshua* itself are conflicting;

and elsewhere in the Hexateuch it is said that Jehovah forbade the extermination of the population, lest the land relapse to wilderness (*Deuteronomy*
7: 22, 23). Outside the Hexateuch also, in *Judges,* we discover that, generations after the conquest, Israel is in possession of only the highlands of the
south, while the Canaanites are still in the valleys and farther north the
Canaanites and Hebrews are mingling in one population.

There are many such contradictions; and it is now generally recognized
that the books of the Hexateuch do not provide a trustworthy history or a
consistent handbook of religion. This is not strange to one who knows their
literary history. They are centuries later than the events they describe; and
they are compilations from earlier writings, that were themselves of different
times and of different points of view. Moreover the writers follow a literary
practice common among ancient authors, especially the Arabs, in borrowing
from earlier writers without acknowledging their borrowings or combining
them well with their own materials. The ethics of writing were not modern;
there was no sentiment against plagiarism.

The problems presented by the Hexateuch confront one elsewhere
throughout the Old Testament. Books that write the same history do not
always tell the same story. The books from *Genesis* to *Kings* attempt a continuous record of events from the creation of the world until the Exile.
Chronicles, Ezra and *Nehemiah* cover the same period but extend it to the
years after the Exile. These two histories, where they are parallel, often disagree. The author of *Chronicles* tries to improve the story told in *Kings,*
omitting what he finds unedifying and magnifying the institutions of the
past. By the time of the Chronicler the priestly party in Israel had risen to
control and had developed an elaborate ritual of worship. The Chronicler
writes as if this had existed from the beginning, having come down from
Moses himself.

More difficult still is the fact that one finds in the Old Testament, sometimes in the same book, conflicting views of God, of religion, of the future
life, of the destiny of the Hebrew nation. The prophet Samuel thinks of
Jehovah as the violent partisan of the Hebrews; Deutero-Isaiah thinks of
him as the God of all nations. *Leviticus* presents religion as a matter of ritual
observances, of tithes and offerings; *Micah* says religion is to "do justly, and
love kindness, and walk humbly with God." As a Jewish scholar has said,
"In the realm of ideas which he conceived as belonging to his tradition the
Jew was not logical; he did not pick and choose; he absorbed the whole. In
Jewish theology of all ages we find the most obvious contradictions." [1]

As for the Hexateuch, a safe general conclusion is this, that we have no
reliable history of the Hebrews before the conquest of Canaan, that the
stories of Abraham and the Patriarchs are basically tribal traditions, told
around the campfires for generations before they were committed to writing.
Such traditions cannot be complete, or accurate, or even self-consistent. Some

[1] Israel Abrahams, *Judaism,* Constable & Co., p. 6.

events will be forgotten, some distorted, some magnified. The history back of the Hexateuch would seem to be somewhat as follows, that some section of Israel was connected in prehistoric times with the East; that some clan of Israel sojourned also in Egypt; that this clan left Egypt under the leadership of Moses and was by him introduced to the worship of Jehovah, or *Yahweh,* a storm god of Midian, with a seat at Mt. Sinai, which may be identical with Mt. Horeb; that Moses led his followers from Midian to Canaan, where they combined with other Hebrew clans from Arabia, the ancestral home of the Hebrews. Moses came in time to overshadow everyone else in the early history of the Hebrews; and the events connected with him dominated the tradition of ancient Hebrew life, because his deity *Yahweh* became the national god of Israel in Palestine. His ethical teaching, too, founded the tradition of Israelite morality carried forward by the great prophets.

THE SYNOPTIC PROBLEM

Matthew, Mark and *Luke* are Synoptic Gospels, synoptic in the sense that they present the same general picture of Jesus, in contrast with *John,* which is rather a philosophy than a biography.

Studying the Synoptic Gospels together, one finds that if *Matthew* and *Luke* are placed in parallel columns with *Mark* between, sometimes all three, sometimes two, are seen to report the same event or teaching in exactly the same words. Sometimes they report the same thing, but in different words and with a different sense. Sometimes only one Gospel reports an event or teaching.

The problem presented by these agreements and differences is called the Synoptic Problem. It was the central problem of New Testament study for fifty years, but is now practically solved. There is general agreement that *Mark* is the earliest of the Gospels, and that the authors of *Matthew* and *Luke* used *Mark*. But *Matthew* and *Luke* are much longer than *Mark*, the additional material being concerned mainly with the teaching of Jesus. This teaching is largely the same in the two Gospels, and is often verbally identical. It is clear that the authors of *Matthew* and *Luke* used, in addition to *Mark*, some collection of sayings of Jesus; and scholars call this collection *Q* (German *Quelle,* source).

Matthew and *Luke* include still other materials, not found in either *Mark* or *Q,* one valuable document quoted in *Luke* being a collection of parables and anecdotes. The parables of the Good Samaritan, the lost sheep, the prodigal son, the rich man and Lazarus, the Pharisee and the publican, and several others, are found only in *Luke,* as are the stories of the raising of the widow's son of Nain, the anointing of Jesus in the house of Simon the Pharisee, the visit of Jesus to Martha and Mary.

Then, in addition to all written documents, there were stories passed on by word of mouth. These stories would change with time; and so the oral tradition would not be trustworthy in quite the same way as written documents. Such stories are those in the opening chapters of *Matthew* and *Luke,* of marvels attending the birth of John the Baptist and Jesus, stories that do not appear in *Mark* and *Q,* and that differ from each other in *Matthew* and *Luke.*

From what has been said it is plain that the Synoptists are not so much authors as editors of earlier materials. Yet they have together provided a likeness of Jesus that is vivid and self-consistent. And indeed they were more directly in touch with the facts than might be supposed. Scholarly studies confirm the ancient Christian tradition that the author of *Mark* is John Mark, cousin of Barnabas. His mother's house in Jerusalem, soon after the crucifixion of Jesus, was a place of assembly for his disciples and a place of retreat for the apostles in times of danger (*Acts* 12: 11–17). John Mark must have heard in boyhood what the apostles had to say about Jesus. In manhood he travelled with Barnabas and Paul. Later, so tradition says, he became the permanent travelling companion of Peter. At the end he was the devoted and trusted attendant of both Peter and Paul, when they were awaiting death at Rome (I *Peter* 5: 13; *Col.* 4: 10–14). If Mark's Gospel is thirty or forty years later than the events he describes, he nevertheless writes out of his own knowledge and that of eye-witnesses.

As for the third Gospel, the ancient ascription of it to Luke, physician and companion of Paul, has been re-examined in our time, and philologists have compared the Gospel with *Acts*. The ancient view is confirmed, that the third Gospel and *Acts* are from the same hand, and that the author of both is Luke. He was in a position to gather good evidence. He shared the travels of Paul. He would hear the folklore and read the documents preserved in the Christian communities they visited. As we have seen, he uses in his Gospel both *Mark* and *Q*, and at least one other collection of parables and anecdotes; and he tells, very beautifully and poetically, certain stories of the birth and infancy of Jesus, that were circulating by word of mouth.

Concerning the Gospel of Matthew, it is almost certainly not the work of an apostle or an eye-witness of the Lord. It does not speak with such first-hand knowledge as Mark and Luke. It seems to have been called *Matthew* because it was known to incorporate many sayings of Jesus, that had been committed to writing by the apostle Matthew. The author is a Christian archeologist of Palestine, who speaks Greek and who has combined into one work much of *Mark*, many sayings of Jesus preserved by Matthew, and other materials from sources unknown.

The sum of the matter, therefore, is this, that while the authors of the Synoptic Gospels had little, if any, personal acquaintance with Jesus, they knew those who had. They report what eye-witnesses have said, together with some little popular tradition, less valuable as evidence.

JUDAISM AFTER THE THIRD JEWISH
WAR, 132-135 A. D.

THE Jewish rebellion against Rome in 132, inspired by the Rabbi Akiba and led by Simon bar Cochba, determined the Emperor Hadrian to suppress Judaism. When therefore the rebellion was crushed in 135 and a Roman city, *Aelia Capitolina,* built on the site of Jerusalem, the rites and ceremonies of Judaism were made illegal everywhere. The scholastic centre at Jamnia was destroyed.

It was in vain. Akiba, from a prison cell in Caesarea, continued to direct the religious life of the people, and died by torture. Hanina, son of Teradion, was convicted of teaching the Law and was burned at the stake, wrapped in the scroll of the Law. Ten disciples of Akiba suffered martyrdom; and others fled to the Dispersion in Babylonia. Only two courses were open to Rome—to exterminate the Jewish people or return to the policy of conciliation. Hadrian's successor, Antoninus Pius, chose the latter. The intolerant edicts were revoked. The disciples of Akiba returned to Palestine, this time to Usha in Galilee. They re-established the Sanhedrin, and restored Jewish worship and education. Schools of the Law revived; and those in Galilee again became the most influential throughout all Jewry.

The president of the Sanhedrin was now recognized by the imperial government as the head of Jewry. He was the *Nasi,* or Patriarch, and received almost royal honours. The earliest, Judah I, was a great scholar, educated by the disciples of Akiba. He directed the nation, in Palestine and the Dispersion, for fifty years, honoured alike for his learning and his piety. He revived the use of Hebrew by scholars, and made it the daily language of his own household, instead of Aramaic.

Meanwhile Jewish religious legalism approached completion. The rabbis at Jamnia had already begun to commit to writing their traditional lore, the Oral Law; and this became the habit of scholars everywhere. This written tradition was the *Mishnah,* or rehearsal; and for a time every great scholar had his own. Judah and his associates, however, pooled their wealth of traditional lore and codified it; and their *Mishnah* gradually superseded all others in Jewry. It cites one hundred and forty-eight ancient scholars; and these, with the codifiers, have remained ever since the great teachers of Judaism. They are the *Tannaim,* the "repeaters of the tradition."

The *Mishnah* was meant to be a text-book for the guidance of judges and teachers. It was in Hebrew, the language of the ancient Law. That gave to the *Mishnah* the flavour of antiquity and the odour of sanctity.

The classical age of Judaism closed with the *Tannaim*. Rabbinical schools thereafter were satisfied to discuss the existing *Mishnah,* its meaning and application. The records of their discussions became another vast literature, a supplementary legal authority. It too had to be codified if it was to be usable; and its codified form is called the *Talmud,* or teaching.

The *Talmud* is the last stage in a legal development that began nearly fifteen hundred years before, when Moses enunciated a few principles of universal application, the Decalogue, and gave them greater authority by making them a covenant with Yahweh. The Decalogue grew into the Code of the Covenant, into *Deuteronomy,* into the Pentateuch; and was enlarged generation after generation by "the tradition of the Elders" as to the meaning of the Pentateuch and its application. Now at last the tradition had itself been codified in the *Mishnah;* and professional scholars were busy with the *Mishnah,* thus producing the *Talmud. Talmud* and *Mishnah* had not quite the authority of the Pentateuch; but they also were binding.

During all this march of the legislators voices of protest were occasionally heard, prophets crying from the roadside, "Who hath required this?" They were sometimes silenced, sometimes ignored, sometimes noticed in new legislation, as in *Deuteronomy;* but Israel, in the main, paid little heed to the greater prophets, except when they predicted a glorious future for the nation. She valued them later, as she valued her poets and sages, as exhibiting aspects of the racial genius; but the Law was her national charter, the divine pledge of her future greatness. Deprived at last of nationhood, Israel went forth, to Mesopotamia and Persia and Armenia, Asia Minor and Egypt and Europe, hugging the Law to her breast, superior to all others and so disliked by all others, exclusive and so excluded.

So Judaism remains to this day. Many Jews have fallen out and been lost in the crowd. Some, like Saadia, attempted a philosophical defence of Judaism, a defence which the rabbis thought unnecessary and the Gentiles did not read. Some, like the mystic Bahya ibn Pakuda, continued devoted to the Law, while finding their real satisfaction where mystics have always found it, in contemplation and illumination. Some, like Moses Mendelssohn, laboured to overcome the isolation of the Jew and introduce him to contemporary life and culture. A few, like Baal Shem, became aware that the rabbis "through study of the Law had no time to think about God," and attempted the reformation of Judaism itself. So Reformed Synagogues arose after long centuries, rejecting the *Talmud,* abandoning Messianic expectations, rationalizing Sabbath laws, accepting the dispersion of the Jews as their destiny, while still revering the ancient Law; but the hard nucleus of Jewish legalism has endured, an atom that no spiritual physics can split.

RELIGION IN GREEK PHILOSOPHY

More than five hundred years before Christ philosophy began to be systematized in the Greek colonies of Asia Minor, and especially in Ionia. Miletus, the wealthy capital of Ionia, had the earliest school of Greek philosophy, a school which was therefore called the Milesian School. In it originated the fundamental terms and distinctions, by which the human mind still attempts to explain the Universe. In it philosophy first recognized that a thing may be real without being material. And from Ionia to Athens came Anaxagoras, to become a member of the brilliant circle of Pericles and Euripides and Thucydides, and to teach that the moving force in all the Universe is mind.

Side by side with philosophical speculation, there was always some ethical reflection among the Greeks. It was stimulated by the rise of the Tyrants, setting up their private wills as superior to the State and to customary morality. It was more difficult thereafter for men to accept the *status quo,* since laws were changing every year. The thoughtful were bound to look beyond laws, to the nature of justice and morality. And so the Sophists arose. They wandered from city to city, instructing chiefly the sons of the rich. Greatest of them all was Socrates, a tattered saint, with thick lips and snub nose, who felt himself divinely appointed to be gadfly of the State. Socrates declared that all man really needs to know is how to live, that every man has within him the capacity for such knowledge, and that, beneath all the individual prejudices and opinions that make men disagree, there are universal truths about which they can agree. The method of philosophy is to get beyond individual idiosyncrasies to the essential nature of man.

This idea was developed by Plato, who came under the influence of Socrates at twenty and remained with him until the master's execution eight years later. In his study of the nature of man, Plato made the first serious attempt in history at an adequate psychology, or science of the soul. There are in man, he said, sensations and appetites, that are mere functions of the body; and a spirit, or active will, which is the seat of the heroic virtues; and the reason, or soul, where wisdom dwells and whose right it is to rule. These faculties are distinct and often at war with each other, reason fighting against desire. Reason must rule because man is man, because there is for him no enduring satisfaction, except as he realises his essential nature.

In Plato individuality is disparaged, in the search for the universal, rational element, that each man has in common with all other men and that makes each a member of the state and a part of the universe. It is not the actual state, however, but the ideal state, Utopia, of which Plato thinks, the state he portrays in the *Republic*. It is not a democracy but a paternalism, in which common men submit to the wise man, the philosopher-king, in the interest of the whole.

But how, in an imperfect and changing world, is the ideal to be found? In reply Plato begins by affirming that truth is not relative, as Heraclitus taught; there is an absolute standard of truth. The very idea of knowledge implies permanent reality somewhere. How shall one know anything, where everything is changing? Philosophy has to do with the permanent, what Plato calls the "general Idea," that which is common to all things of the same sort. Thus, if philosophy undertakes to say what man is, it does not describe an individual, but rather those characteristics which belong to man as such.

Permanent and universal "Ideas" then are "the truth," of which both science and philosophy are in search. Shall one say that it does not exist? No! Plato affirms that, over against the changing world of sensation, is a realm of Ideas, of permanent existence. Thus there are two worlds—the world of individual things, met through the senses, subject to the Heraclitan flux; and the world of true Being, the world of Ideas, unchanging, absolute.

It was the work of Plato to find the world of eternal, immutable Ideas, and to teach men to judge individual men and things by its standards. How does one find it? Plato replies that knowledge itself is recollection, it is the impress left on the soul by a previous existence, an existence before it became a wanderer from its home in the realm of true reality, immersed in the world of sense. The earlier vision of reality may be recalled to consciousness by faithful thought.

This is Plato's theory of knowledge; and it includes one truth that philosophy still affirms—the truth that the universe we know is not an aggregate of sense perceptions but an interpretation by the mind.

There are visible defects in all this. Plato saw a great gulf fixed between the world of experience and the world of Ideas. The "lilies of the field," the "birds of the heaven," all the world of things, was too confused a shadow of the world of Ideas to be of use to either science or religion. So also with the nature of man. There is hostility between body and soul. "The soul when using the body as an instrument of perception, that is to say, when using the sense of sight or hearing or some other sense . . . is then dragged by the body into the region of the changeable, and wanders and is confused; the world spins round her, and she is like a drunkard when under their influence." So that, to reach the Ideal, one must strive to close eyes and ears, and follow only the pure light of the mind. "When returning into herself (the soul) reflects; then she passes into the realm of purity, and eternity, and immortality, and unchangeableness, which are her kindred, . . . then she ceases from her erring ways, and being in communion with the unchanging is unchanging. And this state of the soul is called wisdom." [1] One may not hope to attain it here in fulness, hampered as one is by the senses; but in another life the faithful will gather the perfect fruits of wisdom. Plato thus teaches the immortality of the soul.

Here in Plato are all the elements of asceticism. The philosopher must flout the body, isolate himself from the common life, and become absorbed in the beatific vision. It is a world renunciation that was to reappear in many a Christian anchorite and monk, who would think he had learned it from Jesus.

Plato's thought was developed by his great disciple Aristotle, who nevertheless departed in important particulars from the master's teaching, and notably in psychology. Aristotle denied that man is constitutionally a divided being, necessarily at war with himself. The human body, Aristotle said, quite in the manner of modern psychology, is the servant of the soul; and virtue is the reward, not of suppressing the natural impulses, but of regulating them. Aristotle says many things about consciousness, sensation, memory, the association of ideas, that anticipate the teaching of modern science; but he was not widely influential in Roman society, his optimistic view of human nature being ill-suited to its pessimism. [2]

With Aristotle the era of speculative philosophy in Greece came to an end. Greek independence was lost to Macedonia; and the sentence of death upon Greece was confirmed two centuries later, when the Roman general Mummius captured Corinth in 146 B.C., and Greece became a Roman province, Achaia. Thoughtful men were in desperate need of individual satisfactions, independent of the state. They could not take refuge in the gods of the ancestral religion. Skepticism had undermined belief in them. Men turned therefore to new philosophies, and to Oriental religious cults.

Of the new philosophies, Epicureanism and Stoicism were most influential. The philosophy of Epicurus was Hedonism. The good life is the pleasant life. Virtue itself is justified by the pleasures that it brings. But one must select his pleasures, avoiding those that have an aftermath of pain, preferring simple and natural joys before those of luxury and excess. Epicurus was thus an ancient Rousseau, calling men back from the complexities of civilization to natural pleasures, and from the Platonic struggle after truth to the joy of refined conversation and friendly intercourse. He was interested in physical science only in so far as a knowledge of the world is necessary to a quiet mind. It rids one, Epicurus says, of that great hindrance to inward peace, religion. This is the function of science, to sweep away the fears and scruples of religion. There are no gods near enough and interested enough to torment

---

[1] Plato, *Phaedo*, 79, Jowett's translation.

[2] The greatest single achievement of Aristotle is his logic, set forth in a group of writings known as the *Organon*. It dominated the mediaeval Christian mind, which had lost the will for original thought but revelled in logic; and Formal Logic to-day, the analysis of the processes of deductive argument, differs little from that of Aristotle.

men. There is no hereafter, no woes of Tartarus, that need affright the human spirit.

Epicureanism was a creed for the leisurely. It could satisfy neither the scientific mind nor the ardent conscience. In science it was dogmatic, interested to support its own view of life, uninterested in truth for truth's sake. In ethics it was without enthusiasm and indifferent to mankind. It was, as Cicero said, a bourgeois philosophy, of cheerfulness and good taste.

Better suited to human needs was Stoicism, the philosophy of Zeno, a Semite from the island of Cyprus, who was teaching in the Stoa, or painted corridor on the north side of the market-place of Athens, in the days of Epicurus. Stoicism was more ascetic, reflecting Oriental ideals; and it produced a type of character nobler than any of the other schools. It differed from its rival in that it made virtue, not pleasure, the highest good. And virtue is conformity to Nature. All reality, Zeno said, is an organic whole, whether one call it Nature or God. True knowledge is to understand Nature. Virtuous conduct, which is also rational conduct, is that which furthers the purposes of Nature. And Nature herself is not a mere collection of atoms, but a living soul. This soul is everywhere present in the world, as a more active and refined kind of matter, just as the human soul is present in the body.[3] Indeed the human soul, being but a part of the world soul, will in the end lose its individuality and be received again into the world soul.

Stoicism, however, pursued speculative philosophy only far enough to find a theoretical basis for ethics; and a reasoned view of ethics requires some view of human psychology. Here the Stoics introduced an innovation. Human desires and emotions, they said, are not a legitimate part of the soul, to be directed by reason; they are a disease, to be destroyed. The Stoic ethical ideal, therefore, includes freedom from emotion. One will not be sad in adversity; nor will one pity a friend in adversity, though one will relieve him, since he also is a part of Nature. But emotion is a disturbance of the mind, which easily becomes ungovernable; and in yielding to it one opens the gate to the enemy. The virtuous man will stand fast against all pressure from without.

The harshness of Stoic ethics was mitigated, however, by the principle already mentioned, that all reality is an organic whole. The sage, therefore, will not regard other men as fools, since all are parts of Nature and are brothers. Quite suitably, therefore, the two most famous Stoics of the second Christian century were an emperor and a slave, Marcus Aurelius and Epictetus.

The religious spirit, too, was in Stoicism, when at its best. Man was not only a citizen of the world; he was a part of its very substance. This would be a hard, relentless fact, where Nature was regarded as a play of atoms; but since the Stoic regarded Nature as soul, his own relation to Nature was

---

[3] This soul, or rational principle, Zeno calls the *Logos* (Greek *speech,* or *utterance*), a term the Christian Church was later to use to describe the place of Christ in the universe.

that of kinship. If he could not turn Nature to his purposes, the purposes of Nature were at least the expression of his own true being and needs. True Stoics could say, with Marcus Aurelius, "To her who gives and takes back all, to Nature, the man who is instructed and modest says: 'Give what thou wilt, take back what thou wilt.' And he says this, not proudly but obediently, and as well pleased with her."

Occasionally the sentiment of the Stoic for Nature approached pure monotheism. Epictetus said, as naturally as any Christian or Jew or Moslem, "Dare to look up to God and say: 'Deal with me for the future as thou wilt, I refuse nothing that pleases thee.'" Stoic and Christian had much in common, too, in their ideas of worthy conduct. "Never value anything as profitable to thyself," said Marcus Aurelius, "which compels thee to break thy promise, to lose thy self-respect, to hate any man, to suspect, to curse, to act the hypocrite, to desire anything that needs walls and curtains."

Such integrity of soul, the Stoic said, is its own reward. Other delights are trivial when compared with it. Serene in possession of himself, a man can welcome the buffetings of fortune, confident that all things work together for his good. In short, the world is a perfect world, expressing in everything a divine purpose.

Here was an ideal of life and character more profound than any the Greek world had known; and it was a genuine refuge to noble minds. It served also, in Roman society, both to prepare the minds of men for Christian monotheism and to provide an alternative. Stoicism, indeed, had some resemblances to the young religion from Palestine, that was first to supplant it and then to suppress it.

There were, of course, in the Mediterranean world, systems of thought that were not Greek. In intellectual centres like Rhodes and Tarsus, Antioch and Alexandria, men had an ancient Oriental inheritance of their own, in addition to the more recently acquired Hellenic culture. Inevitably some of them attempted to combine Hellenism with their ancestral systems and cults. So there arose eclectic philosophies and religions, systems, that is, which combined elements drawn from various sources.

Eclecticism was congenial to the governing Romans, who had little interest in philosophy as such and were disposed to regard the metaphysical distinctions of keener minds as foolishness. Cicero is best known of the Roman eclectics, labouring diligently to popularize Greek ideas and adjust them to Roman.

The Eclecticism of most importance for the history of religion arose at Alexandria. That city had, for three centuries before Christ, an influential Jewish colony; and after the eclipse of Greece Jewish Hellenism became the dominant intellectual force. Here Philo, a Jew of the time of Christ, attempted to prove an essential harmony between Jewish religious thought and Greek philosophy, especially that of Plato. The oppositions between He-

brew Scriptures and Greek ideas were overcome by allegorical interpretations of the Scriptures. In particular, God was kept as remote as Greek
thought required and as accessible as Hebrew religion required by positing
a series of lesser beings, sometimes Platonic Ideas, sometimes Hebrew
angels, who are the messengers of God to the world. Foremost among
them was the *Logos,* or Word, of God, the medium of divine revelation in
history.

This conception was to enter Christian theology, through the adoption of
the *Logos* idea by a certain John, who wrote the Gospel of John. The author
adopts the idea to explain the mystery of Christ, and his place and function
in the universe: "In the beginning was the *Logos,* and the *Logos* was with
God, and the *Logos* was God."

Greek philosophy, too, yielded more and more to the need for religion.
We have seen that late Stoicism tended to regard Nature as God, and men
as sons of God and brothers.[4] It was outside Stoicism, however, that most
was done, in two new developments of Greek philosophy, Neo-Pythagorism
and Neo-Platonism.

Neo-Platonism was the more influential. It was both the last great system
and the culmination of the religious tendency in Greek philosophy. Its
founder, as we have seen (p. 145), was Ammonius Saccas of Alexandria,
its most distinguished exponent Plotinus, a native of Egypt, who came to
Rome as a teacher in 244 A.D., and soon acquired a great reputation. Plotinus
regarded matter as the constitutional enemy of spirit, and salvation therefore
as the extermination of physical desires. It is to rise superior to normal feelings and emotions, and live the pure life of the soul.

Not only did Plotinus disparage the life of sense, however, and praise
the life of contemplation, as Plato had done; he went further, teaching that
one must get beyond thought itself, if one would know God. One yields to
the feeling of something real, that is beyond all thought, and is rewarded
with ecstasy, in which one's individuality falls away and one melts into unity
with the Absolute.

But how did the physical world come into being? What has the Absolute
to do with a world so alien? Plotinus advances a theory not unlike the *Logos*
doctrine of Philo, or the angelology of later Judaism. It is the theory of
Emanations. All finite existence, Plotinus says, is a progressive falling away
from an original perfection. As the light of the sun shines into the darkness,
without thereby diminishing in its own being, though the darkness itself be
less and less illuminated, in proportion as it is more and more remote, so

---

[4] The philosopher, not the priest, was the real spiritual guide, tending to fill the place
of the modern clergyman. With long beard and wearing a cloak, he was distinctive in
appearance. He was looked to for advice in difficult moral situations, was called to the
bedside of the dying, delivered discourses in the clerical manner. He did what he could
to meet the demand for some cure for the ills of life and release from the sense of sin.
But the ideal of virtue was beyond the reach of the masses; and Greek philosophy provided no Saviour.

the Absolute overflows, through ever lessening gradations of being, until it reaches the lowest of all, the material world, the shadow of a shadow. The evil of the world is not so much positive as negative; it is exhaustion of being. Such beauty as there is in the world is the shining through of the spiritual reality, the Absolute.

Here then, as we have said (p. 168), is "Platonism, influenced by the best things in other systems. It was one more composite creation of the Hellenistic Age, with its eagerness for religious satisfaction from any source." It is "a mysticism that conceives the Universe pantheistically, as animated by a divine soul, and that sees also, beyond the Universe, a Being, the Absolute, who cannot be intellectually perceived and described but may be known in mystical ecstasy."

Neo-Platonism in the third century, when Christianity was advancing irresistibly through all the Mediterranean world, was still a vital alternative in intellectual circles. Still later it seemed for a moment that it might triumph, when the Emperor Julian, a Neo-Platonist, tried to turn back the Christian tide. Julian failed, however; and Greek philosophy survived only in so far as it could be turned to the uses of the Christian Church.

INDEX